Autodesk® Revit® 2015 MEP Fundamentals

ASCENT – Center for Technical Knowledge®

AUTODESK.
Authorized Author

Publications

SDC Publications
P.O. Box 1334
Mission, KS 66222
913-262-2664
www.SDCpublications.com
Publisher: Stephen Schroff

Examination Copies:
Books received as examination copies are for review purposes only and may not be made available for student use. Resale of examination copies is prohibited.

Electronic Files:
Any electronic files associated with this book are licensed to the original user only. These files may not be transferred to any other party.

Trademarks:
Autodesk, Autodesk Revit Structure, Autodesk Revit Architecture, Autodesk Revit MEP, Autodesk Inventor, AutoCAD, and DWG are registered trademarks of Autodesk, Inc., and/or its subsidiaries and/or affiliates in the USA and/or other countries. All other brand names, product names, or trademarks belong to their respective holders.

The author and publisher of this book have used their best efforts in preparing this book. These efforts include the development, research and testing of the material presented. The author and publisher shall not be liable in any event for incidental or consequential damages with, or arising out of, the furnishing, performance, or use of the material.

ISBN-13: 978-1-58503-888-6
ISBN-10: 1-58503-888-1

Printed and bound in the United States of America.

Table of Contents

Preface

To take full advantage of Building Information Modeling, the *Autodesk® Revit® 2015 MEP Fundamentals* training guide has been designed to teach the concepts and principles of creating 3D parametric models of MEP systems from engineering design through construction documentation. The training guide is intended to introduce students to the software's user interface and the basic HVAC, electrical, and plumbing/piping components that make the Autodesk Revit software a powerful and flexible engineering modeling tool. The objective is to familiarize students with the tools necessary to create, document, and print the parametric model. The examples and practices are designed to take the students through the basics of a full MEP project from linking in an architectural model to construction documents.

The main topics covered in the course include:

- Introduction to the Autodesk Revit software, its interface, including viewing, drawing, and editing commands.

- Working with linked architectural files.

- Creating and modifying views.

- Understanding MEP systems in general.

- Creating spaces and zones.

- Analyzing heating and cooling loads.

- Working with the HVAC module to add air terminals, mechanical equipment, and create HVAC systems.

- Working with the Piping module to add mechanical equipment as well as creating hydronic piping systems.

- Working with fixtures and piping systems in the Plumbing module.

- Working with fire protection systems.

- Working with components, circuits, cable tray, and conduits in the Electrical module.

- Creating and annotating construction documents.

- Adding tags and creating schedules.

- Detailing in the Autodesk Revit software.

Icon Reference Chart

The following icons are used throughout this training guide to help you to quickly and easily find helpful information.

(checkmark icon)	Indicates the Learning Objectives that are covered in the current chapter or section of the training guide.
Enhanced in 2015 (magnifier icon)	Indicates items that have been enhanced in the AutoCAD 2015 software.
New in 2015 (lightbulb icon)	Indicates items that are new in the AutoCAD 2015 software.

Students and Educators can Access Free Autodesk Software and Resources

Free products are subject to the terms and conditions of the end-user license and services agreement that accompanies the software. The software is for personal use for education purposes and is not intended for classroom or lab use.

Autodesk challenges you to get started with free educational licenses for professional software and creativity apps used by millions of architects, engineers, designers, and hobbyists today. Bring Autodesk software into your classroom, studio, or workshop to learn, teach, and explore real-world design challenges the way professionals do.

Get started today - register at the Autodesk Education Community and download one of the many Autodesk software applications available.

Visit www.autodesk.com/joinedu/

Class Files

To download the Class Files that are required for this training guide, type the following in the address bar of your web browser:

SDCpublications.com/downloads/978-1-58503-888-6

Setting up the Interface

The Autodesk® Building Design Suite version of the Autodesk® Revit® software is designed to be used with all building disciplines but the interface can be modified to suit each user's need. In this topic you learn how to modify the discipline-specific interface that is used in this training guide.

Discipline Specific Interface

The Autodesk Revit software has three disciplines: Architecture, Structure, and MEP (Mechanical, Electrical, and Plumbing, which is also know as Systems). When using the Autodesk Building Design Suite, all of the tools for these disciplines are installed in one copy of the software. By default, all of the tools, templates, and sample files are available, as shown in Figure 1. Most users only need access to their specific set of tools and the interface can be customized to suit those needs.

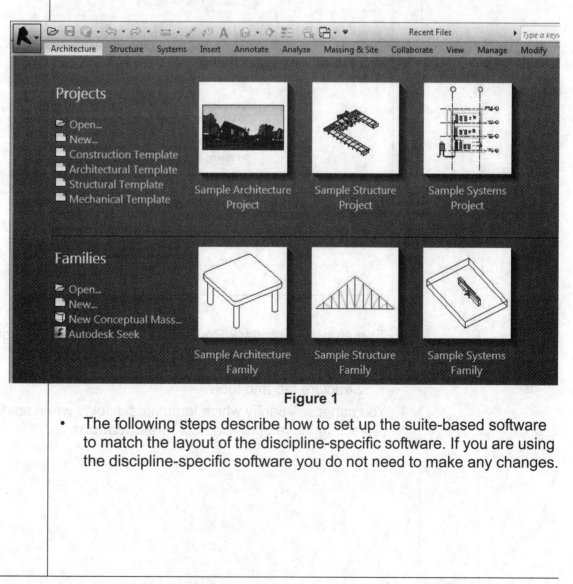

Figure 1

- The following steps describe how to set up the suite-based software to match the layout of the discipline-specific software. If you are using the discipline-specific software you do not need to make any changes.

How To: Setup the Autodesk Revit Interface by Discipline

1. In the upper left corner of the screen, expand ![Application Menu icon] (Application Menu) and click Options .
2. In the Options dialog box, in the left pane, select **User Interface**.
3. In the *Configure* area, under *Tools and analyses* (as shown in Figure 2), clear all of options that you do not want to use.

You are not deleting these tools, just removing them from the current user interface.

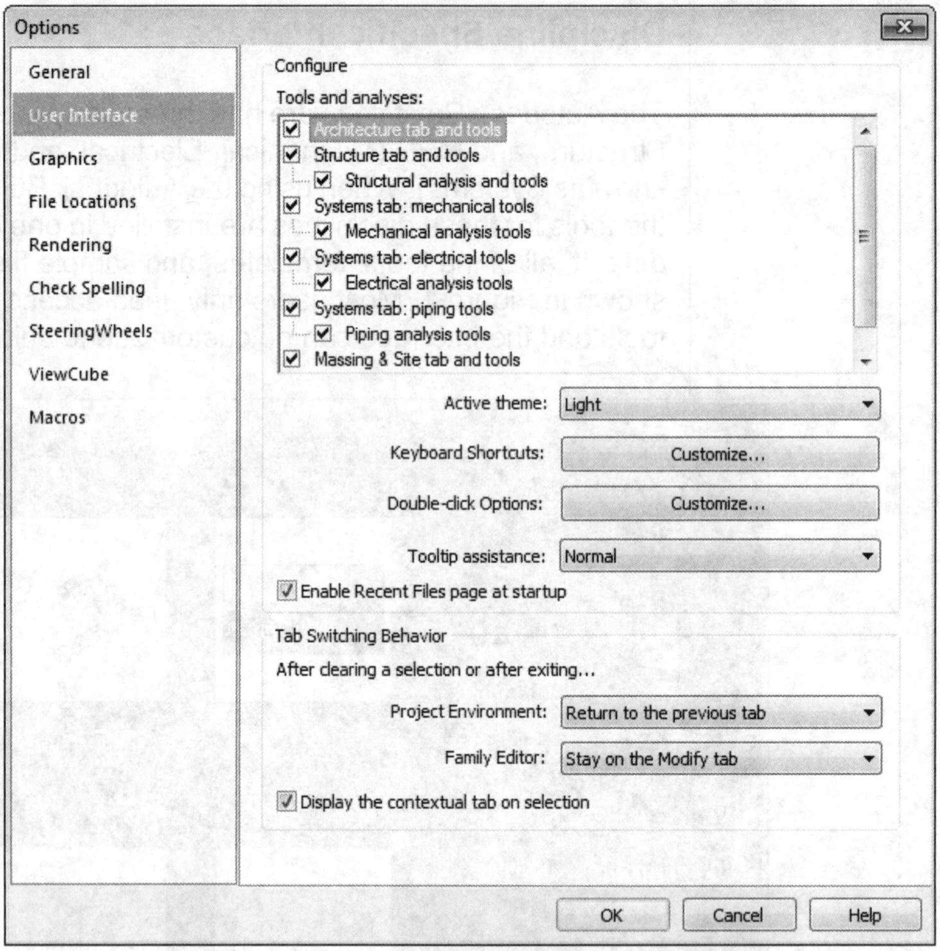

Figure 2

- To match the Autodesk Revit MEP interface, clear the following option:

  - *Structure* tab and tools.

4. You can also specify which templates display when starting a new project. In the left pane, select **File Locations**.

5. In the right pane (as shown in Figure 3), select and order the templates that you want to display. Typically, these are set up by the company.

Project template files: The first five project templates will appear as links on the Recent Files page.

Name	Path
Construction Tem...	C:\ProgramData\Autodesk\RVT 2014\Tem...
Architectural Tem...	C:\ProgramData\Autodesk\RVT 2014\Tem...
Structural Template	C:\ProgramData\Autodesk\RVT 2014\Tem...
Mechanical Templ...	C:\ProgramData\Autodesk\RVT 2014\Tem...

Figure 3

*   To match the Autodesk Revit MEP interface, remove the **Construction Template**, **Architectural Template,** and **Structural Template**. Add the **Electrical Template** (**Electrical-Default.rte**), **Plumbing Template (Plumbing-Default.rte)**, and **Systems Template** (**Systems-Default.rte**) found in the RVT 2015>Templates>*<appropriate units>* folder. Place them in the order shown in Figure 4.

New Project

Template file

Mechanical Template   Browse...

<None>
Mechanical Template
Electrical Template
Plumbing Template
Systems Template

OK   Cancel   Help

Figure 4

6. Click [OK]. The interface and template locations update for this installation of the software.

*   You might also need to move the tabs to a different order. To do so, select the tab, hold <Ctrl> and drag the tab to the new location.

*   To match the Autodesk Revit MEP interface, select the *Systems* tab, hold <Ctrl> and drag it to the front of the tabs.

Chapter 1

Introduction to BIM and Autodesk Revit

In this chapter you learn about Building Information Modeling (BIM) and how it is used in the Autodesk® Revit® software. You investigate the software interface and terminology, learn how to start projects, and work with the viewing commands including zoom controls, 3D isometric, and perspective views.

This chapter contains the following topics:

- **Building Information Modeling**
- **Overview of the Interface**
- **Standard Terminology**
- **Starting Projects**
- **Viewing Commands**

1.1 Building Information Modeling

 Learning Objective

- Describe the concept of Building Information Modeling and its workflow in relation to the Autodesk Revit software.

Building Information Modeling (BIM) is an approach to the entire building life cycle. The BIM process supports the ability to coordinate, update, and share design data with team members throughout the design, construction, and management phases of a building's life.

The Autodesk Revit software is a *Parametric Building Modeler*, and is an important part of the BIM process. *Parametric* means you can establish a relationship between two building elements; when one element changes the other element changes as well. *Building* signifies that this software is designed for working with buildings, as opposed to gears or roads. *Modeler* signifies how a project is built in a single file around the building model (as shown on the left in Figure 1–1). All views, such as plans (as shown on the right in Figure 1–1), elevations, sections, details, schedules, as well as all design sheets printed for construction documents, are automatically generated based on the model.

When a change is made anywhere in the model, all of the views update automatically. For example, if you add an element in a plan view, it displays in the related section view and in schedules (if applicable).

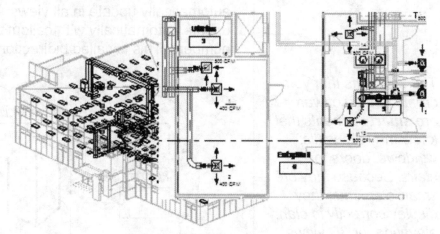

Figure 1–1

- The Autodesk® Revit® software includes tools for architectural, mechanical, electrical, plumbing, and structural design.

- It is important that everyone works in the same version and build of the software.

Workflow and BIM

BIM has changed the process of how a building is designed. The Autodesk Revit software is a true BIM product in that it is much more than a drafting software. By creating complete models and associated views of those models, the software takes much of the tediousness out of producing a building design.

In the traditional design process, plans create the basis for the model, from which you then create sections and elevations, as shown in Figure 1–2. Construction Documents (CDs) can then be created. In this workflow, changes are made at the plan level and then coordinated with other documents in the set.

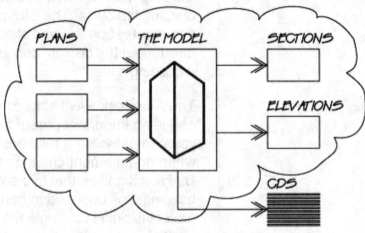

Figure 1–2

In the BIM, the design process revolves around the model, as shown in Figure 1–3. Plans, elevations, and sections are simply 2D versions of the 3D model. Changes made in one view automatically update in all views. Even Construction Documents update automatically with callout tags in sync with the sheet numbers. This is called bidirectional associativity.

*The elements that you create in the software are **smart** elements that know they are walls, windows, doors, or stairs. Because they are smart elements, they display correctly in plan, elevation, or 3D views. This ensures that drawings are coordinated across the project because the same model generates all of the necessary views.*

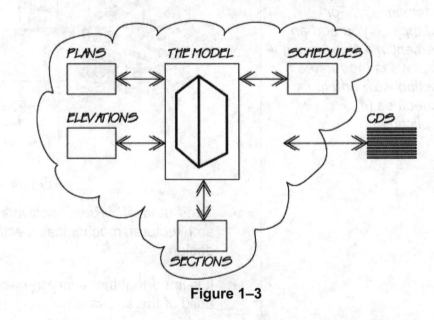

Figure 1–3

Views and Sheets

In the traditional workflow, the most time-consuming part of the project is the construction documents. With BIM, the base views of those documents (i.e., floor plans, ceiling plans, elevations, sections, and schedules) are produced automatically and update as the model is updated, saving hours of work. The views are then placed on sheets that form the construction document set.

For example, a floor plan is duplicated to create a Lighting Plan. In the new view, certain categories of elements are automatically turned off (such as grids) or on (such as lighting fixtures). Annotation is added as required, and the plan is then placed on a sheet, as shown in Figure 1–4.

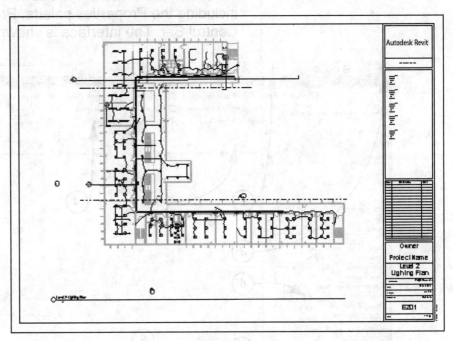

Figure 1–4

- Work can continue on a view and is automatically updated on the sheet.

- Annotating views in the preliminary design phase is often not required. You might be able to wait until you are further along in the project.

1.2 Overview of the Interface

 Learning Objective

- Navigate the graphic user interface.

The Autodesk Revit interface is designed for intuitive and efficient access to commands and views. It includes the Ribbon, Quick Access Toolbar, Application Menu, Navigation Bar, and Status Bar, which are common to the Autodesk® software. It also includes tools that are specific to the Autodesk Revit software, including the Properties palette, Project Browser, and View Control Bar. The interface is shown in Figure 1–5.

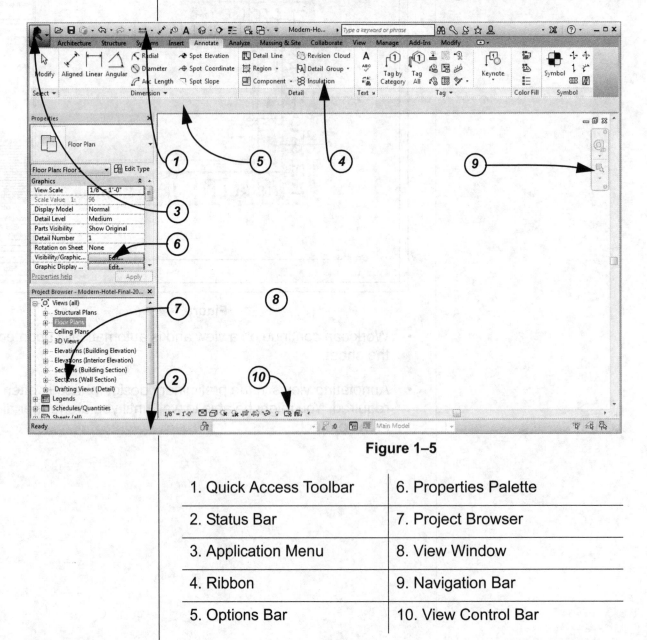

Figure 1–5

1. Quick Access Toolbar	6. Properties Palette
2. Status Bar	7. Project Browser
3. Application Menu	8. View Window
4. Ribbon	9. Navigation Bar
5. Options Bar	10. View Control Bar

1. Quick Access Toolbar

The Quick Access Toolbar provides access to commonly used commands, such as **Open**, **Save**, **Undo** and **Redo**, **Dimension**, and **3D View**, as shown in Figure 1–6.

Figure 1–6

- The Quick Access Toolbar is easily customizable. Select the arrow at the end of the toolbar. You can choose from the list of commands or click **Customize Quick Access Toolbar** to bring up a dialog box where you can modify the location of the tools on the toolbar as shown in Figure 1–7.

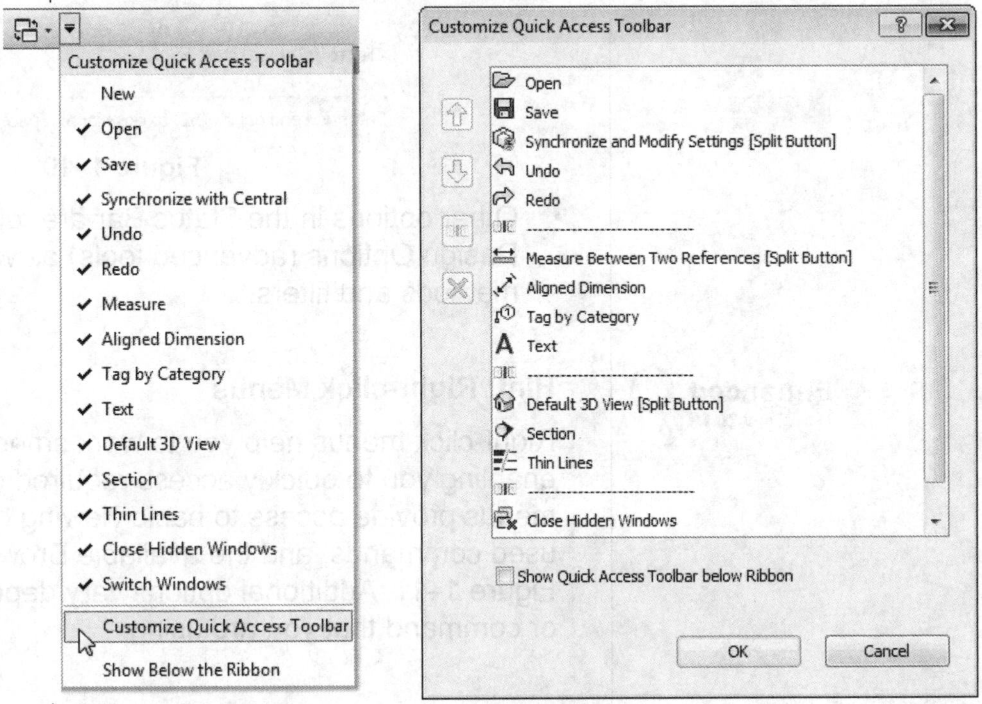

Figure 1–7

- You can also customize it by adding commands from any of the Ribbon tabs. Right-click on the command in the Ribbon and select **Add to Quick Access Toolbar** as shown in Figure 1–8.

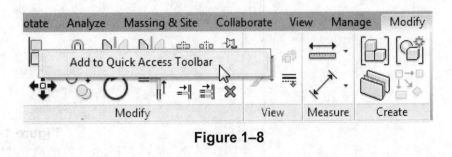

Figure 1–8

The other end of the Quick Access Toolbar hosts the InfoCenter, which enables you to quickly search for help on the web, as shown in Figure 1–9. You can specify which Help documents to search and collapse or expand the *Search* field to save screen space. You can also sign into the Autodesk 360 service to access additional on-line services.

You can collapse or expand the Search field to save screen space.

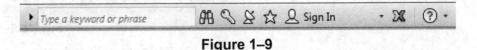

Figure 1–9

2. Status Bar

The Status Bar provides information about the current process, such as the next step for a command, as shown in Figure 1–10.

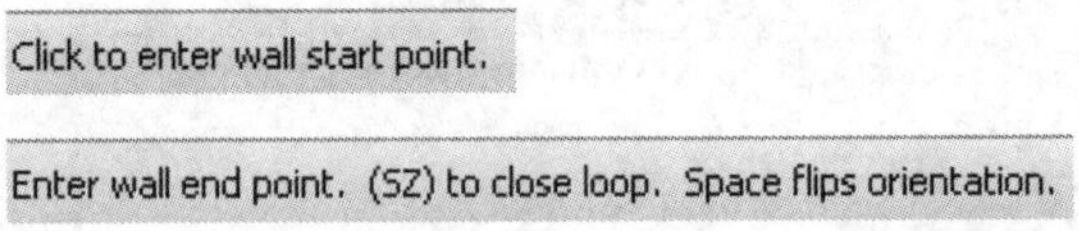

Click to enter wall start point.

Enter wall end point. (SZ) to close loop. Space flips orientation.

Figure 1–10

- Other options in the Status Bar are related to Worksets and Design Options (advanced tools) as well as selection methods and filters.

Enhanced in 2015

Hint: Right-click Menus

Right-click menus help you to work smoothly and efficiently by enabling you to quickly access required commands. These menus provide access to basic viewing commands, recently used commands, and the available Browsers, as shown in Figure 1–11. Additional options vary depending on the element or command that you are using.

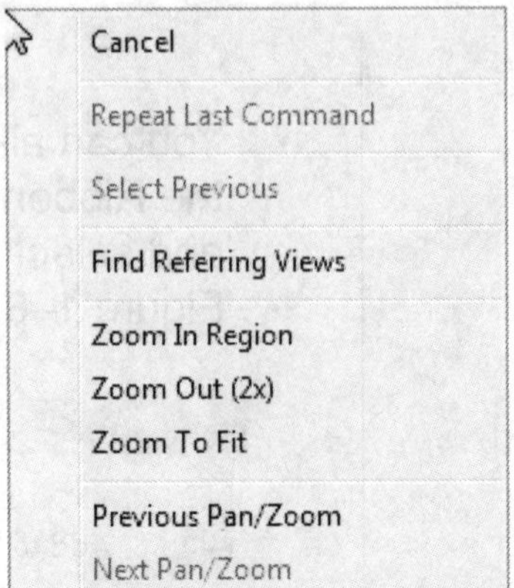

Cancel

Repeat Last Command

Select Previous

Find Referring Views

Zoom In Region
Zoom Out (2x)
Zoom To Fit

Previous Pan/Zoom
Next Pan/Zoom
Browsers ▶
✓ Properties

Figure 1–11

3. Application Menu

The Application Menu provides access to file commands, settings, and documents, as shown in Figure 1–12. Hover the cursor over a command to display a list of additional tools.

If you click the primary icon, rather than the arrow, it starts the default command.

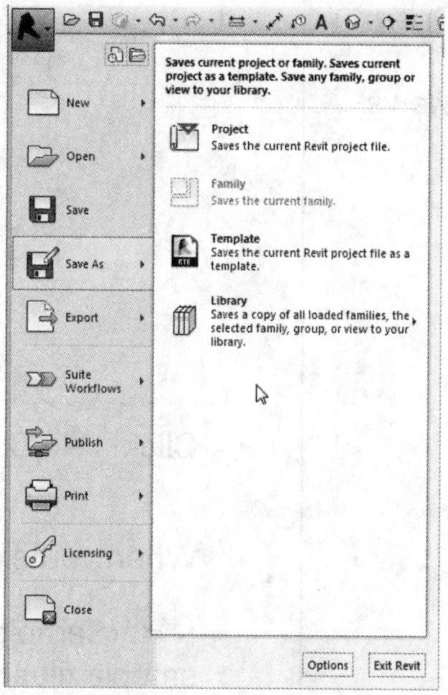

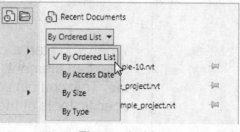

Figure 1–12

- At the bottom of the menu, click to open the Options dialog box or click Exit Revit to exit the software.

How To: Recent Documents

To display a list of recently used documents, click ⬜ (Recent Documents) in the Application menu. The documents can be reordered as shown in Figure 1–13.

Figure 1–13

- Click (Pin) next to a document name to keep it available, even if more documents are opened than can be displayed. It displays with the push pin tacked in (⬤).

How To: Open Documents

To display a list of open documents and views, click

 (Open Documents). The list displays the open documents and each view that is open, as shown in Figure 1–14.

You can use the Open Documents list to change between views.

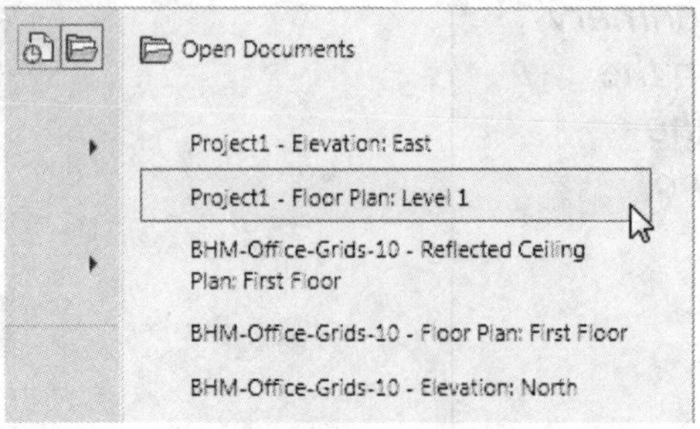

Open Documents

> Project1 - Elevation: East

Project1 - Floor Plan: Level 1

> BHM-Office-Grids-10 - Reflected Ceiling Plan: First Floor

BHM-Office-Grids-10 - Floor Plan: First Floor

BHM-Office-Grids-10 - Elevation: North

Figure 1–14

* Click (Close) to close the current project.

* When you expand (Open) there is an option

((Sample Files)), which opens a folder containing the sample files supplied with the software.

4. Ribbon

The Ribbon contains tools in a series of tabs and panels as shown in Figure 1–15. Selecting a tab displays a group of related panels. The panels contain a variety of tools, grouped by function.

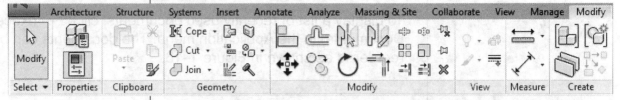

Figure 1–15

When you start a command that creates new elements or you select an element, the Ribbon displays the *Modify |* contextual tab. This contains general editing commands and command specific tools at the end of the tab, as shown in Figure 1–16.

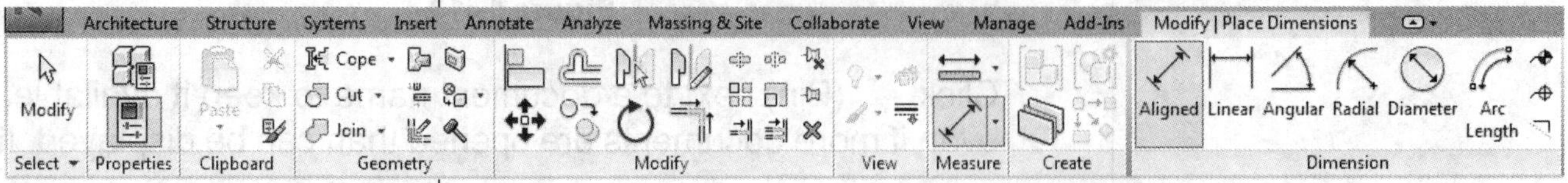

Figure 1–16

- When you hover over a tool on the Ribbon, tooltips display the tool's name and a short description. If you continue hovering over the tool, a graphic displays (and sometimes a video), as shown in Figure 1–17.

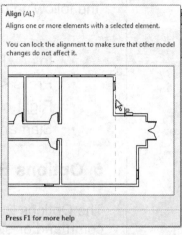

Figure 1–17

- Many commands have shortcut keys. For example, press <A> and then press <L> for **Align** or press <M> and then press <V> for **Move**. They are listed next to the name of the command in the tooltips. Do not press <Enter> to execute shortcuts.

- The order in which the Ribbon tabs are displayed can be modified. Select the tab, hold <Ctrl>, and drag it to a new location. The location is remembered when you restart the software.

- Any panel can be dragged by its title into the drawing area to become a floating panel. Click the **Return Panels to Ribbon** button as shown in Figure 1–18 to replace the panel.

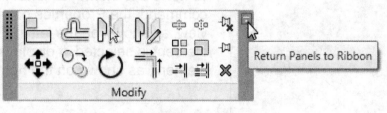

Figure 1–18

Hint: You are always in a command when using the Autodesk Revit software.

When you are finished working with a tool, you typically default back to the **Modify** command. To end a command, use one of the following methods:

- In any Ribbon tab, click (Modify).
- Press <Esc> once or twice to revert to **Modify**.
- Right-click and select **Cancel...** once or twice.
- Start another command.

5. Options Bar

The Options Bar displays options that are related to the selected command or element. For example, when the **Rotate** command is active it displays options for rotating the selected elements, as shown at the top in Figure 1–19. When the **Place Dimensions** command is active it displays dimension related options, as shown at the bottom in Figure 1–19.

| Modify | Multi-Select | ☐ Disjoin ☐ Copy   Angle: 45| | Center of rotation: Place | Default |

| Modify | Place Dimensions | Wall centerline ▾   Pick: Individual Reference ▾ | Options |

Figure 1–19

6. Properties Palette

In the Properties palette you can make extensive modifications to views and elements. If nothing is selected and you are not in a command, the Properties palette displays options for the current view, as shown on the left in Figure 1–20. If a command or element is selected, it displays options for the associated element, as shown on the right in Figure 1–20.

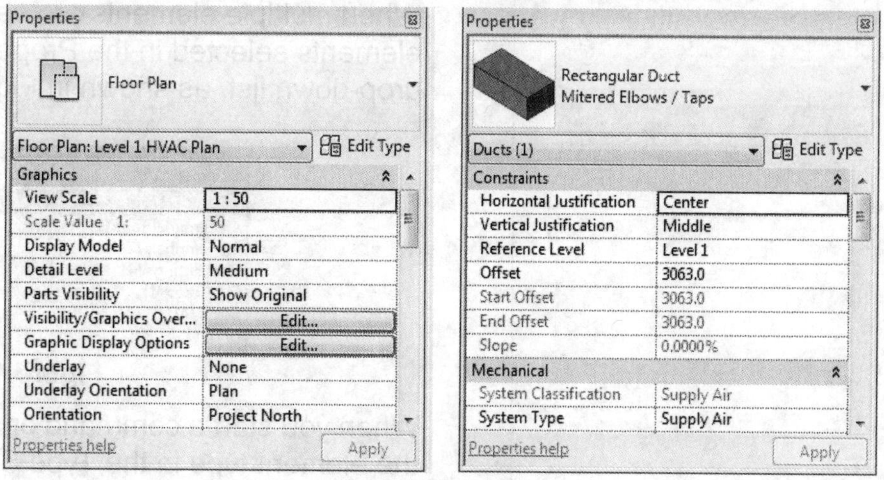

Figure 1-20

- Items that are grayed out are read-only.

- The Properties palette is usually kept open while working on a project to easily permit modifications at any time. It can be placed on a second monitor as well as floated, resized, and docked on top of the Project Browser or other dockable palettes.

- If the Properties palette and other palettes are docked on top of each other, the tabs are displayed at the bottom of the combined palette, as shown in Figure 1-21. Click the tab to display its associated panel.

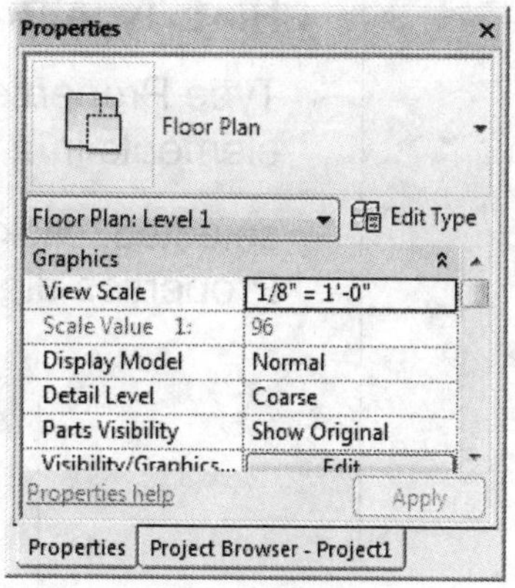

Figure 1-21

- If the Properties palette does not display, click

  (Properties) in the *Modify* tab>Properties panel, or press <P> twice.

- You can also access the user interface options by selecting the *View* tab>Windows panel, expanding (User Interface), and selecting an option.

- When multiple elements are selected, you can filter the elements selected in the Properties palette using the drop-down list, as shown in Figure 1–22.

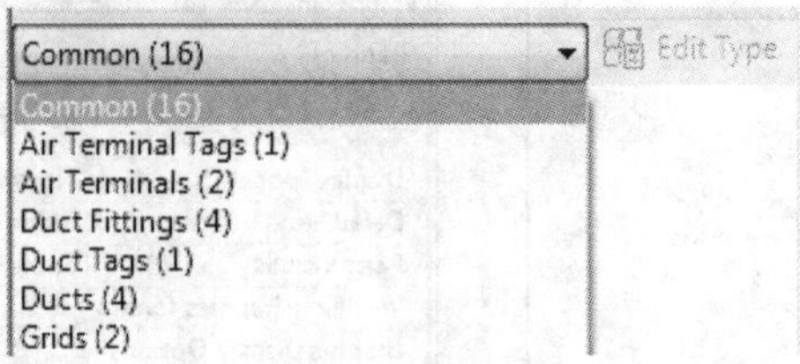

Figure 1–22

- When you start a command or select an element, you can set the element type in the Type Selector as shown in Figure 1–23.

Right-click on the Type Selector to add it to the Quick Access Toolbar and/or to the Ribbon Modify tab.

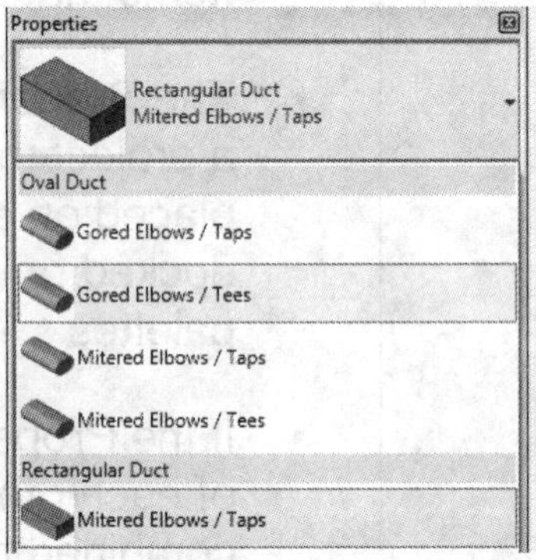

Figure 1–23

Hint: Type Properties

Type Properties are parameters that are common to all of the elements in a specific family. When a single type of element is selected, click ▦ (Edit Type) in Properties to open the Type Properties dialog box, as shown in Figure 1–24.

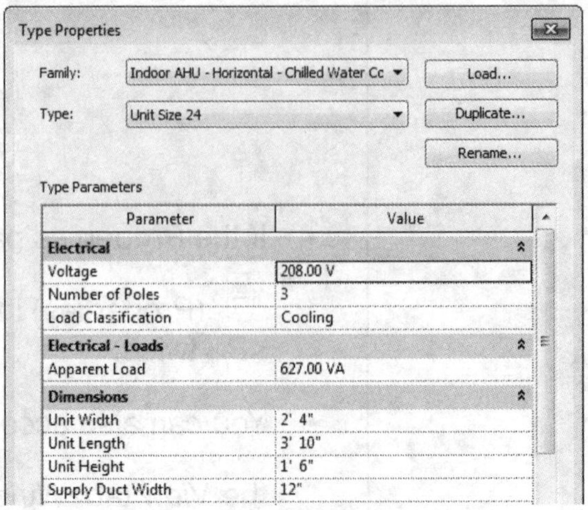

Figure 1–24

---

7. Project Browser

The Project Browser lists the views that can be opened in the software as shown in Figure 1–25. This includes all views of the model in which you are working and any additional views that you create, such as floor plans, ceiling plans, 3D views, elevations, sections, etc. It also includes views of schedules, legends, sheets (for plotting), groups, and Autodesk Revit Links.

The Project Browser displays the name of the active project.

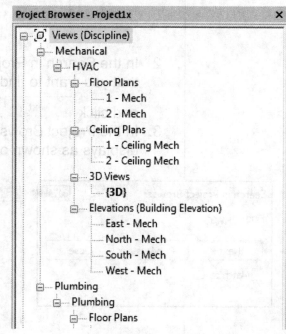

Figure 1–25

- Double-click on an item in the list to open the associated view.

- To display the views associated with a view type, click ⊞ (Expand) next to the section name. To hide the views in the section, click ⊟ (Contract).

- Right-click on a view and select **Rename** or press <F2> to rename a view in the Project Browser.

- If you no longer need a view, you can remove it. Right-click on its name in the Project Browser and select **Delete**.

- The Project Browser can be floated, resized, docked on top of the Properties palette, and customized. If the Properties palette and the Project Browser are docked on top of each other, use the appropriate tab to display the required panel.

How To: Search the Project Browser

1. In the Project Browser, right-click on the top level Views node as shown in Figure 1–26.

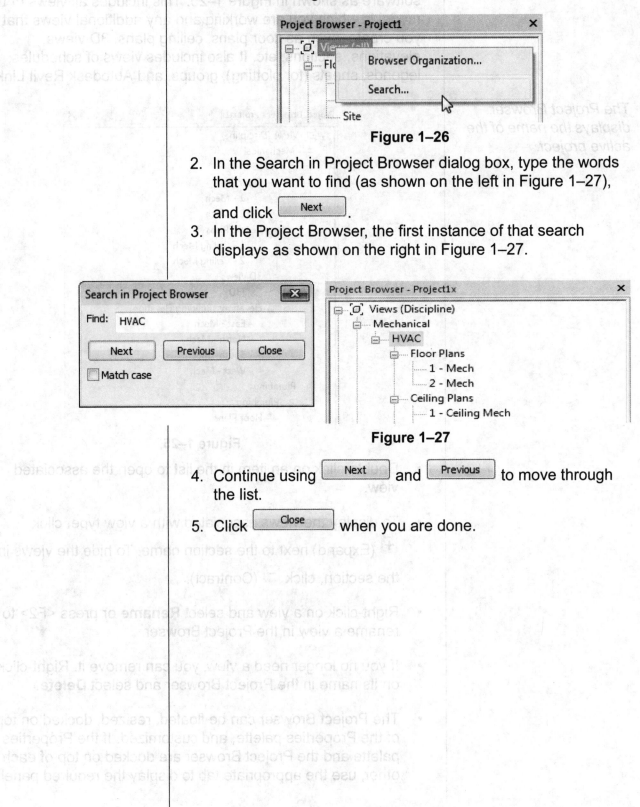

Figure 1–26

2. In the Search in Project Browser dialog box, type the words that you want to find (as shown on the left in Figure 1–27), and click [Next].

3. In the Project Browser, the first instance of that search displays as shown on the right in Figure 1–27.

Figure 1–27

4. Continue using [Next] and [Previous] to move through the list.

5. Click [Close] when you are done.

8. View Window

Each view of a project opens in its own window, as shown in Figure 1–28. Each view displays a Navigation Bar (for quick access to viewing tools) and the View Control Bar.

In 3D views you can also use the ViewCube to rotate the view.

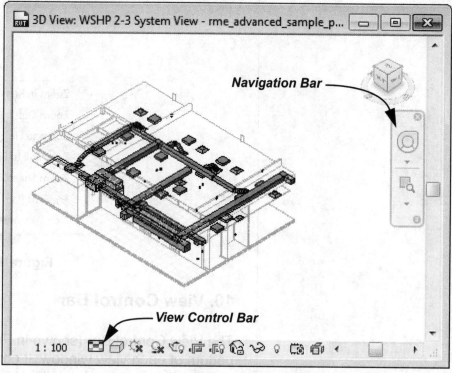

Navigation Bar

View Control Bar

Figure 1–28

- Each view of a project opens in its own window. You can use the Project Browser or press <Ctrl>+<Tab> to cycle through the open views.

- If you have multiple views open you can select a view by name. In the Quick Access Toolbar or *View* tab>Windows panel, expand ⬚ (Switch Windows) and select from the list.

- If you have more than one view open, click ⬚ (Cascade) or ⬚ (Tile) in the *View* tab>Windows panel to arrange them in the selected order on the screen. You can also use the shortcut keys by pressing <W> and then pressing <C> for **Cascade** or pressing <W> and then pressing <T> for **Tile**.

9. Navigation Bar

The Navigation Bar enables you to access various viewing commands, as shown in Figure 1–29.

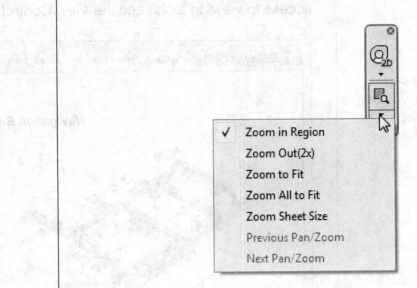

Figure 1–29

10. View Control Bar

The View Control Bar (shown in Figure 1–30), displays at the bottom of each view window. It controls aspects of that view, such as the scale and detail level. It also includes tools that display parts of the view and hide or isolate elements in the view.

Figure 1–30

1.3 Standard Terminology

 Learning Objective

- Use typical terms and concepts found in the software.

As you start working with BIM based software, you should know the typical terms used to describe items in the Autodesk Revit software. There are several types of elements, as shown in Figure 1–31, and described in the following table.

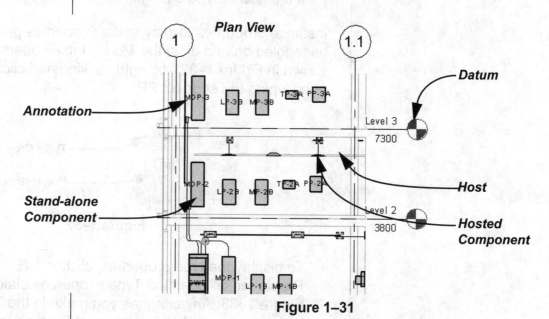

Figure 1–31

Host	*Built-in-place* construction elements (e.g., walls, floors, roofs. and ceilings). They can stand alone in the project.
Components	Elements that need to be attached to host elements (e.g., ceiling mounted lighting fixtures and air terminals), as well as stand-alone items (such as some mechanical equipment).
Views	Enables you to display and manipulate the project. For example, you can view and work in floor plans, ceiling plans, elevations, sections, schedules, and 3D views. You can change a design from any view. All views are stored in the project.
Datum	Elements that define the project context. These include levels for the floors, column grids, and reference planes that help you draw.
Annotation	2D elements that are placed in views to define the information drawn in the project. These include dimensions, text, tags, and symbols. The view scale controls their size.

Property Types

There are two types of properties for most elements in the software:

- **Instance Properties:** Parameters that can be set for the individual element you are drawing or modifying. They display in the Properties palette.

- **Type Properties:** Control options for all elements of the same type. If you modify these parameters, all elements of the selected type change.

Instance properties display in the Properties palette, which can be toggled on and off in the *Modify* tab>Properties panel (as shown in Figure 1–32), by right-clicking and clicking **Properties**, or by typing the shortcut **PP**.

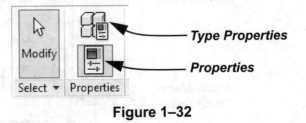

Figure 1–32

- To display the type properties, click 🔲 (Edit Type) in Properties, to open the Type Properties dialog box, shown in Figure 1–33. Any changes you make in the Type Properties dialog box impact all instances of the type in the project.

The parameters shown in the dialog boxes vary according to the type of element selected.

Type Properties	
Family:	M_Lighting and Appliance Panelboard - ▾	Load...
Type:	400 A ▾	Duplicate...
		Rename...

Type Parameters

Parameter	Value
Constraints	⌃
Default Elevation	1200.0
Electrical	⌃
Voltage	
Wattage	
Dimensions	⌃
Width	508.0
Depth	146.1

Figure 1–33

1.4 Starting Projects

Learning Objectives

- Open and save existing projects.
- Start new projects using templates.

File operations to open existing files, create new files from a template, and save files in the Autodesk Revit software are found in the Application Menu, as shown in Figure 1–34.

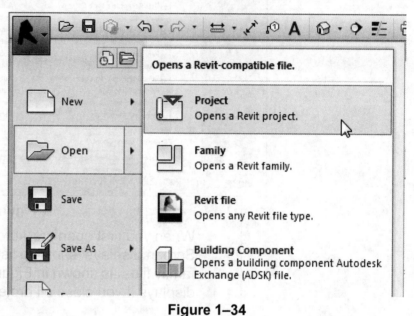

Figure 1–34

There are three main file types:

- **Project files (.rvt):** Your primary drawing files. This is where you do the majority of your work in the building model with views and sheets. They are initially based on template files.

- **Family files (.rfa):** Separate components that can be inserted in a project. For example, an air handling unit or lighting fixture family could include a variety of sizes. Title block and Annotation Symbol files are special types of family files.

- **Template files (.rte):** Designed to hold standard information and settings for creating new project files. The software includes several templates for residential, commercial, and structural projects. You can also create custom templates.

Opening Projects

To open an existing project, in the Quick Access Toolbar or Application Menu click 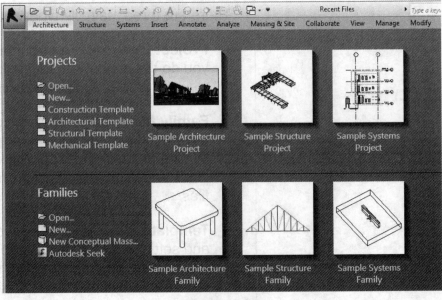 (Open), or press <Ctrl>+<O>. The Open dialog box opens (as shown in Figure 1–35), in which you can navigate to the required folder and select a project file.

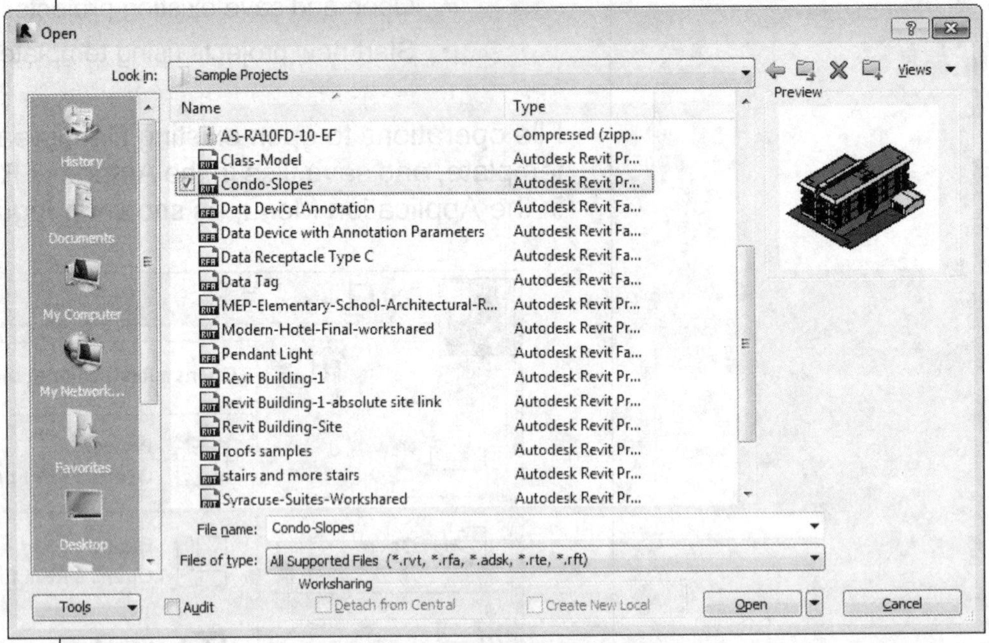

Figure 1–35

- When you first open the Autodesk Revit software, the Startup Screen displays, showing lists of recently used projects and family files as shown in Figure 1–36. This screen also displays if you close all projects.

Figure 1–36

- You can select the picture of a recently opened project or use one of the options on the left to open or start a new project using the default templates.

Hint: Opening Workset-Related Files

Worksets are used when the project becomes large enough for multiple people to work on it at the same time. At this point, the project manager creates a central file with multiple worksets (such as element interiors, building shell, and site) that are used by the project team members.

When you open a workset related file it creates a new local file on your computer as shown in Figure 1–37. Do not work in the main central file.

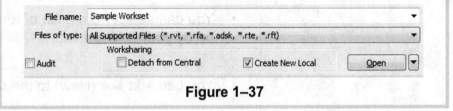

Figure 1–37

Starting New Projects

New projects are based on a template file. The template file includes preset levels, views, and some families, such as wall styles and text styles. Check with your BIM Manager about which template you need to use for your projects. Your company might have more than one based on the types of building that you are designing.

How To: Start a New Project

1. In the Application Menu, expand ⬜ (New) and click
   ⬜ (Project) (as shown in Figure 1–38), or press
   <Ctrl>+<N>.

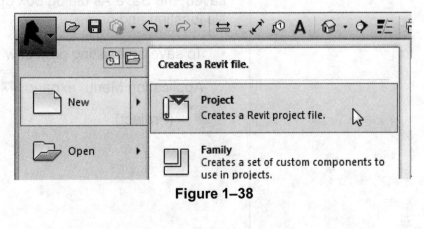

Figure 1–38

The list of Template files is set in the Options dialog box in the File Locations pane. It might vary depending on the installed product and company standards.

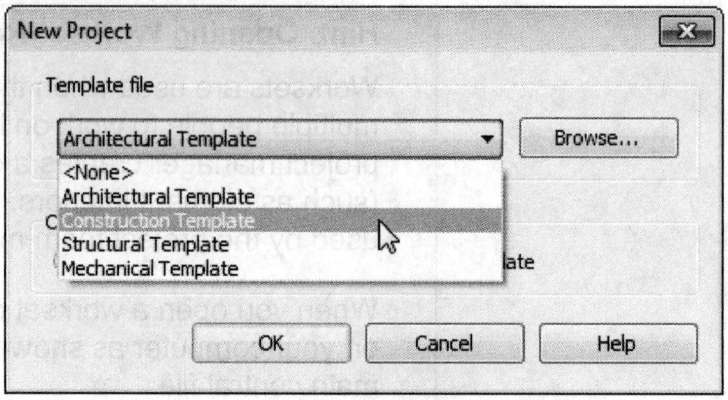

2. In the New Project dialog box (shown in Figure 1–39), select the template that you want to use and click .

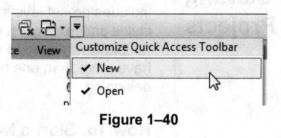

Figure 1–39

- You can select from a list of templates if they have been set up by your BIM Manager.

- You can add ☐ (New) to the Quick Access Toolbar. At the end of the Quick Access Toolbar, click ▼ (Customize Quick Access Toolbar) and select **New**, as shown in Figure 1–40.

Figure 1–40

Saving Projects

Saving your project frequently is a good idea. In the Quick Access Toolbar or Application Menu click 💾 (Save), or press <Ctrl>+<S> to save your project. If the project has not yet been saved, the Save As dialog box opens, where you can specify a file location and name.

- To save an existing project with a new name, in the Application Menu, expand 💾 (Save As) and click 📄 (Project).

- If you have not saved in a set amount of time, the software opens the Project Not Saved Recently alert box, as shown in Figure 1–41. Select **Save the project**. If you want to set reminder intervals or not save at this time, select the other options.

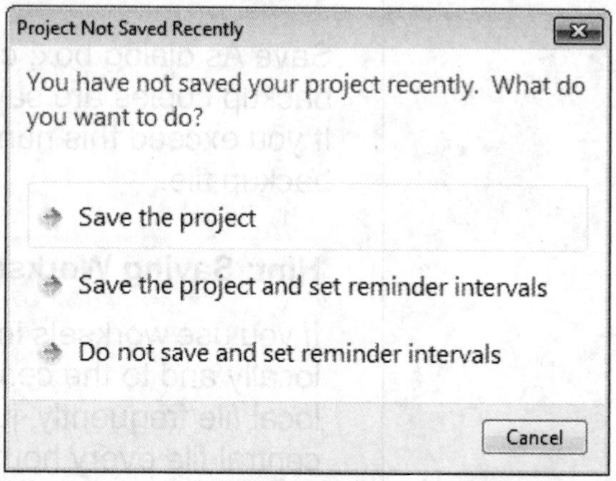

Figure 1–41

- You can set the *Save Reminder interval* to **15** or **30 minutes**, **1**, **2**, or **4 hours**, or to have **No reminders** display. In the

  Application Menu, click Options to open the Options dialog box. In the left pane, select **General** and set the interval as shown in Figure 1–42.

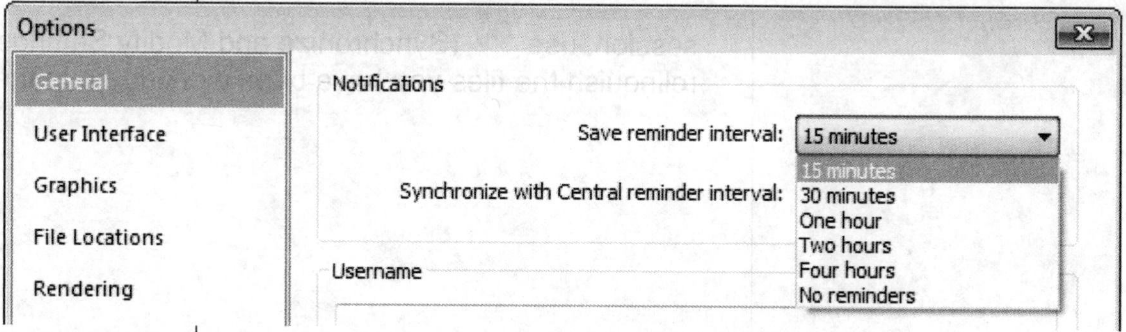

Figure 1–42

Saving Backup Copies

By default, the software saves a backup copy of a project file when you save the project. Backup copies are numbered incrementally (e.g., **My Project.0001.rvt**, **My Project.0002.rvt**, etc.) and are saved in the same folder as the original file. In the

Save As dialog box, click [Options...] to control how many backup copies are saved. The default number is three backups. If you exceed this number, the software deletes the oldest backup file.

> ### Hint: Saving Workset-Related Projects
>
> If you use worksets in your project, you need to save the project locally and to the central file. It is recommended to save the local file frequently, just like any other file, and save to the central file every hour or so.
>
> To synchronize your changes with the main file, in the Quick Access Toolbar expand ⬡ (Synchronize and Modify Settings) and click ⬡ (Synchronize Now). After you save to the central file, save the file locally again.
>
> At the end of the day, or when you are finished with the current session, use ⬡ (Synchronize and Modify Settings) to relinquish the files you have been working on to the central file.

1.5 Viewing Commands

Learning Objectives

- Manipulate 2D and 3D views by zooming and panning.
- Create 3D Isometric and Perspective views.
- Set the Visual Style of a view.

Zoom commands are crucial to working efficiently in most drawing programs and the Autodesk Revit software is no exception. Once in a view, you can use the Zoom controls to navigate within it. You can zoom in and out and pan in any view. There are also special tools for viewing in 3D.

Zooming and Panning

Using The Mouse to Zoom and Pan

Use the mouse wheel (as shown in Figure 1–43) as the main method of moving around the drawing.

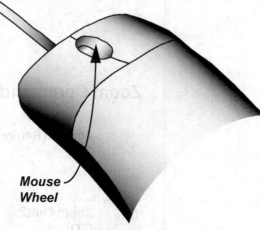

Mouse Wheel

Figure 1–43

- Scroll the wheel on the mouse up to zoom in and down to zoom out.

- Hold the wheel and move the mouse to pan.

- Double-click on the wheel to zoom to the extents of the drawing.

- In a 3D view, hold <Shift> and the mouse wheel and move the mouse to rotate around the model.

Zoom Controls

A number of additional zoom methods enable you to control the screen display. **Zoom** and **Pan** can be performed at any time while using other commands.

- You can access the **Zoom** commands in the Navigation Bar in the upper right corner of the view (as shown in Figure 1–44). You can also access them from most right-click menus and by typing the shortcut commands.

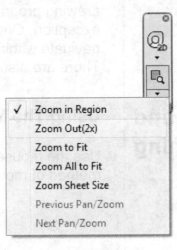

(2D Wheel) provides cursor-specific access to Zoom and Pan.

Figure 1–44

Zoom Commands

	Zoom In Region (ZR)	Zooms into a region that you define. Drag the cursor or select two points to define the rectangular area you want to zoom into. This is the default command.
	Zoom Out(2x) (ZO)	Zooms out to half the current magnification around the center of the elements.
	Zoom To Fit (ZF or ZE)	Zooms out so that the entire contents of the project only display on the screen in the current view.
	Zoom All To Fit (ZA)	Zooms out so that the entire contents of the project display on the screen in all open views.
	Zoom Sheet Size (ZS)	Zooms in or out in relation to the sheet size.
N/A	**Previous Pan/Zoom (ZP)**	Steps back one **Zoom** command.
N/A	**Next Pan/Zoom**	Steps forward one **Zoom** command if you have done a **Previous Pan/Zoom**.

Viewing in 3D

There are two types of 3D views: isometric views created by the 3D View command and perspective views created by the Camera command.

Even if you started a project entirely in plan views, you can quickly create 3D views of the model, as shown in Figure 1–45.

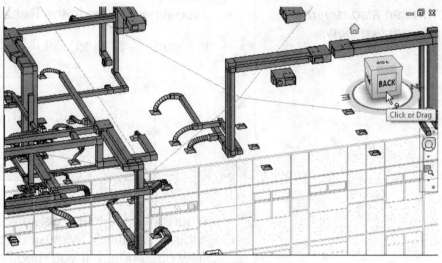

Figure 1–45

Working in 3D views helps you visualize the project and position some of the elements correctly. You can create and modify elements in 3D views just as in plan views.

- Once you have created a 3D view, you can save it and easily return to it.

How To: Create and Save a 3D Isometric View

1. In the Quick Access Toolbar or *View* tab>Create panel, click (Default 3D View). The default 3D Southeast isometric view opens, as shown in Figure 1–46.

You can spin the view to a different angle using the mouse wheel or the middle button of a three-button mouse. Hold <Shift> as you press the wheel or middle button and drag the cursor.

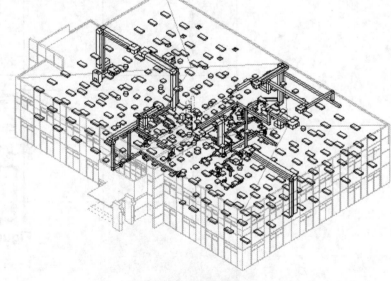

Figure 1–46

You can also rename perspective views.

2. Modify the view to display the building from other directions.
3. In the Project Browser, right-click on the {3D} view and select **Rename...**
4. Type a new name in the Rename View dialog box, as shown in Figure 1–47, and click .

Rename View	✕
Name: Mechanical Layout	
OK	Cancel

Figure 1–47

- When changes to the default 3D view are saved and you start another default 3D view, it displays the Southeast isometric view once again. If you modified the default 3D view but did not save it to a new name, the **Default 3D View** command opens the view in the last orientation you specified.

How To: Create a Perspective View

1. Switch to a Floor Plan view.
2. In the Quick Access Toolbar or *View* tab>Create panel, expand (Default 3D View) and click (Camera).
3. Place the camera on the view.
4. Point the camera in the direction in which you want it to shoot by placing the target on the view, as shown in Figure 1–48.

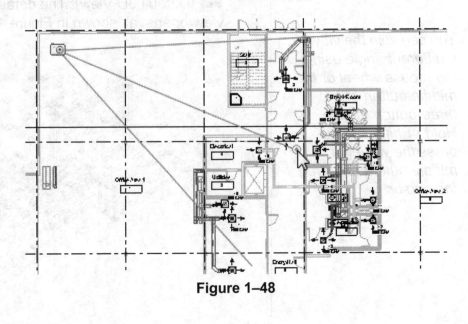

Figure 1–48

A new view is displayed, as shown in Figure 1–49.

Use the round controls to modify the display size of the view and press <Shift> + the mouse wheel to change the view.

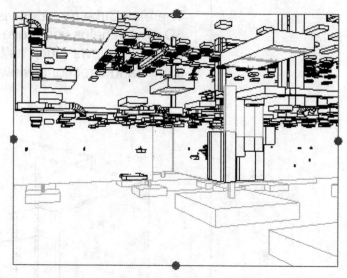

Figure 1–49

- You can further modify a view by adding shadows, as shown in Figure 1–50. In the View Control Bar, toggle ⚬✕ (Shadows Off) and ⚬ (Shadows On). Shadows display in any model view, not just in the 3D views.

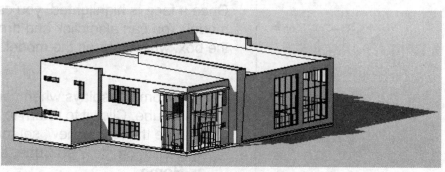

Figure 1–50

Hint: Using the ViewCube

The ViewCube provides visual clues as to where you are in a 3D view. It helps you move around the model with quick access to specific views (such as top, front, and right), as well as corner and directional views, as shown in Figure 1–51.

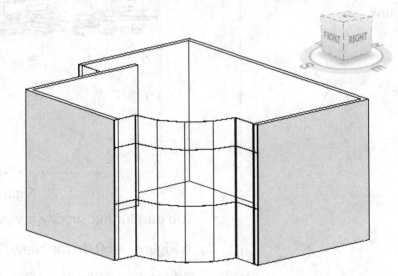

Figure 1–51

Move the cursor over any face of the ViewCube to highlight it. Once a face is highlighted, you can select it to reorient the model. You can also click and drag on the ViewCube to rotate the box, which rotates the model.

- ⌂ (Home) displays when you roll the cursor over the ViewCube. Click it to return to the view defined as **Home**. To change the Home view, set the view as you want it, right-click on the ViewCube, and select **Set Current View as Home**.

- The ViewCube is available in isometric and perspective views.

Visual Styles

Any view can have a visual style applied. The **Visual Style** options found in the View Control Bar (as shown in Figure 1–52), specify the shading of the building model. These options apply to plan, elevation, section, and 3D views.

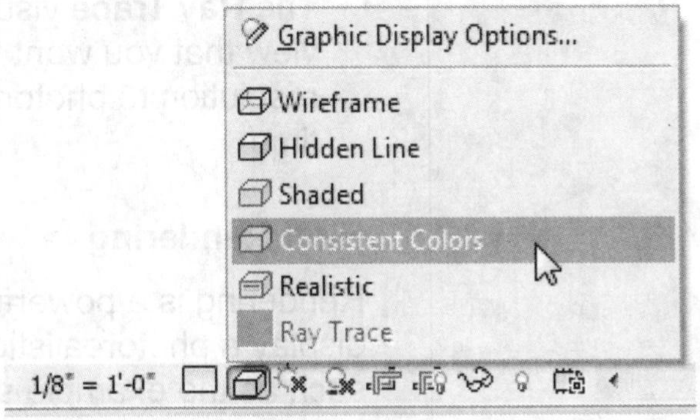

Graphic Display Options...

Wireframe
Hidden Line
Shaded
Consistent Colors
Realistic
Ray Trace

1/8" = 1'-0"

Figure 1–52

The **Wireframe** visual style displays the lines and edges that form elements, but hides the surfaces. This can be useful when you are dealing with complex intersections.

The **Hidden Line** visual style displays the lines, edges, and surfaces of the elements, but it does not display any colors. This is the most common visual style to use while working on a design.

The **Shaded** and **Consistent Colors** visual styles give you a sense of the materials, including transparent glass, as shown in Figure 1–53.

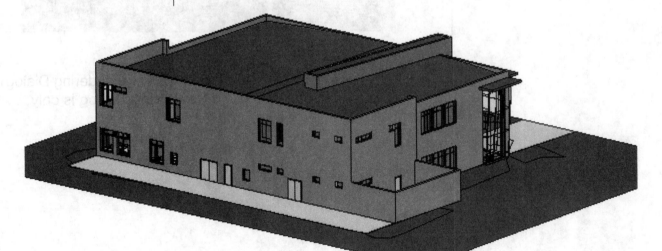

Figure 1–53

- The **Realistic** visual style displays what is shown when you render the view, including RPC (Rich Photographic Content) components and artificial lights. It takes a lot of computer power to execute this visual style. Therefore, it is better to use the other visual styles most of the time as you are working.

- The **Ray Trace** visual style is useful if you have created a 3D view that you want to render. It gradually moves from draft resolution to photorealistic. You can stop the process at any time.

Hint: Rendering

Rendering is a powerful tool in BIM which enables you to display a photorealistic view of the model you are working on, such as the example shown in Figure 1–54. This can be used to help clients and designers to understand a building's design in better detail.

Figure 1–54

- In the View Control Bar, click  (Show Rendering Dialog) to set up the options. **Show Rendering Dialog** is only available in 3D views.

Practice 1a | Open and Review a Project

Learning Objectives

- Navigate the graphic user interface.
- Manipulate 2D and 3D views by zooming and panning.
- Create 3D Isometric and Perspective views.
- Set the Visual Style of a view.

Estimated time for completion: 15 minutes

In this practice you will open a project file and display each of the various parts of the Autodesk Revit MEP interface as shown in Figure 1–55. You will open views through the Project Browser, and switch between different views. You will also select elements and display the information about them in the Properties palette. Finally you will create and save 3D views.

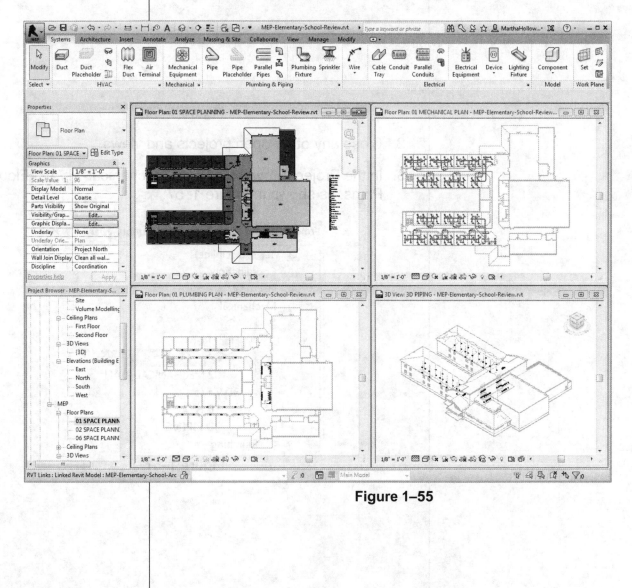

Figure 1–55

Task 1 - Open an Autodesk Revit MEP project and review it.

1. In the *C:\Autodesk Revit 2015 MEP Fundamentals Class Files\Introduction* folder, open **MEP-Elementary-School-Review.rvt**. The project opens in the **3D PIPING** view, as shown in Figure 1–56.

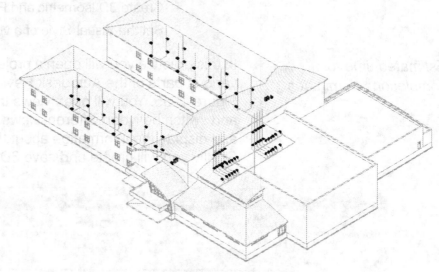

Figure 1–56

2. Close any other open projects and views.

3. In the Project Browser, expand Mechanical>HVAC>Floor Plans, as shown in Figure 1–57.

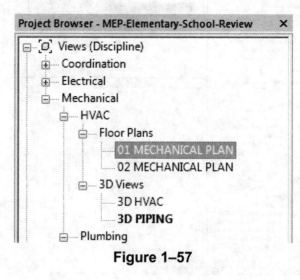

Figure 1–57

4. Double-click on **01 MECHANICAL PLAN**. The applicable view opens as shown in Figure 1–58.

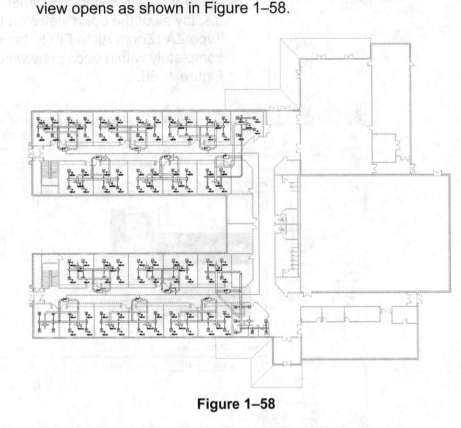

Figure 1–58

5. Use the scroll wheel to zoom and pan around the view.

6. Double-click on the scroll wheel or type **ZF** (Zoom to Fit) to return to the full view.

7. Expand Mechanical>Plumbing>*Floor Plans*. Double-click on the **01 PLUMBING PLAN** view to open it.

8. Expand Coordination>MEP>*Floor Plans*. Double-click on **01 SPACE PLANNING** to open this view.

9. All of the previous views are still open. In the Quick Access

Toolbar (or *View* tab>Windows panel), expand 🗗 (Switch Windows), as shown in Figure 1–59, and select one of the previous views to which to switch.

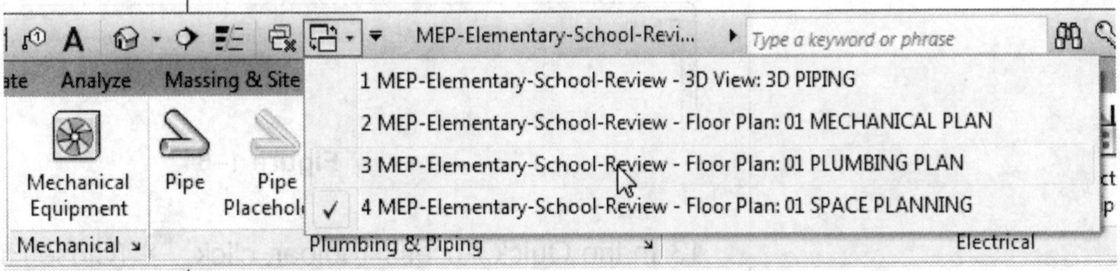

| 1 MEP-Elementary-School-Review - 3D View: 3D PIPING |
| 2 MEP-Elementary-School-Review - Floor Plan: 01 MECHANICAL PLAN |
| 3 MEP-Elementary-School-Review - Floor Plan: 01 PLUMBING PLAN |
| ✓ 4 MEP-Elementary-School-Review - Floor Plan: 01 SPACE PLANNING |

Figure 1–59

10. In the *View* tab>Windows panel, click ⊟ (Tile) or type **WT** to display all of the open views on the screen at the same time. Type **ZA** (Zoom All to Fit) to have the model display completely within each view window, as shown in Figure 1–60.

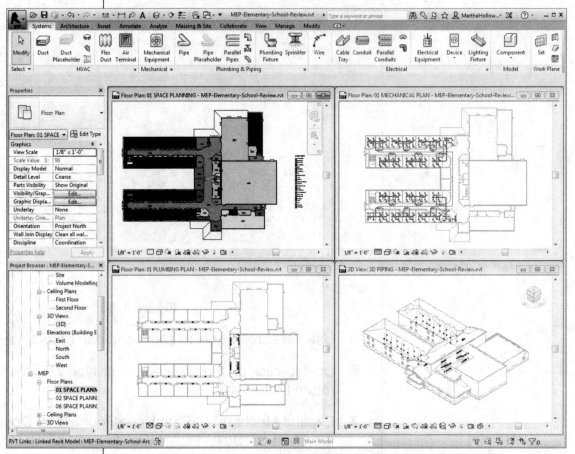

Figure 1–60

11. Click in the open **01 MECHANICAL PLAN** view to make it active.

12. In the upper left corner, click ▣ (Maximize), as shown in Figure 1–61, so that this view fills the drawing area. Then use one of the zoom commands so that the model fills the view.

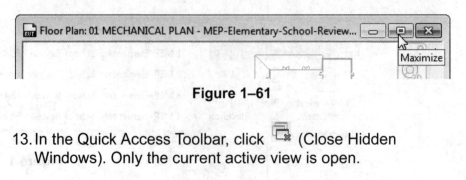

Figure 1–61

13. In the Quick Access Toolbar, click 🗗 (Close Hidden Windows). Only the current active view is open.

Task 2 - Display the Element Properties.

1. In the **01 MECHANICAL PLAN** view, hover over a duct without selecting it first. The duct highlights and a tooltip displays as shown in Figure 1–62. Information about the element also displays in the Status Bar but not in Properties.

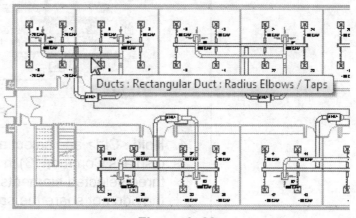

Figure 1–62

2. Click on the duct to select it. The selection color and Ribbon tabs at the top of the screen change. Properties now displays information about this piece of ductwork, as shown in Figure 1–63.

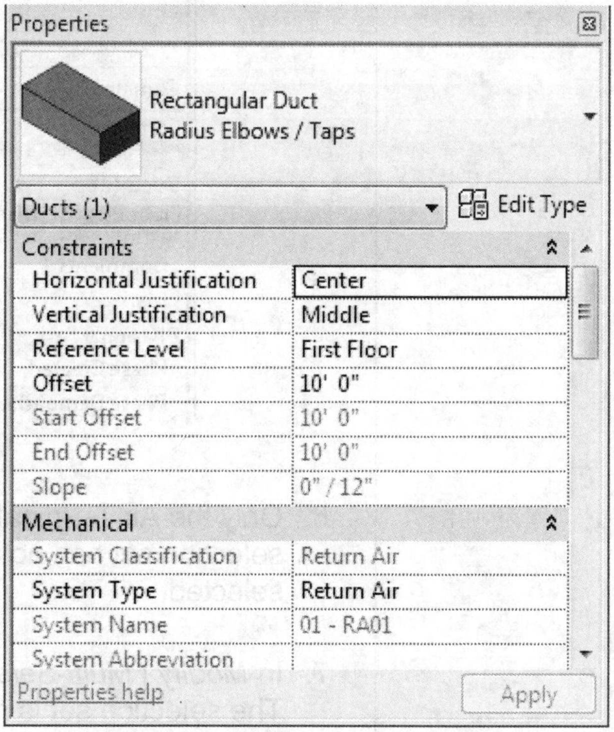

Figure 1–63

3. Hold <Ctrl> and in the view, select another, similar Duct element, as shown in Figure 1–64. Properties now displays that two ducts (Ducts(2)) are selected with the same information.

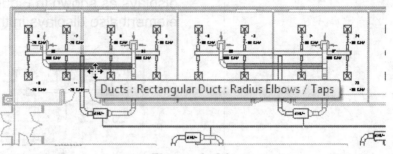

Figure 1–64

4. Hold <Ctrl> and select an air terminal. Properties now displays Common (3) in the Filter drop-down list, because the three selected elements are not of the same type. Therefore they do not share the same type of properties.

5. In Properties, expand the Filter drop-down list and select **Air Terminals**, as shown in Figure 1–65.

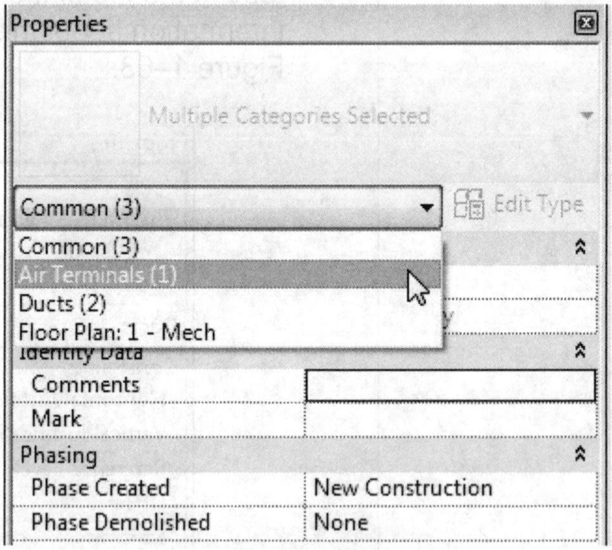

Figure 1–65

6. Only the Air Terminal properties are displayed, but the selection set has not changed. In the view they are all still selected.

7. In *Modify | Multi-Select* tab>Select panel, click (Modify). The selection set is released. You can also press <Esc> twice or click in the drawing window without selecting an element to clear the selected objects.

Task 3 - Create 3D Views.

1. In the Quick Access Toolbar, click 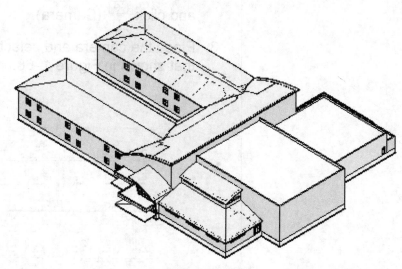 (Default 3D View).

2. A **3D Isometric** view displays, as shown in Figure 1–66.

Figure 1–66

3. Press and hold <Shift> and press the middle mouse (scroll) button to orbit the view.

4. In the View Control Bar, select several different Visual Styles to see how they impact the view, as shown in Figure 1–67.

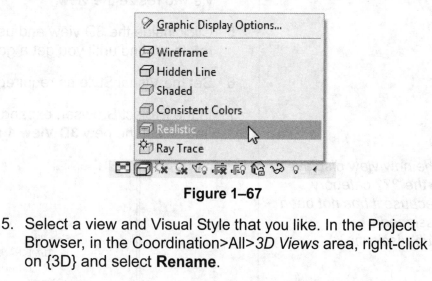

Graphic Display Options...

- Wireframe
- Hidden Line
- Shaded
- Consistent Colors
- Realistic
- Ray Trace

Figure 1–67

5. Select a view and Visual Style that you like. In the Project Browser, in the Coordination>All>*3D Views* area, right-click on {3D} and select **Rename**.

6. Name the view as required and click ⌷ OK ⌷.

Task 4 - Create a Camera View.

1. Switch back to the **01 Mechanical Plan** view.

2. In the Quick Access Toolbar, expand ⌂ (Default 3D View) and click 📷 (Camera).

3. Place the camera and select a point for the target similar to that shown in Figure 1–68.

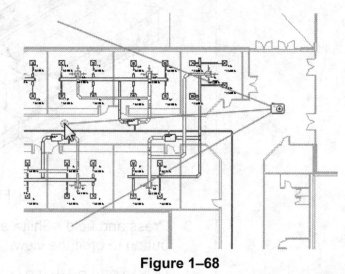

Figure 1–68

4. The new view displays. Use the controls on the outline of the view to resize the view.

5. Click inside the 3D view and use <Shift>+ mouse wheel to rotate around until you get a good view of the ductwork.

6. Set the Visual Style as required.

7. In the Project Browser, expand Mechanical>???>*3D Views* and select the new **3D View 1** as shown in Figure 1–69.

The new view displays in the ??? category because it has not been assigned a Sub-discipline.

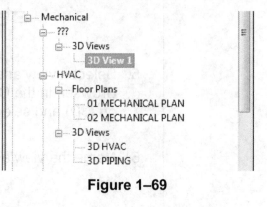

Figure 1–69

8. In Properties, in the *Graphics* area, expand Sub-Discipline and select **HVAC** as shown in Figure 1–70.

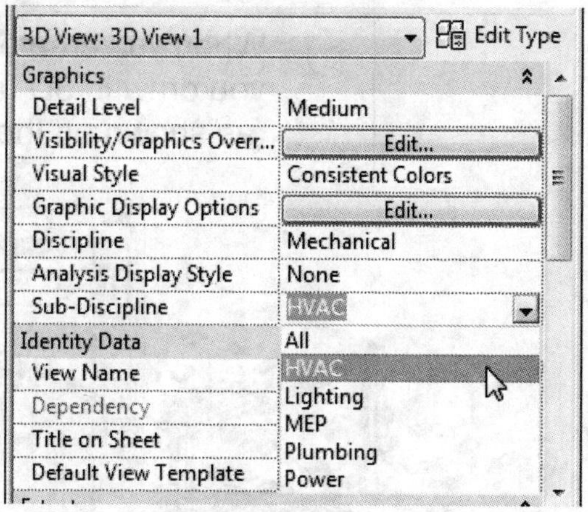

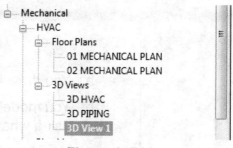

Figure 1–70

9. Click . The view moves to the correct sub-discipline group as shown in Figure 1–71. Rename the view as required.

```
⊟── Mechanical
   ⊟── HVAC
      ⊟── Floor Plans
          ──── 01 MECHANICAL PLAN
          ──── 02 MECHANICAL PLAN
      ⊟── 3D Views
          ──── 3D HVAC
          ──── 3D PIPING
          ──── 3D View 1
```

Figure 1–71

10. Save the project.

11. In the Application Menu, click (Close).

Chapter Review Questions

1. When you create a project in the Autodesk Revit software, do you draw in 3D (as shown on the left in Figure 1–72) or 2D (as shown on the right in Figure 1–72)?

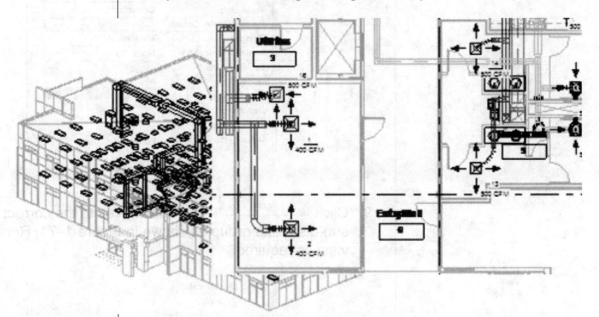

Figure 1–72

   a. You draw in 2D in plan views and in 3D in non-plan views.

   b. You model in 3D almost all of the time, even when you are using what looks like a flat view.

   c. You draw in 2D or 3D depending on how you toggle the 2D/3D control.

   d. You draw in 2D in plan and section views and model in 3D in isometric views.

2. What is the purpose of the Project Browser?

   a. It enables you to browse through the building project, similar to a walk through.

   b. It is the interface for managing all of the files that are needed to create the complete architectural model of the building.

   c. It manages multiple Autodesk Revit projects as an alternative to using Windows Explorer.

   d. It is used to access and manage the views of the project.

3. Which part(s) of the interface changes according to the command you are using?

   a. Ribbon

   b. View Control Bar

   c. Options Bar

   d. Properties Palette

4. The difference between Type Properties and Properties (the Ribbon location is shown in Figure 1–73) is...

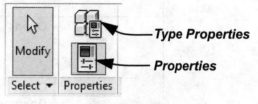

Figure 1–73

   a. Properties stores parameters that apply to the selected individual element(s). Type Properties stores parameters that impact every element of the same type in the project.

   b. Properties stores the location parameters of an element. Type Properties stores the size and identity parameters of an element.

   c. Properties only stores parameters of the view. Type Properties stores parameters of model components.

5. When you start a new project, how do you specify the base information in the new file?

   a. Transfer the base information from an existing project.

   b. Select the right template for the task.

   c. The Autodesk Revit software automatically extracts the base information from imported or linked file(s).

6. What is the main difference between a view made using (3D View) and a view made using (Camera)?

   a. Use **3D View** for exterior views and **Camera** for interiors.

   b. **3D View** creates a static image and a **Camera** view is live and always updated.

   c. **3D View** is isometric and a **Camera** view is perspective.

   d. **3D View** is used for the overall building and a **Camera** view is used for looking in tight spaces.

Command Summary

Button	Command	Location
General Tools		
	Modify	• **Quick Access Toolbar** • **Ribbon:** All tabs>Select panel • **Shortcut:** <M> and <D>
	New	• **Quick Access Toolbar** (Optional) • **Application Menu** • **Shortcut:** <Ctrl>+<N>
	Open	• **Quick Access Toolbar** • **Application Menu** • **Shortcut:** <Ctrl>+<O>
	Open Documents	• **Application Menu**
	Properties	• **Ribbon:** *Modify* tab>Properties panel • **Shortcut:** <P> and <P>
	Recent Documents	• **Application Menu**
	Save	• **Quick Access Toolbar** • **Application Menu** • **Shortcut:** <Ctrl>+<S>
	Synchronize and Modify Settings	• **Quick Access Toolbar**
	Synchronize Now/	• **Quick Access Toolbar**>expand Synchronize and Modify Settings
	Type Properties	• **Ribbon:** *Modify* tab>Properties panel • **Properties Palette**
Viewing Tools		
	Camera	• **Quick Access Toolbar**> Expand Default 3D View • **Ribbon:** *View* tab>Create panel> expand Default 3D View
	Default 3D View	• **Quick Access Toolbar** • **Ribbon:** *View* tab>Create panel
	Home	• **ViewCube**
N/A	Next Pan/Zoom	• **Navigation Bar** • **Shortcut Menu**
N/A	Previous Pan/Zoom	• **Navigation Bar** • **Shortcut Menu** • **Shortcut:** <Z> and <P>

Icon	Command	Access
	Shadows On/Off	• **View Control Bar**
	Zoom All to Fit	• **Navigation Bar** • **Shortcut:** <Z> and <A>
	Zoom In Region	• **Navigation Bar** • **Shortcut Menu** • **Shortcut:** <Z> and <R>
	Zoom Out 2x	• **Navigation Bar** • **Shortcut Menu** • **Shortcut:** <Z> and <O>
	Zoom Sheet Size	• **Navigation Bar** • **Shortcut:** <Z> and <S>
	Zoom to Fit	• **Navigation Bar** • **Shortcut Menu** • **Shortcut:** <Z> and <F>, <Z> and <E>
	Show Rendering Dialog/ Render	• **View Control Bar** • **Ribbon:** *View* tab>Graphics panel • **Shortcut:** <R> and <R>

Visual Styles

Icon	Command	Access
	Consistent Colors	• **View Control Bar:**
	Hidden Line	• **View Control Bar** • **Shortcut:** <H> and <L>
	Ray Trace	• **View Control Bar:**
	Realistic	• **View Control Bar**
	Shaded	• **View Control Bar** • **Shortcut:** <S> and <D>
	Wireframe	• **View Control Bar** • **Shortcut:** <W> and <F>

Chapter 2

Basic Drawing and Modify Tools

In this chapter you learn how to use the basic drawing and modify tools that apply to almost all types of elements. These tools include alignment lines, temporary dimensions, snaps, and the Properties palette. You learn how to select elements for editing and how to move, copy, rotate, mirror, and array them. You also learn to align, split, trim, extend, and offset elements.

This chapter contains the following topics:

- **Using General Drawing Tools**
- **Editing Elements**
- **Working with Basic Modify Tools**
- **Working with Additional Modify Tools**

2.1 Using General Drawing Tools

 Learning Objectives

- Use contextual Ribbon tabs, the Options Bar and Properties as you draw and modify.
- Draw elements using draw and pick tools.
- Use drawing aids including alignment lines, temporary dimensions and snaps.

When you start a command, the contextual Ribbon tab, Options Bar, and Properties palette enable you to set up features for each new element you are placing in the project. As you are drawing, several features called *drawing aids* display, as shown in Figure 2–1. They help you to create designs quickly and accurately.

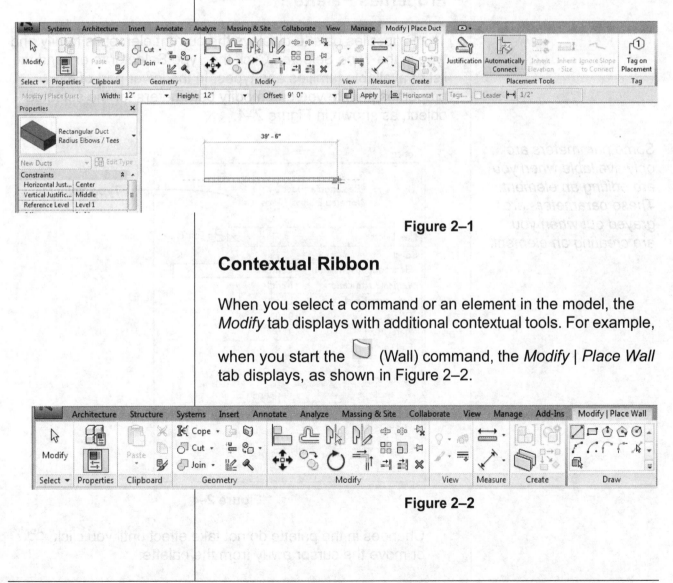

Figure 2–1

Contextual Ribbon

When you select a command or an element in the model, the *Modify* tab displays with additional contextual tools. For example, when you start the (Wall) command, the *Modify | Place Wall* tab displays, as shown in Figure 2–2.

Figure 2–2

- The standard Modify tools are always displayed to the left in the ribbon, while the contextual tools are displayed to the right with a green panel title.

- To finish a command and return to the standard ribbon tabs at any time, in the *Select* panel, click ⌖ (Modify).

Options Bar

The Options Bar, located just below the ribbon, displays the most used options for the element, as shown in Figure 2–3. Some of these options are also found in the Properties palette.

| Modify | Place Wall | Height ▾ Unconi ▾ | 20' 0" | | Location Line: Wall Centerline ▾ | ☑ Chain | Offset: 0' 0" | | ☐ Radius: 1' 0" |

Figure 2–3

Properties Palette

The Properties palette displays the current element's family and type in the *Type Selector*. Click the Type Selector to expand the list of available families and types. In the lower part of the properties palette you can modify parameters for the selected object, as shown in Figure 2–4.

Some parameters are only available when you are editing an element. These parameters are grayed out when you are creating an element.

Properties	
	Rectangular Duct — *Type Selector*
	Mitered Elbows / Taps
New Ducts	▾ 🔲 Edit Type
Constraints	▴
Horizontal Justification	Center
Vertical Justification	Middle
Reference Level	Level 1
Offset	9' 0"
Start Offset	9' 0"
End Offset	9' 0"
Slope	0" / 12"
Mechanical	▴
System Type	Undefined
System Name	
Bottom Elevation	8' 8"
Top Elevation	9' 4"
Equivalent Diameter	9.105/256"
Properties help	Apply

Figure 2–4

- Changes in the palette do not take effect until you click Apply or move the cursor away from the palette.

- The Properties palette can be floated and moved around the interface. You can also dock it on top of other browsers and then switch between them using the tabs at the bottom of the palette, as shown in Figure 2–5.

To dock the palette, drag the titlebar over the titlebar of the other browser.

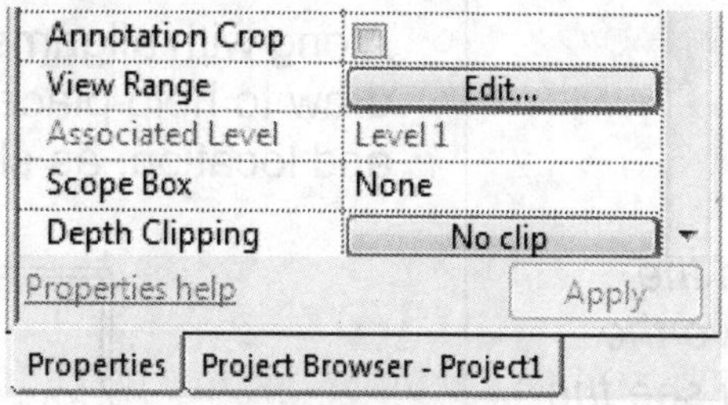

Annotation Crop	☐
View Range	Edit...
Associated Level	Level 1
Scope Box	None
Depth Clipping	No clip
Properties help	Apply
Properties	Project Browser - Project1

Figure 2–5

The Properties palette can be toggled on and off using the following methods:

- Right-click and select **Properties** in the contextual menu.

- In the *Modify* tab>Properties panel click ⬚ (Properties).

- In the *View* tab, expand ⬚ (User Interface), and select **Properties**.

- Use the shortcut by pressing <P> twice.

Drawing Aids

As soon as you start drawing in the software, three drawing aids display: *alignment lines*, *temporary dimensions*, and *snaps*. These are available with most drawing and many modification commands.

Alignment Lines

Dashed *alignment lines* display as soon as you select your first point, as shown in Figure 2–6. They help keep lines horizontal, vertical, or at a specified angle. They also line up with the implied intersections of walls and other elements.

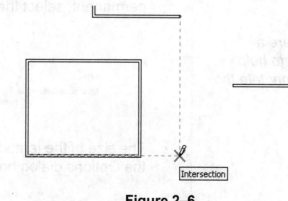

Intersection

Figure 2–6

• Hold <Shift> to force the alignments to be orthogonal (90 degree angles only).

Temporary Dimensions

Along with alignment lines, *temporary dimensions* display as you draw to help place linear elements at the correct length, angle and location, as shown in Figure 2–7.

You can type in the dimension, move the cursor until you see the dimension you want, or place the element and then modify the dimension as required.

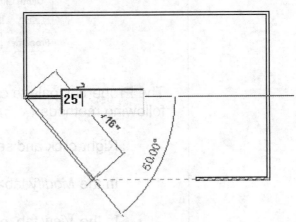

Figure 2–7

• For Imperial measurements (feet and inches), the software understands a default of feet. For example, when you type **4** and press <Enter>, it assumes 4'-0".For a distance such as 4'-6", you can type any of the following: **4'-6", 4'6, 4-6, or 4 6** (the numbers separated by a space). To indicate distances less that one foot, type the inch mark (") after the distance, or enter **0**, a space, and then the distance.

• The increments displayed for temporary dimensions change as you zoom in or out on the elements. These *dimension snap* increments are for both linear and angular dimensions, and can be set in the Snaps dialog box.

• Temporary dimensions disappear as soon as you finish drawing linear elements. If you want to make them permanent, select the control shown in Figure 2–8.

Dimensions are a powerful tool to help create and annotate the model.

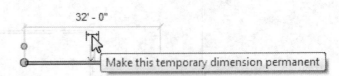

Figure 2–8

• The size of the temporary dimensions, in pixels, can be set in the Options dialog box on the *Graphics* tab.

Snaps

Snaps are key points that help you reference existing elements to exact points when drawing, as shown in Figure 2–9.

Endpoint

Figure 2–9

They include *Endpoints*, *Midpoints*, *Nearest*, *Work Plane Grid*, *Quadrants*, *Intersections*, *Centers*, *Perpendicular*, *Tangents*, and *Points*. When you move the cursor over an element, the **Snap** symbol displays. Each snap location type displays with a different symbol.

- To modify the snap settings, in the *Manage* tab>Settings panel, click 🧲 (Snaps). This opens the Snaps dialog box, where you can set which snap points are active, as well as the snap distances (for dimension and angular increments). It also displays the keyboard shortcuts for each snap, which you can use to override the automatic snapping.

> **Hint: Snap Overrides**
>
> You can use shortcut key combinations (displayed in the Snaps dialog box) or right-click and select **Snap Overrides** to temporarily override snap settings. Temporary overrides only affect a single pick but can be very helpful when there are snaps nearby other than the one you want to use.

Reference Planes

As you develop designs in Autodesk Revit, there are times when you need lines that don't print to help you define certain locations. You can draw *reference planes* (displayed as dashed green lines) to host the height of sinks or to help you define the centerlines and paths for ductwork, as shown in Figure 2–10.

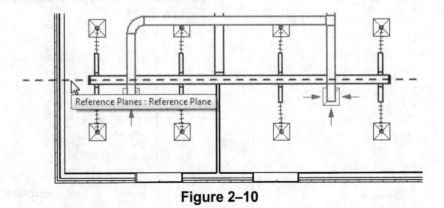

Figure 2–10

- Reference lines display in associated views because they are infinite planes, and not just lines. However, reference planes do not display in 3D views.

How To: Sketch with Reference Planes

1. In the *Architecture* tab>Work Plane panel, click ✎ (Ref Plane) or use the shortcut by pressing <R> and then pressing <P>.
2. In the *Modify | Place Reference Plane* tab>Draw panel, click ✎ (Line) or ✎ (Pick Lines).

   - For ✎ (Line), select two points that define the reference plane.

   - For ✎ (Pick Lines), select any linear element and a reference plane is created that matches the length of that element.

   - In the Options Bar, the *Offset* field enables you to enter values to draw the reference plane at a specified distance from a selected point. For example, set *Offset* to **10'-0"** and select the end points of an existing wall to create a reference plane 10'-0" away. You can also use *Offset* with **Pick Lines**.

3. When you have created all of the required reference planes, end the command by clicking ↳ (Modify) or by using one of the other options.

   - To change the length of a reference plane, drag the circle at either end.

   - You can name reference planes to keep track of their purpose. This also enables you to use a reference plane as a work plane when creating or placing other elements in the project. Select the reference plane and in the Properties palette, in the *Identity Data* area, enter a name, as shown in Figure 2–11.

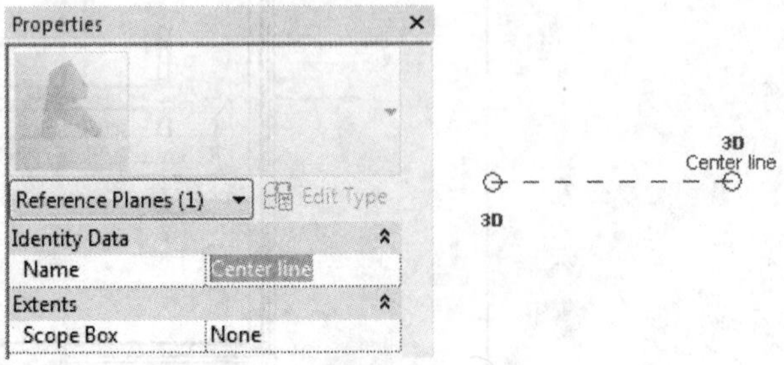

Figure 2–11

Draw Tools

MEP tools (i.e., ducts, pipes, and conduits) are strictly straight, linear elements that are automatically connected to elbows or tees. However, if you are working with walls (as shown in Figure 2–12) or lines used in details, legends, and schematic drawings, additional tools are available. These tools display in the contextual Ribbon, and vary according to the element being drawn.

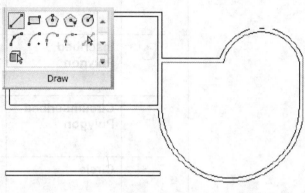

Figure 2–12

- Two styles of tools are available: one where you *draw* the element using a geometric form, and another where you *pick* an existing element (such as a line, face, or wall) as the basis for the new element's geometry.

How To: Draw Linear Elements

1. Start the command you want to use, such as ▢ (Wall).
2. In the contextual tab>Draw panel, select a drawing tool, such as ✎ (Line), as shown in Figure 2–13. Select points to define the elements using other drawing aids, such as temporary dimensions, alignment lines, and snaps.

Figure 2–13

You can change from one Draw tool shape in the middle of a command.

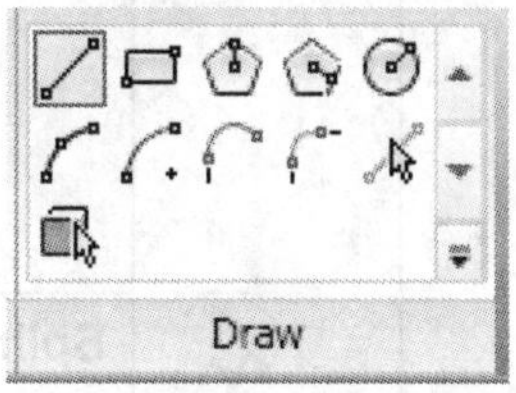

- Use ⬚ (Pick Lines) to create an element by selecting an existing wall, line or edge. This is often used with an offset distance to add the element a specified distance away from the selected element.

⬚ *(Pick Face) is used with conceptual mass elements and is only available in a 3D view.*

3. Finish the command. You can click ⬚ (Modify), press <Esc> twice, or right-click and select **Cancel** twice.

Draw Tools

⟋	**Line**	Draws a straight linear element defined by the first and last points. If Chain is enabled, you can continue selecting end points for multiple segments.
▱	**Rectangle**	Draws four linear elements defined from two opposing corner points. You can adjust the dimensions after selecting both points.
⬠	**Inscribed Polygon**	Draws a polygon inscribed in a hypothetical circle with the number of sides specified in the Options Bar.
⬠	**Circumscribed Polygon**	Draws a polygon circumscribed around a hypothetical circle with the number of sides specified in the Options Bar.
⊙	**Circle**	Draws a circular linear element defined by a center point and radius.
⌒	**Start-End-Radius Arc**	Draws a curved linear element defined by a start, end, and radius of the arc. The outside dimension shown is the included angle of the arc. The inside dimension is the radius.
⌒	**Center-ends Arc**	Draws a curved linear element defined by a center, radius, and included angle. The selected point of the radius also defines the start point of the arc.
⌒	**Tangent End Arc**	Draws a curved linear element tangent to another element. Select an end point for the first point, but do not select the intersection of two or more elements. Then select a second point based on the included angle of the arc.
⌒	**Fillet Arc**	Draws a curved linear element defined by two other linear elements and a radius. Because it is difficult to select the correct radius by clicking, this command automatically moves to edit mode. Select the dimension and then modify the radius of the fillet.
∿	**Spline**	Draws a curved linear element based on selected points. The curve does not actually touch the points (Model and Detail Lines only).
⬭	**Ellipse**	Draws an ellipse from a primary and secondary axis (Model and Detail Lines only).
⌒	**Partial Ellipse**	Draws only one side of the ellipse, like an arc. A partial ellipse also has a primary and secondary axis (Model and Detail Lines only).

Pick Tools

	Pick Lines	Use this option to select existing linear elements in the project. This is useful when you start the project from an imported 2D drawing.
	Pick Face	Use this option to select the face of a 3D massing element (walls and 3D views only).
	Pick Walls	Use this option to select an existing wall in the project to be the basis for a new sketch line (floors, ceilings, etc.).

Draw Options

When you are in Drawing mode, several options display in the Options Bar, as shown in Figure 2–14.

☑ Chain   Offset: 0' 0"   ☐ Radius: 1' 0"

Figure 2–14

- The **Chain** option controls how many segments are drawn in one process. If it is not selected, the **Line** and **Arc** tools only draw one segment at a time. If it is selected, you can continue drawing segments until you select the command again.

- The *Offset* field enables you to enter values to draw the linear elements at a specified distance from the selected points.

- When using a radial draw tool, you can select the **Radius** option and add a radius in the edit field.

- To draw angled lines, move the cursor to the desired angle shown by the temporary dimensions, and type the distance value. The angle increments shown vary depending on how far in or out the view is zoomed.

Different options display according to the type of element that is selected, or the command that is active.

2.2 Editing Elements

 Learning Objectives

- Select elements to modify.
- Modify elements using the Ribbon, Properties, temporary dimensions, and controls.
- Filter selection sets.

Building design projects typically involve extensive changes to the positions of walls, doors, and other elements. The Autodesk Revit software was designed to make such changes quickly and efficiently. When you select an element there are a number of ways to change it, as shown in Figure 2–15:

When you hover the cursor over an element, a tooltip displays its family and type.

- *Controls* enable you to drag, flip, lock, and rotate the element.
- *Temporary dimensions* enable you to change the element's dimensions.
- Modify commands and element-specific tools display in the contextual tab in the Ribbon.
- The Properties palette displays the Type Selector and associated parameters.

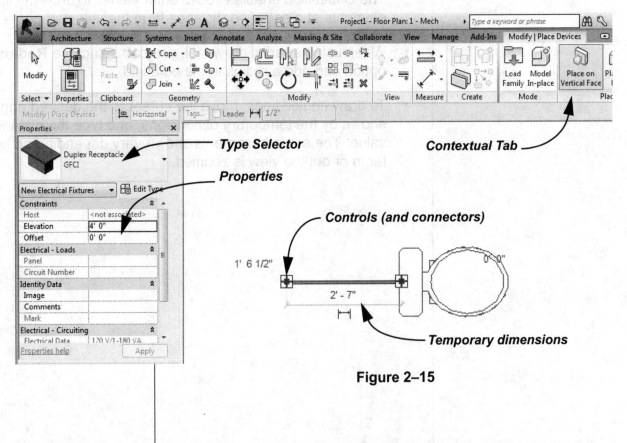

Figure 2–15

- Connectors are frequently linked to controls. When a control is moved, the connector is moved with it. You should not disconnect systems when moving a control.

- To delete an element, select it and press <Delete>, right-click and select **Delete**, or in the Modify panel, click ✖ (Delete).

- When working with temporary dimensions, the default location of the dimension line might not be where you need it to be. You can click on the circular control to move the witness line to another part of the element (such as a different layer in a multilayer wall), or drag it to a new element. In the example shown on the left in Figure 2–16, the dimension is from the center of the left wall to the selected wall. To change the dimension so that it touches the grid line, drag the circular control (also called the witness line) so that it touches the grid line, as shown on the right in Figure 2–16.

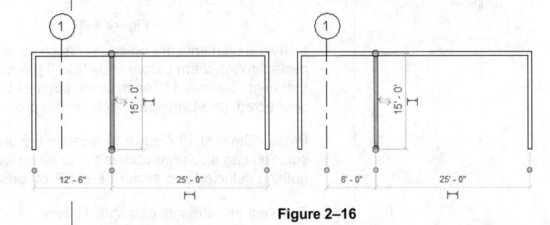

Figure 2–16

- The new location of a temporary dimension for an element is remembered as long as you are in the same session of the software.

Hint: Nudge

Nudge enables you to move an element in short increments. When an element is selected, you can press one of the four arrow keys to move the element in that direction. The distance the element moves depends on how far in or out you are zoomed. This is very useful with annotation elements.

Selecting Elements

You can select elements in several ways:

- To select a single element, place the cursor on the edge of the element and click to select.

- To add another element to a selection set, hold <Ctrl> and select another item.

- To remove an element from a selection set, hold <Shift> and select the element.

- If you click and drag the cursor to *window* around elements, you have two selection options, as shown in Figure 2–17. If you drag from left to right, you only select the elements completely inside the window. If you drag from right to left, you select elements both inside and crossing the window.

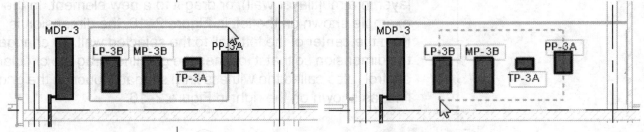

Figure 2–17

- If several elements are on or near each other, press <Tab> to cycle through them before you click. If there are elements that might be linked to each other, such as walls that are connected, pressing <Tab> selects the chain of elements.

- Press <Ctrl>+<Left Arrow> to reselect the previous selection set. You can also right-click in the drawing window with nothing selected and select **Select Previous**.

- To select all elements of a specific type, right-click on an element and select **Select All Instances>Visible in View** or **In Entire Project**, as shown in Figure 2–18.

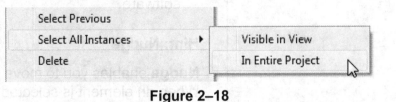

Figure 2–18

Hint: Selection Options

You can control how the software selects specific elements in a project by toggling them on and off on Status Bar, or in any Ribbon tab expand the *Select* panel's title as shown in Figure 2–19.

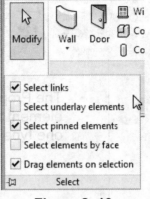

Figure 2–19

- **Select links:** When toggled on, you can selected linked drawings or Autodesk Revit models. When it is toggled off you cannot select them when using **Modify** or **Move**.

- **Select underlay elements:** When toggled on, you can select underlay elements. When toggled off, you cannot select them when using **Modify** or **Move**.

- **Select pinned elements:** When toggled on, you can selected pinned elements. When toggled off, you cannot select them when using **Modify** or **Move**.

- **Select elements by face:** When toggled on you can select elements (such as the floors or walls in an elevation) by selecting the interior face or selecting an edge. When toggled off, you can only select elements by selecting an edge.

- **Drag elements on selection:** When toggled on, you can hover over an element, select it, and drag it to a new location. When toggled off, the Crossing or Box select mode starts when you press and drag, even if you are on top of an element. Once elements have been selected they can still be dragged to a new location.

Selecting Multiple Elements

When multiple element types are selected, the *Multi-Select* contextual tab opens in the Ribbon, as shown in Figure 2–20. This gives you access to all of the Modify tools, as well as the **Filter** command.

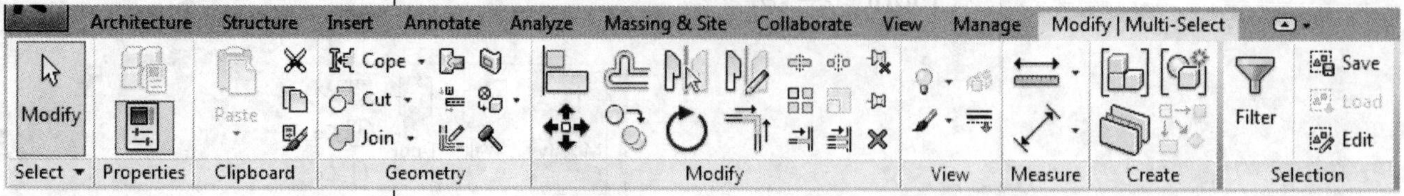

Figure 2–20

- The Properties palette displays tools that are common to all element types if they are available. You can also select just one type and make modifications, as shown in Figure 2–21.

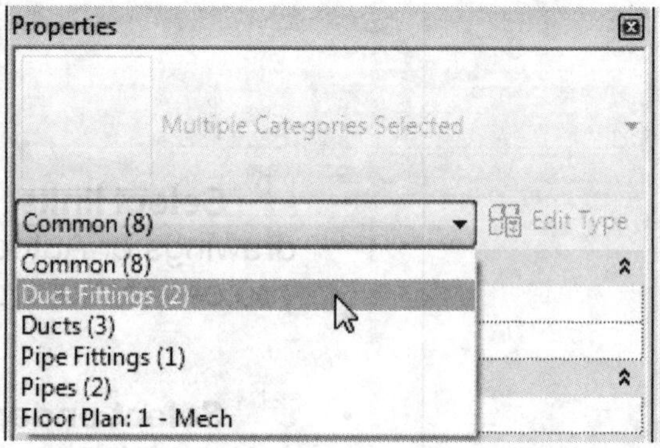

Figure 2–21

Filtering Selection Sets

The **Filter** command enables you to specify the types of elements to select. For example, you might only want to select lighting fixtures, as shown in Figure 2–22.

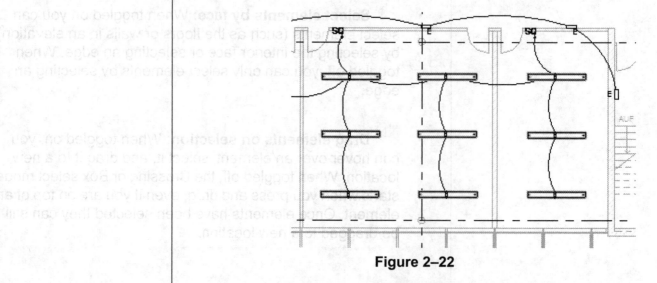

Figure 2–22

How To: Filter a Selection Set

1. Select everything in the required area.
2. in the *Modify | Multi-Select* tab>Selection panel, or in the Status Bar, click ⛛ (Filter). The Filter dialog box opens, as shown in Figure 2–23.

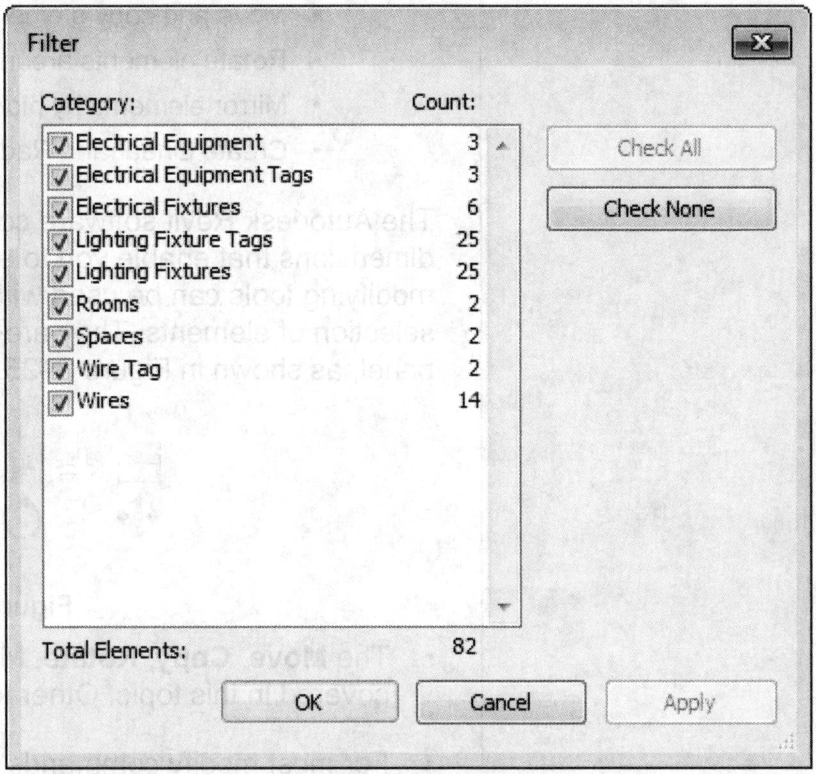

The Filter dialog box displays all types of elements in the original selection.

Category:	Count:	
☑ Electrical Equipment	3	Check All
☑ Electrical Equipment Tags	3	
☑ Electrical Fixtures	6	Check None
☑ Lighting Fixture Tags	25	
☑ Lighting Fixtures	25	
☑ Rooms	2	
☑ Spaces	2	
☑ Wire Tag	2	
☑ Wires	14	

Total Elements: 82

OK   Cancel   Apply

Figure 2–23

3. Click [Check None] to clear all of the options and then select the element types that you want included in the selection.

4. Click [OK]. The selection set is now limited to the elements you specified.

- In the Status Bar, the number of elements selected displays beside the Filter icon, as shown in Figure 2–24. You can also see the number of selected elements in the Properties palette.

Figure 2–24

2.3 Working with Basic Modify Tools

 Learning Objectives

- Move and copy elements.
- Rotate elements around the center or an origin.
- Mirror elements by picking an axis or by drawing an axis.
- Create Linear and Radial Arrays of elements.

The Autodesk Revit software contains controls and temporary dimensions that enable you to edit elements. Additional modifying tools can be used with individual elements or any selection of elements. They are found in the *Modify* tab>Modify panel, as shown in Figure 2–25, and in contextual tabs.

Figure 2–25

- The **Move**, **Copy**, **Rotate**, **Mirror**, and **Array** commands are covered in this topic. Other tools are covered later.

- For most modify commands, you can either select the elements and start the command, or start the command, select the elements, and press <Enter> to finish the selection and move to the next step in the command.

Moving and Copying Elements

The **Move** and **Copy** commands enable you to select the element(s) and move or copy them from one place to another. You can use alignment lines, temporary dimensions, and snaps to help place the elements, as shown in Figure 2–26.

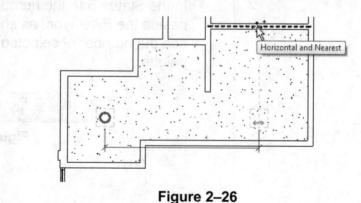

Figure 2–26

How To: Move or Copy Elements

1. Select the elements you want to move or copy.
2. In the Modify panel, click ✛ (Move) or ⟳ (Copy). A boundary box displays around the selected elements.
3. Select a move start point on or near the element.
4. Select a second point. Use alignment lines and temporary dimensions to help place the elements.
5. When you are finished, you can start another modify command using the elements that remain selected, or switch back to **Modify** to end the command.

* If you start the **Move** command and hold <Ctrl>, the elements are copied.

*You can also use the shortcut for the **Move** command by pressing <M> and pressing <V>, or for the **Copy** command by pressing <C> and pressing <O>.*

Move/Copy Elements

The **Move** and **Copy** commands have several options that display in the Options Bar, as shown in Figure 2–27.

☐ Constrain   ☐ Disjoin   ☐ Multiple

Figure 2–27

Constrain	Restricts the movement of the cursor to horizontal or vertical, or along the axis of an item that is at an angle. This keeps you from selecting a point at an angle by mistake. **Constrain** is off by default.
Disjoin (Move only)	Breaks any connections between the elements being moved and other elements. If **Disjoin** is on, the elements move separately. If it is off, the connected elements also move or stretch. **Disjoin** is off by default.
Multiple (Copy only)	Enables you to make multiple copies of one selection. **Multiple** is off by default.

* These commands only work within the current view, not between views or projects. To copy between views or projects, use 🗐 (Copy to Clipboard) and 📋 (Paste).

Hint: Pinning Elements

If you do not want elements to be moved, you can pin them in place, as shown in Figure 2–28. Select the elements and in the

Modify tab, in the Modify panel, click <img> (Pin). Pinned elements can be copied, but not moved. If you try to delete a pinned element, a warning dialog displays reminding you that you must unpin the element before the command can be started.

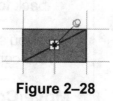

Figure 2–28

Select the element and click <img> (Unpin) or use the shortcut by pressing <U> and pressing <P> to free it.

Rotating Elements

The **Rotate** command enables you to rotate selected elements around a center point or origin. You can use alignment lines, temporary dimensions, and snaps to help specify the center of rotation and the angle. You can also create copies of the element as it is being rotated.

How To: Rotate Elements

1. Select the element(s) you want to rotate.

2. In the Modify panel, click ○ (Rotate) or use the shortcut by pressing <R> and pressing <O>.

3. The center of rotation is automatically set to the center of the element or group of elements, as shown on the left in Figure 2–29. To change the center of rotation, as shown on the right in Figure 2–29, use the following:

   - Drag the ○ (Center of Rotation) control to a new point.

   - In the Options Bar, next to **Center of rotation**, click `Place` and use snaps to move it to a new location.

   - Press the <Spacebar> to select the center of rotation and click to move it to a new location.

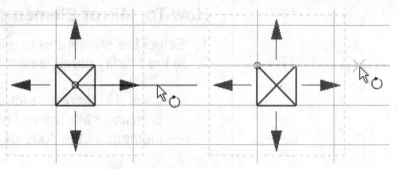

Figure 2–29

- To start the **Rotate** command with an automatic prompt to select the center of rotation, select the elements first and type **R3**.

4. In the Options Bar, specify if you want to make a Copy (select **Copy** option), type an angle in the *Angle* field (as shown in Figure 2–30), and press <Enter>. You can also specify the angle on screen.

*To specify the angle on screen, select a point for the **rotate start ray** (the reference line for the rotation angle). Then select a second point, using the temporary dimension to help you set the angle.*

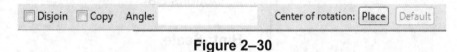

Figure 2–30

5. The rotated element(s) remain highlighted, enabling you to start another command, or return to **Modify** to finish.

- The **Disjoin** option breaks any connections between the elements being rotated and other elements. If **Disjoin** is on (selected), the elements rotate separately. If it is off (cleared), the connected elements also move or stretch. **Disjoin** is off by default.

Mirroring Elements

The **Mirror** command enables you to mirror elements about an axis defined by a selected element, as shown in Figure 2–31, or by selected points.

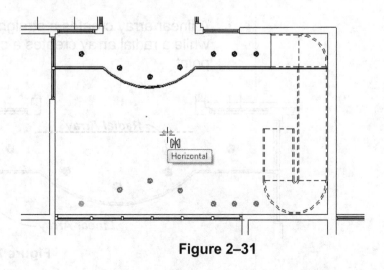

Figure 2–31

How To: Mirror Elements

1. Select the element(s) to mirror.
2. In the Modify panel, select the method you want to use:

- Click 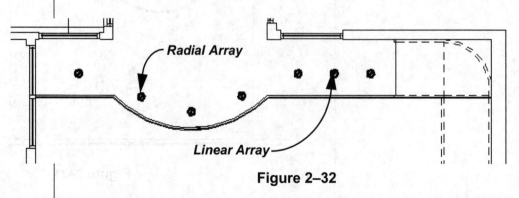 (Mirror - Pick Axis) or use the shortcut by pressing <M> twice. This prompts you to select an element as the **Axis of Reflection** (mirror line).

- Click (Mirror - Draw Axis) or use the shortcut by pressing <D> and pressing <M>. This prompts you to select two points to define the axis about which the elements mirror.

3. The new mirrored element(s) remain highlighted, enabling you to start another command, or return to **Modify** to finish.

- By default, the original elements that were mirrored remain. To delete the original elements, clear the **Copy** option in the Options Bar.

> **Hint: Scale**
>
> The Autodesk Revit software is designed with full-size elements. Therefore, not much can be scaled. However, you can use (Scale) in reference planes, images, and imported files from other programs.

Creating Linear and Radial Arrays

The **Array** command creates multiple copies of selected elements in a linear or radial pattern, as shown in Figure 2–32. For example, you can array a row of columns to create a row of evenly spaced columns on a grid, or array a row of parking spaces. The arrayed elements can be grouped or placed as separate elements.

- A linear array creates a straight line pattern of elements, while a radial array creates a circular pattern around a center point.

Radial Array

Linear Array

Figure 2–32

How To: Create a Linear Array

1. Select the element(s) to array.
2. In the Modify panel, click ⬚⬚ (Array).
3. In the Options Bar, click 🔟 (Linear).
4. Specify the other options as required.
5. Select a start point and an end point to set the spacing and direction of the array. The array is displayed.
6. If the **Group and Associate** option is selected, you are prompted again for the number of items, as shown in Figure 2–33. Type a new number or click on the screen to finish the command.

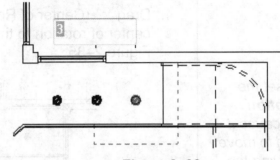

Figure 2–33

- To make a linear array in two directions, you need to array one direction first, select the arrayed elements, and then array them again in the other direction.

Array Options

In the Options Bar, set up the **Array** options for **Linear Array** (top of Figure 2–34) or **Radial Array** (bottom of Figure 2–34).

| 🔟 🔄 | ☑ Group And Associate | Number: 2 | Move To: ◉ 2nd ○ Last |

| 🔟 🔄 | ☐ Group and Associate | Number: 3 | Move To: ○ 2nd ◉ Last | Angle: | Center of rotation: Place Default |

Figure 2–34

Group and Associate	Creates an array group element out of all arrayed elements. Groups can be selected by selecting any elements in the group.
Number	Specifies how many instances you want in the array.
Move To:	**2nd** specifies the distance or angle between the center points of the two elements.
	Last specifies the overall distance or angle of the entire array.

Constrain	Restricts the direction of the array to only vertical or horizontal (Linear only).
Angle	Specifies the angle (Radial only).
Center of rotation	Specifies a location for the origin about which the elements rotate (Radial only).

How To: Create a Radial Array

1. Select the element(s) to array.
2. In the Modify panel, click ⊞ (Array).
3. In the Options Bar, click ⟳ (Radial).
4. Drag ⟳ (Center of Rotation) or use `Place` to the move the center of rotation to the appropriate location, as shown in Figure 2–35.

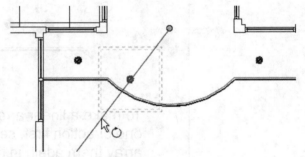

Figure 2–35

*Remember to set the **Center of Rotation** control first, because it is easy to forget to move it before specifying the angle.*

5. Specify the other options as required.
6. In the Options Bar, type an angle and press <Enter>, or specify the rotation angle by selecting points on the screen.

Modifying Array Groups

When you select an element in an array that has been grouped, you can change the number of instances in the array, as shown in Figure 2–36. For radial arrays you can also modify the distance to the center.

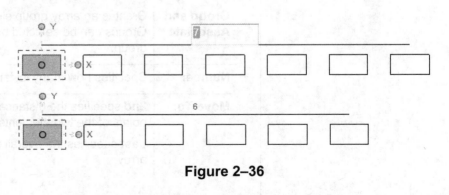

Figure 2–36

- Dashed lines surround the element(s) in a group, and the XY control lets you move the origin point of the group

If you move one of the elements within the array group, the other elements move in response based on the distance and/or angle, as shown in Figure 2–37

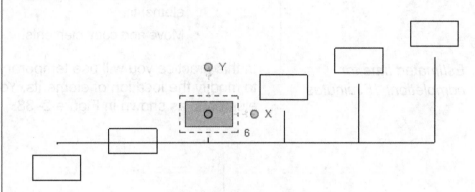

Figure 2–37

- To remove the array constraint on the group, select all of the elements in the array group and, in the *Modify* contextual

    tab>Group panel, click ![ungroup icon] (Ungroup).   .

- If you select an individual element in an array and click

    ![ungroup icon] (Ungroup), the element you selected is removed from the array, while the rest of the elements remain in the array group.

- You can use ![filter icon] (Filter) to ensure that you are selecting only **Model Groups**.

Practice 2a

Work with Basic Modify Tools

Learning Objectives

- Use various drawing aids to modify the location of elements.
- Move and copy elements.

Estimated time for completion: 15 minutes

In this practice you will use temporary dimensions and controls to modify the location of elements. You will than move and copy elements, as shown in Figure 2–38.

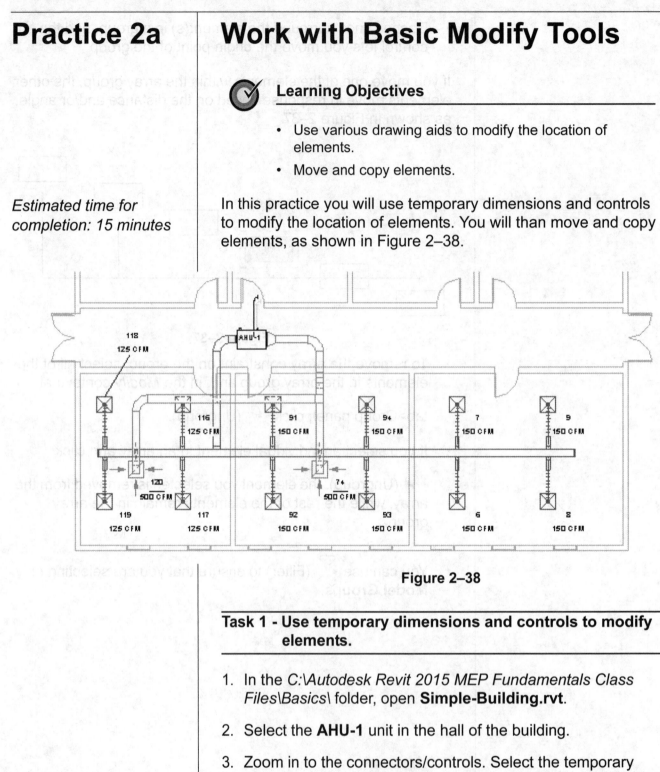

Figure 2–38

Task 1 - Use temporary dimensions and controls to modify elements.

1. In the *C:\Autodesk Revit 2015 MEP Fundamentals Class Files\Basics* folder, open **Simple-Building.rvt**.

2. Select the **AHU-1** unit in the hall of the building.

3. Zoom in to the connectors/controls. Select the temporary dimension above the unit and change the *distance* to **3'-0"**, as shown in Figure 2–39.

The temporary dimensions work with the walls in this project because they are part of the project, not linked in.

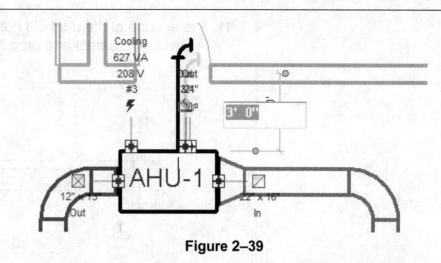

Figure 2–39

4. The unit moves and the ducts move with it because the connectors control the location of the duct fittings and ducts.

5. Pan over to the lower left room in the building. Select the tag that overlaps the ductwork as shown on the left in Figure 2–40.

6. In the Options Bar, select **Leader**.

7. Use the **Move** control to move the tag outside the room to a position in which it is not overlapping anything as shown on the right in Figure 2–40.

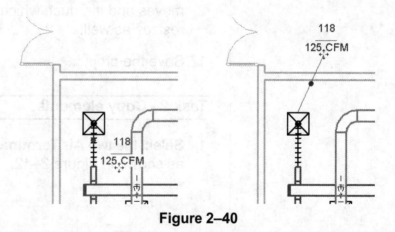

Figure 2–40

8. Zoom out to display the entire building. (Hint: Double-click the mouse wheel.)

9. Select the blue horizontal duct and use the Drag control to lengthen the duct so that it reaches into the room on the far right.

10. Click in empty space to clear the duct selection.

11. The endcap of the duct did not move, as shown in Figure 2–41. Select and drag it to the endpoint of the duct.

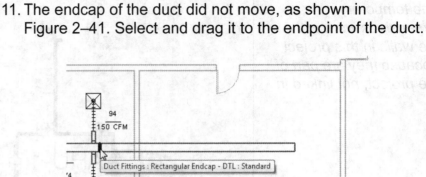

Figure 2–41

12. Undo the change in duct length.

13. Select the duct endcap.

14. In the *Modify | Duct Fittings* tab>Modify panel, click
    ✛ (Move).

15. For the base point, select the duct endpoint.

16. Move it into the other room again. This time the endcap moves and the duct, which has a connector to the endcap, resizes as well.

17. Save the project.

Because there is only one type of element selected, the specific type of element is displayed in the contextual tab.

Task 2 - Copy elements.

---

1. Select the two **Air Terminals**, associated ductwork, and tags, as shown in Figure 2–42.

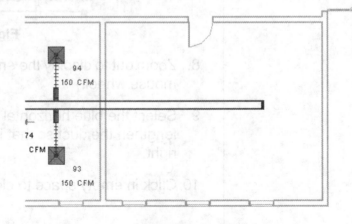

Figure 2–42

Because there is more than one type of element selected the contextual tab displays as Multi-Select.

2. In the *Modify | Multi-Select* tab>Modify panel, click (Copy).

3. In the Options Bar, select the **Multiple** option.

4. For the base point, select the endpoint of one of the vertical ducts as shown in Figure 2–43.

5. Copy the elements into the last room, as shown in Figure 2–43.

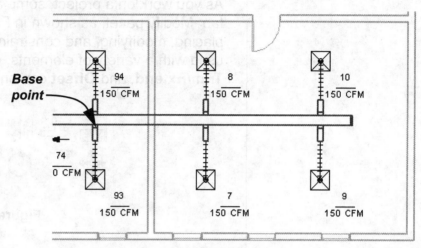

Figure 2–43

*To end a command, you can also right-click and select **Cancel** twice, or in the Select panel, click*

(Modify). Some commands require you to cancel twice, while others end after one cancel command.

6. Press <Esc> twice to end the command

7. Save the project.

2.4 Working with Additional Modify Tools

 Learning Objective

- Use modify tools to align, split, trim, and offset walls and other elements.

As you work on a project, some additional tools on the *Modify* tab>Modify panel, as shown in Figure 2–44, can help you with placing, modifying, and constraining elements. **Align** can be used with a variety of elements, while **Split Element**, **Trim/Extend**, and **Offset** can only be used with linear elements.

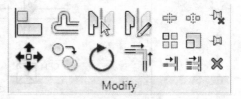

Figure 2–44

Aligning Elements

The **Align** command enables you to line up one element with another. Most elements in the Autodesk Revit software can be aligned. For example, you can line up an air terminal with ceiling grids, as shown in Figure 2–45.

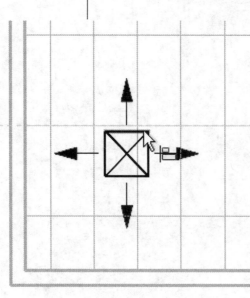

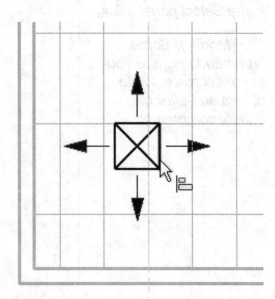

Figure 2–45

How To: Align Elements

1. In the *Modify* tab>Modify panel, click 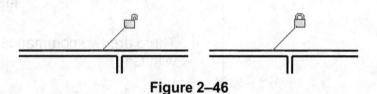 (Align) or use the shortcut by pressing <A> and then pressing <L>.
2. Select a line or point on the element that is going to remain stationary. For walls, press <Tab> to select the correct wall face.
3. Select a line or point on the element to be aligned. The second element moves into alignment with the first one.

- The **Align** command works in both plan and elevation views.

- The **Align** command also works in 3D views. Ensure you select the correct component of the elements to align. For example, to line up two windows vertically select the side of the frame of each window. Zoom in if needed.

Locking elements enlarges the size of the project file, so use this option carefully.

- You can lock alignments so that the elements move together if either one is moved. Once you have created the alignment, a padlock is displayed. Click on the padlock to lock it, as shown in Figure 2–46.

Figure 2–46

- Select the **Multiple Alignment** option to select multiple elements to align with the first element, as shown in Figure 2–47. You can also hold <Ctrl> to make multiple alignments.

- For walls, you can specify if you want the command to prefer **Wall centerlines**, **Wall faces**, **Center of core**, or **Faces of core**, as shown in Figure 2–47. The core refers to the structural members of a wall as opposed to facing materials, such as sheetrock.

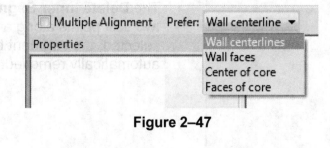

Figure 2–47

Splitting Linear Elements

The **Split** Element command enables you to break a linear element at a specific point. You can use alignment lines, snaps, and temporary dimensions to help place the split point. After you have split the linear element, you can use other editing commands to modify the two parts, or change the type of one part, as shown with walls in Figure 2–48.

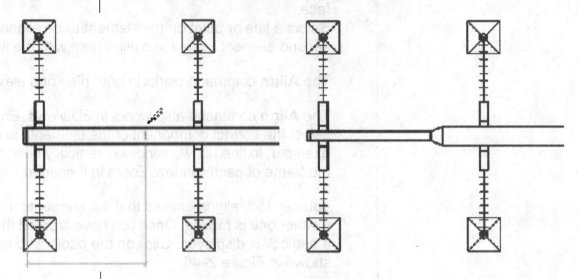

Figure 2–48

- There are two commands: ⊕ (Split Element) and ⊕ (Split with Gap).

How To: Split Linear Elements

1. In the *Modify* tab>Modify panel, click ⊕ (Split Element) or use the shortcut by pressing <S> and pressing <L>.
2. In the Options Bar, select or clear the **Delete Inner Segment** option.
3. Move the cursor to the point you want to split and select the point.
4. Repeat for any additional split locations.
5. Modify the elements that were split, as required.

- The **Delete Inner Segment** option is used when you select two split points along a linear element. When the option is selected, the segment between the two split points is automatically removed.

- (Split with Gap) splits the linear element at the point you select (as shown in Figure 2–49), but also creates a *Joint Gap* specified in the Options Bar.

This command is typically used with structural precast slabs.

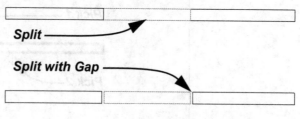

Split

Split with Gap

Figure 2–49

Trimming and Extending

There are three trim/extend methods that you can use with linear elements: **Trim/Extend to Corner**, **Trim/Extend Single Element**, and **Trim/Extend Multiple Elements**.

- When selecting elements to trim, click the part of the element that you want to keep. The opposite part of the line is then trimmed.

How To: Trim/Extend to Corner

1. In the *Modify* tab>Modify panel, click ⬚ (Trim/Extend to Corner) or use the shortcut by pressing <T> and pressing <R>.
2. Select the first linear element on the side you want to keep.
3. Select the second linear element on the side you want to keep, as shown in Figure 2–50.

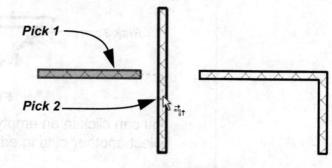

Pick 1

Pick 2

Figure 2–50

How To: Trim/Extend a Single Element

1. In the *Modify* tab>Modify panel, click ⬚ (Trim/Extend Single Element).
2. Select the cutting or boundary edge.

3. Select the linear element to be trimmed or extended, as shown in Figure 2–51.

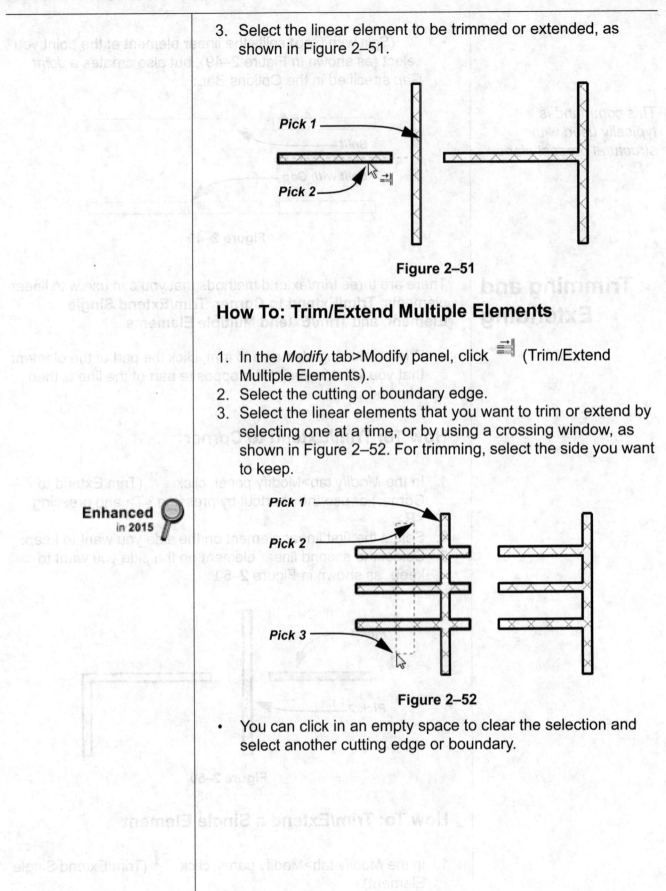

Figure 2–51

How To: Trim/Extend Multiple Elements

1. In the *Modify* tab>Modify panel, click ⇉‖ (Trim/Extend Multiple Elements).
2. Select the cutting or boundary edge.
3. Select the linear elements that you want to trim or extend by selecting one at a time, or by using a crossing window, as shown in Figure 2–52. For trimming, select the side you want to keep.

Figure 2–52

- You can click in an empty space to clear the selection and select another cutting edge or boundary.

Enhanced
in 2015

Offsetting Elements

The **Offset** command is an easy way of creating parallel copies of linear elements at a specified distance, as shown in Figure 2–53. Walls, beams, braces, and lines are among the elements that can be offset.

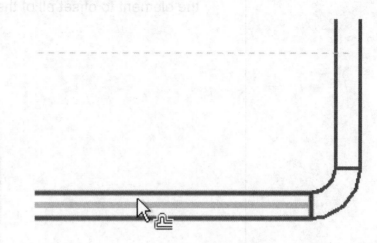

Figure 2–53

- If you offset a wall that has a door or window embedded in it, the elements are copied with the offset wall.

The offset distance can be set by typing the distance (**Numerical** method shown in Figure 2–54) or by selecting points on the screen (**Graphical** method).

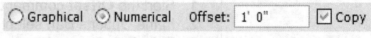

○ Graphical ◉ Numerical   Offset: 1' 0"   ☑ Copy

Figure 2–54

How To: Offset using the Numerical Method

1. In the *Modify* tab>Modify panel, click (Offset) or use the shortcut by pressing <O> and pressing <F>.
2. In the Options Bar, select the **Numerical** option.
3. In the Options Bar, type the desired distance in the *Offset* field.
4. Move the cursor over the element you want to offset. A dashed line previews the offset location. Move the cursor to flip the sides, as required.
5. Click to create the offset.
6. Repeat Steps 4 and 5 to offset other elements by the same distance, or to change the distance for another offset.

*The **Copy** option (which is on by default) makes a copy of the element being offset. If this option is not selected, the **Offset** command moves the element the set offset distance.*

- With the **Numerical** option, you can select multiple connected linear elements for offsetting. Hover the cursor over an element and press <Tab> until the other related elements are highlighted, as shown in Figure 2–55. Select the element to offset all of the elements at the same time.

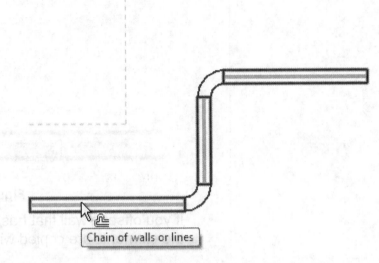

Chain of walls or lines

Figure 2–55

How To: Offset using the Graphical Method

1. Start the **Offset** command.
2. In the Options Bar, select the **Graphical** option.
3. Select the linear element to offset.
4. Select two points that define the distance of the offset and which side to apply it. You can type an override in the temporary dimension for the second point.

- When working with MEP elements, the offset element might not automatically connect to other nearby elements, as shown on the left in Figure 2–56. To form the connection, drag the end of the new element away from the other element and then back again. It should connect as shown on the right in Figure 2–56.

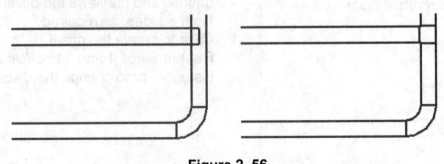

Figure 2–56

Hint: Hiding Elements in Views

As you are working, you can hide individual elements or entire categories of elements to clarify the display. They remain hidden until you display them again. Hidden elements do not print.

- Select the element(s) you want to hide, right-click and select **Hide in view>Elements** or **Hide in view>Category**.

- The **Elements** option hides only the elements that you selected, while the **Category** option hides all elements in that category. For example, you can select one grid line and use **Hide in view>Category** to hide all of the grid lines.

- To display the elements or category again, in the View Control Bar, click 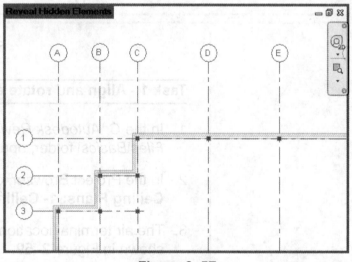 (Reveal Hidden Elements). The border and all hidden elements are displayed in magenta, while displayed elements in the view are grayed out, as shown in Figure 2–57. Select the hidden elements you want to restore, right-click, and select **Unhide in View>Elements** or **Unhide in View>Category** or in the *Modify |* contextual

  tab> Reveal Hidden Elements panel click (Unhide

  Element) or (Unhide Category).

Figure 2–57

When you are finished, in the View Control Bar, click (Close Reveal Hidden Elements) or, in the *Modify |* contextual tab>

Reveal Hidden Elements panel click (Toggle Reveal Hidden Elements Mode).

Practice 2b

Work with Additional Modify Tools

Learning Objective

- Align and rotate elements.

Estimated time for completion: 10 minutes

In this practice you will align air terminals to the ceiling grid, as shown in Figure 2–58.

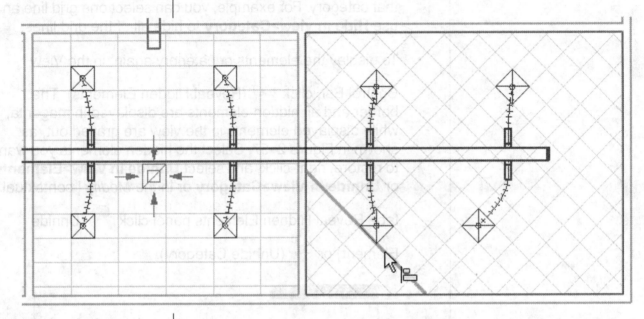

Figure 2–58

Task 1 - Align and rotate elements.

1. In the *C:\Autodesk Revit 2015 MEP Fundamentals Class Files\Basics* folder, open **Simple-Building-1.rvt**.

2. In the Project Browser, open the view Mechanical>HVAC> **Ceiling Plans: 1- Ceiling Mech**.

3. The air terminal locations do not match the ceiling grids as shown in Figure 2–59.

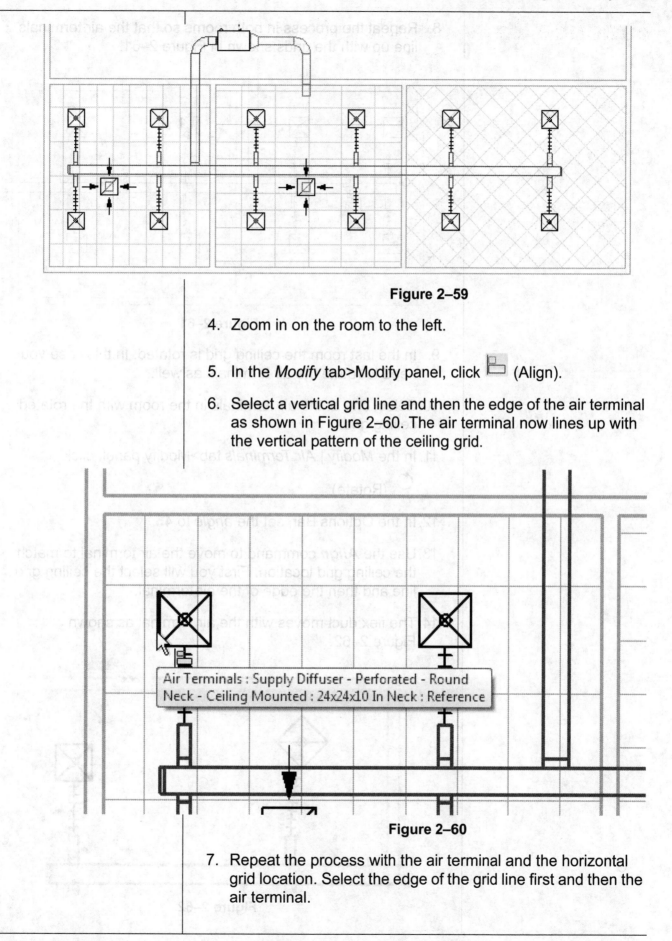

Figure 2–59

4. Zoom in on the room to the left.

5. In the *Modify* tab>Modify panel, click ⬜ (Align).

6. Select a vertical grid line and then the edge of the air terminal as shown in Figure 2–60. The air terminal now lines up with the vertical pattern of the ceiling grid.

Air Terminals : Supply Diffuser - Perforated - Round Neck - Ceiling Mounted : 24x24x10 In Neck : Reference

Figure 2–60

7. Repeat the process with the air terminal and the horizontal grid location. Select the edge of the grid line first and then the air terminal.

8. Repeat the process in both rooms so that the air terminals line up with the grids shown in Figure 2–61.

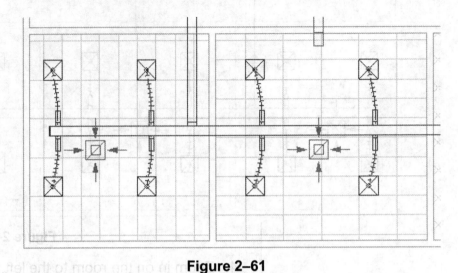

Figure 2–61

9. In the last room the ceiling grid is rotated. In this case you need to rotate the air terminals as well.

10. Select one of the air terminals in the room with the rotated ceiling grid.

11. In the *Modify | Air Terminals* tab>Modify panel, click

    ↻ (Rotate).

12. In the Options Bar, set the *angle* to **45**.

13. Use the ***Align*** command to move the air terminal to match the ceiling grid location. First you will select the ceiling grid line and then the edge of the air terminal.

14. The flex duct moves with the air terminal as shown Figure 2–62.

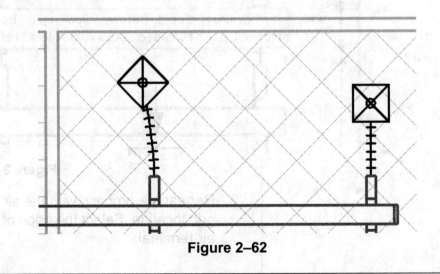

Figure 2–62

15. Without rotating the air terminal, click 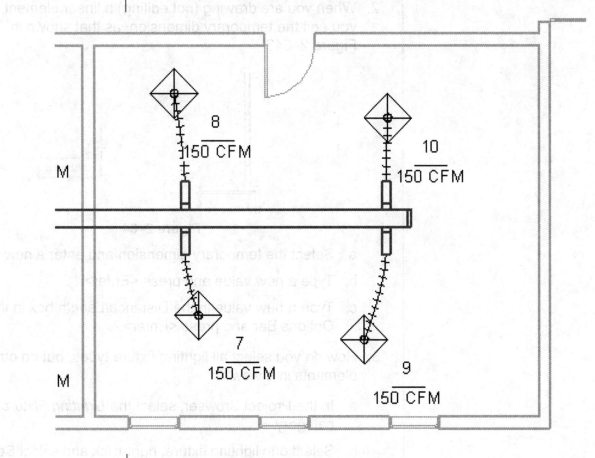 (Align).

16. Select a grid line close to one of the other air terminals and then select the edge of the air terminal. The air terminal moves to touch the grid line and also rotates to match the angle of the grid line.

17. Finish aligning all of the air terminals in this room. The exact location is up to you.

18. Zoom out to display the entire building.

19. Switch to the Mechanical>HVAC>Floor Plans>**1 - Mech** view. The rotated terminals and flex duct display correctly in this view as well as shown in Figure 2–63.

Figure 2–63

20. Zoom out to display the entire building.

21. Save and close the model.

Chapter Review Questions

1. What is the purpose of an alignment line?

    a. Displays when the new element you are placing or drawing is aligned with the grid system.

    b. Indicates that the new element you are placing or drawing is aligned with an existing object.

    c. Displays when the new element you are placing or drawing is aligned with a selected tracking point.

    d. Indicates that the new element is aligned with true north rather than project north.

2. When you are drawing (not editing) a linear element, how do you edit the temporary dimension, as that shown in Figure 2–64?

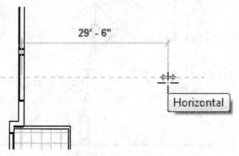

Figure 2–64

    a. Select the temporary dimension and enter a new value.

    b. Type a new value and press <Enter>.

    c. Type a new value in the Distance/Length box in the Options Bar and press <Enter>.

3. How do you select all lighting fixture types, but no other elements in a view?

    a. In the Project Browser, select the *Lighting Fixture* category.

    b. Select one lighting fixture, right-click and select **Select All Instances>Visible in View**.

    c. Select all of the objects in the view and use (Filter) to clear the other categories.

    d. Select one lighting fixture, and click (Select Multiple) in the Ribbon.

4. What are the two methods for starting (Move) or 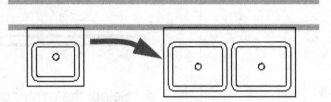 (Copy)?

   a. Start the command first and then select the objects, or select the objects and then start the command.

   b. Start the command from the *Modify* tab, or select the object and then select **Move** or **Copy** from the shortcut menu.

   c. Start the command from the *Modify* tab, or select the objects and select **Auto-Move**.

   d. Use the **Move/Copy** command or **Cut/Copy** and **Paste** using the Clipboard.

5. Where do you change the type for a selected element, as shown in Figure 2–65?

Figure 2–65

   a. In the *Modify* | *<contextual>* tab> Properties panel, click (Type Properties) and select a new type in the dialog box.

   b. In the Options Bar, click `Change Element Type ▾`.

   c. Select the dynamic control next to the selected element and select a new type in the drop-down list.

   d. In Properties, select a new type in the Type Selector drop-down list.

6. Both ⟳ (Rotate) and ⊞ (Array) with ⟲ (Radial) have a center of rotation that defaults to the center of the element or group of elements you have selected. How do you move the center of rotation to another point as shown in Figure 2–66? (Select all that apply.)

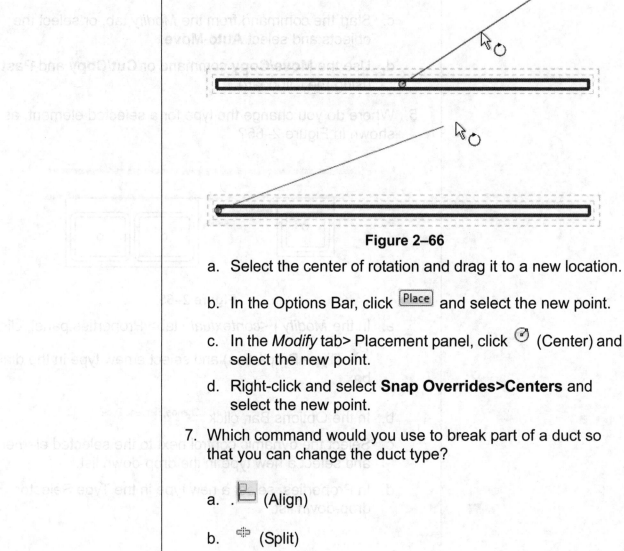

Figure 2–66

a. Select the center of rotation and drag it to a new location.

b. In the Options Bar, click Place and select the new point.

c. In the *Modify* tab> Placement panel, click ⟲ (Center) and select the new point.

d. Right-click and select **Snap Overrides>Centers** and select the new point.

7. Which command would you use to break part of a duct so that you can change the duct type?

a. ⊟ (Align)

b. ⊹ (Split)

c. ⇥ (Trim)

d. ⟰ (Offset)

8. All of the **Trim** commands can also be used to extend elements.

    a. True

    b. False

9. In the **Mirror** command, how do you remove the original element(s) if you do not want to keep them?

    a. You must delete them separately from the command.

    b. Use the **Demolish** tool.

    c. Clear the **Copy** option in the Options Bar.

    d. Select the **Delete Original** option in the Options Bar.

10. Which command do you use if you want two pipes that are not touching to come together, as shown in Figure 2–67?

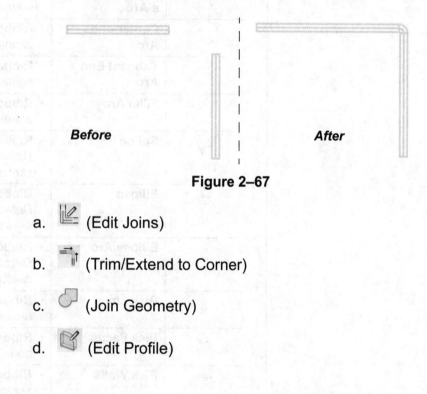

Before   *After*

Figure 2–67

    a.   (Edit Joins)

    b.   (Trim/Extend to Corner)

    c.   (Join Geometry)

    d.   (Edit Profile)

Command Summary

Button	Command	Location
Draw Tools		
	Line	• **Ribbon:** *Modify	(various linear elements)* tab>Draw panel
	Rectangle	• **Ribbon:** *Modify	(various linear elements)* tab>Draw panel
	Inscribed Polygon	• **Ribbon:** *Modify	(various linear elements)* tab>Draw panel
	Circumscribed Polygon	• **Ribbon:** *Modify	(various linear elements)* tab>Draw panel
	Circle	• **Ribbon:** *Modify	(various linear elements)* tab>Draw panel
	Start-End-Radius Arc	• **Ribbon:** *Modify	(various linear elements)* tab>Draw panel
	Center-ends Arc	• **Ribbon:** *Modify	(various linear elements)* tab>Draw panel
	Tangent End Arc	• **Ribbon:** *Modify	(various linear elements)* tab>Draw panel
	Fillet Arc	• **Ribbon:** *Modify	(various linear elements)* tab>Draw panel
	Spline	• **Ribbon:** *Modify	Place Lines, Place Detail Lines, and various boundary sketches*>Draw panel
	Ellipse	• **Ribbon:** *Modify	Place Lines, Place Detail Lines, and various boundary sketches*>Draw panel
	Ellipse Arc	• **Ribbon:** *Modify	Place Lines, Place Detail Lines, and various boundary sketches*>Draw panel
	Pick Lines	• **Ribbon:** *Modify	(various linear elements)* tab>Draw panel
	Pick Faces	• **Ribbon:** *Modify	Place Wall*> Draw panel
	Pick Walls	• **Ribbon:** *Modify	(various boundary sketches)*>Draw panel
Modify Tools		
	Align	• **Ribbon:** *Modify* tab>Modify panel • **Shortcut:** <A> and <L>
	Array	• **Ribbon:** *Modify* tab>Modify panel • **Shortcut:** <A> and <R>
	Copy	• **Ribbon:** *Modify* tab>Modify panel • **Shortcut:** <C> and <O>
	Copy to Clipboard	• **Ribbon:** *Modify* tab>Clipboard panel • **Shortcut:** <Ctrl>+<C>

	Delete	• **Ribbon:** *Modify* tab>Modify panel • **Shortcut:** <D> and <E>
	Mirror - Draw Axis	• **Ribbon:** *Modify* tab>Modify panel • **Shortcut:** <D> and <M>
	Mirror - Pick Axis	• **Ribbon:** *Modify* tab>Modify panel • **Shortcut:** <M> and <M>
	Move	• **Ribbon:** *Modify* tab>Modify panel • **Shortcut:** <M> and <V>
	Offset	• **Ribbon:** *Modify* tab>Modify panel • **Shortcut:** <O> and <F>
	Paste	• **Ribbon:** *Modify* tab>Clipboard panel • **Shortcut:** <Ctrl>+<V>
	Pin	• **Ribbon:** *Modify* tab>Modify panel • **Shortcut:** <P> and <N>
	Rotate	• **Ribbon:** *Modify* tab>Modify panel • **Shortcut:** <R> and <O>
	Scale	• **Ribbon:** *Modify* tab>Modify panel • **Shortcut:** <R> and <E>
	Split Element	• **Ribbon:** *Modify* tab>Modify panel • **Shortcut:** <S> and <L>
	Split with Gap	• **Ribbon:** *Modify* tab>Modify panel
	Trim/Extend to Corner	• **Ribbon:** *Modify* tab>Modify panel • **Shortcut:** <T> and <R>
	Trim/Extend Multiple Elements	• **Ribbon:** *Modify* tab>Modify panel
	Trim/Extend Single Element	• **Ribbon:** *Modify* tab>Modify panel
	Unpin	• **Ribbon:** *Modify* tab>Modify panel • **Shortcut:** <U> and <P>

Select Tools

	Drag elements on selection	• **Ribbon:** All tabs>Expanded Select panel • **Status Bar**
	Filter	• **Ribbon:** *Modify	Multi-Select* tab>Filter panel>Filter • **Status Bar**
	Select Elements By Face	• **Ribbon:** All tabs>Expanded Select panel • **Status Bar**
	Select Links	• **Ribbon:** All tabs>Expanded Select panel • **Status Bar**

	Select Pinned Elements	• **Ribbon:** All tabs>Expanded Select panel • **Status Bar**
	Select Underlay Elements	• **Ribbon:** All tabs>Expanded Select panel • **Status Bar**
	Selection Sets: Add to Selection	• **Ribbon:** *Edit Selection Set* tab>Edit Selection panel
	Selection Sets: Load	• **Ribbon:** *Modify	Multi-Select* tab> Selection panel or *Manage* tab> Selection panel
	Selection Sets: Edit	• **Ribbon:** *Modify	Multi-Select* tab> Selection panel or *Manage* tab> Selection panel
	Selection Sets: Remove from Selection	• **Ribbon:** *Edit Selection Set* tab>Edit Selection panel
	Selection Sets: Save	• **Ribbon:** *Modify	Multi-Select* tab> Selection panel or *Manage* tab> Selection panel

Chapter 3

Starting Autodesk Revit MEP Projects

In this chapter you learn how to link and manage an architectural model created in Autodesk® Revit® into an MEP project. You then learn how to use the Copy/Monitor tools, and run a Coordination Review. You also learn how to add, copy, and monitor levels.

This chapter contains the following topics:

- **Linking in Autodesk Revit Models**
- **Copying and Monitoring Elements**
- **Setting Up Levels**
- **Batch Copy and Monitor**
- **Coordination Review**

3.1 Linking in Autodesk Revit Models

Learning Objectives

- Link an architectural or structural model into an MEP project.
- Manage links including reloading the linked file and modifying the reference type.

When you are working with firms that use the Autodesk® Revit® software, you can link architectural and structural models directly into your MEP systems project. A linked model automatically updates if the original file is changed. When the model is linked to the systems project, the architectural and structural elements display in halftone, as shown in Figure 3–1.

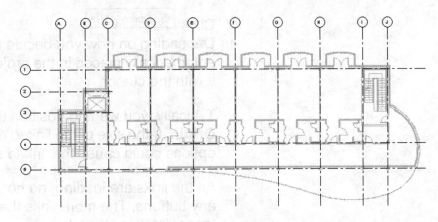

Figure 3–1

- Architectural, structural, and MEP models created in the Autodesk Revit software can be linked to each other as long as they are from the same release cycle.

- When you use linked models, clashes between disciplines can be detected and information can be passed between disciplines.

- Elements can be copied and monitored for even better coordination. For example, if the architect has established levels, the engineer can copy the levels into their model. As elements are copied, they are also monitored for changes. If a level is modified, the software provides a report. You then have the option of permitting the software to adjust the host project to coordinate with the change in the architectural model.

How To: Add a Linked Model to a Host Project

1. In the *Insert* tab>Link panel, click 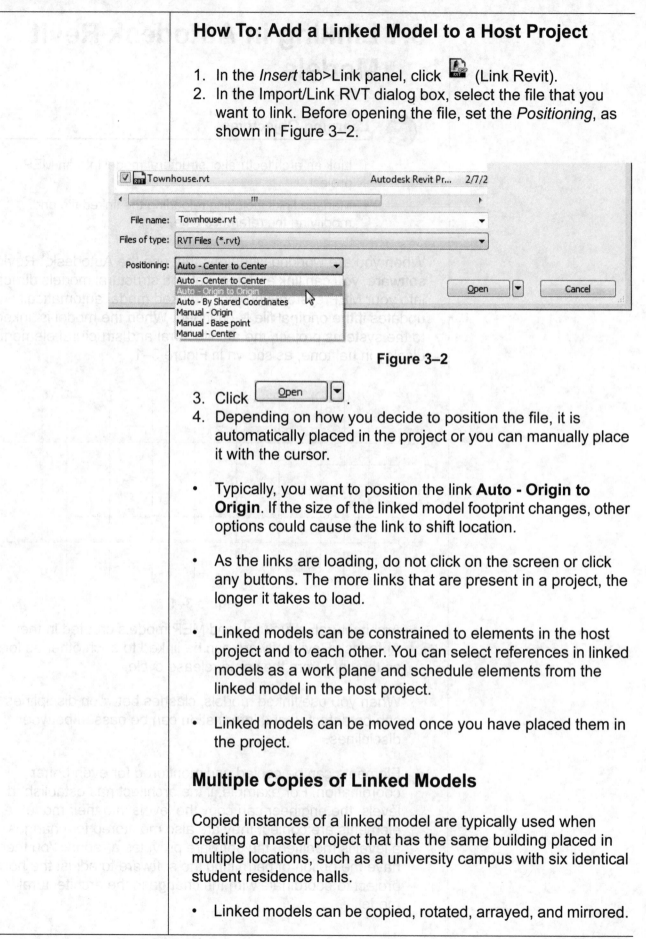 (Link Revit).
2. In the Import/Link RVT dialog box, select the file that you want to link. Before opening the file, set the *Positioning*, as shown in Figure 3–2.

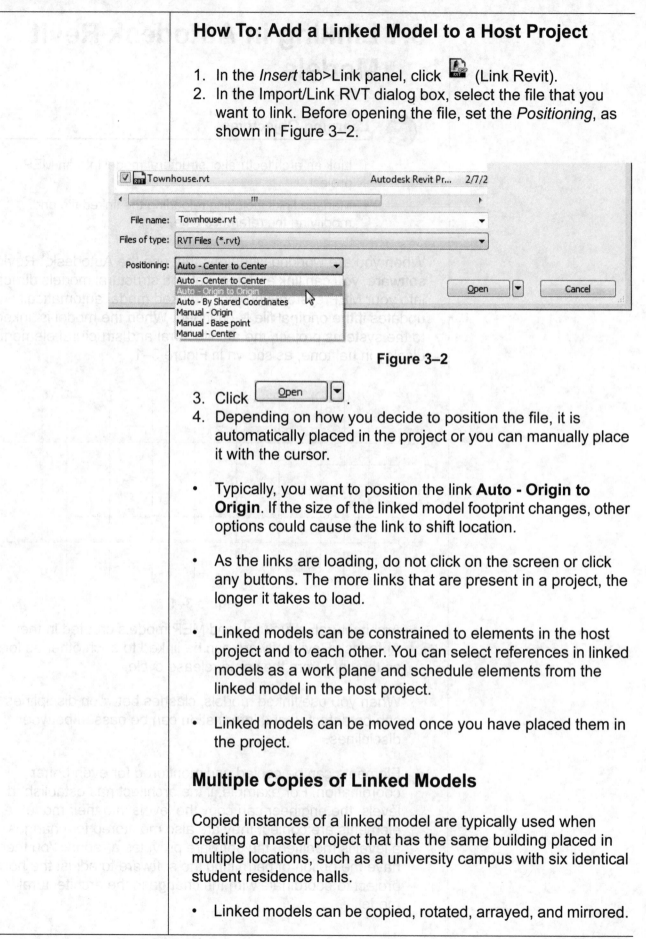

Figure 3–2

3. Click [Open].
4. Depending on how you decide to position the file, it is automatically placed in the project or you can manually place it with the cursor.

- Typically, you want to position the link **Auto - Origin to Origin**. If the size of the linked model footprint changes, other options could cause the link to shift location.

- As the links are loading, do not click on the screen or click any buttons. The more links that are present in a project, the longer it takes to load.

- Linked models can be constrained to elements in the host project and to each other. You can select references in linked models as a work plane and schedule elements from the linked model in the host project.

- Linked models can be moved once you have placed them in the project.

Multiple Copies of Linked Models

Copied instances of a linked model are typically used when creating a master project that has the same building placed in multiple locations, such as a university campus with six identical student residence halls.

- Linked models can be copied, rotated, arrayed, and mirrored.

- You only need to link a model once, but you can place as many copies into the host project as required. The copies are numbered automatically, and the name can be changed in the Properties when the instance is selected. There is only one linked model, while the copies are additional instances of that link.

- When you have placed a linked model in a project, you can use the Project Browser, as shown in Figure 3–3, to drag and drop additional copies of the link into the project.

⊟╌🖘 Revit Links
　　⬇ Warehouse Layout.rvt

Figure 3–3

Hint: Cleaning up Linked Files

Linked files can be very large and include a lot of unnecessary information when all you need is the base building model. Depending on the standards of your office, it can help to clean up the linked file by deleting views, sheets, and unused families. Sometimes you can request the original creator to setup coordination views that can be used specifically as base views in the MEP project.

Managing Links

If the architectural model changes as you are working on the host project, it can be managed in one of two ways. You can reload the model by right-clicking on the Revit Link in the Project Browser and selecting **Reload** or **Reload From...** as shown in Figure 3–4.

Figure 3–4

You can also manage the link using the *Revit* tab in the Manage Links dialog box as shown in Figure 3–5.

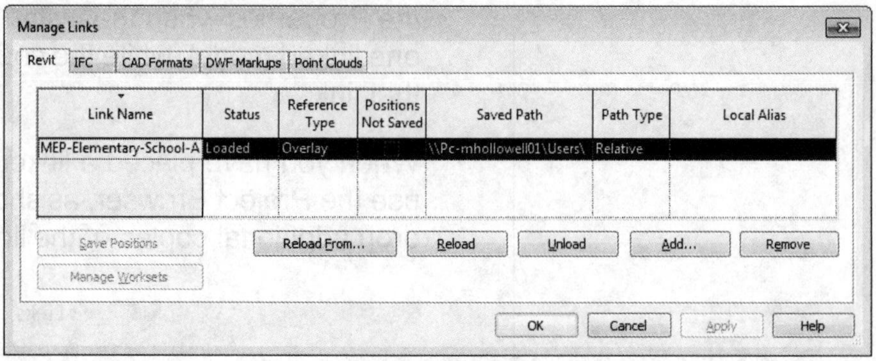

Figure 3–5

- To open the dialog box, select the link and in the *Modify>RVT Links* tab> Link panel, click (Manage Links). You can also access the dialog box through the *Insert* tab>Link panel or *Manage* tab>Manage Project panel. Alternatively, you can right-click on Revit Links in the Project Browser and select **Manage Links**.

Manage Links Options

- **Status:** Displays the status of the linked model (**Loaded** or **Not Loaded**). This is read-only.

- **Reference Type:** Linked models can be nested in one another. How a linked model responds when the host project is linked into another project depends on the **Reference Type**. If the type is set to **Overlay**, the linked model is not referenced in the new host project. If the type is set to **Attach**, it displays in the new host project.

- **Positions Not Saved:** Works in conjunction with **Save Positions**. It is active if the linked model is part of a shared coordinate environment.

- **Saved Path:** Displays the location of the original linked model.

- **Path Type:** The path type can be set to **Relative** (which searches the root folder of the current project) or **Absolute** (which searches only the folder where it was originally saved). Typically, it is set to **Relative** so that if the linked model is moved, the software still searches for it. If it is set to **Absolute** and the original linked model is moved, the software is unable to find it.

- **Local Alias:** Displays an additional name for models linked to Worksets.

- **Save Positions:** Works with shared coordinate systems to save a linked model to a position in the host project.

- **Reload From:** If the file location has changed, use this option to find the new location.

- **Reload:** Reloads the linked model without needing to close and reopen the project.

- **Unload:** Unloads the linked model so that it is not seen or calculated in the project but is still linked. Use **Reload** to restore it.

- **Add:** Opens the Import/Link RVT dialog box where you can link additional models into the host project.

- **Remove:** Deletes the link to the model.

Hint: Visibility Graphics and Linked Files

When you open the Visibility/Graphics dialog box (type **VV** or **VG**), you can modify the graphic overrides for Revit links as shown in Figure 3–6. This can help you clean up the view or assign a view to build on.

Visibility/Graphic Overrides for Floor Plan: 1 - Mech

| Model Categories | Annotation Categories | Analytical Model Categories | Imported Categories | Filters | Revit Links |

Visibility	Halftone	Underlay	Display Settings
☑ BHM-Office-Final-12.rvt			By Host View
☑ 1 (<Not Shared>)	☐	☐	Not Overridden

Figure 3–6

The *Display Settings* include:

- **By host view:** The display of the Revit link is based on the view properties of the current view in the host model.

- **By linked view:** The appearance of the Revit link is based on the view properties of the selected linked view and ignores the view properties of the current view.

- **Custom:** You can override all of the graphical elements.

Practice 3a

Start an MEP Project

✔ Learning Objectives

- Start a new project from a template.
- Link an architectural model into a MEP project.
- Modify the Display Settings of the view.

In this practice you will create a new project file and link an architectural Autodesk Revit model into it. You will then modify the display settings to show only the base building elements in two floor plan views, as shown for the first floor in Figure 3–7.

Estimated time for completion: 10 minutes

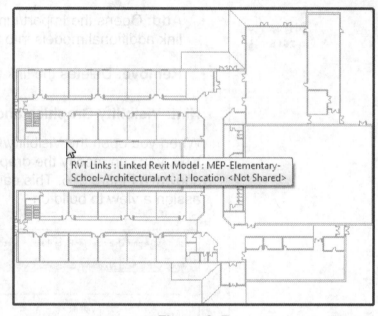

RVT Links : Linked Revit Model : MEP-Elementary-School-Architectural.rvt : 1 : location <Not Shared>

Figure 3–7

Task 1 - Create a new project.

1. In the Quick Access Toolbar or Application Menu, click ▢ (New).

2. In the New Project dialog box, select the *Template file:* **Systems Template** and click `OK`. If the **Systems Template** is not available in the drop-down list, click `Browse...`.

3. In the Choose Template dialog box, select **Systems-Default**, click `Open`, and then click `OK`.

*Click ▼ (Customize Quick Access Toolbar) at the end of the Quick Access Toolbar and select **New** if it is not displayed.*

4. Save the project as **Elementary-School.rvt** in the *Starting* folder of your class files folder.

Task 2 - Link in a architectural model.

1. In the *Insert* tab>Link panel, click 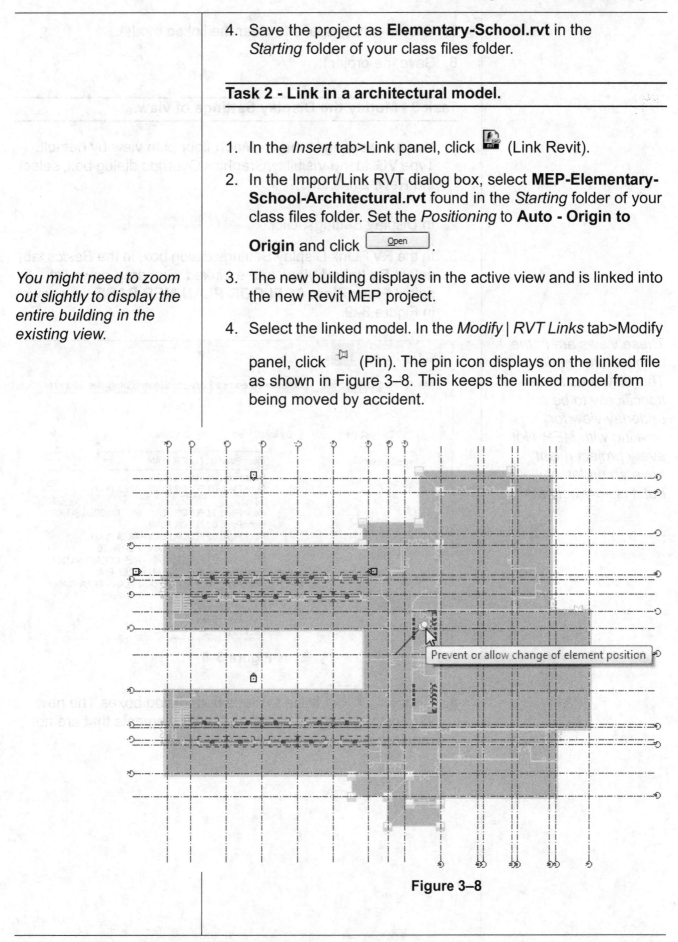 (Link Revit).

2. In the Import/Link RVT dialog box, select **MEP-Elementary-School-Architectural.rvt** found in the *Starting* folder of your class files folder. Set the *Positioning* to **Auto - Origin to Origin** and click ⎡ Open ⎤.

3. The new building displays in the active view and is linked into the new Revit MEP project.

You might need to zoom out slightly to display the entire building in the existing view.

4. Select the linked model. In the *Modify | RVT Links* tab>Modify panel, click (Pin). The pin icon displays on the linked file as shown in Figure 3–8. This keeps the linked model from being moved by accident.

Figure 3–8

5. Click in empty space to clear the linked model.

6. Save the project.

Task 3 - Modify the Display Settings of view.

1. You are working in the **1 - Mech** floor plan view by default. Type **VG**. In the Visibility/Graphics Override dialog box, select the *Revit Links* tab.

2. In Display Settings, click [By Host View].

3. In the RVT Link Display Settings dialog box, in the *Basics* tab, select **By linked view**. In the Linked view drop-down list, select **Floor Plan: 01 FLOOR PLAN-MEP BASE**, as shown in Figure 3–9.

These views are in the architectural model. This view was made specifically to be an underlay view for working with MEP. Not every project might have an underlay view but it is very helpful.

RVT Link Display Settings

| Basics | Model Categories | Annotation Categories | Analytical Model Categories | Import Categories |

○ By host view   ● By linked view   ○ Custom

Linked view: Floor Plan: 01 FLOOR PLAN ▼

View filters: Floor Plan: 01 FLOOR PLAN
                      Floor Plan: 01 FLOOR PLAN - AREA PLAN
View range: Floor Plan: 01 FLOOR PLAN - MEP BASE
                      Floor Plan: 01 FLOOR PLAN - MEP COORDINATION
                      Floor Plan: 02 FLOOR PLAN
Phase: Floor Plan: 02 FLOOR PLAN - AREA PLAN
                      Floor Plan: 02 FLOOR PLAN - MEP BASE
Phase filter: Floor Plan: 02 FLOOR PLAN - MEP COORDINATION
                      Floor Plan: 06 FLOOR PLAN - AREA PLAN
Detail level: Floor Plan: Copy of 01 FLOOR PLAN - AREA PLAN
                      Floor Plan: Level 1
Discipline: Floor Plan: Level 2
                      Floor Plan: Site Plan
Color fill: Floor Plan: TOF

Figure 3–9

4. Click [OK] twice to close both dialog boxes. The new view displays without grids and other elements that are not required.

5. Move the elevation markers outside of the building, as shown in Figure 3–10.

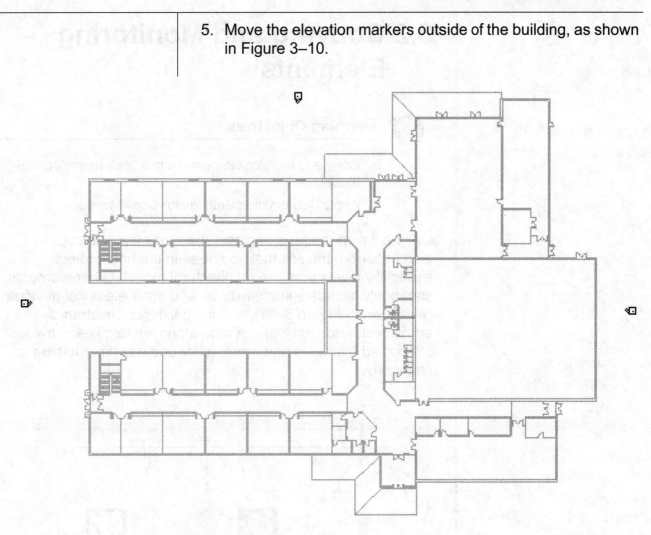

Figure 3–10

6. Open the Mechanical>HVAC>Floor Plans>**2 - Mech** view.

7. Modify the view display using the Visibility Graphics Override dialog box, as you did for the first floor. Use the linked view **Floor Plan: 02 FLOOR PLAN - MEP BASE**.

8. Open the default 3D view and zoom in to look at it. All of the MEP related elements in the architectural model display in black, while the architectural elements are grayed out.

9. Zoom out to fit the view (type **ZF**).

10. Save the project.

3.2 Copying and Monitoring Elements

Learning Objectives

- Copy and monitor elements from a linked architectural model.
- Apply Coordination Settings for Copy/Monitor.

Once a linked model is in place, the next step is to copy elements from the link that you need in the host project, especially levels from the architectural model. Other elements commonly include lighting fixtures and other electrical devices (as shown in Figure 3–11), plumbing fixtures, mechanical equipment, and sprinklers. A monitoring system keeps track of the copied elements and prompts for updates if something is changed.

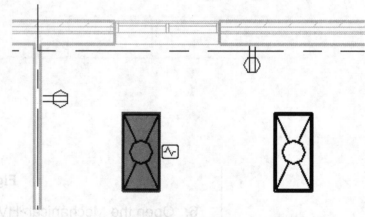

Figure 3–11

- Items that are monitored, display ⚡ (Monitor) when selected, as shown in Figure 3–11.

How To: Copy and Monitor from a Linked Model

1. In the *Collaborate* tab>Coordinate panel, expand

   ⚡ (Copy/Monitor) and click ⚡ (Select Link).

Typically, Copy and Monitor as explained here is used primarily to monitor levels and grids. Fixtures are more easily copy/monitored using the Coordination Settings and Batch Copy described later in this chapter.

2. Hover the cursor over the linked model. A frame displays around the linked model and a tooltip also displays as shown in Figure 3–12. When they are displayed, select the linked model.

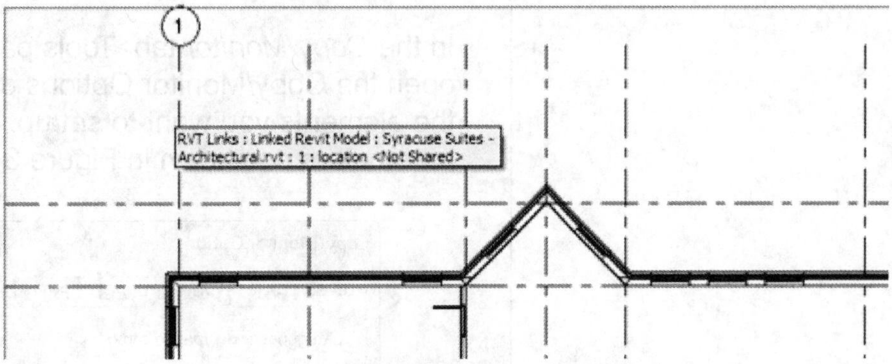

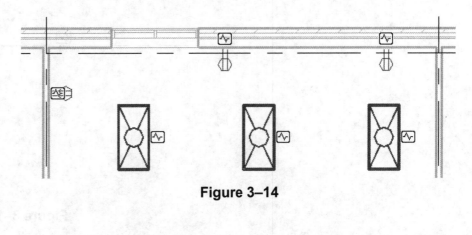

Figure 3–12

3. In the *Copy/Monitor* tab>Tools panel, click ⟳ (Copy).
4. Select each element you want to copy or, in the Options Bar, select the **Multiple** option as shown in Figure 3–13.

| Copy/Monitor | ▼ | ☑ Multiple [Finish] [Cancel] |

Figure 3–13

5. Hold the <Ctrl> key (and/or use a window selection) and select all of the elements that you want to copy into your model.

6. In the Options Bar, click [Finish].
7. Repeat the process with any other elements that you want to copy.

Warnings about duplicated or renamed types might display.

8. Click ✓ (Finish) to end the session of Copy/Monitor. The elements are physically copied into your model and

⟳ (Monitor) displays indicating that the elements are actively monitored as shown in Figure 3–14.

Figure 3–14

Hint: Copy/Monitor Options

Copy/Monitor Options are similar to **Coordination Settings**, except that they work with architectural and structural elements, such as Levels, Grids, Columns, Walls, and Floors.

In the *Copy/Monitor* tab>Tools panel, click (Options) to open the Copy/Monitor Options dialog box. Select the tab for the elements you want to set up. You can then specify the parameters as shown in Figure 3–15.

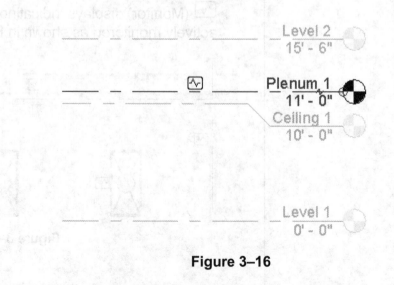

Copy/Monitor Options

| Levels | Grids | Columns | Walls | Floors |

Categories and Types to copy:

Original type	New type
1/4" Head	1/4" Head
No Head	1/4" Head

Additional Copy Parameters:

Parameter	Value
Offset Level	0' 0"
Reuse Levels with the same name	✓
Reuse matching Levels	Don't reuse
Add suffix to Level Name	
Add prefix to Level Name	

Figure 3–15

Monitoring Elements

Sometimes you need to model elements in the host project and then check them against changes in the architectural model. For example, you might need to add a level for the base of a plenum that you want to be monitored against a ceiling level in the linked model as shown in Figure 3–16.

Level 2
15' - 6"

Plenum 1
11' - 0"

Ceiling 1
10' - 0"

Level 1
0' - 0"

Figure 3–16

How To: Monitor Elements

1. In the *Collaborate* tab>Coordinate panel, expand ![icon] (Copy/ Monitor) and click ![icon] (Select Link) to monitor elements between the MEP project and the linked model. You can also click ![icon] (Use Current Project) to monitor elements within the MEP project.

2. In the *Copy/Monitor* tab>Tools panel, click ![icon] (Monitor).

3. Select the first element that you want to monitor. If you are working with a linked model, select the element that is in your host project first. (Hint: the order in which the software requires you to select the elements is displayed in the Status Bar, as shown in Figure 3–17.)

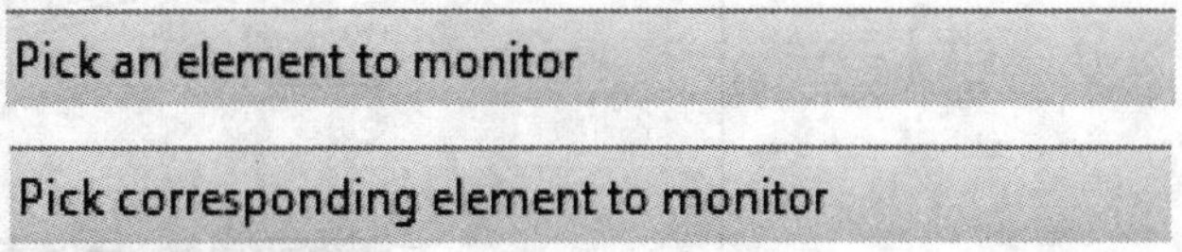

Pick an element to monitor

Pick corresponding element to monitor

Figure 3–17

4. Select the corresponding element to monitor.
5. The two elements are now monitoring each other. If one is modified, an alert displays indicating the change.
6. Repeat the process for any additional elements.

7. Click ![icon] (Finish) when you are done.

- The elements do not have to be at the same elevation or location for the software to monitor them.

3.3 Setting Up Levels

 Learning Objectives

- Add and modify levels.
- Create Plan views from levels.

Levels define stories and other vertical heights (such as a plenum or a reference height), as shown in Figure 3–18. The default templates include two levels, but you can define as many levels in a project as required. They can go down (for basements) as well as up.

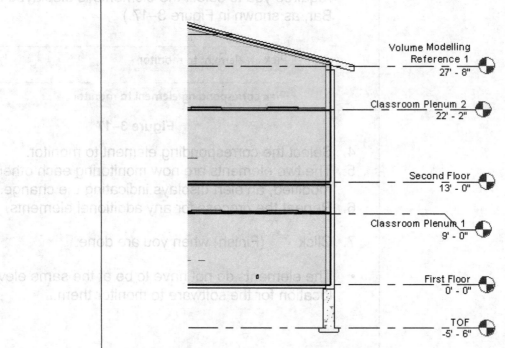

Volume Modelling
Reference 1
27' - 8"

Classroom Plenum 2
22' - 2"

Second Floor
13' - 0"

Classroom Plenum 1
9' - 0"

First Floor
0' - 0"

TOF
-5' - 6"

Figure 3–18

- You must be in an elevation or section view to define levels.

- Levels can be drawn or copied and monitored.

- It is recommended to copy and monitor levels from the linked architectural model into a MEP project first. Then the required levels can be drawn in the MEP project.

How To: Draw Levels

1. Open an elevation or section view.

2. In the *Architecture* tab>Datum panel, click (Level), or type **LL**.

- Click (Add Elbow) to add a jog to the level line as shown in Figure 3–22. Drag the blue sizing handles to new locations as required. This is a view-specific change.

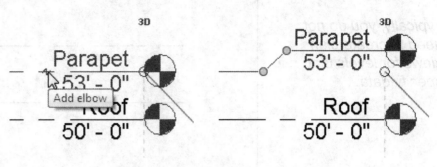

Figure 3–22

Renaming Levels

You can rename a level by double-clicking on the name next to the level head or by selecting the level and modifying the *Name* in Properties.

- If you rename a Level, an alert box opens, prompting you to rename the corresponding views as shown in Figure 3–23.

Click ⌐ Yes ⌐. The view is renamed in the Project Browser and all other associated views.

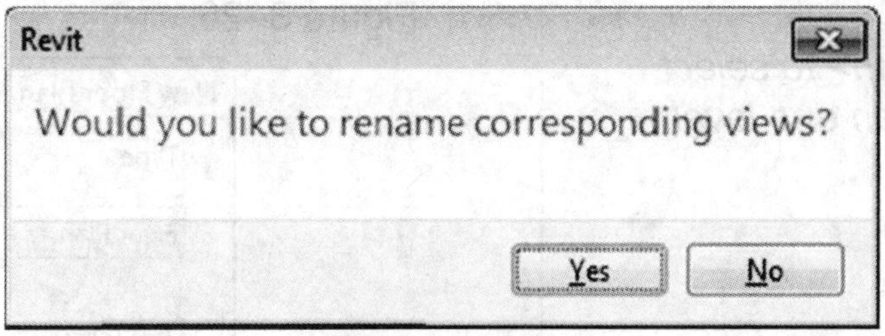

Figure 3–23

Creating Plan Views

If you do not want the plan views to be created, clear the option.

When you place a level, a Floor Plan and Ceiling Plan view for that level is automatically created if the **Make Plan View** option is selected in the Options Bar, as shown in Figure 3–24.

| Place Level | ☑ Make Plan View | Plan View Types... | Offset: 0' 0" |

Figure 3–24

• You can identify if a plan view is created for a level, by the color of the level head. Level heads with views are blue, such as Level 1 and Level 2 in Figure 3–25, and level heads without views are black, such as Level 3 in Figure 3–25.

Typically, you do not need to create plan views for levels that specify data.

| Level 3 |
| 24' - 0" |

| Level 2 |
| 13' - 0" |

| Level 1 |
| 0' - 0" |

Figure 3–25

• You can add plan views to match levels if they were not already created.

How To: Create Plan Views

1. In the *View* tab>Create panel, expand ▣ (Plan Views) and click ▭ (Floor Plan) or ▣ (Reflected Ceiling Plan).

Hold <Ctrl> to select more than one level.

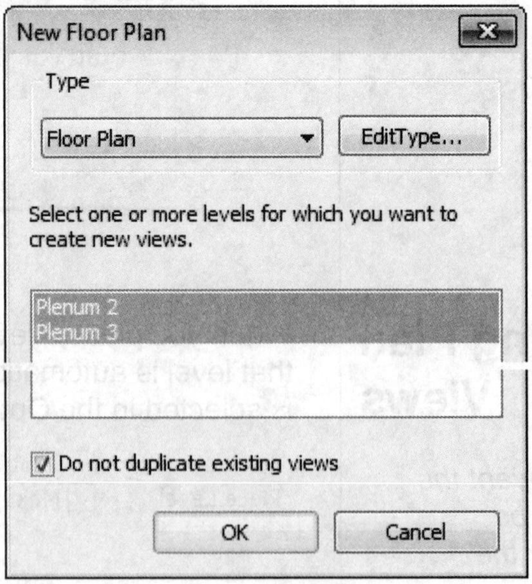

2. In the New Floor (or Ceiling) Plan dialog box, select the levels for which you want to create plan views, as shown in Figure 3–26.

New Floor Plan

Type

Floor Plan ▼   Edit Type...

Select one or more levels for which you want to create new views.

Plenum 2
Plenum 3

☑ Do not duplicate existing views

OK   Cancel

Figure 3–26

3. Click OK .

Practice 3b

Copy, Add, and Monitor Levels

 Learning Objectives

- Copy and monitor levels.
- Add and monitor levels.

Estimated time for completion: 10 minutes.

In this practice, you will use **Copy/Monitor** to copy and monitor levels from the architectural model to the MEP project, as shown in Figure 3–27. You will also add levels and then monitor them against other levels.

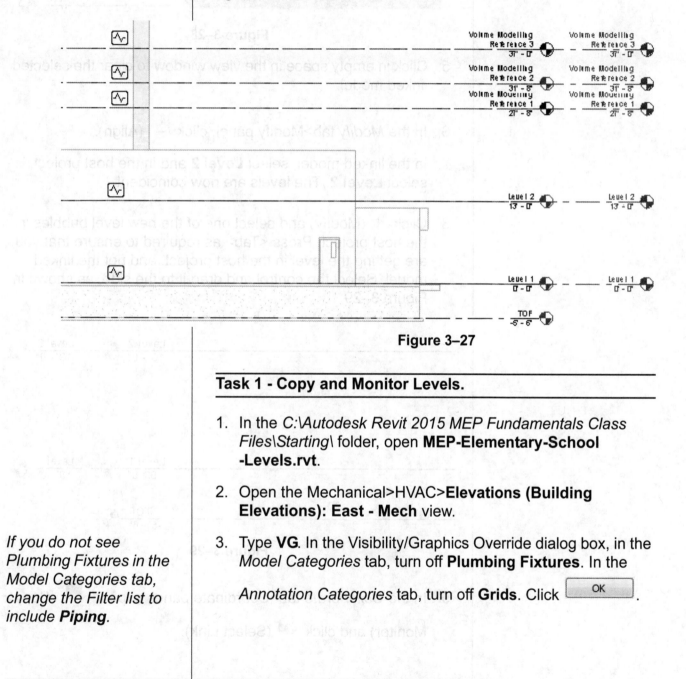

Figure 3–27

Task 1 - Copy and Monitor Levels.

1. In the *C:\Autodesk Revit 2015 MEP Fundamentals Class Files\Starting* folder, open **MEP-Elementary-School -Levels.rvt**.

2. Open the Mechanical>HVAC>**Elevations (Building Elevations): East - Mech** view.

*If you do not see Plumbing Fixtures in the Model Categories tab, change the Filter list to include **Piping**.*

3. Type **VG**. In the Visibility/Graphics Override dialog box, in the *Model Categories* tab, turn off **Plumbing Fixtures**. In the *Annotation Categories* tab, turn off **Grids**. Click ☐ OK ☐.

4. There are two levels in the host project. Select the linked architectural model to help you distinguish between them, as shown in Figure 3–28.

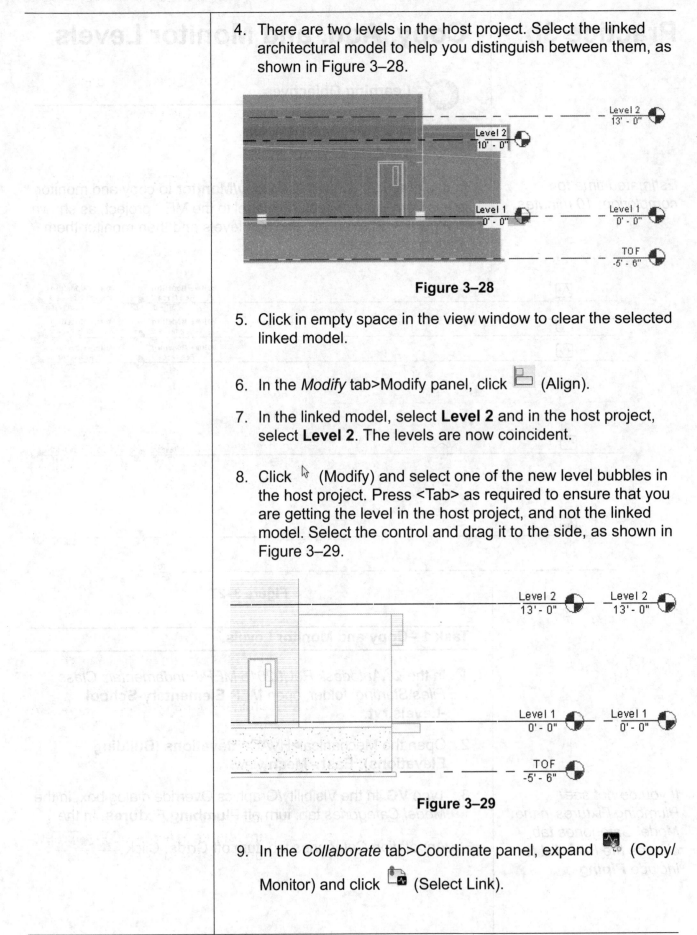

Figure 3–28

5. Click in empty space in the view window to clear the selected linked model.

6. In the *Modify* tab>Modify panel, click ⊡ (Align).

7. In the linked model, select **Level 2** and in the host project, select **Level 2**. The levels are now coincident.

8. Click ⌖ (Modify) and select one of the new level bubbles in the host project. Press <Tab> as required to ensure that you are getting the level in the host project, and not the linked model. Select the control and drag it to the side, as shown in Figure 3–29.

Figure 3–29

9. In the *Collaborate* tab>Coordinate panel, expand (Copy/ Monitor) and click (Select Link).

10. Select the linked model.

11. In the *Copy/Monitor* tab>Tools panel, click (Monitor).

12. In the host project, select **Level 1**. In the linked model, select **Level 1**. Repeat for **Level 2.**

13. In the Copy/Monitor panel, click (Finish). The levels are now monitored as shown in Figure 3–30.

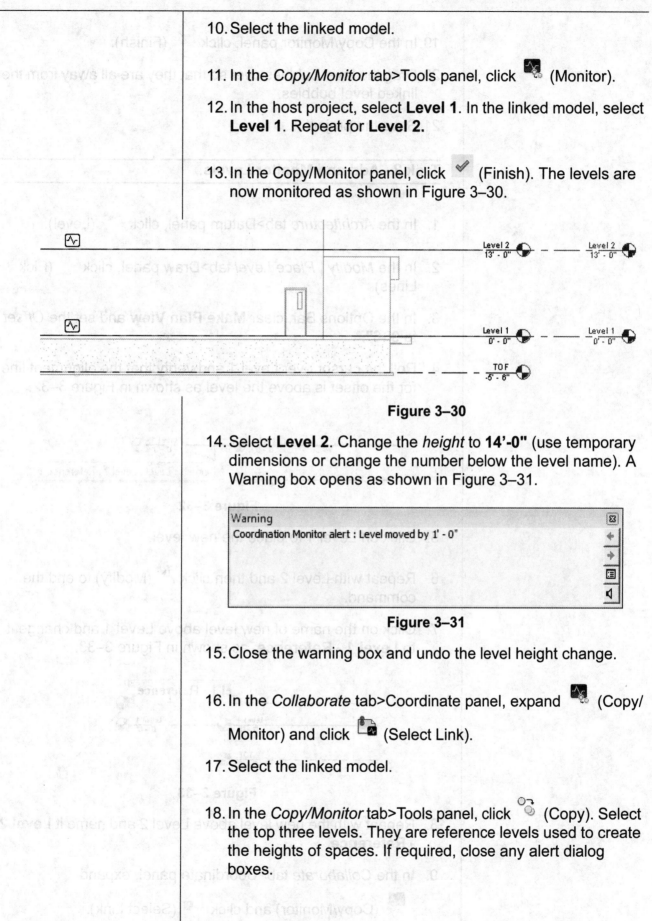

Figure 3–30

14. Select **Level 2**. Change the *height* to **14'-0"** (use temporary dimensions or change the number below the level name). A Warning box opens as shown in Figure 3–31.

Figure 3–31

15. Close the warning box and undo the level height change.

16. In the *Collaborate* tab>Coordinate panel, expand (Copy/ Monitor) and click (Select Link).

17. Select the linked model.

18. In the *Copy/Monitor* tab>Tools panel, click (Copy). Select the top three levels. They are reference levels used to create the heights of spaces. If required, close any alert dialog boxes.

19. In the Copy/Monitor panel, click ✓ (Finish).

20. Drag the level bubbles over so that they are all away from the linked level bubbles.

21. Save the project.

Task 2 - Add and Monitor Levels.

1. In the *Architecture* tab>Datum panel, click ⌖ (Level).

2. In the *Modify | Place Level* tab>Draw panel, click ⤢ (Pick Lines).

3. In the Options Bar, clear **Make Plan View** and set the *Offset* to **3'-6"**.

4. Roll the cursor over Level 1 and verify that the alignment line for the offset is above the level as shown in Figure 3–32.

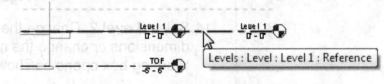

Figure 3–32

5. Click on Level 1 to place the new level.

6. Repeat with Level 2 and then click ⌖ (Modify) to end the command.

7. Click on the name of new level above Level 1 and change it to **Level 1 - Reference**, as shown in Figure 3–33.

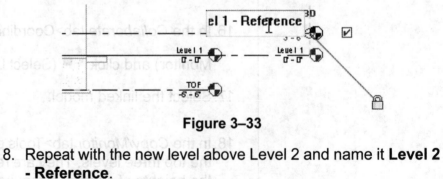

Figure 3–33

8. Repeat with the new level above Level 2 and name it **Level 2 - Reference**.

9. In the *Collaborate* tab>Coordinate panel, expand
   ⬚ (Copy/Monitor) and click ⬚ (Select Link).

10. Select the linked model.

11. In the *Copy/Monitor* tab>Tools panel, click ![icon] (Monitor).

12. In the host project, select **Level 1 - Reference**. In the linked model, select **Level 1**. Repeat for **Level 2 - Reference** and **Level 2.**

13. In the Copy/Monitor panel, click ![icon] (Finish).

14. Zoom out and save the project.

3.4 Batch Copy and Monitor

 Learning Objectives

- Apply Coordination Settings for Copy/Monitor.
- Copy and monitor elements using **Batch Copy**.

Fixtures that can be copied and monitored from linked models include air terminals, lighting fixtures, electrical fixtures, mechanical equipment, plumbing fixtures and others. To make the process of copy/monitor more effective, you can setup the behavior of various categories as they are copied, as shown in the Coordination Settings dialog box in Figure 3–34. In this dialog box, you can also prepare elements to be batch copy/monitored.

Coordination Settings - MEP-Elementary-School-Architectural.rvt : 1 (<Not Shared>)

Apply settings to: MEP-Elementary-School-Architectura ▾

Category	Behavior	
Air Terminals	Copy behavior	Copy individually
Communication Devices	Mapping behavior	Copy original
Data Devices		
Electrical Equipment		
Electrical Fixtures		
Fire Alarm Devices		
Lighting Devices		
Lighting Fixtures		
Mechanical Equipment		
Nurse Call Devices		
Plumbing Fixtures		
Security Devices		
Sprinklers		
Telephone Devices		

Figure 3–34

- Only Autodesk Revit MEP fixtures in the linked model can be copied and monitored. This process cannot be used for non-MEP elements in the host project.

- If a linked model has nested links you can only copy and monitor fixtures from primary linked model.

- Create the default settings before you start to copy and monitor. This saves you time and reduces errors.

How To: Define Default Coordination Settings

1. In the *Collaborate* tab>Coordinate panel, expand
   (Copy/Monitor) and click (Select Link).
2. Select the linked model you want to work with.

Coordination Settings are also accessible in the Collaborate tab> Coordinate panel.

3. In the *Copy/Monitor* tab>Tools panel, click (Coordination Settings).
4. In the Coordination Settings dialog box, set the *Behavior* for each category of MEP fixtures, as shown in Figure 3–35 for Air Terminals. In the *Category* area, select the type of fixtures you want to modify. In the *Behavior* area, specify the **Copy behavior** and the **Mapping behavior**.

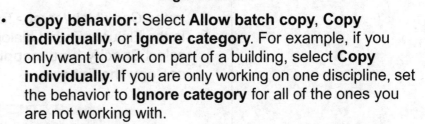

Figure 3–35

- **Copy behavior:** Select **Allow batch copy**, **Copy individually**, or **Ignore category**. For example, if you only want to work on part of a building, select **Copy individually**. If you are only working on one discipline, set the behavior to **Ignore category** for all of the ones you are not working with.

  - **Mapping behavior:** Select **Copy original** or **Specify type mapping**.

5. If you select **Specify type mapping**, under the Category, select Type Mapping. Then you can set up the coordination between the linked model and the host project as shown in Figure 3–36.

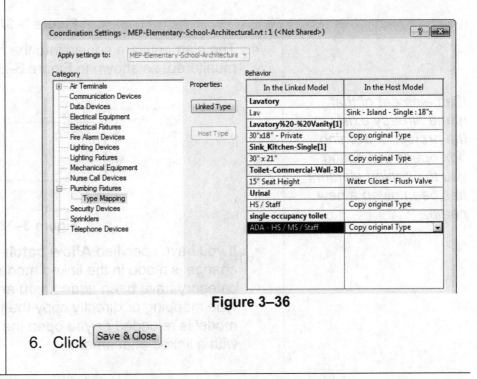

Figure 3–36

6. Click Save & Close .

Batch Copying Fixtures

When working with a project in which the architect has placed most of the fixtures and devices, you can use a batch copying process that saves you the time it would take to select each element.

- It is recommended that you set up the Coordination Settings for the linked model before you start the process. However, you can also do this before copying in the fixtures.

- Levels should be copied first before you copy fixtures into the project.

How To: Batch Copy Fixtures

1. Start the **Copy/Monitor** process and set the **Coordination Settings** for a selected linked model.

2. In the *Copy/Monitor* tab>Tools panel, click (Batch Copy).

3. In the Fixtures Found dialog box shown in Figure 3–37, select **Specify type mapping behavior and copy fixtures** or **Copy the fixtures**.

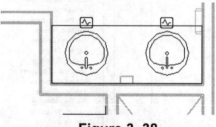

Figure 3–37

4. The elements are copied into the host project and set to be monitored, as shown in Figure 3–38.

Figure 3–38

If an element of that name already exists in the project, a warning box opens prompting you the copied element has been given a new name.

- If you have specified **Allow batch copy** for a category and a change is made in the linked model to which elements of that category have been added, you are prompted to specify the type mapping or directly copy the fixtures when the linked model is reloaded or you open the Autodesk Revit MEP file with a linked attachment.

3.5 Coordination Review

Learning Objective

- Run a Coordination Review.

Monitoring elements identifies changes in the data (such as level names) as well as changes in placement. For example, if you move a plumbing fixture, it prompts a Coordination Monitor alert, as shown in Figure 3–39. To correct or accept these changes you can run a Coordination Review.

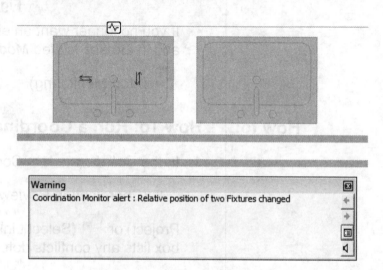

Figure 3–39

- If you open a project with a linked model, which contains elements that have been modified and monitored, the Warning shown in Figure 3–40 displays.

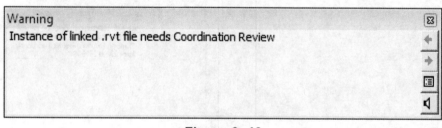

Figure 3–40

- If you move an element that is copied into the host file, a Warning displays as shown in Figure 3–41. This does not prevent you from making the change but alerts you that this is a monitored element that needs further coordination with other disciplines.

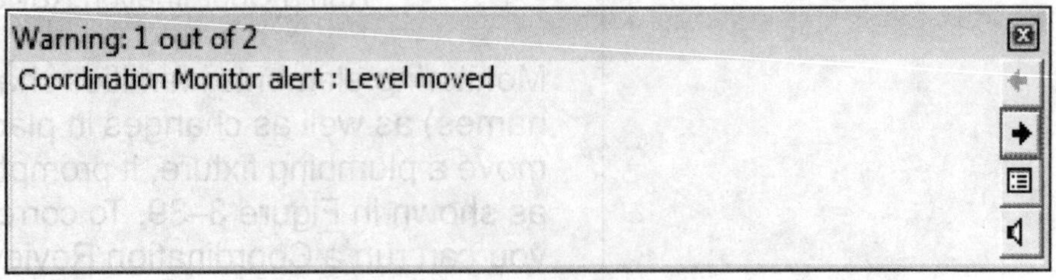

Warning: 1 out of 2

Coordination Monitor alert : Level moved

Figure 3–41

- If you no longer want an element to be monitored, select it and in the associated *Modify* tab>Monitor panel, click

  (Stop Monitoring).

How to:

How To: Run a Coordination Review

1. In the *Collaborate* tab>Coordinate panel, expand

   (Coordination Review) and click (Use Current

   Project) or (Select Link). The Coordination Review dialog box lists any conflicts detected as shown in Figure 3–42.

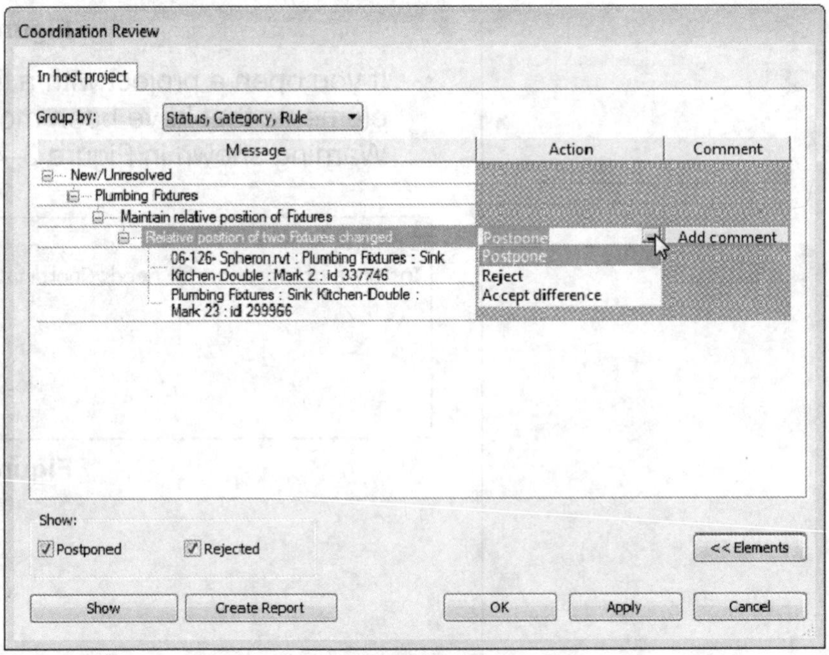

Figure 3–42

- If there are no conflicts the *Message* area is empty.

- You can group the information by **Status**, **Category**, and **Rule** in a variety of different ways in the Group by: drop-down list. This is important if you have many elements to review.

- Beside each conflict is a place for an Action. The Action can be: **Postpone**, **Reject**, **Accept Difference** (as shown in Figure 3–43), or **Rename/Modify/Move** in relationship to the elements involved.

Message	Action	Comment
New/Unresolved		
Levels		
Maintain Position		
Level moved by 50	Postpone	Add comment
Level moved by 50	Postpone	
	Reject	
	Accept difference	
	Move Level 'Level 2'	
	Move Level 'Level 1'	

Figure 3–43

- To add a comment, click Add comment in the column to the right. This enables you to make a note about the change, such as the date of the modification

- You can select the element names or click Show to display any items in conflict where the view changes to center the elements in your screen. Selecting the name does not change the view.

- Click Create Report to create an HTML report that you can share with other users, such as the example shown in Figure 3–44.

Revit Coordination Report

In host project

New/Unresolved	Plumbing Fixtures	Maintain relative position of Fixtures	Relative position of two Fixtures changed	Plumbing Fixtures : Sink_Kitchen-Single[1] : Mark 1 : id 734856 MEP-Elementary-School-Architectural.rvt : Plumbing Fixtures : Sink_Kitchen-Single[1] : Mark 80 : id 329165

Figure 3–44

Practice 3c

Estimated time for completion: 15 minutes.

Batch Copy and Coordination Review

 Learning Objective

- Make changes to monitored levels and use Coordination Review to resolve the changes.

In this practice you will copy and monitor MEP fixtures using **Batch Copy**, and coordinate a level change between the architectural model and MEP project, as shown in Figure 3–45.

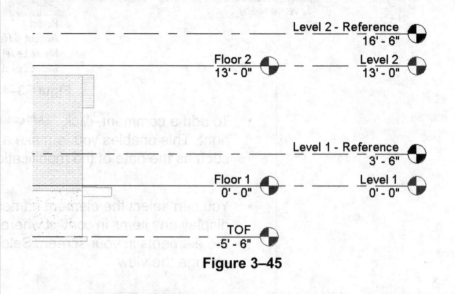

Figure 3–45

Task 1 - Copy and Monitor MEP Fixtures.

1. In the *C:\Autodesk Revit 2015 MEP Fundamentals Class Files\Starting* folder, open **MEP-Elementary-School -Batch.rvt**.

2. In the Project Browser, open the Mechanical>Plumbing> Floor Plans> **1 - Plumbing** view.

3. Type the shortcut **VG**. In the *Annotation Categories* tab, toggle off **Grids**. Note that the MEP base linked view does not work because you need to see the plumbing elements in the architectural model. Click OK.

4. Plumbing fixtures in the linked model display darker in this view but are not yet copied into the host project.

5. In the *Collaborate* tab>Coordinate panel, expand
   ⬛ (Copy/Monitor) and click ⬛ (Select Link).

6. Select the linked model.

7. In the *Copy/Monitor* tab>Tools panel, click ⬛ (Coordination Settings).

8. Select the **Plumbing Fixtures** category and set the *Copy behavior* to **Allow batch copy** and the *Mapping behavior* to **Specify type mapping** as shown in Figure 3–46.

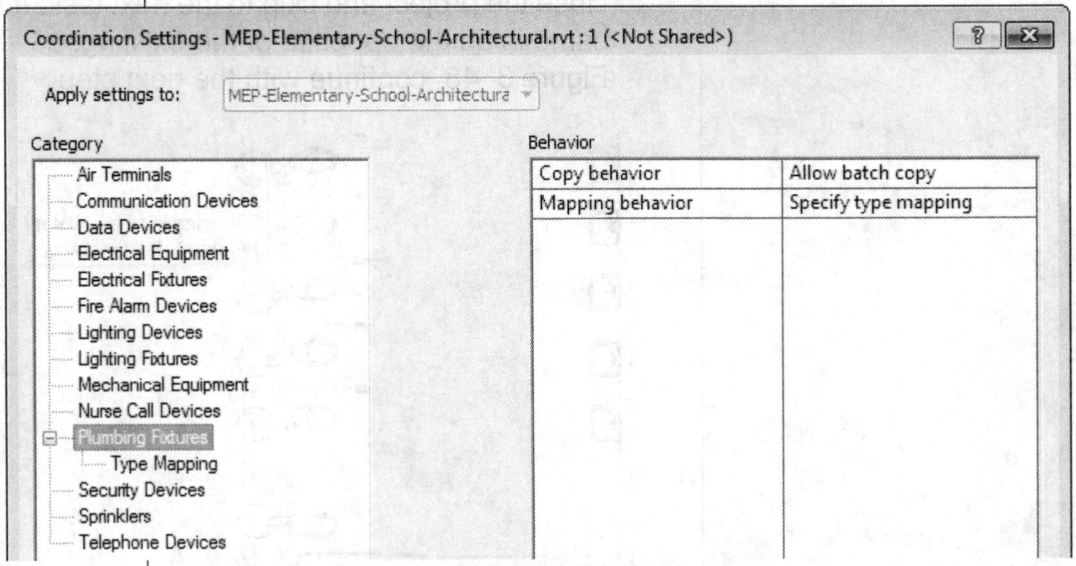

Figure 3–46

9. In the *Category* area, under the **Plumbing Fixtures** category, select **Type mapping**.

10. In the Behavior area, change the *Host Model* type for both of the toilet types to **Water Closet - Flush Valve - Wall Mounted: Public - 1.6 gpf** as shown in Figure 3–47.

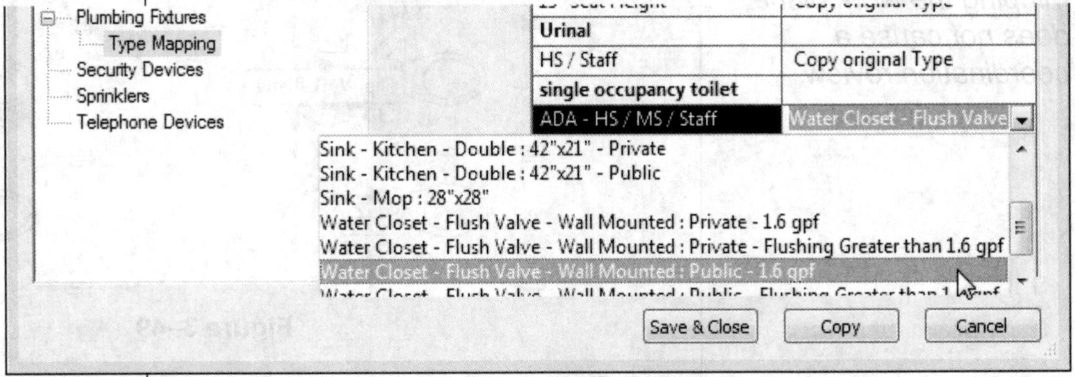

Figure 3–47

11. Click Save & Close .

12. In the *Copy/Monitor* tab>Tools panel, click (Batch Copy).

13. In the Fixtures Found dialog box, select **Copy the fixtures**. Wait while the fixtures are being pasted.

14. In the Copy/Monitor panel, click (Finish).

15. Zoom in on one of the restrooms. If the Water Closet that was specified in the Type Mapping came in correctly, save and close the project and skip to the next task. If the Water Closet came in as the opposite of the existing, as shown in Figure 3–48, continue with the next step.

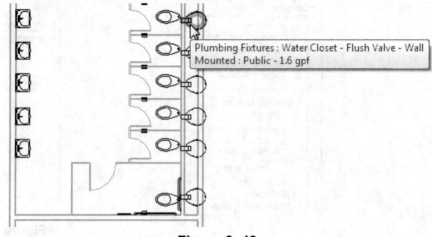

Figure 3–48

16. Select one of the water closets. (Flip Workplane) displays as shown on the left in Figure 3–49. Click on the control. The water closet is placed in the correct direction as shown on the right in Figure 3–49.

Flipping the work plane does not cause a coordination review.

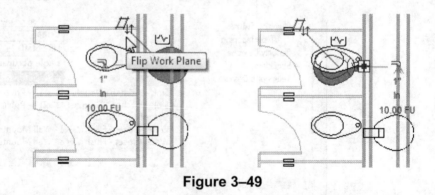

Figure 3–49

17. Repeat this process for each of the water closet fixtures. This must be done one at a time.

18. Double-click the mouse wheel to zoom out to the full view.

19. Save and close the project. Note that you cannot open a linked project while the host project is open.

Task 2 - Coordinate the architectural and MEP models.

1. Open the file **MEP-Elementary-School-Architectural.rvt** found in the *Starting* folder of your class files folder. This is the file that is linked into the Autodesk Revit MEP project.

2. In the Project Browser, open the Elevations (Building Elevation)>Architectural: **East** view.

3. Zoom in on the Level names to the right of the elevation.

4. Select **Level 1** and change the *name* to **Floor 1** as shown in Figure 3–50. When prompted to rename the corresponding views, click .

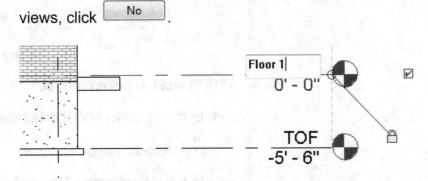

Figure 3–50

5. Repeat with **Level 2** and rename it **Floor 2**.

6. Save and close the project.

7. Reopen **MEP-Elementary-School-Batch.rvt**. A Warning box opens, prompting you that the linked model needs a Coordination Review, as shown in Figure 3–51.

Autodesk Revit 2015

Warning - can be ignored

Instance of link needs Coordination Review

| Show | More Info | Expand >> |

| OK | Cancel |

Figure 3–51

8. Click   OK   .

9. Open the Mechanical>HVAC>Elevation (Building Elevation): **East - Mech** view and zoom in on the level names. The linked model displays the updated names but the host file has not yet been updated as shown in Figure 3–52.

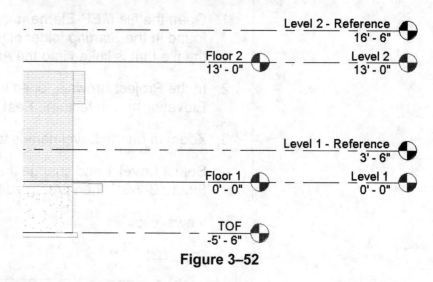

Figure 3–52

10. Select the linked model.

11. In the *Modify | RVT Links* tab>Monitor panel, click

    (Coordination Review).

12. In the Coordination Review dialog box, expand each of the New/Unresolved>Levels>Maintain Name>*Name changed* categories to display the proposed changes.

13. Select one of the **Name changed** options to display the related levels highlighted in the view as shown in Figure 3–53. In the example, the software recognizes the monitoring connection between Level 2 in the host project with Floor 2 in the linked model.

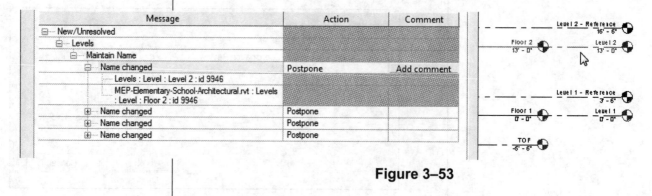

Figure 3–53

14. Next to each N*ame changed* message, expand the list in the *Action* column and select **Rename Element** as shown for Level 2 in Figure 3–54.

In host project

Group by:	Status, Category, Rule ▾		
Message		**Action**	**Comment**
⊟ New/Unresolved			
⊟ Levels			
⊟ Maintain Name			
⊞ Name changed		Postpone ▭	Add comment
⊞ Name changed		Postpone	
⊞ Name changed		Reject	
⊞ Name changed		Accept difference	
		Rename Element 'Level 2'	

Figure 3–54

15. Click [OK].

16. The levels in the host project are renamed as shown in Figure 3–55.

Floor 2 - Reference
16' - 6"

Floor 2 — Floor 2
13' - 0"   13' - 0"

Floor 1 - Reference
3' - 6"

Floor 1 — Floor 1
0' - 0"   0' - 0"

Figure 3–55

17. Save and close the model.

If the second level does not change you might have missed monitoring it earlier in the practice.

Chapter Review Questions

1. Which of the following elements can be copied and monitored? (Select all that apply.)

    a. Plumbing Fixtures

    b. Levels

    c. Ducts

    d. Electrical Devices

2. On which of the following element types can a coordination review with the host project be performed?

    a. CAD link

    b. CAD import

    c. Revit link

    d. Revit import

3. When linking an architectural model into a systems project, which of the positioning methods, as shown in Figure 3–56, keeps the model in the same place if the extents of the linked model change in size?

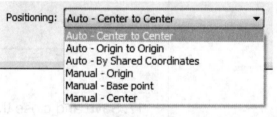

Figure 3–56

    a. Auto - Center-to-Center

    b. Auto - Origin-to-Origin

    c. Manual - Basepoint

    d. Manual - Center

4. How many times can one project be linked into another project?

    a. Once

    b. It is limited by the size of the link.

    c. As many as you want.

5. How many different levels, such as those shown in Figure 3–57, can you have in a project?

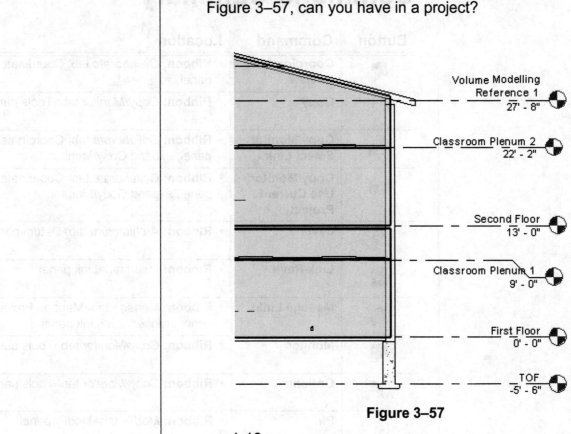

Figure 3–57

a. 1-10

b. 10 up and 10 down from Level 1.

c. As many as there are in the template file.

d. As many as you want.

Command Summary

Button	Command	Location
	Coordination Review	• **Ribbon:** *Collaborate* tab>Coordinate panel
	Copy	• **Ribbon:** *Copy/Monitor* tab>Tools panel
	Copy/Monitor> Select Link	• **Ribbon:** *Collaborate* tab>Coordinate panel, expand Copy/Monitor
	Copy/Monitor> Use Current Project	• **Ribbon:** *Collaborate* tab>Coordinate panel, expand Copy/Monitor
	Level	• **Ribbon:** *Architecture* tab>Datum panel
	Link Revit	• **Ribbon:** *Insert* tab>Link panel
	Manage Links	• **Ribbon:** *Manage* tab>Manage Projects panel or *Insert* tab>Link panel
	Monitor	• **Ribbon:** *Copy/Monitor* tab>Tools panel
	Options	• **Ribbon:** *Copy/Monitor* tab>Tools panel
	Pin	• **Ribbon:** *Modify* tab>Modify panel
	Visibility/ Graphics	• **Ribbon:** *View* tab>Graphics panel • **Shortcut Key:** VG or VV

Chapter 4

Working with Views

In this chapter you learn how to create duplicate views, callout views, elevations, and sections. You also learn how to setup views using underlays and view range as well as by overriding graphics in views.

This chapter contains the following topics:

- **Duplicating Views**
- **Adding Callout Views**
- **Setting the View Display**
- **Elevations and Sections**

4.1 Duplicating Views

Learning Objective

- Duplicate views so that you can modify what displays in each view.

Once you have created a model, you do not have to redraw the elements at different scales or copy them so that they can be used on more than one sheet. Instead, duplicate views and modify them to suit your needs. For example, a view or callout of the First Floor plan can be duplicated and modified to create a dimension plan, HVAC plan, etc., as shown in Figure 4–1.

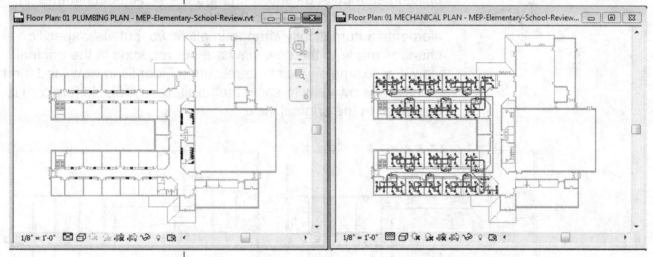

Figure 4–1

How To: Create Duplicate Views

1. Open the view you want to duplicate.
2. In the *View* tab>Create panel, expand **Duplicate View** and select the type of duplicate view you want to create, as shown in Figure 4–2.

Most types of views can be duplicated.

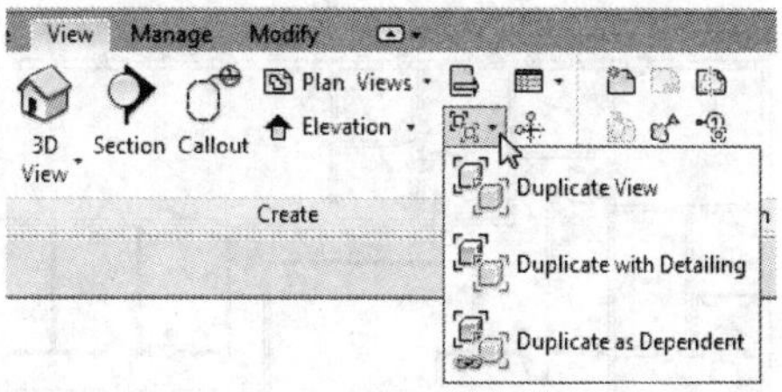

Figure 4–2

• Alternatively, you can right-click on a view in the Project Browser and select the type of duplicate that you want to use, as shown in Figure 4–3.

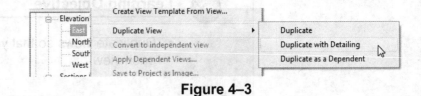

Figure 4–3

• When you duplicate a view, it is named after the original view name with "Copy x" appended to the end (x stands for the number of the copy).

Duplication Types

Duplicate creates a copy of the view that only includes the building elements, as shown in Figure 4–4. Annotation and detailing are not copied into the new view. Building model elements automatically change in all views, but view-specific changes made to the new view are not reflected in the original view. For example, you can duplicate a Floor Plan view, and then modify the new view to show the furniture layout. No furniture is displayed in the original view.

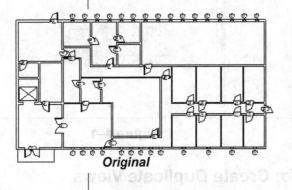
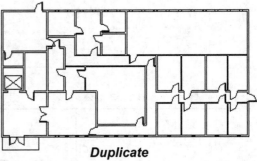

Original   *Duplicate*

Figure 4–4

Duplicate with Detailing creates a copy of the view and includes all annotation and detail elements (such as tags), as shown in Figure 4–5. Any annotation or view-specific elements created in the new view are not reflected in the original view.

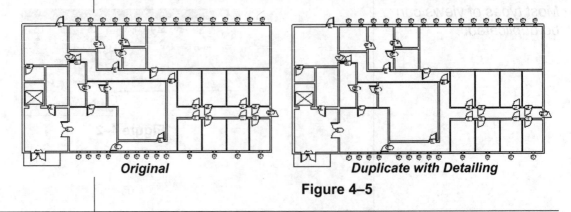

Original   *Duplicate with Detailing*

Figure 4–5

Duplicate as a Dependent creates a copy of the view and links it to the original (parent) view. View-specific changes made to the original view are also reflected in the dependent (child) view and vice-versa. Any updates to View Properties, View Display, or Visibility/Graphic Overrides display in both the original and dependent views.

Hint: Common Uses of Duplicate as a Dependent

Use dependent views when the building model is so large that you need to split the building onto separate sheets, with views that are all same scale. Having one overall view with dependent views makes viewing changes (i.e., scale or detail level) easier.

Dependent views display in the Project Browser under the top-level view, as shown in Figure 4–6.

Figure 4–6

- If you need a plan displayed at a smaller scale, create a regular duplicate view, change the scale, and then create dependent views of this new view if needed.

- If you want to separate a dependent view from the original view, right-click on the dependent view and select **Convert to independent view**.

- The building model always updates in every view, but annotation elements (such as door tags, window tags, and dimensions) are view-specific.

- You can use View Properties, View Display, and Visibility/Graphic Overrides to make the duplicate view different from the original view.

You can also press <F2> to start the Rename command.

- Once you create a new view, you probably want to assign a new name to it. Right-click on the new view in the Project Browser and select **Rename**. In the Rename View dialog box, type in the new name in place of the copy, as shown in Figure 4–7.

Figure 4–7

4.2 Adding Callout Views

Learning Objectives

- Create callout views for detailed plans and sections.
- Modify callout views in the main view and in the callout view including setting the Annotation Crop Region.

Callouts are details of plan, elevation, or section views. When you place a callout in a view, it automatically creates a new view clipped to the boundary of the callout, as shown in Figure 4–8. If you change the size of the callout box in the original view, it automatically updates the callout view and vice-versa. You can create rectangular or sketched callout boundaries.

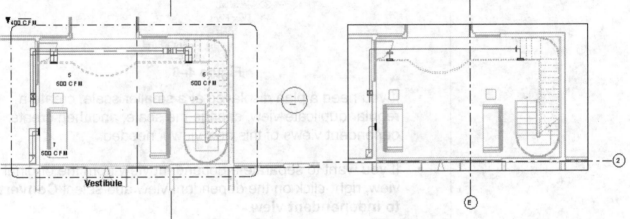

Figure 4–8

How To: Create a Rectangular Callout

1. In the *View tab>Create panel,* click **(Callout)**.
2. Select points for two opposite corners to define the callout box around the area you want to detail.
3. Select the callout and use the shape handles to modify the location of the bubble and any other edges that might need changing.
4. In the Project Browser, rename the callout as required.

How To: Create a Sketched Callout

1. In the *View tab>Create panel,* expand (Callout), and click (Sketch).

2. Sketch the shape of the callout using the tools in the *Modify | Edit Profile* tab>Draw panel, as shown in Figure 4–9.

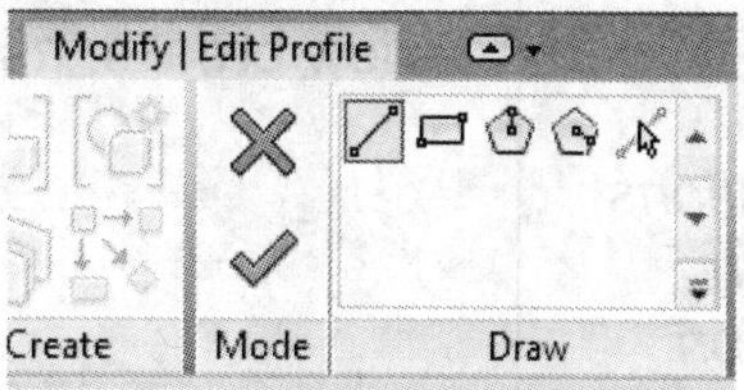

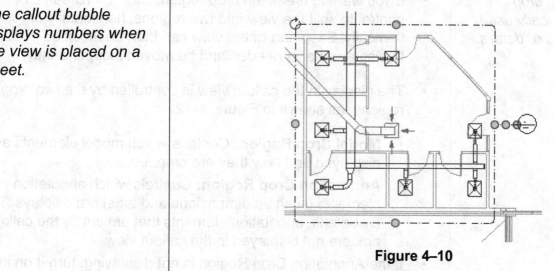

Figure 4–9

3. Click ✓ (Finish) to complete the boundary.
4. Select the callout and use the shape handles to modify the location of the bubble and any other edges that might need to be changed.
5. In the Project Browser, rename the callout as required.

- To open the callout view, double-click on its name in the Project Browser or double-click on the callout bubble (verify that it is not selected before you double-click on it).

- The callout bubble information automatically populates when you place the callout on a sheet.

Modifying Callouts

Modifying Callout Boundaries

In the original view where the callout is created, you can use the shape handles to modify the callout boundary and bubble location, as shown in Figure 4–10. You can also rotate the callout box by dragging ○ (Rotate).

The callout bubble displays numbers when the view is placed on a sheet.

Figure 4–10

Modifying Callout Views

In the callout view, you can modify callouts with controls and view breaks, as shown in Figure 4–11.

The crop region options are also available in section and elevation views.

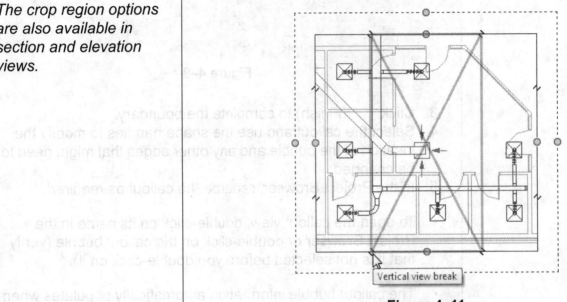

Figure 4–11

- The crop region must be displayed if you want to modify the size of the view. In the View Control Bar, click ⊞ (Show Crop Region) if it is not displayed.

- Resize the crop region using the ○ control on each side of the region.

Breaking the crop region is typically used with sections or details.

- If you want to break the crop region, click ⤲ (Break Line) control to split the view into two regions, horizontally or vertically. Each part of the view can then be modified in size to display what is needed and be moved independently.

- The display in the callout view is controlled by the two crop regions, as shown in Figure 4–12.

    - **Model Crop Region:** Controls which model elements are displayed and how they are cropped.

    - **Annotation Crop Region:** Controls which annotation elements (such as dimensions and tags) are displayed. By default, annotation elements that are cut by the callout box are not displayed in the callout view.

    - If the Annotation Crop Region is not displaying, turn it on in the Properties of the view. Scroll down to the *Extents* area and select **Annotation Crop**, as shown in Figure 4–12.

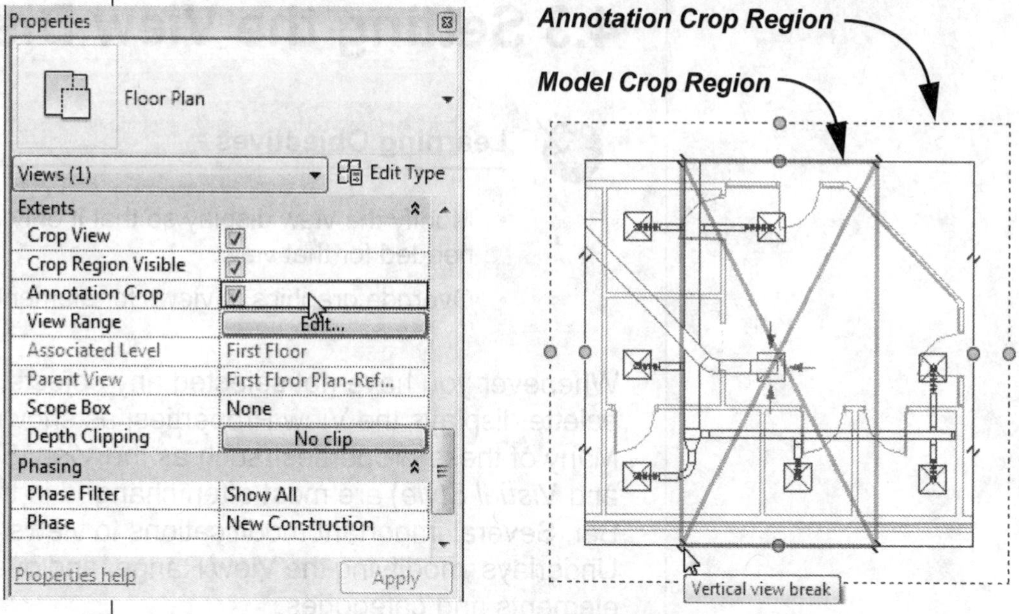

Figure 4–12

- The annotation crop region remains rectangular even if the original callout boundary was created by a sketch.

- If you want to edit the crop region to reshape the boundary of the view, select the crop region and, in the *Modify | Floor Plan* tab>Mode panel, click (Edit Crop). If you want to return a modified crop region to the original rectangular configuration, click ⌐ (Reset Crop).

- You can also resize the crop region and the annotation crop region using the Crop Region Size dialog box as shown in Figure 4–13. In the *Modify | Floor Plan* tab>Crop panel, click ⌐ (Size Crop) to open the dialog box.

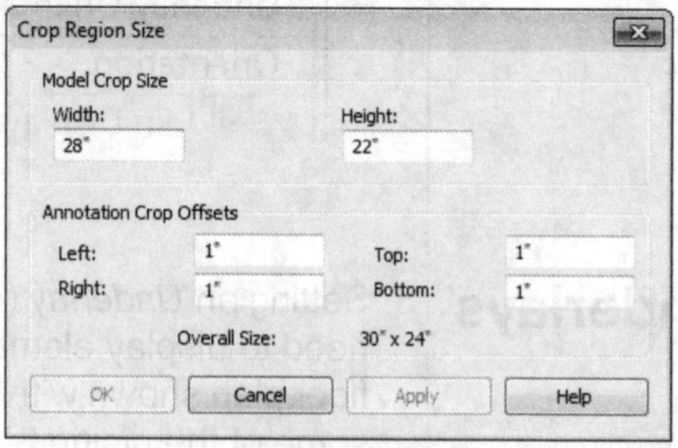

Figure 4–13

- It is a good idea to hide a crop region before placing a view on a sheet. Doing so minimizes the viewport size. In the View Control Bar, click ⊞ (Hide Crop Region).

4.3 Setting the View Display

 Learning Objectives

- Modify the view display so that it only displays what is needed for that view.
- Override graphics in views for elements and categories.

Whenever you have not selected any objects, the Properties palette displays the View Properties, as shown in Figure 4–14. Many of these properties (such as the *View Scale*, *Detail Level*, and *Visual Style*) are most often changed in the View Control Bar. Several important modifications to views include setting Underlays, modifying the View Range, and overriding graphics of elements and categories.

The options in View Properties vary according to the type of view. A floor plan has some different parameters than a 3D view.

Properties	⊠
Floor Plan	▾

Floor Plan: 1 - Mech	▾	🔲 Edit Type

Display Model	Normal
Detail Level	Medium
Parts Visibility	Show Original
Visibility/Graphics Overr...	Edit...
Graphic Display Options	Edit...
Underlay	None
Underlay Orientation	Plan
Orientation	Project North
Wall Join Display	Clean all wall joins

Figure 4–14

Underlays

Setting an *Underlay* (*Graphics* area in Properties) is helpful if you need to display elements on a different level, such as the first floor plan shown with an underlay of the second floor plan, where some of the piping is located in Figure 4–15. You can then use the elements to trace over or even copy to the current level of the view.

Underlays are only available in Floor Plan and Ceiling Plan views.

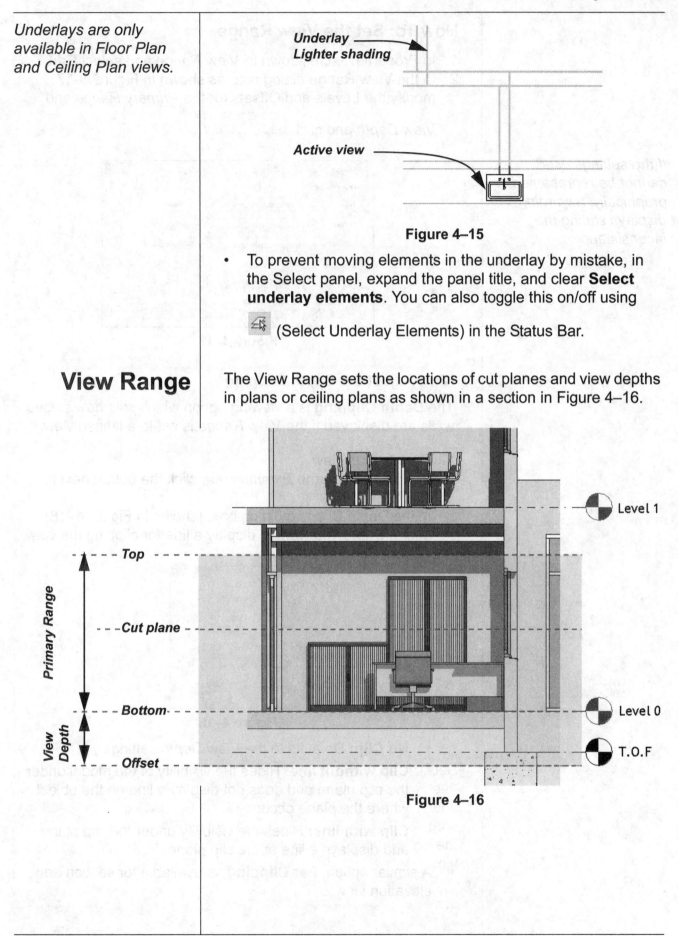

Figure 4–15

- To prevent moving elements in the underlay by mistake, in the Select panel, expand the panel title, and clear **Select underlay elements**. You can also toggle this on/off using

    (Select Underlay Elements) in the Status Bar.

View Range

The View Range sets the locations of cut planes and view depths in plans or ceiling plans as shown in a section in Figure 4–16.

Figure 4–16

How To: Set the View Range

1. In Properties, scroll down to *View Range* and select **Edit...**.
2. In the View Range dialog box, as shown in Figure 4–17, modify the Levels and Offsets for the *Primary Range* and

   View Depth and click | OK |.

If the settings used cannot be represented graphically, a warning displays stating the inconsistency.

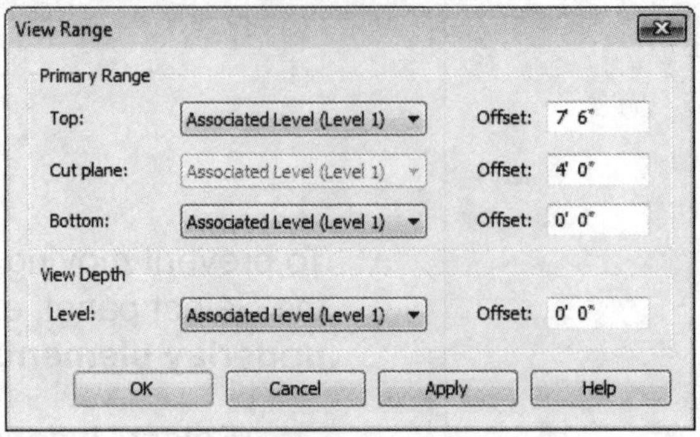

Figure 4–17

Hint: Adjust the Depth Clipping

The **Depth Clipping** is a viewing option which sets how sloped walls are displayed if the *View Range* is set to a limited view.

1. Open a plan view.
2. In Properties, in the *Extents* area, click the button next to *Depth Clipping*.
3. In the Depth Clipping dialog box, (shown in Figure 4–18) define where you want to display a line for clipping the view.

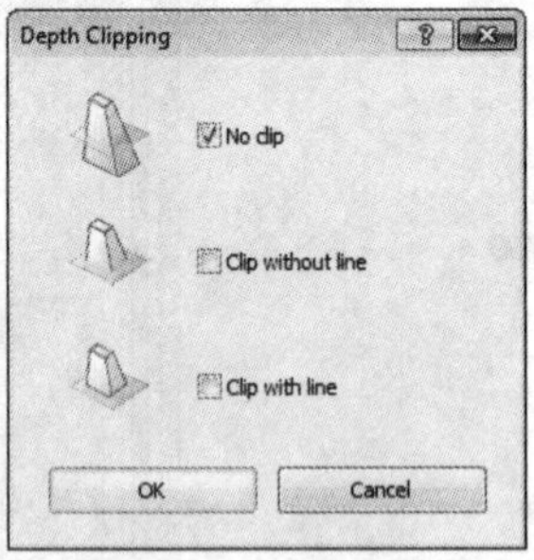

Figure 4–18

- **No Clip:** Defaults to the *View Depth* setting.
- **Clip without line:** Hides the visibility of the model under the clip plane and does not display a line on the object where the plane occurs.
- **Clip with line:** Hides the visibility under the clip plane and displays a line at the clip plane.
- A similar option, **Far Clipping**, is available for section and elevation views.

Overriding Graphics in a View

If you want to change the way the graphics (such as lineweight, color, or pattern) display for elements or categories, you can override them in a view. For example, you can change the grid category in a Floor Plan to halftone, as shown in Figure 4–19.

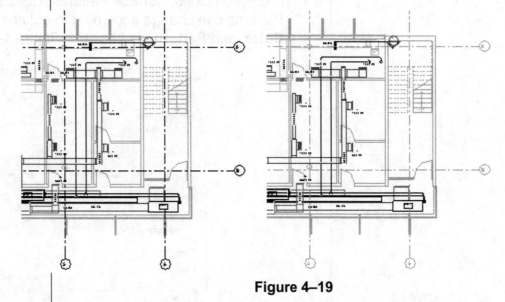

Figure 4–19

- Hiding or overriding by element in a dependent view impacts only that view. If you hide or override by category, it impacts the primary view and all dependent views.

How To: Override Graphics of Individual Elements

1. Select the element(s) you want to modify.
2. Right-click and select **Override Graphics in View>By Element**. The View-Specific Element Graphics dialog box opens, as shown in Figure 4–20.

View-Specific Element Graphics
☑ Visible ☐ Halftone
▶ Projection Lines
▶ Surface Patterns
▶ Surface Transparency
▶ Cut Lines
▶ Cut Patterns
Reset OK Cancel Apply

Figure 4–20

3. Select the changes you want to make and click OK.

- The options in the dialog box vary depending on the type of elements selected.

- Clearing the **Visible** option is the same as hiding elements.

- Projection Lines, Surface Patterns, Cut Lines, and Cut Patterns can change according to options, such as **Weight**, **Color**, and **Pattern**, as shown in Figure 4–21.

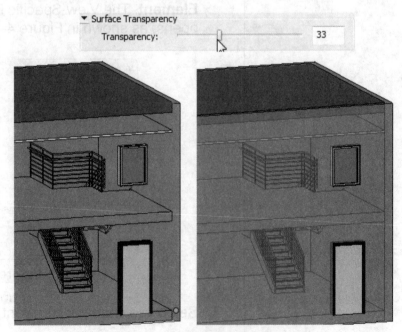

Figure 4–21

- You can modify the transparency of a surface by moving the Surface Transparency slider bar. For example, the transparency of the wall shown on the left in Figure 4–22 is set all of the way to the right of the bar, while that of the wall on the right is set at a 33% transparency.

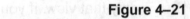

Figure 4–22

How To: Override Graphics of Entire Categories

1. Select an element in the category you want to modify.
2. Right-click and select **Override Graphics in View>By Category**.
3. In the View-Specific Category Graphics dialog box (shown in Figure 4–23), modify the options as you would modify the element graphics and click OK.

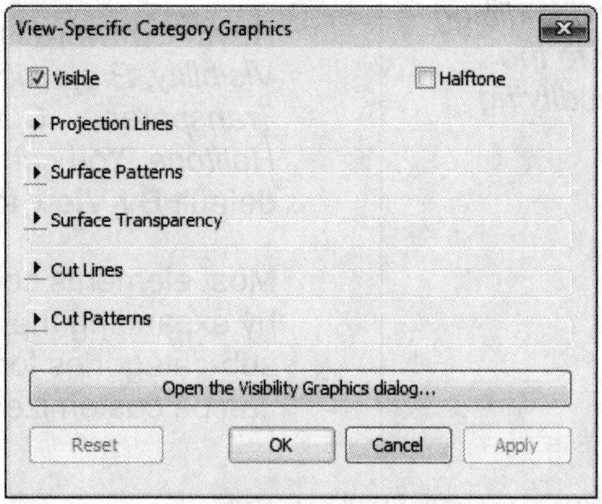

Figure 4–23

- To have more control over the categories click Open the Visibility Graphics dialog... . The Visibility/ Graphic Overrides dialog box opens, as shown in Figure 4–24.

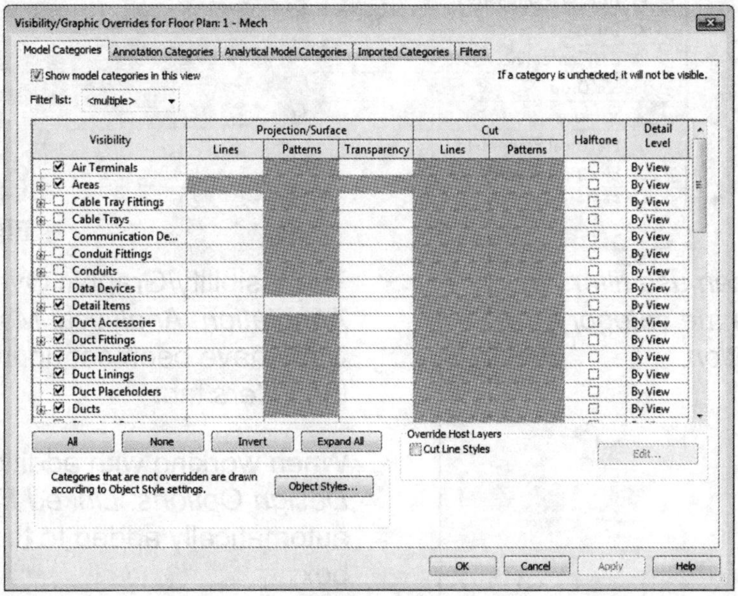

Figure 4–24

For AutoCAD software users, modifying categories in this dialog box is similar to the concept of modifying layers.

- You can also open the Visibility/Graphic Overrides dialog box without opening the View-Specific Category Graphics dialog box first. The quickest way is to use the shortcut by pressing <V> and then pressing <V> or <G>. It is also available in a view's Properties: in the *Graphics* section, beside Visibility/Graphic Overrides, click [Edit...   ].

- The options in the Visibility/Graphic Overrides dialog box control how every element and sub-element in the Autodesk® Revit® software is displayed per view. You can control the *Visibility*, *Projection/Surface for Lines*, *Patterns and Transparency*, *Cut Lines*, and *Patterns*, as well as set *Halftone*. You can also override the *Detail Level* from the default **By View** to **Coarse**, **Medium**, or **Fine**.

- Most elements contain sub-categories that can be modified by expanding the category. For example, ducts include sub-categories for Center line, Drop, and Rise, each of which can be customized, as shown in Figure 4–25.

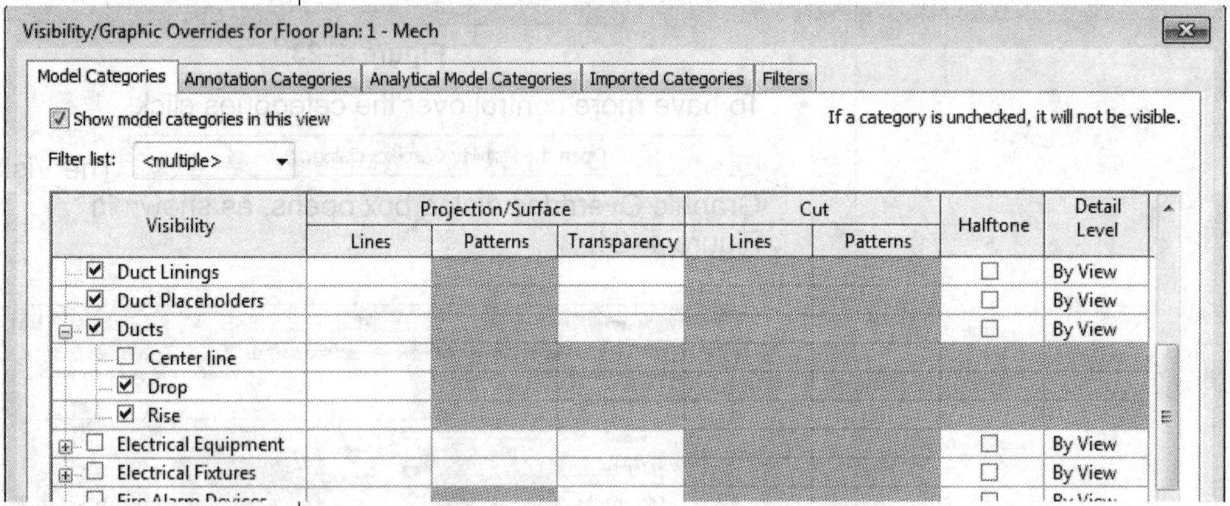

Figure 4–25

You can use filters to refine the category selection.

- The Visibility/Graphic Overrides are divided into *Model*, *Annotation*, *Analytical Model*, and *Imported* categories. If filters have been set up in the project, they are included on the *Filters* tab.

- When working with additional information or data (such as *Design Options*, *Linked Files*, or *Worksets*), new tabs are automatically added to the Visibility/Graphic Overrides dialog box.

Hint: Applying View Templates

A powerful way to use views effectively is to set up a view and then save it as a View Template. To apply a View Template, right-click on a view in the Project Browser and select **Apply View Template Properties....** Then, in the Apply View Template dialog box, select a *Name* in the list (as shown in Figure 4–26) and click OK .

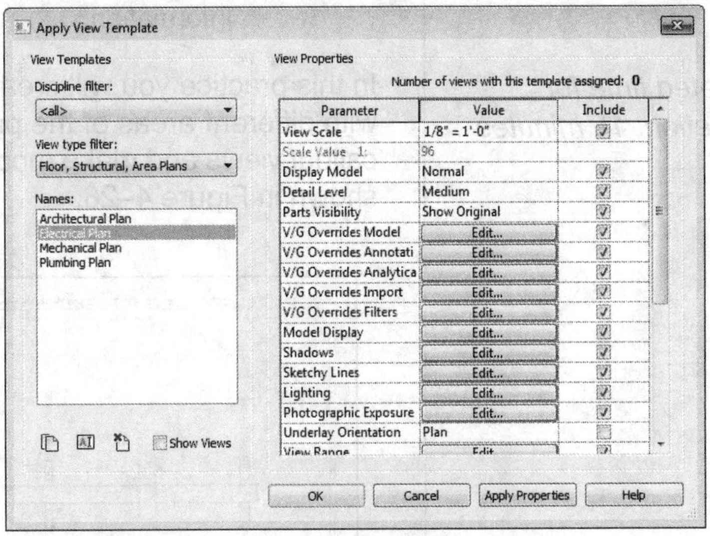

Figure 4–26

- View Templates can also be preset in the View Properties as shown in Figure 4–27.

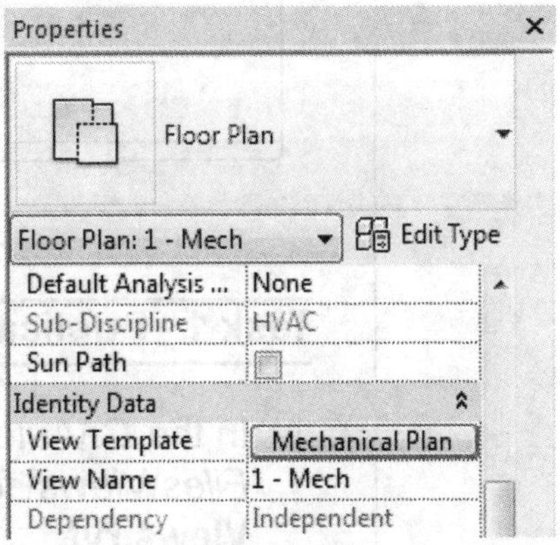

Figure 4–27

- To modify the view without long term changes, click

(Temporary View Properties) in the View Control Bar, enable the temporary View Properties, and select a different view template from the same menu. When finished, select **Restore View Properties**.

Practice 4a

Set Up Duplicate Views and Callouts

 Learning Objectives

- Duplicate and crop views.
- Add a callout view and modify the visibility and graphics so that duplicates of the call out display different information.

Estimated time for completion: 15 minutes

In this practice you will create duplicate views at different scales with different areas of the project cropped. You will also create callout views and make modifications to the visibility graphics, as shown in Figure 4–28.

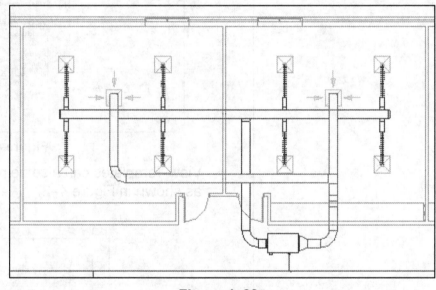

Figure 4–28

Task 1 - Duplicate views.

1. In the *C:\Autodesk Revit 2015 MEP Fundamentals Class Files\Views* folder, open **MEP-Elementary-School-Views.rvt**.

2. In the Project Browser, open the Coordination>All>Floor Plans>**Level 1** view.

3. In the Project Browser, right-click on the **Level 1** view and select **Duplicate View>Duplicate with Detailing**. A copy of the view is created, including the tags that display the room names.

4. Right-click on the new view and rename it as **01 NORTH WING**.

5. In the View Control Bar, click 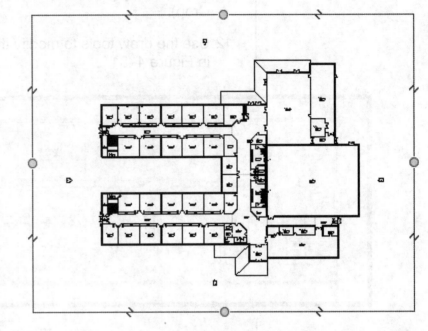 (Show Crop Region).

6. Zoom out to display the full extents of the crop region and select it, as shown in Figure 4–29.

Figure 4–29

7. Change the crop region so that only the upper left wing of the building displays, as shown in Figure 4–30.

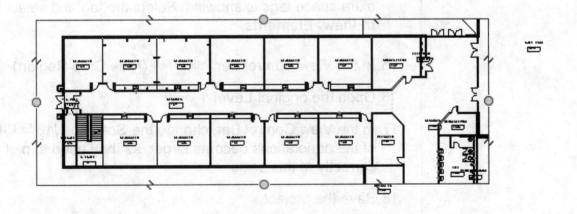

Figure 4–30

8. There are several tags outside the crop region that still display. Select the crop region.

9. In Properties, in the *Extents* area, select **Annotation Crop**, and click [Apply] .

10. Modify the *Annotation Crop* region so the room/space tags do not display.

11. In the *Modify | Floor Plan* tab>Mode panel, click ✏ (Edit Crop).

12. Use the draw tools to modify the crop window to that shown in Figure 4–31.

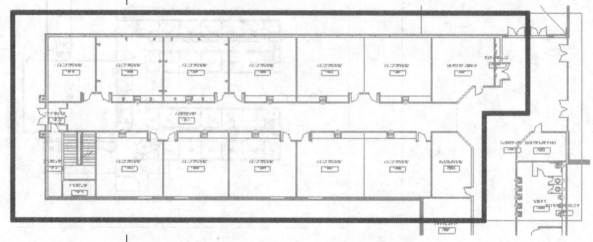

Figure 4–31

13. Click ✓ (Finish Edit Mode).

14. The *Annotation Crop* region is not modified and one of the extra space tags is showing. Select the tag and select **Hide in View>Elements**.

15. In the View Control Bar, click ▣ (Hide Crop Region).

16. Open the original **Level 1** view.

17. In the View Control Bar, change the *Scale* to **1/16"=1'-0"**. All of the annotations become larger, as they need to plot correctly at this scale.

18. Save the project.

Task 2 - Add callout views.

1. In the Project Browser, collapse the *Coordination* group and expand the Mechanical>HVAC>*Floor Plans* group. Open the **02 MECHANICAL PLAN** view.

2. Type **VG**.

3. In the Visibility Graphics Overrides dialog box, in the *Annotation Categories* tab, clear **Grids**.

4. In the *View* tab>Create panel, click 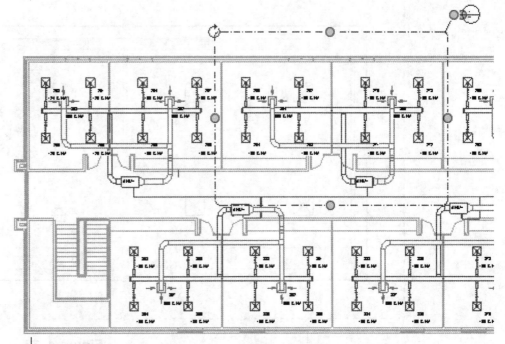 (Callout).

5. Place a callout around the two classrooms in the north wing of the building, as shown in Figure 4–32. Move the bubble as required. Click in empty space to clear the selection.

Figure 4–32

6. Double-click on the callout view bubble to open the view.

7. In the Project Browser, rename the view as **Typical HVAC System - Air Terminals**.

8. Duplicate the callout view and rename it as **Typical HVAC System - Ductwork**.

Task 3 - Hide and override graphics in views.

---

1. Open the **Typical HVAC System - Air Terminals** view.

2. Close all open views.

3. Select one of the ducts, right-click and select **Hide in View> Elements**. Only the selected duct is turned off.

Autodesk Revit 2015 MEP Fundamentals

4. Select another duct, right-click and select **Hide in View> Category**. All of the ducts are turned off.

5. Select at least one of the Duct Fittings and Flex Ducts. Right-click and select **Hide in View>Category**. The rest of the ducts and associated fittings are turned off.

6. Modify the crop region so the Air Handling Unit (AHU) is not displayed, as shown in Figure 4–33.

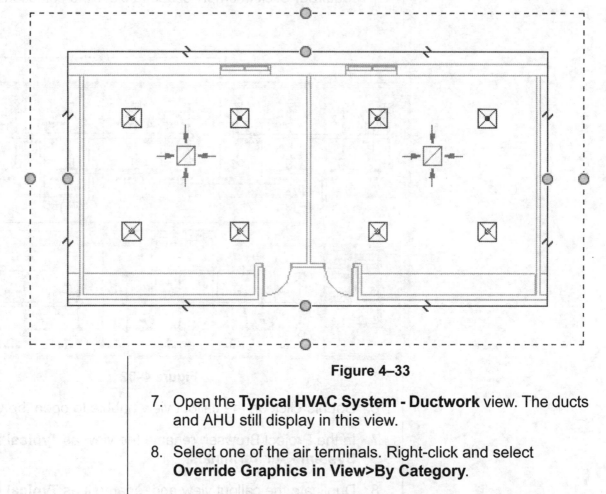

Figure 4–33

7. Open the **Typical HVAC System - Ductwork** view. The ducts and AHU still display in this view.

8. Select one of the air terminals. Right-click and select **Override Graphics in View>By Category**.

9. In the View-Specific Category Graphics dialog box, select **Halftone**. Click OK to close the dialog box.

10. In the View Control Bar, change the *Detail Level* to (Medium). The ducts display full size, as shown in Figure 4–34.

The view should display with all of the air terminals in halftone.

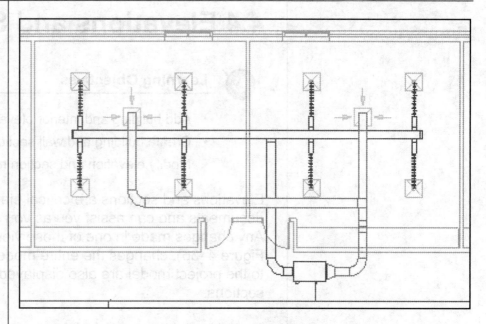

Figure 4–34

11. In the *View* tab>Windows panel, click 🔲 (Tile). The two views should display. If there are any other projects open, close them and tile the windows again so that only the two callout views are displayed.

12. Move one of the air terminals slightly. The ductwork automatically updates as shown in Figure 4–35. What is done in one view replicates in all other related views.

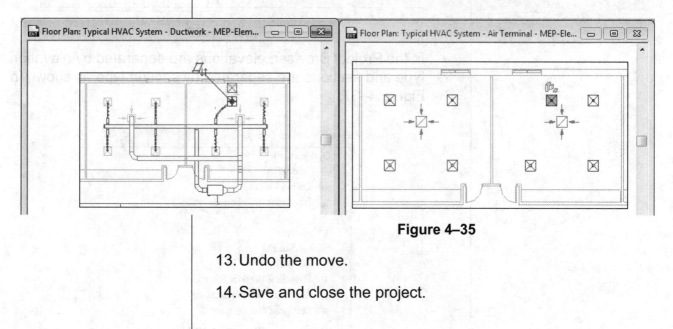

Figure 4–35

13. Undo the move.

14. Save and close the project.

4.4 Elevations and Sections

Learning Objectives

- Add building and interior elevations.
- Create building and wall sections.
- Modify elevation and section markers and views.

Elevations and sections are critical elements of construction documents and can assist you as you are working on a model. Any changes made in one of these views (such as the section in Figure 4–36), changes the entire model and any changes made to the project model are also displayed in the elevations and sections.

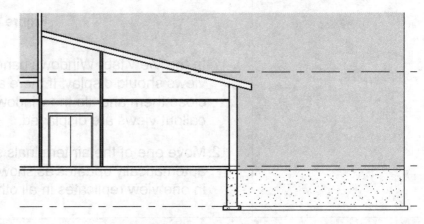

Figure 4–36

- In the Project Browser, elevations are separated by elevation type and sections are separated by section type as shown in Figure 4–37.

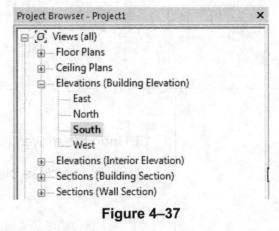

Figure 4–37

- To open an elevation or section view, double-click on the marker arrow or on its name in the Project Browser.

- To give the elevation or section a new name, right-click on it in the Project Browser and select **Rename...**

- When you add an elevation or section to a sheet, the detail number and sheet number are automatically added to the view title.

Elevations

Elevations are *face-on* views of the interiors and exteriors of a building. Four Exterior Elevation views are defined in the default template: **North**, **South**, **East**, and **West**. You can create additional building elevation views at other angles or for Interior Elevation views, such as the elevation shown in Figure 4–38.

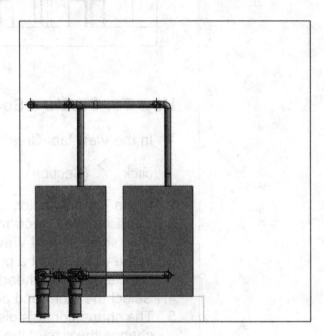

Figure 4–38

- Elevations must be created in plan views.

How To: Create an Elevation

1. In the *View* tab>Create panel, expand ⬆ (Elevation) and click ⬆ (Elevation).
2. In the Type Selector, select the elevation type. Two options that come with the templates are **Building Elevation** and **Interior Elevation**.
3. Move the cursor near one of the walls that defines the elevation. The marker follows the angle of the wall.
4. Click to place the marker.

- The length, width, and height of an elevation are defined by the wall(s) at which the elevation marker is pointing.

The software remembers the last elevation type used, so you can click the top button if you want to use the same elevation command.

Sections

Sections can be created in plan, elevation, and other section views.

Sections are slices through a model. You can create a section through an entire building, as shown in Figure 4–39, or through one wall for a detail.

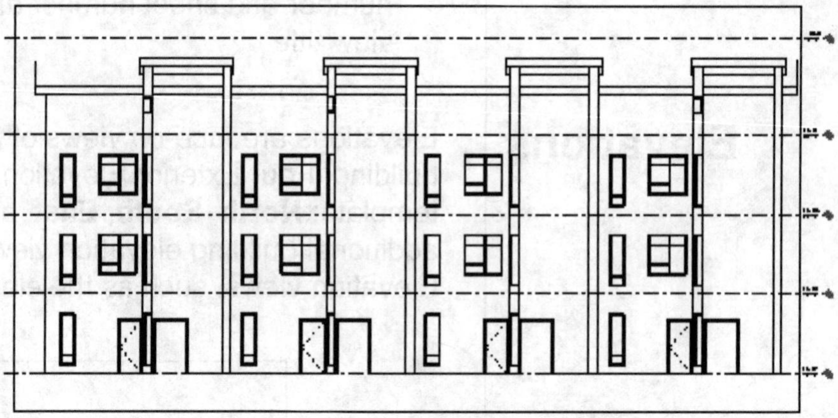

Figure 4–39

How To: Create a Section

1. In the *View* tab>Create panel or in the Quick Access Toolbar, click 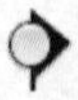 (Section).
2. In the Type Selector, select **Section: Building Section** or **Section: Wall Section.** If you want a section in a Drafting view select **Detail View: Detail.**
3. In the view, select a point where you want to locate the bubble and arrowhead.
4. Select the other end point that describes the section.
5. The shape controls display. You can flip the arrow and change the size of the cutting plane, as well as the location of the bubble and flag.

Hint: 3D Section Views

You can modify a 3D view to display in the section, as shown in Figure 4–40.

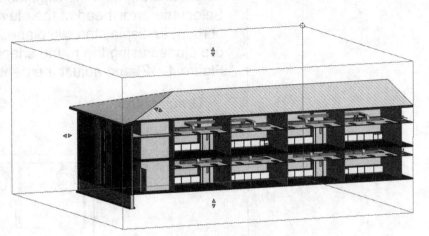

Figure 4–40

1. In a 3D view and without any elements selected, in Properties, in the *Extents* section, select **Section Box**.

2. Click [Apply], or press <Enter>, or click in the view.

3. Select **Section Box** in the 3D view and use the shape handles to modify the plane of the box.

• You can rotate the box to achieve the required cut. Select and drag the ○ (Rotate) control until the cut that you want is displayed.

Modifying Elevations and Sections

There are two parts to modifying elevations and sections, modifying the markers (as shown in Figure 4–41), and modifying the view. The markers have slightly different options, but the views have the same options.

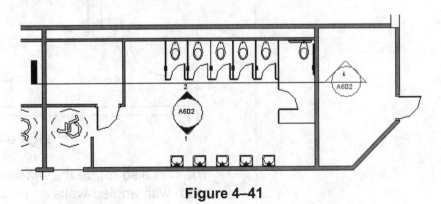

Figure 4–41

Modifying Elevation Markers

When you modify the elevation markers you can specify the length and depth of the clip plane as well as split the section line. Select the arrowhead of the elevation marker (not the circle portion) to display the clip plane. You can adjust the length of the clip planes using the round shape handles (as shown in Figure 4–42) and adjust the depth of the elevation using the

▲
▼ Drag control.

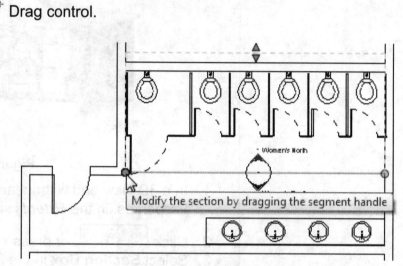

Figure 4–42

To display additional interior elevations from one marker, place an elevation marker and select the circle portion (not the arrowhead). With the elevation marker selected, place a checkmark in the directions that you want to display, as shown in Figure 4–43.

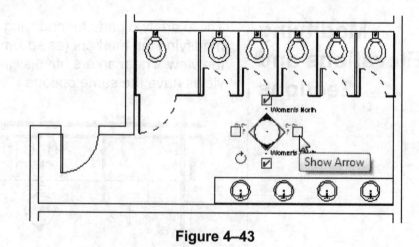

Figure 4–43

- You can also rotate the marker using ↻ (Rotate) (i.e., for a room with angled walls).

Modifying Section Markers

When you modify the section markers, you can specify the length and depth of the clip plane, flip the orientation, and create a gap as well as split the section line. Various shape handles and controls enable you to modify a section, as shown in Figure 4–44.

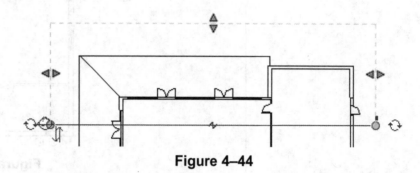

Figure 4–44

- Change the size and location of the cut plane by dragging ▲▼ (Arrow) on the dashed lines in or out.

- Change the location of the arrow or flag without changing the cut boundary by dragging the circular controls at either end of the section line.

- Click ⇔ (Flip) to change the direction of the arrowhead, which also flips the entire section.

- Cycle between an arrowhead, flag, or nothing on each end of the section by clicking ↻ (Cycle Section Head/Tail).

- Create gaps in section lines by clicking ⤙ (Gaps in Segments), as shown in Figure 4–45. Select it again to restore the full section cut.

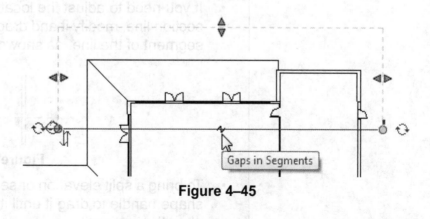

Figure 4–45

How To: Split an Elevation or Section Line

In some cases, you need to create additional jogs in an elevation or section line so that it displays the most important information along the cut, as shown for a section in Figure 4–46.

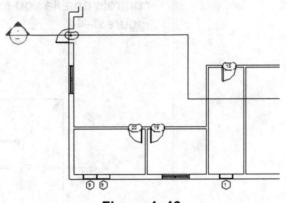

Figure 4–46

1. Select the elevation or section line you want to split.

2. In the Section panel, click (Split Segment).
3. Select the point along the line where you want to create the split, as shown in Figure 4–47.

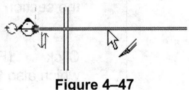

Figure 4–47

4. Specify the location of the split line, as shown in Figure 4–48.

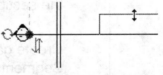

Figure 4–48

*   If you need to adjust the location of any segment on the section line, modify it and drag the shape handles along each segment of the line, as shown in Figure 4–49.

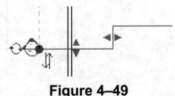

Figure 4–49

*   To bring a split elevation or section line back into place, use a shape handle to drag it until it is in line with the rest of the elevation or line.

Modifying Elevation and Section Views

Modifying elevation and section views includes the same methods as the callout views, including adjusting the crop region to specify what needs to be seen. You can modify the view by dragging the segment handles and use the break controls as shown for an elevation view in Figure 4–50.

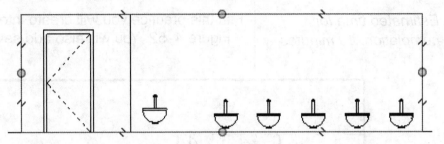

Figure 4–50

- You can also edit the crop region to reshape the boundary of the view. Select the crop region and, in the *Modify | Views* tab>Mode panel, click ⬚ (Edit Crop).

- If you want to return a modified crop region to the original rectangular configuration, click ⬚ (Reset Crop).

Hint: Using Thin Lines

The software automatically applies line weights to views, as shown for a section on the left in Figure 4–51. If a line weight seems heavy or obscures your work on the elements, turn off the line weights. In the Quick Access Toolbar or in the *View* tab>Graphics panel, click ⬚ (Thin Lines). The lines display with the same weight, as shown on the right in Figure 4–51.

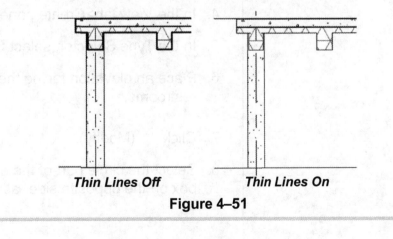

Thin Lines Off   *Thin Lines On*

Figure 4–51

Practice 4b

Create Elevations and Sections

Learning Objectives

- Create interior elevations.
- Add building sections

Estimated time for completion: 10 minutes

In this practice you will create interior elevations, as shown in Figure 4–52. You will also add several building sections.

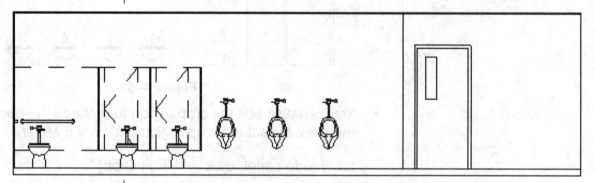

Figure 4–52

Task 1 - Add interior elevations.

1. In the *C:\Autodesk Revit 2015 MEP Fundamentals Class Files\Views* folder, open **MEP-Elementary-School -Elevations.rvt**.

2. Open the Mechanical>Plumbing>Floor Plans> **01 PLUMBING PLAN** view.

3. Zoom in on the restrooms near the basketball court.

4. In the *View* tab>Create panel, click (Elevation).

5. In the Type Selector, select **Elevation: Interior Elevation**.

6. Place an elevation facing the wall of sinks in one of the restrooms.

7. Click ⬚ (Modify).

8. Select the circle part of the elevation marker and check the box on the opposite side, as shown in Figure 4–53.

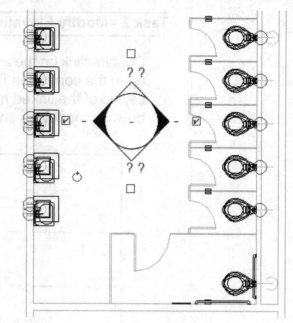

Figure 4–53

9. Press <Esc> to release the selection.

10. Select one of the arrows and zoom out to see the full length and depth of the section.

11. Drag the ends back to the restroom and modify the depth as required as shown in Figure 4–54.

The elevation does not reflect the size of the room automatically because it cannot read the location of the walls in the linked model.

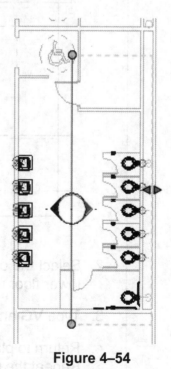

Figure 4–54

12. Repeat with the other direction.

Task 2 - Modify Elevation Views.

1. Double-click on the arrow pointing toward the water closets to open the corresponding view. The elevation cannot find the ceiling of the linked model so it selects the extents of the building model, as shown in Figure 4–55.

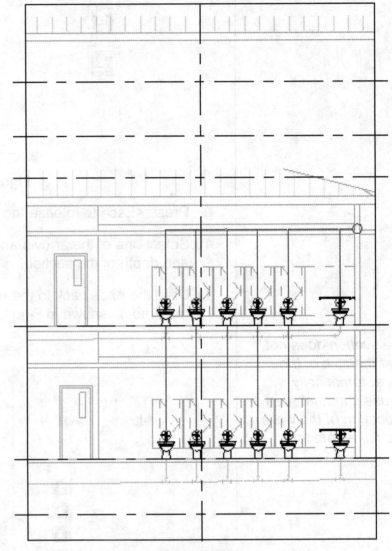

Figure 4–55

2. Select the crop region and resize the view so that only the lower floor restroom is displayed.

3. Type **VG** and turn off the Grids category.

4. Return to plan view and open the arrow in the other direction. Repeat the process of resizing the crop region and turning off the grid as shown in Figure 4–56.

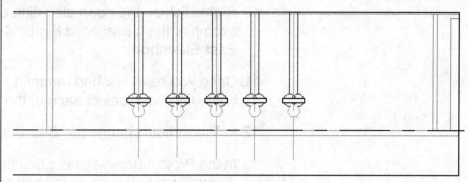

Figure 4–56

5. Return to plan view.

6. Select the entire elevation marker (the circle and both arrows).

7. Hold <Ctrl> and drag a copy of the marker up to the other restroom.

8. Open each of the new elevation views and modify the crop regions as required. The example in Figure 4–57 was lengthened to show the full sanitary line.

By setting up one elevation and then copying it to a location, you can save some steps.

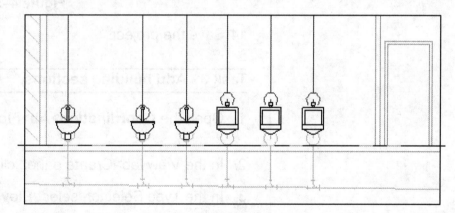

Figure 4–57

9. In the Project Browser expand **Mechanical>???>Elevations (Interior Elevation)**. Note that the four new elevations have generic names and are in an unknown sub-category, as shown in Figure 4–58.

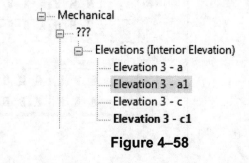

Figure 4–58

10. Right-click on the open elevation and give it a new title. For example, the elevation in Figure 4–57 would be **01 Men's East Elevation**.

11. Once you have finished renaming each of the elevations, hold <Ctrl> and select each of the new elevations.

12. In Properties, change the *Sub-Discipline* to **Plumbing**.

13. In the Project Browser, note that the elevations are now in the Plumbing sub-category, as shown in Figure 4–59.

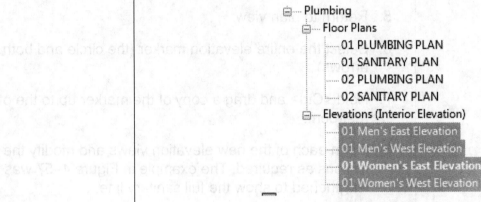

Figure 4–59

14. Save the project.

Task 3 - Add building sections.

---

1. Open the **Coordination>All>Floor Plans Level 1** view.

2. In the *View* tab>Create panel, click (Section).

3. In the Type Selector, select **Elevation: Building Section**.

4. Draw a section through the north wing, as shown in Figure 4–60.

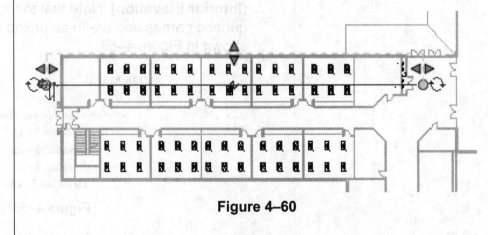

Figure 4–60

5. Press <Esc> and then double-click on the arrow of the section marker to open the section view.

6. Type **VG** and turn off the grids and levels.

7. Expand the crop region so that the first floor and the full height of the roof is displayed, as shown in Figure 4–61

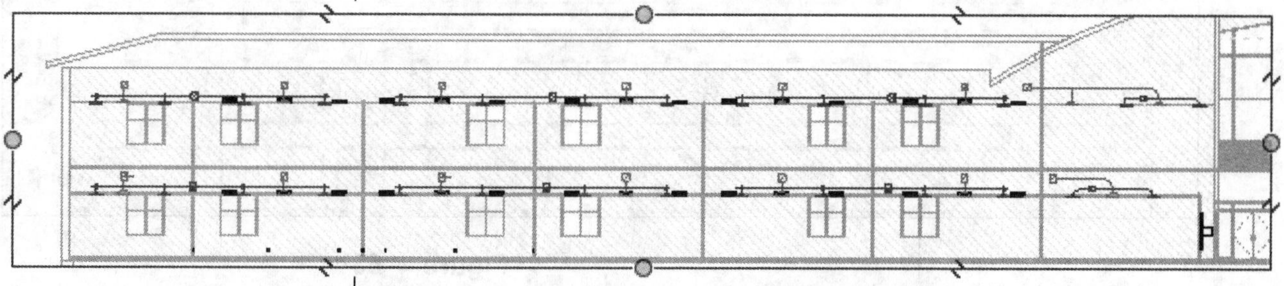

Figure 4–61

8. Type **VG** again and select the *Filters* tab. There are no filters.

9. Click [Add].

10. In the Add Filters dialog box, select **Hydronic Return**, **Hydronic Supply**, **Mechanical - Return**, and **Mechanical - Supply**, as shown in Figure 4–62. Click [OK].

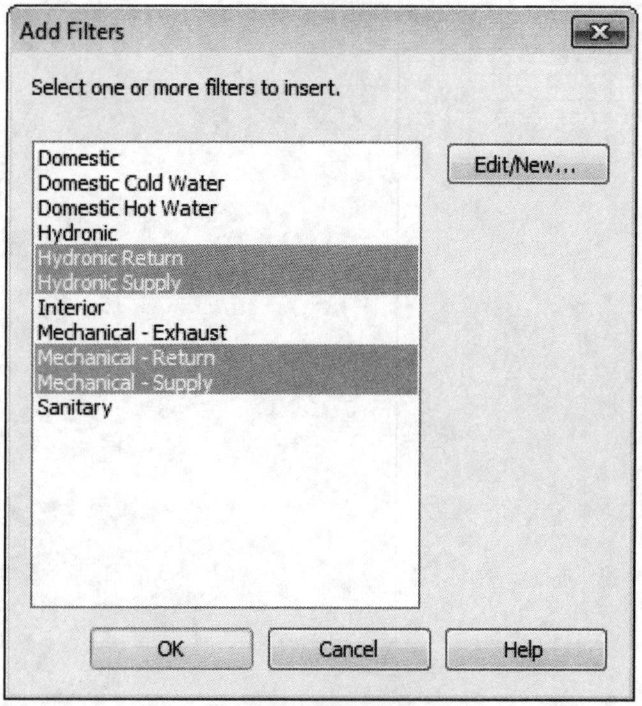

Figure 4–62

11. In the *Visibility* column, clear each of these filters and click

    OK .

12. The view now displays with only the lighting and power elements displayed, as shown in Figure 4–63.

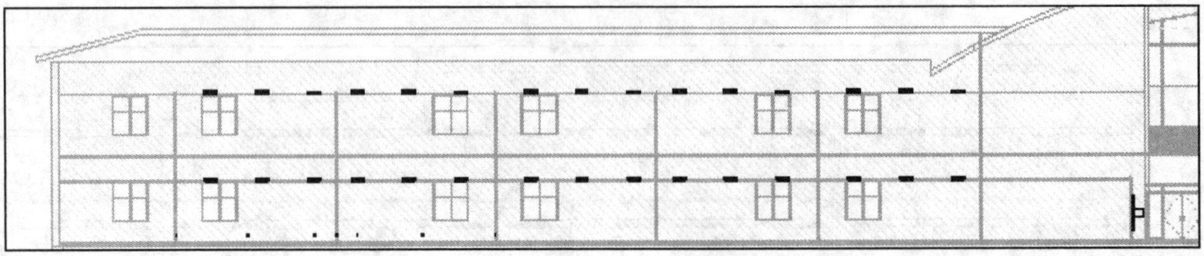

Figure 4–63

13. In the plan view, draw several other sections and review the section views.

14. In the Project Browser, under the *Sections* group, rename the sections as required.

15. Save the project.

Chapter Review Questions

1. Which of the following commands shown in Figure 4–64, creates a view that results in an independent view displaying the same model geometry and containing a copy of the annotation?

3D section	**Duplicate View**	▶	**Duplicate**	
3D View 1	Convert to independent view		**Duplicate with Detailing**	
3D View 2	Apply Dependent Views...		**Duplicate as a Dependent**	
Breakroom	Save to Project as Image...			
Conference	Delete			
Front Entr	Copy to Clipboard			
Massing S	Rename...			
Perspectiv	Select All Instances	▶		
Rear Isome				
Stair1 Pers	✓ Properties			
Studio	Save to New File...			
{3D}	Search...			
Elevations (Bu				
East Eleva				
East-Prelir				
North Ele				

Figure 4–64

a. Duplicate

b. Duplicate with Detailing

c. Duplicate as a Dependent

2. Which of the following is true about the Visibility Graphic Overrides dialog box? (Select all that apply.)

a. Changes made in the dialog box only affect the current view.

b. It can only be used to turn categories on and off.

c. It can be used to turn individual elements on and off.

d. It can be used to change the color of categories.

3. The purpose of callouts is to create a...

a. Boundary around part of the model that needs revising, similar to a revision cloud.

b. View of part of the model for export to the AutoCAD® software for further detailing.

c. View of part of the model that is linked to the main view from which it is taken.

d. 2D view of part of the model.

4. You placed dimensions in a view and some of them display and others do not (as shown on the left in Figure 4–65) but you were expecting the view to display as shown on the right in Figure 4–65. To display the missing dimensions you need to modify the...

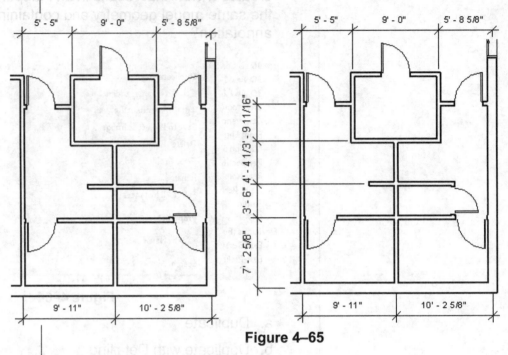

Figure 4–65

a. Dimension Settings

b. View Properties

c. Visibility Graphic Overrides

d. Annotation Crop Region

5. How do you create multiple interior elevations in one room?

a. Using the **Interior Elevation** command, place the elevation marker.

b. Using the **Elevation** command, place the first marker, select it and select the appropriate Show Arrow boxes.

c. Using the **Interior Elevation** command, place an elevation marker for each wall of the room you want to display.

d. Using the **Elevation** command, select a Multiple Elevation marker type, and place the elevation marker.

6. How do you create a jog in a building section, such as that shown in Figure 4–66?

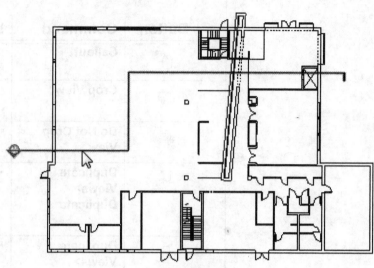

Figure 4–66

a. Use the **Split Element** tool in the *Modify* tab>Modify panel.

b. Select the building section and then click the **Split Segment** icon in the contextual tab.

c. Select the building section and click the blue control in the middle of the section line.

d. Draw two separate sections, and use the **Section Jog** tool to combine them into a jogged section.

Command Summary

Button	Command	Location
	Callout	• **Ribbon:** *View* tab>Create panel>Callout
	Crop View	• **View Control Bar** • **View Properties:** Crop View (*check*)
	Do Not Crop View	• **View Control Bar** • **View Properties:** Crop View (*clear*)
	Duplicate Views> Duplicate	• **Ribbon:** *View* tab>Create panel> Duplicate View>Duplicate View • **Right-click:** (*on a view in the Project Browser*) Duplicate View>Duplicate
	Duplicate Views> Duplicate as Dependent	• **Ribbon:** *View* tab>Create panel> Duplicate View>Duplicate as Dependent • **Right-click:** (*on a view in the Project Browser*) Duplicate View>Duplicate as Dependent
	Duplicate Views> Duplicate with Detailing	• **Ribbon:** *View* tab>Create panel> Duplicate View>Duplicate with Detailing • **Right-click:** (*on a view in the Project Browser*) Duplicate View>Duplicate with Detailing
	Edit Crop	• **Ribbon:** (*when the crop region of a callout, elevation, or section view is selected*) Modify	*Views* tab>Mode panel>Edit Crop
	Elevation	• **Ribbon:** *View* tab>Create panel> Elevation>Elevation
	Hide Crop Region	• **View Control Bar** • **View Properties:** Crop Region Visible (*clear*)
	Hide in View	• **Ribbon:** *Modify* tab>View Graphics panel>Hide>Elements *or* By Category • **Right-click:** (*when an element is selected*) Hide in View>Elements *or* Category
	Override Graphics in View	• **Ribbon:** *Modify* tab>View Graphics panel>Hide>Elements *or* By Category • **Right-click:** (*when an element is selected*) Override Graphics in View>By Element *or* By Category • **Shortcut:** (*category only*) <V> and <V>, <V> and <G>

	Reset Crop	• **Ribbon:** *(when the crop region of a callout, elevation or section view is selected) Modify | Views* tab>Mode panel>Reset Crop
	Reveal Hidden Elements	• **View Control Bar**
	Section	• **Ribbon:** *View* tab>Create panel> Section • **Quick Access Toolbar**
	Show Crop Region	• **View Control Bar** • **View Properties:** Crop Region Visible (*check*)
	Size Crop	• **Ribbon:** *(when the crop region of a callout, elevation or section view is selected) Modify | Views* tab>Mode panel>Size Crop
	Split Segment	• **Ribbon:** *(when the elevation or section marker is selected) Modify | Views* tab>Section panel>Split Segment
	Temporary Hide/Isolate	• **View Control Bar**

Chapter 5

Understanding MEP Systems

In this chapter you learn about the Autodesk® Revit® MEP systems in general, including how to work with components such as air terminals, mechanical equipment, plumbing fixtures, and electrical fixtures. You also get an overview of creating systems, connecting components, and analyzing systems.

This chapter contains the following topics:

- **About MEP Systems**
- **Working with Components**
- **Connecting Components**
- **Creating Systems - Overview**
- **Analyzing Systems**

5.1 About MEP Systems

 Learning Objective

- Identify the systems supplied with the Autodesk Revit software and access the system commands.

MEP systems include duct, piping, and electrical systems that are used in the process of creating and analyzing the various elements. These elements form the HVAC, piping, fire suppression, plumbing, and electrical layouts in a building.

Frequently these systems overlap. For example, a chilled water air handling unit is connected to supply and return duct systems, hydronic supply, and return systems. It also needs electrical input and therefore is connected to an electrical system (circuit) as well, as shown in Figure 5–1.

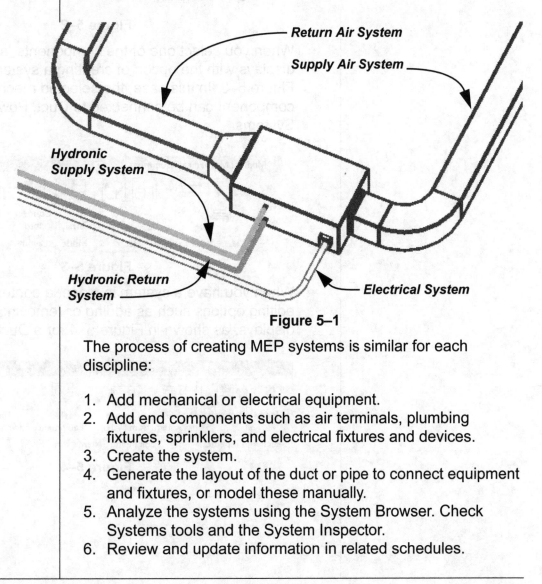

Figure 5–1

The process of creating MEP systems is similar for each discipline:

1. Add mechanical or electrical equipment.
2. Add end components such as air terminals, plumbing fixtures, sprinklers, and electrical fixtures and devices.
3. Create the system.
4. Generate the layout of the duct or pipe to connect equipment and fixtures, or model these manually.
5. Analyze the systems using the System Browser. Check Systems tools and the System Inspector.
6. Review and update information in related schedules.

Accessing MEP System Commands

As you are creating the systems, several similar ribbon tabs hold the commands that you need.

- The system components and connectors (such as ducts and pipes) are found in the *Systems* tab as shown in Figure 5–2.

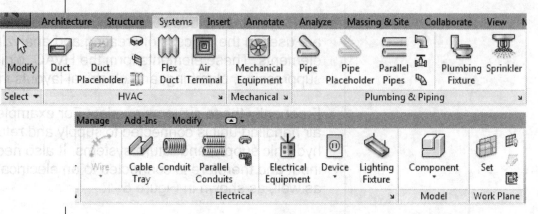

Figure 5–2

- When you select one of the components, a contextual tab displays with the option of creating a system, as shown in Figure 5–3. In this case, the selected mechanical equipment component can be connected to Duct, Power, and Piping Systems.

Figure 5–3

- When you have a system in place, a contextual tab with editing options such as adding or removing components displays, as shown in Figure 5–4 for a Duct system.

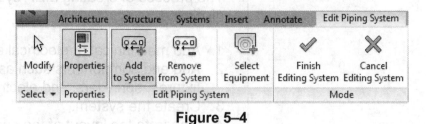

Figure 5–4

5.2 Working with Components

Learning Objective

- Load and insert components used by the various systems.

Air terminals, mechanical equipment, plumbing fixtures, sprinklers, as well as electrical equipment, devices, and lighting fixtures are all considered Autodesk Revit components. They are full 3D elements that can be placed at appropriate locations and heights as shown in Figure 5–5. The general methods for inserting and modifying those are the same for all of the different types of components.

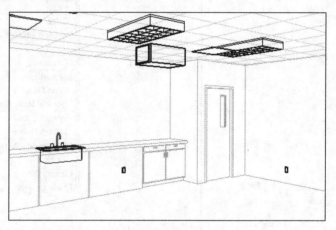

Figure 5–5

How To: Insert Components

1. Start the appropriate command.
2. In the Type Selector, select the type/size you want to use, as shown in Figure 5–6.

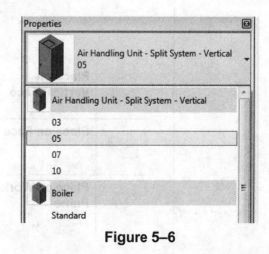

Figure 5–6

3. In the related contextual tab>Tag panel, click (Tag on Placement) to toggle this option on or off.

4. In Properties or in the Options Bar, set appropriate information.

5. Depending on the type of component select the following:

- If the component can be placed on any surface, set the *Level* and *Offset* in Properties, as shown in Figure 5–7, and then click in the model to place it.

Parameters found in Properties are also included in schedules.

Set the Elevation for components hosted by walls.

Properties	
	Air Handling Unit - Split System - Vertical 03
Mechanical Equipment (1)	▼ Edit Type
Constraints	⌃
Level	Level 1
Host	Level : Level 1
Offset	0' 0"
Electrical - Loads	⌃
Panel	
Circuit Number	
Mechanical	⌃
Drain Flow	0 GPM
External Static Pressure	0.5000 in-wg
System Classification	Supply Air,Return Air,Othe...
System Name	Mechanical Supply Air 1
Mechanical - Airflow	⌃
Air Flow	1170 CFM
Identity Data	⌄
Phasing	⌄

Figure 5–7

- If the component can be placed on a face, the options display in the related contextual tab>Placement panel, as shown in Figure 5–8.

Figure 5–8

	Place on Vertical Face	Places the component on a vertical face, such as a wall.
	Place on Face	Places the component on a defined face, such as the ceiling grid.
	Place on Work Plane	Places the component on a defined plane such as a level or ceiling in a linked architectural model.

Loading Family Types

If the required components for mechanical or electrical equipment, air terminals, plumbing fixtures, etc., do not exist in your project, you can load the families from the library. A wide variety of families is stored in library folders for Cable Trays, Conduit, Duct, Electrical Components, Fire Protection, Mechanical Components, Pipe, and Plumbing Components, as shown in Figure 5–9.

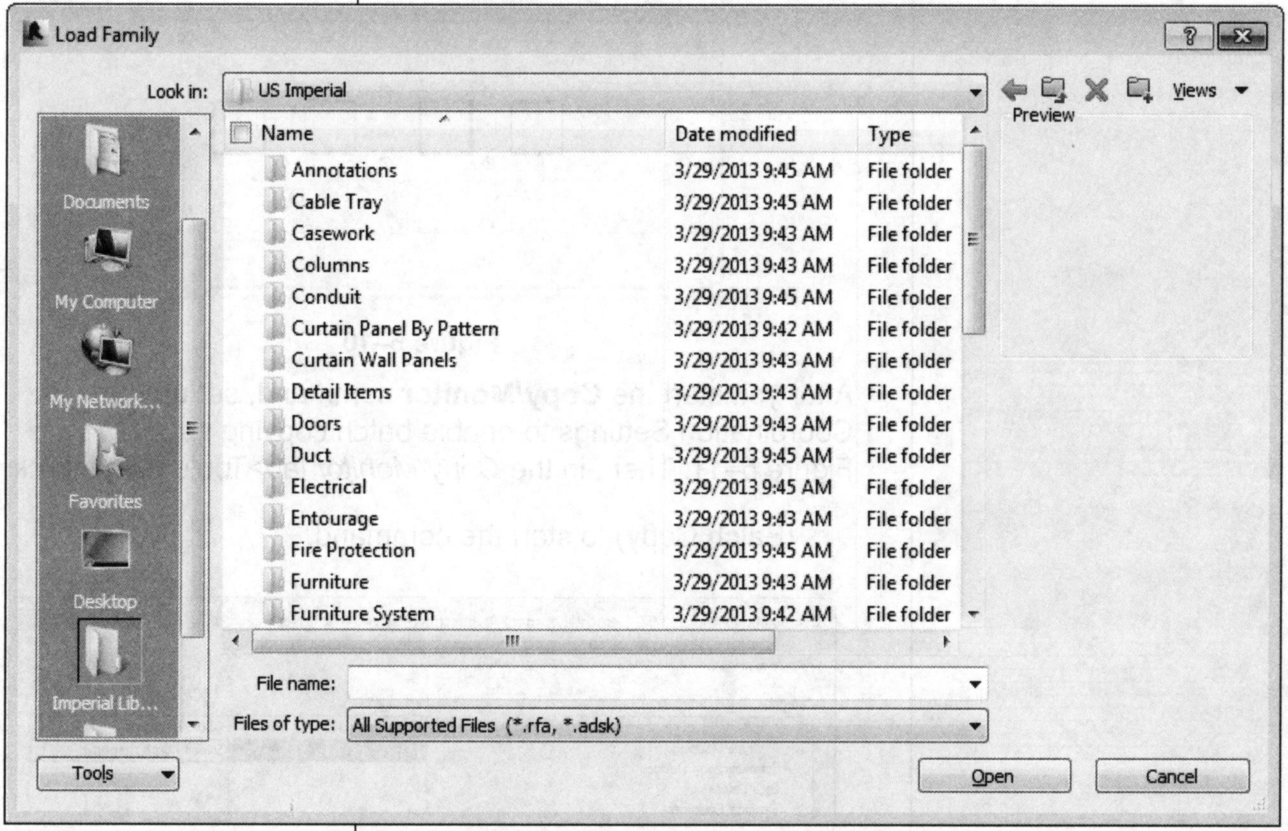

Figure 5–9

How To: Load Family Types

1. If you have started a command such as Air Terminal or Plumbing Fixture, in the *Modify | contextual* tab>Mode panel, click ⬇ (Load Family). If you have not started a command, in the *Insert* tab>Load from Library panel, click ⬇ (Load Family).

2. In the Load Family dialog box, navigate to the appropriate folder, select a type and click ⬇Open . The component is then available for selection in the Type Selector.

   • If a family type or tag for that type has not been loaded, you are prompted to load one.

Hint: Batch Copying

If you are working with a linked model that has components, such as plumbing fixtures or lighting fixtures, already placed, as shown in Figure 5–10, you can batch copy them into the host project using the appropriate MEP families in their place.

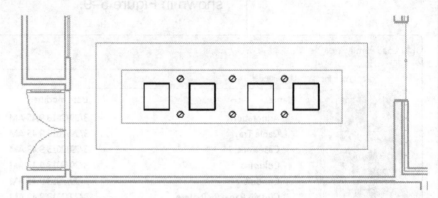

Figure 5–10

After you start the **Copy/Monitor** command, set up the Coordination Settings to enable batch copying as shown in Figure 5–11. Then, in the *Copy/Monitor* tab>Tools panel, click

(Batch Copy) to start the command.

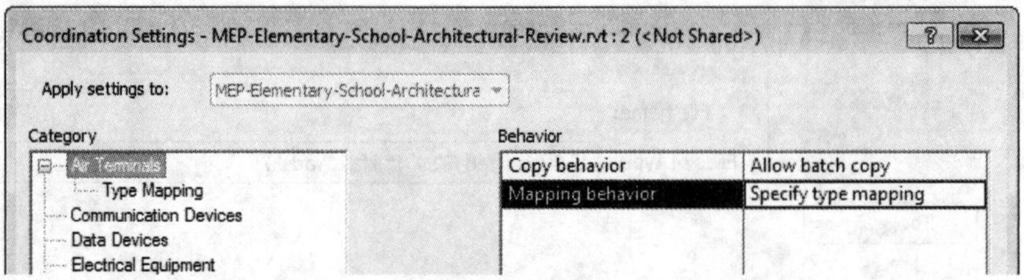

Figure 5–11

5.3 Connecting Components

Learning Objective

- Connect MEP components using ducts, pipes, conduit, cable tray, or wiring.

Once you have components in place, you can start connecting them together using elements such as ducts, as shown in Figure 5–12, pipes, cable tray, and conduit. You can also add duct, pipe, conduit, cable tray, and wiring manually between components as required.

For electrical systems, wiring can also be generated but it is symbolic and annotative.

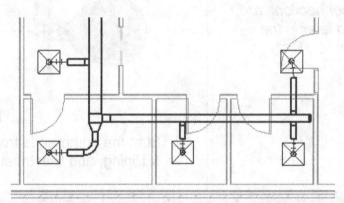

Figure 5–12

- Once systems are created, there are additional layout tools to automatically generate duct or pipe layouts to connect all of the components in a system.

- All of the MEP system elements have connectors. Using the connectors, as shown in Figure 5–13, you can attach ducts, pipe, etc. to the correct point on the component. Then the software can calculate the height and size of the opening and apply the appropriate fittings.

These connectors might also contain options to create systems, draw ducts and pipes, when you right-click on them.

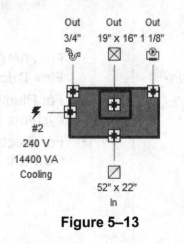

Figure 5–13

- You can connect elements before or after creating systems, but the systems must to be in place to use the automatic layout tools.

Drawing Connections

For each system type, exact steps for creating these connections are covered later in the material.

There are several ways of drawing linear connections between components:

1. Select a component, right-click on a connector and select one of the options, as shown for a plumbing fixture in Figure 5–14. You can also click on the connector icon to start the default option.

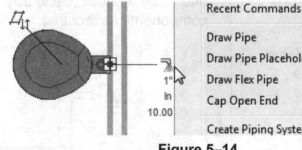

Recent Commands	▶
Draw Pipe	
Draw Pipe Placeholder	
Draw Flex Pipe	
Cap Open End	
Create Piping System	

Figure 5–14

2. Start the commands from the *Systems* tab>HVAC, Plumbing & Piping, and Electrical panels as shown in Figure 5–15.

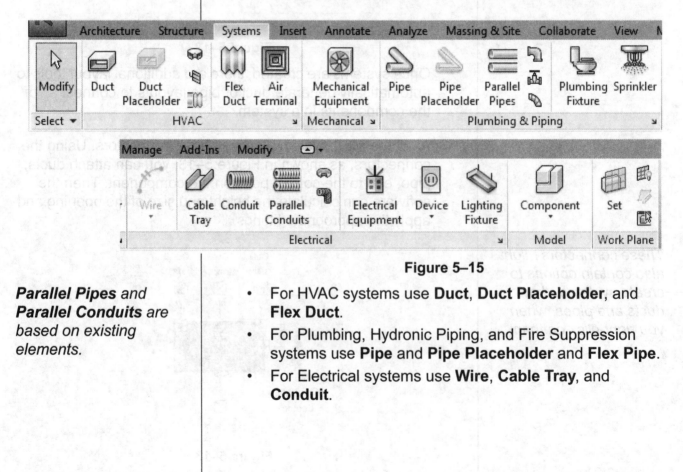

Figure 5–15

Parallel Pipes and Parallel Conduits are based on existing elements.

- For HVAC systems use **Duct**, **Duct Placeholder**, and **Flex Duct**.
- For Plumbing, Hydronic Piping, and Fire Suppression systems use **Pipe** and **Pipe Placeholder** and **Flex Pipe**.
- For Electrical systems use **Wire**, **Cable Tray**, and **Conduit**.

3. Type in the associated shortcut key found by hovering over the tool in the Ribbon, as shown Figure 5–16.

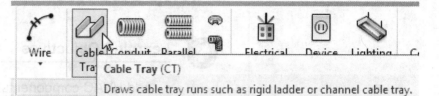

Figure 5–16

- Once you have started one of the drawing commands select the type in the Type Selector and set options such as **Justification**, **Elevation**, and **Size** in the Placement Tools panel or Options Bar, as shown in Figure 5–17. Other tools are available depending on the type of elements you are working with.

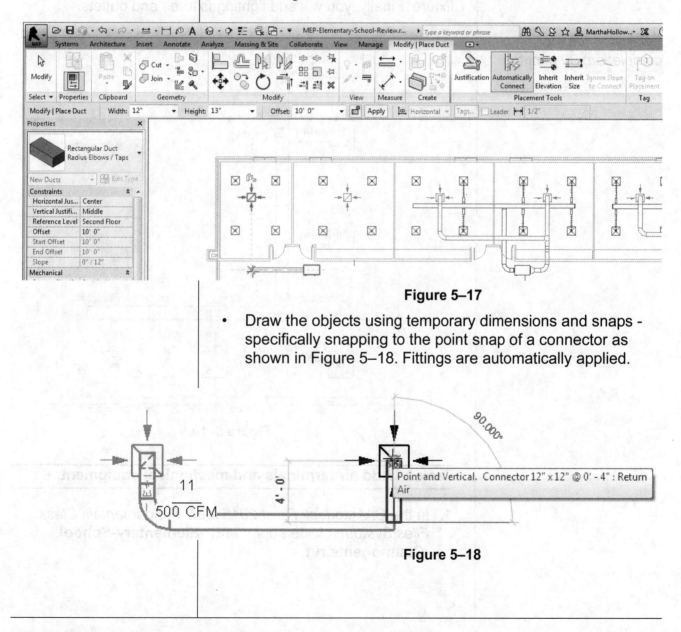

Figure 5–17

- Draw the objects using temporary dimensions and snaps - specifically snapping to the point snap of a connector as shown in Figure 5–18. Fittings are automatically applied.

Figure 5–18

Practice 5a

Insert and Connect MEP Components

 Learning Objectives

- Add HVAC components and ductwork
- Add a plumbing fixture and piping
- Add lights and outlets.

In this practice you will add air terminals and an air handling unit component, and then connect them using rectangular and flexible ducts, as shown in Figure 5–19. You will also add a plumbing fixture and draw hot and cold water pipes from the fixture. Finally, you will add lighting fixtures and outlets.

Estimated time for completion: 30 minutes

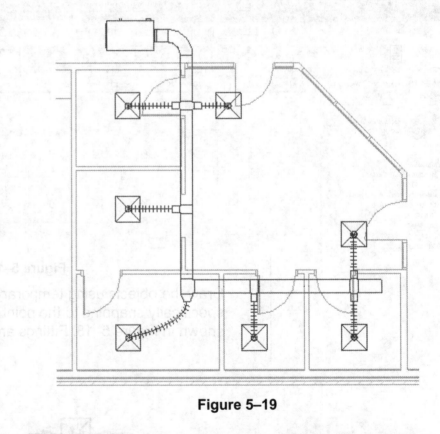

Figure 5–19

Task 1 - Add air terminals and mechanical equipment.

1. In the *C:\Autodesk Revit 2015 MEP Fundamentals Class Files\Systems* folder, open **MEP-Elementary-School -Components.rvt**.

2. Open the Coordination>MEP>Ceiling Plans>**01 RCP** view and zoom in on the office area, as shown in Figure 5–20. Adding the fixtures here insures that they are placed appropriately on the ceiling grid.

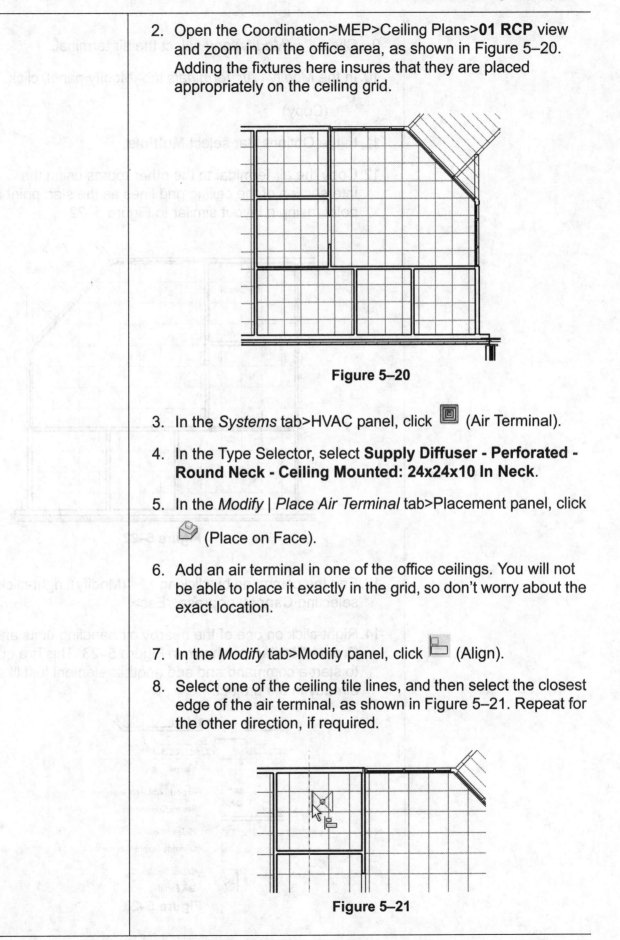

Figure 5–20

3. In the *Systems* tab>HVAC panel, click ▣ (Air Terminal).

4. In the Type Selector, select **Supply Diffuser - Perforated - Round Neck - Ceiling Mounted: 24x24x10 In Neck**.

5. In the *Modify | Place Air Terminal* tab>Placement panel, click ◇ (Place on Face).

6. Add an air terminal in one of the office ceilings. You will not be able to place it exactly in the grid, so don't worry about the exact location.

7. In the *Modify* tab>Modify panel, click ⊟ (Align).

8. Select one of the ceiling tile lines, and then select the closest edge of the air terminal, as shown in Figure 5–21. Repeat for the other direction, if required.

Figure 5–21

9. Click ⌖ (Modify) and select the air terminal.

10. In the *Modify | Air Terminals* tab>Modify panel, click ⌖ (Copy).

11. In the Options Bar select **Multiple**.

12. Copy the air terminal to the other rooms using the intersection of the ceiling grid lines as the start point and end point, using a layout similar to Figure 5–22.

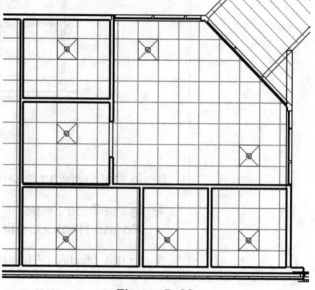

Figure 5–22

13. End the command by clicking ⌖ (Modify), right-clicking and selecting **Cancel**, or press <Esc>.

14. Right-click on one of the nearby air handling units and select **Create Similar**, as shown in Figure 5–23. This is a quick way to start a command and add another element just like one already in the project.

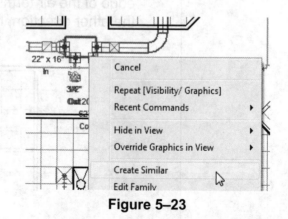

Figure 5–23

15. In Properties, set the *Offset* to **9'-3"**.

16. Press <Spacebar> until the pipe outlets face up, and then click to place it outside of the office, as shown in Figure 5–24.

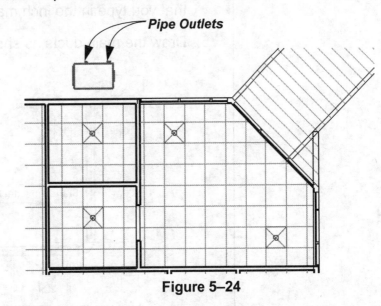

Figure 5–24

17. End the command and save the project.

Task 2 - Add ductwork

1. Open the Mechanical>HVAC>Floor Plans> **01 MECHANICAL PLAN** view and zoom in on the office. The air handling unit (AHU) and air terminals display, but the lighting fixtures do not.

2. Select the AHU and then select **Create Duct** on the supply air duct symbol, as shown in Figure 5–25.

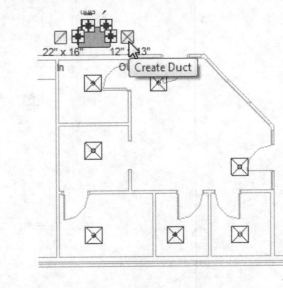

Figure 5–25

3. In the Type Selector, verify that the *Type* is set to **Rectangular Duct: Radius Elbow and Taps**.

4. In the Options Bar set the *Width* and *Height* to **12"** (Ensure that you type in the inch mark.)

5. Draw the main ducts as shown in Figure 5–26.

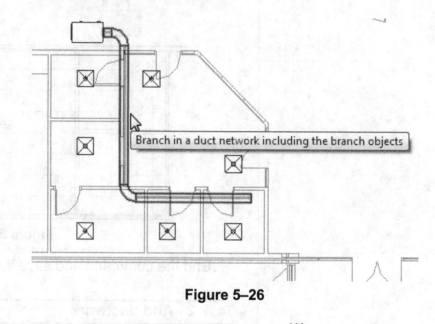

Branch in a duct network including the branch objects

Figure 5–26

6. In the *System* tab>HVAC panel, click (Flex Duct).

7. Draw flex duct from the air terminals to the main duct branch for those shown in Figure 5–27.

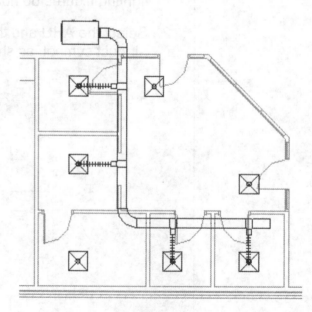

Figure 5–27

8. Click on the main duct elbow and select **Tee,** as shown in Figure 5–28.

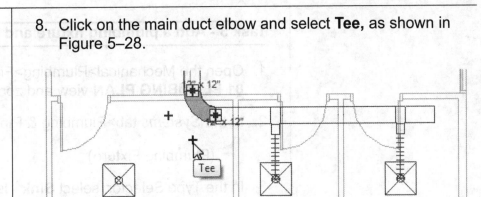

Figure 5–28

9. Type **FD** to start the flex duct command again and draw duct from the new tee location to the air terminal, as shown in Figure 5–29

10. Modify the other two fittings and draw flex duct from these connectors to the air terminals, as shown in Figure 5–29.

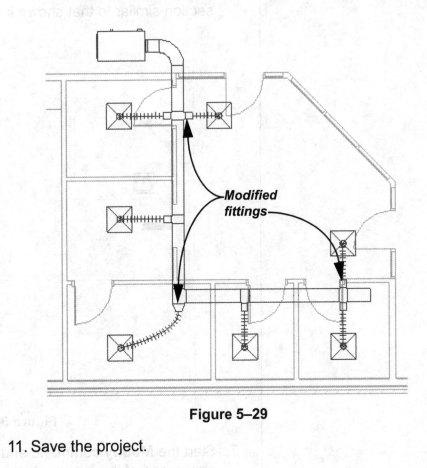

Modified fittings

Figure 5–29

11. Save the project.

Task 3 - Add a plumbing fixture and piping

1. Open the Mechanical>Plumbing>Floor Plans>
   01 PLUMBING PLAN view and zoom in on the office.

2. In the *Systems* tab>Plumbing & Piping pane, click
   ![toilet icon] (Plumbing Fixture).

3. In the Type Selector, select **Sink - Island - Single: 18" x 18"
   - Public**.

4. In the *Modify | Place Plumbing Fixture* tab>Placement panel
   click ![icon] (Place on Face). This fixture is designed to attach to
   a counter, not the wall.

5. Place the sink on the counter in the copy room, as shown in
   Figure 5–30.

6. In the Quick Access Toolbar, click ![section icon] (Section), and draw a
   section similar to that shown in Figure 5–30.

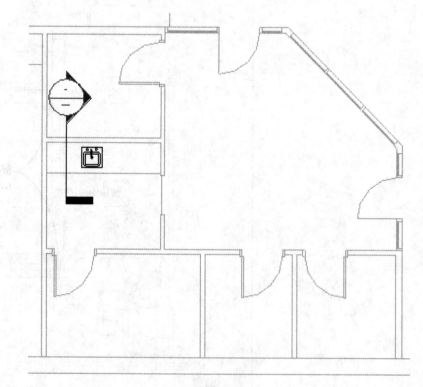

Figure 5–30

7. Start the **Modify** command and then double-click on the
   arrowhead of the new section.

8. In the section view, expand the crop region so that the full height of the room is displayed. Zoom in on the sink.

9. In the View Control Bar, set the *Detail Level* to 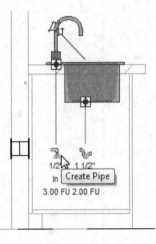 (Fine). The faucet displays and the pipes will display at full size instead, of in schematic.

10. In the Quick Access Toolbar, turn off ▤ (Thin Lines) so that you can see the pipes better.

11. Select the sink and then click on the **Create Pipe** icon, as shown in Figure 5–31.

Figure 5–31

12. Because there are two connectors close to each other, the Select Connector dialog box opens, as shown in Figure 5–32. Select the Cold Water connector and click [OK].

Figure 5–32

13. In the Type Selector, change the *Pipe Type* to **Copper.** The dialog box opens again and you need to reselect the connector.

14. Draw the pipe down into the wall, and then up into the plenum space above the ceiling, as shown in Figure 5–33.

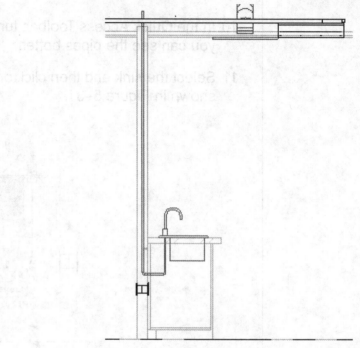

Figure 5–33

15. Repeat the process with the Hot Water connector. You can draw the pipe along the same path as the cold water pipes because they are actually separated. But do not end the pipe runs at the same point, as they will automatically connect.

16. Return to the associated plan view. The pipes display as shown in Figure 5–34.

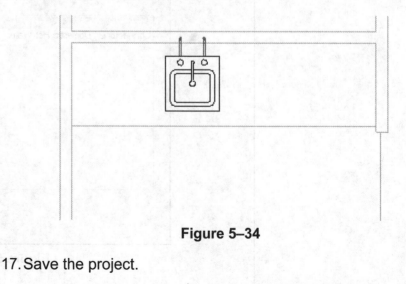

Figure 5–34

17. Save the project.

Task 4 - Add light fixtures.

1. Open the Coordination>MEP>Ceiling Plans>**01 RCP** view and zoom in on the office area. Adding the fixtures here insures that they are placed appropriately on the ceiling grid.

2. In the *Systems* tab> Electrical panel click ⬦ (Lighting Fixture).

3. Open the *Type Selector* list. Note that there are no 2x2 fixtures, so you must load a new one.

4. In the *Modify | Place Fixture* tab>Mode panel click 🗁 (Load Family).

5. In the Load Family dialog box, navigate to the *Lighting>MEP>Internal* folder, and select **Troffer Light - 2x2 Parabolic**. The connectors and light source for the lighting fixture display in the preview, as shown in Figure 5–35.

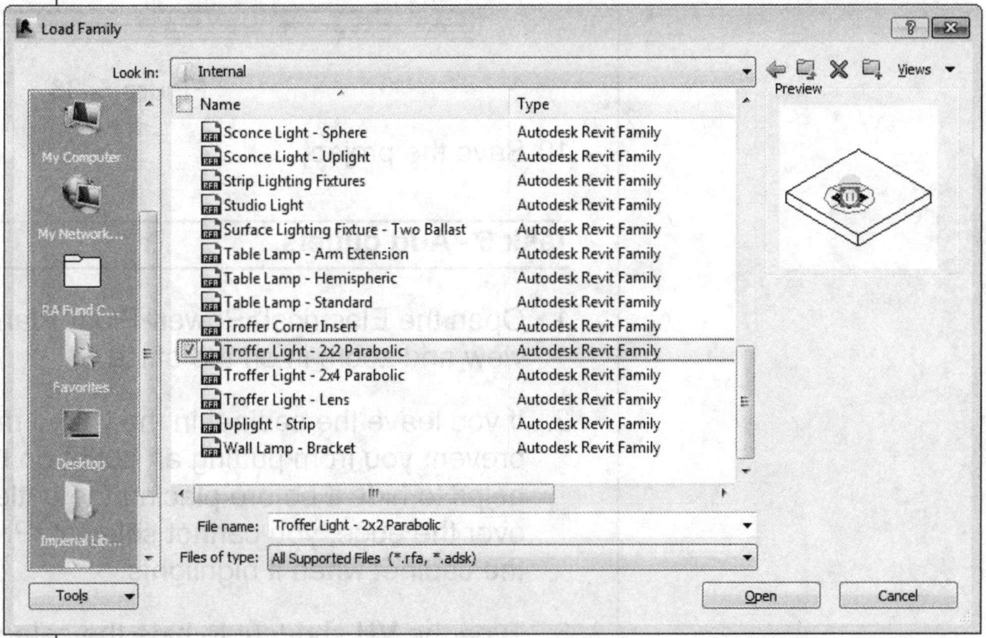

Figure 5–35

6. Click [Open].

7. In the Type Selector, verify that **Troffer Light - 2x2 Parabolic: 2'x2' (2 Lamp) - 120V** is selected.

8. In the *Modify | Place Fixture* tab>Placement panel click ⬦ (Place on Face).

The ducts are hidden in this image for printing clarity.

9. Add the light fixtures to the office area and use (Align) as required to move them into the correct position, as shown in Figure 5–36

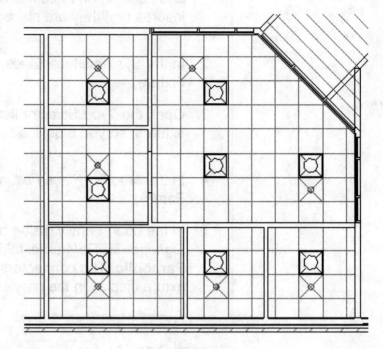

Figure 5–36

10. Save the project.

Task 5 - Add outlets.

---

1. Open the Electrical>Power>Floor Plans>**01 POWER PLAN** view and zoom in on the office.

2. If you leave the cabinet in the linked model displayed, it will prevent you from putting an outlet on the wall. Therefore, it helps to hide it before placing the outlets. Hover the cursor over the edge, you cannot select it. Press <Tab> and select the cabinet when it highlights.

3. Type the **VH** shortcut to hide the category.

4. In the *Systems* tab>Electrical panel, expand ⬚ (Device), and then click ⬚ (Electrical Fixture).

5. In the Type Selector, select **Duplex Receptacle: Standard**.

6. In the *Modify | Place Devices* tab>Placement panel, verify that (Place on Vertical Face) is selected. This device is typically placed on a wall.

7. Place outlets around the rooms, as shown in Figure 5–37.

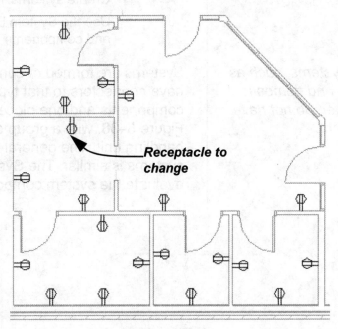

Receptacle to change

Figure 5–37

8. Select the receptacle (near the sink) shown in Figure 5–37. In the Type Selector, change the *Type* to **Duplex Receptacle: GFCI.**

9. In Properties, set the *Elevation* to **4'-0"** so that it will be above the cabinet.

10. Save the project.

5.4 Creating Systems - Overview

 Learning Objectives

- Create systems.
- Use the System Browser to identify and select systems and components of systems.

Some systems, such as sanitary and domestic cold water, do not have equipment.

Systems are formed of components that are of the same type or have connectors to that type of system. Most systems have end components and one piece of source equipment, as shown in Figure 5–38, with a group of supply air terminals and an air handling unit. The general method for creating all different systems is similar. The System Browser helps you identify and evaluate the system components.

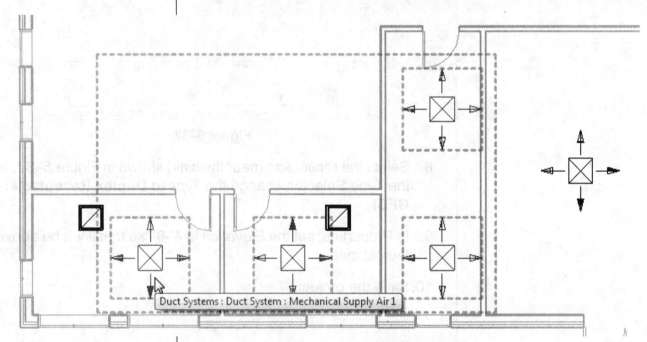

Duct Systems : Duct System : Mechanical Supply Air 1

Figure 5–38

- Components can be part of several systems. For example, if an air handling unit is using hot water from a central boiler, then that boiler and all of the air handling units receiving water from it would be part of a separate hydronic supply system, as shown in Figure 5–39.

Creating systems correctly is critical for the Autodesk Revit software to understand and calculate flow, pressure, etc.

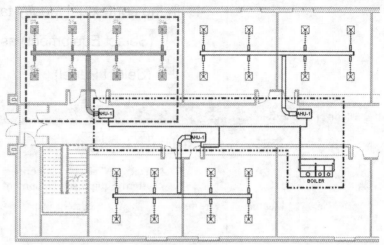

Figure 5–39

Hint: Dealing with Warnings

Warnings might display as you are working or in one of the contextual tabs. These are situations that can be ignored and

dealt with at a later time. Click 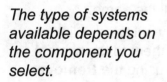 (Show Related Warnings) to open a dialog box displaying messages about what is not working. Often, these are corrected as you continue working in a system and complete the full connection. However, some need to be corrected before the system works as required.

How To: Create a System

1. Select one or more related components. (For example, you can select supply air terminals but not supply and return air terminals or not supply terminals and a light switch.) Do not select source equipment at this point.

The type of systems available depends on the component you select.

2. In the *Modify | contextual* tab> Create Systems panel, click (Duct), (Power), (Piping), (Data), (Fire Alarm, (Controls) or other system types.

3. For Duct and Piping Systems, you are prompted to select the *System type* and assign a *System name,* as shown in

*If you know you want to add the source equipment or more components to the system at this time, select **Open in System Editor**.*

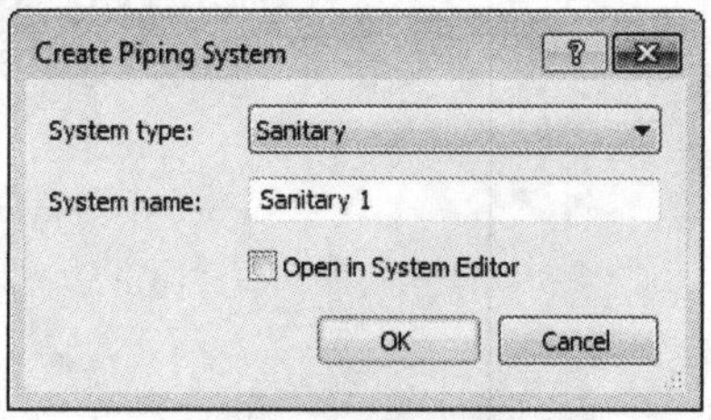

Figure 5–40. Then click .

Figure 5–40

---

4. In the contextual *Modify* tab>System Tools panel, click
   (Select Equipment) as shown in Figure 5–41, or click
   (Select Panel).

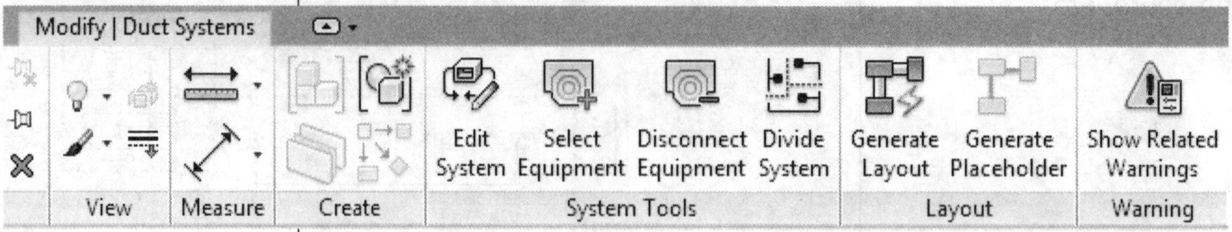

Figure 5–41

- The number of options that display in the *Modify* tab
  depends on where you are in the system creation.

5. If you want to add additional end components (and did not
   select **Open** in System Editor, for ducts or pipes), in the
   contextual *Modify* tab>System Tools panel, click the related

   Edit tool such as (Edit Circuit). The related contextual tab
   displays, as shown in Figure 5–42.

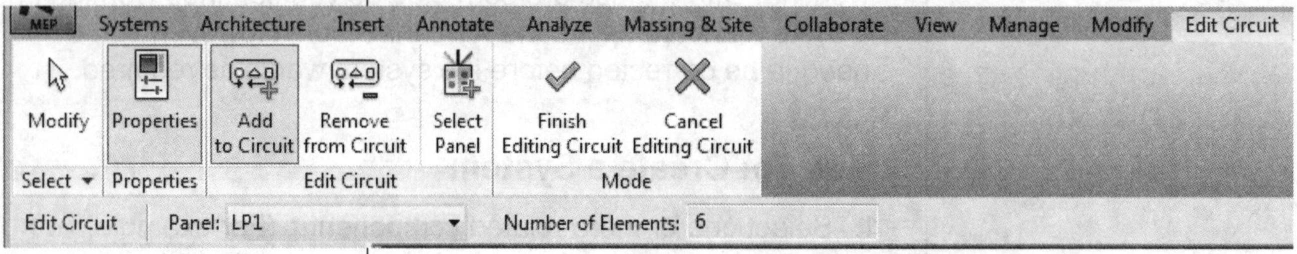

Figure 5–42

- While the icon and name for each system type is different,
  the processes and locations are still the same.

6. The related **Add to** tool is automatically selected. Click on
   other components in the model to add them to the system.
   Remove components from the system using the **Remove
   from** tool.

7. To add mechanical equipment or an electrical panel to a
   system, you can use the related **Select** tool or in the Options
   Bar, select the equipment from a list.

8. When you have completed your selection, click (Finish
   Editing System/Circuit).

- Whenever you select a component that is assigned to a system, you can return to editing the system by clicking on the contextual tabs, as shown for an air handling unit in Figure 5–43.

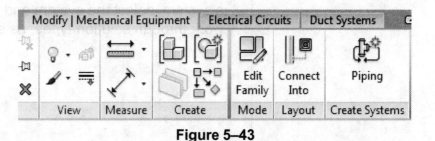

Figure 5–43

- When drawing piping or ductwork, you do not have to create a system or select mechanical equipment first. For example, if you draw ductwork between two Return Air Terminals, all of the elements are automatically placed in a new Return Air System.

- If you started to draw duct or pipe from an element in an existing system, and then selected an element that has not been added to the system, the selected element is automatically added to the existing system.

- You can select a system by hovering over one component and pressing <Tab> until the system highlights.

Hint: Creating Automatic Layouts

Once you have setup a system you can use the information to generate automatic connections. For example, after you create a system, select the system and click 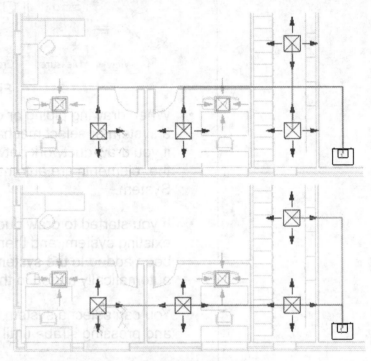 (Generate Layout) to work through solution types, as shown in Figure 5–44.

Figure 5–44

- When you have completed the routing, finish the layout and the connecting ducting or piping is automatically created as shown in Figure 5–45.

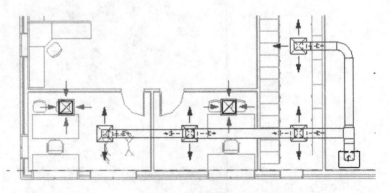

Figure 5–45

- You can use settings to modify the heights and other aspects of the layout.

Using the System Browser

The System Browser, as shown in Figure 5–46, is an important part of determining the relationships between components and the systems they are a part of. It also enables you to identify and select the components, especially those not assigned to a system.

BHM office sample - System Browser					
View: Systems ▾ All Disciplines ▾					
Systems	Flow	Size	Space Name	Space Number	
⊞ 🗐 Unassigned (31 items)					
⊟ 🗀 Mechanical (1 systems)					
⊟ ⊠ Supply Air					
⊟ 🗀 Air Handling Unit - ...	2000 CFM	15" x 12"	Mech/Elec	104	
⊟ 🗐 Mechanical Sup...	2000 CFM				
🗐 Supply Diff...	500 CFM	12" x 12"	Product Library	103	
🗐 Supply Diff...	500 CFM	12" x 12"	Product Library	103	
🗐 Supply Diff...	500 CFM	12" x 12"	Office	102	
🗐 Supply Diff...	500 CFM	12" x 12"	Office	101	
🗀 Piping (0 systems)					
🗀 Electrical (0 systems)					

Figure 5–46

Enhanced in 2015

- You can open the System Browser using any of the following methods:

  - Press <F9>.
  - In the view, right-click, expand **Browsers**, and select **System Browser**.
  - In the *View* tab>Windows panel, expand ⬛ (User Interface), and select **System Browser**, as shown in Figure 5–47.

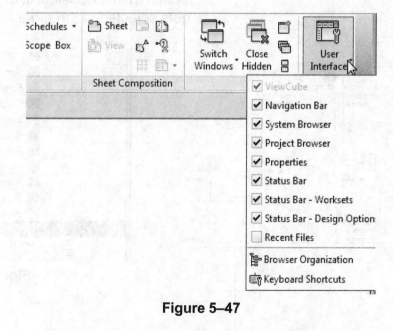

Figure 5–47

- You can float or dock the System Browser to any side of the screen. You can also place it on a second monitor.

- The System Browser can be docked with Properties and the Project Browser to save screen space.

- At the top of the System Browser you can select **Systems** or **Zones** (used in HVAC analysis) to display the drop-down list. When working with Systems, select the discipline in which you want to work, as shown in Figure 5–48. Selecting a discipline limits the display of elements to that specific discipline both in the system names and in the *Unassigned* area.

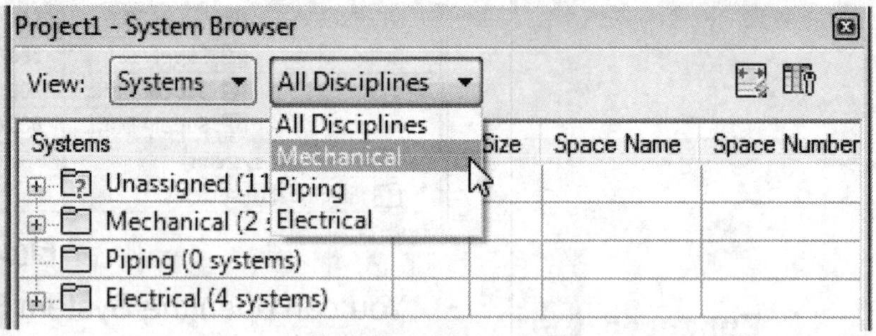

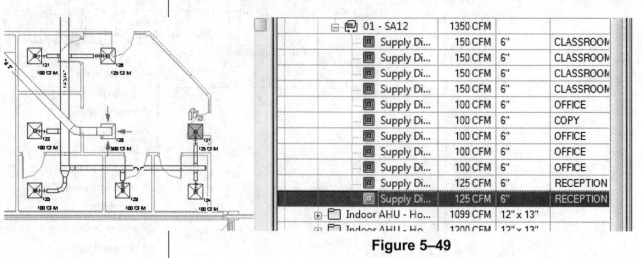

Figure 5–48

- The System Browser is setup with a multiple level tree structure for clarity. Expand the nodes down to the components level to view all of the components found in each system. Components that are not in a system, display in the Unassigned list which is also setup in the tree structure.

- In the System Browser, when you hover the cursor over the system name or select it, or select an individual component, it gets selected in the model as shown in Figure 5–49.

Figure 5–49

- You can select multiple items in the System Browser by holding down <Ctrl> or <Shift> while selecting.

- If you select a component in the model, it is also selected in the System Browser.

- If you select a component that is referenced to multiple systems, it is highlighted in each of those systems as shown in Figure 5–50.

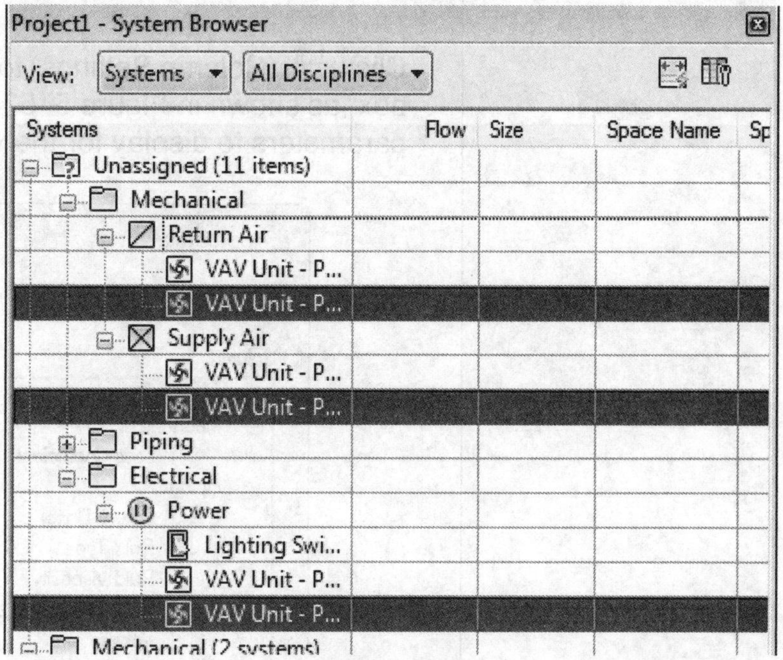

Figure 5–50

- When a component or system is selected in the System Browser, it also displays in Properties where you can modify parameters associated with the items.

- If you want to get a close-up view of a component, select it in the System Browser, right-click and select **Show**. If a view with the component is already open, it zooms into that view. In the Show Element(s) In View dialog box, as shown in Figure 5–51, click [Show] to search for other views.

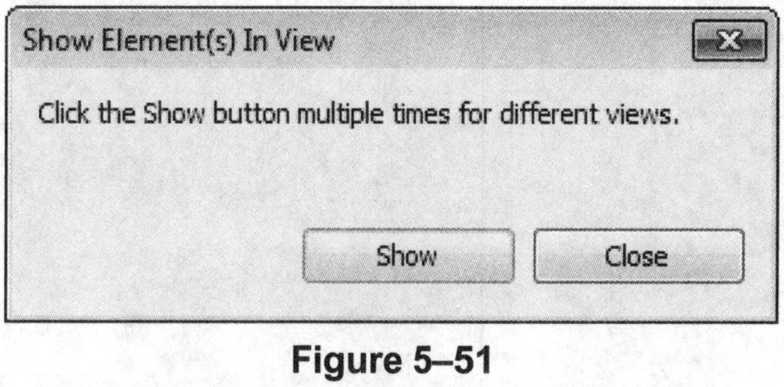

Figure 5–51

- To delete a component through the System Browser, right-click on it and select **Delete**. This deletes it from the project.

Hint: What is displayed in the System Browser?

Two buttons in the System Browser help display what you need to see. Click 📑 (Autofit all Columns) to change the width of the columns so that the contents fit exactly in the column.

Click 🔠 (Column Settings) to open the Column Settings dialog box, as shown in Figure 5–52, in which you can select the parameters to display for the various system types.

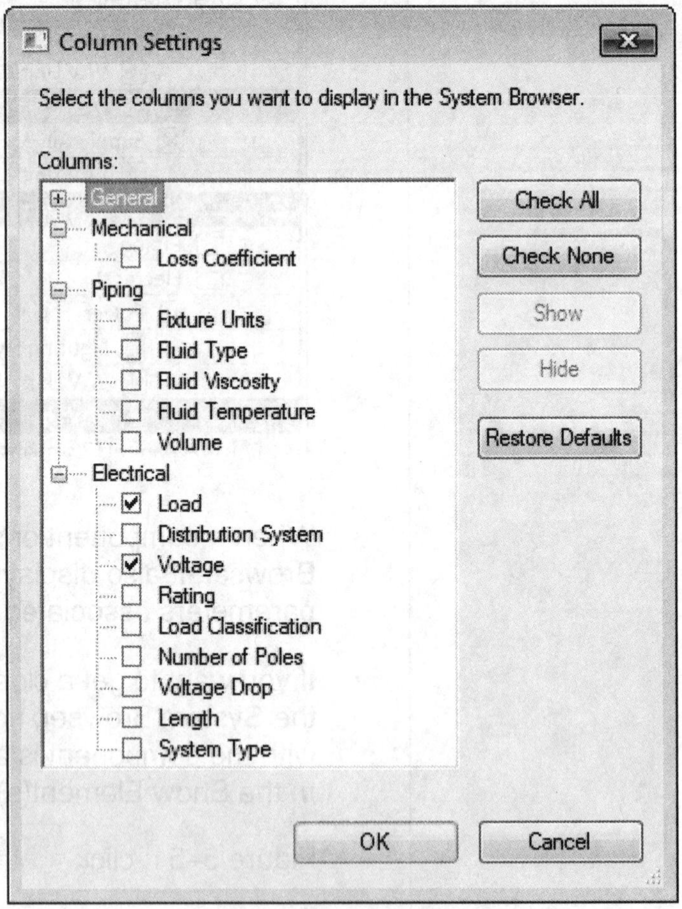

Figure 5–52

Practice 5b

View and Create Systems

Learning Objectives

- Attach piping to an existing system
- Investigate systems using the System Browser
- Create an electrical switch system.

Estimated time for completion: 20 minutes

In this practice you will create a section view to help you attach piping into an existing piping system, as shown in Figure 5–53. You will review this system and others in the System Browser. Finally, you will add switches and create switch systems.

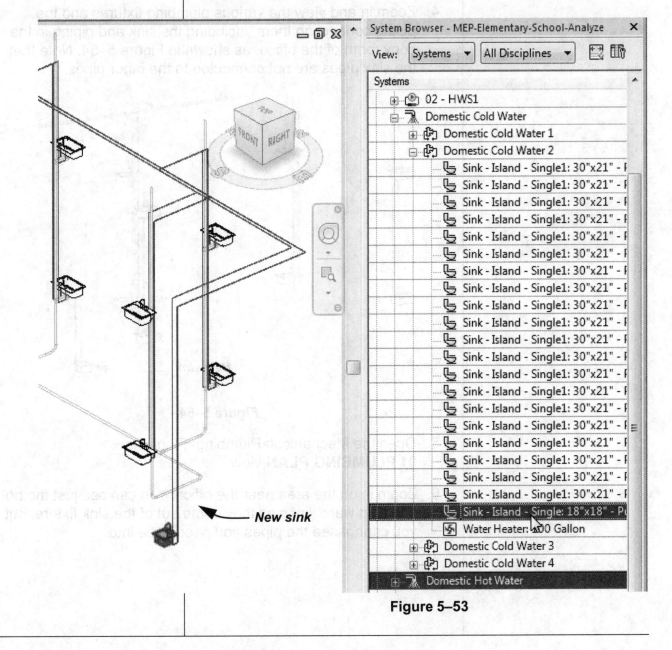

Figure 5–53

Many elements are automatically placed in a system type because of the connectors they are attached to.

Task 1 - Attach new plumbing to an existing system.

1. In the *C:\Autodesk Revit 2015 MEP Fundamentals Class Files\Systems* folder, open **MEP-Elementary-School -Systems.rvt**.

2. Open the Mechanical>Plumbing>3D Views>**3D PLUMBING** view. You can see the colors indicating the various systems: blue for *Cold Water*, red for *Hot Water*, and green for *Sanitary*.

3. To make the MEP elements easier to view, select the linked architectural model and, in the View Control Bar, click ⤳ (Temporary Hide/Isolate), and select **Hide Element**.

4. Zoom in and view the various plumbing fixtures and the piping connecting them, including the sink and piping in the copy room of the office, as shown in Figure 5–54. Note that the sink pipes are not connected to the other pipes.

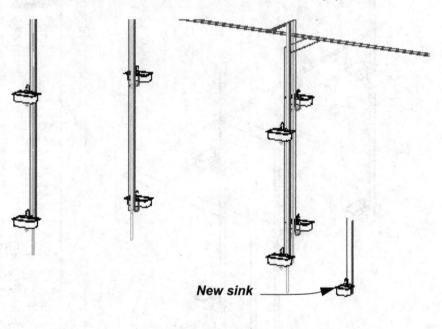

New sink

Figure 5–54

5. Open the Mechanical>Plumbing>Floor Plans> **01 PLUMBING PLAN** view.

6. Zoom in on the area near the office. You can see just the hot and cold water lines as they come out of the sink fixture, but you cannot see the pipes you need to tie into.

7. In Properties, set the *Underlay* to **Level 2**. The pipes are now displayed, as shown in Figure 5–55.

8. Draw a section facing the new sink and expanded to incorporate the pipes on Level 2, as shown in Figure 5–55.

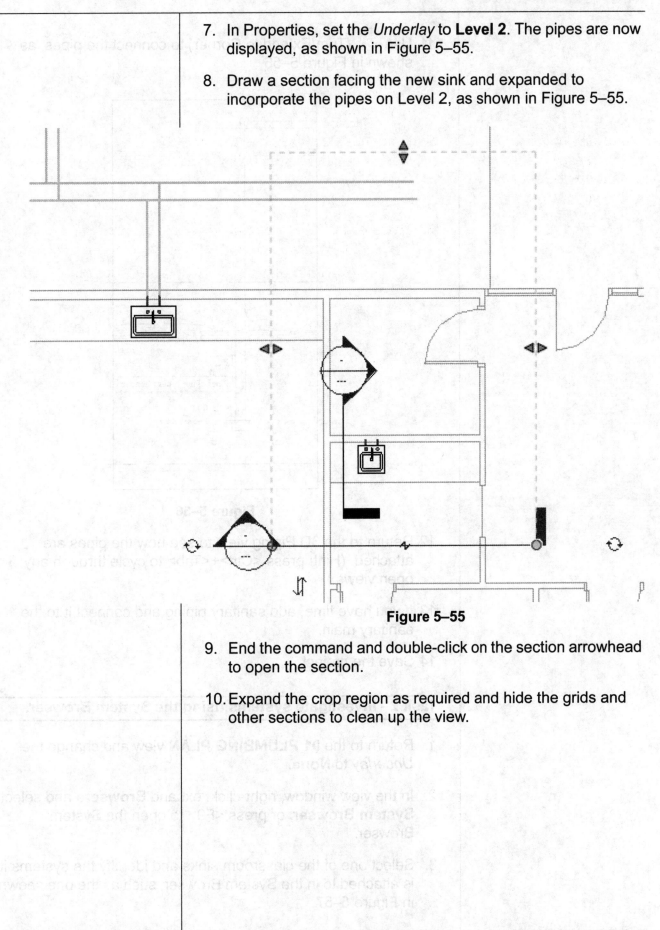

Figure 5–55

9. End the command and double-click on the section arrowhead to open the section.

10. Expand the crop region as required and hide the grids and other sections to clean up the view.

11. Use 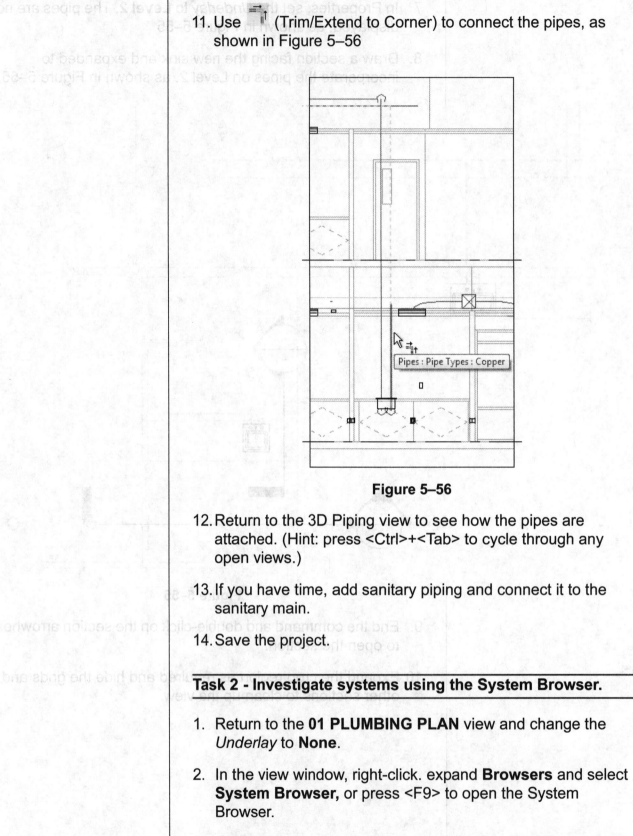 (Trim/Extend to Corner) to connect the pipes, as shown in Figure 5–56

Figure 5–56

12. Return to the 3D Piping view to see how the pipes are attached. (Hint: press <Ctrl>+<Tab> to cycle through any open views.)

13. If you have time, add sanitary piping and connect it to the sanitary main.

14. Save the project.

Task 2 - Investigate systems using the System Browser.

1. Return to the **01 PLUMBING PLAN** view and change the *Underlay* to **None**.

2. In the view window, right-click. expand **Browsers** and select **System Browser,** or press <F9> to open the System Browser.

3. Select one of the classroom sinks and identify the systems it is attached to in the System Browser, such as the one shown in Figure 5–57.

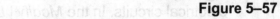

Figure 5–57

4. Select the sink in the copy room. It is automatically connected to the *Domestic Cold Water 2* and *Domestic Hot Water 2* systems when it was tied into the piping.

5. Zoom out to see the entire floor plan.

6. In the Systems Browser, select one of the *Sanitary* systems. The system displays in the model, as shown in Figure 5–58.

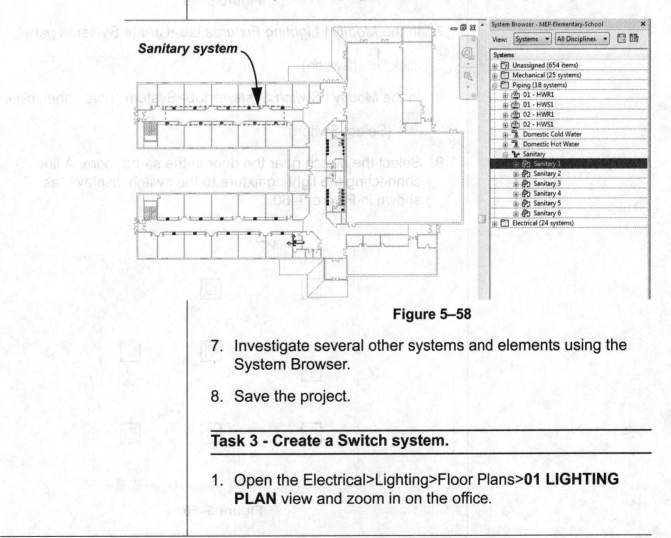

Sanitary system

Figure 5–58

7. Investigate several other systems and elements using the System Browser.

8. Save the project.

Task 3 - Create a Switch system.

1. Open the Electrical>Lighting>Floor Plans>**01 LIGHTING PLAN** view and zoom in on the office.

2. In the *Systems* tab>Electrical panel, expand (Device), and then select (Lighting).

3. In the Type Selector, select **Lighting Switches: Single Pole**.

4. Add switches near the door to each room, but no switch in the copy room.

5. Select one of the light fixtures in the main room.

6. Lighting fixtures can be connected to switch systems and electrical circuits. In the *Modify | Lighting Fixtures* tab>Create Systems panel (shown in Figure 5–59), **Power** and **Switch** are the two choices for related systems.

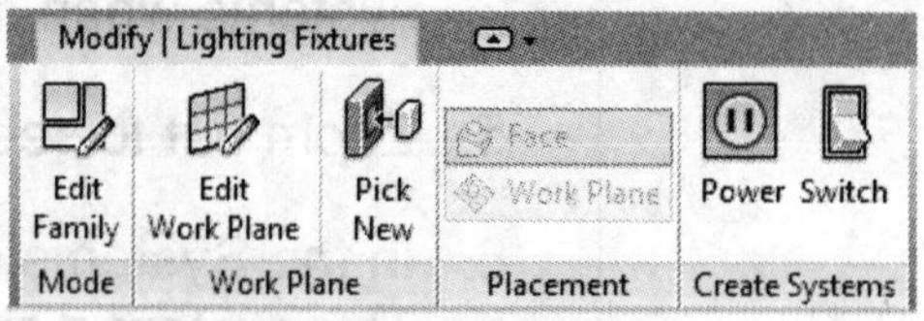

Figure 5–59

7. In the *Modify | Lighting Fixtures* tab>Create Systems panel, click (Switch).

8. In the *Modify | Switch Systems* tab>System Tools panel, click (Select Switch).

9. Select the switch near the door in the same room. A line connecting the lighting fixture to the switch displays, as shown in Figure 5–60.

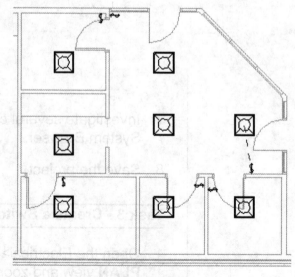

Figure 5–60

10. The new switch system is still selected. In the *Modify | Switch System* tab>System Tools panel, click (Edit Switch System).

11. (Add to System) is automatically selected.

12. Click on the other lighting fixtures in the main room, as well as the copy room and then click (Finish Editing System).

13. Hover over one of the lighting fixtures and <Tab> through the options until the Switch System displays as shown in Figure 5–61.

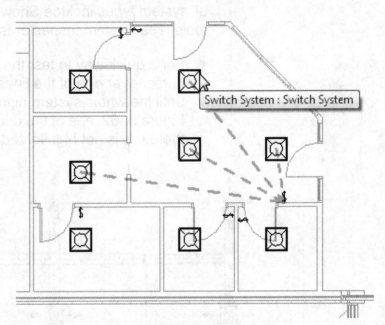

Figure 5–61

14. Move the cursor away from the selection.

15. Add switch systems to each of the other rooms.

16. Type **ZF** (for Zoom to Fit the view).

17. Save the project.

5.5 Analyzing Systems

Learning Objectives

- Check systems by displaying disconnects and running the **Check Systems** tool.
- Use the System Inspector to display information about the system.

The Autodesk Revit software is not only a drawing tool but a full BIM (Building Information Modeling) type of software. Therefore, the elements used in each model are smart elements and can be used to analyze the different types of systems. The tools used by all system types include Show Disconnects and various Check tools. The System Inspector is used for duct and pipe systems.

- For a quick way to test the continuity of a system, hover the cursor over one of the linear connections and press <Tab> until the whole system highlights. For example, in Figure 5–62, one of the ducts is not attached to the fitting and therefore is not highlighted.

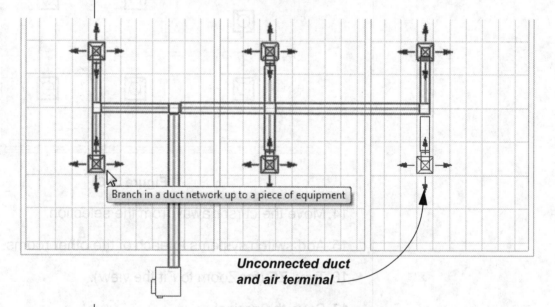

Branch in a duct network up to a piece of equipment

Unconnected duct and air terminal

Figure 5–62

If there are issues with a selected system, the Warning panel displays in the related *Modify* toolbar, as shown in Figure 5–63.

Click ![icon] (Show Related Warnings) to bring up the dialog box and review the issues.

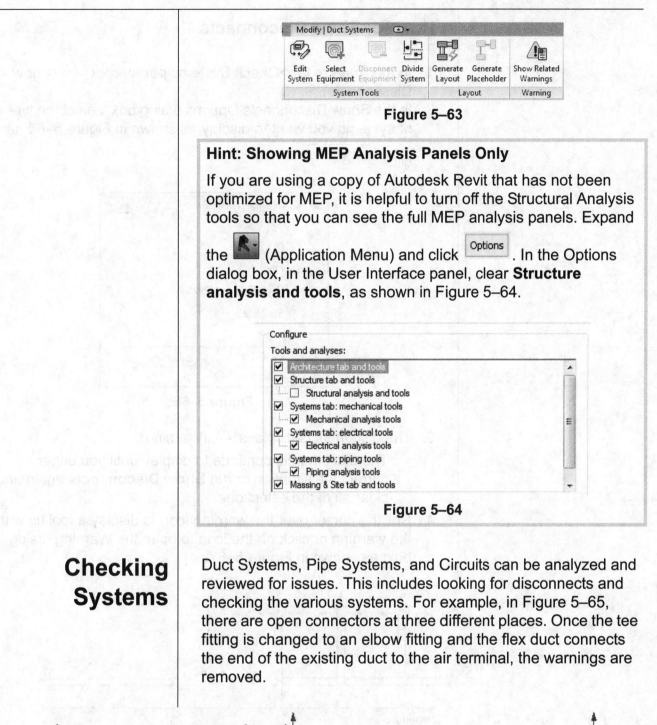

Figure 5–63

Hint: Showing MEP Analysis Panels Only

If you are using a copy of Autodesk Revit that has not been optimized for MEP, it is helpful to turn off the Structural Analysis tools so that you can see the full MEP analysis panels. Expand the (Application Menu) and click Options . In the Options dialog box, in the User Interface panel, clear **Structure analysis and tools**, as shown in Figure 5–64.

Figure 5–64

Checking Systems

Duct Systems, Pipe Systems, and Circuits can be analyzed and reviewed for issues. This includes looking for disconnects and checking the various systems. For example, in Figure 5–65, there are open connectors at three different places. Once the tee fitting is changed to an elbow fitting and the flex duct connects the end of the existing duct to the air terminal, the warnings are removed.

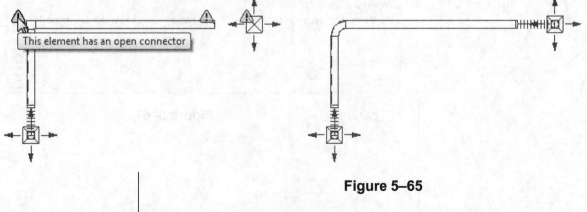

Figure 5–65

How To: Show Disconnects

1. In the *Analyze* tab>Check Systems panel, click ⚓ (Show Disconnects).
2. In the Show Disconnects Options dialog box, select the types of systems you want to display as shown in Figure 5–66 and click ▢ OK ▢.

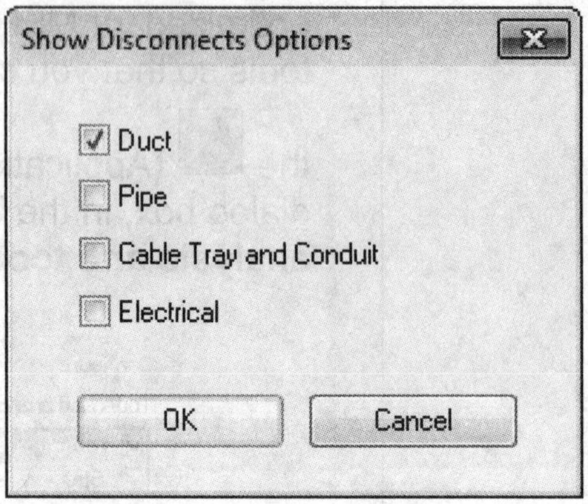

Show Disconnects Options

☑ Duct
☐ Pipe
☐ Cable Tray and Conduit
☐ Electrical

OK   Cancel

Figure 5–66

3. The disconnects displays ⚠ (Warning).
   • The disconnects continue to display until you either correct the situation or run **Show Disconnects** again and clear all of the selections.
4. Roll the cursor over the warning icon to display a tool tip with the warning or click on the icon to open the Warning dialog box, as shown in Figure 5–67.

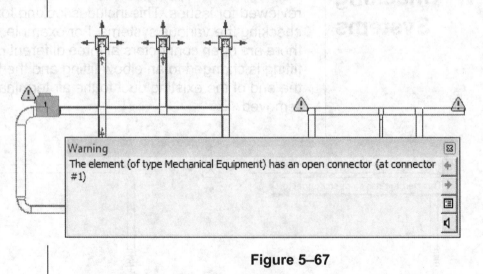

Warning

The element (of type Mechanical Equipment) has an open connector (at connector #1)

Figure 5–67

How To: Use the Check Systems Tools

1. In the *Analyze* tab>Check Systems panel, click 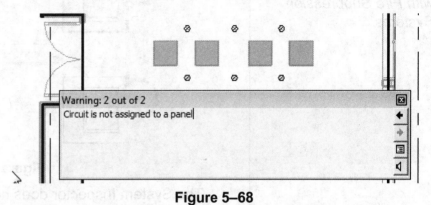 (Check Duct Systems), (Check Pipe Systems, or (Check Circuits). These are on/off toggles.

2. (Warning) displays. Click one of the icons to open the Warning alert box as shown in Figure 5–68.

Figure 5–68

- For icons that have more than one warning, in the Warning alert box, click (Next Warning) and (Previous Warning) to search through the list.

- Click (Expand Warning Dialog) to open the dialog box as shown in Figure 5–69. You can expand each node in the box and select elements to show or delete.

If there are a lot of warnings to review, you can click 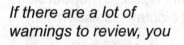 and save the HTML report to review separately.

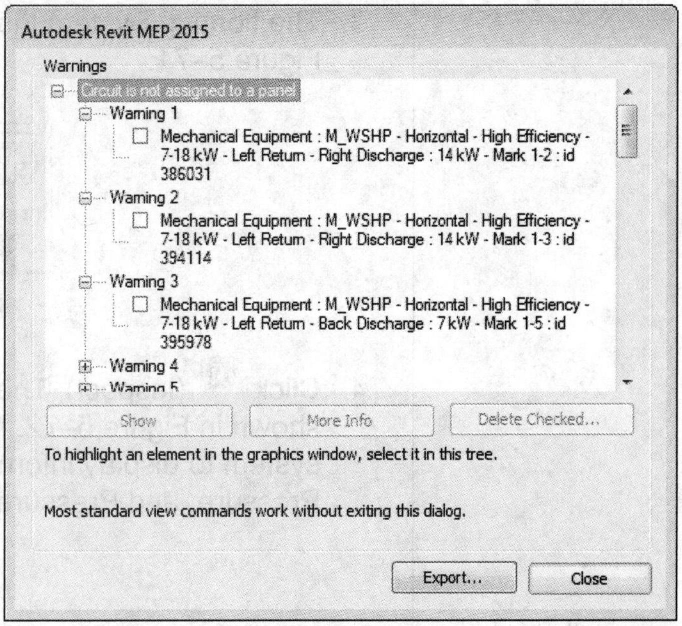

Figure 5–69

System Inspector

The System Inspector works with all Duct and Piping Systems except with Fire Suppression Systems.

The System Inspector provides information such as flow rate, static pressure, and pressure loss at every point in a system, as shown in Figure 5–70 for a Domestic Cold Water system. It also enables you to make changes to components of the system, while you are inspecting.

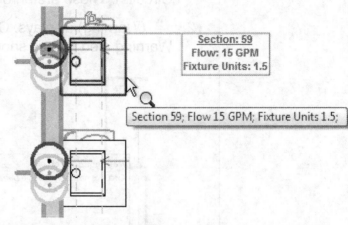

Figure 5–70

- The System Inspector does not display in the Ribbon if an open system is selected.

How To: Use the System Inspector

1. Select any part of a system including air terminals, ductwork, piping, mechanical equipment, or plumbing fixtures.
2. In the contextual *Modify* tab>Analysis panel, click

   (System Inspector) or in the System Browser, right-click on the top level of a system and select **System Inspector**.
3. The floating System Inspector panel displays, as shown in Figure 5–71.

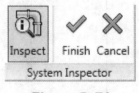

Figure 5–71

4. Click (Inspect). The air flow displays in the system, as shown in Figure 5–72. Move the cursor over a section of system to display information, such as the Flow, Static Pressure, and Pressure Loss for duct systems.

The red path displays the greatest static pressure.

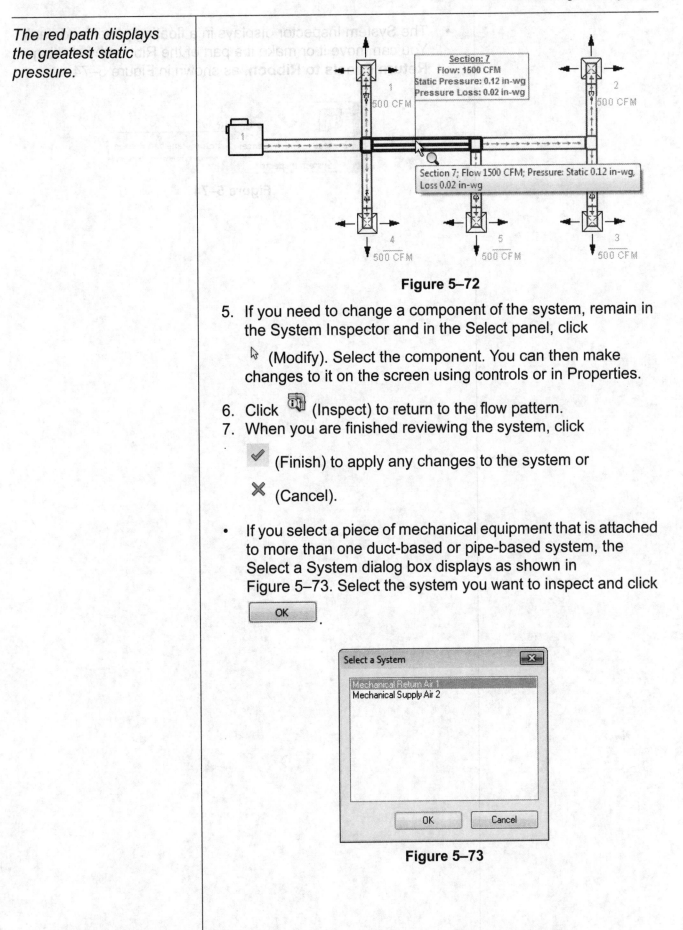

Figure 5–72

5. If you need to change a component of the system, remain in the System Inspector and in the Select panel, click

   ▷ (Modify). Select the component. You can then make changes to it on the screen using controls or in Properties.

6. Click 🗠 (Inspect) to return to the flow pattern.

7. When you are finished reviewing the system, click

   ✓ (Finish) to apply any changes to the system or

   ✕ (Cancel).

- If you select a piece of mechanical equipment that is attached to more than one duct-based or pipe-based system, the Select a System dialog box displays as shown in Figure 5–73. Select the system you want to inspect and click

   OK .

Figure 5–73

- The System Inspector displays in a floating panel by default. You can move it or make it a part of the Ribbon by clicking **Return Panels to Ribbon**, as shown in Figure 5–74.

Figure 5–74

Practice 5c

Analyze Systems

Learning Objectives

- Check a duct system, correct problems and then use the System Inspector to analyze it.
- Review pipe disconnects in a plumbing system.
- Check electrical systems and correct a problem.

Estimated time for completion: 15 minutes

In this practice you will review warnings, and run **Check Duct Systems** (as shown in Figure 5–75) and **Show Disconnects**. You will then correct any problems and run the **System Inspector**. You will view disconnects in a plumbing system. Finally you will check an electrical system and correct a problem.

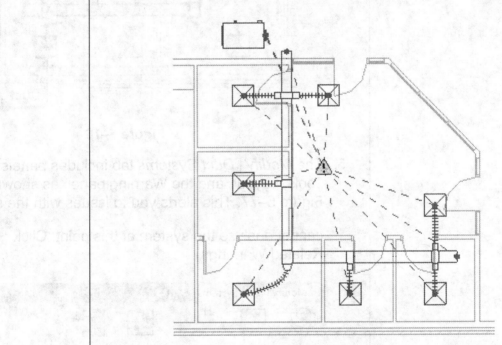

Figure 5–75

Task 1 - Review warnings and check duct systems

1. In the *C:\Autodesk Revit 2015 MEP Fundamentals Class Files\Systems* folder, open **MEP-Elementary-School -Analyze.rvt**.

2. Open the Mechanical>HVAC>Floor Plans> **01 MECHANICAL PLAN** view.

3. Zoom in on the office area.

4. Hover over a duct and press <Tab> until you see the duct system highlight, as shown in Figure 5–76. Click to select it.

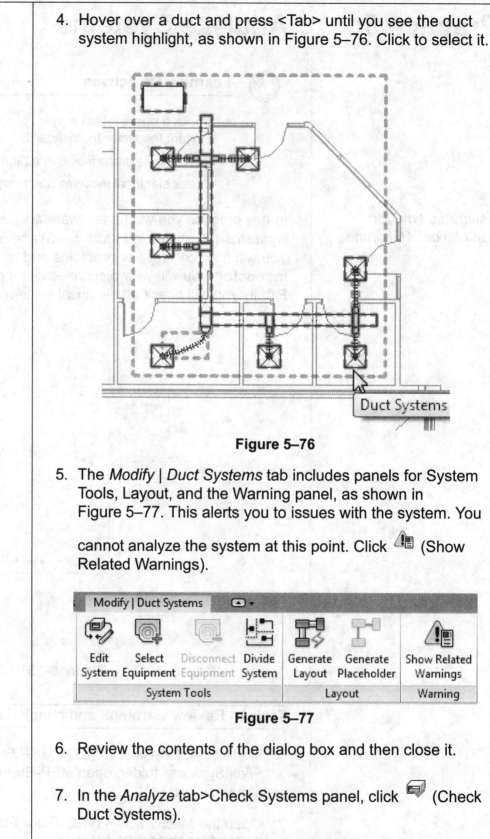

Figure 5–76

5. The *Modify | Duct Systems* tab includes panels for System Tools, Layout, and the Warning panel, as shown in Figure 5–77. This alerts you to issues with the system. You cannot analyze the system at this point. Click 🔺 (Show Related Warnings).

Figure 5–77

6. Review the contents of the dialog box and then close it.

7. In the *Analyze* tab>Check Systems panel, click 🗐 (Check Duct Systems).

8. Zoom in on the office area where there is a duct system that is not working, as shown in Figure 5–78.

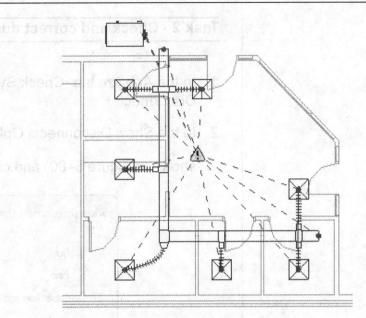

Figure 5–78

9. There is a missing duct coming out of the air handling unit. Use the **Draw Duct** tool and add this back in. Draw a horizontal duct coming from the AHU (as shown in

   Figure 5–79), and then use 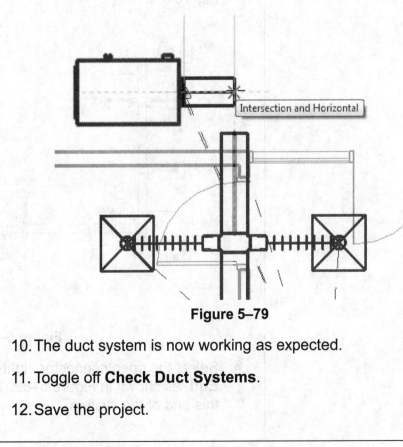 (Trim/Extent to Corner) to clean up the intersection and automatically apply the needed elbow fitting.

Figure 5–79

10. The duct system is now working as expected.

11. Toggle off **Check Duct Systems**.

12. Save the project.

Task 2 - Check and correct duct disconnects.

1. In the *Analyze* tab>Check Systems panel, click ⚠️ (Show Disconnects)

2. In the Show Disconnects Options dialog box, select **Duct** (as shown in Figure 5–80) and click [OK].

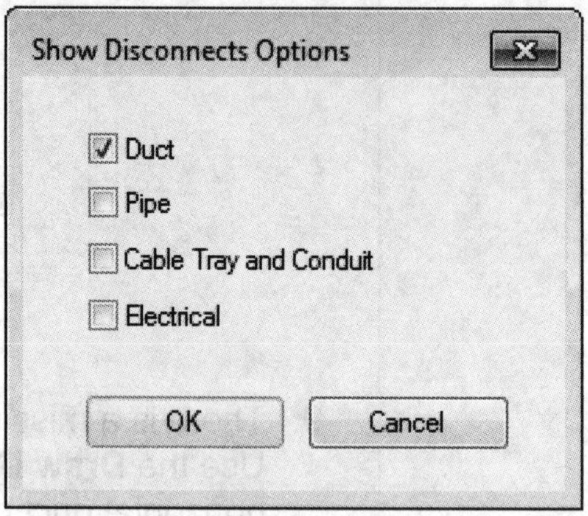

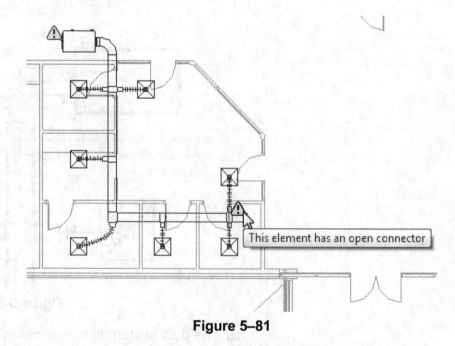

Figure 5–80

3. While the system is now connected correctly there are still disconnects at both ends of the system, as shown in Figure 5–81.

Figure 5–81

4. Select the open connector, right-click and select **Cap Open End**, as shown in Figure 5–82. This solves the problem on this end of the system.

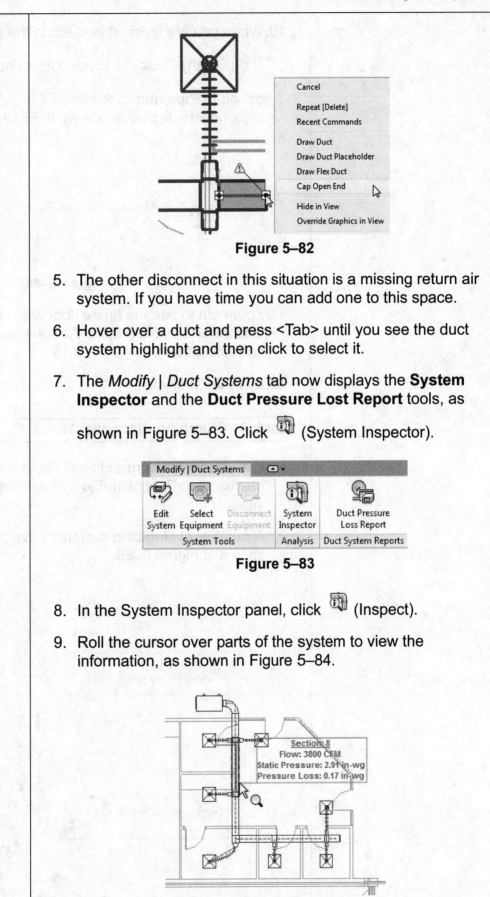

Figure 5–82

5. The other disconnect in this situation is a missing return air system. If you have time you can add one to this space.

6. Hover over a duct and press <Tab> until you see the duct system highlight and then click to select it.

7. The *Modify | Duct Systems* tab now displays the **System Inspector** and the **Duct Pressure Lost Report** tools, as shown in Figure 5–83. Click (System Inspector).

Figure 5–83

8. In the System Inspector panel, click (Inspect).

9. Roll the cursor over parts of the system to view the information, as shown in Figure 5–84.

Figure 5–84

10. When you are finished inspecting the system, click

    (Finish). Click 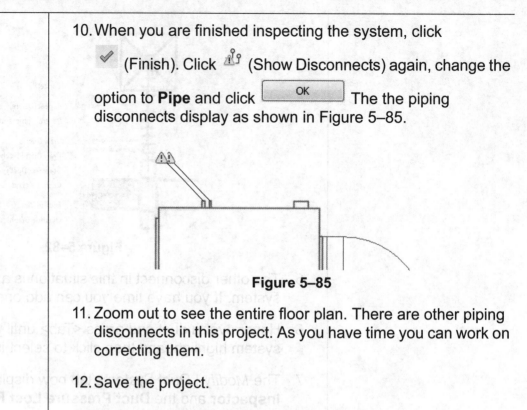 (Show Disconnects) again, change the

    option to **Pipe** and click [OK] The the piping
    disconnects display as shown in Figure 5–85.

Figure 5–85

11. Zoom out to see the entire floor plan. There are other piping
    disconnects in this project. As you have time you can work on
    correcting them.

12. Save the project.

Task 3 - Plumbing disconnects.

1. With **Show Disconnects** still set to **Piping** open the
   Mechanical>Plumbing>Floor Plans>**01 PLUMBING PLAN**
   view.

2. A number of plumbing systems have open connectors, as
   shown in Figure 5–86.

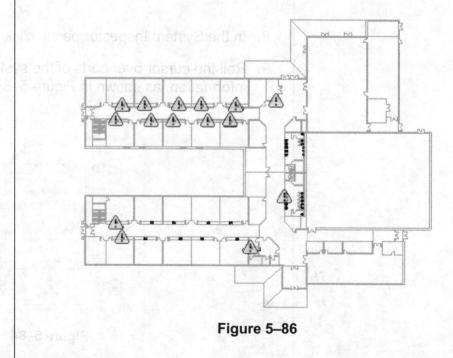

Figure 5–86

3. Zoom in on the office and select the sink in the copy room. You can see the open connector is for *Sanitary* piping.

4. Open the side facing section where you can see the disconnect more clearly, as shown in Figure 5–87.

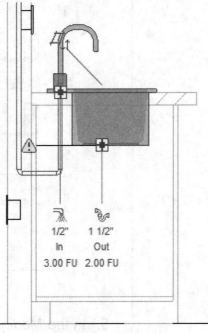

Figure 5–87

5. As you have time you can draw sanitary piping and connect into the existing system. You can also see what is needed to fix the other disconnects.

6. Save the project.

Task 4 - Check circuits and correct a problem.

---

1. Open the view Electrical>Lighting>Floor Plans>**01 LIGHTING PLAN**.

2. In the *Analyze* tab>Check Systems panel, click 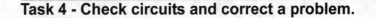 (Check Circuits).

3. A Warning dialog box displays with the message **Circuit is not assigned to a panel**. The elements in the circuit are also highlighted, (This is in another part of the building from the office.)

---

4. Hover the cursor over one of the lighting fixtures and press <Tab> to display the circuit, as shown in Figure 5–88. Click to select the circuit.

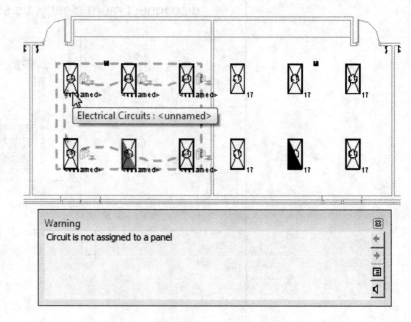

Figure 5–88

5. In the *Modify | Electrical Circuits* tab>System Tools panel, click 🔲 (Select Panel).

6. Zoom/Pan to the electrical room (in the upper right corner of the top classroom wing, as shown in Figure 5–90) and select panel **LP1** as shown in Figure 5–89.

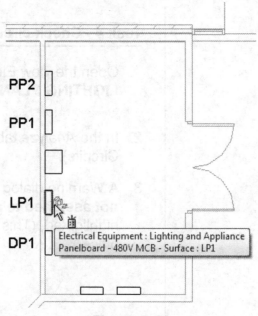

Figure 5–89

7. Zoom out to see the circuit outline including the panel, as shown in Figure 5–90.

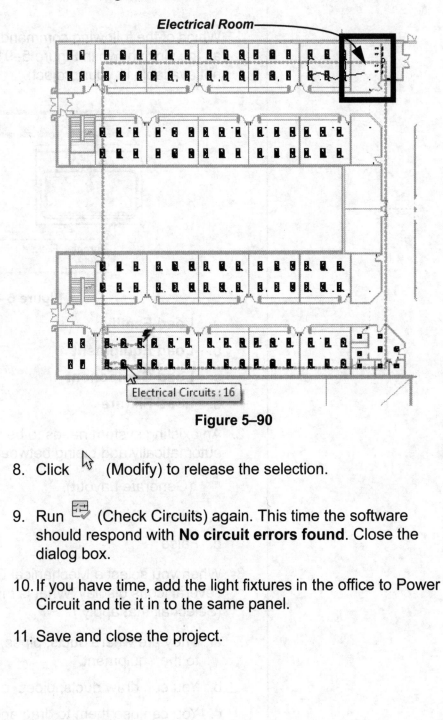

Electrical Room

Electrical Circuits : 16

Figure 5–90

8. Click ⬚ (Modify) to release the selection.

9. Run ⬚ (Check Circuits) again. This time the software should respond with **No circuit errors found**. Close the dialog box.

10. If you have time, add the light fixtures in the office to Power Circuit and tie it in to the same panel.

11. Save and close the project.

Chapter Review Questions

1. Which of the following commands imports a component, such as the sink shown in Figure 5–91, that you want to use that is not available in your project.

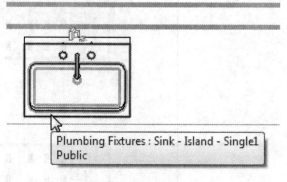

Plumbing Fixtures : Sink - Island - Single1 Public

Figure 5–91

a. **Load Family**

b. **Load Equipment**

c. **Load Component**

d. **Load Fixture**

2. An existing system needs to be in place before you can automatically add piping between plumbing fixtures using

    ![icon] (Generate Layout).

a. True

b. False

3. When you select a Mechanical Equipment component several icons display. What is the purpose of these icons? (Select all that apply.)

a. They are where ducts, pipes, or electrical circuits connect to the equipment.

b. You can draw ducts, pipes, or circuits from them.

c. You can use them to drag and align to other features in the project.

d. They establish the size or power of the connection.

4. Which of the following happens when you select components in the System Browser, as shown in Figure 5–92? (Select all that apply.)

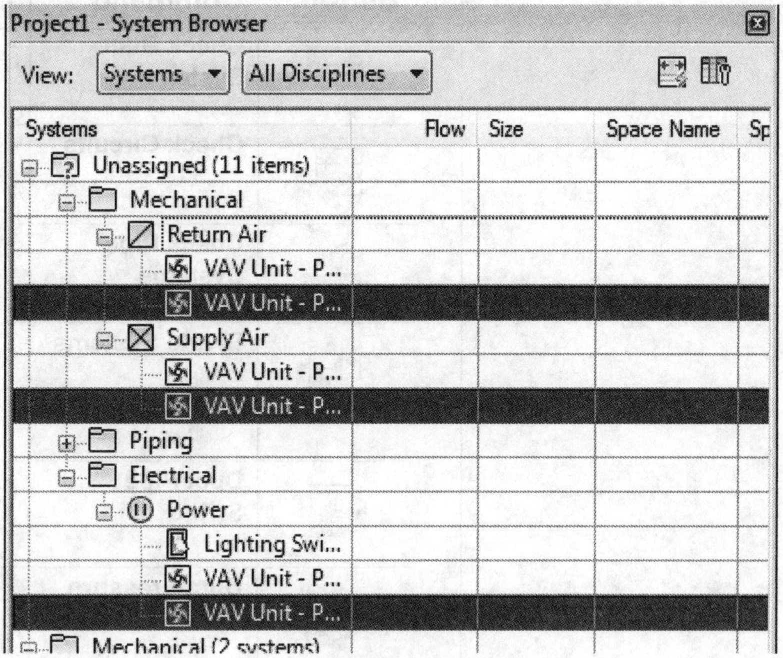

Figure 5–92

a. The components highlight in the current view.

b. The parameters of the components display in Properties.

c. If the components are attached to more than one system they also highlight in the other nodes in the System Browser.

d. The appropriate Ribbon tab displays.

5. When analyzing a project how do you specify that you see places where the ducts or pipes are not closed?

a. Use **Check Duct/Pipe Systems**.

b. Use **Show Disconnects**.

c. Create a Duct/Pressure Loss Report.

d. Open the Review Warnings dialog box

Command Summary

Button	Command	Location
	Check Duct Systems	• **Ribbon:** *Analyze* tab>Check Systems panel
	Check Circuits	• **Ribbon:** *Analyze* tab>Check Systems panel
	Check Pipe Systems	• **Ribbon:** *Analyze* tab>Check Systems panel
	Divide Systems	• **Ribbon:** (*when a duct or pipe system with more than one network is selected*) *Modify	varies* tab>System Tools panel
	Duct/Pipe Sizing	• **Ribbon:** (*when ducts or pipes are selected*) *Modify	varies* tab>Analysis panel
	Duct Pressure Loss Report	• **Ribbon:** *Analyze* tab>Reports & Schedules panel
	Load Family	• **Ribbon:** (*when a command that uses components is selected*) *Modify	varies* tab>Mode panel • **Ribbon:** *Insert* tab>Load from Library panel
	Pipe Pressure Loss Report	• **Ribbon:** *Analyze* tab>Reports & Schedules panel
	Show Disconnects	• **Ribbon:** *Analyze* tab>Check Systems panel
	Show related Warning	• **Ribbon:** varies according to the element selected
N/A	**System Browser**	• **Ribbon:** *View* tab>Window panel, expand (User Interface) • **Shortcut:** <F9>
	System Inspector	• **Ribbon:** (*when a system component is selected*) *Modify	varies* tab >Analysis panel • **System Browser:** *Right-click on a system name*>Inspect

Chapter 6

Spaces and Zones

In this chapter you learn how to add and modify spaces, use space separations, and place space tags. You also learn about zones and how to work with the System Browser with zones and spaces. Finally, you learn to create color-coded diagrams based on zones.

This chapter contains the following topics:

- **Creating Spaces**
- **Working with Spaces**
- **Creating Zones**
- **Creating Color Schemes**

6.1 Creating Spaces

Learning Objectives

- Prepare a model so that you can add spaces by setting room bounding status, volume computations, and creating views and view templates.
- Create spaces individually or automatically.
- Add Space Separation lines to further divide spaces.

The Space element is a critical component in the process of establishing heating and cooling loads. Spaces are also used to calculate the light levels based on the number and types of lighting fixtures in a room. Spaces identify each room in a building providing area, perimeter, and volume information about each space as well as information used in Electrical, Mechanical, and Energy Analysis, as shown in Figure 6–1.

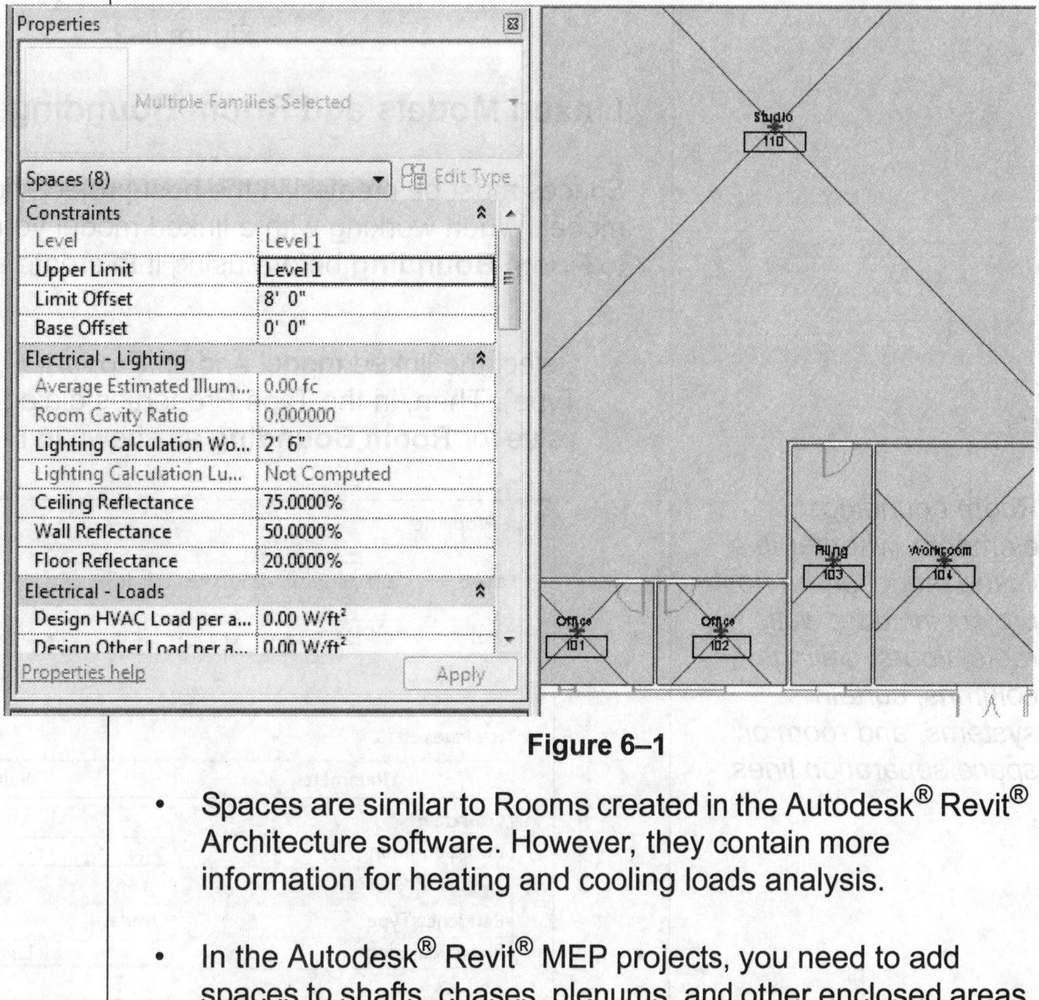

Figure 6–1

- Spaces are similar to Rooms created in the Autodesk® Revit® Architecture software. However, they contain more information for heating and cooling loads analysis.

- In the Autodesk® Revit® MEP projects, you need to add spaces to shafts, chases, plenums, and other enclosed areas that would not normally be assigned a room by the architect.

Preparing a Model for Spaces

Before adding spaces to a project it is helpful to set up the room bounding status of linked models and the area and volume computations, and to create views that display the spaces, as shown in Figure 6–2.

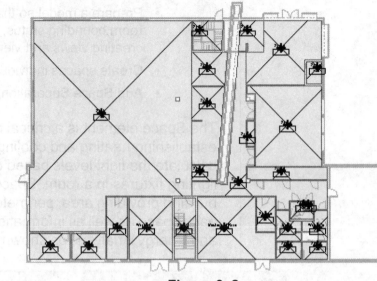

Figure 6–2

Linked Models and Room Bounding Status

Spaces must be created in the host project, not in a linked model. When working with a linked model you first need to set it to **Room Bounding** before using it to create spaces.

- Select the linked model and, in Properties, click ⬚ (Edit Type). Then, in the Type Properties dialog box, select the value for **Room Bounding** as shown in Figure 6–3.

Room bounding elements, whether in a linked model or the host project include: walls, roofs, floors, ceilings, columns, curtain systems, and room or space separation lines.

Type Properties		
Family:	System Family: Linked Revit Model ▼	Load...
Type:	06-126- Spheron.rvt ▼	Duplicate...
		Rename...

Type Parameters

Parameter	Value
Constraints	⌃
Room Bounding	☑
Other	⌃
Reference Type	Overlay
Phase Mapping	Edit...

Figure 6–3

Area and Volume Computations

You can set the way Autodesk Revit calculates volumes and boundary locations. In the *Analyze* tab>Spaces & Zones panel, expand the panel title and click  (Area and Volume Computations) to open the Area and Volume Computations dialog box, as shown in Figure 6–4.

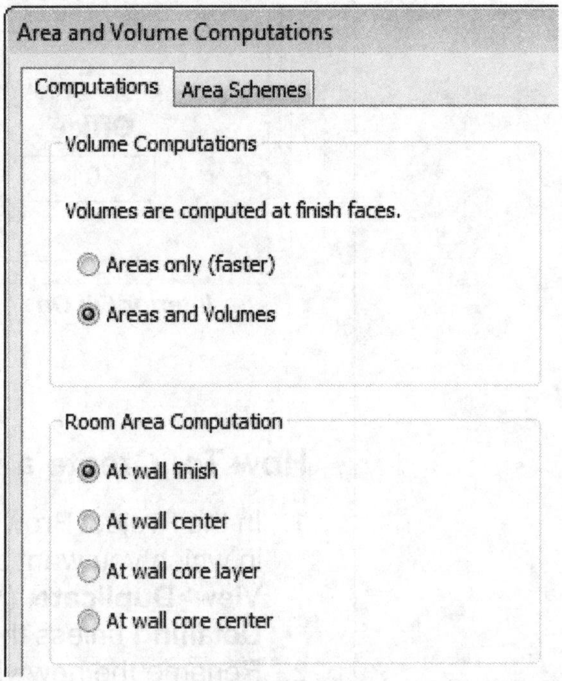

Figure 6–4

- Typically, you have **Areas and Volumes** on when you are working in Autodesk Revit MEP projects. This impacts the spaces that are controlled by bounding elements, such as ceilings and roofs as shown in Figure 6–5.

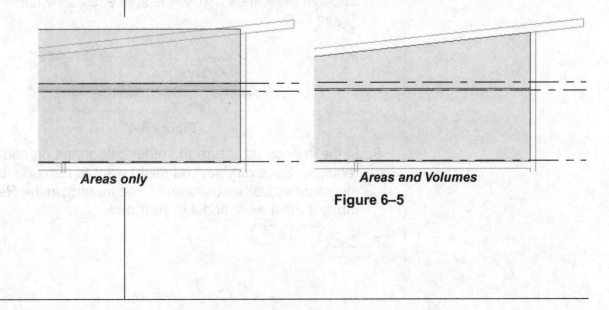

Areas only   *Areas and Volumes*

Figure 6–5

Creating Views for Spaces

By default, spaces only display when you hover the cursor over them or select them. To help you place and view spaces, create a view that displays them and limits the display of other elements. You can set up spaces to display an interior fill and reference lines (as shown in Figure 6–6), in floor plans, and in sections.

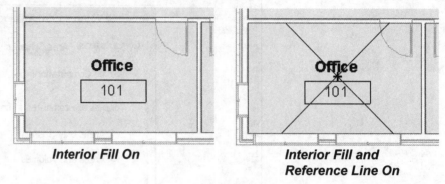

Interior Fill On   *Interior Fill and*
                                      Reference Line On

Figure 6–6

How To: Create a View to display spaces

1. In the Project Browser, right-click on a view similar to the one in which you want to display spaces and select **Duplicate View>Duplicate**. (You do not need to use **Duplicate with Detailing** unless the view you select already has space tags.)
2. Rename the new view.
3. In Properties, assign the *Discipline* (often **Coordination**) and *Sub-Discipline* as required.
4. Type **VG** to open the Visibility/Graphics Overrides dialog box.
5. In the *Model Categories* tab, expand Spaces and select **Interior** as shown in Figure 6–7. The **Reference** option displays the x lines across the space, as shown in Figure 6–6.

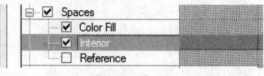

Figure 6–7

6. In the various tabs, turn the other categories on and off as required. For example, you might want to turn off most MEP elements as well as grids and furniture and, in the *Revit Links* tab, set the linked model to **Halftone**.

7. Click .

View Templates

View templates can be used to quickly apply not only Visibility/ Graphics Overrides, but also any other View Properties including *Discipline* and *View Range*, as shown in Figure 6–8. You can then apply the view template to views.

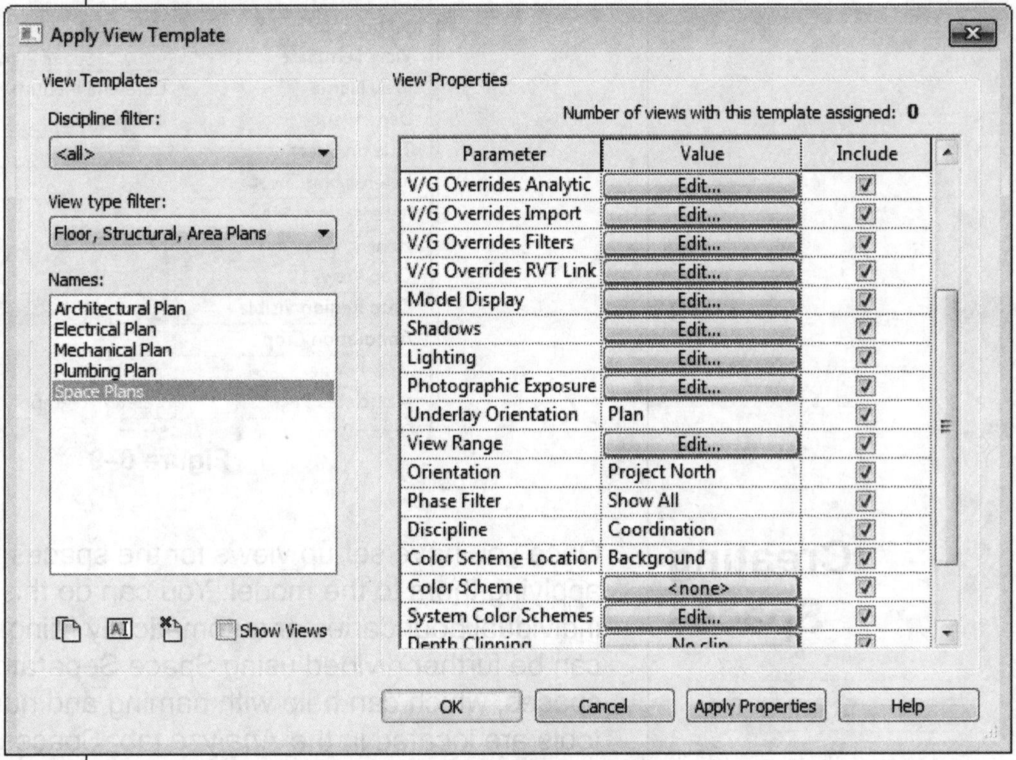

Figure 6–8

- View templates work with all types of model views.

How To: Create and Apply View Templates to Views

1. Setup a view the way you want it.
2. In the Project Browser, right-click on that view and select **Create View Template From View...**
3. In the New View Template dialog box, type a new Name and click OK.
4. To apply a view template to a view, right-click on the view and select **Apply Template Properties.**
5. In the Apply View Template dialog box, select the one you want to use and click OK.

- To have more control over views, in the Properties of the view, in the *Identity Data* area, you can specify a View Template as shown in Figure 6–9. Doing so limits the changes you can make to the view, such as the Scale, Visibility Graphics Overrides, and View Range.

Floor Plan: Cafeteria Plenum ▾   ⊞ Edit Type

Identity Data	⌃
View Template	Space Plan
View Name	Cafeteria Plenum
Dependency	Independent
Title on Sheet	
Referencing Sheet	
Referencing Detail	
Extents	⌃
Crop View	☐
Crop Region Visible	☐
Annotation Crop	☐
View Range	Edit...
Associated Level	Cafeteria Plenum

Figure 6–9

Creating Spaces

Once you have set up views for the spaces you can start applying them to the model. You can do this by selecting individual boundaries or automatically filling each space. Spaces can be further divided using Space Separators. You can also tag spaces, which can help with naming and numbering. The space tools are located in the *Analyze* tab>Spaces & Zones panel as shown in Figure 6–10.

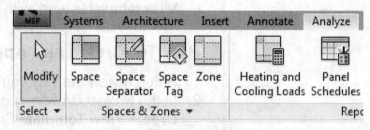

Figure 6–10

How To: Create Spaces by Selecting Boundaries

1. In the *Analyze* tab>Spaces & Zones panel, click ⊞ (Space).

2. In the *Modify | Place Space* tab>Tag panel, click ⌐① (Tag on Placement) if you want to include a tag as you place the space. In the Options Bar, you can set the *Orientation* of the tag and the *Leader*.

3. In the Options Bar, set the *Upper Limit* and *Offset*, which control the volume calculations, and set the height of the space, as shown in Figure 6–11. If space names were previously created in a schedule, you can select a *Space* name from the drop-down list.

| Modify | Place Space | Upper Limit: | Level 1 ▼ | Offset: 9' 0" | 🖿 Horizontal ▼ | ☐ Leader | Space: New ▼ |

Figure 6–11

- Set the *Upper Limit* to the level above and the *Offset* to **0** if you want elements, such as ceilings, to control the height of the space.

4. Move the cursor into a boundary area and click to place the space. Continue adding spaces, as shown in Figure 6–12.

To see the volume of the spaces as you create them it helps to have a floor plan and a section view tiled.

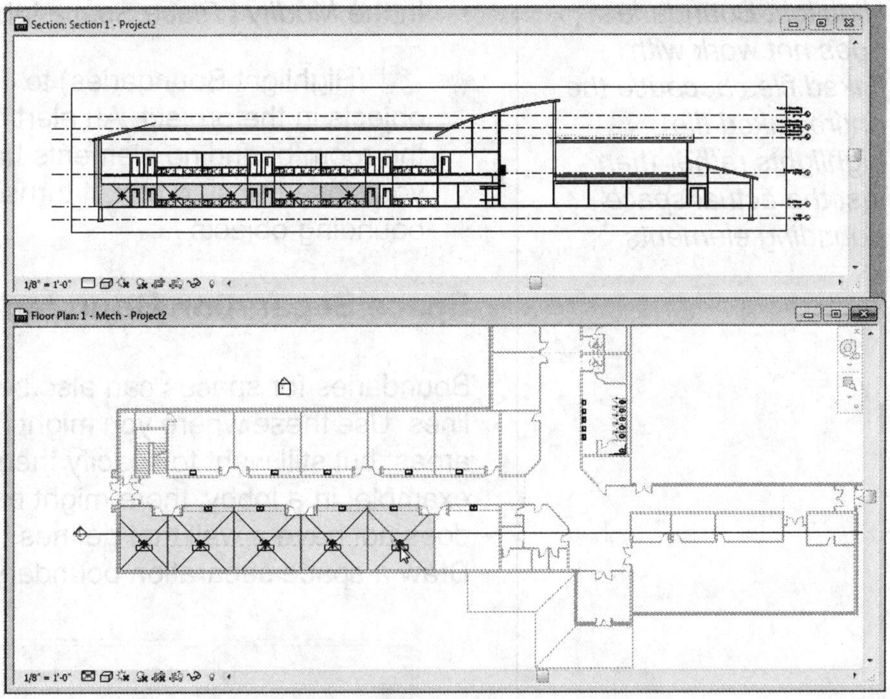

Figure 6–12

5. Click ⌖ (Modify) or press <Esc> to end the command.

How To: Place Spaces Automatically

1. In the *Analyze* tab>Spaces & Zones panel, click ▦ (Space).
2. In the *Modify | Place Space* tab>Spaces panel, click

   ▤ (Place Spaces Automatically).

3. An alert box opens prompting you about the number of spaces created as shown in Figure 6–13. Click .

> **Revit** ⊠
>
> 56 Spaces created automatically.
>
> Close

Figure 6–13

4. Spaces are added in each bounded area and a tag is placed if that option is selected in the Ribbon.

Highlight Boundaries does not work with linked files because the entire linked file highlights rather than just the actual space bounding elements.

- In the *Modify | Place Space* tab>Spaces panel, click ☐ (Highlight Boundaries) to display all of the bounding objects in the project. An alert box opens prompting you that the room bounding elements have been highlighted. When you close the alert box, it turns off the highlighting of the bounding objects.

Space Separation Boundaries

Boundaries for spaces can also be defined by space separation lines. Use these where you might not have a wall to separate the areas, but still want to specify them as different space. For example, in a lobby, there might be an area open to above that does not have a wall that defines the change in space height. Draw a space separation boundary as shown in Figure 6–14.

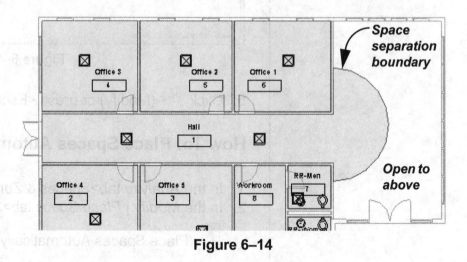

Figure 6–14

How To: Create Space Separation Boundaries

1. In the *Analyze* tab>Spaces & Zones panel, click (Space Separator).

2. In the *Modify | Place Space Separation* tab>Draw panel, use the sketch tools to draw the edges of the boundary.

3. Click (Modify) or press <Esc> to end the command.

4. Use (Space) to add spaces in the areas bounded by the separation lines.

- You can edit space separation lines by splitting, trimming, etc.

6.2 Working with Spaces

Learning Objectives

- Select spaces and modify them graphically and in Properties.
- Set up spaces for specific situations, including shafts, sliver spaces, cavities, and plenums.

As you are working with spaces in a project, it is important to place a space in every open area so that the energy analysis is computed correctly. Check the project in plan and in section to find elements, such as shafts and plenum spaces as shown in Figure 6–15. You also need to set up the properties of each space for correct calculation.

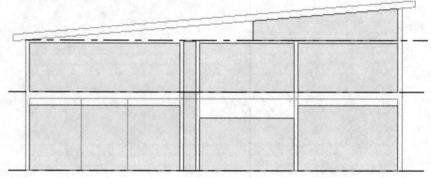

Figure 6–15

- To select a space, hover the cursor over it until you see the crossing line, as shown in Figure 6–16. Select the reference point to pick the space.

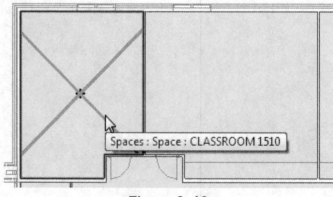

Spaces : Space : CLASSROOM 1510

Figure 6–16

- When a space is selected, you can modify its Properties, as shown in Figure 6–17. These include *Constraints* on the space, including the **Upper Limit** and **Limit Offset**, which display the height of the space, *Electrical-Lighting* and *Loads* information, and *Mechanical Airflow* and *Energy Analysis* features as well as standard *Identity Data* where you set up the *Space Name* and *Space Number*.

This information is critical to setup before doing Heating and Cooling Loads and using various Energy Analysis tools.

Properties	✕
Spaces (1)	▼ Edit Type
Constraints	☆
Level	Level 1
Upper Limit	Level 2
Limit Offset	0' 0"
Base Offset	0' 0"
Electrical - Lighting	☆
Average Estimated Illu...	0.00 lx
Room Cavity Ratio	0.000000
Lighting Calculation W...	2' 6"
Lighting Calculation Lu...	Not Computed
Ceiling Reflectance	75.0000%
Wall Reflectance	50.0000%
Floor Reflectance	20.0000%
Electrical - Loads	☆
Design HVAC Load per ...	0.00 W/ft²
Design Other Load per ...	0.00 W/ft²
Mechanical - Flow	☆
Properties help	Apply

Figure 6–17

- You can select several spaces at once to add the same information to all of them.

- If a linked architectural model includes rooms the associated *Room Name* and *Number* are displayed in the Space Properties and can be set to match as shown in Figure 6–18.

*The **Space Naming Utility** (subscription only tool) automatically updates space names based on the corresponding room name.*

Identity Data	☆
Number	112
Name	Studio
Room Number	112
Room Name	Studio
Comments	

Figure 6–18

- Another way to change the space name or number is to select the tag name or number to modify it, as shown in Figure 6–19.

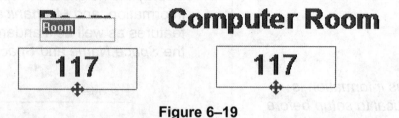

Figure 6–19

- To make a height change visually, open a section and use the controls and temporary dimensions as shown in Figure 6–20.

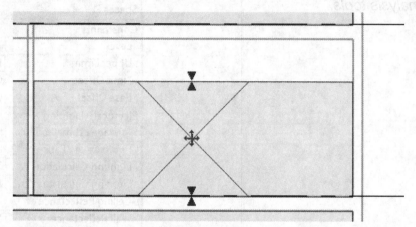

Figure 6–20

- When there are changes in the height of an area the space must be placed at the tallest height as shown on the left in Figure 6–21, where a Plenum level was added. You can then change the *Bottom Offset* in Properties to have the space extend down as shown on the right in Figure 6–21.

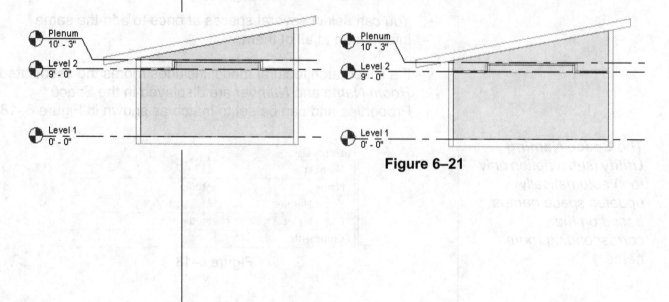

Figure 6–21

Hint: Adding Space Tags

Not all tags are needed until you set up construction documents, but space tags can help you identify and set up the spaces. You can change the space name and number by clicking on the tag.

Space Tags can be added during or after spaces are added to a project. There are three space tag types: **Space Tag**, **Space Tag With Area**, and **Space Tag With Volume**, as shown in Figure 6–22.

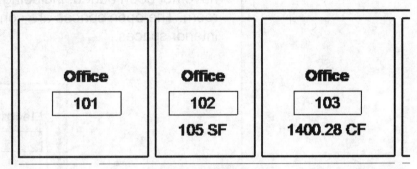

Figure 6–22

If you need to add tags after spaces have been placed, in the *Analyze* tab>Spaces & Zones panel or the *Annotate* tab>Tag panel, click (Space Tag). In the Type Selector, select the tag type and then select the space to tag.

* Spaces can be tagged in plan or section views.

* If you delete a space tag, the space is not deleted.

* If you move a tag outside its space without a leader, it loses the association, as shown in Figure 6–23. You can add a leader or use the alert box buttons to move it back in the space to re-associate it.

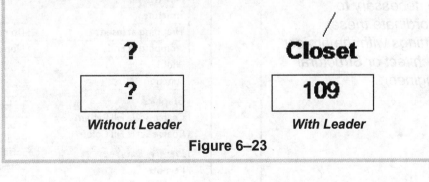

Figure 6–23

Special Space Situations

There are several situations in which you need to make modifications to spaces or the surrounding bounding areas to have them read correctly when analysis is done. These include shafts, sliver spaces, cavities, and plenum spaces.

Shafts and Interior/Exterior Bounding Elements

It is critical to place a space in every area in a building before you try to analyze the heating and cooling load because any wall that is not bounded by another space is considered an exterior wall. In the example in Figure 6–24, there are several spaces that have not been added, including a shaft, an elevator shaft, and a room. The open spaces are considered exterior rather than interior spaces.

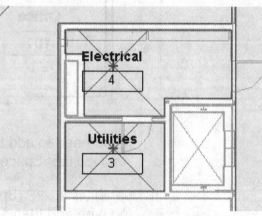

Figure 6–24

- Wall type functions can be specified in the Type Parameters as shown in Figure 6–25. **Interior** and **Core-shaft** *Function* types are considered interior whether they have a space on the other side of the wall or not.

When space boundary objects are contained in linked projects it might be necessary to coordinate these settings with the project Architect or Structural Engineer.

Figure 6–25

- Floor types can also have a *Function* of **Interior** or **Exterior**.

Sliver Spaces

This is useful when the boundary objects have not been set to define core, soffit, interior, or exterior options.

Sliver spaces are shafts or other thin vertical spaces that have parallel walls with spaces on all sides and meet a Sliver Space Tolerance setup in Energy Settings. The default is **1'-0"**. You cannot place a space in such areas.

- To define the Sliver Space Tolerance, in the *Manage* tab>

  Settings panel, click <img (Project Information) and click

  [Edit...] next to the **Energy Settings** parameter.

- Instead of changing the Sliver Space Tolerance, which could cause problems elsewhere in your project, you can clear the Room Bounding status in the wall properties as shown in Figure 6–26. If there is a linked model this must be done directly in the original file.

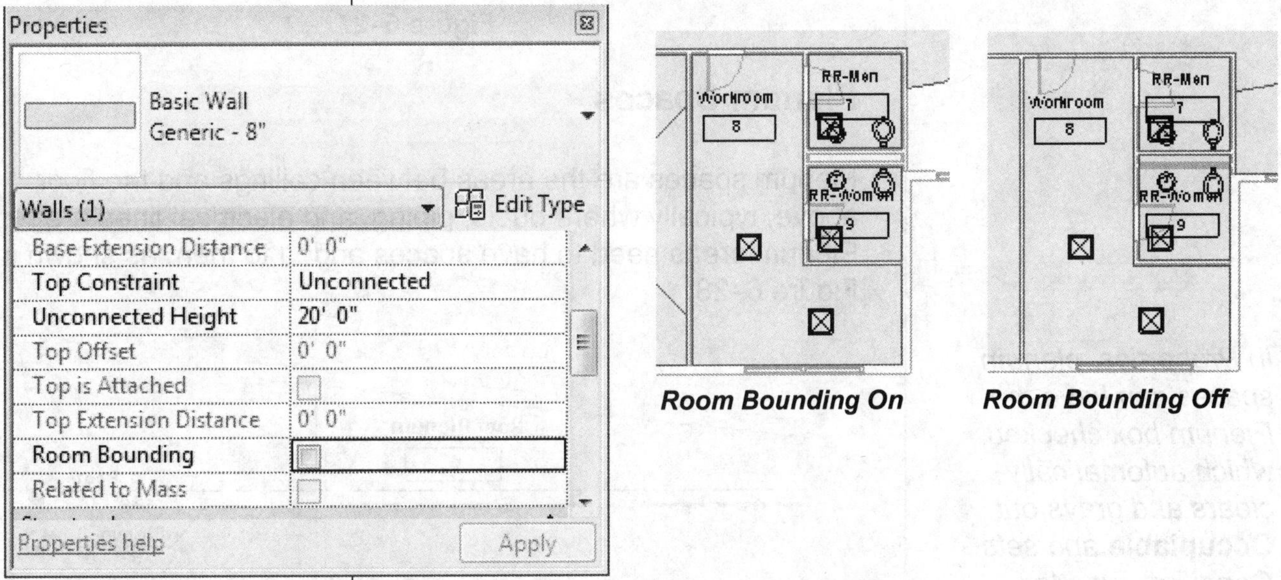

Room Bounding On   *Room Bounding Off*

Figure 6–26

Cavities

Cavities are small areas in which the walls are asymmetrical, such as a curved or triangular space that defines an odd shaped room, as shown in Figure 6–27. Typically, walls that define such spaces only extend to the ceiling or just above the ceiling. If you can add a space, do so. Check the area in section to verify that the entire space has been filled.

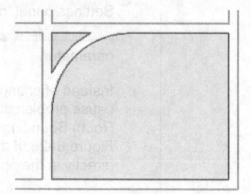

Figure 6–27

Plenum Spaces

Plenum spaces are the areas between ceilings and the floor above, typically where ducts, piping, and electrical lines are run. Plenum areas need to have spaces added to them as shown in Figure 6–28.

In Properties, plenum spaces can have the Plenum box checked, which automatically clears and grays out Occupiable and sets Condition Type to Unconditioned.

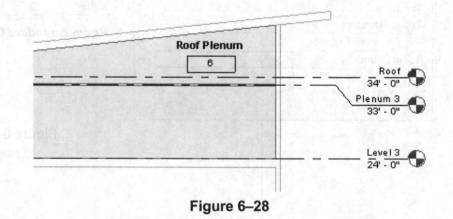

Figure 6–28

How To: Create Spaces in a Plenum

1. Place spaces in the existing areas.
2. In a plan view, create a section that cuts through the area in which the plenum runs.

3. In the section, verify that all of the spaces are touching the ceilings, as shown in Figure 6–29. (Typically, set the space **Upper Limit** to the level above to have the space automatically stop at a boundary, such as a ceiling.)

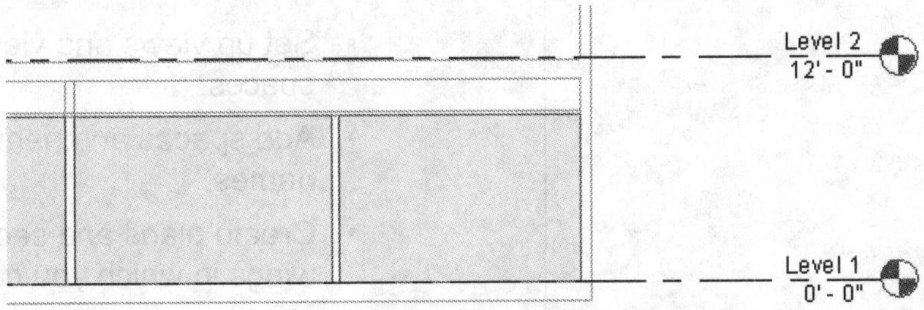

Figure 6–29

Some templates include the Plenum Level type. However, it is not included in all templates and is not a requirement.

4. In the *Architecture* tab>Datum panel, click (Level).
5. In the Type Selector, select **Level: Plenum**.
6. In the Options Bar, select **Make Plan View**.
7. Draw a new level at the height of the ceiling.
8. Rename the level and any associated views with a name that fits the project, such as **Plenum 1** shown in Figure 6–30.

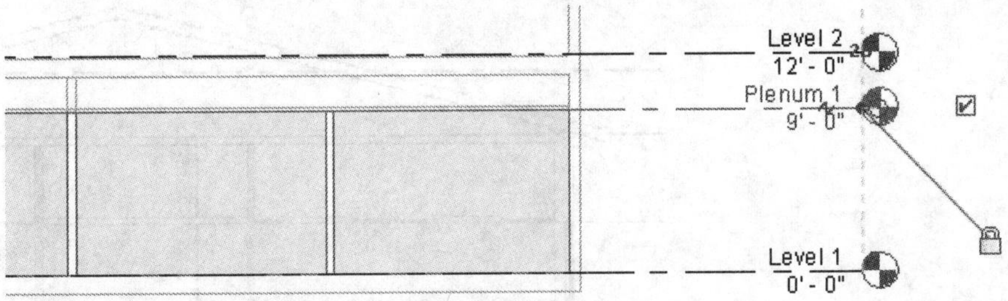

Figure 6–30

9. Open the new floor plan.
10. In Properties, edit the View Range and set the *cut plane offset* to **6"** (or other value that fits the height of the plenum.)
11. In the plan view, place the spaces. They should fill the plenum area as shown in Figure 6–31.

In this example, one wall touches the ceiling and another goes up to the floor above to indicate how the space in the plenum is divided.

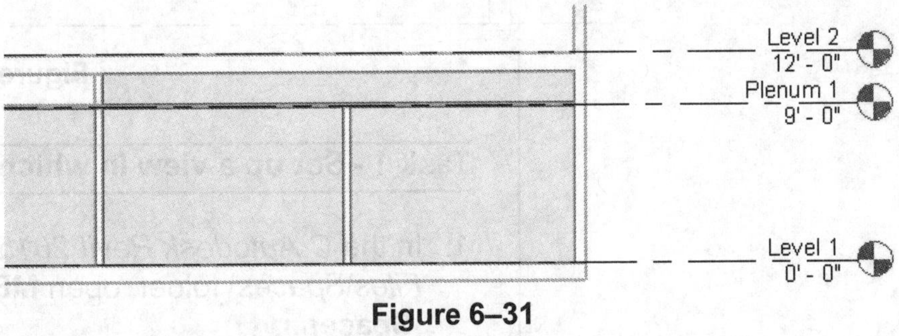

Figure 6–31

12. Repeat as required for all other plenum areas.

Practice 6a

Work with Spaces

Learning Objectives

- Set up views and view templates where you define spaces.
- Add spaces and name them based on existing room names.
- Create plans and sections in the cafeteria and classroom wings in which you can place plenum spaces.
- Investigate and correct problems with overlapping spaces.

Estimated time for completion: 30 minutes

In this practice you will add spaces to a variety of areas, modifying heights and renaming them as required. You will also create plenum levels and add plenum spaces, as shown in Figure 6–32. You will investigate an overlap of spaces and add space separation lines to correct it.

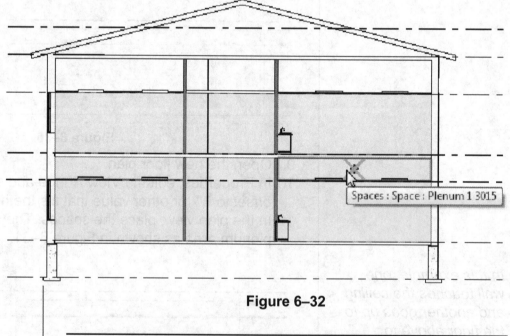

Figure 6–32

Task 1 - Set up a view in which you will define spaces.

1. In the *C:Autodesk Revit 2015 MEP Fundamentals Class Files\Spaces* folder, open **MEP-Elementary-School -Spaces.rvt**.

*Use **Duplicate with Detailing** so existing tags are included.*

2. In the Project Browser, expand Coordination>All>*Floor Plans*. Select the **First Floor** view, right-click and select **Duplicate View>Duplicate with Detailing**.

3. Rename the new view as **01 Space Planning**.

4. In Properties, change the *Sub-Discipline* to **MEP**.

5. The new view moves to the MEP node as shown in Figure 6–33.

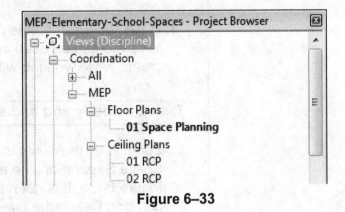

Figure 6–33

6. No spaces display in this view. Type **VG** to open the Visibility/Graphics dialog box.

7. In the *Model Categories* tab, scroll down and expand **Spaces**. Select **Interior** and click OK.

8. Most of the areas in this building have spaces as shown in Figure 6–34 but several still need to be added for the Gym, Cafeteria, and Kitchen.

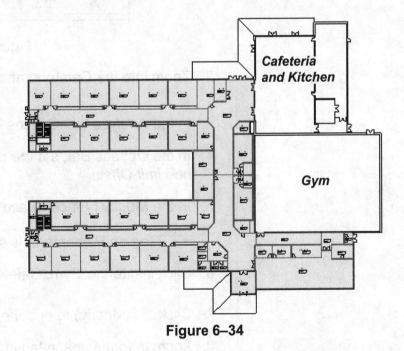

Figure 6–34

You need to apply these view settings to other views as you work with spaces. Therefore, it is a good idea to create a View template.

9. In the Project Browser, right-click on the **01 Space Planning** view and select **Create View Template from View...**

10. In the New View Template dialog box, type **Space Plan** and click OK .

11. In the View Templates dialog box, click OK . This template can be used again for any other plan views that you create while working with spaces.

Task 2 - Modify and add spaces.

1. Zoom in on the Stairs in the North Classroom wing. There is a Space Separation line across the stairwell as shown in Figure 6–35. It is not needed because the stair is open to the corridor. Delete the line and the related Corridor space fills the stairwell.

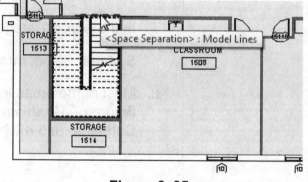

Figure 6–35

2. Zoom into the Cafeteria and Gym areas of the building.

3. In the *Analyze* tab>Spaces & Zones panel, click (Space).

4. In the Options Bar, set the *Upper Limit* to **Second Floor** with no *Limit Offset*.

5. In the *Modify | Place Space* tab>Tag panel, verify that (Tag on Placement) is selected.

6. Click inside the Gym, Cafeteria, and support spaces.

7. Click (Modify) to end the command.

8. Zoom in to the space tag in the gym. The right name and number are not set even though there is an associated room in the linked model.

9. Select the space (not the tag).

10. In Properties, scroll down to the *Identity Data* area. The *Number* and *Name* for the space do not match the *Room Number* and *Room Name* as shown in Figure 6–36.

Spaces (1)		
Identity Data		
Number	210	
Name	Chase	
Room Number	3500	
Room Name	GYM	
Comments		

Figure 6–36

11. Change the space name and number to match the room name and number and click Apply .

12. In the view, note that the space tag updated with the new information.

13. Repeat the process with the other new spaces for the Cafeteria (as shown in Figure 6–37), Kitchen, Kitchen Storage, and Corridor.

To make it easier to see the Identity Data area, collapse the other areas. This modification is remembered for spaces as long as you are working in this session of the software.

Spaces (1)		
Constraints		
Level	First Floor	
Upper Limit	Second Floor	
Limit Offset	0' 0"	
Base Offset	0' 0"	
Electrical - Lighting		
Electrical - Loads		
Mechanical - Flow		
Dimensions		
Identity Data		
Number	3000	
Name	CAFETERIA	
Room Number	3000	
Room Name	CAFETERIA	
Comments		

Figure 6–37

14. Save the project.

Task 3 - Verify the heights of spaces.

1. Draw a section across the part of the gym that extends beyond the rest of the building, as shown in Figure 6–38.

Draw the section so it does not display the far wall. This makes it easier to just display the gym and its space.

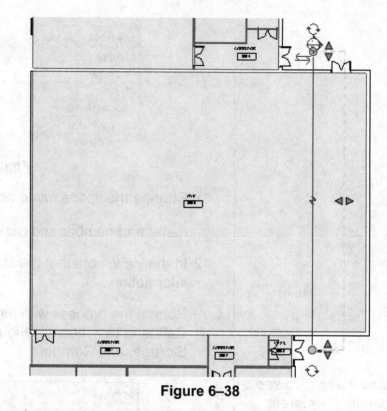

Figure 6–38

2. Click in empty space to clear the selection and then double-click on the arrow of the section marker to open the section.

3. In Properties, set the *Sub-Discipline* to **MEP**.

4. Type **VG**. In the Visibility/Graphics Overrides dialog box, in the *Model Categories* tab, select the **Spaces>Interior** category. In the *Annotation Categories* tab, clear **Grids**.

5. In the Project Browser, right-click on the new section view (Coordination>MEP>Section (Building Section): **Section 1**) and select **Create View Template from View...**

6. In the New View Template dialog box, type **Space Section** and click [OK].

7. In the View Templates dialog box, click [OK]. This template can be used again for any other section views that you create while working with spaces.

8. The space height in the gym is too low as shown in Figure 6–39.

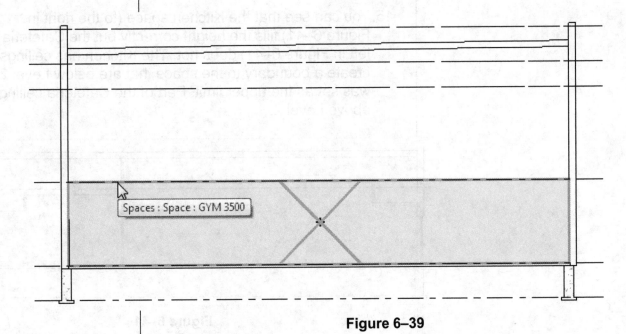

Spaces : Space : GYM 3500

Figure 6–39

9. Select the space. Use the controls to extend the space above the roof of the gym or, in Properties, change the *Upper Limit* to **Volume Modeling Reference 3**.

10. Press <Ctrl>+<Tab> to return to the **First Floor** plan view.

11. Draw a section across the end of the Cafeteria and Kitchen as shown in Figure 6–40.

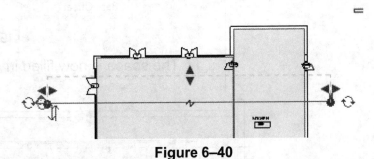

Figure 6–40

12. Click in empty space to clear the selection and then double-click on the arrow of the section marker to open the section.

13. In Properties, scroll down to the *Identity Data* area and click the button next to *View Template.* In the Apply View Template dialog box, select **Space Section** and click $\boxed{\text{OK}}$. The view inherits the settings of the View Template that you created earlier.

14. The **Library Entrance Reference** level is not needed in this view. Right-click and select **Hide in View>Elements**.

15. You can see that the Kitchen space (to the right in Figure 6–41) fills the height correctly but the Cafeteria (to the left in Figure 6–41) does not. The Kitchen has ceilings that create a boundary to the space that are below Level 2 which was set as the upper limit. Part of the Cafeteria ceiling is above Level 2.

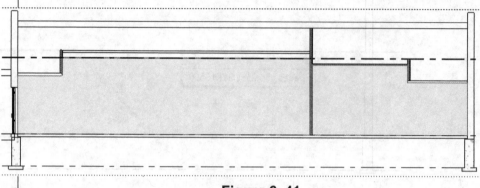

Figure 6–41

16. Select the Cafeteria space. In Properties, change the *Limit Offset* to **5'-0"** as shown in Figure 6–42.

Figure 6–42

17. The space is now filled in correctly as shown in Figure 6–43.

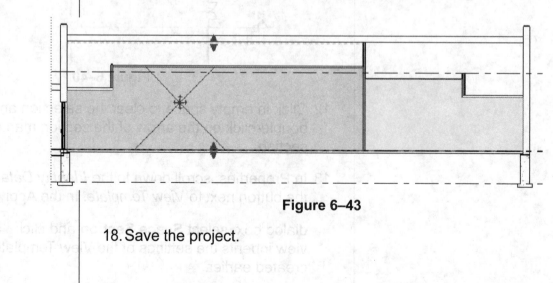

Figure 6–43

18. Save the project.

Task 4 - Add Plenum Spaces.

As you can see in the section of the Cafeteria and Kitchen, there is an open area above the ceilings that also needs a space. To do this you need to add an additional level and its associated plan view.

1. In the *Architecture* tab>Datum panel, click 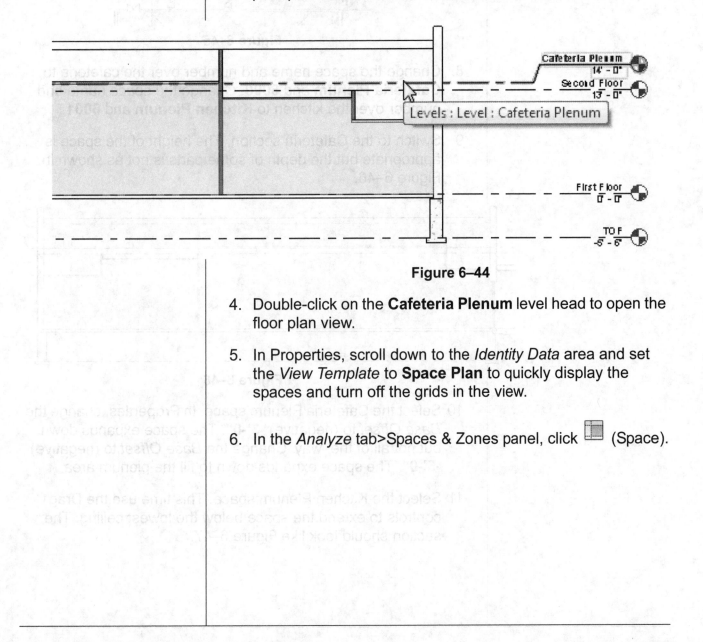 (Level).

2. In the Type Selector, select **Level: Plenum** and, in Properties, clear the **Building Story** option.

3. Draw a level line **14'-0"** above the First Floor and rename it as **Cafeteria Plenum** as shown in Figure 6–44. When prompted, rename all of the associated views.

Figure 6–44

4. Double-click on the **Cafeteria Plenum** level head to open the floor plan view.

5. In Properties, scroll down to the *Identity Data* area and set the *View Template* to **Space Plan** to quickly display the spaces and turn off the grids in the view.

6. In the *Analyze* tab>Spaces & Zones panel, click (Space).

7. Add spaces to the Cafeteria and Kitchen areas. The Kitchen space fills the entire area, as shown in Figure 6–45, because the base of the space is at the Cafeteria Plenum level, which is above all of the interior walls.

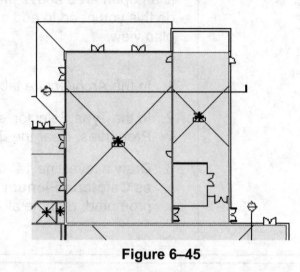

Figure 6–45

8. Change the space name and number over the cafeteria to **Cafeteria Plenum** and **6000**. Change the space name and number over the kitchen to **Kitchen Plenum** and **6001**.

9. Switch to the Cafeteria section. The height of the space is appropriate but the depth of some parts is not as shown in Figure 6–46.

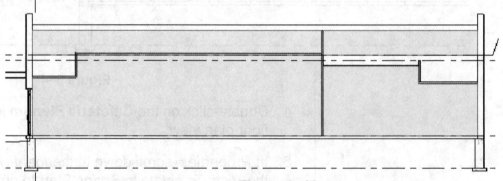

Figure 6–46

10. Select the Cafeteria Plenum space. In Properties, change the *Base Offset* to (negative) **-3'-0"**. The space expands down but not all of the way. Change the *Base Offset* to (negative) **-5'-0"**. The space expands down to fill the plenum area.

11. Select the Kitchen Plenum space. This time use the Drag controls to extend the space below the lowest ceiling. The section should look like Figure 6–47.

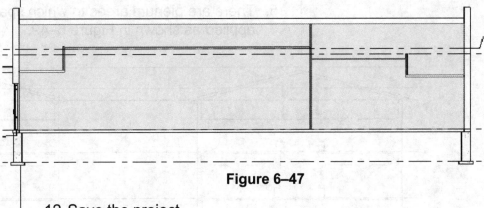

Figure 6–47

12. Save the project.

Task 5 - Add plenum spaces to the Classroom Wings.

1. Return to the **01 Space Planning** view.

2. Draw a section that cuts across both Classroom Wings as shown in Figure 6–48.

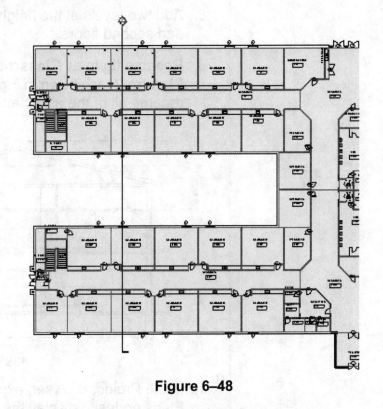

Figure 6–48

3. Verify that the section is pointing to the left.

4. Open the section view and, in Properties, set the *View Template* to **Space Section**.

5. There are plenum areas to which spaces have not been applied as shown in Figure 6–49.

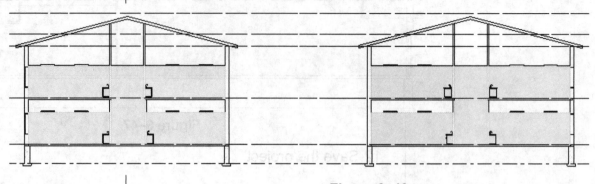

Figure 6–49

6. In the *Architecture* tab>Datum panel, click (Level).

7. In the Type Selector, select **Level: Plenum** and, in Properties, clear the **Building Story** option.

8. Add two levels at the height of the ceilings (**9'-0"**) on the first and second floors.

9. Rename them as **Classroom Plenum 1** and **Classroom Plenum 2**, as shown in Figure 6–50. When prompted, rename all of the associated views.

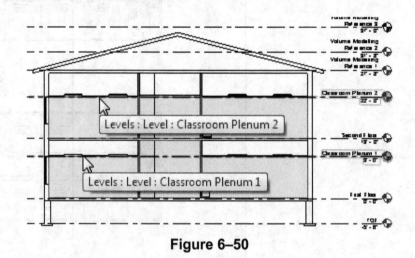

Figure 6–50

10. In the Project Browser, expand the Coordination>???>Floor Plans nodes to display the new Classroom Plenum views.

11. Hold <Ctrl> and select both of them.

12. Right-click and select **Apply View Template...**

13. In the Apply View Template dialog box, select **Space Plan** and click OK.

14. The plans are now moved to the Coordination>MEP>Floor Plans node, the grids are turned off and spaces are turned on as specified in the view template

15. Open the **Classroom Plenum 1** view.

16. In Properties, scroll down to the *Extents* area, and edit the *View Range*. Change the *Cut Plane Offset* to **1'-0"** and click OK . Some spaces are already expanded through the plenum areas as shown in Figure 6–51.

If you set the View Template in Properties you cannot change the View Range at this point.

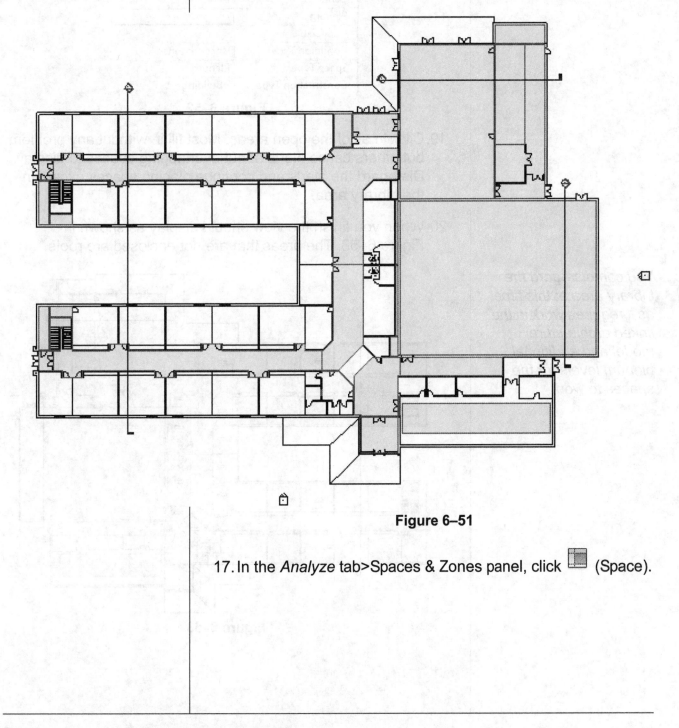

Figure 6–51

17. In the *Analyze* tab>Spaces & Zones panel, click (Space).

18. In Properties, set the *Upper Limit* to **Second Floor** and the *Offset* to **0**. Scroll down to the *Identity Data* area and change the *Name* to **Plenum 1**. Scroll down to *Energy Analysis* and select **Plenum** as shown in Figure 6–52. Doing so means that all of the spaces you place in this command have these properties.

New Spaces	▼	Edit Type
Phase	New Construction	
Energy Analysis		≫
Zone	Default	
Plenum	☑	
Occupiable	☐	
Condition Type	Unconditioned	
Space Type	Plenum	
Construction Type	<Building>	

Figure 6–52

19. Click in all of the open areas. Most fill in without any problem but others cause alerts about overlapping spaces to display. Disregard the alerts and continue placing spaces except in the Library area.

20. When you finish the view should display as shown in Figure 6–53. The areas that are not enclosed are roofs.

You can disregard the Library area at this time as it requires work in the linked architectural model and additional plenum levels for the spaces to work.

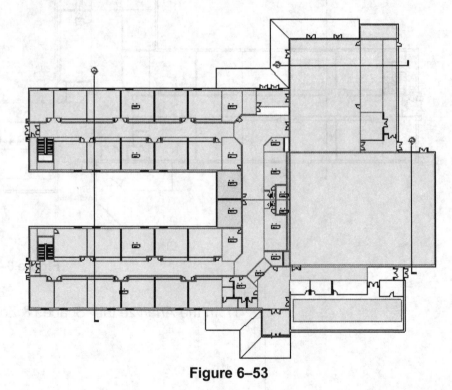

Figure 6–53

21. Zoom in on the Office area near the Front Entrance, as shown in Figure 6–54. There are two issues in this area. There is a small triangular area that does not have a space. Start the **Space** command again and add a space to the area.

Verify the properties of the new space before or after placing it.

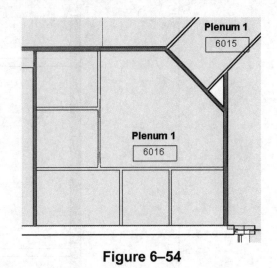

Figure 6–54

22. Select the space in the office.

This option displays if there is a problem with the selected space.

23. In the *Modify | Spaces* tab>Warnings panel, click (Show Related Warnings).

24. In the dialog box, expand the warnings as shown in Figure 6–55. The issues are with the Copy and Reception spaces on the first floor and the plenum space above.

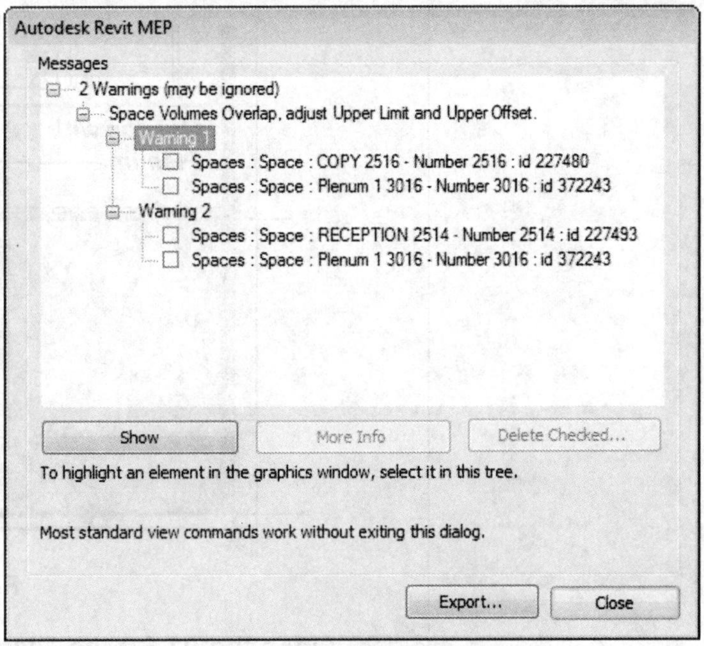

Figure 6–55

25. In Warning 1, select the Copy space and click [Show]. Read any alerts and continue. The view zooms in and displays the problems as shown in Figure 6–56.

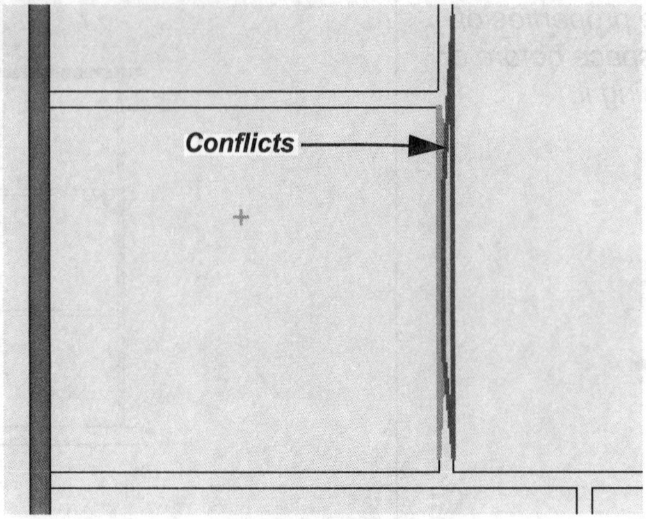

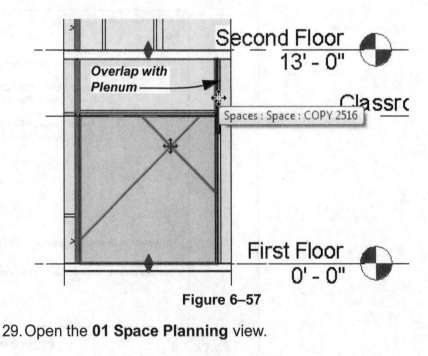

Figure 6–56

26. Close the dialog box.

27. Draw a short section through this area. Open the section and apply the **Space Section** view template to it.

28. When you select the copy space you can see how it extends into the plenum area as shown in Figure 6–57 but you cannot tell why.

Figure 6–57

29. Open the **01 Space Planning** view.

30. There is an opening rather than a door between the Copy and Reception areas. This is creating an issue with the wall and therefore with the plenum space. To solve this problem you need to add a Space Separator so that the software treats this opening like any other door.

31. In the *Analyze* tab>Spaces and Zones panel, click (Space Separator).

32. In the Options Bar, clear **Chain** and draw two lines on each side of the framed opening as shown in Figure 6–58.

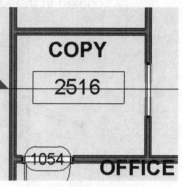

Figure 6–58

33. Select the Copy space again. The Warning no longer displays.

34. Display the related section and the **Classroom Plenum 1** plan view. None of the overlaps exist.

35. Save the project.

Task 6 - Add other spaces (optional).

---

1. Create a copy of the Coordination>All>Floor Plans>**Second Floor** view and rename it **02 Space Planning** and apply the Space Plan view template to it.

2. Look for areas in which there are no spaces and add any if needed.

3. Open the **Classroom Plenum 2** floor plan view and add plenum spaces.

4. There are other plenums in the project and spaces with overlaps. If you have time you can investigate the problems and figure out the solutions. Use sections and additional levels as required to modify the spaces.

5. Save the project.

6.3 Creating Zones

Learning Objectives

- Add zones to connect spaces for analysis.
- Use the System Browser with Zones.

The next step in preparing to compute heating and cooling loads is to divide the building into zones, as shown in Figure 6–59. Each zone consists of similar spaces that would be heated and cooled in the same manner.

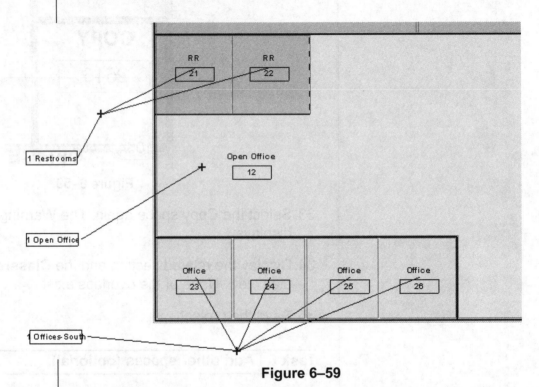

Figure 6–59

- There is always one **Default** zone in a project. All spaces are automatically attached to that zone when they are created.

- While you can add typical zones into a template, you usually add spaces first and then create zones and add spaces to the zones.

- You can create zones in plan and section views.

How To: Add Zones

You can set up a view template for zones in the same manner as you set up one for spaces.

1. Open a plan view that contains the spaces you want to work with. (If you have a zone that stretches across two levels, open a section view as well.)
2. For each view, type **VG**. In the Visibility/Graphic Overrides dialog box, expand **HVAC Zones** and select all of the options as shown in Figure 6–60.

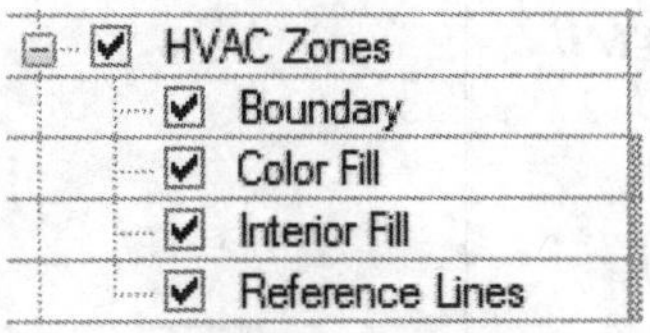

☐–☑ HVAC Zones
 ☑ Boundary
 ☑ Color Fill
 ☑ Interior Fill
 ☑ Reference Lines

Figure 6–60

3. In the *Analyze* tab>Spaces & Zones panel, click ▦ (Zone).
4. In Properties, under *Identity Data*, type a name for the Zone. By default, they are numbered incrementally.
5. In the *Edit Zone* tab, as shown in Figure 6–61, ▦ (Add Space) is automatically selected.

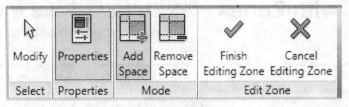

Figure 6–61

6. Select the spaces that you want to add to the zone.

7. Click ✓ (Finish Editing Zone).

• Another quick way to add a zone is to select the spaces first and then, in the *Analyze* tab>Spaces & Zones panel, click

 ▦ (Zone). The spaces are automatically added to the zone.

• To edit an existing zone, select one of the zone lines and, in

 the *Modify | HVAC Zones* tab>Zone panel, click ▦ (Edit Zone). The *Edit Zone* tab displays in which you can add more spaces.

• Click ▦ (Remove Space) to detach a space from the zone or modify the zone properties.

- Zones do not automatically have a tag placed but it is helpful to display these as you are working, as shown in

  Figure 6–62. In the *Annotate* tab>Tag panel, click 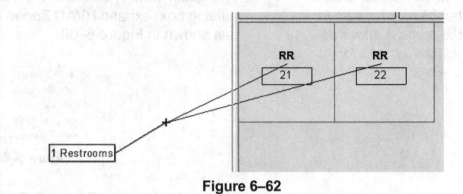 (Tag by Category) and select on the zone(s) that you want to tag.

You can change the name of a zone by selecting the tag and selecting the blue text. If Zone tags are not loaded, you can find them in the Autodesk Revit library in the Annotations> Mechanical folder.

Figure 6–62

Using the System Browser with Zones

The System Browser is a useful tool when working with spaces and zones. When you select a space in the System Browser, it displays in the project and the System Browser, as shown in Figure 6–63. The selected zone or space is automatically made active in the Properties. This enables you to modify names for spaces and zones and assign information such as electrical loads and mechanical airflow.

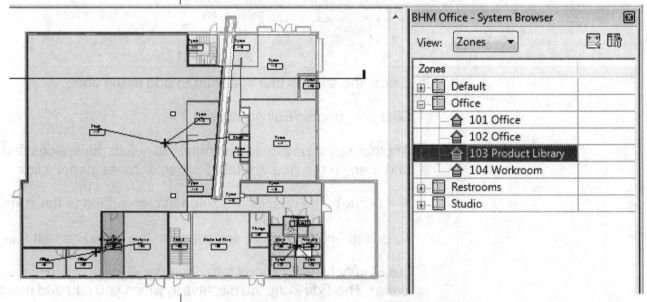

Figure 6–63

- As with other palettes, the System Browser can be floated or docked. If you have dual screens you can move it to the other monitor and can remain open as long as required.

How To: Use the System Browser with Zones

1. In the *Analyze* tab>System Browser panel, click ![icon] (System Browser).
2. If the zones are not displayed, open the View drop-down list and select **Zones** as shown in Figure 6–64.

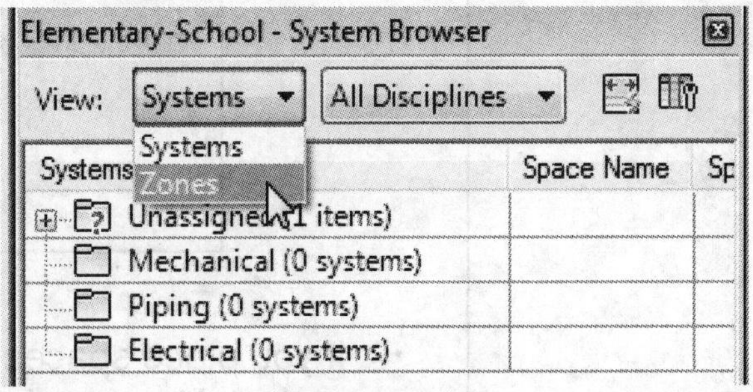

Figure 6–64

3. All of the spaces are listed under the Default zone, as shown in Figure 6–65, until they are added to a specific zone.

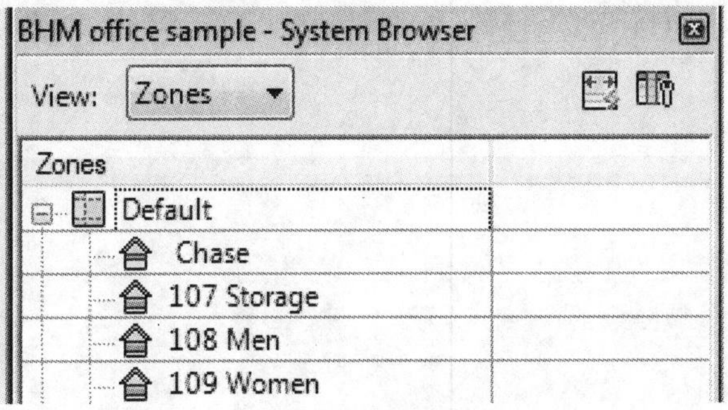

Figure 6–65

- Each space displays an icon showing its status:

  ![icon] (Occupiable), ![icon] (Not Occupiable), and ![icon] (Space not placed).

- As new zones are added the spaces are moved into the new zones.

4. Select a space or zone. It is highlighted in the project and becomes active in the Properties.

- You can select more than one space or zone at a time using <Ctrl> and <Shift>.

- In the System Browser, if you right-click on a space or zone and select **Show**, the software zooms in on the selected elements. If there is more than one view in which the space can be displayed, the Show Element(s) in View dialog box opens as shown in Figure 6–66.

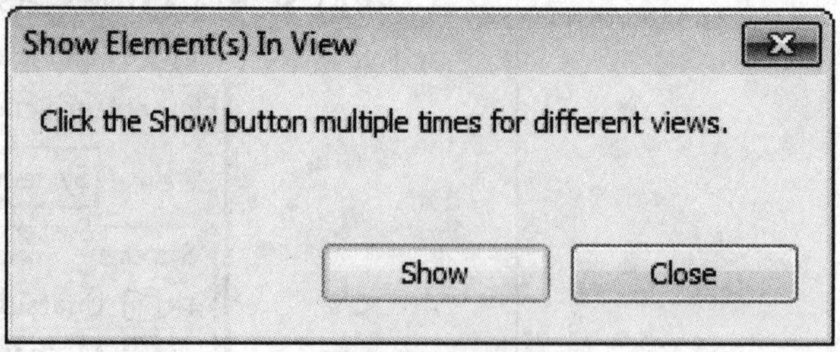

Show Element(s) In View

Click the Show button multiple times for different views.

Show   Close

Figure 6–66

- If you place spaces and then delete them, they remain in the project. You can delete them entirely in the System Browser, by right-clicking on the name and selecting **Delete**.

- You can also delete spaces in a space schedule view.

6.4 Creating Color Schemes

Learning Objective

- Create Color Schemes and Color Fill Legends for spaces and zones.

When working with Zones and Spaces, it is useful to have a view that displays color coding for individual zones, spaces, or rooms as shown in Figure 6–67. You can include a color fill legend in the same view to clarify the use of the colors.

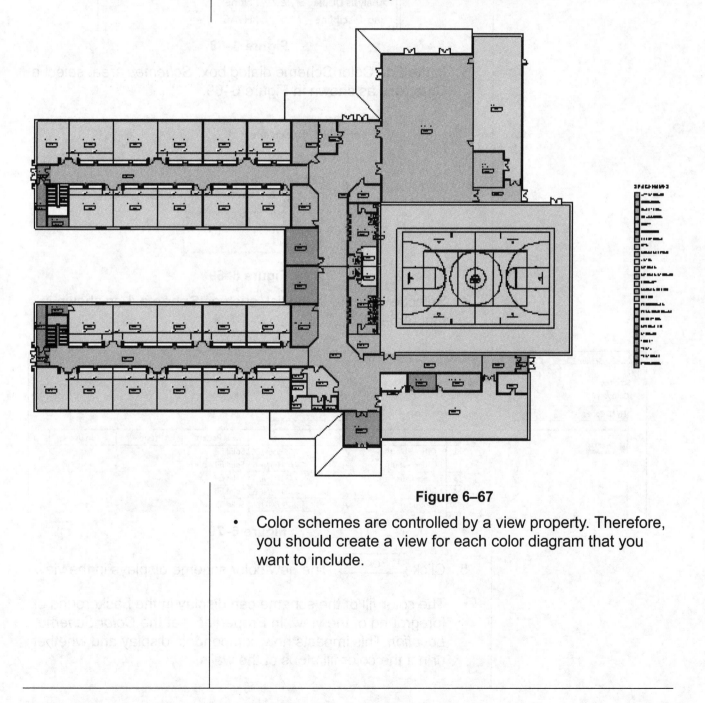

Figure 6–67

- Color schemes are controlled by a view property. Therefore, you should create a view for each color diagram that you want to include.

How To: Set Up a Color Scheme in a View

1. Create or duplicate a view that you want to use for the color scheme.
2. In Properties, click the button next to the **Color Scheme** parameter, as shown in Figure 6–68.

Floor Plan: 1 - Mech Spaces and Zones ▼	⊞ Edit Type
Discipline	Mechanical
Color Scheme Location	Background
Color Scheme	Schema 1
System Color Schemes	Edit...
Analysis Display Style	None
Sub-Discipline	HVAC

Figure 6–68

3. In the Edit Color Scheme dialog box, *Schemes* area, select a **Category** as shown in Figure 6–69.

Edit Color Scheme

Schemes

Category:

HVAC Zones ▼
HVAC Zones
Rooms
Spaces

Figure 6–69

4. Select a scheme in the list, such as **Schema 1** as shown in Figure 6–70.

Edit Color Scheme

Schemes
Category:
HVAC Zones ▼

(none)
Schema 1

Scheme Definition
Title: Schema 1 Legend   Color: Name ▼   ◉ By value ○ By range   Edit Format...

	Value	Visible	Color	Fill Pattern	Preview	In Use
1	1 Offices-North	✓	RGB 156-185	Solid fill		Yes
2	1 Offices-South	✓	PANTONE 6	Solid fill		Yes
3	1 Open Office	✓	PANTONE 3	Solid fill		Yes
4	1 Plenum	✓	PANTONE 6	Solid fill		Yes
5	1 Restrooms	✓	RGB 139-166	Solid fill		Yes

Figure 6–70

5. Click OK . The new color scheme displays in the view.

• The color fill of the scheme can display in the background or foreground of the view. In Properties, set the *Color Scheme Location*.This impacts how components display and whether or not the color fill stops at the walls.

Type Properties for the Color Fill Legend control the appearance of the legend, including swatch size and text styles.

• You can add a legend that matches the Color Scheme, as shown in Figure 6–71. In the *Analyze* tab>Color Fill panel, click (Color Fill Legend) and place the legend where you want it.

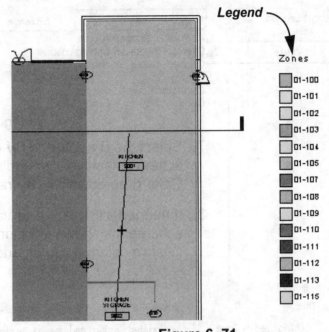

Figure 6–71

• If you change the **Color Scheme** in the View Properties dialog box, it also updates the associated legend.

How To: Define a Color Scheme

1. In Properties, click the button next to the **Color Scheme** parameter.
2. In the Edit Color Scheme dialog box, *Schemes* area, select a **Category**.
3. Select an existing scheme and click ⎗ (Duplicate).
4. In the New color scheme dialog box, enter a new name and click ⎡ OK ⎤. If the Colors Not Preserved warning displays, click ⎡ OK ⎤ again.
5. In the Edit Color Scheme dialog box, in the *Scheme Definition* area, type a name for the *Title* of the color scheme. This displays when the legend is placed in the view.

6. In the Color drop-down list, select an option, as shown in Figure 6–72. The available parameters depend on the type of scheme you are creating.

Scheme Definition

Title: Schema 1 Legend

Color: Occupied Area ▼

● By value
○ By range
Edit Format...

	Value	Vis		Preview	In Use

Air Volume Calculation Type
Calculated Area per Cooling Load
Calculated Area per Heating Load
Calculated Cooling Load
Calculated Cooling Load per area
Calculated Heating Load

Figure 6–72

7. Select the **By value** or **By range** options to set how the color scheme displays. Depending on the selection made in the Color drop-down list, **By range** might not be available.

8. If needed, click ✛ (Add Value) to add more rows to the scheme, as shown in Figure 6–73. Modify the visibility (*Visible* column), *Color*, and *Fill Pattern* as required.

Scheme Definition

Title: Cooling Load By Zone

Color: Calculated Cooling Load ▼

○ By value
● By range
Edit Format... 1235 kW

At Least	Less Than	Caption	Visible	Color	Fill Pattern	Preview	In Use
	7.00000 kW	Less than 7 k	☑	RGB 156-	Solid fill		Yes
7.00000 kW	11.00000 kW	7 kW - 11 k	☑	PANTO	Solid fill		Yes
11.00000 kW	14.00000 kW	11 kW - 14 k	☑	RGB 096-	Solid fill		Yes
14.00000 kW	18.00000 kW	14 kW - 18 k	☑	Blue	Solid fill		Yes
18.00000 kW	20.00000 kW	18 kW - 20 k	☑	Magenta	Solid fill		Yes
20.00000 kW		20 kW or mo	☑	Red	Solid fill ▼		No

Figure 6–73

9. In the *Options* area, select the **Include elements from linked files** option if you are using linked models.

10. Click ⟨ OK ⟩ to end the command.

Color Schemes By Value

If you select the **By value** option, you can modify the visibility, color, and fill pattern of the scheme. The value is assigned by the parameter data in the room or area object.

- Values are automatically updated when you add data to the parameters used in the color scheme. For example, if you create a color by space name and then add another space name in the project, it is also added to the color scheme.

- Click ⬆E (Move Rows Up) and ⬇E (Move Rows Down) to change the order of rows in the list.

- To remove a row, select it and click ▬ (Remove Value). This is only available if the parameter data is not being used in the room or area elements in the project.

Color Schemes By Range

If you select the **By range** option, you can modify the *At Least* variable and the *Caption*, as well as the visibility, color, and fill pattern, as shown in Figure 6–74.

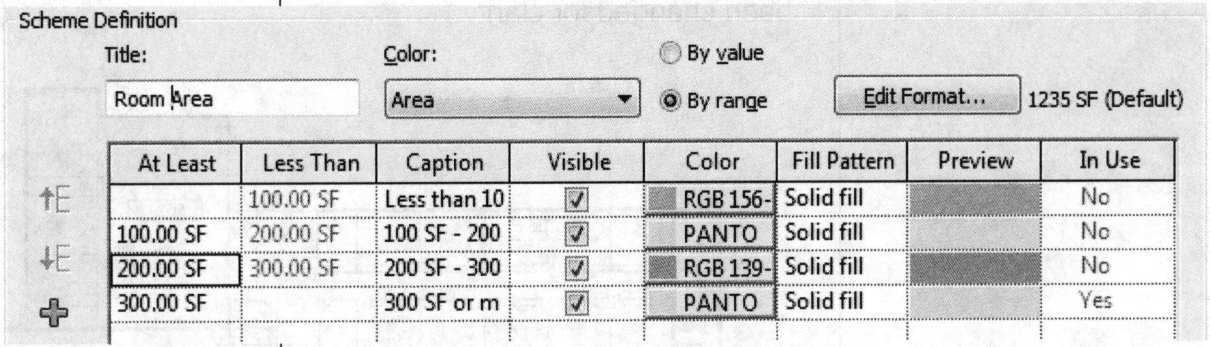

Scheme Definition

Title: Room Area

Color: Area

○ By value ● By range   [Edit Format...]   1235 SF (Default)

	At Least	Less Than	Caption	Visible	Color	Fill Pattern	Preview	In Use
⬆E		100.00 SF	Less than 10	☑	RGB 156-	Solid fill		No
⬇E	100.00 SF	200.00 SF	100 SF - 200	☑	PANTO	Solid fill		No
	200.00 SF	300.00 SF	200 SF - 300	☑	RGB 139-	Solid fill		No
✚	300.00 SF		300 SF or m	☑	PANTO	Solid fill		Yes

Figure 6–74

- Click [Edit Format...] to modify the units display format.

- To add rows, select the row above the new row and click

    ✚ (Add Value). The new row increments according to the previous distances set or by double the value of the first row.

Practice 6b

Estimated time for completion: 15 minutes

Create Zones

Learning Objectives

- Create views and add zones to the new views.
- Use the System Browser to identify and modify zone information.
- Create a color scheme showing the zones.

In this practice you will add zones to the project. You will examine the zones and spaces in the System Browser and you set up a view that displays the zone names by color as shown in Figure 6–75 with optional zone tags. (The scale of this view has been changed for clarity.)

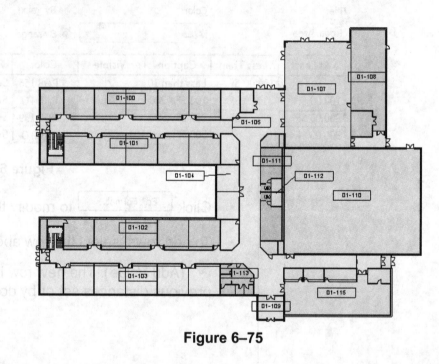

Figure 6–75

Task 1 - Add zones.

1. In the *C:\Autodesk Revit 2015 MEP Fundamentals Class Files\Spaces* folder, open **MEP-Elementary-School -Zones.rvt**.

2. In the Project Browser, Coordination>MEP>*Floor Plans* area, right-click on the **01 Space Planning** view and create a **Duplicate with Detailing** view named **01 Zoning**.

3. Repeat the process with **02 Space Planning** and name it **02 Zoning**.

You can create a view template after modifying the first view and apply it to any other plan views.

4. In each view, open the Visibility/Graphics Overrides dialog box and in the *Model Categories* tab, expand **HVAC Zones** and select **Interior Fill** and **Reference Lines.**

5. Open the **01 Zoning** view.

6. In the *Analyze* tab>Spaces & Zones panel, click 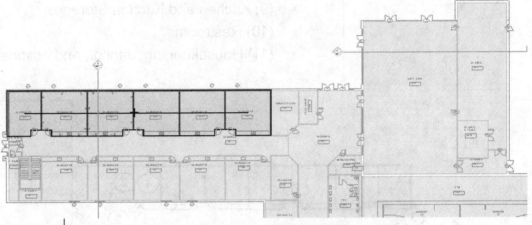 (Zone).

7. In the *Edit Zone* tab, verify that (Add Space) is selected.

8. Select the spaces across the top group of Classrooms as shown in Figure 6–76.

Figure 6–76

9. In Properties, change the *Name* to **01-100**.

10. In the *Edit Zone* tab>Edit Zone panel, click (Finish Editing Zone).

11. Add another zone to the Classrooms and Storage Areas on the other side of the hall as shown in Figure 6–77.

The name of the zone automatically increments as each zone is added.

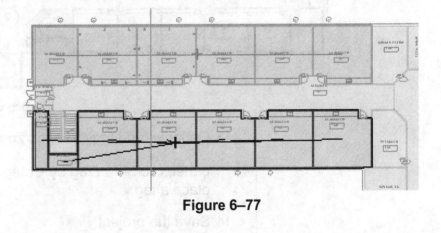

Figure 6–77

12. Continue adding zones as listed below and shown in Figure 6–78. This figure uses different shades for clarity.

- (1) Two sets of Classroom zones in the South Wing.
- (2) All of the corridors plus the Electrical Room.
- (3) All of the vestibules.
- (4) Nurse's Office, Bookroom, Special Ed rooms, and Workroom.
- (5) Reception, Offices, and Copy Room.
- (6) Library and associated rooms.
- (7) Gym.
- (8) Cafeteria.
- (9) Kitchen and Kitchen Storage.
- (10) Restrooms.
- (11) Housekeeping, Janitor, and associated chases.

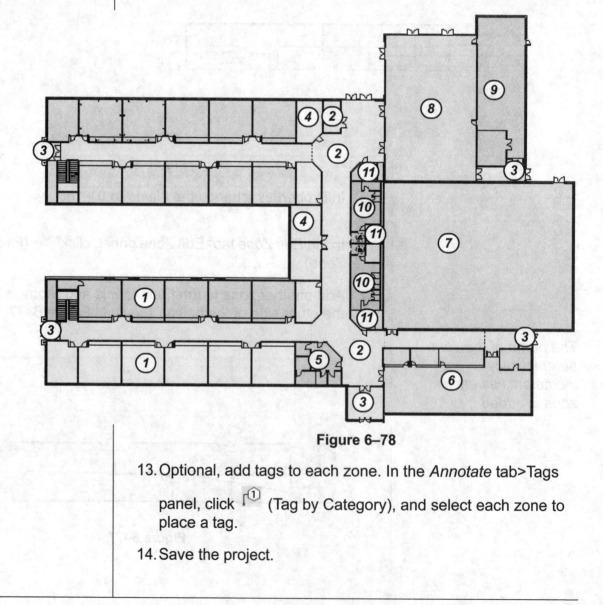

Figure 6–78

13. Optional, add tags to each zone. In the *Annotate* tab>Tags panel, click (Tag by Category), and select each zone to place a tag.

14. Save the project.

Task 2 - Use the System Browser.

1. Open the System Browser if it is not already open.

2. In the System Browser, set the view so it displays **Zones**. It should display as shown in Figure 6–79.

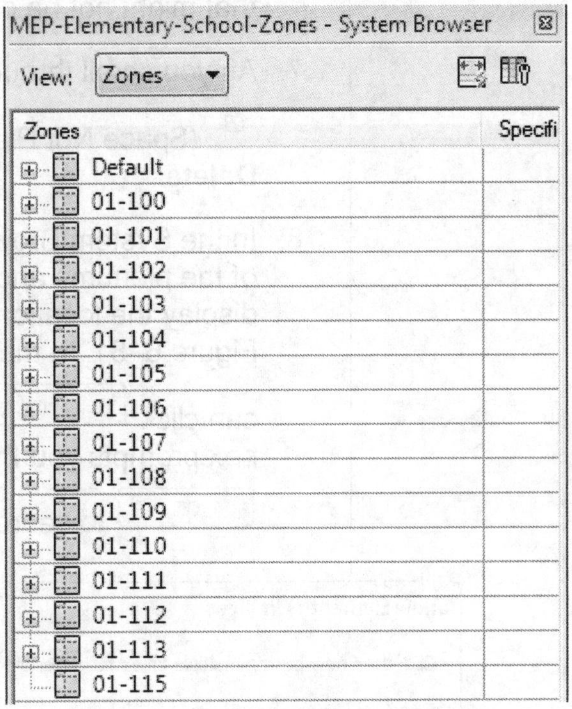

Figure 6–79

3. Expand the various zone names to display the spaces.

4. There are still a lot of spaces in the Default Zone as shown in Figure 6–80. There are two different types of icons for spaces displaying occupied and unoccupied spaces.

Your list might look different than the one shown in Figure 6–80.

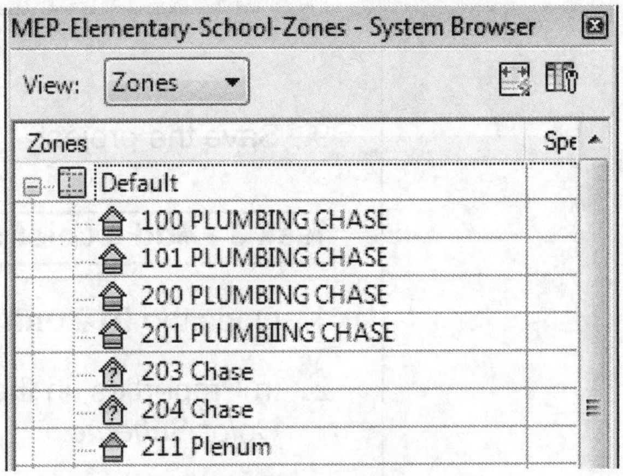

Figure 6–80

5. Some of the spaces that should be unoccupied, such as the Plumbing Chases shown in Figure 6–80, are not set correctly. In the System Browser, hold <Ctrl> and select several plumbing chases.

6. In Properties, scroll down to the *Energy Analysis* area and clear **Occupiable**. Repeat this for other chases or plenums that might not be correctly.

7. As you scroll through the spaces, note that some display

   ⬆ (Space Not Placed). Right-click on them and click **Delete**.

8. In the System Browser, in the default zone, right-click on one of the plenums and select **Show**. The view changes to display the location of the plenum, such as the one shown in Figure 6–81. In the Show Element(s) in View dialog box, you

   can click [Show] to display multiple views. If the alert box prompts you that no other views are open, click

   [OK] to search the closed views.

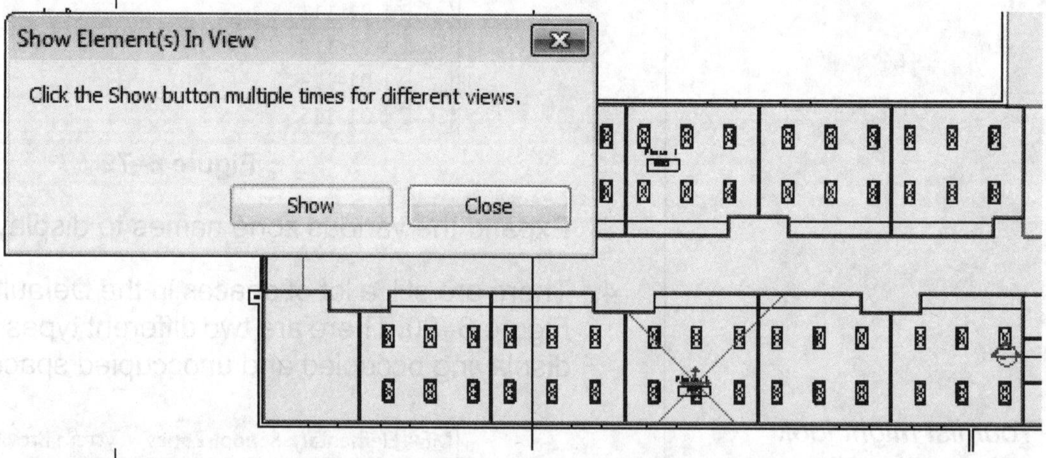

Figure 6–81

9. Save the project.

Task 3 - Add a color scheme.

1. Open the **01 Zoning** view and close any hidden windows.

2. In Properties, in the *Graphics* area, click the button next to *Color Scheme*.

3. In the Edit Color Scheme dialog box, in the *Schemes* area, change the *Category* to **HVAC Zones**.

4. Select the default **Schema 1**. The Scheme Definition automatically populates by zone name as shown in Figure 6–82.

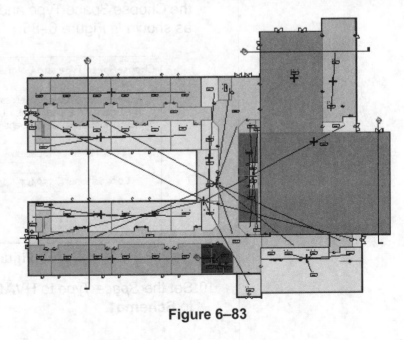

Edit Color Scheme

Schemes
Category:

HVAC Zones

(none)
Schema 1

Scheme Definition

Title: Schema 1 Legend   Color: Name   ◉ By value   ○ By range   Edit Format...

	Value	Visible	Color	Fill Pattern	Preview	In Use
1	1-North-1	☑	RGB 156-18	Solid fill		Yes
2	1-North-2	☑	PANTONE	Solid fill		Yes
3	1-North-3	☑	PANTONE	Solid fill		Yes
4	1-North-4	☑	RGB 139-16	Solid fill		Yes
5	1-North-5	☑	PANTONE	Solid fill		Yes
6	1-North-6	☑	RGB 096-17	Solid fill		Yes
7	1-South-1	☑	RGB 209-20	Solid fill		Yes
8	1-South-2	☑	RGB 173-11	Solid fill		Yes
9	1-South-3	☑	RGB 194-16	Solid fill		Yes
10	1-South-4	☑	PANTONE	Solid fill		Yes
11	1-South-5	☑	RGB 192-06	Solid fill		Yes
12	1-South-6	☑	RGB 064-06	Solid fill		Yes
13	1-South-7	☑	RGB 064-19	Solid fill		Yes
14	2-North-1	☑	RGB 064-06	Solid fill		Yes
15	2-North-2	☑	RGB 096-22	Solid fill		Yes
16	2-North-3	☑	RGB 160-09	Solid fill		Yes

Options

☐ Include elements from linked files

OK   Cancel   Apply   Help

Figure 6–82

5. Change the *Title* of the Scheme to **Zones**.

6. Click [OK]. The color scheme is applied to the view. The display will be similar to that shown in Figure 6–83.

Your zone colors might vary.

Figure 6–83

7. In the *Analyze* tab>Color Fill panel, click 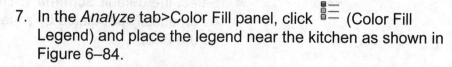 (Color Fill Legend) and place the legend near the kitchen as shown in Figure 6–84.

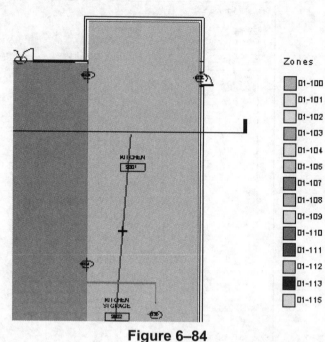

Figure 6–84

8. To turn off the lines that connect the zones, type **VG**. In the Visibility/Graphics dialog box, expand HVAC Zones and clear **Reference Lines**. This can make the color fill easier to read.

9. Open the **02 Zoning** view and add a Color Fill Legend. Because a Color Scheme has not been assigned to the view the Choose Space Type and Color Scheme dialog box opens as shown in Figure 6–85.

Figure 6–85

10. Set the *Space Type* to **HVAC Zones** and the *Color Scheme* to **Schema1**.

11. Some of the Zones display because they penetrate the second floor.

12. If the HVAC Zone Reference Lines from the first floor display and make the view difficult to understand, turn them off.

13. Add a zone to the group of classrooms in the North Wing similar to that on the first floor. In Properties, change the name to **02-100**.

14. The zone is automatically filled with color and added to the zone name list as shown in Figure 6–86.

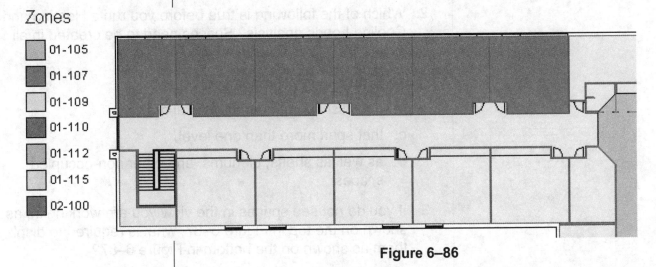

Figure 6–86

15. Continue adding zones to the second floor.

16. If you have time, add other zones including those in the plenums.

17. Save the project.

Chapter Review Questions

1. When you want to add spaces to a project that uses a linked model, what is required for the spaces to work as expected?

   a. The linked model needs to have rooms.

   b. The linked model needs to be set to Room Bounding.

   c. The MEP project needs to be set to Room Bounding.

   d. The MEP project needs to have rooms.

2. Which of the following is true before you run a Heating and Cooling Loads analysis? Spaces need to be created in all rooms...

   a. that have heating and cooling.

   b. established in the architectural drawing.

   c. that span more than one level.

   d. as well as shafts, plenums, and other non-occupied spaces.

3. If you do not see spaces in the view you are working in, as shown on the top in Figure 6–87, what is required to display them as shown on the bottom in Figure 6–87?

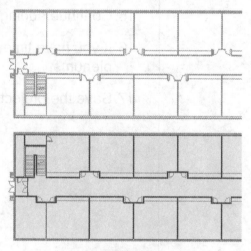

Figure 6–87

   a. Open the Visibility/Graphics dialog box and turn on the **Interior** option under *Spaces*.

   b. Before placing spaces, set the *Space Visibility* to **Interior** in the Option Bar.

   c. In Properties, select the **Space View** option.

   d. In the View Control Bar, toggle on **Spaces**.

4. If a space is not reaching the ceiling, as shown in a section in Figure 6–88, which of the following methods can you use to fix the issue? (Select all that apply.)

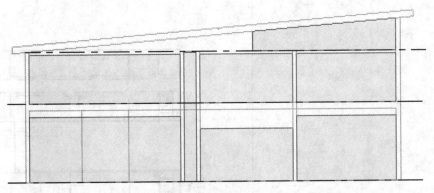

Figure 6–88

a. Change the height of the room because the space reflects room size.

b. Select the space and use the controls to move the top edge above the ceiling.

c. Change the *Space Settings* to **Height by Ceiling**.

d. Verify that the ceiling is set to **Room Bounding**.

5. When you have a space that is not defined entirely by walls, such as a balcony in a 2-story lobby, how do you control the size of the space?

a. Sketch the boundaries of the space.

b. Add space separation lines.

c. Modify the size in Properties.

d. Change the Room Bounding status of the other walls.

6. If the colors for spaces or zones (such as the zones shown in Figure 6–89) are not displayed, how do you display them?

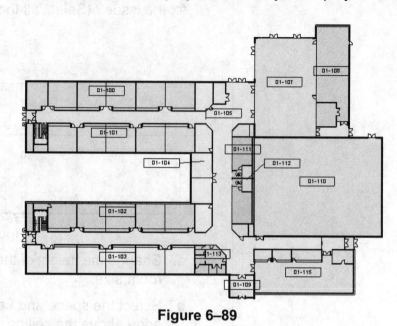

Figure 6–89

a. Modify the Color Scheme in Visibility/Graphics.

b. Assign a Color Scheme in Properties.

c. Toggle on Color Schemes in the View Control Bar.

d. Add a Color Fill Legend.

7. Zones, as shown in Figure 6–90, are formed of spaces that can be heated and cooled in the same manner.

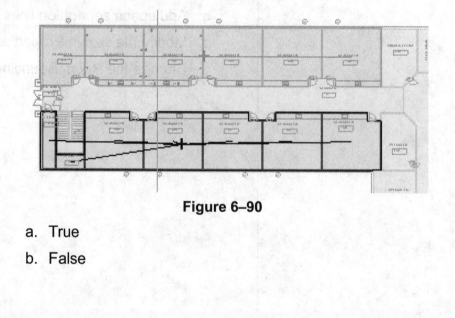

Figure 6–90

a. True

b. False

Command Summary

Button	Command	Location
	Area and Volume Computations	• **Ribbon:** *Analyze* tab>Spaces & Zones panel>expand the panel title
	Color Fill Legend	• **Ribbon:** *Analyze* tab>Color Fill panel
	Space	• **Ribbon:** *Analyze* tab>Spaces & Zones panel
	Space Separator	• **Ribbon:** *Analyze* tab>Spaces & Zones panel
	Space Tag	• **Ribbon:** *Analyze* tab>Spaces & Zones panel or *Annotate* tab>Tag panel
	System Browser	• **Ribbon:** *View* tab>Windows panel, expand User Interface • **Shortcut:** <F9>
	Zone	• **Ribbon:** *Analyze* tab>Spaces & Zones panel

Chapter 7

Energy Analysis

In this chapter you learn how to prepare a project to analyze Heating and Cooling Loads, run the Heading and Cooling Loads tool, and export a project to gbXML for additional energy analysis.

This chapter contains the following topics:

- **Preparing a Project for Energy Analysis**
- **Analyzing the Heating and Cooling Loads**
- **Exporting for Secondary Analysis**

7.1 Preparing a Project for Energy Analysis

 Learning Objective

- Set up the specifics of the Energy Settings and Building Type Settings for the project.

Before adding HVAC systems to a project you need to analyze the heating and cooling loads. To do this you first must have spaces and zones in place. Then you can either use the **Heating and Cooling Loads** tool that comes with the Autodesk® Revit® MEP software, as shown in Figure 7–1, or export the project to gbXML (Green Building XML) which can then be imported into a third-party analysis software.

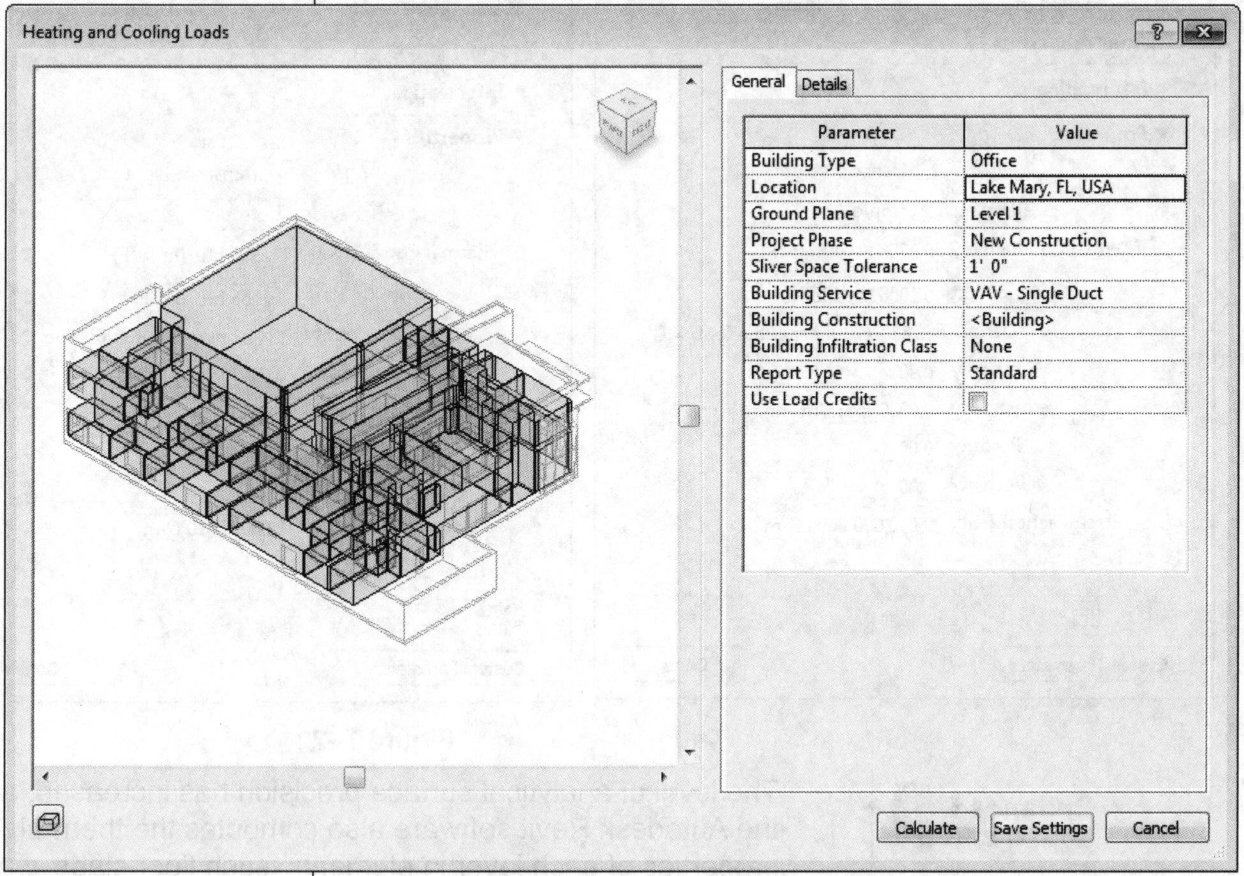

Heating and Cooling Loads

Parameter	Value
Building Type	Office
Location	Lake Mary, FL, USA
Ground Plane	Level 1
Project Phase	New Construction
Sliver Space Tolerance	1' 0"
Building Service	VAV - Single Duct
Building Construction	<Building>
Building Infiltration Class	None
Report Type	Standard
Use Load Credits	

General | Details

Calculate   Save Settings   Cancel

Figure 7–1

- Before running the energy analysis software, verify that all areas in the project are set up with space elements, including unoccupied shafts, plenums, and sliver spaces.

- Add spaces to zones other than the default zone. The default zone is calculated but might not work correctly as spaces in the default zone can be far apart.

- Sliver spaces do not display in plan views but do display in the analytical model.

- Materials have Thermal Properties, as shown in Figure 7–2, which can be used for analysis in an Autodesk Revit project or when exported to GbXML. These need to be set up in the architectural model.

▶ Gypsum Wall Board	
Assets	≣ ▾
Name	Aspect
Gypsum Wall Board	Graphics
Gypsum Board - Painted White	Appearance
Gypsum Wall Board	Physical
Gypsum Plasterboard	Thermal

Thermal Properties

▶ Information

▼ Properties

☐ Transmits Light	
Behavior	Isotropic ▾
Thermal Conductivity	0.3756 btu/(hr·ft·°F) ▲▼
Specific Heat	0.2006 btu/(lb·°F) ▲▼
Density	68.67 pound per cubic foot ▲▼
Emissivity	0.90 ▲▼
Permeability	0.0000 grain/(ft²·hr·inHg) ▲▼
Porosity	0.00 ▲▼
Reflectivity	0.00 ▲▼
Electrical Resistivity	2,000,000.0000 Ω·m ▲▼

Custom Parameters   Done

▶ Glass, Clear Glazing	
Assets	≣ ▾
Name	Aspect
Glass, Clear Glazing	Graphics
Clear	Appearance
Glass - Soda Lime	Physical
Glass - Lime Window	Thermal

Thermal Properties

▶ Information

▼ Properties

☑ Transmits Light	
Behavior	Isotropic ▾
Thermal Conductivity	0.6356 btu/(hr·ft·°F) ▲▼
Specific Heat	0.2006 btu/(lb·°F) ▲▼
Density	154.82 pound per cubic foo ▲▼
Emissivity	0.95 ▲▼
Permeability	0.0000 grain/(ft²·hr·inHg) ▲▼
Porosity	0.00 ▲▼
Reflectivity	0.00 ▲▼
Electrical Resistivity	1.0000E+10 Ω·m ▲▼

Custom Parameters   Done

Figure 7–2

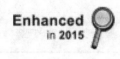
Enhanced in 2015

- The level of analytical surface precision has increased, and the Autodesk Revit software also computes the thermal properties of each layer in elements, such floor slabs, walls and roofs.

Preparing Energy Analysis

After adding spaces and zones you need to take more steps to prepare the entire project for analysis, including **Energy Analysis Settings** and **Building/Space Type Settings**. These settings can be as detailed as the opening and closing time of a retail building type as shown in Figure 7–3.

Parameter	Value
Energy Analysis	⌃
Area per Person	71.76 SF
Sensible Heat Gain per person	250.00 Btu/h
Latent Heat Gain per person	200.00 Btu/h
Lighting Load Density	0.90 W/ft²
Power Load Density	1.50 W/ft²
Plenum Lighting Contribution	20.0000%
Occupancy Schedule	Warehouse Occupancy - 7 A
Lighting Schedule	Retail Lighting - 7 AM to 8 PM
Power Schedule	Retail Lighting - 7 AM to 8 PM
Opening Time	8:00 AM
Closing Time	6:00 PM
Unoccupied Cooling Set Point	82.00 °F

Figure 7–3

Energy Settings

Energy Settings are critical components because a multi-story office in a tropical climate has different heating and cooling requirements than a warehouse in a cold climate. In the *Analyze* tab>Energy Analysis panel, click 🛠 (Energy Settings) to open the Energy Settings dialog box as shown in Figure 7–4.

Parameter	Value
Common	⌃
Building Type	Office ▼
Location	Boston, MA
Ground Plane	First Floor
Detailed Model	⌃
Export Category	Spaces
Export Complexity	Simple with Shading Surfaces
Project Phase	New Construction
Sliver Space Tolerance	1' 0"
Building Service	Radiant Heater - No Flue
Building Construction	<Building>
Building Infiltration Class	None
Export Default Values	☑
Report Type	Standard
Energy Model	⌃
Analytical Space Resolution	1' 6"
Analytical Surface Resolution	1' 0"

Figure 7–4

Common Settings

Building Type: Select a building type from a list of types, as shown in Figure 7–5. Additional information about these types can be set in the **Building/Space Type Settings**.

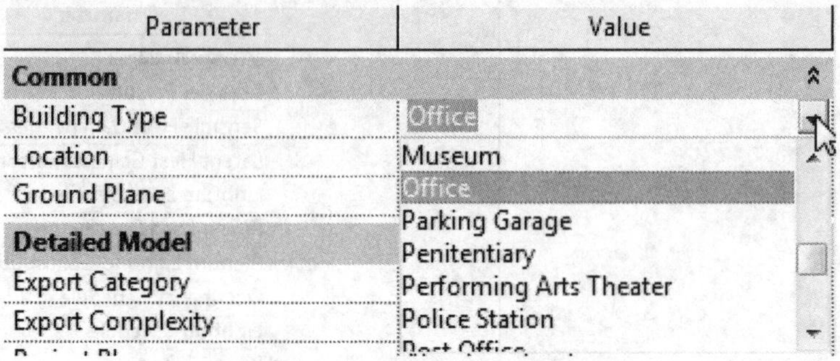

Parameter	Value
Common	⊗
Building Type	Office
Location	Museum
Ground Plane	Office
	Parking Garage
Detailed Model	Penitentiary
Export Category	Performing Arts Theater
Export Complexity	Police Station
	Post Office

Figure 7–5

Location: Define the location using the **Internet Mapping Service**, as shown in Figure 7–6, or use **Default City List** in which you can select from a list of cities or specify the exact **Latitude** and **Longitude** for the site.

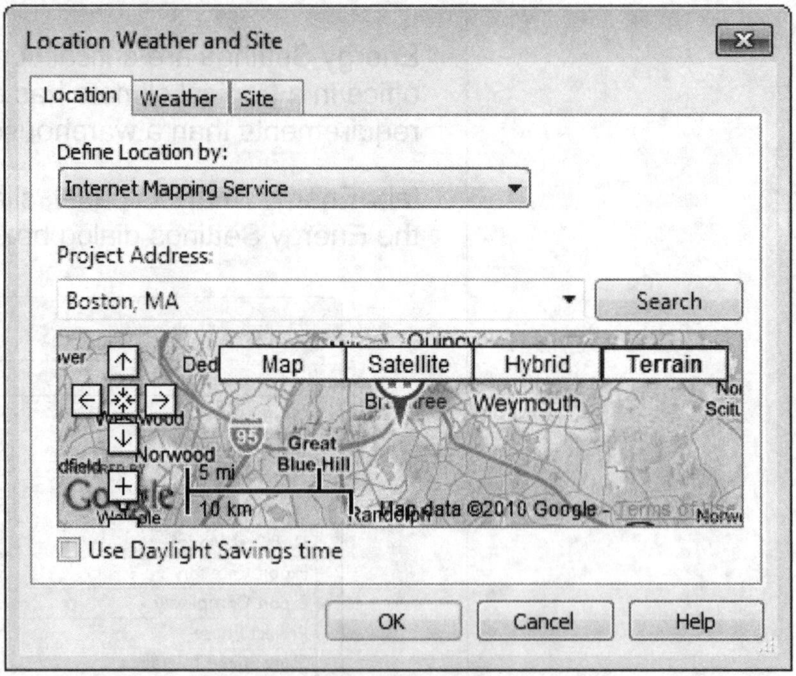

Figure 7–6

- Select the *Weather* tab to set precise information about the Weather. By default, the software automatically selects the closest weather station to your location. You can override the weather settings if needed.

Ground Plane: Specifies the level that is considered the ground plane for the project. All elements below this level are considered underground.

Detailed Model Settings

Export Category: Select Spaces or Rooms.

Export Complexity: Specify how much detailed information you need for analysis. When using the analysis tools that come with the software, use **Simple**. **Simple with Shading Surfaces** (shown in Figure 7–7) and **Complex** are only used when you export to gbXML and want to indicate how the building behaves with sun obstructions.

Detailed Model		⌃
Export Category	Spaces	
Export Complexity	Simple with Shading Surfaces	▼
Project Phase	Simple	
Sliver Space Tolerance	Simple with Shading Surfaces	
Building Service	Complex	
Building Construction	Complex with Shading Surfaces	
Building Infiltration Class	Complex with Mullions and Shading Surfaces	

Figure 7–7

Project Phase: Specify the phase the project is in for this analysis. (For renovation and multi-phase projects).

Sliver Space Tolerance: Specify the opening size of shafts, etc. that are considered sliver spaces.

Building Service: Specifies the type of heating and cooling service used in the building as shown in Figure 7–8.

Building Service	VAV - Single Duct	▼
Building Construction	Radiant Heater - No Flue	
Building Infiltration Class	Radiant Heater - Multi-burner	
Export Default Values	Forced Convection Heater - Flue	
Report Type	Forced Convection Heater - No Flue	
	VAV - Single Duct	
Energy Model	VAV - Dual Duct	
Core Offset	VAV - Indoor Packaged Cabinet	

Figure 7–8

Building Construction: By default, the materials of model elements provide the properties for analysis but you can add overrides, as shown in Figure 7–9.

Building Construction

Construction Types

<Building>

Analysis Properties

By default, analysis properties are generated from information in model elements.
Properties of Analytic Constructions are used when override is selected or model information is missing.

Category	Override	Analytic Construction
Roofs	✓	4 in lightweight concrete (U=0.2245 BTU/(h·ft²·°F))
Exterior Walls	✓	8 in lightweight concrete block (U=0.1428 BTU/(h·ft²·°F))
Interior Walls	✓	Frame partition with 3/4 in gypsum board (U=0.2595 BTU/(h
Ceilings	✓	8 in lightweight concrete ceiling (U=0.2397 BTU/(h·ft²·°F))
Floors	✓	Passive floor, no insulation, tile or vinyl (U=0.5210 BTU/(h·ft²
Slabs	✓	Un-insulated solid (U=0.1243 BTU/(h·ft²·°F))
Doors	✓	Metal (U=0.6520 BTU/(h·ft²·°F))
Exterior Windows	✓	Large double-glazed windows (reflective coating) - industry
Interior Windows	✓	Large single-glazed windows (U=0.6498 BTU/(h·ft²·°F), SHG
Skylights	✓	Large double-glazed windows (reflective coating) - industry

All   None   Shading factor for exterior windows: 0

OK   Cancel

Figure 7–9

Building Infiltration Class: Indicates the amount of outdoor air that leaks into the building envelope. Specify **Loose** (0.076 cfm/sqft), **Medium** (0.038 cfm/sqft), **Tight** (0.019 cfm/sqft) or **None** (information excluded from calculation of loads).

Export Default Values: For gbXML export only. When cleared, only user-specified values are exported. When selected it also includes default values for **People and Electrical Loads**, **Occupancy**, **Lighting**, and **Power Schedules**, and building/space type **Construction Types**.

Report Type: Specifies the amount of information in the heating and cooling loads report. You can select **Simple**, **Standard**, or **Detailed**.

• The Energy Model and Energy Model - Building Services areas are for use when doing an energy analysis of the Conceptual Model, a feature that is available to subscription customers.

Building Type Settings

When you set energy setting options, the building type is included, such as an office, theater, or warehouse. The settings for building types can be managed in Building/Space and Types Settings dialog box as shown in Figure 7–10.

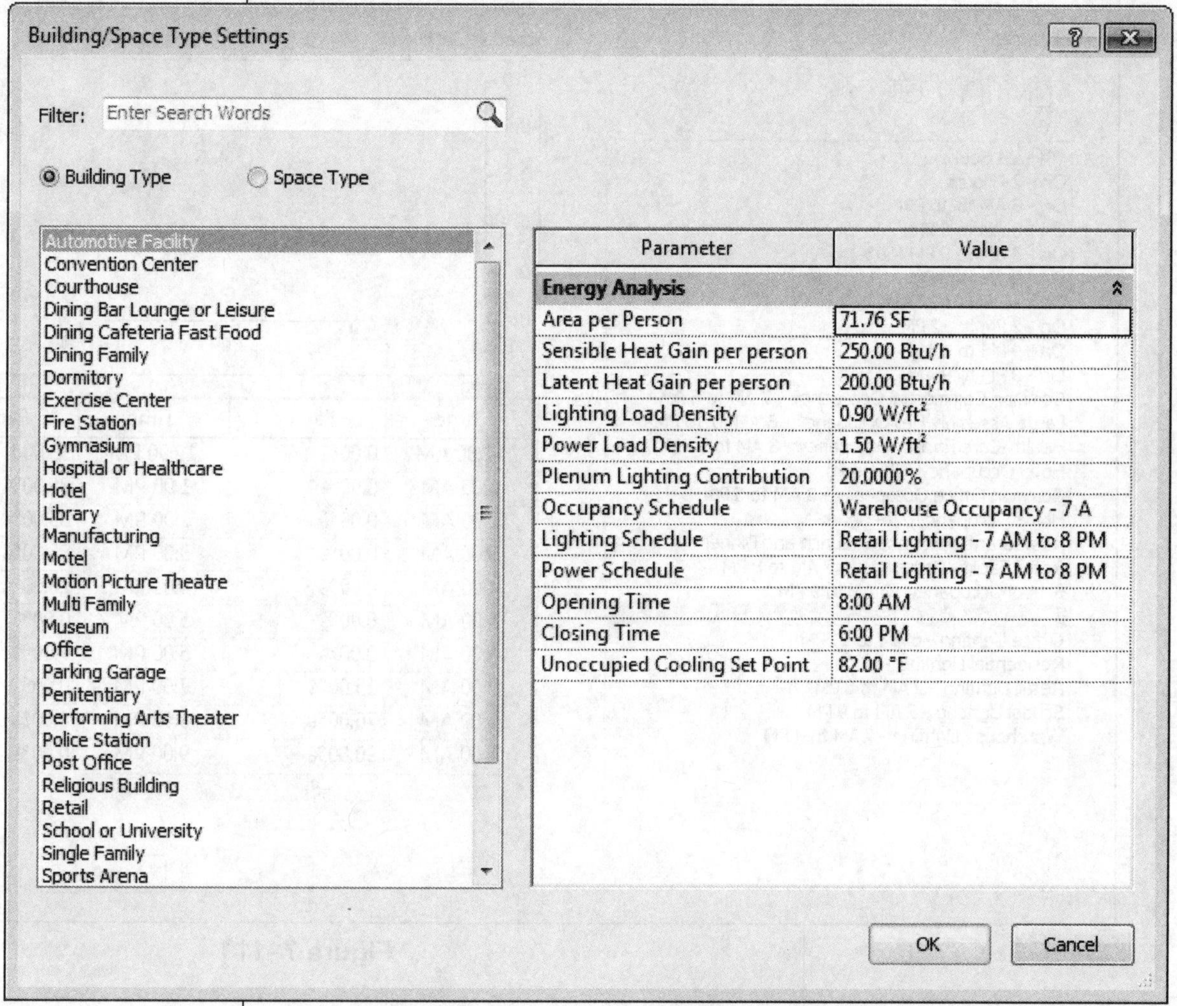

Building/Space Type Settings

Filter: Enter Search Words

◉ Building Type   ○ Space Type

Automotive Facility
Convention Center
Courthouse
Dining Bar Lounge or Leisure
Dining Cafeteria Fast Food
Dining Family
Dormitory
Exercise Center
Fire Station
Gymnasium
Hospital or Healthcare
Hotel
Library
Manufacturing
Motel
Motion Picture Theatre
Multi Family
Museum
Office
Parking Garage
Penitentiary
Performing Arts Theater
Police Station
Post Office
Religious Building
Retail
School or University
Single Family
Sports Arena

Parameter	Value
Energy Analysis	
Area per Person	71.76 SF
Sensible Heat Gain per person	250.00 Btu/h
Latent Heat Gain per person	200.00 Btu/h
Lighting Load Density	0.90 W/ft^2
Power Load Density	1.50 W/ft^2
Plenum Lighting Contribution	20.0000%
Occupancy Schedule	Warehouse Occupancy - 7 A
Lighting Schedule	Retail Lighting - 7 AM to 8 PM
Power Schedule	Retail Lighting - 7 AM to 8 PM
Opening Time	8:00 AM
Closing Time	6:00 PM
Unoccupied Cooling Set Point	82.00 °F

OK   Cancel

Figure 7–10

- To open the dialog box, in the *Manage* tab>Settings panel, expand 🎴 (MEP Settings) and click 🔧 (Building/Space and Type Settings) or in the *Analyze* tab, click ⬛ in the Reports & Schedules panel title.

- For each type of building or space you can specify energy analysis information, such as the number of people and expected heat gain per person, as well as the schedules of typical times that the building is occupied as shown for a Warehouse in Figure 7–11.

Schedule Settings

Schedules

Off - 24 Hours
On - 24 Hours
On - 6 AM to 10 PM
On - 8 AM to 6 PM
On - 8 AM to 6 PM (50%)
On - 9 AM to 9 PM
On - 10 AM to 12 AM
On - 2 PM to 12 PM
On - 4 PM to 4 AM
On - 9 PM to 9 AM
Common Commercial Occupancy - 7 AM to 6 PM
Large Assembly Hall Occupancy - 8 AM to 10 PM
Health-Care Facility Occupancy - 8 AM to 9 PM
Hotel Occupancy - 24 Hours
Common Office Occupancy - 8 AM to 5 PM
Home Occupancy - 24 Hours
Restaurant Occupancy - Lunch and Dinner
Retail Facility Occupancy - 7 AM to 8 PM
School Occupancy - 8 AM to 9 PM
Warehouse Occupancy - 7 AM to 4 PM
Office Lighting - 6 AM to 11 PM
Residential Lighting - All Day
Retail Lighting - 7 AM to 8 PM
School Lighting - 7 AM to 9 PM
Warehouse Lighting - 7 AM to 4 PM

Schedule Settings

Time	Factor	Time	Factor
12:00 AM	0.00%	12:00 PM	50.00%
1:00 AM	0.00%	1:00 PM	85.00%
2:00 AM	0.00%	2:00 PM	85.00%
3:00 AM	0.00%	3:00 PM	85.00%
4:00 AM	0.00%	4:00 PM	20.00%
5:00 AM	0.00%	5:00 PM	0.00%
6:00 AM	0.00%	6:00 PM	0.00%
7:00 AM	15.00%	7:00 PM	0.00%
8:00 AM	70.00%	8:00 PM	0.00%
9:00 AM	90.00%	9:00 PM	0.00%

OK   Cancel   Help

Figure 7–11

7.2 Analyzing the Heating and Cooling Loads

Learning Objective

• Run a Heating and Cooling Loads analysis.

Using the power of BIM technology in the Autodesk Revit software, the information you set in spaces, zones, and other energy analysis parameters is used as the basis of the loads analysis for the project. Use the **Heating and Cooling Loads** tool to verify the spaces and zones, as shown in Figure 7–12, and verify the parameters before calculating a Loads Report.

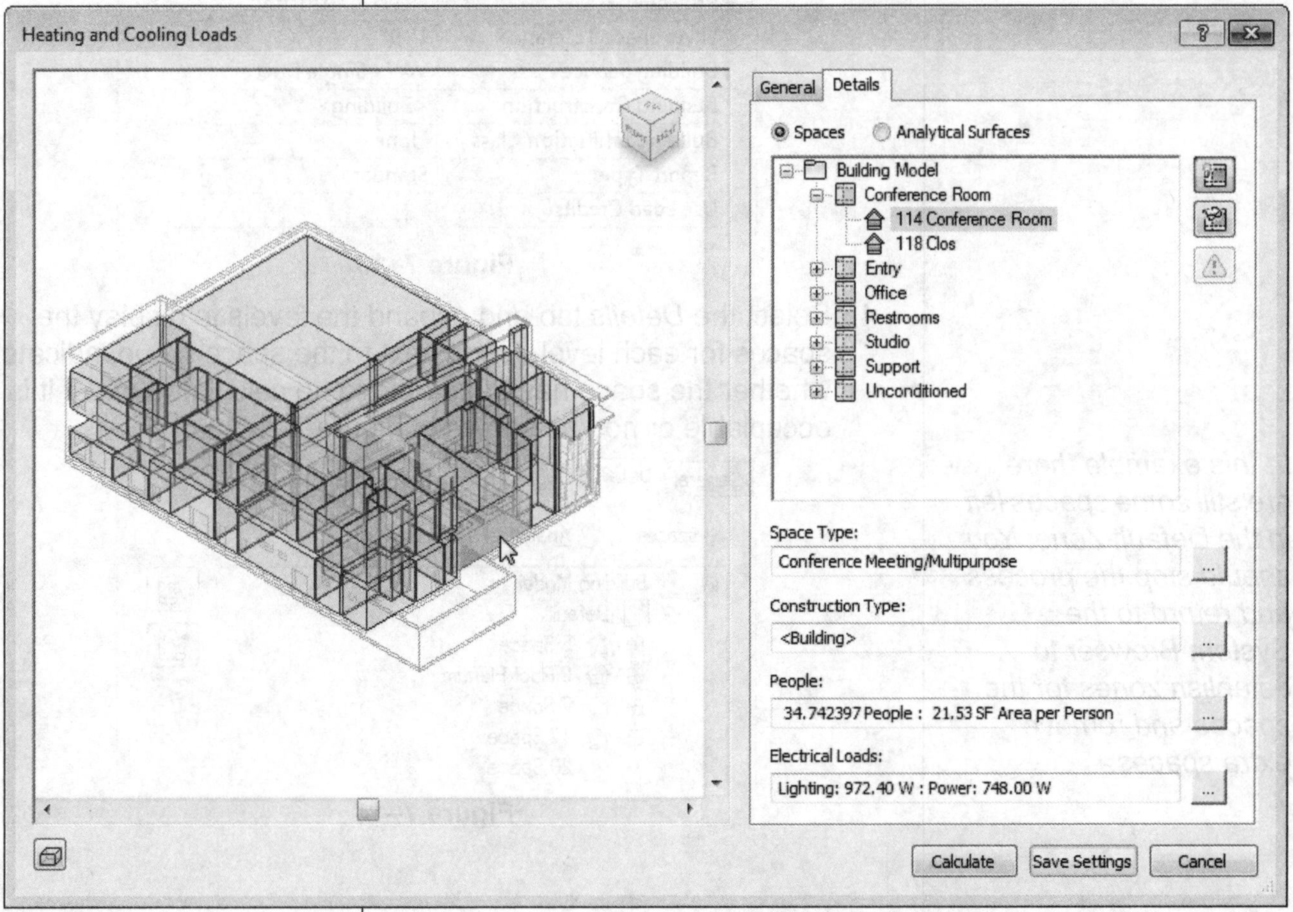

Heating and Cooling Loads

General | Details

◉ Spaces   ○ Analytical Surfaces

- Building Model
  - Conference Room
    - 114 Conference Room
    - 118 Clos
  - Entry
  - Office
  - Restrooms
  - Studio
  - Support
  - Unconditioned

Space Type:

Conference Meeting/Multipurpose

Construction Type:

\<Building\>

People:

34.742397 People : 21.53 SF Area per Person

Electrical Loads:

Lighting: 972.40 W : Power: 748.00 W

Calculate | Save Settings | Cancel

Figure 7–12

How To: Run a Heating and Cooling Loads Analysis

1. In the *Analyze* tab>Reports & Schedules panel, click

   (Heating and Cooling Loads).

2. The Heating and Cooling Loads dialog box opens as shown in Figure 7–12. It contains a 3D view of the space volumes and displays information in the *General* and *Details* tabs.

3. In the *General* tab, verify or apply the **Project Information** parameters, as shown in Figure 7–13.

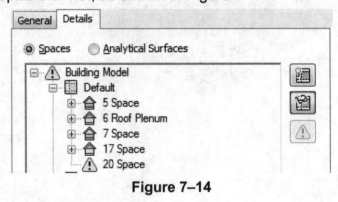

Parameter	Value
Building Type	Office
Location	Orlando, FL
Ground Plane	Level 1
Project Phase	New Construction
Sliver Space Tolerance	1' 0"
Building Service	VAV - Single Duct
Building Construction	<Building>
Building Infiltration Class	None
Report Type	Standard
Use Load Credits	

Figure 7–13

4. Select the *Details* tab and expand the levels to display the spaces for each level. Icons next to the space name indicate whether the space has been able to be calculated and if it is occupiable or not, as shown in Figure 7–14.

General | **Details**

◉ Spaces   ○ Analytical Surfaces

⊟ ⚠ Building Model
  ⊟ ▦ Default
    ⊞ 🏠 5 Space
    ⊞ 🏠 6 Roof Plenum
    ⊞ 🏠 7 Space
    ⊞ 🏠 17 Space
    —— ⚠ 20 Space

Figure 7–14

In this example there are still some spaces left in the Default Zone. You should stop the process and return to the System Browser to establish zones for the spaces and remove extra spaces.

5. To display an error, select the room name and click
⚠ (Show Related Warnings). The Warning box opens as
shown in Figure 7–15, indicating the cause of the warning.

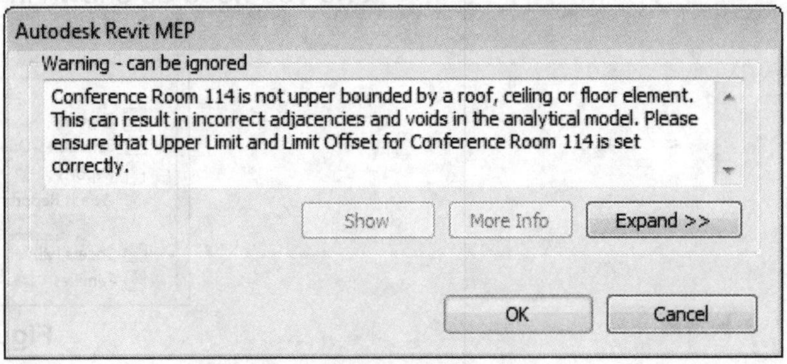

> **Autodesk Revit MEP**
>
> Warning - can be ignored
>
> Conference Room 114 is not upper bounded by a roof, ceiling or floor element.
> This can result in incorrect adjacencies and voids in the analytical model. Please
> ensure that Upper Limit and Limit Offset for Conference Room 114 is set
> correctly.
>
> [Show] [More Info] [Expand >>]
>
> [OK]   [Cancel]

Figure 7–15

6. To display visual information about the space, select the
space name and click 📖 (Highlight) to highlight the space

in the 3D view. You can also click 📖 (Isolate) to turn off the
display of all of the other spaces in the 3D view.
   • Click the icons again to turn them off.

7. Select **Analytical Surfaces** to display the surface calculation
planes, as shown in Figure 7–16.

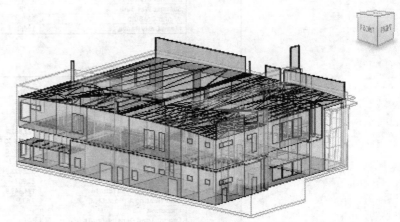

Figure 7–16

   • You can use the cursor or the ViewCube to zoom, pan,
   and rotate around the model.

8. If you need to make changes to the model, click `Save Settings` to
save any changes you have made and return to the model.

9. When you are ready to run the report, click Calculate . The
   Loads Report displays and is also available in the Project
   Browser. Expand **Reports>Loads Reports** and select the
   one you need as shown in Figure 7–17.

Project Browser - New Office Building.rvt
- 3D Plumbing
- Legends
- Schedules/Quantities
- Reports
  - Loads Reports
    - Loads Report (1)
- Sheets (all)
- Families

Figure 7–17

- The name of the report can be changed in Properties
  when the report is selected in the Project Browser.
- The Loads Report (shown in Figure 7–18), includes
  summaries for the Project, Building, and each Zone.

Project Summary

Location and Weather	
Project	Project Name
Address	
Calculation Time	Wednesday, May 23, 2012 10:58 AM
Report Type	Standard
Latitude	28.50°
Longitude	-81.37°
Summer Dry Bulb	97 °F
Summer Wet Bulb	79 °F
Winter Dry Bulb	39 °F
Mean Daily Range	16 °F

Building Summary

Inputs	
Building Type	Office
Area (SF)	15,086
Volume (CF)	249,638.16
Calculated Results	
Peak Cooling Total Load (Btu/h)	522,862.2
Peak Cooling Month and Hour	June 3:00 PM
Peak Cooling Sensible Load (Btu/h)	507,407.0
Peak Cooling Latent Load (Btu/h)	15,455.2
Maximum Cooling Capacity (Btu/h)	522,923.9
Peak Cooling Airflow (CFM)	23,907
Peak Heating Load (Btu/h)	194,349.9
Peak Heating Airflow (CFM)	7,632
Checksums	
Cooling Load Density (Btu/(h·ft²))	34.66
Cooling Flow Density (CFM/SF)	1.58
Cooling Flow / Load (CFM/ton)	548.69
Cooling Area / Load (SF/ton)	346.23
Heating Load Density (Btu/(h·ft²))	12.88
Heating Flow Density (CFM/SF)	0.51

Zone Summary - Conference Room

Inputs	
Area (SF)	775
Volume (CF)	7,743.26
Cooling Setpoint	74 °F
Heating Setpoint	70 °F
Supply Air Temperature	54 °F
Number of People	35
Infiltration (CFM)	0

Figure 7–18

7.3 Exporting for Secondary Analysis

 Learning Objective

- Export information contained in a project to gbXML that can be used in other energy analysis software.

The process of exporting a file to gbXML is the same as running the internal heating and cooling load analysis, except that you create a gbXML file that can then be imported into another energy analysis software. Numerous types of software do this type of analysis. Most of this third-party software can also analyze shading for the seasons and time of day that impacts energy consumption, as shown in the shadow study in Figure 7–19.

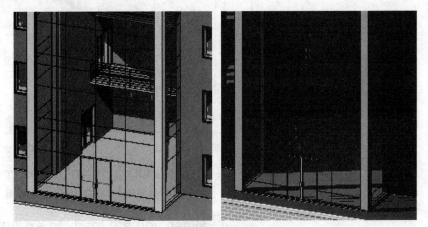

Figure 7–19

- gbXML stands for **G**reen **B**uilding E**x**tensible **M**arkup **L**anguage. It is a standard used to transfer building information from a BIM model to an engineering analysis tool.

- Engineering analysis tools include HVAC manufacturer software (such as Trane or Carrier), and the United States Department of Energy's simulation tool.

- **Subscription-Only Feature**. You can enable the energy model directly in the Autodesk Revit software and run energy simulations in the cloud using Autodesk 360 and Autodesk Green Building Studio. This can be done early in a project using the conceptual mass elements or building elements without the spaces in place. This does not require exporting to gbXML The results are also hosted in the cloud and you can compare results from different runs of the software.

How To: Export a File to gbXML

1. In the Application Menu, expand 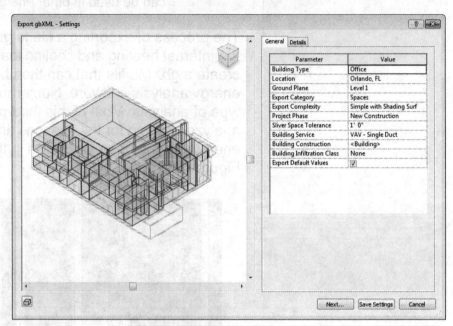 (Export) and click (gbXML).

2. The Export gbXML - Settings dialog box opens as shown in Figure 7–20, displaying a 3D view of the space volumes and information in the *General* and *Details* tabs.

Figure 7–20

3. Review all of the values as you would if you were using the **Heating and Cooling Loads** tool.

4. When you are ready to export, click 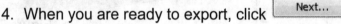 Next...

5. In the Export gbXML - Save to Target Folder dialog box, select the folder location and the file, and click Save.

6. The resulting .XML file can then be imported into an energy analysis software.

The beginning of the .XML file contains project information about the building, as shown in Figure 7–21. Each room is listed with its name, description, area, volume, and coordinate points.

```
<?xml version="1.0" encoding="UTF-8" ?>
- <gbXML temperatureUnit="F" lengthUnit="Feet" areaUnit="SquareFeet" volumeUnit="CubicFeet" useSIUnitsForResults="false"
  xmlns="http://www.gbxml.org/schema" version="0.37">
- <Campus id="cmps-1">
  - <Location>
    <Name>Boston, MA, USA</Name>
    <Latitude>42.358300</Latitude>
    <Longitude>-71.060300</Longitude>
  </Location>
  - <Building id="bldg-1" buildingType="Office">
```

Figure 7–21

Practice 7a

Heating and Cooling Analysis

 Learning Objectives

- Prepare a project for energy analysis with Energy Settings.
- Review the details of zones and spaces in the Heating and Coolings Loads dialog box and fix any warnings.
- Calculate the analysis and export the file to gbXML.

Estimated time for completion: 20 minutes

In this practice you will run the Heating and Cooling Loads software and review the details of the zones and spaces in the project. You will identify problems, as shown in Figure 7–22, return to the model to solve them and then rerun the software and calculate the analysis. You will then export the file to gbXML.

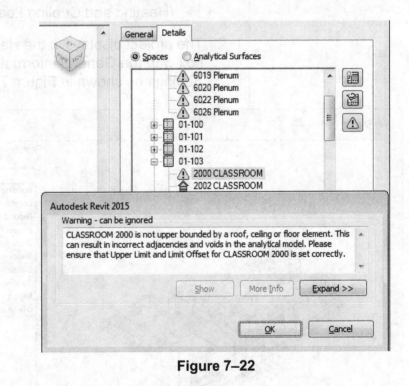

Figure 7–22

Task 1 - Prepare the project for energy analysis.

1. In the *C:\Autodesk Revit 2015 MEP Fundamentals Class Files\Analysis* folder, open **MEP-Elementary-School -Analysis.rvt**.

2. In the *Analyze* tab>Energy Analysis panel, click (Energy Settings).

3. In the Energy Settings dialog box, set the following values:

- *Building Type*: **School or University**.
- *Location*: your home town
- *Building Service*: **VAV - Single Duct**
- *Building Infiltration Class*: **Medium**

4. If time permits, set the *Building Construction* values in the associated dialog box.

5. Click [OK] to close the dialog box.

Task 2 - Test the project.

1. In the *Analyze* tab>Reports & Schedules panel, click (Heating and Cooling Loads).

2. The project displays in the Heating and Cooling Loads dialog box with the General information that you set in the Energy Settings as shown in Figure 7–23.

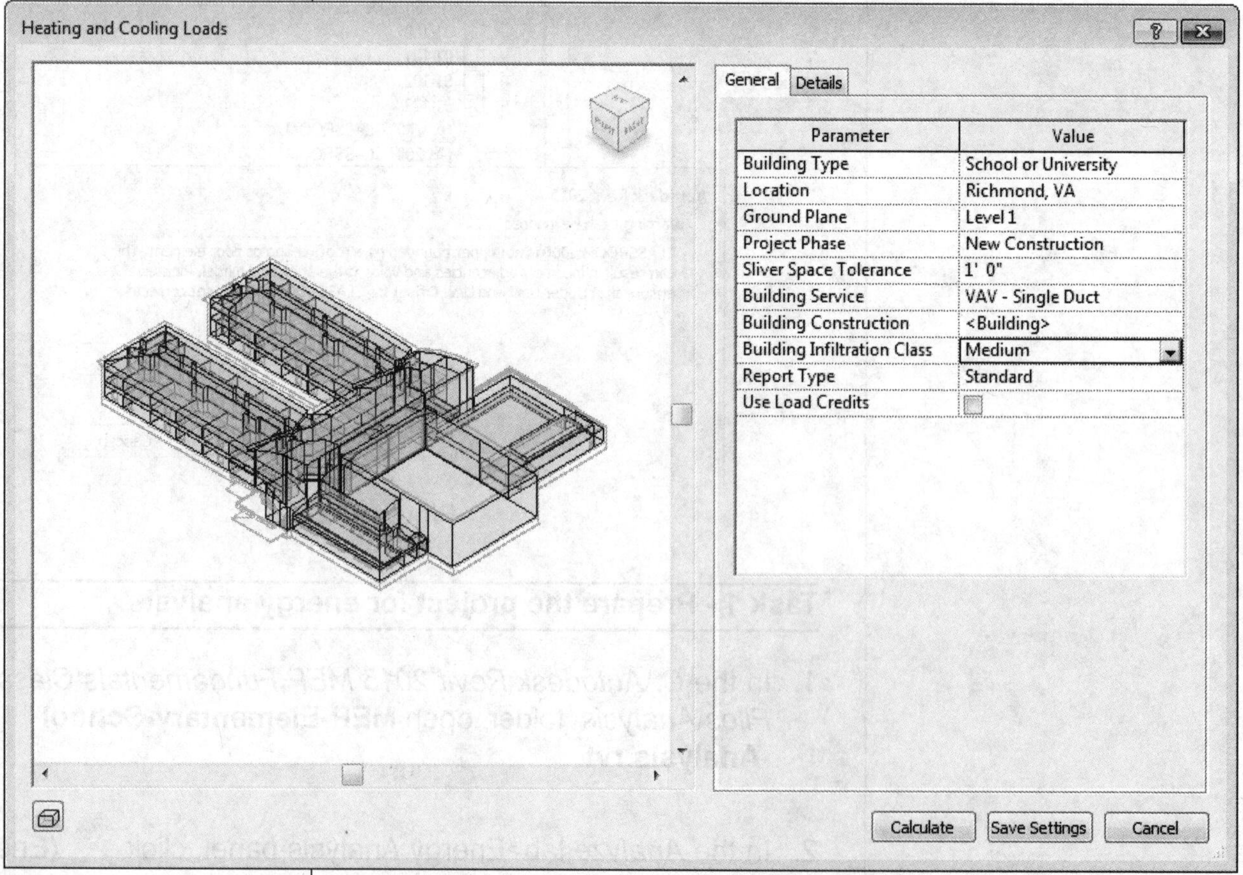

Parameter	Value
Building Type	School or University
Location	Richmond, VA
Ground Plane	Level 1
Project Phase	New Construction
Sliver Space Tolerance	1' 0"
Building Service	VAV - Single Duct
Building Construction	<Building>
Building Infiltration Class	Medium
Report Type	Standard
Use Load Credits	

Figure 7–23

3. Select the *Details* tab.

4. Several issues need to be resolved before you can calculate the loads starting with a Warning at the top of the building model as shown in Figure 7–24.

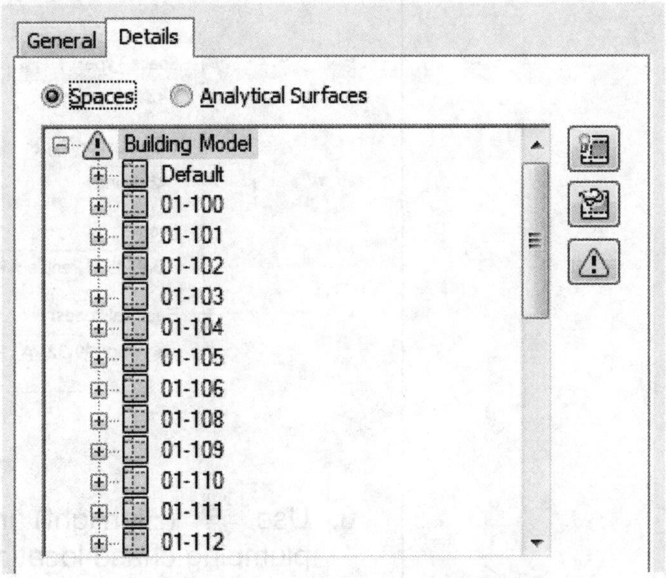

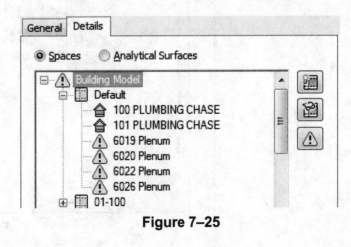

Figure 7–24

If your company includes a space schedule in your templates you can use it as mentioned in the Warning. You can also delete empty spaces in the Zone view of the System Manager.

5. Click ⚠ (Show Related Warnings). The Warning indicates that there are undefined spaces in the model. Click Cancel .

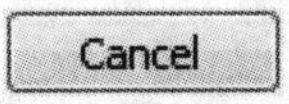

6. Expand the Default Zone. There are several spaces in this zone that need to be modified and moved to other zones, as shown in Figure 7–25.

Figure 7–25

7. Select **100 Plumbing Chase**. The information about the space indicates that there are People and Electrical Loads associated with this space when they should not be, as shown in Figure 7–26. This is also indicated by the (Occupiable) icon beside the space name.

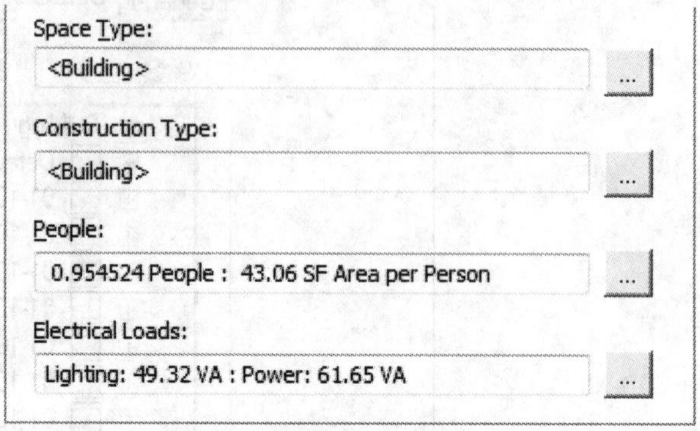

Figure 7–26

8. Use 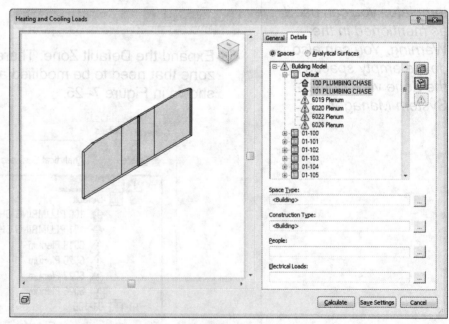 (Highlight) and (Isolate) to identify the plumbing chase locations. For example, you might want to select both chases and isolate them first as shown in Figure 7–27. Then switch to **Highlight** to indicate their location within the building. They are hard to identify because they are very thin.

Figure 7–27

9. Turn off **Highlight** and **Isolate**.

10. Select the four plenum spaces by holding down <Ctrl> as you select.

11. Click 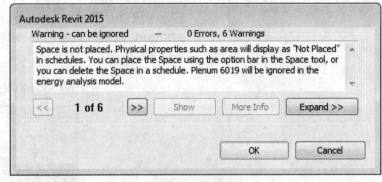 (Show Related Warnings). These spaces have not been placed and are ignored in the energy analysis as shown in Figure 7–28.

Autodesk Revit 2015

Warning - can be ignored   --   0 Errors, 6 Warnings

Space is not placed. Physical properties such as area will display as "Not Placed" in schedules. You can place the Space using the option bar in the Space tool, or you can delete the Space in a schedule. Plenum 6019 will be ignored in the energy analysis model.

<<   **1 of 6**   >>   Show   More Info   Expand >>

OK   Cancel

Figure 7–28

12. Scroll down through the zones to check for other problems, such as the one shown in Figure 7–29. Write down this zone and the space number so you can correct it in the model.

General   **Details**

⦿ Spaces   ○ Analytical Surfaces

⚠ 6019 Plenum
⚠ 6020 Plenum
⚠ 6022 Plenum
⚠ 6026 Plenum
⊞ 01-100
⊞ 01-101
⊞ 01-102
⊟ 01-103
   ⚠ 2000 CLASSROOM
   ⬆ 2002 CLASSROOM

Autodesk Revit 2015

Warning - can be ignored

CLASSROOM 2000 is not upper bounded by a roof, ceiling or floor element. This can result in incorrect adjacencies and voids in the analytical model. Please ensure that Upper Limit and Limit Offset for CLASSROOM 2000 is set correctly.

Show   More Info   Expand >>

OK   Cancel

Figure 7–29

13. Click Save Settings to close the Heating and Cooling Loads dialog box and return to the model so that it can be modified.

Task 3 - Modify the model.

1. Open the System Browser (press the <F9> key) in the Zones view.

2. Expand the Default zone. Select the four unplaced plenum spaces, right-click and select **Delete**, as shown in Figure 7–30.

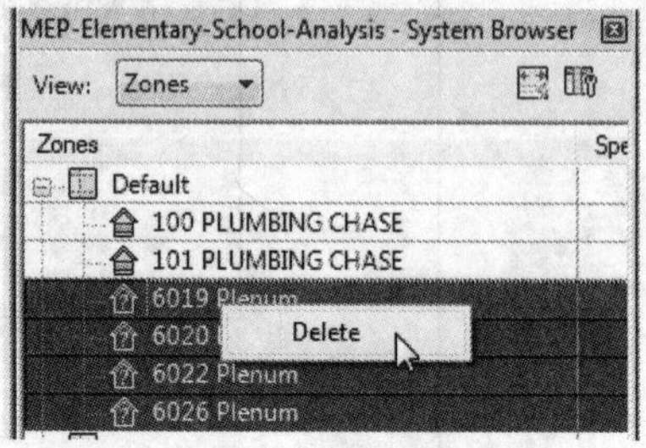

Figure 7–30

3. When prompted to delete the spaces, click .

4. If they do not get deleted, in the Project Browser, open the Schedules/Quantities>**SPACE SCHEDULE** view.

5. At the top of the schedule, note the four spaces that were not placed. Hold <Ctrl> and select all four of them.

6. Right-click and select **Delete Row**. Click . This time they are deleted from the schedule as well as from the project.

7. Return to the previous view.

8. In the System Browser, select one of the plumbing chase spaces.

If you want see it is in the project, right-click and select Show. The view zooms in to the location with the space selected.

9. The information about the space also displays in Properties. In Properties, scroll down to the *Energy Analysis* area, clear **Occupiable** and click Apply. The icon in the System Browser changes as shown in Figure 7–31.

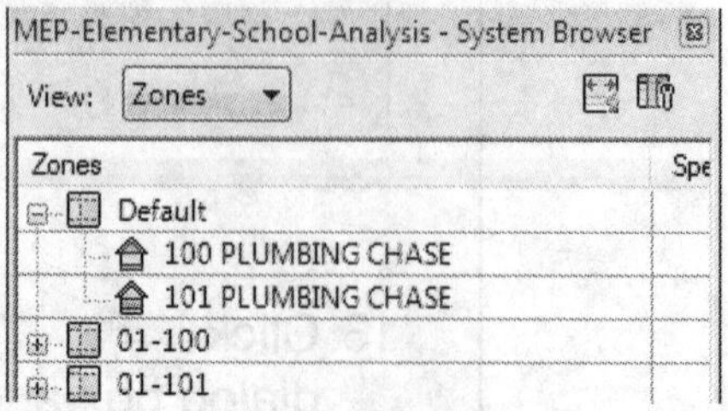

Figure 7–31

10. Select the other plumbing chase and repeat the process.

11. These two chases need to be added to the same zone as the other chases nearby. Roll the cursor over one of the other chase spaces until the Zone highlights, as shown in Figure 7–32. Select the Zone.

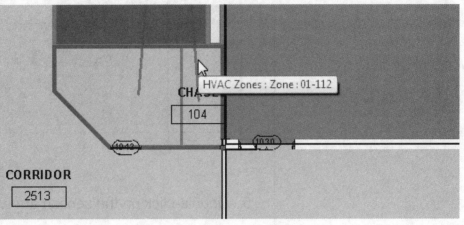

Figure 7–32

12. In the *Modify | HVAC Zones* tab>Zones panel, click 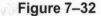 (Edit Zone).

13. In the *Edit Zone* tab>Mode panel, click (Add Space).

14. Zoom in as required and select the two plumbing chase spaces. They should change to the color of the selected zone. Click (Finish Editing Zone).

15. In the System Browser, there should no longer be any spaces in the default zone.

Task 4 - Fix a Space.

1. In the Systems Browser, find the other space (Zone **01-103** Space **2000 Classroom**) that had a problem with HVAC Loads. It does not display any warnings.

2. Right-click on the space and select **Show**. The view zooms in on the space but there are no warnings that anything is wrong.

3. In the View Control Panel, click (Reveal Hidden Elements). (This temporarily displays the section markers which have been hidden in this view.)

4. Draw a section through the space as shown in Figure 7–33.

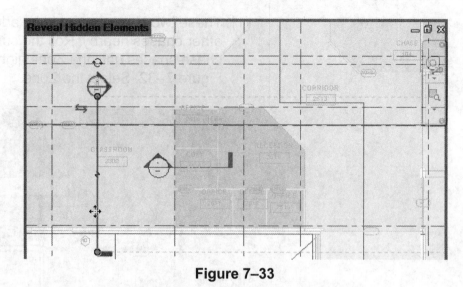

Figure 7–33

5. Double-click on the section arrow to open the section.

6. Modify the crop region of the view to show the lower classroom and hide categories to clean up the view. Type **VG** and turn on **Spaces>Interior**. The space does not extend up to the ceiling as it should as shown in Figure 7–34.

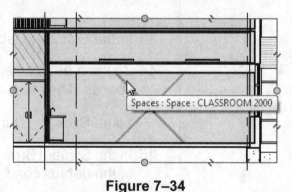

Figure 7–34

7. In the section view, select the space. In Properties, change the *Limit Offset* to **10'-0"**. The space now extends up to touch the ceiling as shown in Figure 7–35.

You can also use the drag controls to modify the height of the space.

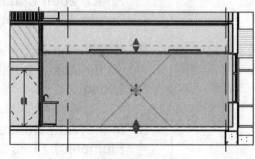

Figure 7–35

8. Return to the previous plan view. In the View Control Bar, click ⬚ (Close Reveal Hidden Elements) and zoom out to display the entire plan.

9. Save the project.

Task 5 - Run the Heating and Cooling Loads.

1. Type **LO** (the shortcut key) or in the *Analyze* tab>Reports & Schedules panel, click ⬚ (Heating and Cooling Loads).

2. In the Heating and Cooling Loads dialog box, in the *Details* tab, expand the zones. The problems have been taken care of as shown in Figure 7–36.

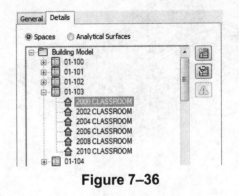

Figure 7–36

3. Click ⬚ Calculate . The progress displays in the Status bar as shown in Figure 7–37. This takes time.

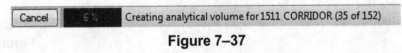

Figure 7–37

4. Review the Loads analysis document as shown in part in Figure 7–38.

Project Summary

Location and Weather	
Project	MEP Elementary School
Address	1234 Schoolhouse Road Richmond, VA 23225
Calculation Time	Wednesday, November 10, 2010 4:59 PM
Report Type	Standard
Latitude	37.54°
Longitude	-77.47°
Summer Dry Bulb	96 °F
Summer Wet Bulb	80 °F
Winter Dry Bulb	14 °F
Mean Daily Range	19 °F

Figure 7–38

5. Save the project.

Task 6 - Export the project to gbXML.

1. In the Application Menu, expand ⬚ (Export) and click
   ⬚ (gbXML). A dialog box similar to the Heating and Cooling
   Loads dialog box opens, as shown in Figure 7–39.

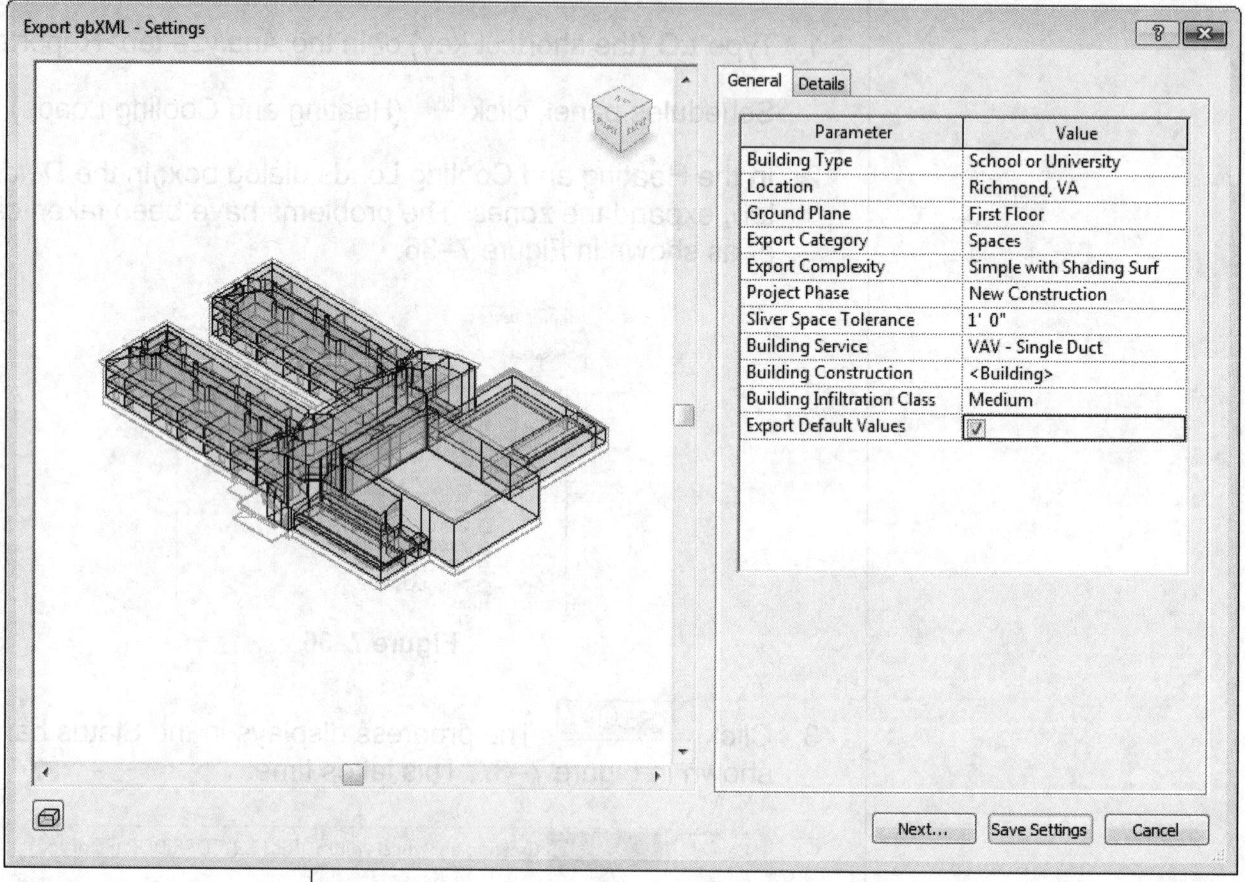

Export gbXML - Settings

Parameter	Value
Building Type	School or University
Location	Richmond, VA
Ground Plane	First Floor
Export Category	Spaces
Export Complexity	Simple with Shading Surf
Project Phase	New Construction
Sliver Space Tolerance	1' 0"
Building Service	VAV - Single Duct
Building Construction	<Building>
Building Infiltration Class	Medium
Export Default Values	✓

Next...   Save Settings   Cancel

Figure 7–39

2. Click Next... .

3. In the Export gbXML - Save to Target Folder dialog box,
   specify the class folder as the location for the file and click
     Save .

4. You can now import the resulting .XML file into an energy
   analysis software, or view it with Internet Explorer.

5. Save and close the project.

Chapter Review Questions

1. Which of the following are Energy Settings that impact Energy Analysis? (Select all that apply.)

    a. Geographic location of the building.

    b. Exterior wall construction.

    c. Number of spaces in the model.

    d. Plenum heights.

2. In the System Browser, in the Zones view, 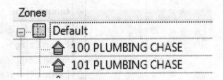 displays next to the name of the space. It indicates that the space...

    a. occupancy has not been defined.

    b. does not have an upper boundary.

    c. has not been placed.

    d. is not part of a zone.

3. When running the Heating and Cooling Loads analysis, the *Details* tab indicates that there are still spaces listed under Default, as shown in Figure 7–40. What needs to be done?

Figure 7–40

    a. Delete those spaces from the model.

    b. Verify the height of the spaces.

    c. Move the spaces to another zone.

    d. Change the status of the spaces to unoccupied.

4. The primary purpose of exporting a file to gbXML, as shown in Figure 7–41, is to import the information into spreadsheet software for manual review of the energy analysis information.

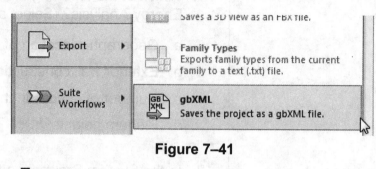

Figure 7–41

a. True

b. False

5. When establishing the Energy Settings before running the Heating and Cooling Loads, set the *Export Complexity,* as shown in Figure 7–42, to...

Figure 7–42

a. **Simple**

b. **Simple with Shading Surfaces**

c. **Complex**

d. **Complex with Shading Surfaces**

6. Before running the energy analysis, all areas in the project need to be set up with...

a. light fixtures

b. spaces

c. heating equipment

d. sun shade devices

Command Summary

Button	Command	Location
	Export gbXML	• **Application Menu:** expand Export
	Heating and Cooling Loads	• **Ribbon:** *Analyze* tab>Reports & Schedules panel
	Energy Settings	• **Ribbon:** *Analyze* tab>Energy Analysis panel

Chapter 8

HVAC Systems

In this chapter you learn about HVAC Systems including how to add air terminals and mechanical equipment. You also learn to add ductwork manually or automatically and create duct systems.

This chapter contains the following topics:

- **About HVAC Systems**
- **Adding Air Terminals and Mechanical Equipment**
- **Adding Ductwork**
- **Modifying Ducts**
- **Creating Duct Systems**
- **Automatic Ductwork Layouts**

8.1 About HVAC Systems

 Learning Objectives

- Understand the steps required for creating an HVAC system.
- Prepare Mechanical Settings.

HVAC Systems consist of components to provide heating, ventilation, and air conditioning to a building, as shown in Figure 8–1. Autodesk® Revit® MEP software provides tools to help you correctly design these systems.

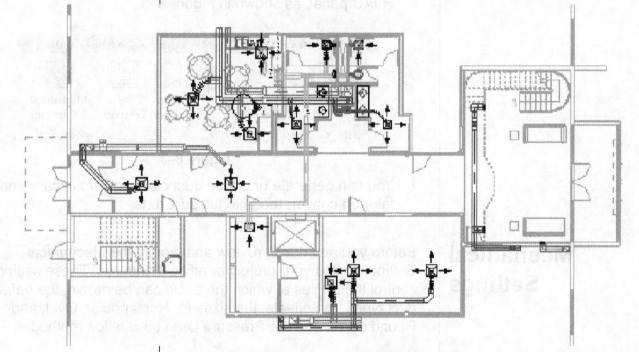

Figure 8–1

There are several steps in the process of creating HVAC systems:

1. Add air terminals and mechanical equipment.
2. Create a supply or return air system. Some of them get created automatically when you insert the components.
3. Generate ductwork automatically or add it manually. When adding ductwork manually, you can attach it to connectors on the air terminals and mechanical equipment as well as to other ducts.
4. Check and modify the system.

- Fittings between changes of height or size are automatically applied, as shown in Figure 8–2.

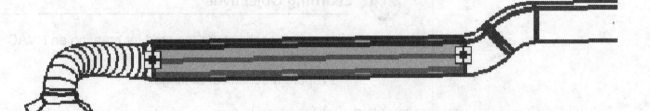

Figure 8–2

- The tools to begin creating and placing HVAC components and systems are located in the Ribbon, in the *Systems* tab> HVAC panel, as shown in Figure 8–3.

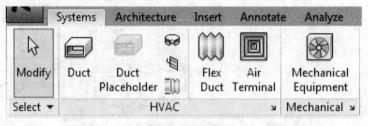

Figure 8–3

- You can generate or create duct placeholders initially and later on convert those to full duct runs.

Mechanical Settings

Before you add ducts, review and modify the Mechanical Settings to suit your project or office standards. These settings control the angles at which the ducts can be drawn, the default duct types and offsets, the sizes for Rectangular, Oval, and Round ducts, and the Pressure Drop calculation method.

In the *Systems* tab>Mechanical panel title, click ⌐ (Mechanical Settings) or type **MS** to open the Mechanical Settings dialog box. In the left pane, select the options you want to review. For example, in the *Conversion* category, you can set the Duct Type and Offset for each System Classification, as shown in Figure 8–4.

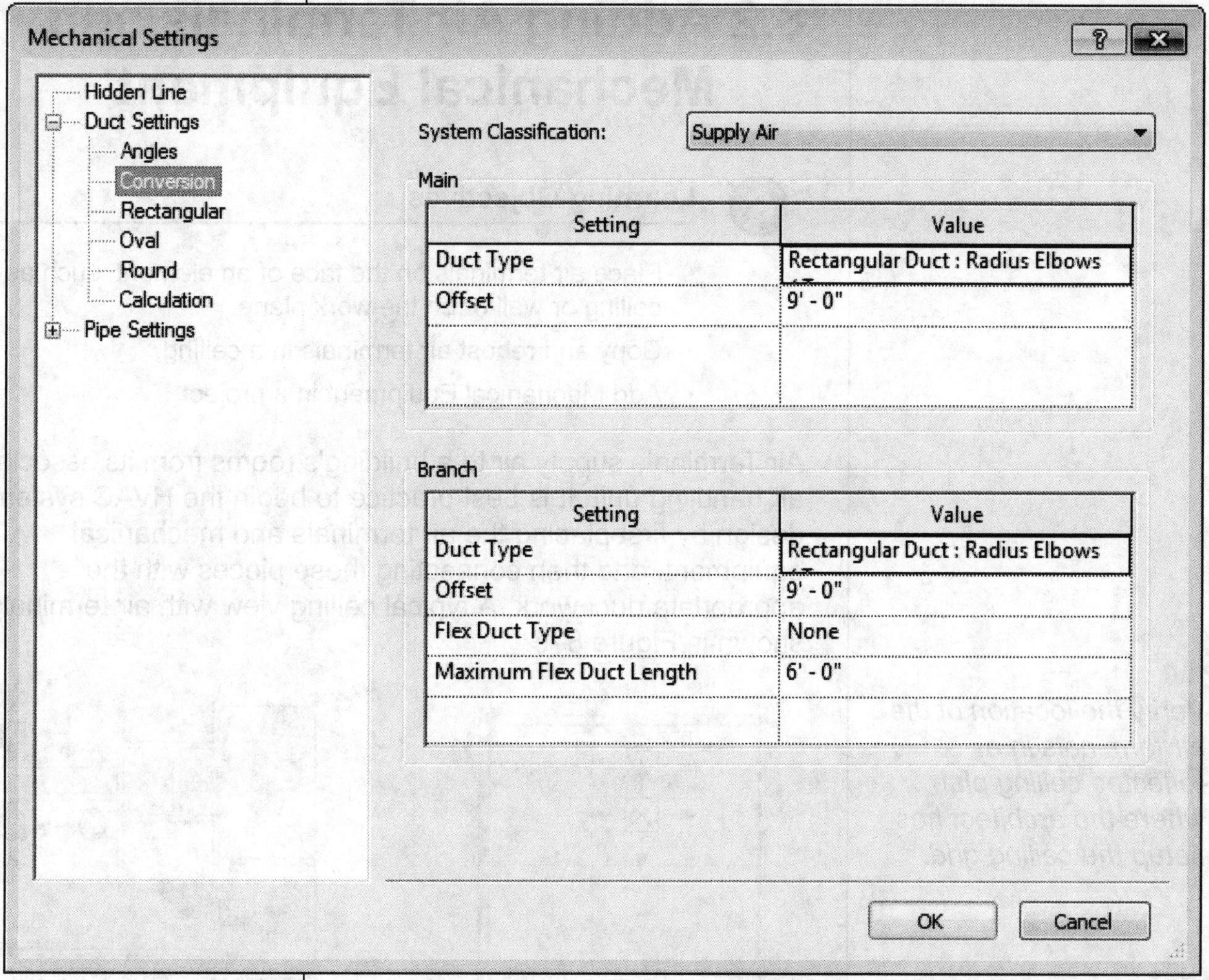

Mechanical Settings

Hidden Line
Duct Settings
  Angles
  Conversion
  Rectangular
  Oval
  Round
  Calculation
Pipe Settings

System Classification: Supply Air

Main

Setting	Value
Duct Type	Rectangular Duct : Radius Elbows
Offset	9' - 0"

Branch

Setting	Value
Duct Type	Rectangular Duct : Radius Elbows
Offset	9' - 0"
Flex Duct Type	None
Maximum Flex Duct Length	6' - 0"

OK   Cancel

Figure 8–4

- Duct Settings are set by project and can be included in templates or imported into a project from another project using **Transfer Project Standards**.

8.2 Adding Air Terminals and Mechanical Equipment

 Learning Objectives

- Place air terminals on the face of an element, such as a ceiling or wall or on the work plane.
- Copy and rehost air terminals in a ceiling.
- Add Mechanical Equipment in a project.

Air Terminals supply air to a building's rooms from its associated air handling unit. It is best practice to begin the HVAC system design by first placing the air terminals and mechanical equipment, and then connecting these pieces with the appropriate duct work. A typical ceiling view with air terminals is shown in Figure 8–5.

Verify the location of the air terminals in a reflected ceiling plan where the architect has setup the ceiling grid.

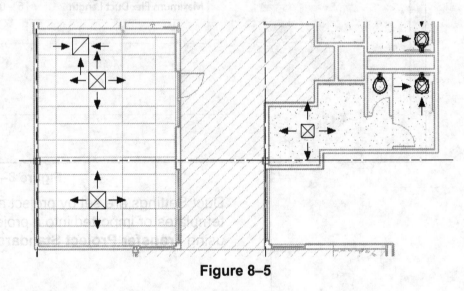

Figure 8–5

Air Terminals

Air terminals can be used in supply, return or exhaust air systems. You can place individual air terminals or batch copy them from a linked file.

- Typically, air terminals are placed on a host, such as a ceiling. Therefore when placing an air terminal, use a reflected ceiling plan view.

- Some air terminal types can also be placed directly on ducts.

- Air terminals display regardless of the cut plane of the view.

- Air terminals that are hosted by a ceiling in a linked model (as shown in Figure 8–6), move automatically with any changes that the architects make to the ceiling height. This can be an advantage of using hosted fixtures.

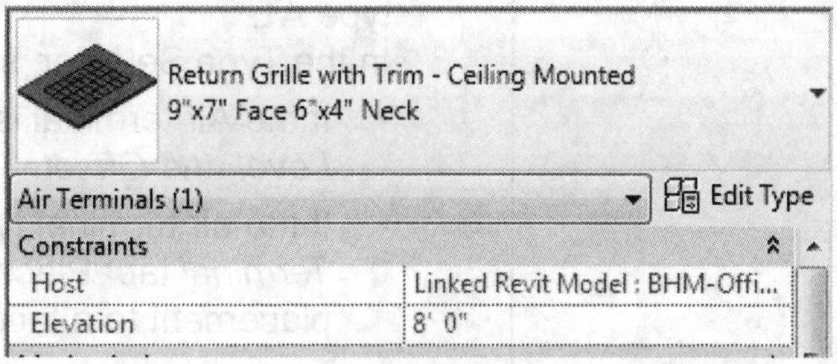

Figure 8–6

- If the architect deletes the ceiling and puts a new one in the linked model, the hosted air terminals are orphaned and do not move with changes in the ceiling height. A warning box opens when you reload the linked model or reopen the MEP project, as shown in Figure 8–7. Use the **Coordination Monitoring** tools to address the issue.

Some firms add reference planes and place the hosted families on them instead of in the ceiling. This gives them control over the height of the families. If the architect moves the ceilings up or down, the engineer adjusts the height of the reference plane to match.

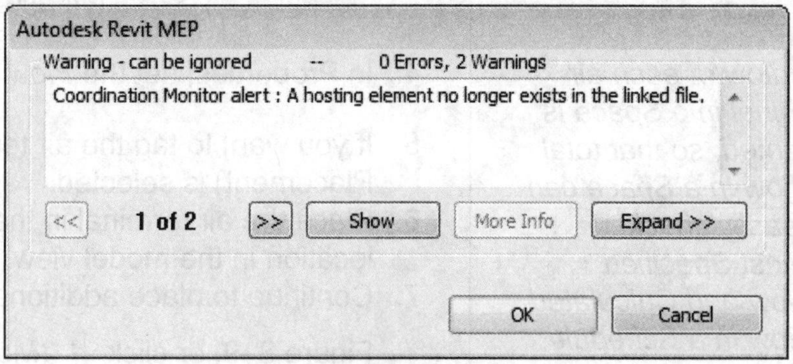

Figure 8–7

- When using a non-hosted air terminal it is placed at a specified height above the level of the current view, as shown in Figure 8–8. It is not modified if the linked architectural model is modified.

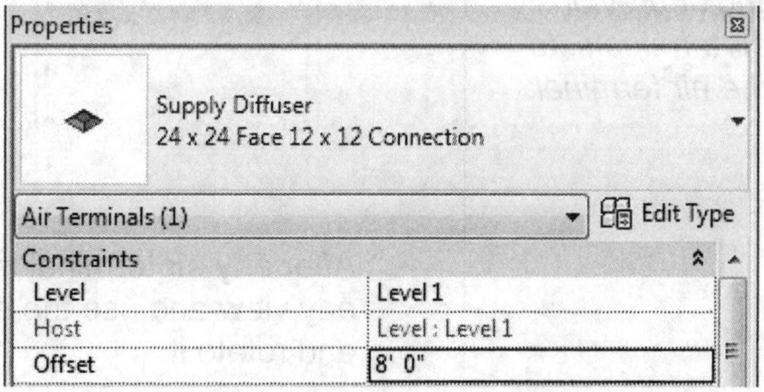

Figure 8–8

How To: Place an Air Terminal

1. Open the view where you want to place the air terminals.

2. In the *Systems* tab>HVAC panel, click ▣ (Air Terminal) or type **AT**.

3. In the Type Selector, select an air terminal type.
   - If the Air terminal is not hosted, in Properties, set the *Level* and *Offset*.
   - If the air terminal type is hosted, in the *Modify | Place Air Terminal* tab>Placement panel, select the type of placement to a face or a plane.

	Place on Vertical Face	Places air terminal on a vertical face, such as a wall.
	Place on Face	Places the air terminal on a defined face, such as the ceiling grid.
	Place on Work Plane	Places the air terminal on a defined plane such as a level or ceiling in a linked architectural model.

4. In Properties, set the *Flow* and other parameters.

5. If you want to tag the air terminal, verify that ↱① (Tag on Placement) is selected.

6. Place the air terminal in the model by clicking at the desired location in the model view.

7. Continue to place additional air terminals, as shown in Figure 8–9, or click ⬉ (Modify) to exit the command.

The flow of each air terminal in a Space is summed, so that total air flow in a Space can be easily checked against Specified Airflow and Calculated Airflow in a Schedule.

Use other objects in the model, such as the ceiling grid or previously placed air terminals, to line up the air terminal.

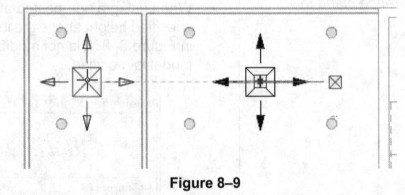

Figure 8–9

- After any air terminal is initially placed, you can modify it in any view and use the standard modify tools to move, align, and rotate it.

- If the air terminal you want does not exist in your project, you can load one from the Library>*Mechanical>MEP>Air-Side Components>Air Terminals* folder. Some air terminal types prompt you to select sizes as shown in Figure 8–10.

Specify Types

Family:

Supply Diffuser - Perforated

Types:

Type	Diffuser Heigh	Diffuser Width	Duct Diameter	Flow	Pressure D
(all)	(all)	(all)	(all)	(all)	(all)
20x20x6 In Neck	1' 8"	1' 8"	15/64"	275	0.258
16x16x8 In Neck	1' 4"	1' 4"	81/256"	490	0.350
20x20x8 In Neck	1' 8"	1' 8"	81/256"	490	0.295
24x24x8 In Neck	2' 0"	2' 0"	81/256"	490	0.295
48x24x8 In Neck	4' 0"	2' 0"	81/256"	8000	0.320
16x16x10 In Nec	1' 4"	1' 4"	101/256"	760	0.475

Select one or more types on the right for each family listed on the left

[OK] [Cancel] [Help]

Figure 8–10

- You can modify Air Terminal sizes. In Properties, click

  ⊞ (Edit Type) and duplicate it before making changes.

How To: Place an Air Terminal on a Duct

1. Have a duct in place. If it is a round or oval duct, verify the diameter before selecting the air terminal.
2. Start the **Air Terminal** command.
3. In the Type Selector, select the required air terminal. There are different types for curved and rectangular duct faces. Curved face air terminals are created by duct diameter as shown in Figure 8–11.

Ensure that you are selecting an air terminal that matches the system type of the duct.

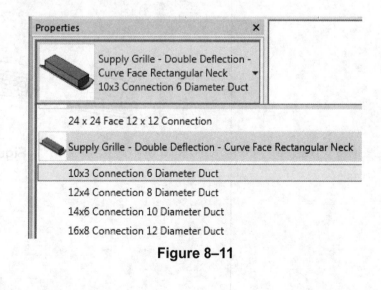

Figure 8–11

4. In the *Modify | Place Air Terminal* tab>Layout panel, verify that 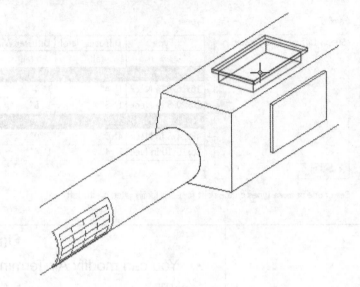 (Air Terminal on Duct) is toggled on.

5. Move the cursor over to the duct where you want to place the air terminal. The air terminal automatically rotates to the face you are closest to, as shown in Figure 8–12.

Figure 8–12

6. Click to place the air terminal.

Copying Air Terminals

You can also batch copy fixtures from a linked file into the host file.

If you have air terminals in a project with similar parameters including the type, elevation, and flow, you can place one and then copy it to the other locations. This works with independently placed air terminals and those placed directly on ducts, as shown in Figure 8–13.

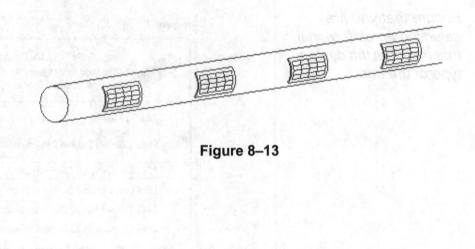

Figure 8–13

Rehosting Air Terminals

While working with linked models, if air terminals are copied from one ceiling to other ceilings of the same height, the copied air terminals are hosted by their respective new ceilings. However, if the ceilings are a different height than the ceiling that hosts the original air terminal, the copied fixtures are not associated with the ceiling. They end up at the same elevation as the original air terminal, as shown in Figure 8–14. Therefore, you need to rehost the air terminal.

If the ceilings are in the host project you are not permitted to copy a hosted air terminal from one ceiling to another.

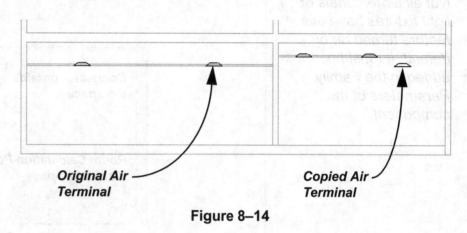

Original Air Terminal

Copied Air Terminal

Figure 8–14

How To: Rehost an Air Terminal

1. Copy the air terminals as required.
2. Select the one(s) that need to be rehosted to a different ceiling.
3. In the *Modify | Air Terminals* tab>Work Plane panel, click
   (Pick New).
4. In the Placement panel, click (Face).
5. Select the ceiling to which you want the air terminal(s) hosted.

• This needs to be done in the reflected ceiling plan view for ceiling hosted fixtures.

- Occasionally, the location of a light fixture or air terminal is such that the software assigns its electrical/mechanical values to the wrong space. This results in faulty heating and cooling load calculations and incorrect space values. To correct this, use a family that has the **Room Calculation Point** turned on. The point is displayed in the project when a fixture is selected, as shown in Figure 8–15. However, the point cannot be manipulated and its visibility is only for review purposes.

Not all air terminals or light fixtures have this feature turned on by default. It must be added in the Family Parameters of the component.

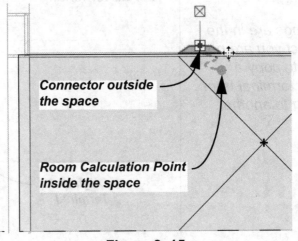

Connector outside
the space

Room Calculation Point
inside the space

Figure 8–15

Mechanical Equipment

Mechanical Equipment supplies the air to the air terminals, and is connected to the air terminals via duct work to complete the system. Mechanical Equipment includes various air handling units, such as fan coil units or variable air volume units. Mechanical equipment families have connectors, as shown in Figure 8–16, where the system components connect.

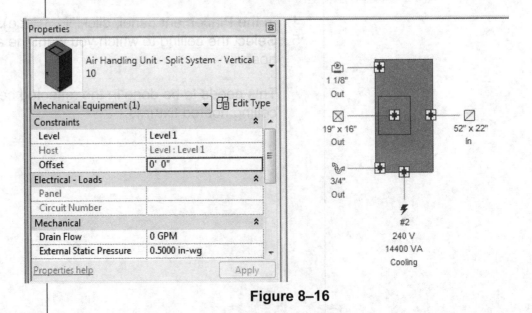

Figure 8–16

- Depending on the component, Mechanical Equipment can be placed in plan, elevation, and 3D views.

How To: Place Mechanical Equipment

1. Open the view where you have to place the mechanical equipment element.

2. In the *Systems* tab>Mechanical panel, click 🔲 (Mechanical Equipment) or type **ME**.

3. In the Type Selector, select a Mechanical Equipment type. In Properties, set any other values such as the *Level* and *Offset* if it is not hosted.

4. Place the Mechanical Equipment in the model by clicking at the required location in the model view. You can use other objects in the model to line the element up and press the <Spacebar> to rotate it before placing it.

5. Continue to place additional Mechanical Equipment elements, or click 🔓 (Modify) to exit the command.

- Additional boilers, radiators, VAV units and more can be loaded from the Library in the *Mechanical>MEP* sub-folders.

- Take time to get to know the types of mechanical equipment that come with the Autodesk Revit MEP software. You can view them in 3D, plan, or elevation/section views. Select them to see the connectors as shown in Figure 8–17.

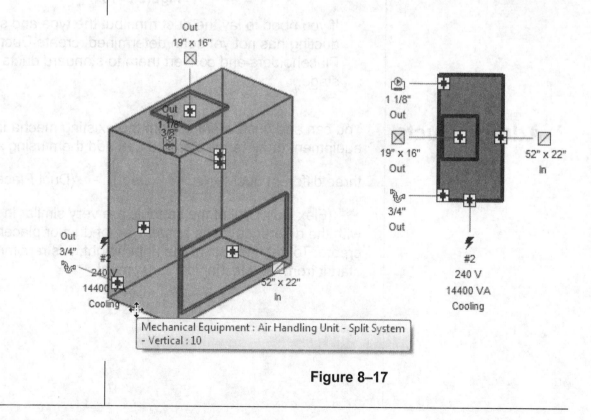

Figure 8–17

8.3 Adding Ductwork

Learning Objective

- Add ductwork to connect mechanical equipment and air terminals.

Duct work connects the mechanical equipment to the air terminals, as shown in Figure 8–18. There are various shapes and sizes that can be used both for regular and flex duct. By using connectors in the equipment and the air terminals you can quickly attach the ducts and have the software automatically calculate any differences in height.

Fittings are automatically added in some cases. You can also modify fittings and add others.

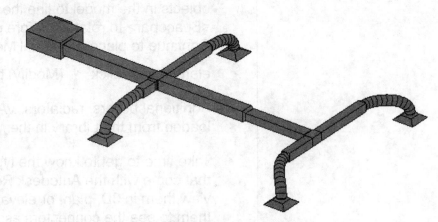

Figure 8–18

- If you need to lay the duct runs but the type and size of ducting has not yet been determined, create Duct Placeholders and convert them to standard ducts at a later stage.

Adding Ducts

You can add ducts starting from the existing mechanical equipment or air terminals. You can add them using any of the three different duct tools: (Duct), (Duct Placeholder), or (Flex Duct). All of the se tools are very similar in creation with the difference in the actual type of duct or placeholder they create. To get the duct at the right height, it is recommended to start it from the Mechanical Equipment.

How To: Add Ducts

1. Open the view where you want to place the duct. Ducts can be drawn in plan, elevation/section, and 3D views.
2. There are several ways to start the **Duct** command:

   - In the *Systems* tab>HVAC panel, click ⬛ (Duct), ⬛ (Duct Placeholder), or ⬛ (Flex Duct).
   - Type **DT** for Duct or **FD** for Flex Duct.
   - Select the mechanical equipment, air terminal, or an existing duct or fitting to display the connectors. Hover over a **Duct Connector** icon and select **Create Duct,** as shown on the left in Figure 8–19.
   - With the element selected, right-click on a duct connector and select **Draw Duct, Draw Duct Placeholder,** or **Draw Flex Duct** as shown on the right in Figure 8–19.

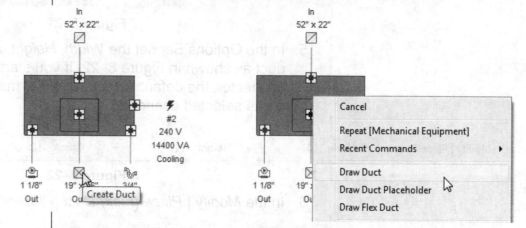

Figure 8–19

3. In the Type Selector, select a duct type as shown in Figure 8–20.

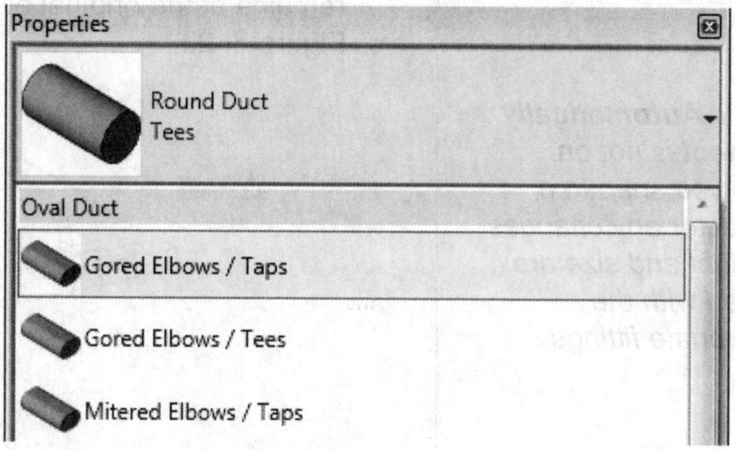

Figure 8–20

4. If you are drawing ducts without selecting mechanical equipment or air terminals, in Properties, specify the *System Type* as shown in Figure 8–21 before you start drawing the duct.

Drawing from existing connectors automatically applies the System Type.

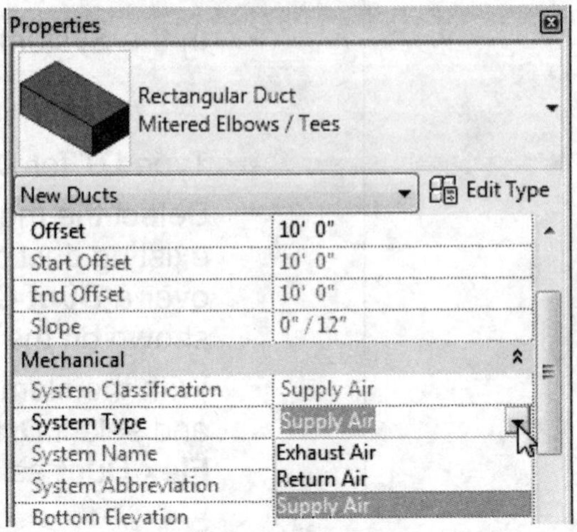

Properties		⊠
	Rectangular Duct Mitered Elbows / Tees	▾
New Ducts		▾ ▦ Edit Type
Offset	10' 0"	
Start Offset	10' 0"	
End Offset	10' 0"	
Slope	0" / 12"	
Mechanical		⊗
System Classification	Supply Air	
System Type	Supply Air	
System Name	Exhaust Air	
System Abbreviation	Return Air	
Bottom Elevation	Supply Air	

Figure 8–21

5. In the Options Bar set the *Width*, *Height*, and *Offset* for the duct as shown in Figure 8–22. If you started from a connector, the default sizes and offset match the parameters of the selected connector.

| Modify | Place Duct | Width: 14" ▾ | Height: 11" ▾ | Offset: 10' 0" ▾ | ⬜ | Apply |

Figure 8–22

6. In the *Modify | Place (Flex) Duct (Placeholder)* tab> Placement Tools panel, click ⬚ (Automatically Connect), if you want a duct to connect to a lower duct and automatically places all of the right fittings, as shown on the left in Figure 8–23. Turn it off, if you want to draw a duct that remains at the original elevation, as shown on the right in Figure 8–23.

*Even if **Automatically Connect** is not on, when you snap to a connector any changes in height and size are applied with the appropriate fittings.*

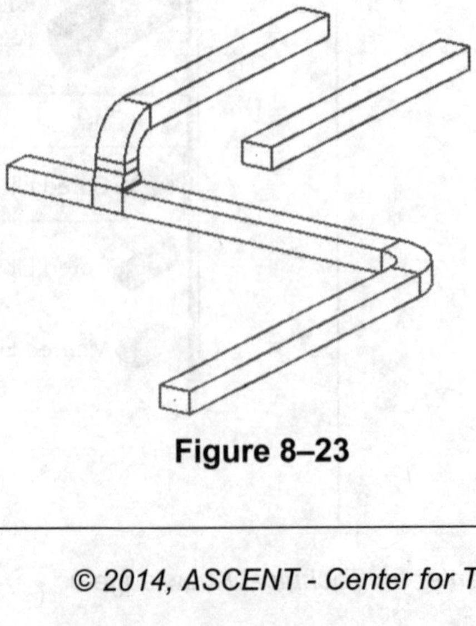

Figure 8–23

7. Draw the ducts using temporary dimensions, snaps, and alignments to locate each point along the path as shown in Figure 8–24.

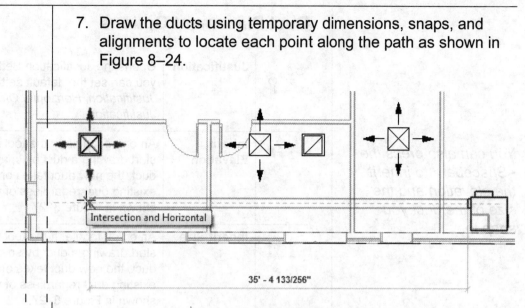

Intersection and Horizontal

35' - 4 133/256"

Figure 8–24

- Press <Esc> once to stay in the command but have a new start location. If you select a point along an existing duct it automatically adds a fitting according to the duct type.

If you change the size or shape, the appropriate duct fitting is automatically added.

- When you change direction an elbow or tee is added. The exact fitting depends on the duct type. This is also true if you change the offset off the level as shown in Figure 8–25.

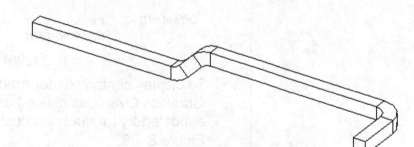

Figure 8–25

- In the example in Figure 8–26, a flex duct is started from the air terminal that is lower than the existing ducts. Ensure that you select the point snap on the end of the other duct to create the connection.

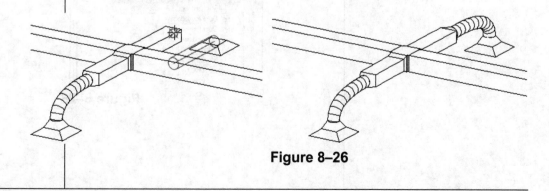

Figure 8–26

Duct Placement Options

![Justification icon]	**Justification**	Opens the Justification Setting dialog box where you can set the default settings for the *Horizontal Justification, Horizontal Offset,* and *Vertical Justification.*
![Inherit Elevation icon]	**Inherit Elevation**	An on/off toggle. If the tool is toggled on and you start drawing a duct by snapping to an existing duct, the new duct takes on the elevation of the existing duct regardless of what is specified, as shown in Figure 8–27
![Inherit Size icon]	**Inherit Size**	An on/off toggle. If the tool is toggled on and you start drawing a duct by snapping to an existing duct, the new duct takes on the size of the existing duct regardless of what is specified, as shown in Figure 8–27.

You can also press the <Spacebar> to inherit the elevation and the size of the duct you snap to.

Horizontal Duct - Offset of 12'-0" and Size of 12" x12"

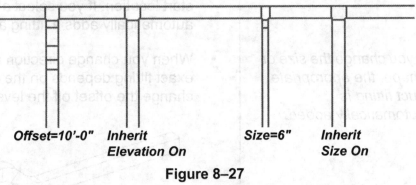

Offset=10'-0" Inherit Elevation On   Size=6"   Inherit Size On

Figure 8–27

- To display centerlines for round ducting, in the Visibility/ Graphics Overrides dialog box, turn on the *Centerline* subcategory for duct and duct fittings, as shown in Figure 8–28.

*Centerlines display in plan and elevation views set to the **Wireframe** or **Hidden Line** visual style.*

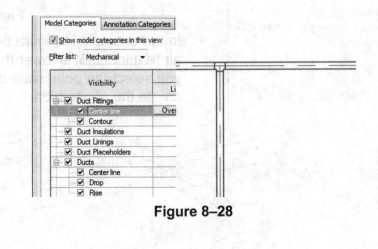

Figure 8–28

8.4 Modifying Ducts

Learning Objectives

- Change ducts using connectors and standard modify tools.
- Convert ducts and duct types by changing the type of duct used in a run, by switching placeholder ducts with standard ducts, and changing rigid ducts to flex ducts.
- Add insulation and lining to ducts.
- Modify duct justifications and work with duct fittings.

Ducts can be modified using a variety of standard modifying tools and other specialty tools, such as duct sizing, converting duct placeholders to ducts, changing rigid ducts to flexible ducts, adding insulation and lining, and modifying the justification of ducts.

Changing Ducts using Standard Tools

You can modify ducts using universal methods by making changes in Properties, in the Options bar, and by using temporary dimensions, controls, and connectors. Modify tools, such as **Move**, **Rotate**, **Trim/Extend**, and **Align** help you place the ducts at the correct locations.

Often a change using these tools automatically applies the correct fittings. For example, in Figure 8–29, the *Edit End Offset* control was changed from **12'-0"** on the left to **10'-0"** on the right and the appropriate duct fittings are automatically placed to facilitate the change in elevation.

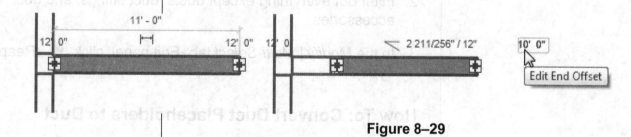

Figure 8–29

Converting Ducts and Duct Types

After placing ducts, you can change the type of the entire duct run including fittings. If the definition of a duct type has been changed you can reapply the type to existing duct runs. You can also convert duct placeholders to ducts and rigid duct to flex duct if it is connected to an air terminal.

How To: Change the Type of Duct Runs

1. Select the duct run and filter out everything except ducts, duct accessories, and duct fittings.

2. In the *Modify | Multi-Select* tab>Edit panel, click (Change Type).

3. In the Type Selector, select a new type of duct run. This changes not only the duct but also any related fittings.

   - In Figure 8–30, the type **Rectangular Duct: Radius Elbows / Tees** was changed to the type **Round Duct: Taps**.

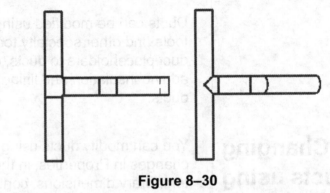

Figure 8–30

How To: Reapply the Type to Duct Runs

1. Select a single duct run. You can select different runs, but they must be all of the same duct type and same system. If you select duct runs in different systems, the software prompts you to select one system to which to reapply the type.

2. Filter out everything except ducts, duct fittings, and duct accessories.

3. In the *Modify | Multi-Select* tab>Edit panel, click (Reapply Type).

How To: Convert Duct Placeholders to Duct

1. Select the duct placeholder(s).

2. In the *Modify | Duct Placeholders* tab>Edit panel, click

   (Convert Placeholder).

3. The placeholder(s) is changed into the duct type that has been selected earlier, as shown in Figure 8–31.

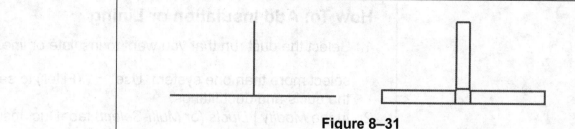

Figure 8–31

How To: Convert Rigid Duct to Flex Duct

1. In the *Systems* tab>HVAC panel, click 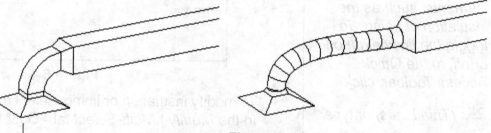 (Convert to Flex Duct) or type **CV**.
2. In the Options Bar set the *Max Length.* The default is **6'-0"**, a standard code requirement.
3. Select the air terminal connected to the rigid duct. The duct is converted as shown in Figure 8–32.

Figure 8–32

- This command only works if the rigid duct is connected to an air terminal.

Adding Insulation and Lining

When you select duct runs, you can add insulation, lining, and specify the type and thickness. This information displays as a thin line outside of the duct for insulation and a dashed line inside the duct for lining, as shown in Figure 8–33.

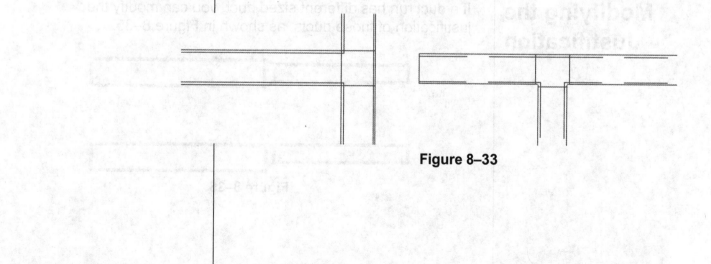

Figure 8–33

How To: Add Insulation or Lining

1. Select the duct run that you want to insulate or line. You can select more than one system. Use 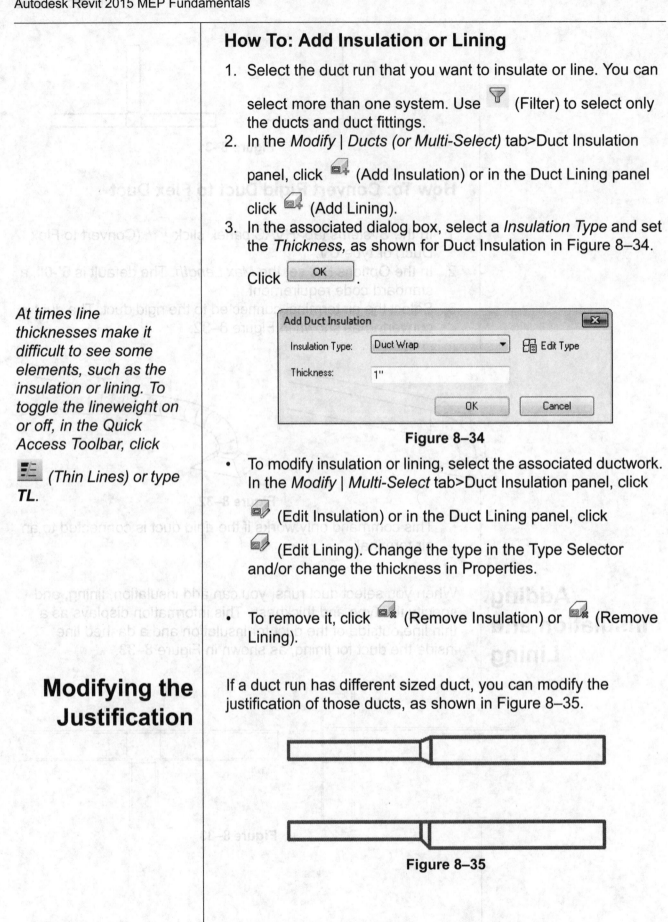 (Filter) to select only the ducts and duct fittings.
2. In the *Modify | Ducts (or Multi-Select)* tab>Duct Insulation panel, click (Add Insulation) or in the Duct Lining panel click (Add Lining).
3. In the associated dialog box, select a *Insulation Type* and set the *Thickness,* as shown for Duct Insulation in Figure 8–34. Click OK .

At times line thicknesses make it difficult to see some elements, such as the insulation or lining. To toggle the lineweight on or off, in the Quick Access Toolbar, click

(Thin Lines) or type **TL**.

Add Duct Insulation

Insulation Type: Duct Wrap ▾ Edit Type

Thickness: 1"

OK   Cancel

Figure 8–34

• To modify insulation or lining, select the associated ductwork. In the *Modify | Multi-Select* tab>Duct Insulation panel, click (Edit Insulation) or in the Duct Lining panel, click (Edit Lining). Change the type in the Type Selector and/or change the thickness in Properties.

• To remove it, click (Remove Insulation) or (Remove Lining).

Modifying the Justification

If a duct run has different sized duct, you can modify the justification of those ducts, as shown in Figure 8–35.

Figure 8–35

How To: Modify Duct Justifications

1. Select the duct run.

2. In the *Modify | Multi-Select* tab>Edit panel, click (Justify).

3. To specify the point on the duct that you want to justify around, in the *Justification Editor* tab>Justify panel, click

   (Control Point) to cycle between the end point references.

   - The alignment location displays as an arrow, as shown in Figure 8–36.

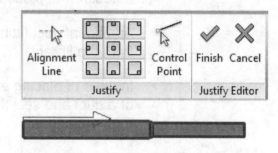

Figure 8–36

4. To indicate the required alignment, either click one of the nine alignment buttons in the Justify panel, or in a 3D view, use

   (Alignment Line) to select the required dashed line, as shown in Figure 8–37.

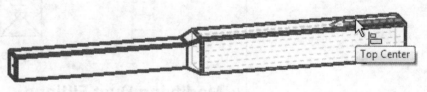

Figure 8–37

Working with Fittings

Many fittings are automatically applied as you create the ductwork, but you might also want to add new ductwork such as the Oval to Round Transition fitting, as shown in Figure 8–38.

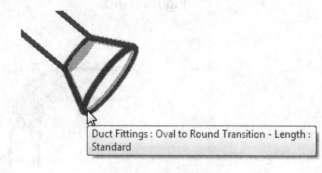

Figure 8–38

How To: Add Duct Fittings

1. In the *Systems* tab>HVAC panel, click 👓 (Duct Fitting).
2. In the Type Selector, select the type of fitting you want to use.
3. Move the cursor over the appropriate connector in the ductwork. Only usable locations are highlighted.
4. Click on the location. The duct fitting resizes to fit the duct.

- 📄 (Duct Accessories) is very similar to Duct Fittings. Select the type of accessory, such as a fire damper, filter, or smoke detector and place it at an appropriate connector.

- Additional duct fittings and duct accessories can be loaded from the library.

- Instead of placing endcap fittings, right-click on the open end of a duct and select **Cap Open End**, as shown in Figure 8–39.

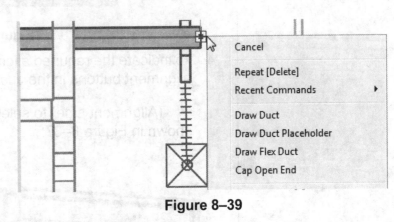

Figure 8–39

Modifying Duct Fittings

Duct Fittings, whether added automatically or manually can be modified using the Type Selector, Properties, the Options Bar, and a variety of connectors and controls. For example, an Elbow can be changed to a Tee by clicking a control, as shown in Figure 8–40.

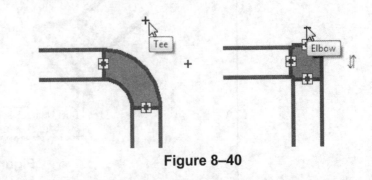

Figure 8–40

Hint: Creating a 3D Section box

When you are working in a multistory building frequently you need to isolate one part of the building in a 3D view, as shown in Figure 8–41, so you can check for interferences and other problems. You can do this by adding a 3D section box created from a plan, elevation, or other 3D view.

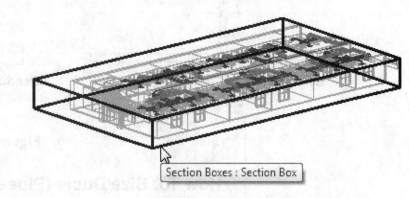

Section Boxes : Section Box

Figure 8–41

Open a 3D view, right-click on the ViewCube and select **Orient to View>Floor Plans>***name of view* as shown in Figure 8–42.

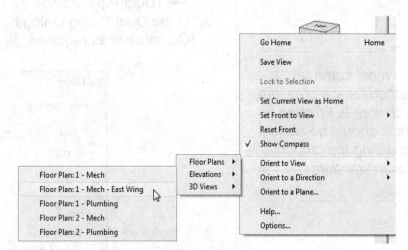

Figure 8–42

The view remains 3D but rotates to the orientation of the selected view. You can then use the ViewCube or mouse to rotate it to an appropriate 3D orientation.

- This works best if you have floor plans with dependent views but also works with callouts of floor plans and elevations. Modify the crop window size if you do not see the model.

Duct Sizing

It is easiest to draw ducts (or pipes) using the default sizes provided by the opening sizes of the equipment, or as preset in the Mechanical Settings, however these are often incorrect for the system. The **Duct/Pipe Sizing** tool uses a specified sizing method and constraints to determine how to correctly size the pipes or ducts, as shown in Figure 8–43.

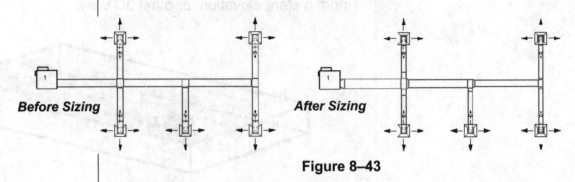

Before Sizing   *After Sizing*

Figure 8–43

How To: Size Ducts (Pipes)

1. Select a duct system.
2. In the *Modify | Multi-Select* tab>Analysis panel, click
   (Duct/Pipe Sizing).
3. In the Duct Sizing dialog box, set the *Sizing Method* and *Constraints* as required, as shown in Figure 8–44.

*The most common method for low pressure duct work is **Friction**. Ducts should be sized according to company design standards.*

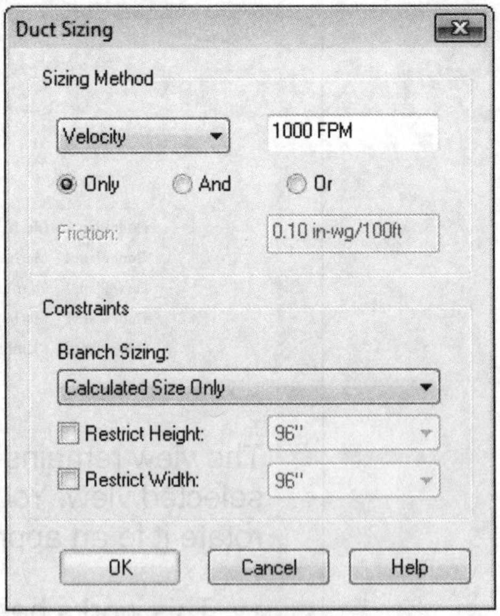

Figure 8–44

4. Click OK .

- If you select only one duct, it analyzes just that one set of connections. Select the entire system to ensure that all of the connections are analyzed.

- Once you make a change to the system, you need to run the software again, as shown in Figure 8–45 where the CFM was changed on two air terminals. Compare this to Figure 8–43.

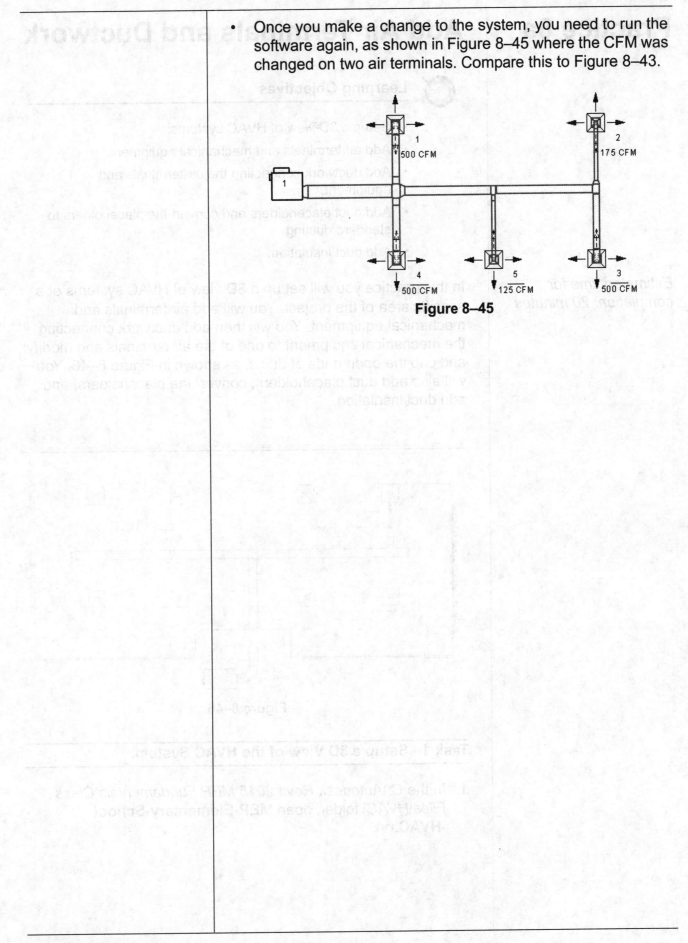

Figure 8–45

Practice 8a

Add Air Terminals and Ductwork

 Learning Objectives

- Setup a 3D view of HVAC systems.
- Add air terminals and mechanical equipment.
- Add ductwork connecting the air terminals and equipment.
- Add duct placeholders and convert the placeholders to standard ducting.
- Add duct insulation.

Estimated time for completion: 20 minutes

In this practice you will set up a 3D view of HVAC systems of a specific area of the project. You will add air terminals and mechanical equipment. You will then add ductwork connecting the mechanical equipment to one of the air terminals and modify and cap the open ends of ducts, as shown in Figure 8–46. You will also add duct placeholders, convert the placeholders, and add duct insulation.

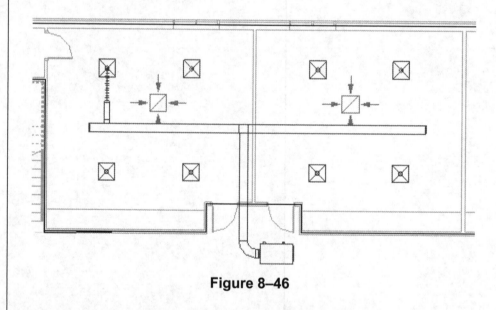

Figure 8–46

Task 1 - Setup a 3D View of the HVAC System.

1. In the *C:\Autodesk Revit 2015 MEP Fundamentals Class Files\HVAC* folder, open **MEP-Elementary-School -HVAC.rvt**.

2. In the Project Browser, expand Mechanical>HVAC>*Floor Plans* and then expand the **01 MECHANICAL PLAN** view to see the dependent views as shown in Figure 8–47.

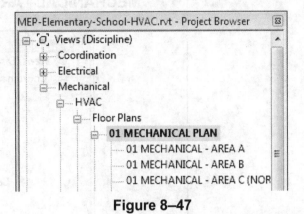

Figure 8–47

3. Open the **01 MECHANICAL - AREA B** view and zoom in on one of the existing systems and review the components of the system.

4. In the Quick Access Toolbar, click 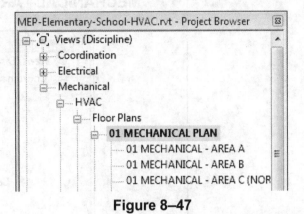 (3D View). The entire building displays and you cannot see the HVAC equipment.

5. Right-click on the ViewCube and select **Orient to View>Floor Plans>Floor Plan: 01 MECHANICAL-AREA B**.

6. Rotate the view using the ViewCube to see it in 3D. The box that *cuts* the view is a section box as shown in Figure 8–48.

The exact orientation of this view and the ones that follow depend on your selection.

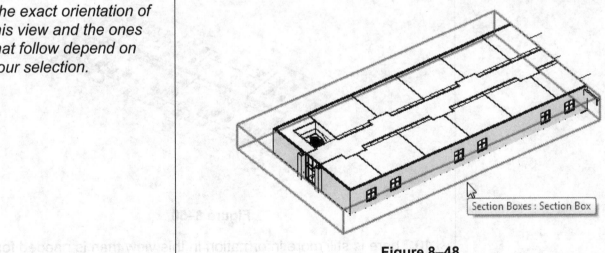

Section Boxes : Section Box

Figure 8–48

7. In the Project Browser, expand Coordination>All>**3D Views** to display the default **{3D}** view, as shown in Figure 8–49. Right-click on it (or press <F2>) and rename it as **01 MECHANICAL - AREA B 3D**.

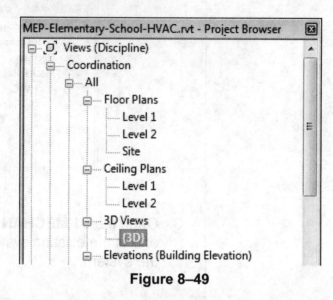

Figure 8–49

8. In Properties, change the *Discipline* to **Mechanical** and the *Sub-Discipline* to **HVAC**.

9. The view moves to Mechanical>HVAC>**3D Views** and the view changes to match the defaults for this type of view as shown in Figure 8–50.

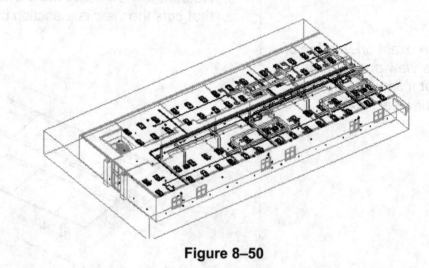

Figure 8–50

10. There is still more information in this view than is needed for the practice including plumbing, electrical, and fire systems. Type **VG**.

11. In the Visibility/Graphics Override dialog box, *Model Categories* tab verify that the *Filter list* is set to **Mechanical**.

12. To select the only elements you want to see, at the bottom of the dialog box, click [All]. Click in one box to clear all of the categories. Click [None] to clear all of the categories.

13. Select the following categories:
    - Air Terminals
    - Duct Accessories
    - Duct Fittings
    - Duct Insulations
    - Duct Linings
    - Duct Placeholders
    - Ducts
    - Flex Ducts
    - Mechanical Equipment

14. Click [OK]. The HVAC Systems are now easier to view as shown in Figure 8–51.

Use this view as required to verify and correct any problems as you create additional systems.

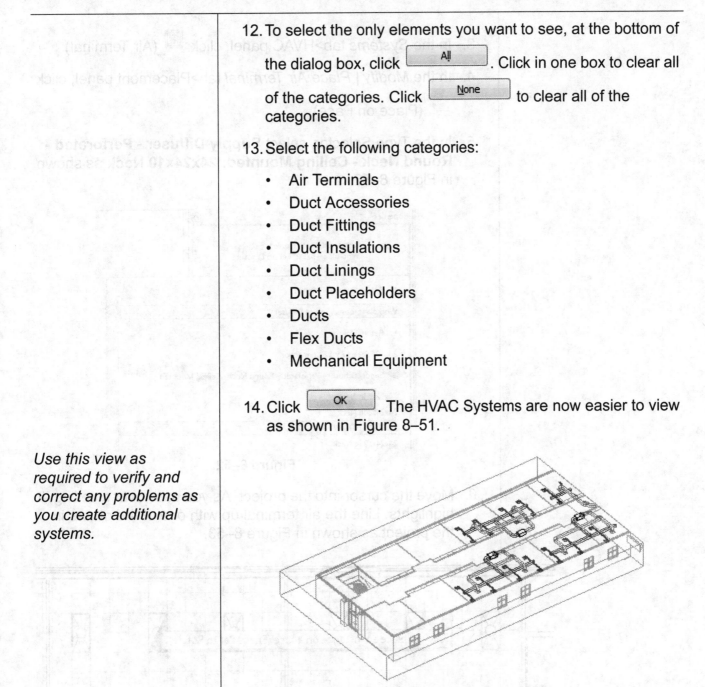

Figure 8–51

Task 2 - Add Air Terminals and Mechanical Equipment.

1. Open the Coordination>MEP>Ceiling Plans**>01 RCP** view. In this view you can see the locations of the ceiling grid and light fixtures provided in the architectural project.

2. Zoom in to the west end of the south wing where there is no HVAC system.

3. In the *Systems* tab>HVAC panel, click 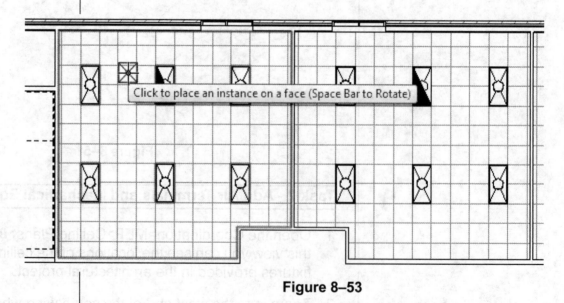 (Air Terminal).

4. In the *Modify | Place Air Terminal* tab>Placement panel, click
(Place on Face).

5. In the Type Selector, select **Supply Diffuser - Perforated - Round Neck - Ceiling Mounted: 24x24x10 Neck** as shown in Figure 8–52.

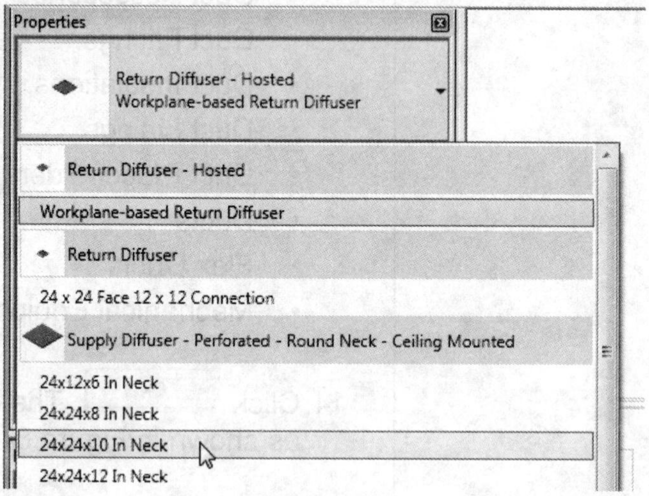

Figure 8–52

6. Move the cursor into the project. As you pass over a ceiling, it highlights. Line the air terminal up with one of the others in the project as shown in Figure 8–53.

Figure 8–53

Use 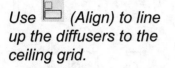 (Align) to line up the diffusers to the ceiling grid.

7. Place the rest of the air terminals as shown in Figure 8–54.

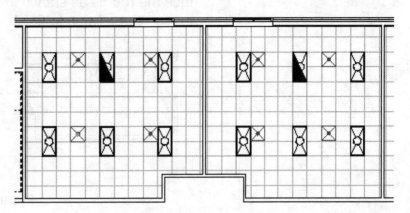

Figure 8–54

8. Select one of the air terminals. In Properties look at the *Elevation*. It is grayed out because the air terminal is attached to the face of the ceiling which is at 9'-0".

You do not need to change the Elevation as it is set by the face.

9. Start the Air Terminal command again and select the type **Return Diffuser - Hosted: Workplane-based Return Diffuser.** In Properties change the *Offset* to **0'-0"** if it is not already set to **0'-0"**.

10. In the *Modify | Place Air Terminal* tab>Placement panel, click (Place on Face). Add two return diffusers as shown in Figure 8–55.

When the return diffusers are inserted, they display in magenta because of the view filters.

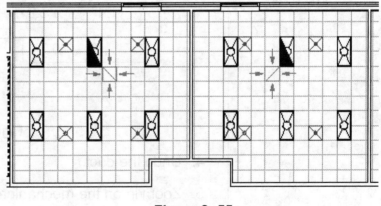

Figure 8–55

11. In the *Systems* tab>Mechanical panel, click 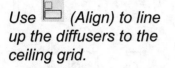 (Mechanical Equipment).

12. In the Type Selector, select **Indoor AHU - Horizontal - Chilled Water Coil: Unit Size 24** and set the *offset* to **9'-3"**.

13. Press <Spacebar> to rotate it around until the connectors face the rooms as shown in Figure 8–56. Click to place it and press <Esc> twice to finish.

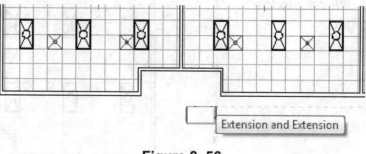

Figure 8–56

14. Save the project.

Task 3 - Add ductwork.

1. Open the Mechanical>HVAC>Floor Plans>01 MECHANICAL PLAN>**01 MECHANICAL - AREA B** view.

2. Select the mechanical equipment and right-click on the left connector and select **Draw Duct**.

3. Start drawing the duct. You can see that the duct is too large and it is a return air duct (magenta) rather than a supply air duct (blue) as shown in Figure 8–57.

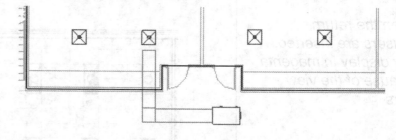

Figure 8–57

4. Undo the duct.

5. Zoom in on the mechanical equipment. In the Quick Access Toolbar, click ![icon](Thin Lines) so you can see the physical of the unit.

6. The unit needs to be mirrored to have the supply air on the left. Select the unit. In the *Modify | Mechanical Equipment* tab>Modify panel, click ![icon](Mirror - Draw Axis).

7. In the Options Bar, clear **Copy**.

8. Draw a vertical axis from the midpoint of the unit as shown in Figure 8–58.

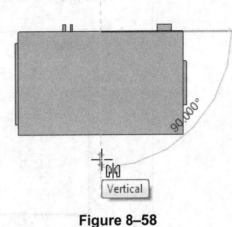

Figure 8–58

9. The unit is flipped over in place. In Properties, verify that the *Offset* is set to **9'-3"**. The unit is reversed in place.

10. Right-click on the left connector again and select **Draw Duct**. This time the size of the duct is smaller. The Width and Height default to the size of the opening in the equipment.

When you type in dimensions for the size of duct you do not need to add the inch mark like you do when drawing dimensions. The software knows that duct sizes are in inches.

11. In the Type Selector, select **Rectangular Duct: Radius Elbows / Taps**.

12. In the Options Bar set the *Width* and the *Height* to **12"** and the *Offset* to **10'-0".**

13. Draw the duct following a path similar to that shown in Figure 8–59. Extend the end of the duct past the air terminals. Press <Esc> twice.

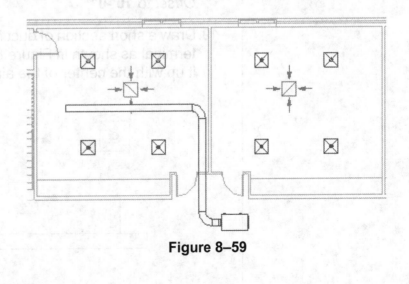

Figure 8–59

14. Select one of the top air terminals in the same room as the ductwork. Right-click on the connector and select **Draw Flex Duct**. Connect the flex duct to the rectangular duct as shown in Figure 8–60.

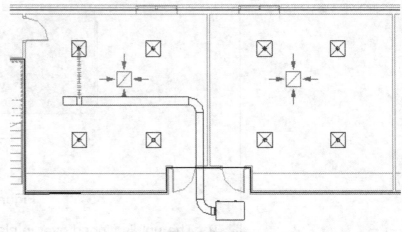

Figure 8–60

15. Select the new flex duct. In the *Modify | Flex Duct* tab, the Warning panel displays because there is a problem. Click

    ⚠️ (Show Related Warnings). You should get a warning stating that the flex duct length exceeds the maximum specified length of 6'-0".

16. There needs to be an additional length of rectangular duct extending out toward the air terminal. Undo the flex duct.

17. In the *Systems* tab>HVAC panel, click 📦 (Duct).

18. In the Options Bar, set the *Width* and *Height* to **8"** and the *Offset* to **10'-0"**.

19. Draw a short section of duct from the main duct toward the air terminal as shown in Figure 8–61. Use alignment lines to line it up with the center of the air terminal.

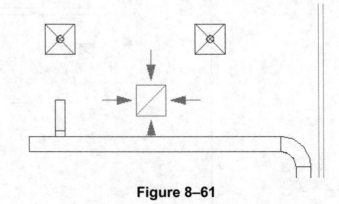

Figure 8–61

20. Repeat the process of selecting the air terminal and drawing flex duct to this new section. Ensure you connect to the *point snap* of the rectangular duct.

21. Select the new flex duct again. This time no warning displays.

Task 4 - Modify and Add Duct Fittings.

1. Zoom in on the rectangular elbow that turns to the left and select it. Click on the Tee control as shown in Figure 8–62.

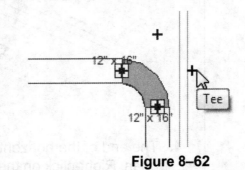

Figure 8–62

2. Right-click on the new tee and draw a duct to the right, as shown in Figure 8–63. Click ⌖ (Modify) to end the command.

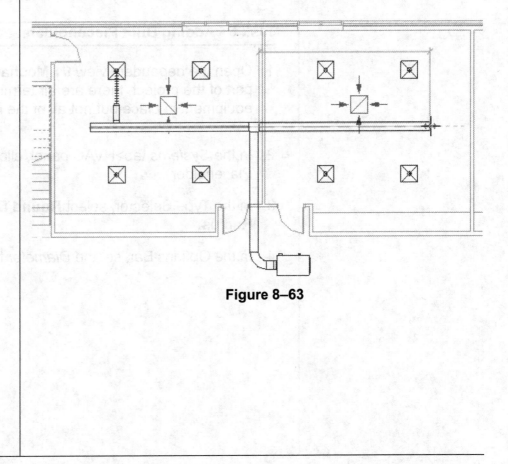

Figure 8–63

3. Open the Mechanical>HVAC>3D Views>**01 MECHANICAL - AREA B 3D** view and review the ductwork you have drawn so far to see the connections as shown in Figure 8–64.

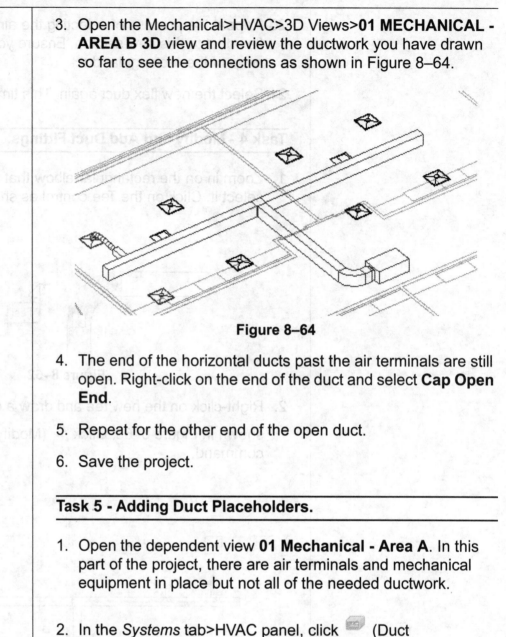

Figure 8–64

4. The end of the horizontal ducts past the air terminals are still open. Right-click on the end of the duct and select **Cap Open End**.

5. Repeat for the other end of the open duct.

6. Save the project.

Task 5 - Adding Duct Placeholders.

---

1. Open the dependent view **01 Mechanical - Area A**. In this part of the project, there are air terminals and mechanical equipment in place but not all of the needed ductwork.

2. In the *Systems* tab>HVAC panel, click 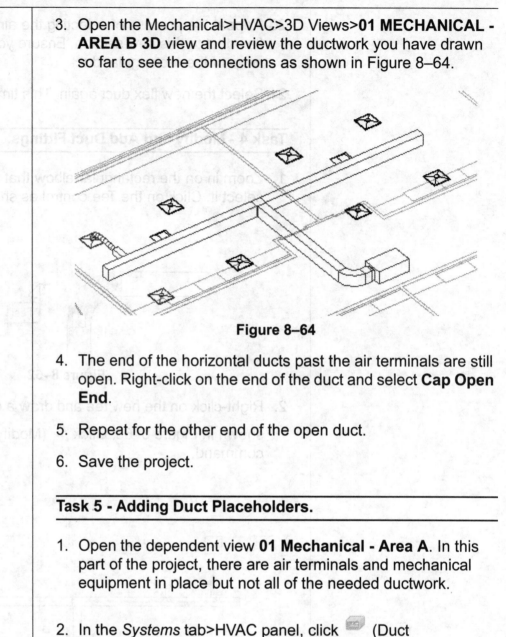 (Duct Placeholder).

3. In the Type Selector, select **Round Duct: Taps / Short Radius.**

4. In the Options Bar, set the *Diameter* to **8"** and *Offset* to **11'-0"**

5. Snap to the Point connector for Supply Air in one of the AHU, as shown in Figure 8–65.

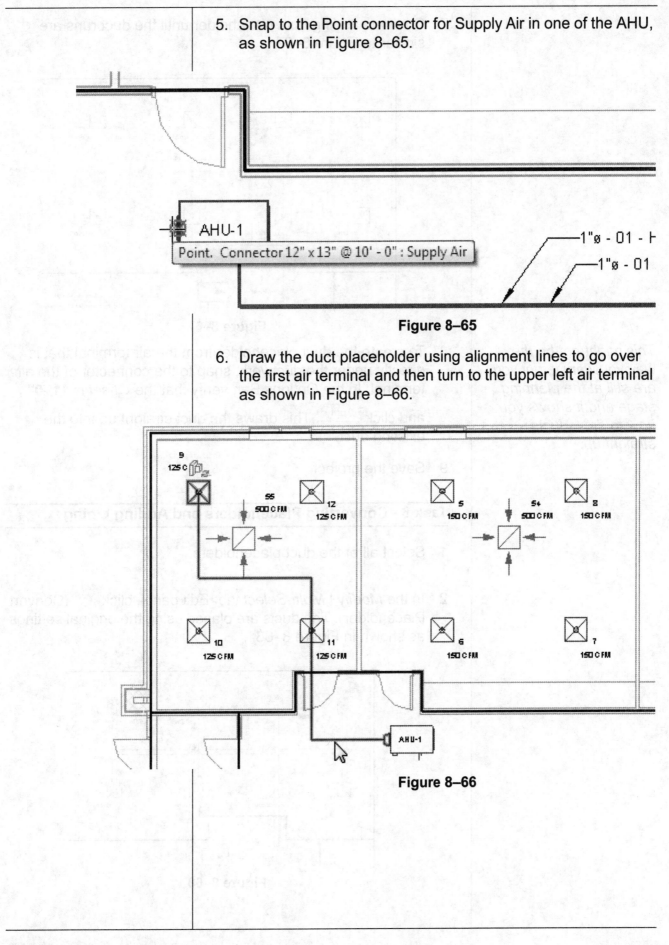

Figure 8–65

6. Draw the duct placeholder using alignment lines to go over the first air terminal and then turn to the upper left air terminal as shown in Figure 8–66.

Figure 8–66

7. Continue adding duct placeholder until the duct runs are similar to Figure 8–67.

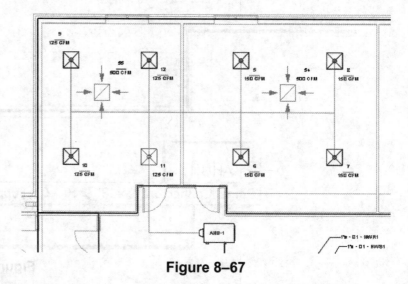

Figure 8–67

This might not be the way you want it, but you are still at the planning stage and it shows you how to draw ducts straight up.

8. To create the duct placeholder from the air terminal that is directly under the ductwork, snap to the connector of the air terminal. In the Options Bar, verify that the *Offset* is **11'-0"** and click Apply. This draws the duct straight up into the existing duct.

9. Save the project.

Task 6 - Converting Placeholders and Adding Lining

1. Select all of the duct placeholders.

2. In the *Modify | Multi-Select* tab>Edit panel, click ⬐ (Convert Placeholder). The ducts are placed using the original settings as shown in Figure 8–68.

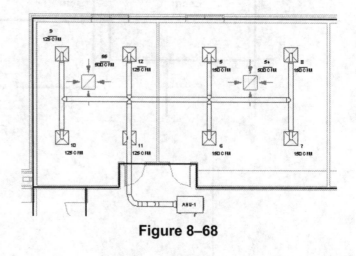

Figure 8–68

3. Select all of the new ducts and fittings.

4. In the *Modify | Multi-Select t*ab>expanded Duct Lining panel, click 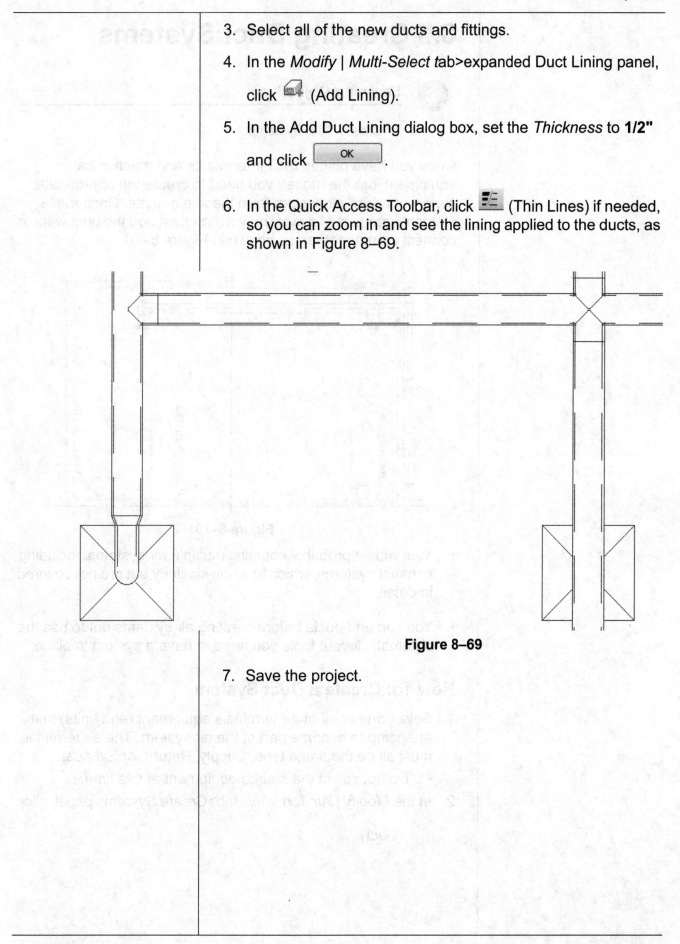 (Add Lining).

5. In the Add Duct Lining dialog box, set the *Thickness* to **1/2"** and click OK .

6. In the Quick Access Toolbar, click (Thin Lines) if needed, so you can zoom in and see the lining applied to the ducts, as shown in Figure 8–69.

Figure 8–69

7. Save the project.

8.5 Creating Duct Systems

Learning Objective

• Create Duct Systems.

Once you have placed the air terminals and mechanical equipment into the model, you need to create the appropriate supply or return air system from these elements. Once the elements are part of a system, you can then add the duct work to connect them together, as shown in Figure 8–70.

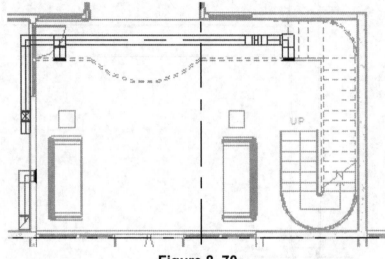

Figure 8–70

• Your model probably contains multiple air systems, including exhaust systems, which function similarly but are not covered in detail.

• You can add ducts before creating air systems but to use the automatic layout tools you need to have a system in place.

How To: Create a Duct System

1. Select one or all of air terminals/equipment (end units) that are going to become part of the air system. The air terminals must all be the same type: Supply, Return, or Exhaust.

   • Do not select the source equipment at this time.

2. In the *Modify | Air Terminals* tab>Create Systems panel, click

   (Duct).

3. In the Create Duct System dialog box, the *System type* is preset if you selected a specific type of air terminal. In the *System name* field, enter a name as shown in Figure 8–71, and click .

You can select a type from the System type drop-down list, if you selected mechanical equipment only.

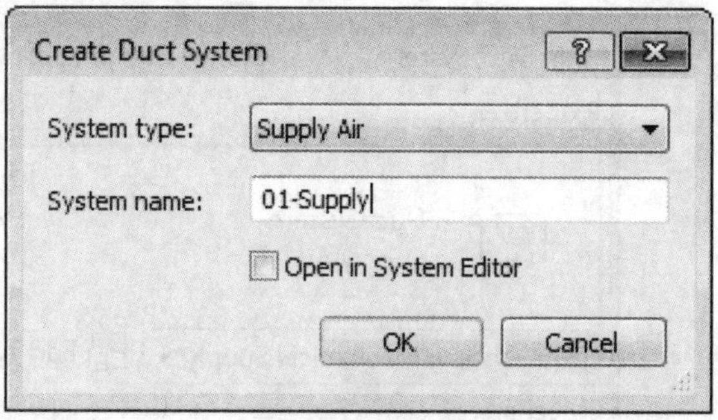

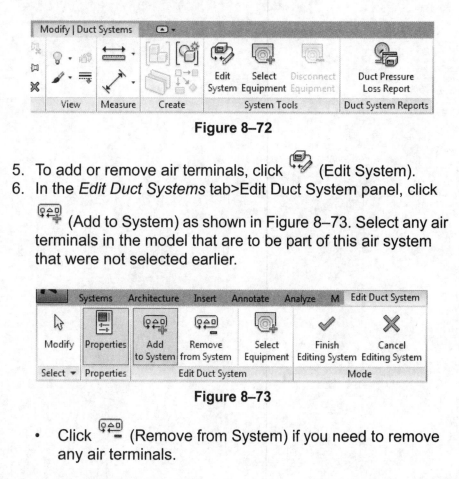

Figure 8–71

- You can also right-click on an air terminal or mechanical equipment connector and select **Create Duct System**.

4. In the *Modify | Duct Systems* tab>System Tools panel, as shown in Figure 8–72, click (Select Equipment) to select the air handling equipment for the system.

Figure 8–72

5. To add or remove air terminals, click (Edit System).
6. In the *Edit Duct Systems* tab>Edit Duct System panel, click (Add to System) as shown in Figure 8–73. Select any air terminals in the model that are to be part of this air system that were not selected earlier.

Figure 8–73

- Click (Remove from System) if you need to remove any air terminals.

7. You can select the mechanical equipment for this air system if you did not select it earlier.

8. In the Options Bar, you can select the *System Equipment* and then modify the *System Name* in Properties, as shown in Figure 8–74.

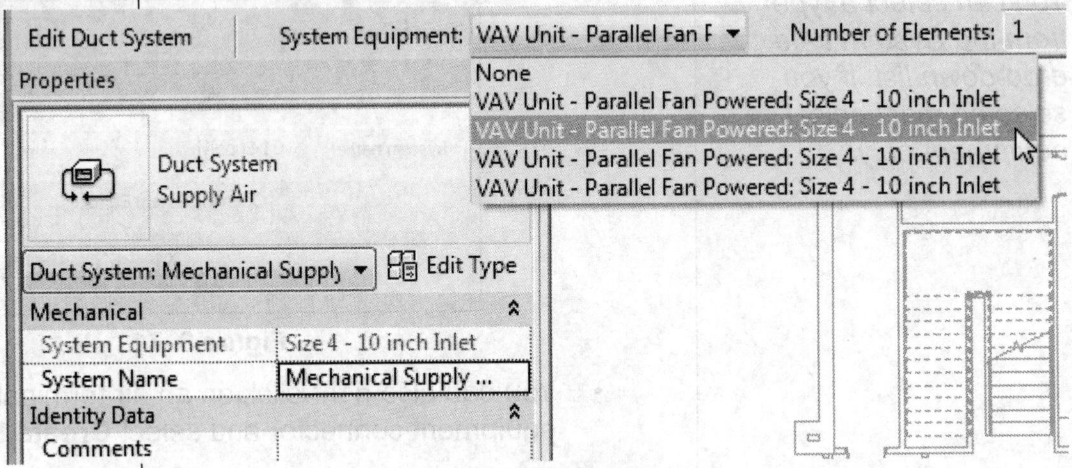

Figure 8–74

9. Click ✓ (Finish Editing System) to accept all components and complete the creation of the air system.

8.6 Automatic Ductwork Layouts

Learning Objectives

- Set up Mechanical Settings related to ductwork.
- Generate automatic ductwork layouts.

Once you have created the duct system, you can automatically create the ductwork layout. These tools create various routes for the ductwork as shown in Figure 8–75.

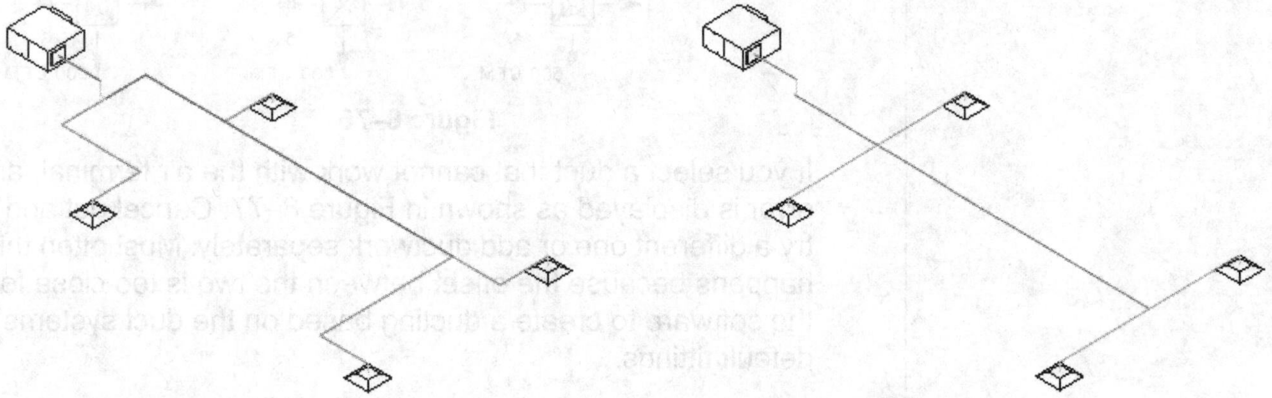

Figure 8–75

Automatic Ductwork

If you have just one or two air terminals that need to be connected to existing ductwork, you can use the **Connect Into** tool. If you have a more complex duct system then use the **Generate Layout** tool.

How To: Connect an Air Terminal to existing Ductwork

1. Select the Air Terminal that needs to be connected to existing ducts.
2. In the *Modify | Air Terminals* tab>Layout panel, click
   (Connect Into).

3. Select the duct to connect as shown in Figure 8–76.

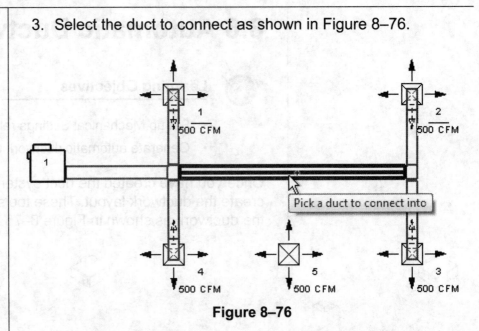

Figure 8–76

- If you select a duct that cannot work with the air terminal, an error is displayed as shown in Figure 8–77. Cancel out and try a different one or add ductwork separately. Most often this happens because the offset between the two is too close for the software to create a ducting based on the duct systems' default fittings.

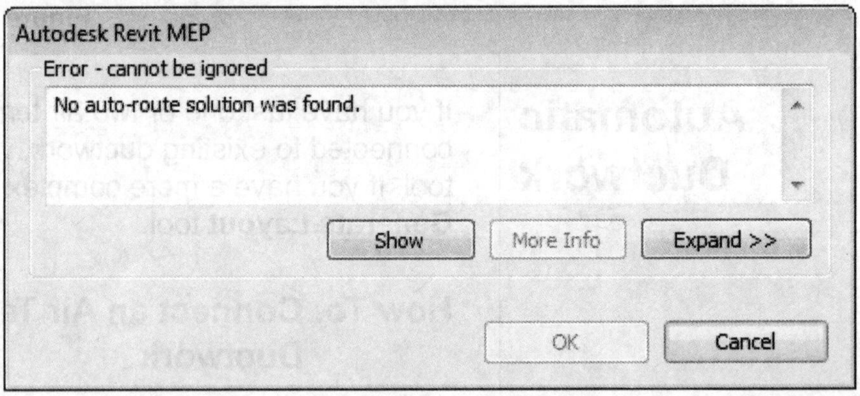

Figure 8–77

- It is also possible that the duct is the wrong system type. The duct *System Type* can be changed in the Properties of the duct if needed.

- This process automatically connects the air terminal to a system.

How To: Generate an automatic ductwork layout

You can view the solutions in the plan or a 3D view.

1. Select one of the air terminals or hover over an air terminal or the mechanical equipment in a system and press <Tab> until you see the outline of the system, as shown in Figure 8–78. Click to select the system.

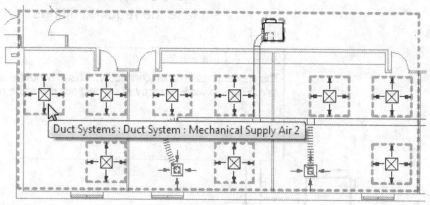

Figure 8–78

2. In the *Modify | Duct Systems* tab>Layout panel, click
   ![icon] (Generate Layout).

3. In the Options Bar, click Settings ... to open the Duct Conversions Settings dialog box and set the duct types and offsets that apply to this layout. (These settings are specific to this system only. Global settings are defined in Mechanical Settings as previously described.)

4. In the Options Bar, select a *Solution Type,* as shown in Figure 8–79, and click ![icon] (Next Solution) or ![icon] (Previous Solution) to cycle through the possible options.

Generate Layout	Solution Type	Network	1 of 2 ◁I I▷	Settings ...
Properties		× Network		
		Perimeter		
		Intersections		

Figure 8–79

Network	Creates a layout with the main segment through the center of a bounding box around the entire system and the branches at 90 degrees from the main branch.
Perimeter	Creates a layout with segments being placed on three of the four sides, and one with segments being placed on all four sides. (The **Inset** value is the offset between the bounding box and components.)
Intersections	Creates a layout with segments extending from each connector of the components. Where they intersect perpendicularly, proposed intersection junctions are created.

- The blue lines identify the main duct system and green lines identify branch systems.

- Gold lines show a potential open connection that could cause problems when the ductwork is added as shown in Figure 8–80, or other issues related to adequate space to place the required fittings.

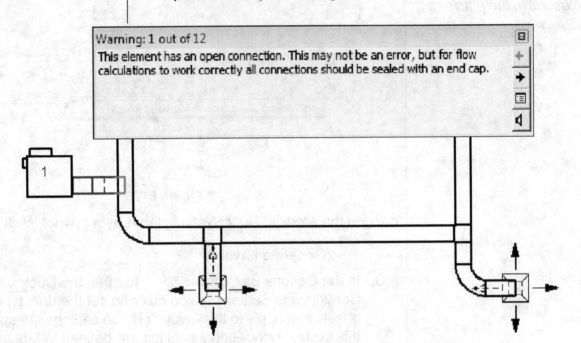

Figure 8–80

5. In the *Generate Layout* tab>Generate Layout panel, click

   (Finish Layout) when you have a solution that looks best.

Settings for Solutions

In the Options Bar, clicking Settings ... opens the Duct Conversion Settings dialog box, as shown in Figure 8–81. You can modify the settings before or as you are selecting solutions to provide the best options. For example, having the *Branch Offset* too low (i.e. 9'-0") can cause issues if the *Offset* of the Air Terminal value is close (i.e. 8'-0"). Also, you should specify a flex duct in the Branch if you want air terminals automatically connected that way.

Duct Conversion Settings	

Main
Branch

System Type: Supply Air

Setting	Value
Duct Type	Rectangular Duct: Radius E
Offset	9' 0"

OK   Cancel

Figure 8–81

How To: Customize the Layout

1. Using 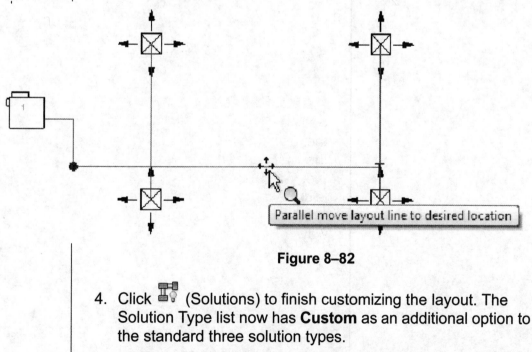 (Solutions), select a layout design similar to what you want to use.
2. In the *Generate Layout* tab>Modify Layout panel, click
   (Edit Layout).
3. Select one of the layout lines. You can use the move control to change the location of the line as shown in Figure 8–82. You can also change the height of the offset by clicking on the number control.

Parallel move layout line to desired location

Figure 8–82

4. Click (Solutions) to finish customizing the layout. The Solution Type list now has **Custom** as an additional option to the standard three solution types.
   - The software only permits one custom option at a time.

5. In the *Generate Layout* tab>Generate Layout panel, click

    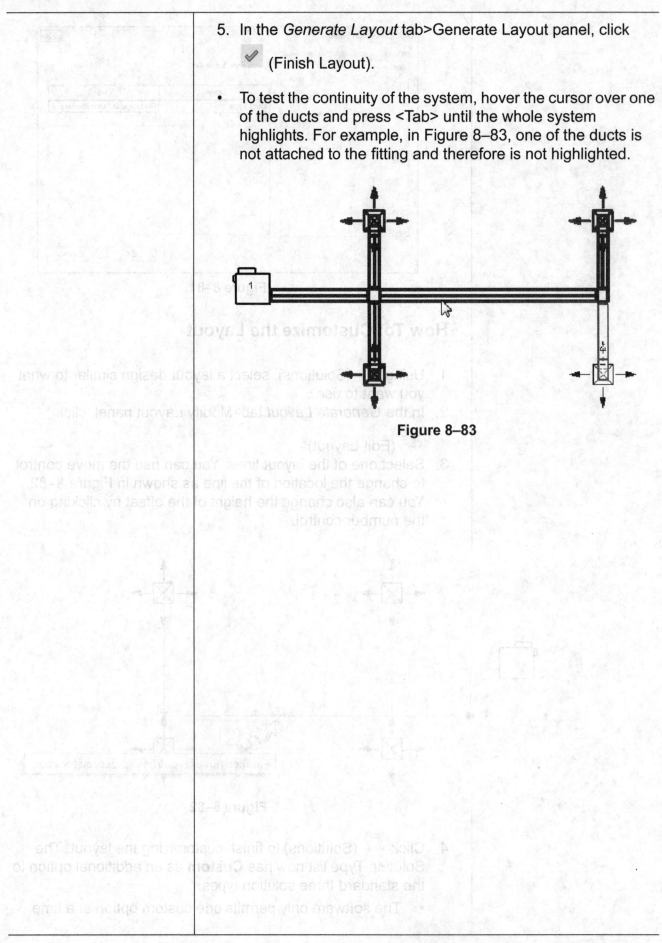 (Finish Layout).

*   To test the continuity of the system, hover the cursor over one of the ducts and press <Tab> until the whole system highlights. For example, in Figure 8–83, one of the ducts is not attached to the fitting and therefore is not highlighted.

Figure 8–83

Practice 8b

Add Duct Systems

Learning Objectives

- Create ducts using the **Generate Layout** tool with both standard and custom layouts.
- Modify ductwork after it has been placed.
- Check the information using existing schedules.

Estimated time for completion: 20 minutes

In this practice you will create supply ducts using the **Generate Layout** tool, and modify the ductwork in the layout and after it has been placed. You will also create a custom layout for the return ducts and modify the ductwork. The final systems are shown in Figure 8–84. You will then check and modify information in premade schedules.

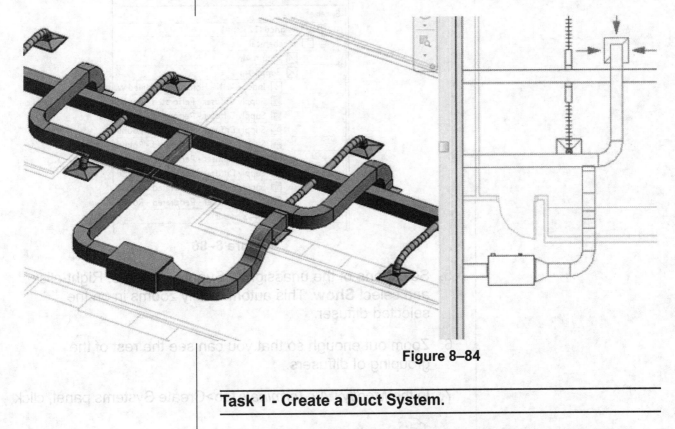

Figure 8–84

Task 1 - Create a Duct System.

1. In the *C:\Autodesk Revit 2015 MEP Fundamentals Class Files\HVAC* folder, open **MEP-Elementary-School -Systems.rvt**.

The System Browser can be docked with the Project Browser and Properties.

2. Open the System Browser. Press <F9> or in the *View* tab>Windows panel, expand 🗗 (User Interface) and select **System Browser**.

---

3. In the System Browser, change the *View* to **Systems** and All Disciplines to **Mechanical,** as shown in Figure 8–85.

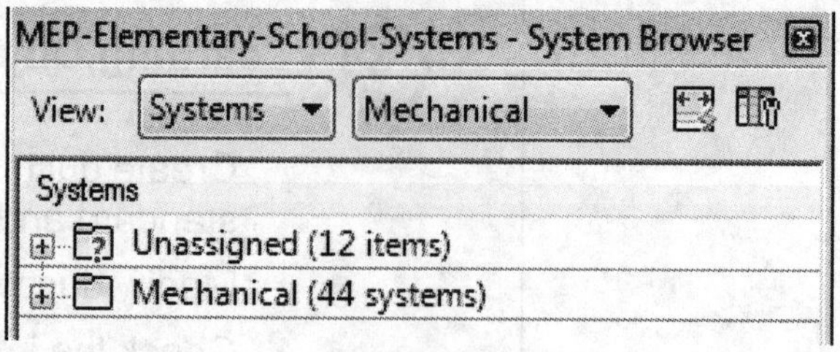

Figure 8–85

4. In the System Browser, expand Unassigned>Mechanical> *Supply Air*. There are several Air Terminals and an AHU listed, as shown in Figure 8–86.

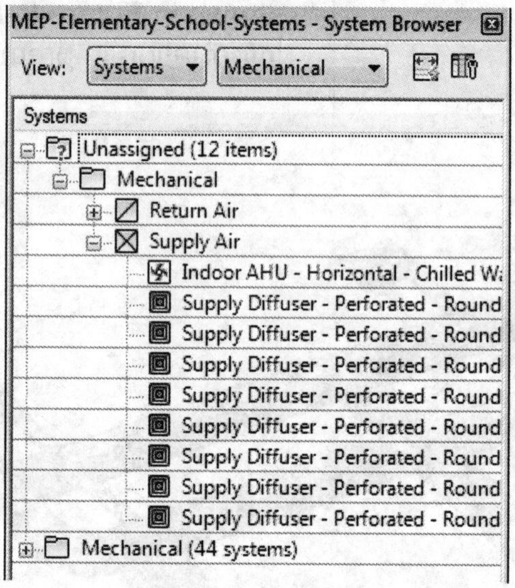

Figure 8–86

5. Select one of the unassigned Supply Diffusers. Right-click and select **Show**. This automatically zooms in on the selected diffuser.

6. Zoom out enough so that you can see the rest of the grouping of diffusers.

7. In the *Modify | Air Terminals* tab>Create Systems panel, click (Duct).

8. In the Create Duct System dialog box, type the name **01 - SA08,** select **Open in System Editor** and click ⬚ OK ⬚.

9. In the *Edit Duct System* tab>Edit Duct System panel, click (Select Equipment) and select the nearby AHU unit.

10. Click 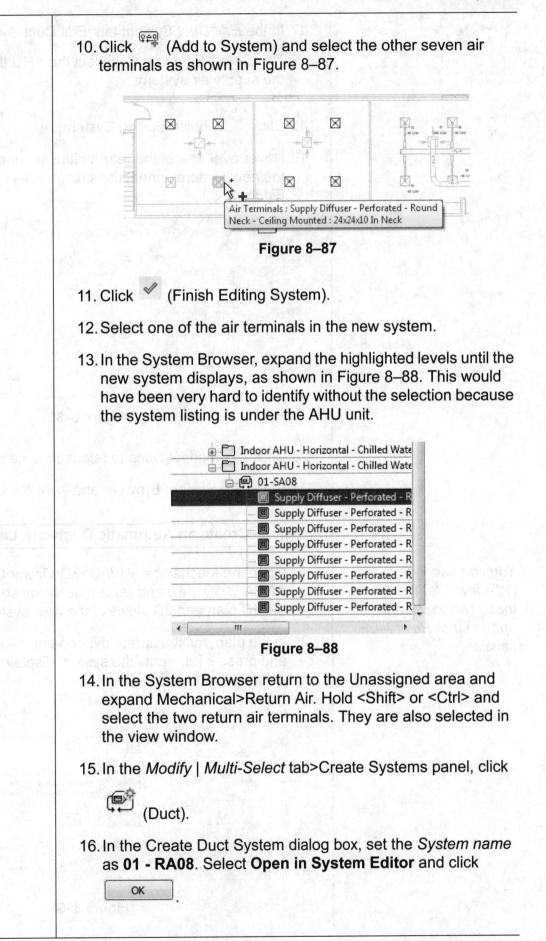 (Add to System) and select the other seven air terminals as shown in Figure 8–87.

Figure 8–87

11. Click ✓ (Finish Editing System).

12. Select one of the air terminals in the new system.

13. In the System Browser, expand the highlighted levels until the new system displays, as shown in Figure 8–88. This would have been very hard to identify without the selection because the system listing is under the AHU unit.

Figure 8–88

14. In the System Browser return to the Unassigned area and expand Mechanical>Return Air. Hold <Shift> or <Ctrl> and select the two return air terminals. They are also selected in the view window.

15. In the *Modify | Multi-Select* tab>Create Systems panel, click 🔲 (Duct).

16. In the Create Duct System dialog box, set the *System name* as **01 - RA08**. Select **Open in System Editor** and click

OK .

17. In the *Edit Duct System* tab>Edit Duct System panel, click (Select Equipment). Select the AHU that you selected for the supply air system.

18. Click (Finish Editing System).

19. Hover over one of the return diffusers and press <Tab> until the new system connections display, as shown in Figure 8–89.

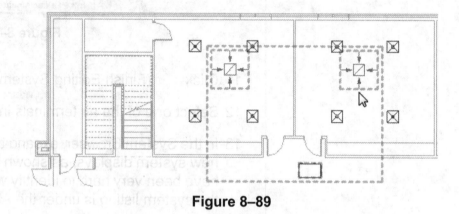

Figure 8–89

20. Click (Modify) twice to release the selection.

21. Close the System Browser and save the project.

Task 2 - Create an Automatic Ductwork Layout.

You can use WT (Window Tile) if only these two views are open in that Revit MEP session.

1. Open the Mechanical>HVAC>3D Views>**01 MECHANICAL - AREA B 3D** view and resize the views so you can see both the 2D plan and 3D views of the new systems area.

2. In the plan, roll the cursor over one of the supply air terminals and press <Tab> until the system displays. Click to select it as shown in Figure 8–90.

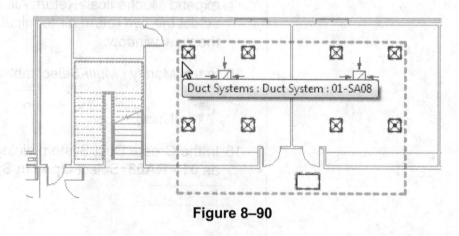

Figure 8–90

3. In the *Modify | Duct Systems* tab>Layout panel, click 
   ![icon] (Generate Layout).

4. In the *Generate Layout* tab>Modify Layout panel, click 
   ![icon] (Solutions).

5. In the Options Bar, click | Settings ... |.

6. In the Duct Conversion Settings dialog box, select **Main** and set the following parameters:

   - *Duct Type - Rectangular Duct*: **Radius Elbows/Taps**
   - *Offset*: **10'-0"**

7. Select **Branch** and set the following parameters, as shown in Figure 8–91:

   - *Duct Type*: **Round Duct: Taps / Short Radius**
   - *Offset*: **10'-0"**
   - *Flex Duct*: **Flex Duct Round: Flex - Round**
   - *Maximum Flex Duct Length*: **6'-0"**

Duct Conversion Settings

Main
Branch

System Type: Supply Air

Setting	Value
Duct Type	Round Duct: Taps
Offset	10' 0"
Flex Duct Type	Flex Duct Round : Flex - Ro
Maximum Flex Duct Length	6' 0"

OK   Cancel

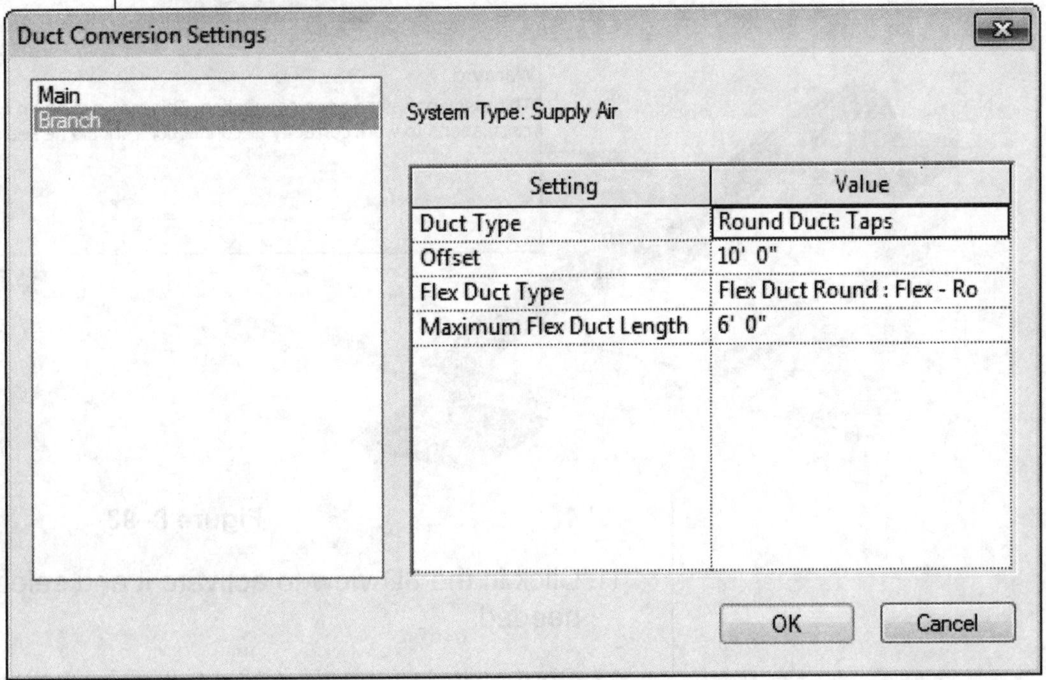

Figure 8–91

8. Click | OK |.

9. In the Options Bar, use the arrow buttons and Solution Types to try out several different solutions. End with the solution Network 1 of 6, shown in Figure 8–92 and click 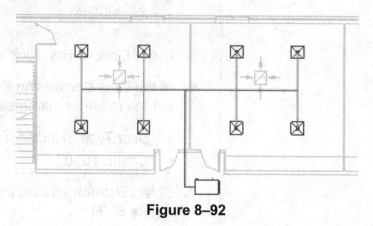 (Finish Layout).

Figure 8–92

10. A Warning displays prompting you that there is an open connection and the horizontal duct is highlighted as shown in Figure 8–93. You can see in the 3D view that it is missing an endcap.

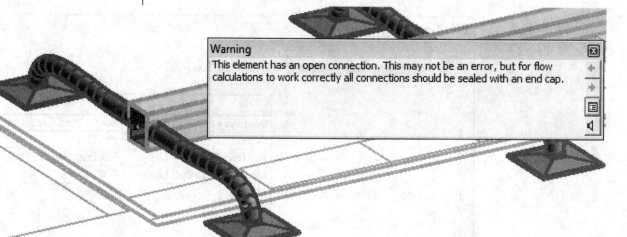

Warning

This element has an open connection. This may not be an error, but for flow calculations to work correctly all connections should be sealed with an end cap.

Figure 8–93

11. Click in the 3D view to activate it and select the duct again, if needed.

12. On the end of the duct, right-click and select **Cap Open End**.

13. Rotate the 3D view or move to 2D view to cap the other open end.

14. Save the project.

Task 3 - Create a Custom Ductwork Layout.

1. Continue working with the same two views open.

2. In the 2D view select the Return Air System.

3. In the *Duct Systems* tab>Layout panel, click ⬛ (Generate Layout).

4. In the *Generate Layout* tab>Modify Layout panel, click ⬛ (Solutions).

5. View the various solutions. Most of them have some problem with the layout. When the gold lines display it is a warning that the layout could fail in those areas.

6. In the Options Bar, click `Settings ...` .

7. In the Duct Conversion Settings dialog box, select **Main** and change the options as follows:

    *   *Duct Type*: **Rectangular Duct: Radius Elbow and Taps**
    *   *Offset*: **11'-6"**

8. Select **Branch** and change the options as follows:

    *   *Duct Type*: **Rectangular Duct: Radius Elbow and Taps**
    *   *Offset*: **11'-6"**
    *   *Flex Duct Type*: **None**

9. Click `OK` . This still didn't correct all of the problems but it solved some by changing the heights of the ducts.

10. Cycle through the solutions to review the options.

11. End with Network 3 of 5. Click ⬛ (Edit Layout).

12. Select the vertical line and move it slightly to the left so that there is more room between the duct to the air terminal and the duct coming from the Air Handling Unit.

13. Click ✓ (Finish Layout). There are still some problems that need to be corrected as shown in Figure 8–94.

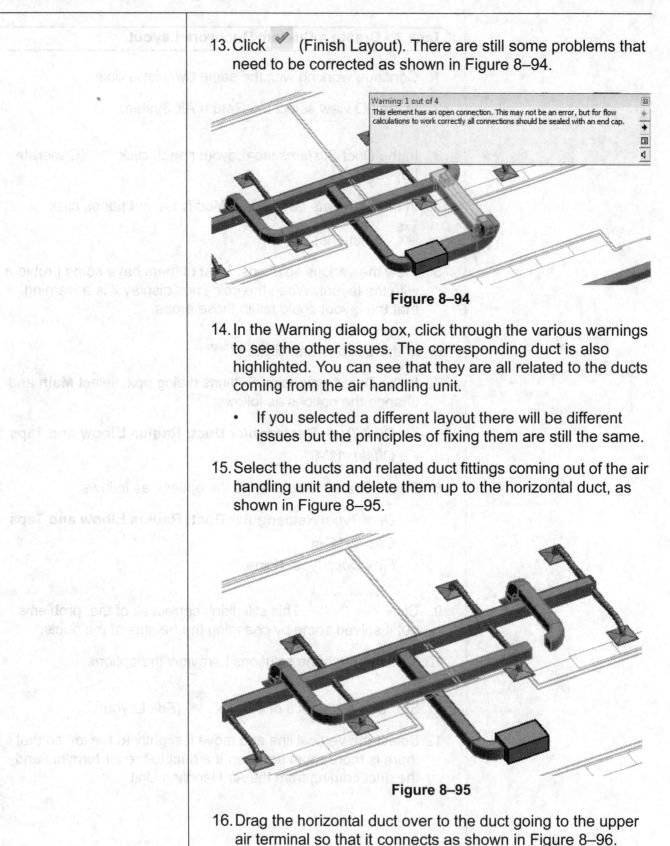

Warning: 1 out of 4
This element has an open connection. This may not be an error, but for flow calculations to work correctly all connections should be sealed with an end cap.

Figure 8–94

14. In the Warning dialog box, click through the various warnings to see the other issues. The corresponding duct is also highlighted. You can see that they are all related to the ducts coming from the air handling unit.

• If you selected a different layout there will be different issues but the principles of fixing them are still the same.

15. Select the ducts and related duct fittings coming out of the air handling unit and delete them up to the horizontal duct, as shown in Figure 8–95.

Figure 8–95

16. Drag the horizontal duct over to the duct going to the upper air terminal so that it connects as shown in Figure 8–96.

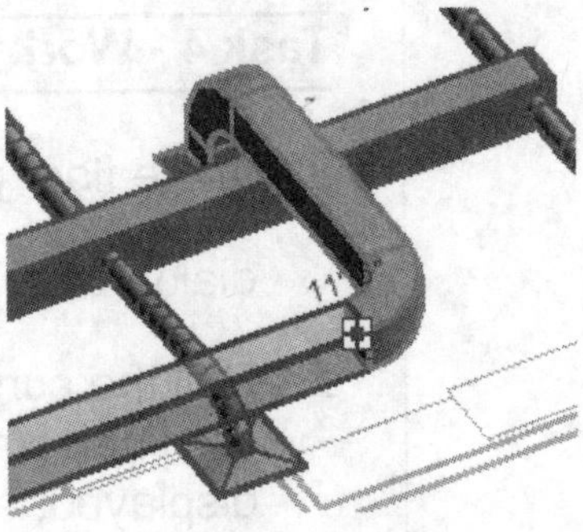

Figure 8–96

17. Select the Mechanical Equipment unit, right-click on the Return Air control and select **Draw Duct**.

18. In the Type Selector verify that the type is set to **Rectangular Duct: Radius Elbows/Taps**.

19. In the Options Bar, set the *Width* and *Height* to **12"** and the *Offset* to **10'-0"** as shown in Figure 8–97.

Figure 8–97

20. Draw the duct out **3'-6"**.

21. In the Options Bar, set *Offset* to **11'-6"** and continue drawing the duct until it connects with the horizontal duct. The appropriate fittings are added to resize the duct coming from the AHU and changing the height going to the other duct, as shown in Figure 8–98.

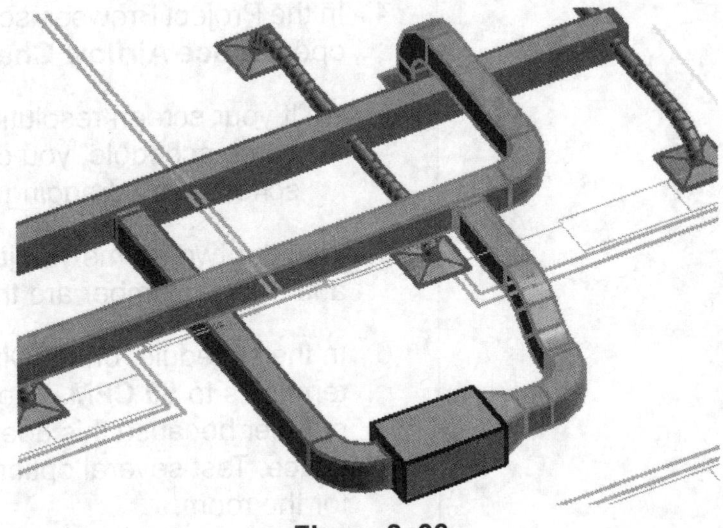

Figure 8–98

22. Save the project.

Task 4 - Work with Schedules.

1. In the floor plan view, type **VV** to open the Visibility/Graphics dialog box. Turn on **Spaces** and click .

2. Roll the cursor over the edge of one of the rooms with air terminals and press <Tab> until you see the room boundary displayed, as shown in Figure 8–99. Click on the room boundary and look at the number and name of the room in Properties.

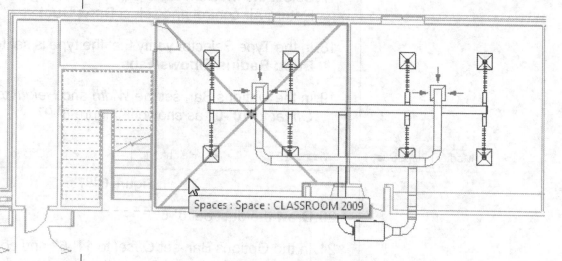

Spaces : Space : CLASSROOM 2009

Figure 8–99

3. Repeat this to find the room number and name for the other room in the system.

4. In the Project Browser, scroll down to the *Schedules* area and open **Space Airflow Check**.

   • If your screen resolution is not high enough to see the entire schedule, you can modify the widths of the schedule by dragging the line between columns.

5. Find the two rooms you just selected. (The Room Number and Space Number are the same.)

6. In the schedule, under Diffuser Airflow, change one of the air terminals to **50 CFM**. The Airflow Check displays a negative number because this does not provide enough airflow for the space. Test several options and end with a positive air flow for the room.

7. Scroll down to Space Number **2008** and **2010**. Neither of these spaces have any air terminals and therefore have a negative Airflow Check number, as shown in Figure 8–100.

2007	CLASSROOM		Heated and cooled	600 CFM	516 CFM	84 CFM
	470	Supply Diffuser – Perforated – Round Neck - Ceil	150 CFM			
	471	Supply Diffuser – Perforated – Round Neck - Ceil	150 CFM			
	472	Supply Diffuser – Perforated – Round Neck - Ceil	150 CFM			
	473	Supply Diffuser – Perforated – Round Neck - Ceil	150 CFM			
2008	CLASSROOM		Heated and cooled	0 CFM	529 CFM	-529 CFM
2009	CLASSROOM		Heated and cooled	600 CFM	552 CFM	48 CFM
	466	Supply Diffuser – Perforated – Round Neck - Ceil	150 CFM			
	467	Supply Diffuser – Perforated – Round Neck - Ceil	150 CFM			
	468	Supply Diffuser – Perforated – Round Neck - Ceil	150 CFM			
	469	Supply Diffuser – Perforated – Round Neck - Ceil	150 CFM			
2010	CLASSROOM		Heated and cooled	0 CFM	411 CFM	-411 CFM
2011	CORRIDOR		Heated and cooled	0 CFM	1068 CFM	-1068 CFM

Figure 8–100

8. Arrange the view windows so you can see the **Space Airflow Check** schedule and the Coordination>MEP>Ceiling Plans**>01 RCP** view with Space 2008 and 2010 showing in each. (The spaces are in the lower left of the south wing of the school.)

9. Select one of the existing supply air terminals. Right-click and select **Create Similar**. This starts the Air Terminal command and sets the type and Properties to match the original.

10. In the *Modify | Place Component* tab>Placement panel, click 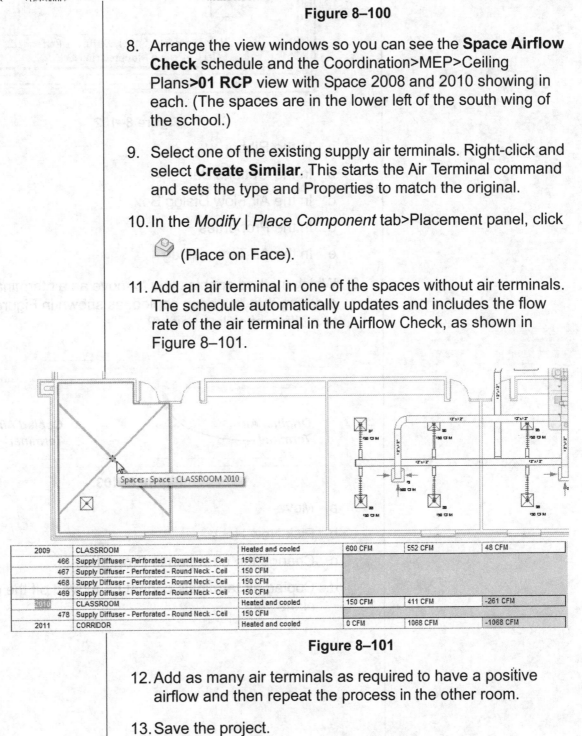 (Place on Face).

11. Add an air terminal in one of the spaces without air terminals. The schedule automatically updates and includes the flow rate of the air terminal in the Airflow Check, as shown in Figure 8–101.

2009	CLASSROOM		Heated and cooled	600 CFM	552 CFM	48 CFM
	466	Supply Diffuser – Perforated – Round Neck - Ceil	150 CFM			
	467	Supply Diffuser – Perforated – Round Neck - Ceil	150 CFM			
	468	Supply Diffuser – Perforated – Round Neck - Ceil	150 CFM			
	469	Supply Diffuser – Perforated – Round Neck - Ceil	150 CFM			
2010	CLASSROOM		Heated and cooled	150 CFM	411 CFM	-261 CFM
	478	Supply Diffuser – Perforated – Round Neck - Ceil	150 CFM			
2011	CORRIDOR		Heated and cooled	0 CFM	1068 CFM	-1068 CFM

Figure 8–101

12. Add as many air terminals as required to have a positive airflow and then repeat the process in the other room.

13. Save the project.

Chapter Review Questions

1. Where do you specify the *Flow* of an air terminal, (i.e.150 CFM) such as that shown in Figure 8–102? (Select all that apply.)

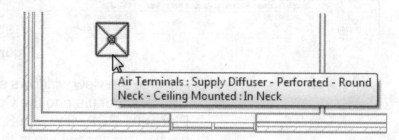

Figure 8–102

   a. In the Ribbon

   b. In the Options Bar

   c. In the Air Flow Dialog Box

   d. In the Properties

   e. In the Air Terminal tag

2. Which method enables you to move an air terminal hosted by a ceiling that has been copied, as shown in Figure 8–103, up to a different ceiling height?

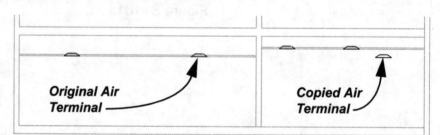

Figure 8–103

   a. Move

   b. Pick New Host

   c. Change the elevation in Properties

   d. Copied air terminals cannot be moved off the original plane

3. The size of the duct drawn from a control on mechanical equipment must remain the same size as the opening on the equipment until it intersects with another duct.

   a. True

   b. False

4. How do you change an elbow fitting to a tee fitting?

   a. Delete the elbow and place a tee instead.

   b. Select the elbow and use the Type Selector to select a tee fitting instead.

   c. Select the elbow and click **+** (Plus).

   d. Select the elbow and click the **Convert to Tee** button in the Ribbon.

5. When can you convert a rigid duct to a flexible duct, such as that shown in Figure 8–104?

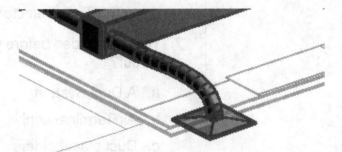

Figure 8–104

   a. When the rigid duct is round.

   b. When the air terminal is already connected to a rigid duct.

   c. When creating a system and sizing the ducting.

   d. When the **Allow Conversion** parameter is selected in the rigid duct's instance properties.

6. Which method enables you to correct the issue mentioned in the warning shown in Figure 8–105 where a Supply Air Terminal was connected to a duct with a Return Air classification.

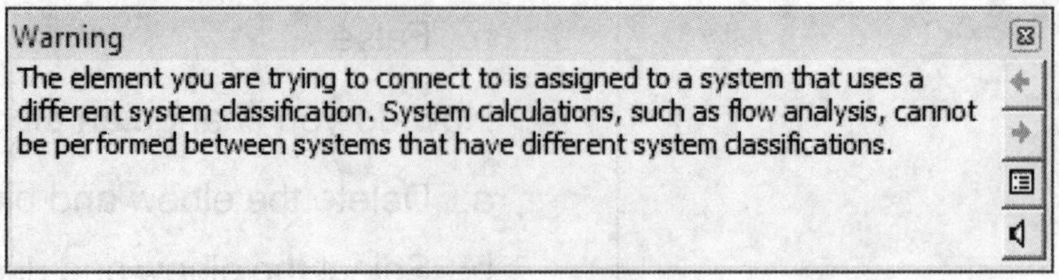

> **Warning**   ☒
> The element you are trying to connect to is assigned to a system that uses a different system classification. System calculations, such as flow analysis, cannot be performed between systems that have different system classifications.

Figure 8–105

a. In Properties, change the System Type to **Supply Air**.

b. In the *Modify | Air Terminal* tab, click ⊞ (Change Type) and change the classification.

c. In the *Duct Systems* tab, click ✎ (Edit System).

d. In the Type Selector, select a Return Air Terminal type.

7. What is needed before you can create an automatic ductwork layout?

a. A Duct System

b. Air Terminals only

c. Duct placeholders

d. All air terminals and equipment placed for the entire project.

Command Summary

Button	Command	Location
	Add Insulation	• **Ribbon:** (*with Ducts and Duct Fittings selected*) *Modify	Multi-Select* tab> Duct Insulation panel
	Add Lining	• **Ribbon:** (*with Ducts and Duct Fittings selected*) *Modify	Multi-Select* tab> Duct Lining panel
	Add to System	• **Ribbon:** *Edit Duct System* tab>Edit Duct System panel
	Air Terminal	• **Ribbon:** *Systems* tab>HVAC panel • **Shortcut:** AT
	Air Terminal on Duct	• **Ribbon:** *Modify	Place Air Terminal* tab>Layout panel
	Change Type	• **Ribbon:** (*with Ducts and Duct Fittings selected*) *Modify	Multi-Select* tab>Edit panel
	Convert to Flex Duct	• **Ribbon:** *Systems* tab>HVAC panel • **Shortcut:** CV
	Disconnect Equipment	• **Ribbon:** *Edit Duct Systems* tab> System Tools panel
	Duct	• **Ribbon:** *Systems* tab>HVAC panel • **Shortcut:** DT
	Duct Accessory	• **Ribbon:** *Systems* tab>HVAC panel • **Shortcut:** DA
	Duct Fitting	• **Ribbon:** *Systems* tab>HVAC panel • **Shortcut:** DF
	Duct Placeholder	• **Ribbon:** *Systems* tab>HVAC panel
	Duct (System)	• **Ribbon:** *Modify	contextual* tab> Create Systems panel • Right-click: Create Duct System
	Edit Layout	• **Ribbon:** *Generate Layout* tab> Modify Layout panel
	Edit Insulation	• **Ribbon:** (*with Ducts and Duct Fittings that have Insulation selected*) *Modify	Multi-Select* tab>Duct Insulation panel
	Edit Lining	• **Ribbon:** (*with Ducts and Duct Fittings that have Lining selected*) *Modify	Multi-Select* tab>Duct Lining panel

	Edit System	• **Ribbon:** *Duct System* tab>System Tools panel
	Flex Duct	• **Ribbon:** *Systems* tab>HVAC panel • **Shortcut:** FD
	Generate Layout	• **Ribbon:** *Duct System* tab>Layout panel and *Modify | Air Terminals* tab> Layout panel
	Inherit Elevation	• **Ribbon:** *Modify | Place Duct* tab> Placement Tools panel
	Inherit Size	• **Ribbon:** *Modify | Place Duct* tab> Placement Tools panel
	Justification (Settings)	• **Ribbon:** *Modify | Place Duct* tab> Placement Tools panel
	Justify	• **Ribbon:** *(with Ducts and Duct Fittings selected) Modify | Multi-Select* tab> Edit panel
	Load Family	• **Ribbon:** *Modify | Place Air Terminal* tab>Mode panel
	Mechanical Equipment	• **Ribbon:** *Systems* tab>Mechanical panel • **Shortcut:** ME
	Mechanical Settings	• **Ribbon:** *Systems* tab>HVAC or Mechanical panel title • **Shortcut:** MS
	Pick New (Work Plane)	• **Ribbon:** *Modify | Air Terminal* tab> Work Plane panel
	Remove from System	• **Ribbon:** *Edit Duct System* tab>Edit Duct System panel and *Generate Layout* tab>Modify Layout panel
	Remove Insulation	• **Ribbon:** *(with Ducts and Duct Fittings that have Insulation selected) Modify | Multi-Select* tab>Duct Insulation panel
	Remove Lining	• **Ribbon:** *(with Ducts and Duct Fittings that have Lining selected) Modify | Multi-Select* tab>Duct Lining panel
	Select Equipment	• **Ribbon:** *Duct System* tab>System Tools and *Edit Duct Systems* tab>Edit Duct System panel
	Solutions	• **Ribbon:** *Generate Layout* tab> Modify Layout panel
	System Browser	• **Ribbon:** *View* tab>Windows panel, expand User Interface • **Shortcut:** <F9>

Chapter 9

Hydronic Piping Systems

In this chapter you learn about Hydronic Piping Systems. You learn to add mechanical equipment, create hydronic systems, and add piping manually or automatically.

This chapter contains the following topics:

- **About Hydronic Piping Systems**
- **Adding Mechanical Equipment**
- **Drawing Piping**
- **Creating Hydronic Systems**
- **Automatic Piping Layouts**

9.1 About Hydronic Piping Systems

 Learning Objectives

- Understand the process of creating hydronic piping systems.
- Review and apply Mechanical settings for piping.

Hydronic Piping Systems use hot and cold water to provide heating and air conditioning to a building. They can include boilers that heat water circulated through radiators or large boiler/chiller equipment that sends hot or cold water to air handling units as shown in Figure 9–1. The software provides tools that help you to correctly design these systems.

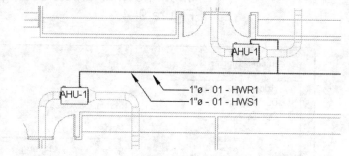

Figure 9–1

There are several steps in the process of creating HVAC systems:

1. Add mechanical equipment.
2. Create a supply or return hydronic system. Some of these are automatically created when you insert the components.
3. Generate piping automatically or add it manually. When adding piping manually, you can attach to connectors on the mechanical equipment and to other pipes. Fittings between different heights or sizes are automatically applied, as shown in Figure 9–2.

Mechanical equipment might already be in place if you are attaching the hydronic piping to air handling units.

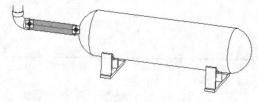

Figure 9–2

4. Check and modify the system.

- The tools used for creating and placing piping components and systems are located in the *Systems* tab>Plumbing & Piping panel, as shown in Figure 9–3.

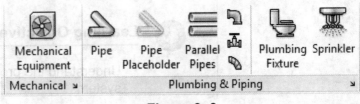

Figure 9–3

Mechanical Settings-Piping

Before you add piping there are defaults that should be set for each type of system (Hydronic Supply, Hydronic Return, and the rest of the types of piping). Similar to the Duct Settings you select the *Pipe Type* and *Offset*. In the *Systems* tab>Plumbing & Piping panel title, click 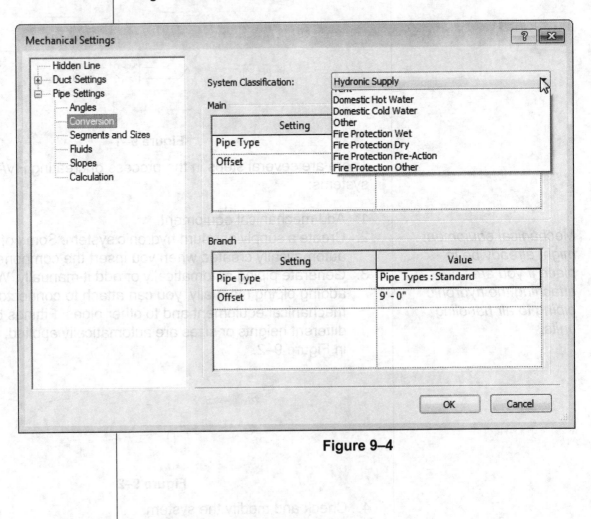 (Mechanical Settings) or type **MS** to open the Mechanical Settings dialog box as shown in Figure 9–4.

Mechanical Settings

Hidden Line
Duct Settings
Pipe Settings
  Angles
  Conversion
  Segments and Sizes
  Fluids
  Slopes
  Calculation

System Classification: Hydronic Supply

Domestic Hot Water
Domestic Cold Water
Other
Fire Protection Wet
Fire Protection Dry
Fire Protection Pre-Action
Fire Protection Other

Main

Setting	
Pipe Type	
Offset	

Branch

Setting	Value
Pipe Type	Pipe Types : Standard
Offset	9' - 0"

OK   Cancel

Figure 9–4

Other options that can be set in this dialog box include the Pipe Rise/Drop Annotation Size and symbols, typical pipe sizes by segment for materials, such as carbon steel, copper, and plastic. You can also set the fluid information where you set the Temperature, Viscosity, and Density of different types of fluids used in the systems and default Slopes for use when you use sloped piping.

Additionally, you can specify limits on the angles that can be used as the pipes are being drawn, as shown in Figure 9–5.

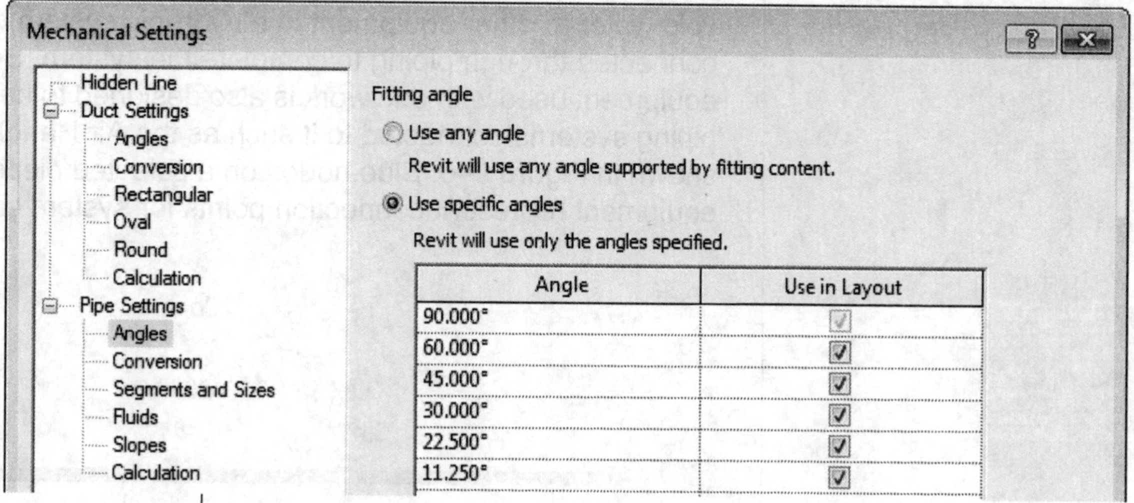

Figure 9–5

9.2 Adding Mechanical Equipment

 Learning Objective

- Place mechanical equipment components for piping systems.

Boilers and chillers or a combination unit supplies the hot and/or cold water to other equipment in a hydronic system. These are connected through piping to complete the system. Some equipment used with ductwork is also designed to have hydronic piping systems connected to it such as the Air Handling Unit, as shown in Figure 9–6. Blue nodes on a selected piece of equipment represent connection points for system components.

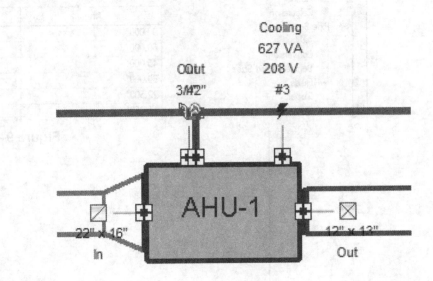

Figure 9–6

- Mechanical Equipment can be placed in any plan view.

How To: Place Mechanical Equipment

1. Open the view where you want to place the mechanical equipment element.

2. In the *Systems* tab>Mechanical panel, click (Mechanical Equipment) or type **ME**.

3. In the Type Selector, select a Mechanical Equipment type. In Properties, set any other values such as the *Level* and *Offset* if it is not hosted.

4. Place the Mechanical Equipment in the model by clicking at the required location in the model view. You can use other objects in the model to line the element up and press the <Spacebar> to rotate it before placing it.

5. Continue to place additional Mechanical Equipment elements, or click ⬉ (Modify) to exit the command.

- Additional boilers, radiators, VAV units and more can be loaded from the Autodesk® Revit® MEP Library in the *Mechanical Components* sub-folders.

- Take time to get to know the types of mechanical equipment that come with the software. You can view them in 3D, plan, or elevation/section views. Select them to display the connectors as shown in Figure 9–7.

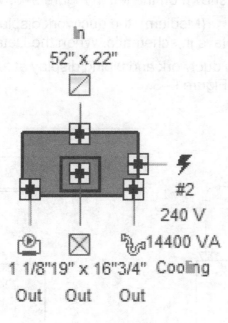
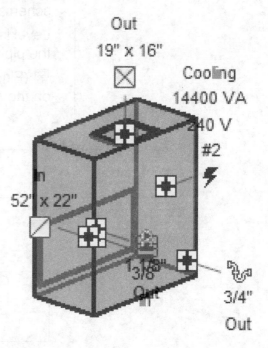

Figure 9–7

9.3 Drawing Piping

Learning Objectives

- Draw piping to connect mechanical equipment that uses fluids including parallel pipe runs.
- Modify pipes including converting pipe placeholders to pipes, changing types in pipe runs, adding insulation, and modifying justification.
- Work with pipe fittings and accessories.

Piping connects the mechanical equipment that heats or cools the fluid to the radiators or air handling units that use the fluid. You can view the piping at different detail levels. When the Detail Level is set to ☐ (Coarse), the pipe and ductwork displays in schematic, as shown on the left in Figure 9–8. When the Detail Level is set to ▨ (Medium), the ductwork displays at full size but the piping displays in schematic. When the Detail Level is set to ▨ (Fine), both ductwork and piping display at full size, as shown on the right in Figure 9–8.

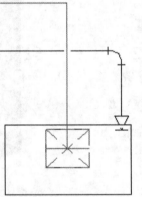 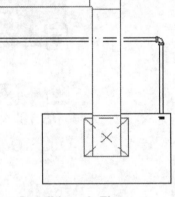

Detail Level: Coarse   *Detail Level: Fine*

Figure 9–8

- Pipes can be drawn in plan, elevation/section, and 3D views.

- Fittings are automatically added according to the system family that has been defined. You can also modify fittings and add others.

- You can draw Pipe Placeholders early in a project and then convert them to standard pipes as the system is further defined.

- Using 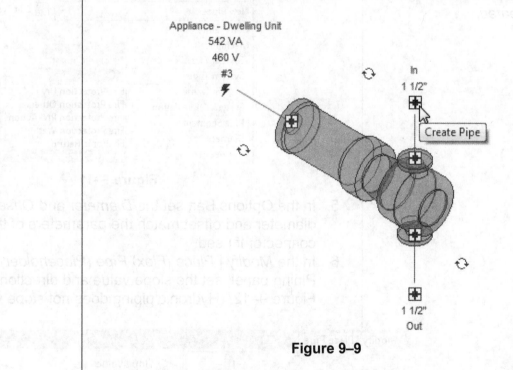 (Pipe), (Pipe Placeholder), and (Flex Pipe) are very similar. The tools are present in the *Systems* tab>Plumbing & Piping panel.

- To display centerlines for piping, in the Visibility/Graphics Overrides dialog box, turn on the *Centerline* subcategory for pipe and pipe fittings. Centerlines display in plan and elevation views set to the **Wireframe** or **Hidden Line** visual style.

How To: Add Piping

1. Open the view where you want to place the pipes.
2. In the *Systems* tab>Plumbing & Piping panel, click

   (Pipe), (Pipe Placeholder), or (Flex Pipe). You can also select the mechanical equipment, plumbing equipment, or an existing pipe or fitting to display the connectors. Click on the connector icon to select **Create Pipe,** as shown in Figure 9–9. You can also right-click while hovering over the appropriate connector and select **Draw Pipe, Draw Pipe Placeholder,** or **Draw Flex Pipe**.

Appliance - Dwelling Unit
542 VA
460 V
#3

In
1 1/2"

Create Pipe

1 1/2"
Out

Figure 9–9

3. In the Type Selector, select a pipe type as shown in Figure 9–10.

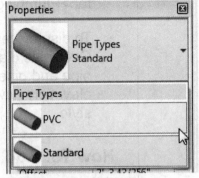

Figure 9–10

4. If you are drawing pipes without starting from a connector, then before you start to draw the pipes, specify the *System Type* in Properties, as shown in Figure 9–11.

Drawing from existing connectors automatically applies the System Type which is setup when the family is created.

Figure 9–11

5. In the Options Bar, set the *Diameter* and *Offset*. The default diameter and offset match the parameters of the selected connector if used.

6. In the *Modify | Place (Flex) Pipe (Placeholder)* tab>Sloped Piping panel, set the slope value and direction, as shown in Figure 9–12. (Hydronic piping does not slope very often.)

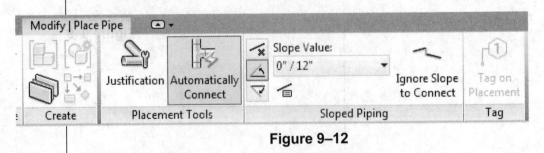

Figure 9–12

7. In the Placement Tools panel, verify that 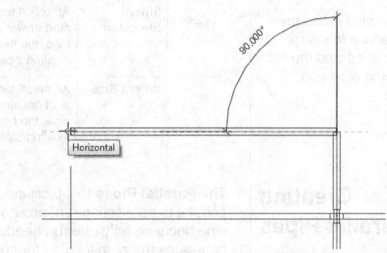 (Automatically Connect) is on.

8. Draw the pipes using temporary dimensions, snaps, and alignments to locate each point along the path as shown in Figure 9–13.

Use reference planes to help you place the piping.

Figure 9–13

- Press <Esc> once to stay in the command but have a new start location. If you select a point along an existing pipe it automatically adds a fitting.

- When you change direction an elbow or tee is added. This is also true if you change the offset of the level as shown in Figure 9–14.

If you change the size or shape, the appropriate pipe fitting is automatically added

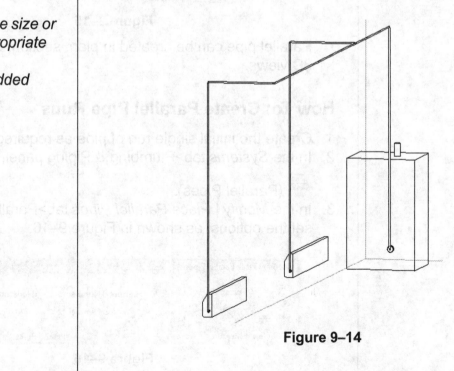

Figure 9–14

Pipe Placement Options

	Justification Settings	Opens the Justification Setting dialog box where you can specify the default settings for the *Horizontal Justification*, *Horizontal Offset*, and *Vertical Justification*.
	Inherit Elevation	An on/off toggle. If the tool is toggled on and you start drawing a pipe by snapping to an existing pipe, the new pipe takes on the elevation of the existing pipe regardless of what is specified.
	Inherit Size	An on/off toggle. If the tool is toggled on and you start drawing a pipe by snapping to an existing pipe, the new pipe takes on the size of the existing pipe regardless of what is specified.

You can also press the <Spacebar> to inherit the elevation and the size of the pipe you snap to.

Creating Parallel Pipes

The **Parallel Pipes** tool facilitates the creation of piping runs parallel to an existing run, as shown in Figure 9–15. This saves time because only one run needs to be laid out, and the tool generates the parallel runs for you.

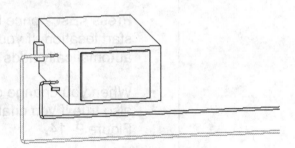

Figure 9–15

- Parallel pipe can be created in plan, section, elevation, and 3D views.

How To: Create Parallel Pipe Runs

1. Create the initial single run of pipe as required.
2. In the *Systems* tab>Plumbing & Piping panel, click (Parallel Pipes).
3. In the *Modify | Place Parallel Pipes* tab>Parallel Pipes panel, set the options, as shown in Figure 9–16.

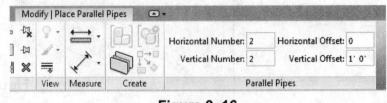

Figure 9–16

If you do not press <Tab>, parallel pipes are only created for the single piece of existing pipe.

4. Hover the cursor over the existing piping, as shown in Figure 9–17, and press <Tab> to select the existing run.

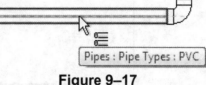

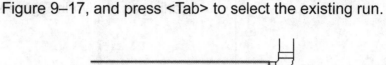

Figure 9–17

5. When the preview displays as required, click to create the parallel runs. The preview varies depending on which side of the existing run you hover the cursor.

Parallel Pipe Creation Options

Horizontal Number	The total number of parallel pipe runs, in the horizontal direction.
Horizontal Offset	The distance between parallel pipe runs, in the horizontal direction.
Vertical Number	The total number of parallel pipe runs, in the vertical direction.
Vertical Offset	The distance between parallel pipe runs, in the vertical direction.

• In section and elevation views, Horizontal refers to parallel to the view (visually up, down, left, or right from the original conduit). Vertical creates parallel conduit runs perpendicular to the view, in the direction of the user.

Modifying Pipes

Pipes can be modified using a variety of standard modifying tools and specialty tools such as pipe sizings, converting pipe placeholders to pipes, adding insulation, and modifying the justification of pipes.

You can modify pipes by making changes in Properties, in the Options Bar, and by using temporary dimensions, controls, and connectors. Modify tools, such as **Move**, **Rotate**, **Trim/Extend**, and **Align** help you place the pipes in the correct locations.

How To: Convert Pipe Placeholders to Pipes

1. Select the pipe placeholder(s).
2. In the *Modify | Pipe Placeholders* tab>Edit panel, click
   (Convert Placeholder).

3. The placeholder(s) is changed into the pipe type selected earlier, as shown in Figure 9–18.

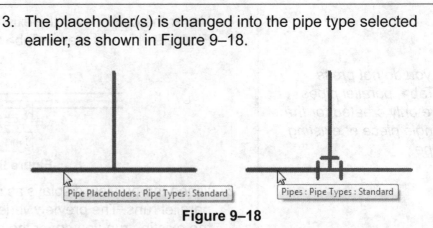

Figure 9–18

- The Detail Level impacts the look of pipes whether it is schematic, as shown in Figure 9–18 or full size, as shown in Figure 9–19.

How To: Change the Type of Pipe Runs

1. Select the pipe run. You can select runs in different systems. Verify that you filter out everything except pipes, pipe fittings, and pipe accessories.
2. In the *Modify | Multi-Select* tab>Edit panel, click (Change Type).
3. In the Type Selector, select a new type of pipe run. This changes the pipe and any related fittings, as shown in Figure 9–19, where the type **Pipe Types: Standard** was changed to the type **Pipe Types: PVC**.

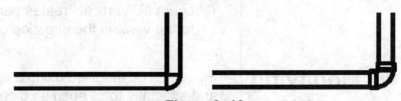

Figure 9–19

How To: Reapply the Type to Pipe Runs

1. Select the pipe run. You can select different runs, but they must be all of the same type of pipe. If you select pipe in different systems, the Autodesk Revit software prompts you to select one system to which to reapply the type. Verify that you filter out everything except pipes, pipe fittings, and pipe accessories.
2. In the *Modify | Multi-Select* tab>Edit panel, click (Reapply Type).

It is sometimes necessary to change the definition of a pipe type after having already created a pipe of that type. This tool enables the user to reapply the type with its new definition to the existing pipe.

Adding Insulation

When you select pipe runs, you can add insulation by specifying the type and thickness. This information displays as a thin line outside of the pipe, as shown in Figure 9–20.

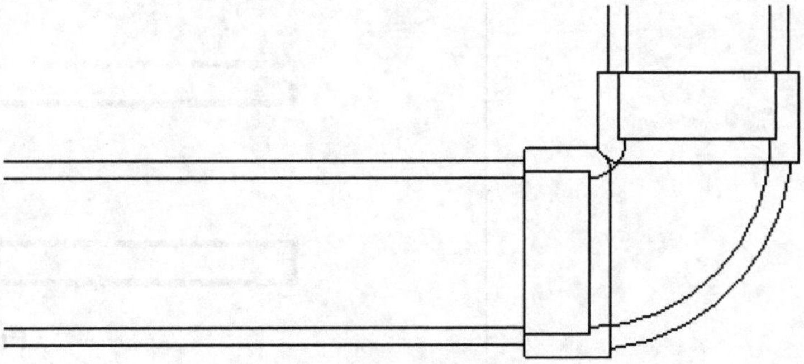

Figure 9–20

How To: Add Insulation

1. Select the pipe run that you want to insulate. You can select more than one system. Use (Filter) to select only the pipes and pipe fittings.
2. In the *Modify | Multi-Select* tab>Pipe Insulation panel, click (Add Insulation).
3. In the associated dialog box, select an *Insulation Type* and set the *Thickness,* as shown for Pipe Insulation in Figure 9–21, and click OK.

Sometimes the line thicknesses make it difficult to see some elements such as the insulation or lining. To toggle on or off the lineweight, in the Quick Access Toolbar, click (Thin Lines) or type TL.

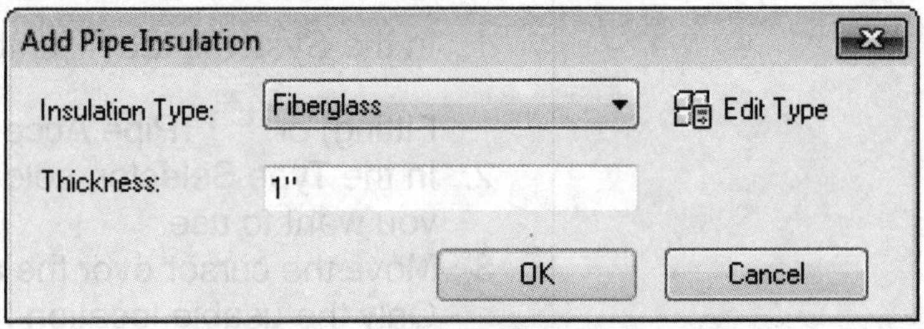

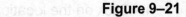

Figure 9–21

- To modify insulation, select the associated piping. In the *Modify | Multi-Select* tab>Pipe Insulation panel, click (Edit Insulation) and change the type in the Type Selector.
- To remove it, click (Remove Insulation).

© 2014, ASCENT - Center for Technical Knowledge®

Modifying the Justification

If a pipe run has different sized pipes, you can modify the justification of those pipes, as shown in Figure 9–22. The process is the same as modifying duct justifications (Refer to HVAC Systems for more information).

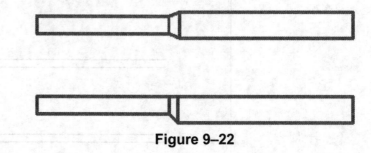

Figure 9–22

Working with Fittings and Accessories

Many fittings are automatically applied as you create the piping. There are times when you need to add your own or add accessories such as the flow meter, as shown in Figure 9–23.

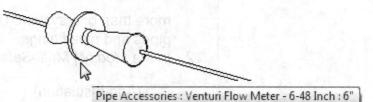

Pipe Accessories : Venturi Flow Meter - 6-48 Inch : 6"

Figure 9–23

How To: Add Pipe Fittings or Accessories

1. In the *Systems* tab>Plumbing & Piping panel, click 🔧 (Pipe Fitting) or 🛠 (Pipe Accessory).
2. In the Type Selector, select the type of fitting or accessory you want to use.
3. Move the cursor over the appropriate connector in the piping. Only the usable location highlights.
4. Click on the location.

• Additional pipe fittings and pipe accessories can be loaded from the *Pipe* folder of the Imperial Library.

Modifying Pipe Fittings

Pipe Fittings, whether added automatically or manually can be modified using the Type Selector, Properties, the Options Bar, and a variety of connectors and controls. For example, an Elbow can be changed to a Tee by clicking a control as shown in Figure 9–24.

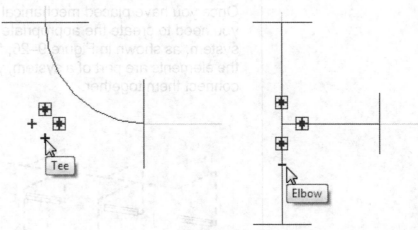

Figure 9–24

- When you trim pipes that intersect, the appropriate fitting is automatically added as part of the **Trim** command.

- Instead of placing endcap fittings, right-click on the open end of a pipe and select **Cap Open End**, as shown in Figure 9–25.

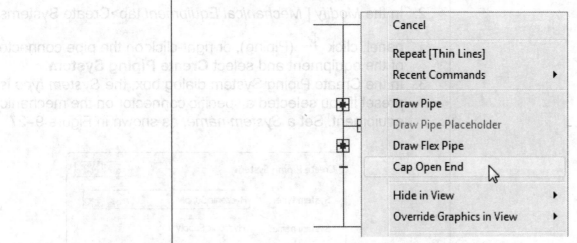

Figure 9–25

9.4 Creating Hydronic Systems

Learning Objective

* Create systems of hydronic piping and mechanical equipment.

Once you have placed mechanical equipment into the model, you need to create the appropriate supply or return hydronic system, as shown in Figure 9–26, from these elements. Once the elements are part of a system, you can then add the piping to connect them together.

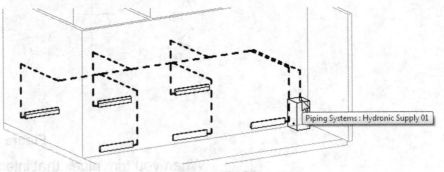

Piping Systems : Hydronic Supply 01

Figure 9–26

How To: Create Hydronic Systems

1. Select one or more end unit components that are going to form the system.
2. In the *Modify | Mechanical Equipment* tab>Create Systems panel, click (Piping), or right-click on the pipe connector of the equipment and select **Create Piping System**.
3. In the Create Piping System dialog box, the *System type* is preset if you selected a specific connector on the mechanical equipment. Set a *System name*, as shown in Figure 9–27.

Create Piping System

System type:	Hydronic Supply
System name:	Hydronic Supply 1

☐ Open in System Editor

OK   Cancel

Figure 9–27

You can also do this while editing the system.

4. In the *Modify | Piping Systems* tab>System Tools panel, click ⊡ (Select Equipment) to select the boiler or chiller for the system, as shown in Figure 9–28.

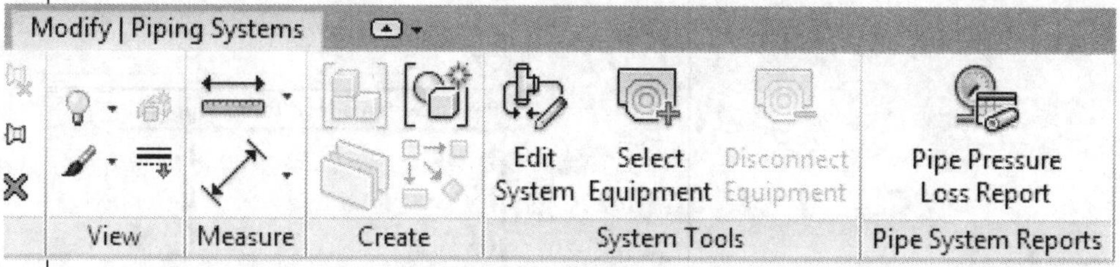

Figure 9–28

5. To add or remove equipment, click ⊡ (Edit System).
6. In the *Edit Piping System* tab>Edit Piping System panel, click ⊡ (Add to System) and select any equipment in the model that is to be part of this system and was not selected earlier.
7. In Properties, change the *System Name,* if needed. In the Options Bar, select the *System Equipment* as shown in Figure 9–29.

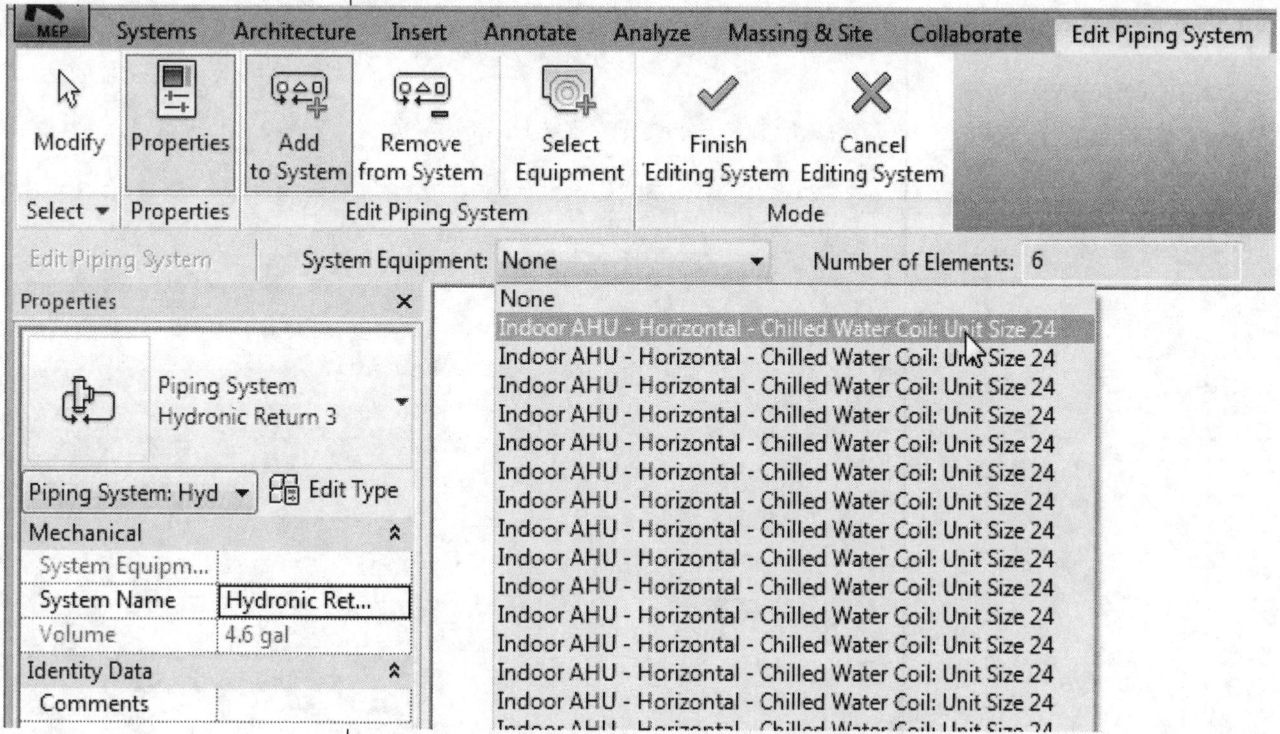

Figure 9–29

- Click ⊡ (Remove from System) if needed to remove any equipment.

8. Click (Finish Editing System) to accept all components and complete the creation of the system as shown in Figure 9–30.

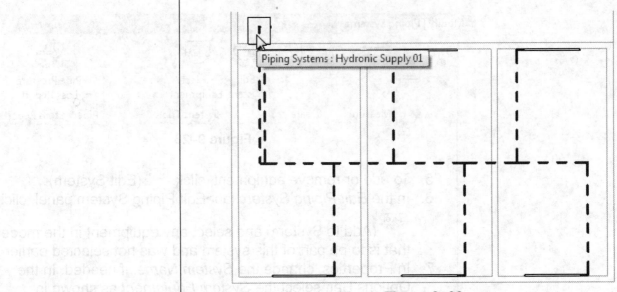

Figure 9–30

9.5 Automatic Piping Layouts

 Learning Objective

• Use the Generate Layout tool to add piping to a piping system.

Once you have created the piping system, you can automatically create the piping layout. These tools create various routes for the piping that you can select from as shown in Figure 9–31

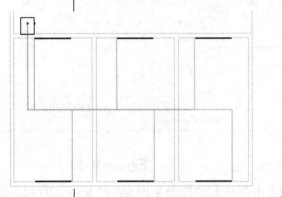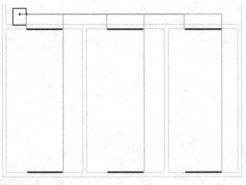

Figure 9–31

If you have just one or two pieces of mechanical equipment that need to be connected to existing piping you can use the **Connect Into** tool. If you have a more complex piping system then use the **Generate Layout** tool.

How To: Connect to existing Hydronic System

1. Select the equipment that needs to be connected to existing pipes.
2. In the *Modify | Mechanical Equipment* tab>Layout panel, click (Connect Into).
3. In the Select Connector dialog box, select the type as shown in Figure 9–32. Click OK .

Select Connector   ✕

Connector 0 : Hydronic Supply : Round : 1"
Connector 1 : Hydronic Return : Round : 1"

Figure 9–32

4. Select the pipe to connect into. This process automatically connects any equipment to a system

Adding a Base to a Layout

This tool is not available for systems in which the source equipment is already specified.

While working in the **Generate Layouts** tool you can add a **Base** (a point of connection to the main system), in cases where the source equipment has not yet been placed or where it is located on a different level of the building. The base can be either rectangular or circular as shown in Figure 9–33. The elevation of the base is set in the Options Bar.

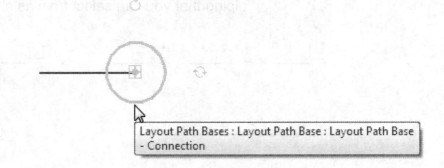

Layout Path Bases : Layout Path Base : Layout Path Base - Connection

Figure 9–33

- Add the base before you cycle through the Solution Types when using the **Layout** tool, as it changes the options.

How To: Generate an automatic piping layout

1. Hover over the hydronic supply or hydronic return outlet in the mechanical equipment and press <Tab> until you see the outline of the system. Click to select the system as shown in Figure 9–34.

You can view the solutions in the plan or a 3D view.

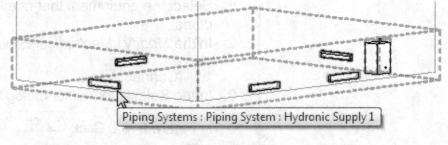

Piping Systems : Piping System : Hydronic Supply 1

Figure 9–34

2. In the *Piping Systems* tab>Layout panel, click (Generate Layout).

3. If you are working with a partial system and need to specify a connection point, in the *Generate Layout* tab>Modify Layout panel, click (Place Base) and place the base in the project. The **Modify Base** command is activated. Set the *Offset* and *Shape*. Also set the *Diameter* of the connection.

   When you are finished, click (Solutions) to return to the layout tool.

4. In the Options Bar, select a *Solution Type,* as shown in Figure 9–35, and click (Next Solution) or (Previous Solution) to cycle through the possible options.

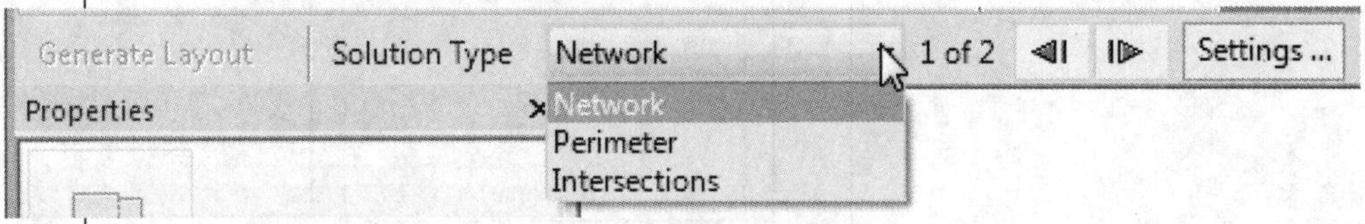

Figure 9–35

Network	Up to six potential solutions, creates a bounding box around entire system, with the main segment through the center of this bounding box, and the branches at 90 degrees off the main branch.
Perimeter	Up to five potential solutions, creates a bounding box around entire system, with segments being placed on three of the four sides, and one with segments being placed on all four sides. (The Inset value determines the offset distance between the bounding box and the components.)
Intersections	Up to eight potential solutions, segments extend from each connector of the components, and where they intersect perpendicularly, proposed intersection junctions are created.

- The blue lines identify the main piping system and green lines identify branch systems.
- Gold lines display a potential open connection that could cause problems when the piping is added.

5. In the *Generate Layout* tab>Generate Layout panel, click (Finish Layout) when you have found the solution that looks best.

- in the Options Bar opens the Pipe Conversion Settings dialog box, as shown in Figure 9–36. You can modify this while selecting solutions to provide the best options.

Pipe Conversion Settings

Main
Branch

System Type: Hydronic Supply

Setting	Value
Pipe Type	Pipe Types: Standard
Offset	9' 0"

OK   Cancel

Figure 9–36

How To: Customize the Layout

1. Click ![icon] (Solutions) and select a layout design similar to what you want to use.
2. In the *Generate Layout* tab>Modify Layout panel, click ![icon] (Edit Layout).
3. Select one of the layout lines. You can use the move control to change the location of the line as shown in Figure 9–37. You can also change the height of the offset by clicking on the number control.

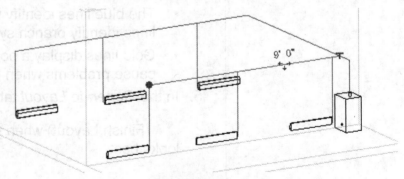

9' 0"

Figure 9–37

The Autodesk Revit software only permits one custom option at a time.

4. Click (Solutions) to finish customizing the layout. The Solution Type list now has **Custom** as an additional option to the standard three solution types.

5. Click ✓ (Finish Layout).

- Once the automatic/custom layout is completed, check through the entire system to verify. Ensure that you include checking slopes if they are used.

- To test the continuity of the system, hover the cursor over one of the pipes and press <Tab> until the whole system highlights. One of the pipes is not attached to the fitting and therefore is not highlighted, as shown in Figure 9–38.

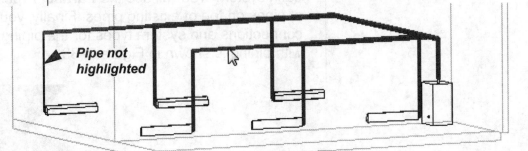

Figure 9–38

Practice 9a

Work with Hydronic Systems

Learning Objectives

- Create Hydronic systems.
- Add pipes, connecting air handling units in the systems and use the **Parallel Pipes** tool to create a set of pipes on the existing pipes.
- Clean up connections between the air handling units and the new pipes and at intersections between pipes.

Estimated time for completion: 25 minutes

In this practice you will create Hydronic Supply and Return Systems and then add pipes to connect the Air Handling Units in each system. You will use the **Parallel Pipes** tool to create a set of pipes on top of existing pipes. Finally, you will verify all of the connections and system types for the piping. One of the AHU with piping is shown in Figure 9–39.

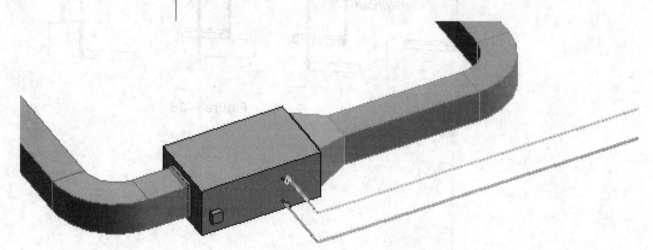

Figure 9–39

Task 1 - Create Hydronic Systems.

1. In the *C:\Autodesk Revit 2015 MEP Fundamentals Class Files\Piping* folder, open **MEP-Elementary-School -Piping.rvt**.

2. In the *Systems* tab> Mechanical panel title bar, click ⌐ (Mechanical Settings).

3. In the Mechanical Settings dialog box, in *Pipe Settings*, click **Angles**.

4. In the right pane, select **Use specific angles** as shown in Figure 9–40. This limits the angles you can use to draw the piping to industry specific fittings.

Mechanical Settings

- Hidden Line
- Duct Settings
  - Angles
  - Conversion
  - Rectangular
  - Oval
  - Round
  - Calculation
- Pipe Settings
  - Angles
  - Conversion
  - Segments and Sizes
  - Fluids
  - Slopes
  - Calculation

Fitting angle

○ Use any angle
  Revit will use any angle supported by fitting content.

◉ Use specific angles
  Revit will use only the angles specified.

Angle	Use in Layout
90.000°	✓
60.000°	✓
45.000°	✓
30.000°	✓
22.500°	✓
11.250°	✓

Figure 9–40

5. In the **01 MECHANICAL PLAN** floor plan view, zoom into the north wing.

6. Select all of the Air Handling Units (AHU) in this wing.

7. In the *Modify | Mechanical Equipment* tab>Create Systems panel, click (Piping).

8. In the Create Piping System dialog box, set the *System type* as **Hydronic Return** and *System name* as **01 - HWR1**. Click OK.

9. Click anywhere in empty space to clear the selection.

10. Repeat the process and create a Hydronic Supply System using the same Air Handling Units. Name this system **01 - HWS1**.

11. If you have time create a Hydronic Return System and a Hydronic Supply System for the Air Handling Units in the south wing. Name the systems **01 - HWR2** and **01 - HWS2**.

12. Save the project.

Ensure that you click the

 *(Hydronic) icon
rather than the*

(Plumbing) icon.

Task 2 - Draw Hydronic Return Pipes.

1. In the north wing, zoom in on the far left AHU and select it. Click on the Hydronic Return control that displays **Create Pipe**, as shown in Figure 9–41.

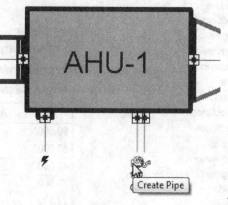

Figure 9–41

2. In the Select Connector dialog box, select **Connector 3: Hydronic Return** and click <kbd>OK</kbd>.

3. In the Type Selector, select **Pipe Types: Copper**.

   • The software might prompt you to reselect the connector after changing the Pipe Type.

4. Toggle (Tag on Placement) off, because the tags obscure the smaller pipe segments.

5. Draw the first pipe segment into the hall **2'-0"**. Then draw the next pipe segment all of the way down the hall until it reaches into the main hall, zooming out as required.

6. Press <Esc> twice to finish the command.

7. Zoom back into the second AHU and draw pipes coming from the Hydronic Return control on the back of the AHU and intersecting with the main horizontal pipe as shown in Figure 9–42.

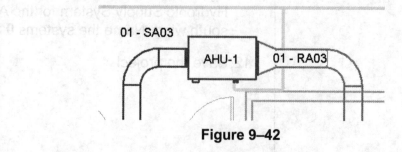

Figure 9–42

8. Repeat the process from each AHU in the wing. You can use

   (Connect Into) for any of the pipes that come directly off the unit to the main pipe. You need to draw the pipes for the ones that come off the back of the AHU.

9. Save the project.

Task 3 - Draw Hydronic Supply Pipes using the Parallel Pipes tool.

1. Open the Mechanical>3D Views>**AREA A 3D** view. In this view you can see the duct systems and the Hydronic Return System you created earlier.

2. Rotate the view to see the 3D information.

3. Select the linked project and temporarily hide it. This makes it easier to select the piping and AHU equipment.

4. In the *Systems* tab>Plumbing & Piping panel, click

   (Parallel Pipes.

5. In the *Modify | Place Parallel Pipes* tab> Parallel Pipes panel, set the *Horizontal Number* to **1**, the *Vertical Number* to **2**, the *Horizontal Offset* and *Vertical Offset* to **1'-0"**, as shown in Figure 9–43.

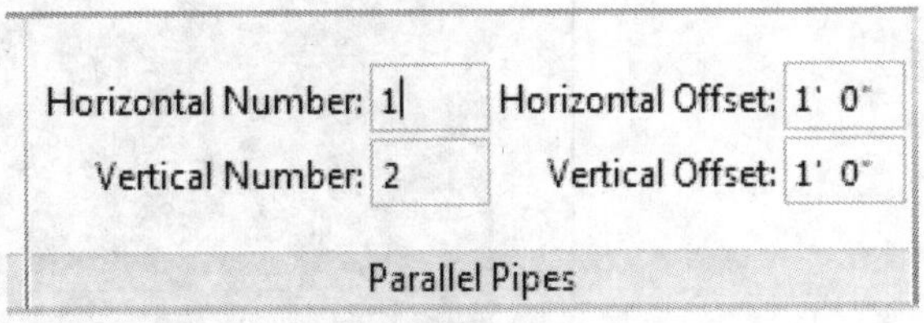

Horizontal Number: 1	Horizontal Offset: 1' 0"
Vertical Number: 2	Vertical Offset: 1' 0"
Parallel Pipes	

Figure 9–43

6. Hover over a pipe and press <Tab> to see if you can select pipe runs (not all of them work). Click on each of the existing pipes or pipe runs. Concentrate first on the north side of the hallway as there are additional issues with connecting the pipes on the south side because of the ductwork.

7. Click   (Modify) to finish the command.

Task 4 - Clean up connections.

1. Zoom in on the AHU at the upper left of the hall. The piping is not attached as shown in Figure 9–44.

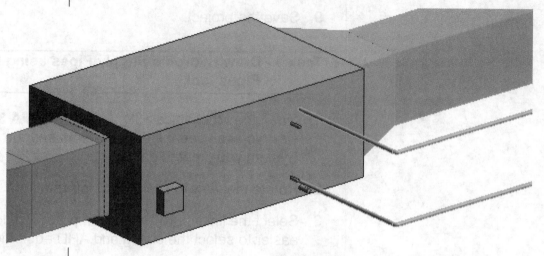

Figure 9–44

2. Select the end of the top pipe closest to the AHU. Drag the end of the pipe to the snap point of the connector on the AHU, as shown in Figure 9–45.

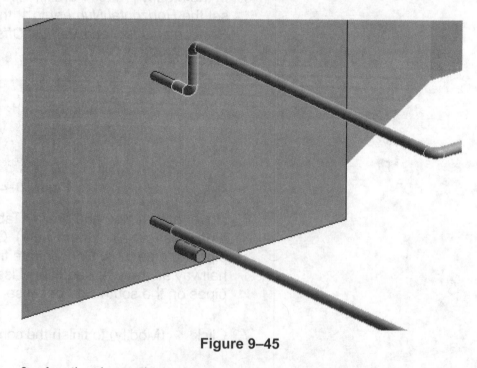

Figure 9–45

3. Another issue that you can see is the color of the pipes. They match the original (Hydronic Return) pipe system type.

4. Select one of the new pipes connected to the supply system.

5. In Properties, in the *Mechanical Section*, change the *System Type* to **Hydronic Supply**.

6. Click out in space and note that the pipes connected to the supply system have now updated.

7. Pan down to the next AHU on the north side of the hallway.

8. Repeat the process of dragging the connector on the pipe to the connector on the AHU and changing the System Type. This time the pipes connected beyond this point do not change.

9. Zoom in on the T intersection as shown in Figure 9–46. Fittings are missing at this point because you could not select a pipe run but only a pipe.

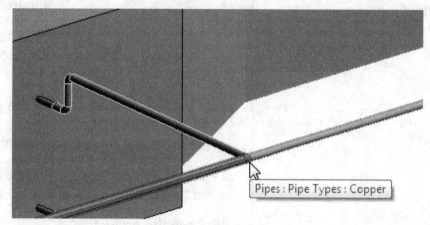

Pipes : Pipe Types : Copper

Figure 9–46

10. Using the connectors, drag the three pipes away from each other, as shown on the left in Figure 9–47. Then drag the two pipes together to touch at connectors. It joins the two pipes together, as shown on the right in Figure 9–47.

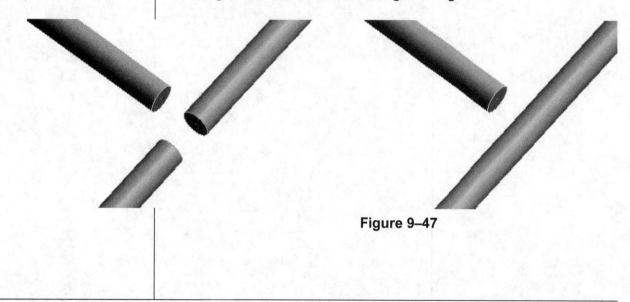

Figure 9–47

11. Finally, drag the vertical pipe to where it intersects with the horizontal pipe. The Tee fitting is automatically applied as shown in Figure 9–48.

Alternately, use

⇉ (Trim/Extend to Corner) and select the two colinear pipes to join them into one. Then

use ⇥ (Trim/Extend Single Element) to force the software to add a Tee fitting where the vertical pipe meets the main run.

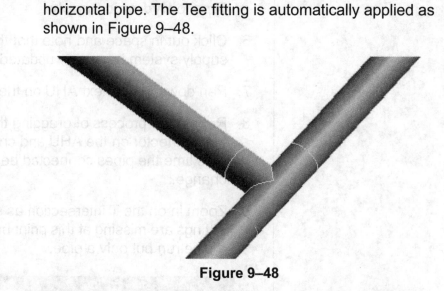

Figure 9–48

12. Continue working down the hall attaching the supply piping correctly to the AHU units. Modify any connections and System Types as required.

13. If you have time, work on the piping from the AHU units on the south side of the hallway. You need to make adjustments so the pipes do not go through the ductwork.

14. Reset **Temporary Hide/Isolate** to display the linked architectural model in the 3D view.

15. Save the project.

Chapter Review Questions

1. Which of the following can you do when modifying pipe? (Select all that apply.)

    a. Change Type

    b. Reapply Type

    c. Add Insulation

    d. Edit Lining

    e. Modify Justification

    f. Modify Material

    g. Change Offset

2. Parallel pipe runs are created automatically at the correct distance from equipment, as shown in Figure 9–49.

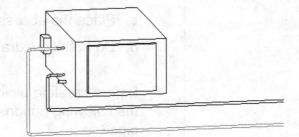

Figure 9–49

    a. True

    b. False

3. Which of the following changes the view shown on the left in Figure 9–50, to the view shown on the right in Figure 9–50?

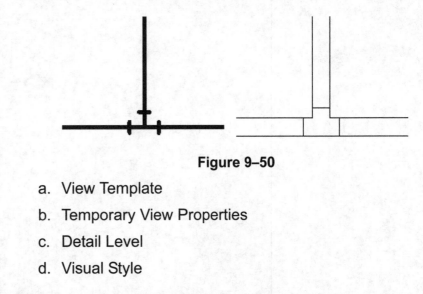

Figure 9–50

    a. View Template

    b. Temporary View Properties

    c. Detail Level

    d. Visual Style

4. When adding pipe accessories, such as the Venturi Flow Meter shown in Figure 9–51, you are first required to:

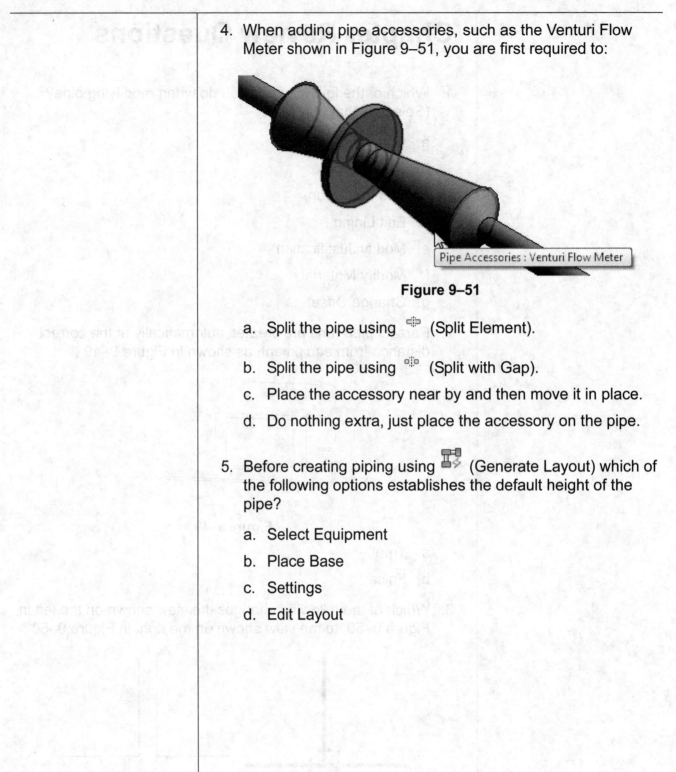

Pipe Accessories : Venturi Flow Meter

Figure 9–51

a. Split the pipe using ⊕ (Split Element).

b. Split the pipe using ⊕ (Split with Gap).

c. Place the accessory near by and then move it in place.

d. Do nothing extra, just place the accessory on the pipe.

5. Before creating piping using ⬚ (Generate Layout) which of the following options establishes the default height of the pipe?

a. Select Equipment

b. Place Base

c. Settings

d. Edit Layout

Command Summary

Button	Command	Location
	Add Insulation	• **Ribbon:** (*with one or more Pipes selected*) *Modify | Pipe* tab>Edit panel or (*with Pipes and Pipe Fittings selected*) *Modify | Multi-Select* tab> Edit panel
	Add to System	• **Ribbon:** *Edit Piping System* tab>Edit Piping System panel
	Change Type	• **Ribbon:** (*with one or more Pipes selected*) *Modify | Pipe* tab>Edit panel or (*with Pipes and Pipe Fittings selected*) *Modify | Multi-Select* tab> Edit panel
	Convert Placeholder	• **Ribbon:** *Modify | Pipe Placeholders* tab>Edit panel
	Disconnect Equipment	• **Ribbon:** *Edit Piping System* tab>Edit Piping System panel
	Edit Insulation	• **Ribbon:** (*with one or more Pipes selected*) *Modify | Pipe* tab>Edit panel or (*with Pipes and Pipe Fittings selected*) *Modify | Multi-Select* tab> Edit panel
	Edit Layout	• **Ribbon:** *Generate Layout* tab>Modify Layout panel
	Edit System (Piping)	• **Ribbon:** *Piping Systems* tab>System Tools panel
	Flex Pipe	• **Ribbon:** *Systems* tab>Plumbing & Piping panel • **Shortcut:** FP
	Generate Layout	• **Ribbon:** *Piping Systems* tab>Layout panel
	Inherit Elevation	• **Ribbon:** *Modify | Place Pipe* tab> Placement Tools panel
	Inherit Size	• **Ribbon:** *Modify | Place Pipe* tab> Placement Tools panel
	Justification (Settings)	• **Ribbon:** *Modify | Place Pipe* tab> Placement Tools panel
	Justify	• **Ribbon:** (*with one or more Pipes selected*) *Modify | Pipe* tab>Edit panel or (*with Pipes and Pipe Fittings selected*) *Modify | Multi-Select* tab> Edit panel

	Mechanical Equipment	• **Ribbon:** *Systems* tab>Mechanical panel • **Shortcut:** ME
	Mechanical Settings	• **Ribbon:** *Systems* tab>Plumbing & Piping panel or Mechanical panel title • **Shortcut:** MS
	Pipe	• **Ribbon:** *Systems* tab>Plumbing & Piping panel • **Shortcut:** PI
	Pipe Accessory	• **Ribbon:** *Systems* tab>Plumbing & Piping panel • **Shortcut:** PA
	Pipe Fitting	• **Ribbon:** *Systems* tab>Plumbing & Piping panel • **Shortcut:** PF
	Pipe Placeholder	• **Ribbon:** *Systems* tab>Plumbing & Piping panel
	Piping (System)	• **Ribbon:** (*with appropriate mechanical equipment selected*) *Modify	Mechanical Equipment* tab>Create Systems panel • **Right-click:** Create Piping System
	Place Base	• **Ribbon:** *Generate Layout* tab>Modify Layout panel
	Remove Insulation	• **Ribbon:** (*with one or more Pipes selected*) *Modify	Pipe* tab>Edit panel or (*with Pipes and Pipe Fittings selected*) *Modify	Multi-Select* tab> Edit panel
	Remove Base	• **Ribbon:** *Generate Layout* tab>Modify Layout panel
	Remove from System	• **Ribbon:** *Edit Piping System* tab>Edit Pipe System panel • **Ribbon:** *Generate Layout* tab>Modify Layout panel
	Select Equipment	• **Ribbon:** *Piping Systems* tab>System Tools panel • **Ribbon:** *Edit Piping System* tab>Edit Piping System panel
	Solutions	• **Ribbon:** *Generate Layout* tab>Modify Layout panel
	Sprinkler	• **Ribbon:** *Systems* tab>Plumbing & Piping panel • **Shortcut:** SK

Chapter 10

Plumbing Systems

In this chapter you learn about plumbing systems, how to add plumbing fixtures, and draw piping for the fixtures. You learn to create sanitary, domestic hot water, and domestic cold water systems as well as review how to use the **Layout** tool with plumbing systems. You also learn to add Fire Protection Systems, including wet and dry sprinklers, with the associated piping and systems.

This chapter contains the following topics:

- **About Plumbing Systems**
- **Adding Plumbing Fixtures**
- **Drawing Piping for Plumbing Systems**
- **Working with Plumbing Systems**
- **Fire Protection Systems**

10.1 About Plumbing Systems

Learning Objective

- Set up views to help you create plumbing systems.

Plumbing Systems include sanitary and domestic hot and cold water. The pipes in a system connect plumbing fixtures together and indicate how the system is laid out. You can draw the pipes directly from the connectors in the fixtures and then create the systems or start with a system and use the automatic layout tools. In either case you need to review the system to verify that the fittings match the direction of the slope as shown in Figure 10–1.

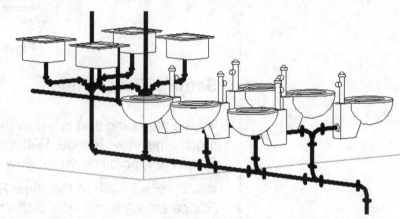

Figure 10–1

There are several steps in creating Plumbing systems:

1. Add plumbing fixtures, such as water closets and lavatories.

2. Create a sanitary or domestic hot or cold water system.

3. Generate piping automatically or add it manually.

4. Check and modify the system.

- The tools to begin creating and placing plumbing fixtures and systems are located in the *Systems* tab>Plumbing & Piping panel, as shown in Figure 10–2.

*You can add **Pipe Placeholders** and **Flex Pipes** using the same methods as placing Pipe.*

Mechanical Equipment	Pipe	Pipe Placeholder	Parallel Pipes		Plumbing Fixture	Sprinkler
Mechanical ⌄			Plumbing & Piping			⌄

Figure 10–2

Modifying Views for Plumbing

Several modifications to views can help you as you create the plumbing systems in a project. These include the View Range where you setup a way to see below the floor in a view, setting the Detail Level to see either schematic or full size views of the piping, using Interior Elevations, Sections, and 3D views to help you as you create the systems. You can also use view filters, as shown in Figure 10–3, to see only the types of systems that are needed at the time.

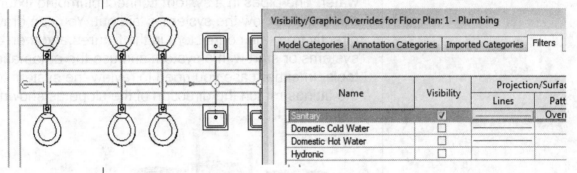

Figure 10–3

Setting View Range

To see plumbing that is below the floor in a plan view you need to modify the View Range. With no elements selected, in Properties, scroll down to *View Range* and click . In the View Range dialog box, in the *Primary Range* area, change the *Bottom Offset* and in the *View Depth* area, change the *Level Offset* to a depth that displays the plumbing but does not display too much of other elements below, as shown in Figure 10–4.

Figure 10–4

Setting the Detail Level

The Coarse and Medium Detail Levels display plumbing piping in schematic while the Fine Detail Level displays the piping at full scale as shown in Figure 10–5. Set the Detail Level on the View Control Bar.

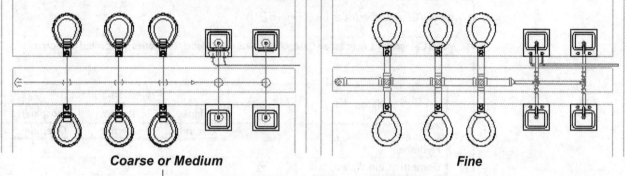

Coarse or Medium   *Fine*

Figure 10–5

Using Interior Elevations, Sections and 3D Views

As you are constructing the plumbing system it is important to work in several views. For example, you might need to create an interior elevation to verify the height of the plumbing fixtures off the floor or a section to ensure that the correct fitting is in place as shown in Figure 10–6.

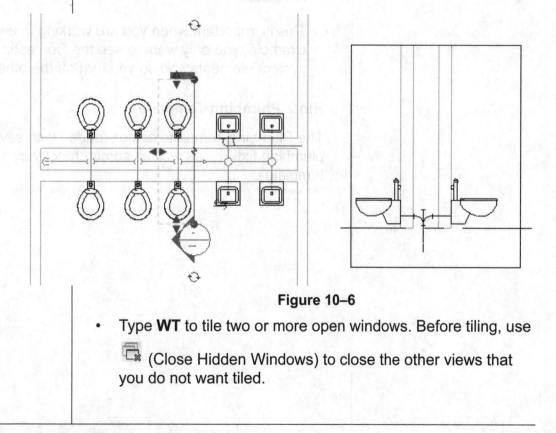

Figure 10–6

- Type **WT** to tile two or more open windows. Before tiling, use

   (Close Hidden Windows) to close the other views that you do not want tiled.

View Filters

You can use View Filters (type **VG** and select the *Filters* tab) to select the type(s) of systems you want to display in a view. For example, in Figure 10–7, Hydronic piping is turned off while the other plumbing related piping types are still displayed.

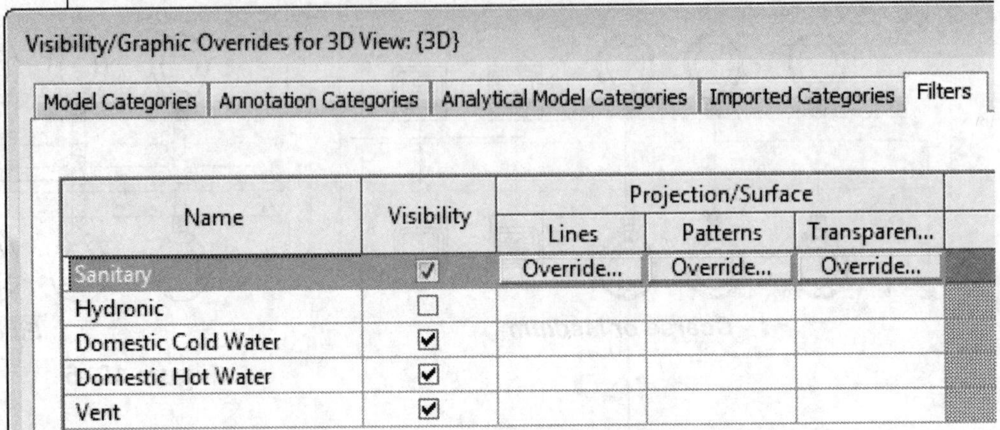

Visibility/Graphic Overrides for 3D View: {3D}

| Model Categories | Annotation Categories | Analytical Model Categories | Imported Categories | Filters |

| Name | Visibility | Projection/Surface | | |
		Lines	Patterns	Transparen...
Sanitary	☑	Override...	Override...	Override...
Hydronic	☐			
Domestic Cold Water	☑			
Domestic Hot Water	☑			
Vent	☑			

Figure 10–7

- If the view filters you want are not present in a view, click [Add] and select from the filters listed.

- These filters and/or views with the filters applied are setup in templates.

- This is important when you are working in a view. For example, you only want to see the Domestic Hot Water system elements and so you turn off the other systems.

Hint: Plumbing Template

The Plumbing Template comes loaded with several different plumbing fixtures as well as some preset views and view templates.

10.2 Adding Plumbing Fixtures

 Learning Objectives

- Add plumbing fixtures to a project.
- Use Named Reference Planes to help you set the right Placement plane for fixtures.

Plumbing fixtures include water closets, sinks, and lavatories as shown in Figure 10–8. They also include bathtubs, drains, drinking fountains and many more. Depending on the type of fixture, there are connectors for sanitary and domestic hot and cold water pipes.

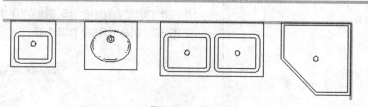

Figure 10–8

How To: Place Plumbing Fixtures

1. Open the view where you want to place the fixtures.
2. In the *Systems* tab>Plumbing & Piping panel, click

   (Plumbing Fixture) or type **PX**.
3. In the Type Selector, select a Plumbing Fixture type. In Properties, set any other values such as the *Level* if it is not hosted.
4. If the fixture is not wall hosted, in the *Modify | Place Plumbing Fixture* tab>Placement panel, select the type of placement for

   the specific fixture. The default is   (Place on Vertical Face), as shown in Figure 10–9.

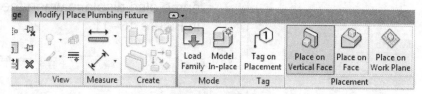

Figure 10–9

5. Place the fixture in the model by clicking at the required location in the model view. Many fixtures are wall based so you need to select a wall to place them. Press <Spacebar> to rotate the fixture before placing it.

6. Continue to place additional fixtures, or click 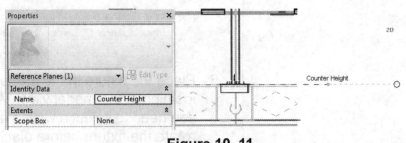 (Modify) to exit the command.

- Additional plumbing fixtures can be loaded from the Autodesk® Revit® MEP Library in the *Plumbing>MEP> Fixtures* sub-folders.

- To place plumbing equipment, such as Hot Water Heaters, use ⊞ (Mechanical Equipment).

Reference Planes

Depending on the type of fixture, you need to place it on a face or a work plane. Faces include walls, ceilings, floors, and counter tops. Use this when you have a face-based component. But, frequently you place fixtures on a workplane. You can specify the *Placement Plane* as shown in Figure 10–10. This can include named reference planes.

Placement Plane: Level : Level 1 ▾
Level : Level 1
Level : Level 2
Pick...
Reference Plane : Counter Height

Figure 10–10

How To: Create a Named Reference Plane

1. Open the view where you want to place the reference plane. For example, to specify a counter height reference you need to be in a section or elevation view.

2. In the *Systems* tab>Work Plane panel, click 📐 (Ref Plane).
3. In the *Modify | Place Reference Plane* tab>Draw panel, click ✏ (Line) or ⤴ (Pick Lines).
4. Draw the reference plane.
5. Click (Modify) and select the new reference plane.
6. In Properties, enter a name for the Reference Plane. The name also displays when the ref plane is selected, as shown in Figure 10–11.

Properties
Reference Planes (1) ▾ 🔲 Edit Type
Identity Data
Name   Counter Height
Extents
Scope Box   None

Counter Height

Figure 10–11

10.3 Drawing Piping for Plumbing Systems

Learning Objectives

- Draw and modify piping between plumbing fixtures.
- Add and modify pipe fittings and accessories.

Piping for plumbing systems is added in the same manner as all other piping. In this case, you work from the plumbing fixtures, as shown in Figure 10–12, instead of mechanical equipment. It is very important to get the direction of flow and slope correct with sanitary systems. There are also fittings that are not applied automatically that need to be added.

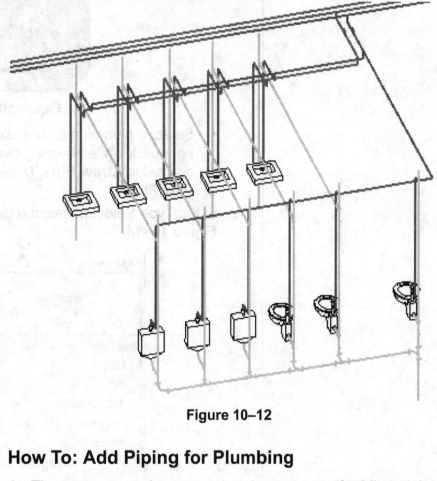

Figure 10–12

How To: Add Piping for Plumbing

1. There are several ways to start the process of adding piping:
   - In the *Systems* tab>Plumbing & Piping panel, click (Pipe), (Pipe Placeholder), or (Flex Pipe).

- Select a plumbing fixture, existing pipe or pipe fitting to display the connectors. Click on one of the connector icons as shown in Figure 10–13.

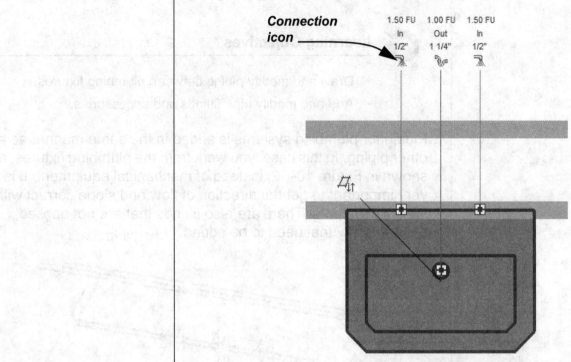

Figure 10–13

- Select a plumbing fixture, existing pipe, or pipe fitting and right-click while hovering over the appropriate connector and select **Draw Pipe, Draw Pipe Placeholder,** or **Draw Flex Pipe**.

2. In the Type Selector, select a pipe type as shown in Figure 10–14.

Figure 10–14

3. If not using a connector to start the command, in the Options Bar, set the *Diameter* and *Offset*. In the Placement Tools panel, you can use (Inherit Elevation) and <img /> (Inherit Size) to set the elevation or size to match a selected pipe.

Connecting the new pipe to the end of an existing pipe at a different offset, is not affected by the Automatically Connect toggle.

- If starting the command from a connector, the default diameter and offset for the new pipe match the parameters of the selected connector.

4. In the *Modify | Place (Flex) Pipe (Placeholder)* tab> Placement Tools panel, use [icon] (Automatically Connect) if you want the pipe you are drawing to connect to the middle of an existing pipe which is at a different offset.

5. Draw the pipes using temporary dimensions, snaps, and alignments to locate each point along the path.

6. Press <Esc> once to stay in the command but have a new start location.

7. Press <Esc> twice or click [cursor] (Modify) to complete the command.

- When drawing pipes with a slope, it helps to identify the direction that *drains to daylight* (the point in the system where it attaches to the exterior drainage pipes). Then, start drawing the pipes from the top most fixture in the system as shown in Figure 10–15.

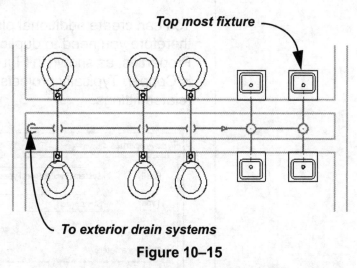

Top most fixture

To exterior drain systems

Figure 10–15

- As you are drawing pipes with slopes, you can set the information in the *Modify | Place Pipe* tab>Sloped Piping panel as shown in Figure 10–16. You can change the direction of the slope, the slope value, and turn the slope off or specify that it be ignored when connecting.

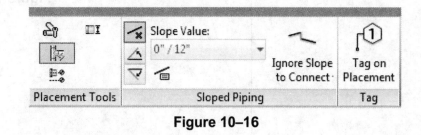

Figure 10–16

- Turn on the Slope Tooltip to see the exact information of the offsets and slope as you draw, as shown in Figure 10–17.

Start Offset	0' 0"
Current Offset	-0' 3 1/8"
Slope	1/4" / 12" Down

Horizontal and Nearest

Figure 10–17

- Another way to draw pipe from a plumbing fixture is using the **Connect Into** tool. It can be used to create piping to connect the plumbing fixture into a main pipe. Select a plumbing fixture which has unconnected connections. In the *Modify |*
Plumbing Fixtures tab>Layout panel, click (Connect Into) and then select the pipe you want to connect the fixture into.

Pipe Types and Settings

You can create additional pipe types. Pipes are a system family therefore you need to duplicate an existing family in the Type Properties, as shown in Figure 10–18. The default Standard pipe is Copper. Typically projects also include PVC piping and its related fittings.

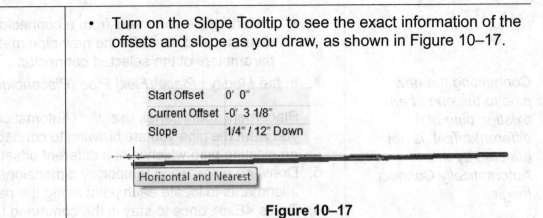

Figure 10–18

Routing Preferences

The Routing Preferences dialog box (shown in Figure 10–19), enables you to specify the kind of pipe and pipe fittings to use. You can have a simple pipe type with one kind of pipe segment used for all sizes and one family for each kind of pipe fitting. Alternatively, you can set up the pipe type so that as the pipe size increases, different pipe and different fittings are used. Use

➕ (Add Row) and ➖ (Remove Row) to create or remove rows, and the arrows to re-order items.

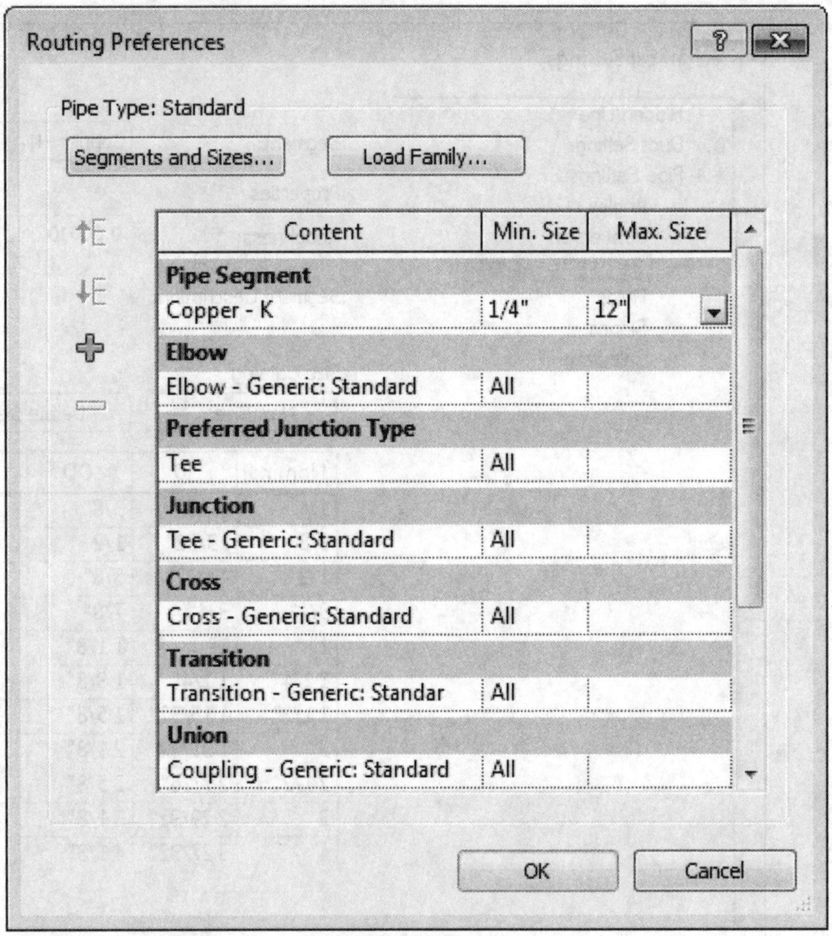

Content	Min. Size	Max. Size
Pipe Segment		
Copper - K	1/4"	12"
Elbow		
Elbow - Generic: Standard	All	
Preferred Junction Type		
Tee	All	
Junction		
Tee - Generic: Standard	All	
Cross		
Cross - Generic: Standard	All	
Transition		
Transition - Generic: Standar	All	
Union		
Coupling - Generic: Standard	All	

Pipe Type: Standard — Segments and Sizes... / Load Family... / OK / Cancel

Figure 10–19

- **Segments and Sizes...** enables you to create named segments with corresponding standard pipe sizes.

- **Load Family...** enables you to load additional pipe fittings as required.

Mechanical Settings

The Mechanical settings for plumbing pipes are similar to other piping systems. In the *Systems* tab>Plumbing & Piping panel title, click ⊌ (Mechanical Settings) or type **MS** to open the Mechanical Settings dialog box.

In this dialog box, you can set general pipe settings, such as annotation, conversion settings for automatic pipe layouts, manage segments and sizes (as shown in Figure 10–20), manage fluid types, and set standard slope values.

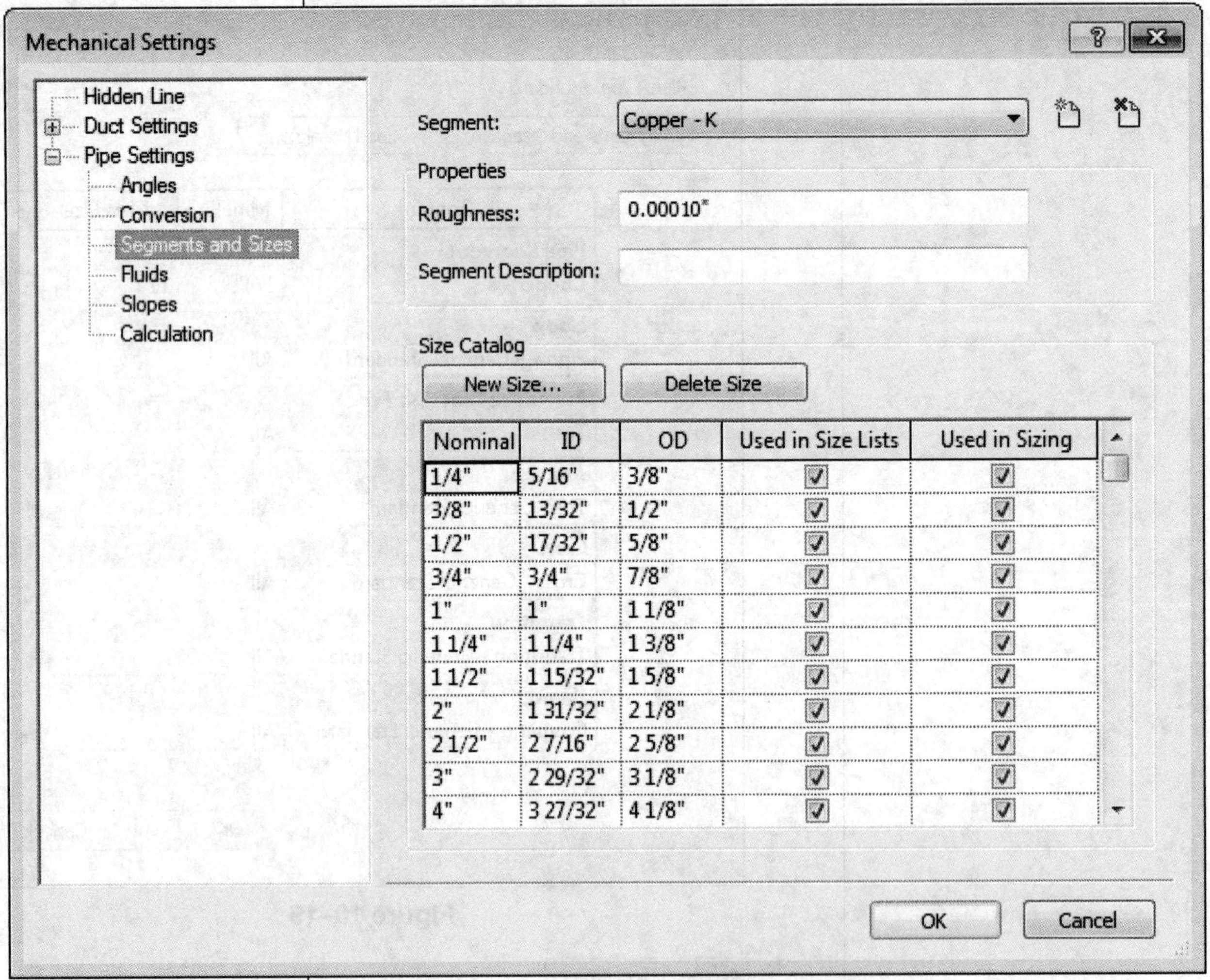

Mechanical Settings

- Hidden Line
- Duct Settings
- Pipe Settings
  - Angles
  - Conversion
  - Segments and Sizes
  - Fluids
  - Slopes
  - Calculation

Segment: Copper - K

Properties

Roughness: 0.00010"

Segment Description:

Size Catalog

New Size...   Delete Size

Nominal	ID	OD	Used in Size Lists	Used in Sizing
1/4"	5/16"	3/8"	✓	✓
3/8"	13/32"	1/2"	✓	✓
1/2"	17/32"	5/8"	✓	✓
3/4"	3/4"	7/8"	✓	✓
1"	1"	1 1/8"	✓	✓
1 1/4"	1 1/4"	1 3/8"	✓	✓
1 1/2"	1 15/32"	1 5/8"	✓	✓
2"	1 31/32"	2 1/8"	✓	✓
2 1/2"	2 7/16"	2 5/8"	✓	✓
3"	2 29/32"	3 1/8"	✓	✓
4"	3 27/32"	4 1/8"	✓	✓

OK   Cancel

Figure 10–20

- Not all settings included in the Autodesk Revit templates have been converted to standard metric sizes.

Modifying Plumbing Pipes

To change the slope of a pipe, select it and modify the slope using the *Edit Slope* control as shown in Figure 10–21. You can also click ✎ (Slope) to open the Slope Editor. The controls are available in plan or section/elevation views.

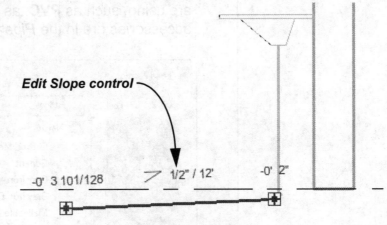

Edit Slope control

Figure 10–21

- You can change the size of the pipe in the Options Bar or Properties. The offset of the pipe ends can be changed using Properties or the *Edit Start/End Offset* controls.

Plumbing Pipe Fittings and Accessories

One of the challenges about working with plumbing is specifying the correct pipe fitting or accessory and verifying that it is working as expected. For example, if a fitting is facing the wrong direction, you can use ⇄ (Flip) to switch it, as shown in Figure 10–22.

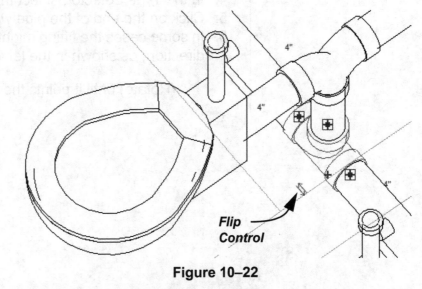

Flip Control

Figure 10–22

- Check various views to verify that you have correctly attached the plumbing fittings to the pipes.

- Some pipe fittings are specified in the Routing Preferences in the Type Properties of the pipe but others have to be added separately. Accessories are always added later.

- Pipe fittings can be loaded from the Library in the *Pipe>Fittings* sub-folder. Select the folder for the type of pipe you are using, such as **PVC**, as shown in Figure 10–23. Pipe accessories are in the *Pipe>Accessories* sub-folder.

Name	Type
Carbon Steel	File folder
Generic	File folder
Gray Iron	File folder
Gray Iron Flanges	File folder
Malleable Iron	File folder
Profiles	File folder
PVC	File folder
Steel Flanges	File folder

Figure 10–23

How To: Add a Pipe Fitting

1. Draw the pipes as required.
2. Load the pipe fitting you want to use.
3. In the *Systems* tab>Plumbing & Piping panel, click (Pipe Fitting.
4. In the Type Selector, select the fitting you want to use.
5. Click on the end of the pipe where you want the fitting.
6. In some cases the fitting might be pointing towards the wrong direction, as shown in the left in Figure 10–24. Click

   (Rotate) until it points the required direction.

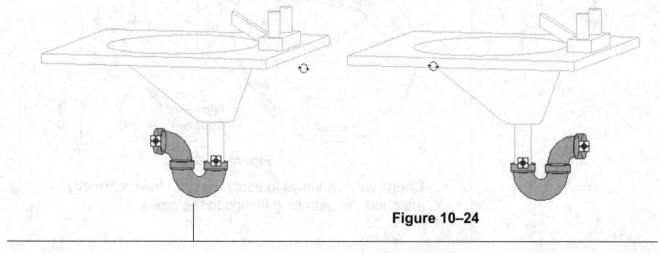

Figure 10–24

10.4 Working with Plumbing Systems

 Learning Objective

- Create plumbing systems for domestic hot and cold water and sanitary piping.

Similar to all other systems, once you have placed plumbing fixtures into the model, you need to create the appropriate sanitary systems, as shown in Figure 10–25, and domestic hot and cold water systems. The processes and tools to create automatic layouts and to analyze them are similar to other systems.

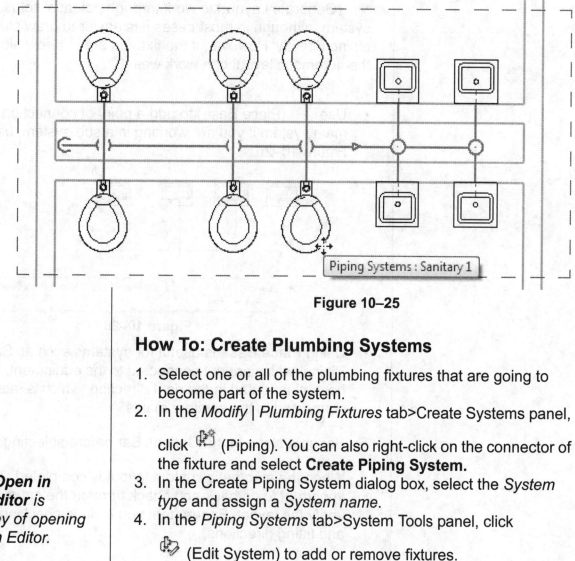

Piping Systems : Sanitary 1

Figure 10–25

How To: Create Plumbing Systems

1. Select one or all of the plumbing fixtures that are going to become part of the system.
2. In the *Modify | Plumbing Fixtures* tab>Create Systems panel, click (Piping). You can also right-click on the connector of the fixture and select **Create Piping System.**
3. In the Create Piping System dialog box, select the *System type* and assign a *System name*.
4. In the *Piping Systems* tab>System Tools panel, click (Edit System) to add or remove fixtures.

*Selecting **Open in System Editor** is another way of opening the System Editor.*

5. In the *Edit Piping Systems* tab>Edit Piping System panel:

- Click ⬚ (Add to System) and select any fixtures that are to be part of this system that were not selected earlier.

- Click ⬚ (Remove from System) if you want to remove any fixtures.

- Click ⬚ (Select Equipment) and select any equipment such as a hot water heater.

6. Click ✓ (Finish Editing System) to accept all components and complete the creation of the system.

Automatic Layouts

The process of creating automatic piping layouts for plumbing systems is the same as for other piping systems. You can use

⬚ (Generate Layout) to work through potential solutions for the system, although in most cases it is easier to draw plumbing piping directly. However, if the fixtures are in a row along a wall the automatic layout can work well.

- Use ⬚ (Place Base) to add a point of connection to the main system if you are working in a sub-system, as shown in Figure 10–26.

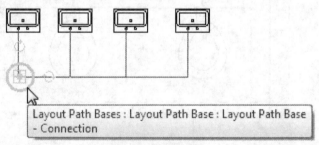

Figure 10–26

- Using **Place Base** is useful for systems such as Sanitary Piping, which are not connected to the equipment, but should have pipe routed in the right direction, which is later connected to the sanitary mains.

- Set up a slope in the Options Bar before selecting a layout.

- When the automatic/custom layout is completed, it is important to go back and check through the entire system to verify the layout. Ensure that you include checking slopes and fitting directions.

Pipe Sizing

It is easiest to draw pipe using the default sizes provided by the opening sizes of the equipment or as preset in the Mechanical Settings. These sizes are often incorrect for the system. The Duct/Pipe Sizing dialog box enables you to specify a sizing method and constraints to determine the way the pipes should be sized, as shown in Figure 10–27.

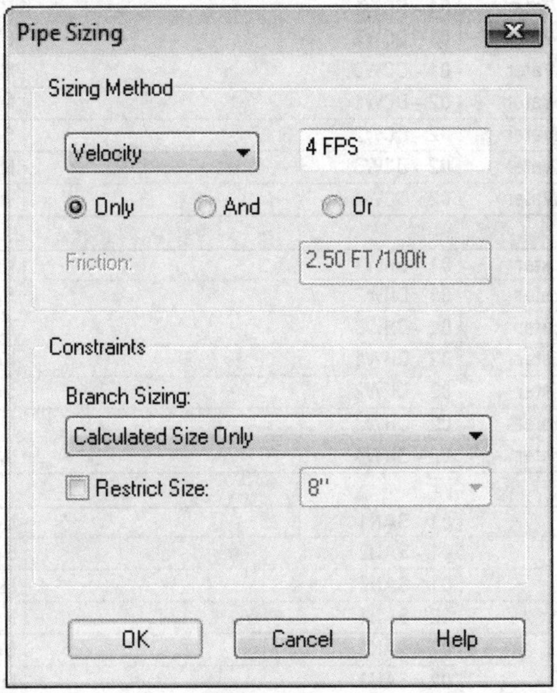

Figure 10–27

- Select a run of piping, in the *Modify | Multi-Select* tab> Analysis panel, click (Duct/Pipe Sizing).

- Plumbing systems are sized using fixture units, the rate of flow within a pipe. As applicable, plumbing fixtures have Waste Fixture Units, Hot Water Fixture Units, and Cold Water Fixture Units assigned to them. All of the connected fixture units in a system are used to size each run of the plumbing line.

- Pipe Sizing cannot be used to size sanitary systems.

- If you add fixtures to the system or change the fixture units of fixtures already included in the system, run the software again as it could impact the pipe sizes.

Plumbing Schedules

No schedules come with the default templates provided by Autodesk® Revit® MEP software, but many firms create typical ones that can be used in most projects. They are helpful for analyzing the systems (such as, displaying the flow rate, keeping track of the systems, etc.) as shown in Figure 10–28.

PLUMBING SYSTEM SCHEDULE			
System Type	System Name	Comments	Flow
Domestic Cold Water	01 – DCW1	North Wing Classroom sinks	42 GPM
Domestic Cold Water	01 – DCW2	South Wing Classroom sinks	42 GPM
Domestic Cold Water	01 – DCW3	Men's Restroom	51 GPM
Domestic Cold Water	02 – DCW1	North Wing Classroom sinks	42 GPM
Domestic Cold Water	02 – DCW2	South Wing Classroom sinks	42 GPM
Domestic Cold Water	02 – DCW3	Men's Restroom	51 GPM
Domestic Cold Water	02 – DCW4	Women's Restroom	57 GPM
Domestic Hot Water	01 – DHW1	North Wing Classroom sinks	23 GPM
Domestic Hot Water	01 – DHW2	South Wing Classroom sinks	23 GPM
Domestic Hot Water	01 – DHW3	Men's Restroom	12 GPM
Domestic Hot Water	02 – DHW1	North Wing Classroom sinks	23 GPM
Domestic Hot Water	02 – DHW2	South Wing Classroom sinks	23 GPM
Domestic Hot Water	02 – DHW3	Men's Restroom	12 GPM
Domestic Hot Water	02 – DHW4	Women's Restroom	12 GPM
Sanitary	01 – SAN1	North Wing Classroom sinks	Not Computed
Sanitary	01 – SAN2	South Wing Classroom sinks	Not Computed
Sanitary	01 – SAN3	Men's Restroom	Not Computed
Sanitary	02 – SAN1	North Wing Classroom sinks	Not Computed
Sanitary	02 – SAN2	South Wing Classroom sinks	Not Computed
Sanitary	02 – SAN3	Men's Restroom	Not Computed
Sanitary	02 – SAN4	Women's Restroom ▼	Not Computed

Figure 10–28

Practice 10a

Work with Plumbing Systems

Learning Objectives

- Set up and review plumbing related views.
- Add Plumbing fixtures.
- Add Domestic Hot and Cold Water piping, as well as sanitary piping and pipe fittings.
- Investigate and create piping systems.

Estimated time for completion: 35 minutes

In this practice you will set up and review several plumbing related views including plans, sections, and 3D views. You will add plumbing fixtures to a restroom and add piping and pipe fittings, as shown in Figure 10–29. You will also use a variety of modify tools to help you connect the plumbing fixtures. You will then investigate the automatically-created systems and create new systems.

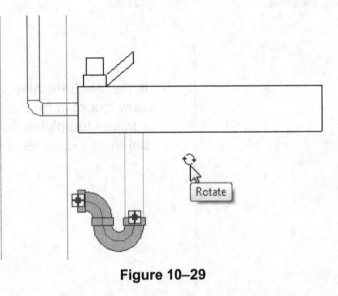

Figure 10–29

Task 1 - Set up and review plumbing related views.

---

1. In the *C:\Autodesk Revit 2015 MEP Fundamentals Class Files\Plumbing* folder, open **MEP-Elementary-School -Plumbing.rvt**.

2. In the *Systems* tab>Mechanical panel title bar, click ⌐ (Mechanical Settings).

3. In the Mechanical Settings dialog box, in *Pipe Settings,* select **Angles**.

4. In the right pane, select **Use specific angles** as shown in Figure 10–30, and click . This limits the angles you can use to draw the piping to industry specific fittings.

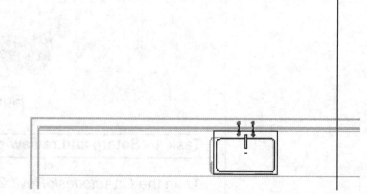

Figure 10–30

5. In the Mechanical>Plumbing>Floor Plans>**01 Plumbing Plan** view, zoom in on the lower left corner of the South wing. You can see the piping coming from the sinks in each classroom, but then it ends as shown in Figure 10–31.

Figure 10–31

6. Double-click on the arrow of the nearby section (or right-click and select **Go to View)**. The piping goes up into the plenum over the ceiling of the second floor, as shown in Figure 10–32.

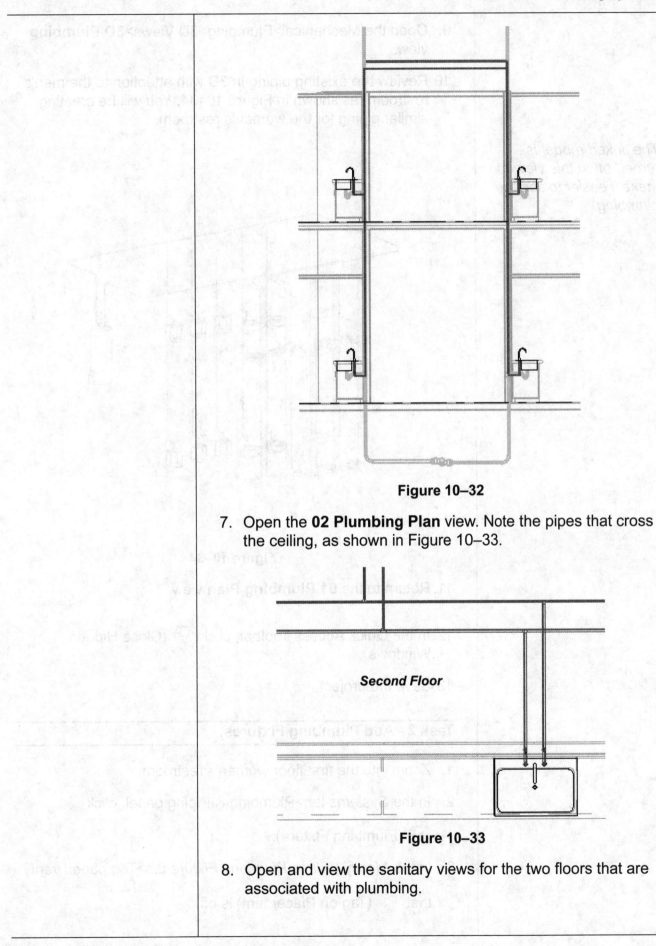

Figure 10–32

7. Open the **02 Plumbing Plan** view. Note the pipes that cross the ceiling, as shown in Figure 10–33.

Second Floor

Figure 10–33

8. Open and view the sanitary views for the two floors that are associated with plumbing.

9. Open the Mechanical>Plumbing>3D Views>**3D Plumbing** view.

10. Review the existing piping in 3D with attention to the men's restroom, as shown in Figure 10–34. You will be creating similar piping for the women's restroom.

The linked model is turned off in this view to make it easier to see the plumbing.

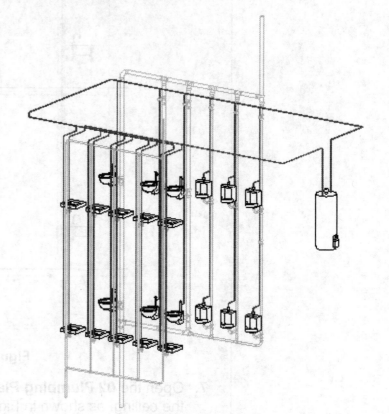

Figure 10–34

11. Return to the **01 Plumbing Plan** view.

12. In the Quick Access Toolbar, click ⬚ (Close Hidden Windows).

13. Save the project.

Task 2 - Add Plumbing Fixtures.

1. Zoom into the first floor women's restroom.

2. In the *Systems* tab>Plumbing & Piping panel, click 🚽 (Plumbing Fixture).

3. In the *Modify | Place Plumbing Fixture* tab>Tag panel, verify that ①⌐ (Tag on Placement) is off.

4. In the Type Selector, select **Water Closet - Flush Valve - Wall Mounted1: Public - 1.6 gpf**.

5. As this is a wall mounted fixture, verify that 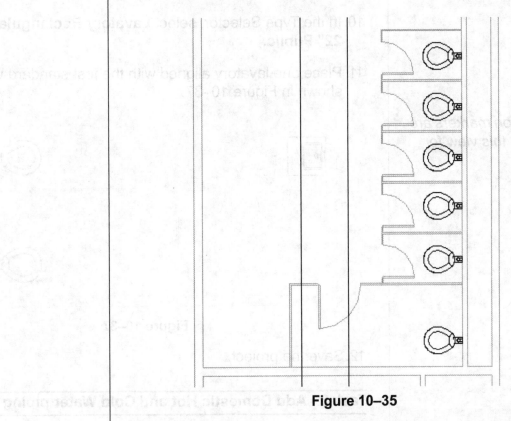 (Place on Vertical Face) is set. Add a WC in each of the stalls, as shown in Figure 10–35. The exact location is not important at this point.

Figure 10–35

6. Start the **Align** command (Hint: the keyboard shortcut is **AL**).

7. For each of the standard stalls, select the alignment line of the stall by hovering over the door, and then the alignment line of the WC, as shown in Figure 10–36.

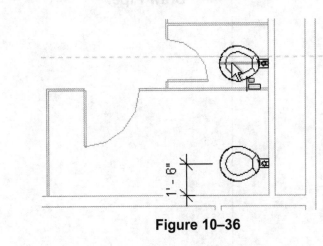

1' - 6"

Figure 10–36

8. For the Handicap WC, draw a dimension from the interior of the wall to the alignment line of the plumbing fixture. Select the plumbing fixture and change the dimension to **1'-6"**, as shown in Figure 10–36. Once the WC is in place you can delete the dimension.

9. Click (Plumbing Fixture) to start the command again.

10. In the Type Selector, select **Lavatory Rectangular1: 22" x 22" Public.**

11. Place one lavatory aligned with the first standard WC, as shown in Figure 10–37.

The section markers are hidden in this view for clarity.

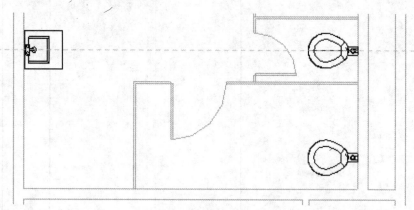

Figure 10–37

12. Save the project.

Task 3 - Add Domestic Hot and Cold Water piping.

1. In the women's restroom, select the lavatory.

2. Click on the Hot Water icon, as shown in Figure 10–38, alternatively, right-click on the Hot Water Control and select **Draw Pipe**.

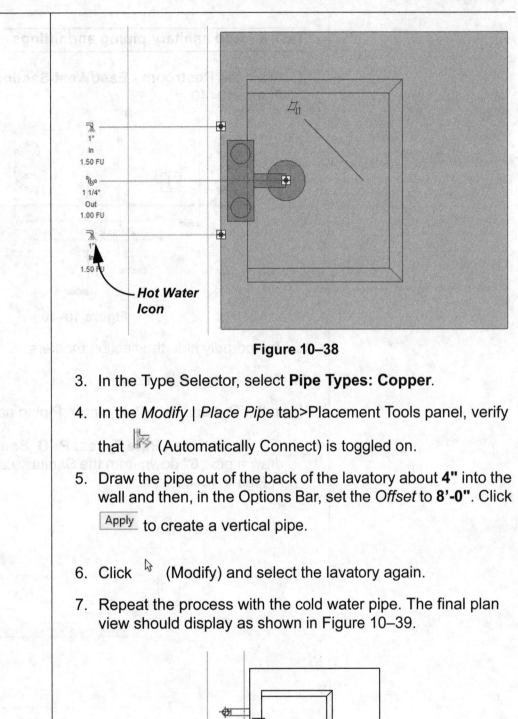

Figure 10–38

3. In the Type Selector, select **Pipe Types: Copper**.

4. In the *Modify | Place Pipe* tab>Placement Tools panel, verify that 🔧 (Automatically Connect) is toggled on.

5. Draw the pipe out of the back of the lavatory about **4"** into the wall and then, in the Options Bar, set the *Offset* to **8'-0"**. Click **Apply** to create a vertical pipe.

6. Click 🔧 (Modify) and select the lavatory again.

7. Repeat the process with the cold water pipe. The final plan view should display as shown in Figure 10–39.

Figure 10–39

8. Save the project.

Task 4 - Add sanitary piping and fittings

1. Open the **Restroom - East/West Section** view shown in Figure 10–40.

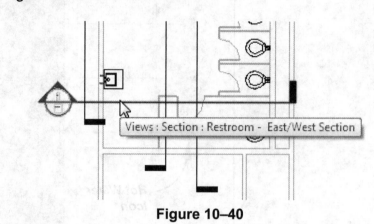

Figure 10–40

2. Temporarily hide the section markers.

3. Zoom in on the lavatory.

4. In the *Systems* tab>Plumbing & Piping panel, click

   (Pipe). Using **Pipe Types: PVC_Sanitary (SR) Glued**, draw a pipe **6"** down from the Sanitary connector, as shown in Figure 10–41.

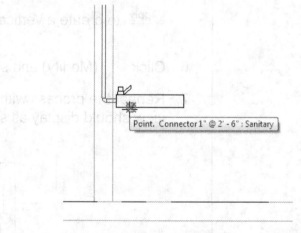

Figure 10–41

5. In the *Systems* tab>Plumbing & Piping panel click (Pipe Fitting).

6. In the Type Selector, select **Trap P - PVC - Sch 40 - DWV: Standard** and place it at the end of the sanitary pipe. Use the **Rotate** control to turn it in the correct direction, as shown in Figure 10–42.

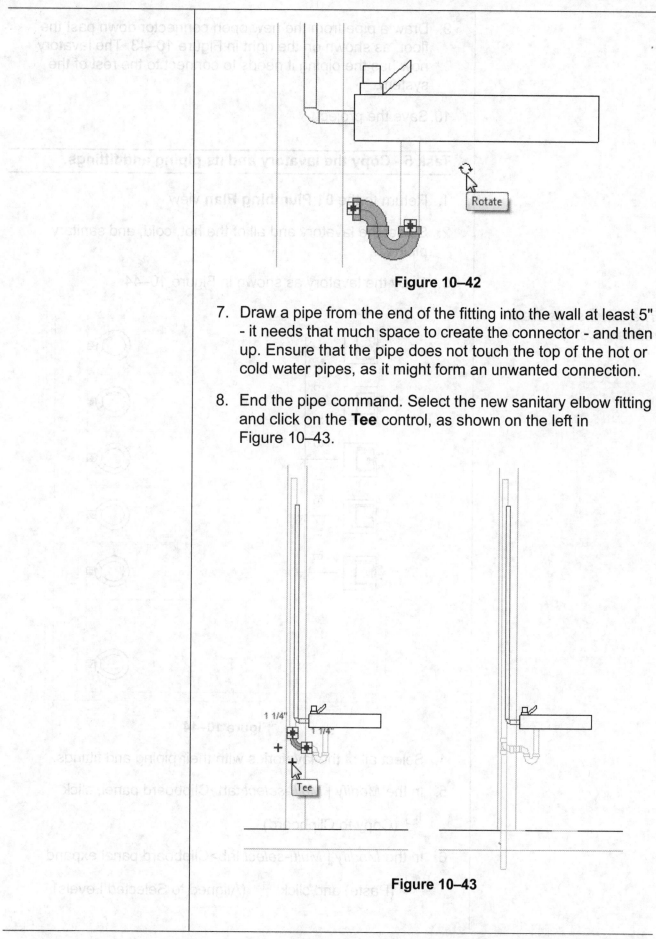

Figure 10–42

7. Draw a pipe from the end of the fitting into the wall at least 5"
   - it needs that much space to create the connector - and then
   up. Ensure that the pipe does not touch the top of the hot or
   cold water pipes, as it might form an unwanted connection.

8. End the pipe command. Select the new sanitary elbow fitting
   and click on the **Tee** control, as shown on the left in
   Figure 10–43.

Figure 10–43

9. Draw a pipe from the new open connector down past the floor, as shown on the right in Figure 10–43. The lavatory now has the piping it needs to connect to the rest of the system.

10. Save the project.

Task 5 - Copy the lavatory and its piping and fittings.

1. Return to the **01 Plumbing Plan** view.

2. Select the lavatory and all of the hot, cold, and sanitary piping.

3. Copy the lavatory as shown in Figure 10–44.

The dimensions are for reference only.

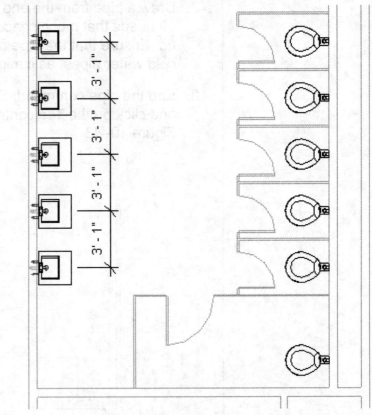

Figure 10–44

4. Select all of the lavatories with their piping and fittings.

5. In the *Modify | Multi-select* tab>Clipboard panel, click

   (Copy to Clipboard).

6. In the *Modify | Multi-select* tab>Clipboard panel expand

   (Paste) and click (Aligned to Selected Levels).

7. In the Select Levels dialog box select Level 2 as shown in Figure 10–45 and click [OK].

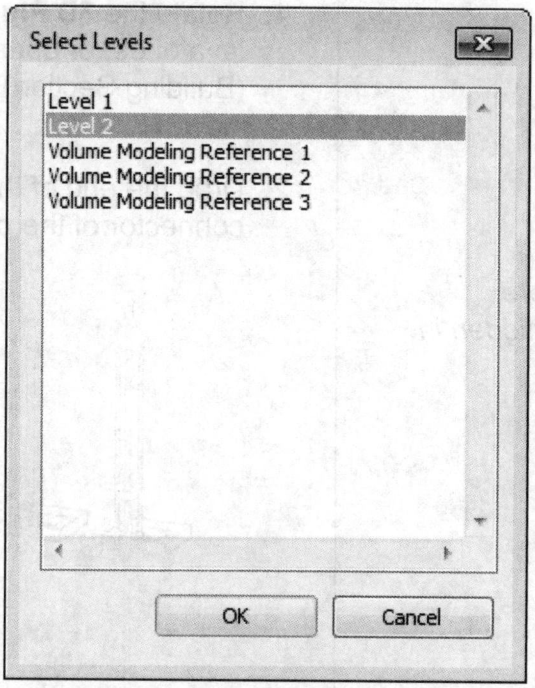

Select Levels

Level 1
Level 2
Volume Modeling Reference 1
Volume Modeling Reference 2
Volume Modeling Reference 3

OK   Cancel

Figure 10–45

8. Open the **3D Plumbing** view and zoom in so that you can see all of the lavatories and connected pipes, as shown in Figure 10–46.

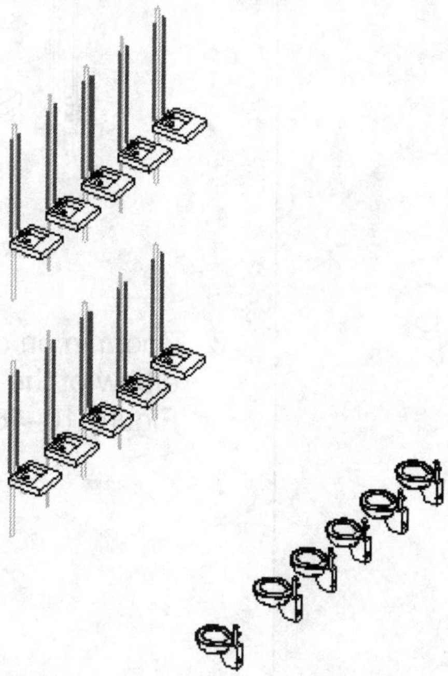

Figure 10–46

9. Save the project.

Task 6 - Clean up the piping runs and connect them to the hot water heater.

1. Rotate the **3D Plumbing** view so you can see the back of the lavatories, or open the Mechanical>Plumbing>Sections (Building Section): Restrooms - **Back of Lavatories Section** view.

2. Drag the end of the lower sanitary pipe until it touches the connector of the pipe above it, as shown in Figure 10–47.

The WCs were temporarily hidden in this view.

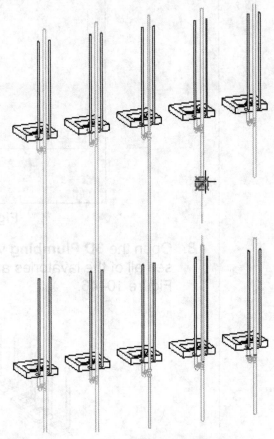

Figure 10–47

3. Zoom in on one of the 2nd Floor lavatories and change the elbow of the hot and cold water pipes to **Tees**, as shown in Figure 10–48.

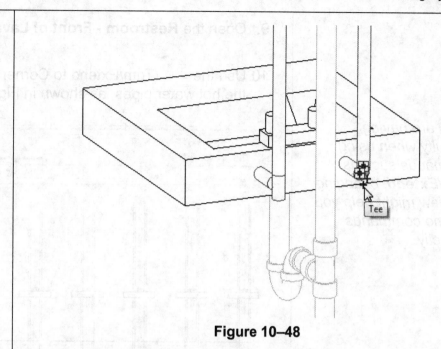

Figure 10–48

4. Extend the hot and cold water pipes from the first floor to the second floor tees.

5. Open the **02 Plumbing Plan** view.

6. Zoom in on the women's restroom, but ensure that you can also see the hot water heater and some of the piping in the men's restroom.

7. Select the hot water heater and the piping coming from the equipment and going into the men's restroom.

8. In the *Modify* | *Multi-select* tab>Modify panel, click 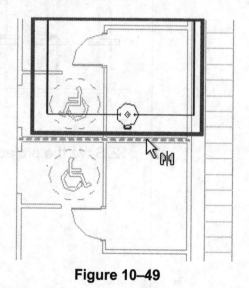 (Mirror - Pick Axis). Select the middle alignment of the wall as the axis, as shown in Figure 10–49.

Figure 10–49

*If you are having difficulty when using commands such as **Trim/Extend**, changing the view might help you use the commands correctly.*

9. Open the **Restroom - Front of Lavatory** section

10. Use the ⬚ (Trim/Extend to Corner) command to connect the hot water pipes, as shown in Figure 10–50.

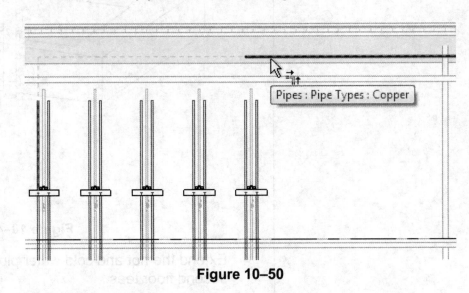

Figure 10–50

11. Use the ⬚ (Trim/Extend Multiple) command to extend the rest of the hot water pipes to the pipe above, as shown in Figure 10–51.

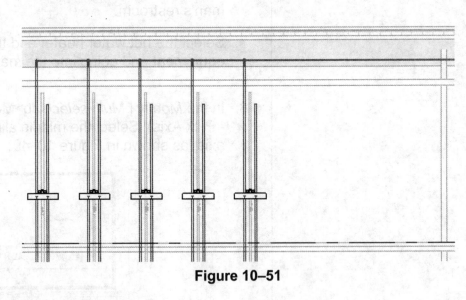

Figure 10–51

12. Save the project.

Task 7 - Investigate and assign Hot and Cold Water Systems.

1. Open the **02 Plumbing Plan** view.

2. Open the System Browser by pressing <F9>, or right-click and select **Browsers>System Browser**.

3. Hover over a lavatory and press <Tab> until it displays the Cold Water system, as shown on the left Figure 10–52. Press <Tab> again until you see the Hot Water system, as shown on the right in Figure 10–52.

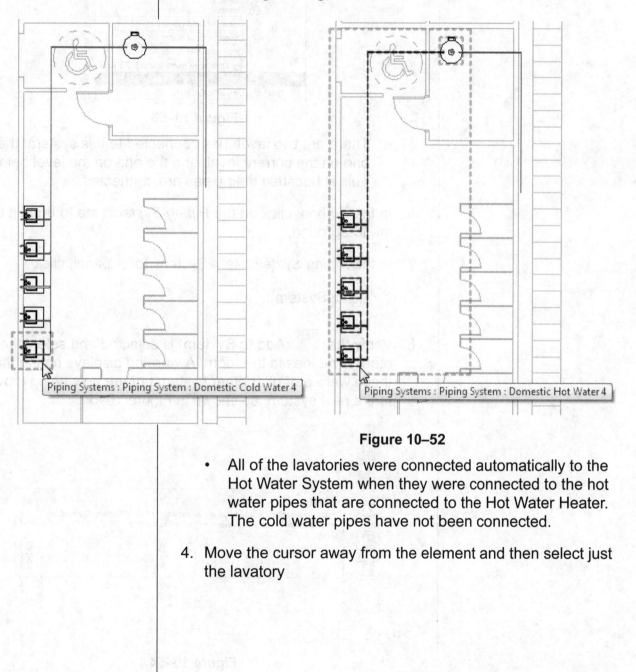

Piping Systems : Piping System : Domestic Cold Water 4

Piping Systems : Piping System : Domestic Hot Water 4

Figure 10–52

- All of the lavatories were connected automatically to the Hot Water System when they were connected to the hot water pipes that are connected to the Hot Water Heater. The cold water pipes have not been connected.

4. Move the cursor away from the element and then select just the lavatory

5. In the System Browser, expand the **Domestic Cold Water** node to see the related system, as shown in Figure 10–53.

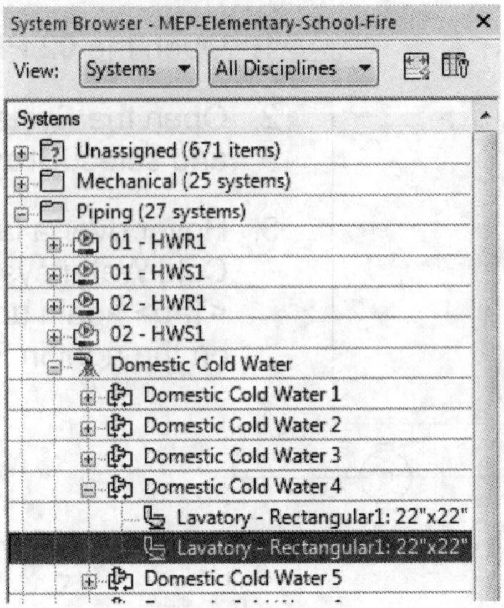

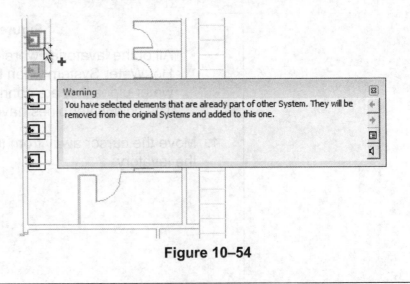

Figure 10–53

- There are two lavatories connected to this system: the one on the current level, and the one on the level below. This is because their pipes are connected.

6. In the Ribbon, click on the *Piping Systems* tab to bring it to the foreground.

7. In the *Piping Systems* tab>System Tools panel, click (Edit System).

8. Verify that (Add to System) is selected and select the other lavatories in the room. A warning displays noting that these were part of another system but are now being moved to the new system, as shown in Figure 10–54.

Figure 10–54

© 2014, ASCENT - Center for Technical Knowledge®

9. Once you have selected all of the lavatories, click ✓ (Finish Editing Systems). All of the lavatories on both levels are now in the same system even though they are not yet connected by piping, as shown in the 3D Plumbing view with the system highlighted in Figure 10–55.

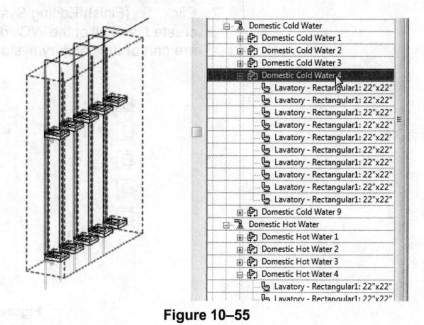

Figure 10–55

10. Save the project.

Task 8 - Create a Sanitary system.

1. Open the **01 Plumbing Plan** view.

2. Select one of the water closets.

3. In the *Modify | Plumbing Fixture* tab>Create Systems panel, click ⬚ (Piping).

4. In the Create Piping System dialog box, verify that the *System Type* is set to **Sanitary**, accept the default name, and select **Open in System Editor** as shown in Figure 10–56.

   Click [OK].

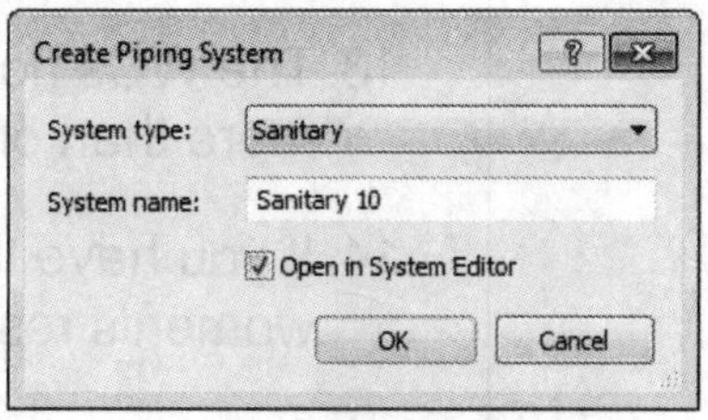

Figure 10–56

5. The *Edit Piping System* tab displays with (Add to System) selected.

6. Select the other WCs in the room.

7. Click ✓ (Finish Editing Systems). The new system is created, and all of the WCs display in green to show that they are part of the sanitary system, as shown in Figure 10–57.

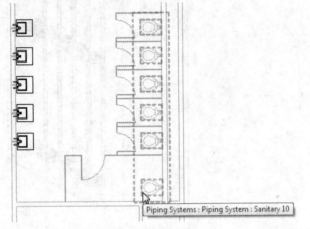

Piping Systems : Piping System : Sanitary 10

Figure 10–57

8. Select the first WC.

9. In the *Modify | Plumbing Fixtures* tab>Create Systems panel, click 🔧 (Piping). This option is available because there is another system that the WC can be assigned to.

10. In the Create Piping System dialog box, set the *System Type* to **Domestic Cold Water**. Accept the default name, select **Open in System Editor**, and click OK .

11. The *Edit Piping System* tab displays with (Add to System) selected.

12. Add the other WCs in the room to the Cold Water System and click ✓ (Finish Editing Systems).

13. The WCs now display black because they are connected to more than one system.

14. If you have time, connect the rest of the piping in the women's restroom to match the men's restroom.

15. Save the project.

10.5 Fire Protection Systems

 Learning Objective

- Add systems, sprinklers, and piping for fire protection systems.

Fire Protection Systems work in much the same way as Hydronic Piping Systems. You place sprinkler heads where they are needed, create a system, and add piping through manual or automatic layout tools as shown in Figure 10–58. Schedules of Fire Protection Systems can be created in a company template. This automatically compiles the total number of sprinkler heads in a project.

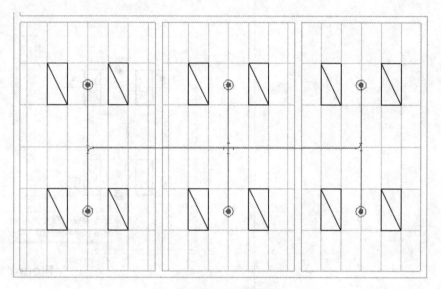

Figure 10–58

- Sprinkler types include wet and dry. All sprinklers in a system must be of the same type.

- To insert sprinklers, in the *Systems* tab>Plumbing & Piping panel, click ⚘ (Sprinkler) or type **SK**.

- You can load sprinklers from the *Fire Protection/Sprinklers* folder of the Library.

- Hosted sprinklers need to be placed on ceilings. Therefore, it is best to use a reflected ceiling plan when adding them.

Practice 10b

Work with Fire Protection Systems

Learning Objectives

- Create a Ceiling Plan view.
- Add two different types of sprinklers and create fire protection systems using the sprinkler types.
- Add piping to the systems using the Layout tools.

In this practice you will create a fire protection ceiling plan view, add both wet and dry sprinklers, as shown in Figure 10–59. You will also create fire protection systems and add piping.

Estimated time for completion: 20 minutes

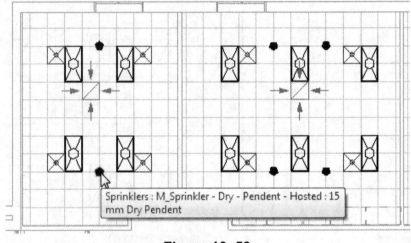

Sprinklers : M_Sprinkler - Dry - Pendent - Hosted : 15 mm Dry Pendent

Figure 10–59

Task 1 - Prepare a Fire Protection Ceiling Plan View.

1. In the *C:\Autodesk Revit 2015 MEP Fundamentals Class Files\Plumbing* folder, open **MEP-Elementary-School -Fire.rvt**.

2. In the *View* tab>Create panel, expand 🗗 (Plan Views) and click 🗗 (Reflected Ceiling Plan).

3. In the New RCP dialog box, clear the **Do not duplicate existing views** option.

4. Select **Level 1** and click [OK]

5. In the Properties, set the *Discipline* to **Mechanical**, for *Sub-Discipline* enter **Fire**, and the *View Name* to **01 Fire RCP** as shown in Figure 10–60.

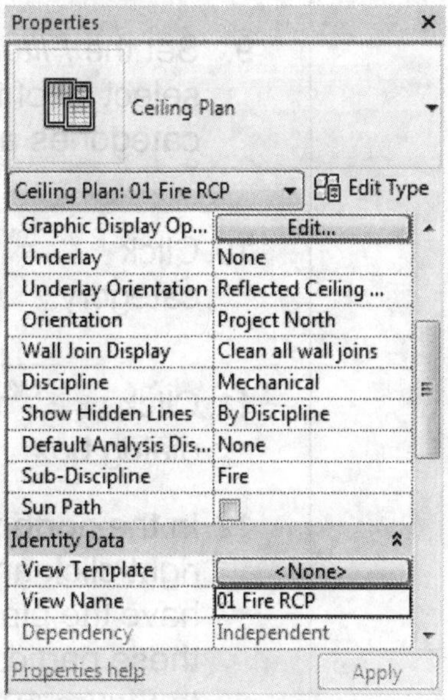

Figure 10–60

• This view displays the light fixtures and air terminals which are required for placing the sprinklers appropriately. It also displays the ducts, mechanical equipment, and piping connected with the HVAC system. The piping category is required to remain displayed so that you can add the piping to the fire protection system.

*If **Pipes** is not listed, expand the Filter list and select **Piping**.*

6. In the Visibility Graphics dialog box, in the *Revit Links* tab, in the *Display Settings* column, select **By Linked View**

7. In the *RVT Links Display Settings* dialog box, in the *Basics* tab, select *By linked view*, and set the *Linked View* to **Reflected Ceiling Plan: 01 RCP MEP BASE** as shown in Figure 10–61. Click Apply.

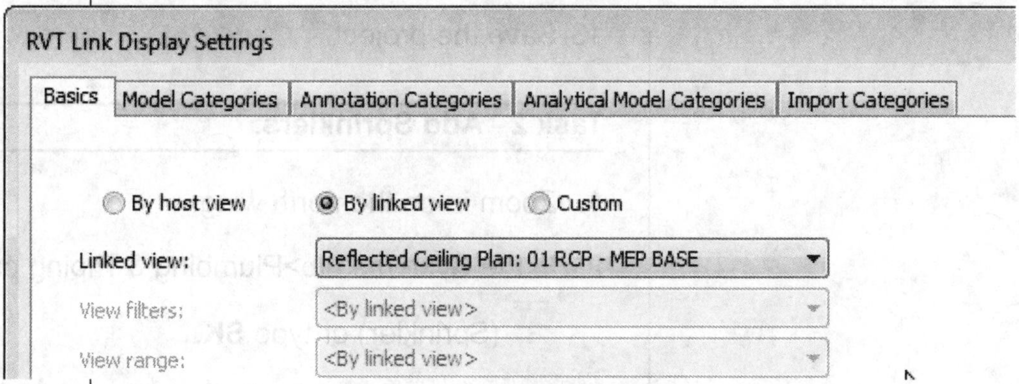

Figure 10–61

8. In the *Model Categories* tab, set the *Filter list* to **Mechanical only** and turn off ducts, flex ducts, duct fittings, and mechanical equipment,

9. Set the *Filter list* to **Electrical** only. Click [All] to select all of the categories. Clear the check from one of the categories and all of the categories are also cleared.

10. Click [None] and select only the **Lighting Fixtures** category.

11. Click [OK] to close the Visibility/Graphic Overrides dialog box.

12. In the north wing, window around the existing piping, right-click and select **Hide in View>Elements**. (You need to have the piping category available but you do not want to see these particular pipes.) The final view should display similar to Figure 10–62.

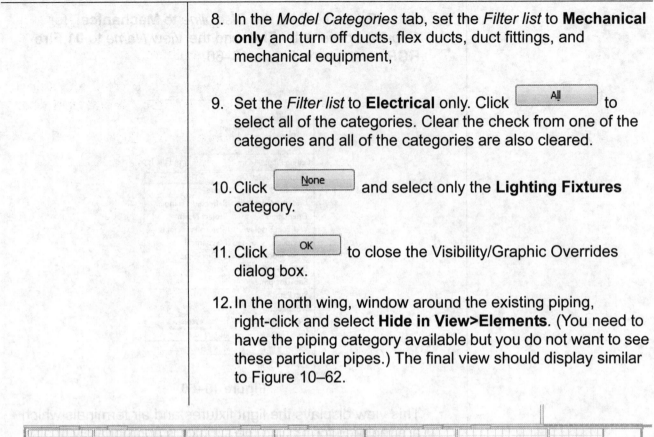

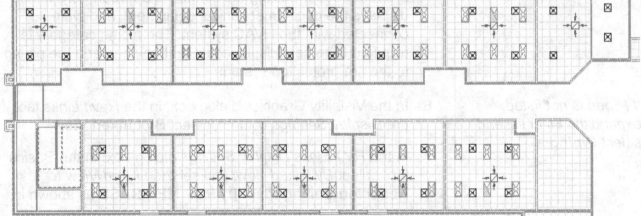

Figure 10–62

13. Save the project.

Task 2 - Add Sprinklers.

1. Zoom in on the north wing.

2. In the *Systems* tab>Plumbing & Piping panel, click (Sprinkler) or type **SK**.

3. A warning displays noting that no sprinklers are loaded in the project yet. Click [Yes] to load them.

4. Navigate to the *Fire Protection>Sprinklers* folder and select both **Sprinkler - Dry - Pendent - Hosted rfa** and **Sprinkler - Pendent.rfa**, as shown in Figure 10–63. Click [Open] .

Figure 10–63

5. In the Type Selector, select **M_Sprinkler - Dry - Pendent - Hosted: 1/2" Dry Pendent**.

6. In the *Modify | Place Sprinkler* tab>Placement panel, click (Place on Face).

7. Move the cursor over the hallway. A ⊘ symbol displays because there is no ceiling in this area.

8. Move the cursor into one of the classrooms where there is a ceiling. Note that you can now place the hosted sprinkler type in the ceiling at the intersections of the grids.

9. Add sprinklers in two classrooms similar to that shown in Figure 10–64.

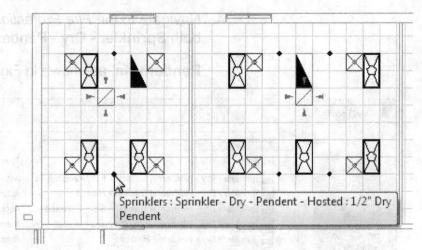

Sprinklers : Sprinkler - Dry - Pendent - Hosted : 1/2" Dry Pendent

Figure 10–64

10. In the Type Selector, select **Sprinkler - Pendent: 1/2" Pendent**. This is a non-hosted sprinkler so you can place it in the hall where there is no ceiling.

11. In Properties, set the *Offset* to **9'-0"**.

You can use Ref Planes to help you place the first sprinkler.

12. Place sprinklers down the hall at a spacing of **6'-0"** off the vestibule door and then **12'-0"** on center, as shown in Figure 10–65. You can place the first one and then array or copy the rest.

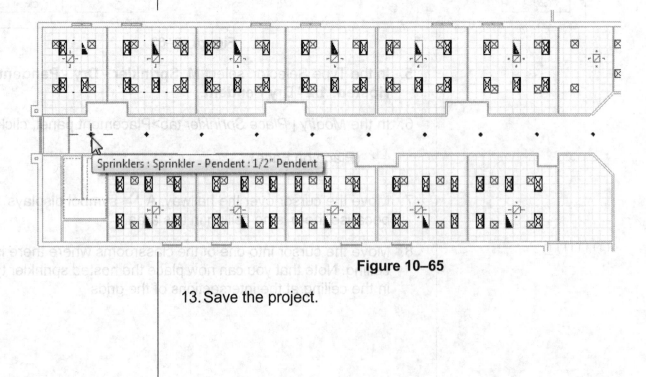

Sprinklers : Sprinkler - Pendent : 1/2" Pendent

Figure 10–65

13. Save the project.

Task 3 - Creating Fire Protection Systems.

1. If you created an array of sprinklers down the hall you need to ungroup them before being able to use the individual controls. Select all of the sprinklers in the array group and in the *Modify | Model Groups* tab>Group panel, click

   (Ungroup). The sprinklers are now independent of each other.

2. Select one of the sprinklers in the hall.

3. In the *Modify | Sprinklers* tab>Create Systems panel, click

   (Piping).

4. In Properties, set the *System Name* to **01-FPW1**.

5. In the *Piping Systems* tab>System Tools panel, click

   (Edit System).

6. Verify that (Add to System) is selected and select the rest of the hall sprinklers. You can select them by drawing a window around them.

7. Click on one of the classroom sprinklers. A warning displays as shown in Figure 10–66. You cannot add this sprinkler to the Wet System because it belongs in a Dry System.

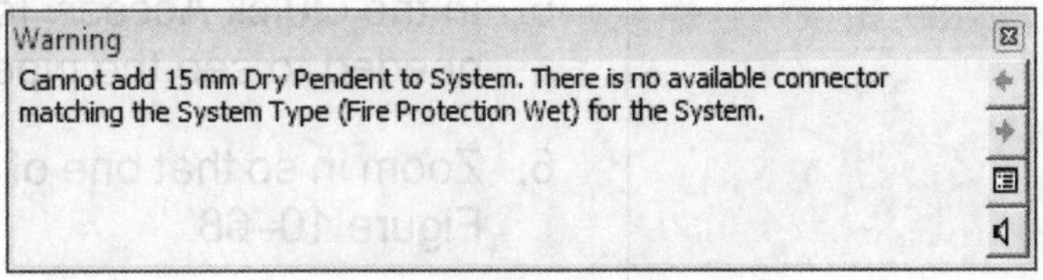

> **Warning**
> Cannot add 15 mm Dry Pendent to System. There is no available connector matching the System Type (Fire Protection Wet) for the System.

Figure 10–66

8. Click (Finish Editing System).

9. Select one of the classroom sprinklers.

10. In the *Modify | Sprinklers* tab>Create Systems panel, click

    (Piping). The software knows that this sprinkler needs to be part of a dry system.

11. Add the dry type sprinklers together in a system named **01-FPD1**.

12. Save the project.

Task 4 - Add Piping for Fire Protection Systems.

1. Select the left most sprinkler in the hallway. Right-click on the connector and select **Draw Pipe**.

2. In the Options Bar, the *Diameter* and *Offset* match the location of the connector. Change the *Offset* to **3000** and press <Enter>. This moves the first segment of the pipe directly up from the sprinkler.

3. Draw the pipe down the hallway and past the last sprinkler as shown in Figure 10–67.

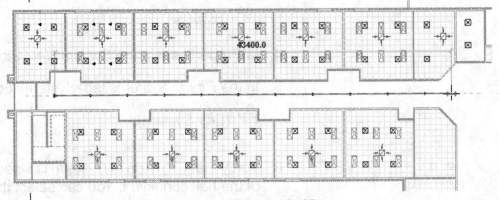

Figure 10–67

4. Open the Mechanical>Fire>Sections (Wall Section)>**Hallway Section** view.

5. In the Quick Access Toolbar, toggle on 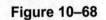 (Thin Lines), if needed to see the pipes and fittings clearly.

6. Zoom in so that one of the sprinklers is displayed as shown in Figure 10–68.

Figure 10–68

7. Select the sprinkler. In the *Modify | Sprinklers* tab>Layout panel, click 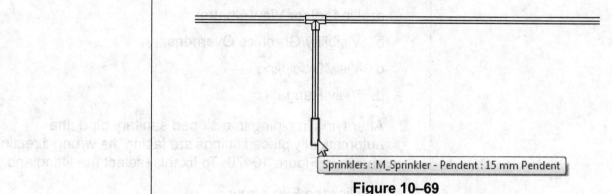 (Connect Into).

8. Select the horizontal pipe to connect into. The new connection is created with appropriate fittings as shown in Figure 10–69.

Sprinklers : M_Sprinkler - Pendent : 15 mm Pendent

Figure 10–69

9. Continue using this method or just draw pipes from each sprinkler to the horizontal piping.

10. If you have time, add piping to the classroom sprinklers. You can draw them using connectors, the **Pipe** command, or with an automatic or custom layout.

11. Save the project.

Chapter Review Questions

1. When you are in a plumbing plan view and the plumbing pipes that you put below a floor are not displayed, which View Property needs to be set to make them display?

   a. Underfloor View Control

   b. Visibility/Graphics Overrides

   c. View Discipline

   d. View Range

2. After tying in piping to a sloped sanitary pipe, the automatically placed fittings are facing the wrong direction, as shown in Figure 10–70. To fix this, select the fitting and...

   a. click the **Flip** arrow.

   b. place its opposite type.

   c. use **Rotate**.

   d. click the **AutoSlope** icon in the Ribbon.

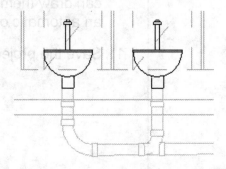

Figure 10–70

3. Which placement option can be used for placing a face based plumbing fixture on the wall, as shown in Figure 10–71?

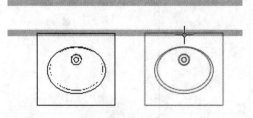

Figure 10–71

   a. **Place on Vertical Face**

   b. **Place on Face**

   c. **Place on Work Plane**

4. How do you specify the direction in which a pipe slopes as you are creating it, as shown in Figure 10–72?

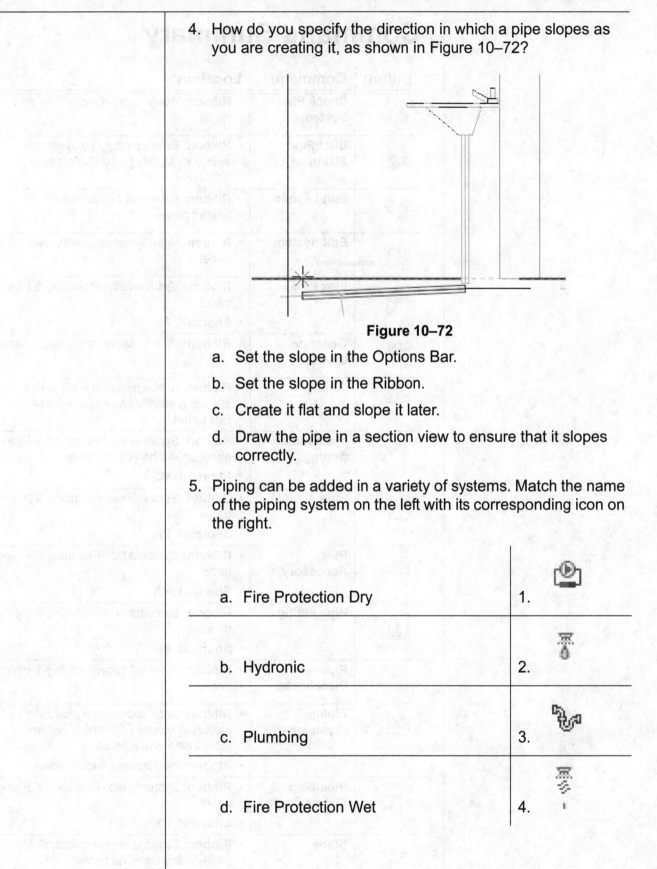

Figure 10–72

a. Set the slope in the Options Bar.

b. Set the slope in the Ribbon.

c. Create it flat and slope it later.

d. Draw the pipe in a section view to ensure that it slopes correctly.

5. Piping can be added in a variety of systems. Match the name of the piping system on the left with its corresponding icon on the right.

a. Fire Protection Dry	1.	
b. Hydronic	2.	
c. Plumbing	3.	
d. Fire Protection Wet	4.	

Command Summary

Button	Command	Location
	Check Pipe Systems	• **Ribbon**: *Analyze* tab>Check Systems panel
	Duct/Pipe Sizing	• **Ribbon**: (*when piping in a system is selected*) *Modify	Multi-Select* tab>Analysis panel
	Edit Layout	• **Ribbon**: *Generate Layout* tab>Modify Layout panel
	Edit System	• **Ribbon**: *Pipe Systems* tab>System Tools panel
	Flex Pipe	• **Ribbon**: *Systems* tab>Plumbing & Piping panel • **Shortcut**: FP
	Generate Layout	• **Ribbon**: *Pipe Systems* tab>Layout panel
	Justify	• **Ribbon**: (*when piping in a system is selected*) *Modify	Multi-Select* tab>Edit panel
	Mechanical Settings	• **Ribbon**: *Systems* tab>Plumbing & Piping panel or Mechanical panel title • **Shortcut**: MS
	Pipe	• **Ribbon**: *Systems* tab>Plumbing & Piping panel • **Shortcut**: PI
	Pipe Accessory	• **Ribbon**: *Systems* tab>Plumbing & Piping panel • **Shortcut**: PA
	Pipe Fitting	• **Ribbon**: *Systems* tab>Plumbing & Piping panel • **Shortcut**: PF
	Pipe Placeholder	• **Ribbon**: *Systems* tab>Plumbing & Piping panel
	Piping (System)	• **Ribbon**: (*with appropriate plumbing selected*) *Modify	Plumbing Fixture* tab>Create Systems panel • **Right-click:** Create Piping System
	Plumbing Fixture	• **Ribbon**: *Systems* tab>Plumbing & Piping panel • **Shortcut**: PX
	Slope	• **Ribbon**: (*when piping is selected*) *Modify	Multi-Select* tab>Edit panel
	Solutions	• **Ribbon**: *Generate Layout* tab>Modify Layout panel

Chapter 11

Electrical Systems

In this chapter you learn about various types of electrical systems, how to place types of electrical components, and create electrical circuits. You also learn how to add cable trays, conduit, and associated fittings. You also create and modify Panel Schedules.

This chapter contains the following topics:

- **About Electrical Systems**
- **Placing Electrical Components**
- **Creating Electrical Circuits**
- **Cable Trays and Conduit**
- **Electrical Panel Schedules**

11.1 About Electrical Systems

Learning Objective

- Prepare to create electrical systems.

Electrical systems in Autodesk® Revit® MEP software are circuits consisting of devices, lighting fixtures, and other electrical equipment. They are elements in a project and are added to the model using the tools in the Ribbon. There can be different types of electrical plan views based on the type of information required. A typical electrical view plan might display power, systems, or lighting layouts as shown in Figure 11–1.

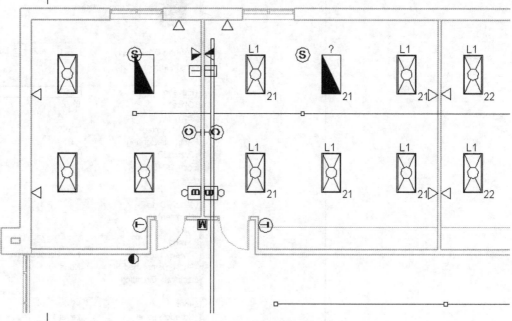

Figure 11–1

There are several steps in the process of creating an Electrical system:

1. Place electrical equipment such as distribution panels.
2. Define the Distribution System in the Properties of the electrical equipment.
3. Place electrical devices, such as receptacles. Each device represents an electrical load in the system.
4. Select an electrical device or lighting fixture, and create a power circuit for it and similar devices in the same room or area of the building.
5. Assign circuits to electrical equipment (e.g. Panel).

The tools for creating and placing Electrical components and circuits are located in the *Systems* tab>Electrical panel, as shown in Figure 11–2.

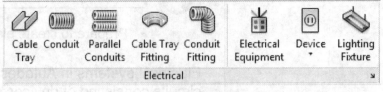

Figure 11–2

When placing Electrical elements in a view, use Properties to set specific information about the element, as shown in Figure 11–3.

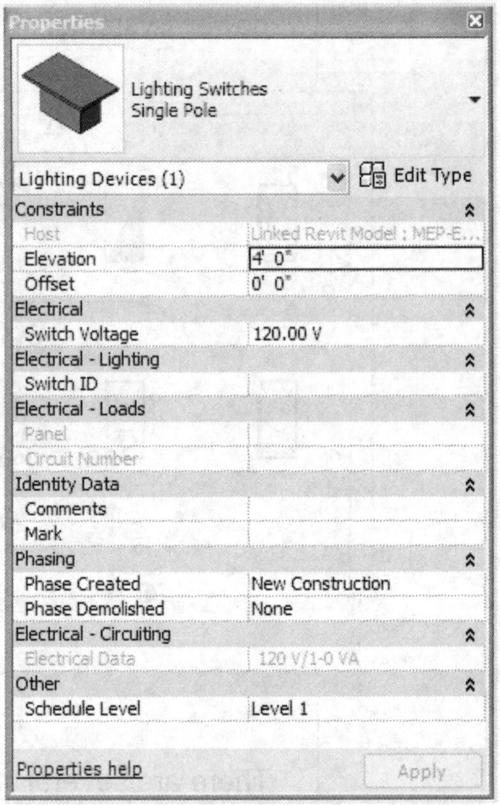

Figure 11–3

In the Type Selector, select a specific family element type. In Properties, other options depend on the type of Electrical element you are placing, and can include offset value, voltage, loads, etc. In the Ribbon, in the Placement panel, you can find options for the face or plane used for placement.

Electrical Settings

Electrical settings contain many parameters used for various electrical component placement and system/circuit creation. They include wiring parameters, voltage definitions, distribution systems, cable tray and conduit settings, load calculation settings, and circuit naming settings.

In *Manage* tab>Settings panel, expand ⚙ (MEP Settings) and click 📋 (Electrical Settings), or in the *Systems* tab>Electrical panel, click ⚡ (Electrical Settings), to open the Electrical Settings dialog box, as shown in Figure 11–4.

Electrical Settings

Setting	Value
Draw MEP Hidden Lines	☑
Line Style	MEP Hidden
Inside Gap	1/64"
Outside Gap	1/64"
Single Line	1/64"

Left pane categories:
Hidden Line, General, Angles, Wiring, Voltage Definitions, Distribution Systems, Cable Tray Settings, Conduit Settings, Load Calculations, Panel Schedules

Figure 11–4

The different categories in the left pane have their own specific settings that are available when the category is selected.

Hidden Line	Settings for cable tray and conduit hidden line styles.
General	Parameters and formats for symbols and styles for various electrical component values, including phase naming.
Angles	Enables to set angle increments or specify the use of specific angles for drawing cable trays and conduit. This is typically used to match industry standards.
Wiring	Determines how wires and wire sizes are displayed and calculated. Includes type of wires available based on material, temperature, and insulation ratings. Specifies which wire types can be used in a project.
Voltage Definitions	Lists the ranges of voltages that can be assigned to the Distribution Systems.
Distributions Systems	Defines available distribution systems.
Cable Tray Settings	Specifies annotative scaling for cable tray fittings and rise/drop symbology and cable tray sizes available.
Conduit Settings	Specifies annotative scaling for conduit fittings, size prefix and suffix, and rise/drop symbology and specifies conduit sizes available.
Load Calculations	Specifies load calculations for loads in spaces, and defines Load Classifications and Demand Factors.
Panel Schedules	Specifies settings for spares and spaces, and for merging multi-poled circuits

11.2 Placing Electrical Components

Learning Objective

- Place electrical equipment, devices, and lighting fixtures.

There are many different types of electrical components that can be added to a model, as shown in Figure 11–5. Components consist of panels, transformers, switches, receptacles, various communication and safety devices, and lighting fixtures. There are different commands for different types of electrical components (devices).

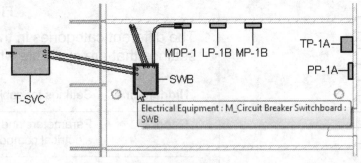

Figure 11–5

- Electrical Components can be placed in any view, including plan, elevation, and 3D.

Electrical Equipment

Electrical equipment includes panels and transformers, which can be placed either as hosted or unhosted components. Panels are typically hosted onto a wall, surface or flush mount, as shown in Figure 11–6, and a transformer could be placed anywhere including ceiling hung. Other electrical equipment includes motor control centers, switchboards, and generators.

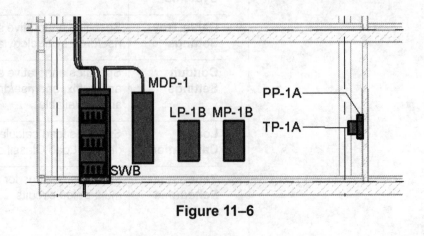

Figure 11–6

How To: Place Electrical Equipment:

1. Open the view where you want to place the electrical equipment.
2. In the *Systems* tab>Electrical panel, click 📺 (Electrical Equipment).
3. In Type Selector, select a panel board or other piece of equipment and then set the required value or option.
4. In the *Modify | Place Equipment* tab>Tag panel, click

   🏷 (Tag on Placement) to select or clear, as required. If you have selected Tag on Placement, set the parameters for the tags in the Options Bar.
5. In the *Modify | Place Equipment* tab>Placement panel, click

   ⬜ (Place on Vertical Face), ⬜ (Place on Face), or

   ◈ (Place on Work Plane).
   - Some equipment does not display the Placement panel. It is placed on the current level with an offset as required.
6. Click on the required location in the model view. Use alignment lines, temporary dimensions, and snaps to aid you in placing the components.
7. Continue to place additional electrical equipment, or click

   ▷ (Modify) to exit the command.

   - After placing a piece of electrical equipment, you can move it to a different location by clicking and dragging it to the new location. Click ▷ (Modify) to exit its selection.

Automatically placing the tags is typically recommended.

Electrical Devices

Electrical devices include a variety of types of devices, including receptacles, switches, telephone/communication/data terminal devices, junction boxes, nurse call devices, wall speakers, starters, smoke detector, and fire alarm manual pull stations, as shown in Figure 11–7. These devices are typically hosted components, as they are usually placed on a wall.

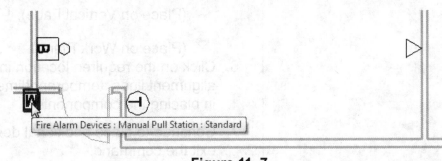

Fire Alarm Devices : Manual Pull Station : Standard

Figure 11–7

How To: Place Electrical Devices:

1. Open the view where you want to place the electrical device.

2. In the *Systems* tab>Electrical panel, expand ⊡ (Device), as shown in Figure 11–8, and click the appropriate command.

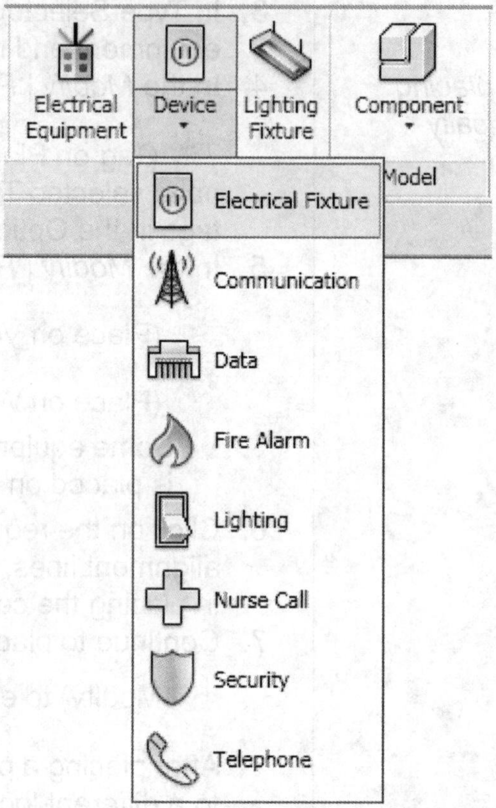

Figure 11–8

3. In Type Selector, select a specific component to insert. In Properties, set any other available required values/options.

4. In the *Modify | Place Devices* tab>Tag panel, click or clear

    ⌐① (Tag on Placement) as required. If you have selected Tag on Placement, set the parameters for the tags in the Options Bar.

5. In the *Modify | Place Devices* tab>Placement panel, click

    ⬚ (Place on Vertical Face), ⬚ (Place on Face), or

    ⬚ (Place on Work Plane).

6. Click on the required location in the model view. Use alignment lines, temporary dimensions, and snaps to aid you in placing the components.

7. Continue to place additional devices, or click ⬚ (Modify) to exit the command.

Hint: Placing Devices Directly Beside or Above Each Other

Electrical device families are model families with an embedded annotation family. This is so that the actual device box displays in sections and 3D views and a symbol displays in plan view, as shown in Figure 11–9.

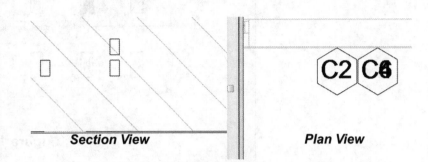

Section View   *Plan View*

Figure 11–9

Some families do not work well if two devices need to be placed directly next to or above each other. For example, in Figure 11–10, devices that are placed correctly in a section view result in overlapping, illegible symbols in plan. Moving the symbol in the plan view also moves the device in the model.

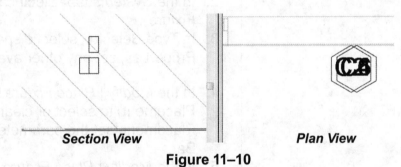

Section View   *Plan View*

Figure 11–10

Many offices create custom device families, which include offset parameters so that the annotation family can move separately from the model family as shown in Figure 11–11.

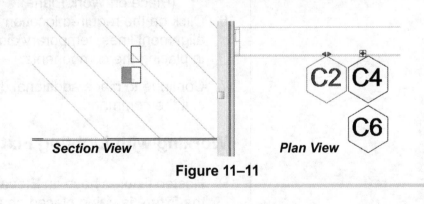

Section View   *Plan View*

Figure 11–11

Lighting Fixtures

Most lighting fixtures, as shown in Figure 11–12, are hosted components, and are therefore placed on a ceiling or on a wall.

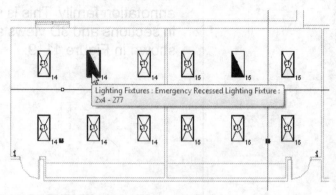

Lighting Fixtures : Emergency Recessed Lighting Fixture : 2x4 - 277

Figure 11–12

- Lighting fixtures can also be copied and monitored from a linked architectural file.

How To: Place Lighting Fixtures:

1. Open the view where you want to place the lighting fixture.

2. In the *Systems* tab>Electrical panel, click (Lighting Fixture).

3. In Type Selector, select a specific component to insert and, in Properties, set any other available required values/options.

4. In the *Modify | Place Fixture* tab>Tag panel, click (Tag on Placement) to select or clear. If you have selected Tag on Placement, set the parameters for the tags in the Options Bar.

5. In the *Modify | Place Fixture* tab>Placement panel, click

    (Place on Vertical Face), (Place on Face), or

    (Place on Work Plane).

6. Click on the required location in the model view. Use alignment lines, temporary dimensions, and snaps to aid you in placing the components.

7. Continue to place additional devices, or click (Modify) to exit the command.

Working with Lighting Fixtures

- Hosted fixtures have an **Elevation** parameter. For example, if the fixture is being placed on a vertical face (e.g., a sconce on a wall), this value can be set to control the height above the level.

- If the fixture is being placed on a face, such as a ceiling, the **Elevation** parameter is automatically determined by the height of the light fixture, which in this case is the same as the ceiling height.

- Some fixtures have an additional **Offset** parameter. This enables you to specify that the fixture be offset from the host, such as a fluorescent fixture, which hangs below the ceiling. In this case, adjust the elevation value to reflect the new elevation of the fixture, as shown in Figure 11–13.

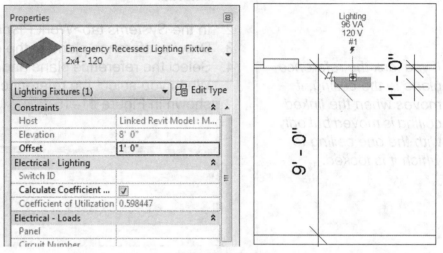

Figure 11–13

- Light fixtures that are hosted by a ceiling in a linked model move automatically with any changes that the architects make to the ceiling height. This can be an advantage of using hosted fixtures.

- If the architect deletes the ceiling and puts a new one in the linked model, the hosted lighting fixtures are orphaned and do not move with changes in the ceiling height. A warning box opens when you reload the linked model or reopen the MEP project, as shown in Figure 11–14. Use the **Coordination Monitoring** tools to address the issue.

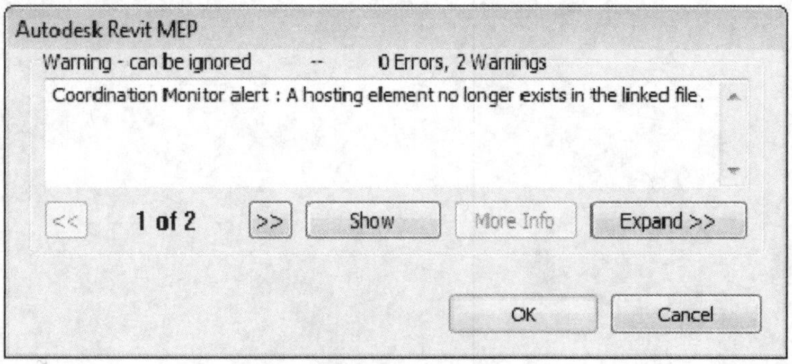

Figure 11–14

- Some firms add reference planes and place the hosted families on them instead of in the ceiling. This gives them control over the height of the families. If the architect moves the ceilings up or down, the engineer adjusts the height of the reference plane to match.

How To: Place a Light Fixture using Reference Planes

1. Cut a section through the area where you are placing the light fixtures.

2. In the *Systems* tab>Work Plane panel, click ✎ (Ref Plane).
3. Draw a reference plane at the ceiling height.
4. Select the reference plane and, in Properties, type in a name. When you select the reference plane the name displays as shown in Figure 11–15.

If you lock the reference plane to the ceiling, it moves when the linked ceiling is moved but only with the one ceiling to which it is locked.

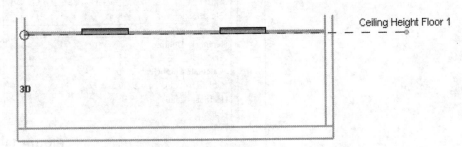

Ceiling Height Floor 1

3D

Figure 11–15

5. Switch to a ceiling plan view.
6. Start the **Lighting Fixture** command.
7. In the Type Selector, select a lighting fixture.
8. In the *Modify | Place Fixture* tab>Placement panel, click

    ◇ (Place on Workplane).

9. In the Work Plane dialog box, select the named reference plane you just created, as shown in Figure 11–16, and click

OK.

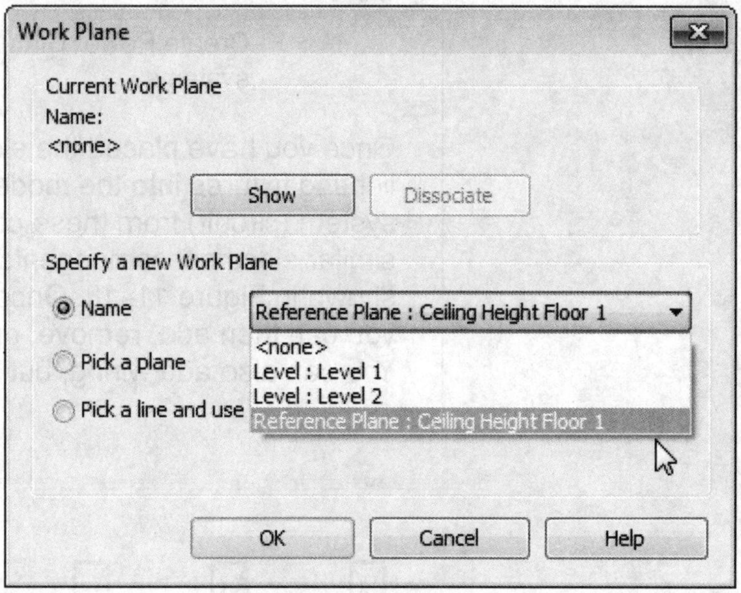

Figure 11–16

10. Add the lighting fixtures. They align to ceiling grids even though they are not hosted by the ceiling.

* Architectural light fixtures cut holes in the architectural ceiling. If the electrical engineer needs to put fixtures in a different place, they usually turn off the visibility of the linked architectural light fixtures first. This results in holes in the ceiling, as shown in Figure 11–17. To correct this issue, the engineer needs to request that the architect move the architectural lighting fixtures to the final, agreed on location.

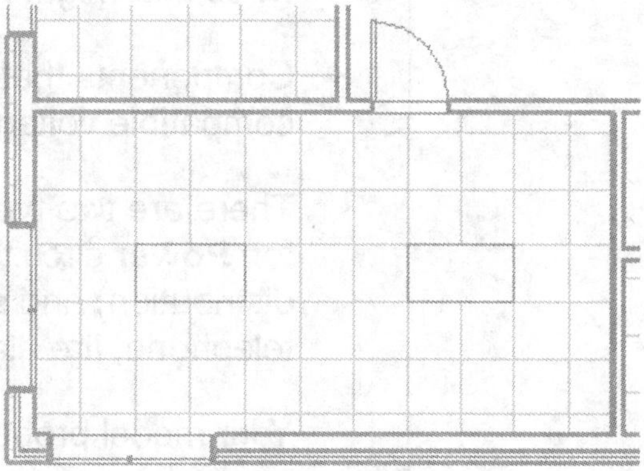

Figure 11–17

11.3 Creating Electrical Circuits

 Learning Objective

- Create Power Circuits, Switch Systems, and other circuit systems.

Once you have placed the electrical equipment, devices, and lighting fixtures into the model, you need to create the electrical system (circuit) from these components. Circuits connect the similar electrical components to form the electrical system, as shown in Figure 11–18. Once the electrical system is created, you can then add, remove, or modify any of the components. You can also add wiring, but it is not necessary.

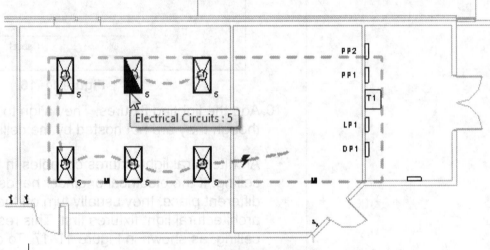

Figure 11–18

- Wiring is typically added to display exposed wires, or other wires that might be necessary for modifications.

- Components that are to be connected in a circuit must be of compatible voltage and distribution system.

- There are two types of systems that circuits can be created for. **Power** circuits (which includes lighting and power distribution) and **signals** and **communications** (data, telephone, fire alarm, nurse call, security, and controls).

- Your model probably contains multiple electrical systems.

Creating Power Circuits

When creating a power circuit, select a component that is to be part of the power circuit. In the Ribbon, use the *Modify* contextual tab to create systems. Power systems connect compatible electrical devices and lighting fixtures, and connects them in a circuit to an electrical equipment panel, as shown in Figure 11–19.

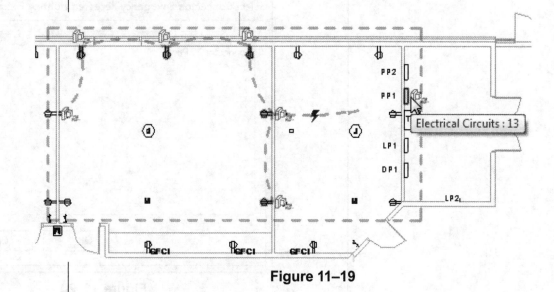

Figure 11–19

How To: Create a Power Circuit

1. Select at least one of the components (electrical device or lighting fixture) that is to be part of the power circuit.
2. In the *Modify | Electrical Fixtures, Lighting Devices, or Lighting Fixtures* tab>Create Systems panel, click

    ⊞ (Power).
3. In the *Electrical Circuits* tab>System Tools panel, click

    (Select Panel) if you need to add the electrical equipment panel. Select an available panel in the model or in the Options Bar. Verify that the panel has a Distribution System specified.
4. In the *Electrical Circuits* tab>System Tools panel, click

    (Edit Circuit).
5. In the *Edit Circuit* tab>Edit Circuit panel, click either (Add to Circuit) or (Remove from Circuit). Select additional components in the model to add them to the same circuit.
6. Click ✓ (Finish Editing Circuit).

- If a component has more than one electrical connector, a Select Connector dialog box opens, as shown in Figure 11–20. Select the connector for which you want to make a circuit and click [OK].

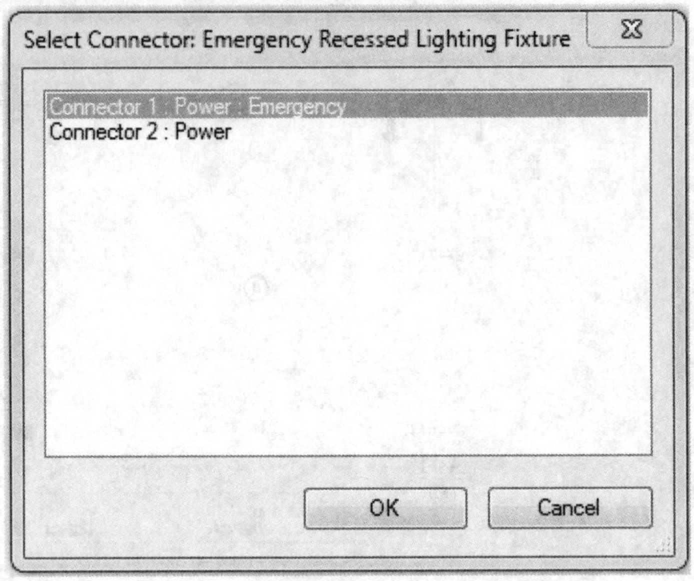

Select Connector: Emergency Recessed Lighting Fixture ⌧

Connector 1 : Power : Emergency
Connector 2 : Power

OK   Cancel

Figure 11–20

Create a Switch System

In addition to power systems, lighting fixtures also have switch systems. Switch systems enable you to indicate which lights are linked to which switch, as shown in Figure 11–21. This is especially useful for those cases where there are multiple lights on the same circuit but controlled by different switches.

These lines are for reference only and do not plot.

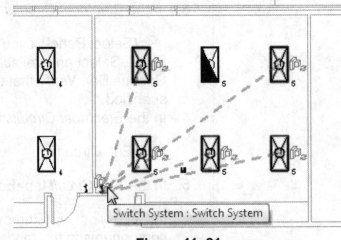

Figure 11–21

How To: Create a switch system

1. Select at least one of the lighting fixtures that is to be part of the switch system.
2. In the *Modify | Lighting Fixture* tab>Create Systems panel, click ⬜ (Switch).
3. In the *Modify | Switch System* tab>System Tools panel, click 🖎 (Edit Switch System).
4. In the *Edit Switch System* tab>Edit Switch System panel, 🔌 (Add to System) is selected by default. In the view, select any other lighting fixtures which are to be part of this switch system.
5. In the Edit Switch System panel, click ⬜₊ (Select Switch).
6. Click ✓ (Finish Editing System).

*   The Switch System is currently only able to have one switch per switch system.

Create Other Circuits

Besides Power circuits, there are other types of circuits that can be created. They are all similar and include data, as shown in Figure 11–22, telephone, fire alarm, communication, nurse call, security, and control systems. When creating these types of circuits, start by selecting a component that is to be part of it. These systems connect compatible devices, and connect them in a circuit to a similar panel.

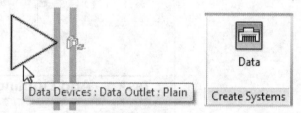

Figure 11–22

*   The process for creating any type of circuit is the same. Select at least one of the components that is to be part of the circuit (such as an ethernet data connector device) and then, in the *Modify | (varies)* tab>Create Systems panel, click the appropriate system type, such as 🖧 (Data).

Practice 11a

Insert Electrical Components and Create Circuits

 Learning Objectives

- Add Lighting fixtures and electrical equipment.
- Create electrical circuits for standard and emergency lighting.
- Display wire connections in a circuit.

Estimated time for completion: 20 minutes

In this practice you will insert lighting fixtures and add two electrical panels, one for standard lights and the other for emergency lights. You will connect light fixtures together in a power circuit, create an emergency power circuit, add light fixtures, and move those, as shown in Figure 11–23. You will also add a transformer and connect panels to it. Finally, you will display wire connections in a circuit.

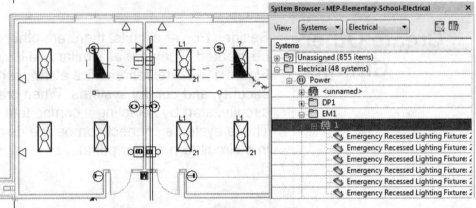

Figure 11–23

Task 1 - Add Lighting Fixtures.

1. In the *C:\Autodesk Revit 2015 MEP Fundamentals Class Files\Electrical* folder, open **MEP-Elementary-School -Electrical.rvt** .

2. In the *Systems* tab>Electrical panel title bar, click ⌐ (Electrical Settings).

3. In the Electrical Settings dialog box, click **Angles**.

4. In the right pane, select **Use specific angles** as shown in Figure 11–24. This limits the angles you can use to draw.

   Click [OK]

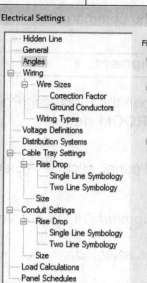

Electrical Settings

- Hidden Line
- General
- Angles
- Wiring
  - Wire Sizes
    - Correction Factor
    - Ground Conductors
  - Wiring Types
- Voltage Definitions
- Distribution Systems
- Cable Tray Settings
  - Rise Drop
    - Single Line Symbology
    - Two Line Symbology
  - Size
- Conduit Settings
  - Rise Drop
    - Single Line Symbology
    - Two Line Symbology
  - Size
- Load Calculations
- Panel Schedules

Fitting angle

○ Use any angle
  Revit will use any angle supported by fitting content.

○ Set an angle increment
  Revit will use the increment to determine the angle values.

  1.000°

◉ Use specific angles
  Revit will use only the angles specified.

Angle	Use in Layout
90.000°	☐
60.000°	☑
45.000°	☑
30.000°	☑
22.500°	☑
11.250°	☑

Figure 11–24

5. Open the Coordination>MEP>Ceiling Plans>**02 ELECTRICAL RCP** view and zoom to the upper left room.

6. In *Systems* tab>Electrical panel, click 🔲 (Lighting Fixture).

7. In Type Selector, select **Troffer Light - 2x4 Parabolic: 2'x4'(2 Lamp) - 277V**.

8. In the *Modify | Place Fixture* tab>Placement panel, click 🔲 (Place on Face).

9. Place three of these lighting fixtures in the upper left room. Then change the type to **Emergency Recessed Lighting Fixture: 2x4 - 277** and place one of these lighting fixtures as shown in Figure 11–25. (Hint: Press <Spacebar> to rotate the fixtures.)

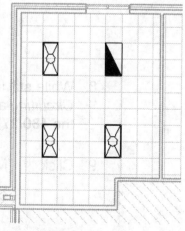

Figure 11–25

10. Click ⏳ (Modify) to exit the command.

Task 2 - Add Electrical Equipment.

1. In the Project Browser, open the Electrical>Power>Floor Plans>**01 ELECTRICAL ROOM** view.

2. In *Systems* tab>Electrical panel, click 📺 (Electrical Equipment).

3. In the *Modify | Place Equipment*>Tag panel, verify that
   🔖 (Tag on Placement) is selected.

4. In Type Selector, select **Lighting and Appliance Panelboard - 480V MCB - Surface: 125 A**.

5. Place one panelboard on the bottom wall of the utility room.

6. Click ⏳ (Modify) and select the newly added panel in the active view.

7. In Properties, scroll down to the *General* area, set *Panel Name* to **LP2**, as shown in Figure 11–26.

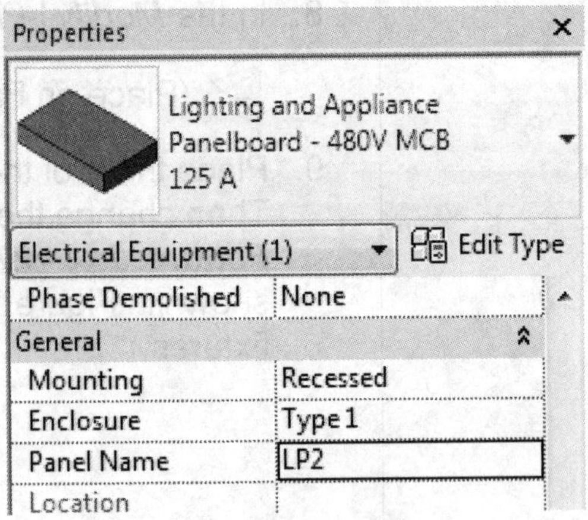

Figure 11–26

8. While still in Properties, scroll further down to the *Electrical - Circuiting* area, expand the *Distribution System* list and select the **480/277 Wye** system.

9. Click ⏳ (Modify) to release the selection.

10. Start the **Electrical Equipment** command again. In the Type Selector, select **Lighting and Appliance Panelboard - 480V MCB - Surface: 400 A**. Place the panel beside the other one you just added.

11. Double-click on the tag and change the name to **EM1**.

12. Select the panel and in Properties, in the *Electrical - Circuiting* area, set *Distribution System* to **480/277 Wye**.

13. Select the tags for the LP2 and EM1 panels and move them above the panels, as shown in Figure 11–27.

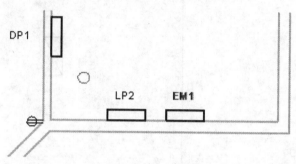

Figure 11–27

14. Save the project.

___

Task 3 - Create an Electrical Circuit System.

1. Open the Electrical>Lighting>Floor Plans> **02 LIGHTING PLAN** view and zoom to the upper left room.

2. Select the upper left light and in the *Modify | Lighting Fixtures* tab>Create Systems panel, click 🔘 (Power).

3. In the *Modify | Electrical Circuits* tab>System Tools panel, click 🖉 (Edit Circuit).

4. In the *Edit Circuit* tab>Edit Circuit panel, verify that 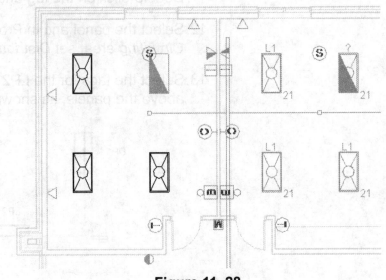 (Add to Circuit) is selected. Select the other two standard lights in the room but not the emergency light, as shown in Figure 11–28.

Do not select the emergency light fixture until the next step.

Figure 11–28

5. Select the emergency light. In the Select Connector dialog box, select **Connector 2: Power** and click ⬛ OK .

6. In the Options Bar, expand the *Panel* list, and select **LP2**.

7. Click ✓ (Finish Editing Circuit) to complete the creation of the Power Circuit.

8. Open the Systems Browser if it is not already open and filter the view so that only the Electrical systems are displayed.

9. Select one of the Troffer light fixtures which you just circuited.

10. In the Systems Browser, expand the highlighted nodes to display the selected light fixtures, as shown in Figure 11–29. Only one light is highlighted in the project.

Figure 11–29

11. In the Systems Browser, select the related circuit **1**. The selection in the view changes to display the circuit outline, as shown in Figure 11–30.

The extents box surrounds the system and has connecting arcs to each fixture in this circuit.

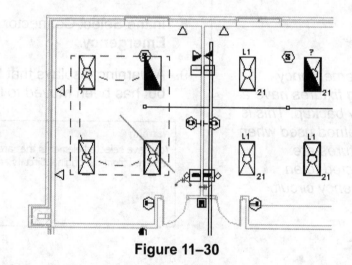

Figure 11–30

12. In Properties, review the circuit properties. In the *Electrical - Loads* area, the *Circuit Number* should be set to **1** as it is the first circuit added to this panel. This field is non-editable.

13. Clear the selection.

14. Select the **Emergency Recessed Lighting Fixture**. In the Systems Browser, note that the Unassigned node highlights as well. This is because the fixture has two connectors, and you have only circuited one of them. This will be resolved in the next task.

15. Save the project

Task 4 - Add and Move Emergency Lighting Fixtures to an Emergency Circuit and Panel.

1. Continue working in the **02 LIGHTING PLAN** view.

2. Select the emergency lighting fixture added earlier.

3. In the *Modify | Lighting Fixtures* tab>Create Systems panel, click ⬛ (Power).

4. In the *Modify | Electrical Circuits* tab>Systems Tools panel, click ▤ (Edit Circuit).

5. In the Options Bar, select the *Panel* **EM1**.

6. In the *Edit Circuit* tab>Edit Circuit panel, verify that ⬚ (Add to Circuit) is selected.

7. Select the emergency fixture in the room directly to the right of the room that you are working in.

8. In the Select Connector dialog box, s elect **Connection 1: Emergency**.

9. A warning displays that the fixture was part of another circuit, but has been moved to this circuit, as shown in Figure 11–31.

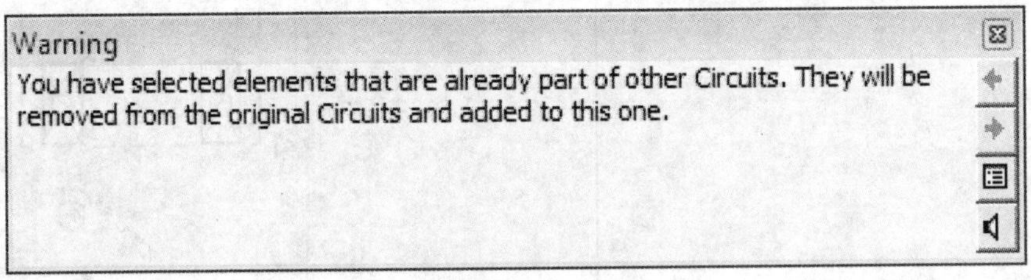

Figure 11–31

10. Click ✓ (Finish Editing Circuit).

11. In the System Browser, in Power>LP1, expand the highlighted nodes as shown in Figure 11–32, and note that it is connected with the rest of the classroom circuit.

   • The system number varies based on the light fixture you selected.

Because there is now only one uncircuited connector on this fixture, the Select Connector dialog box does not open.

Many emergency lighting fixtures have a battery backup. This is the method used when the fixtures are connected to an emergency circuit.

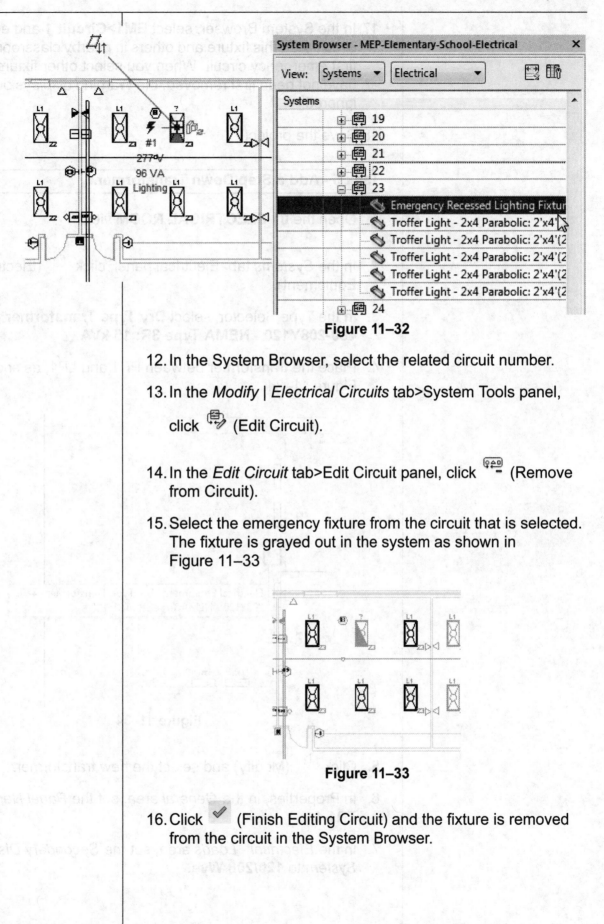

Figure 11–32

12. In the System Browser, select the related circuit number.

13. In the *Modify | Electrical Circuits* tab>System Tools panel, click ⊞ (Edit Circuit).

14. In the *Edit Circuit* tab>Edit Circuit panel, click ⊟ (Remove from Circuit).

15. Select the emergency fixture from the circuit that is selected. The fixture is grayed out in the system as shown in Figure 11–33

Figure 11–33

16. Click ✓ (Finish Editing Circuit) and the fixture is removed from the circuit in the System Browser.

17. In the System Browser, select **EM1>Circuit 1** and edit the circuit. Add this fixture and others in nearby classrooms to the first emergency circuit. When you select other fixtures that have not been first removed, the Warning displays but can be ignored.

18. Save the project.

Task 5 - Add a Step Down Transformer.

1. Open the **01 ELECTRICAL ROOM** view.

2. In the *Systems* tab>Electrical panel, click 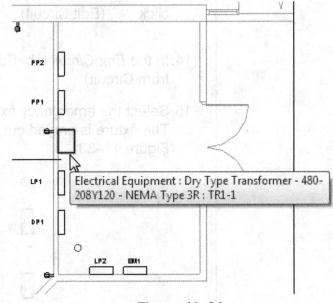 (Electrical Equipment).

3. In the Type Selector, select **Dry Type Transformer - 480-208Y120 - NEMA Type 3R: 15 kVA**.

4. Place the transformer between PP1 and LP1, as shown in Figure 11–34.

Figure 11–34

5. Click ⌨ (Modify) and select the new transformer.

6. In Properties, in the *General* area, set the *Panel Name* to **TR1-1**.

7. In the *Electrical - Loads* area, set the *Secondary Distribution System* to **120/208 Wye**.

The transformer has a primary and secondary distribution system; both are set as properties of the transformer.

8. In the *Electrical - Circuiting* area, set the *Distribution System* to **480/277 Wye**.

9. Click ⬥ (Modify) and select the panel **PP1**.

10. In the *Modify | Electrical Equipment* tab> Create Systems panel, click ⬛ (Power).

11. In the *Modify | Electrical Circuits* tab>System Tools panel, click ⬛ (Select Panel).

12. In the Options Bar, in the *Panel* list select **TR1-1**. The load from panel PP-1 is now assigned to the transformer TR1-1

13. Click ⬥ (Modify) and select **TR1-1**.

14. Right-click and select **Create Power Circuit.**

15. In the *Modify | Electrical Circuits* tab>System Tools panel, click ⬛ (Select Panel).

16. Select the panel **DP1**. The system displays as shown in Figure 11–35.

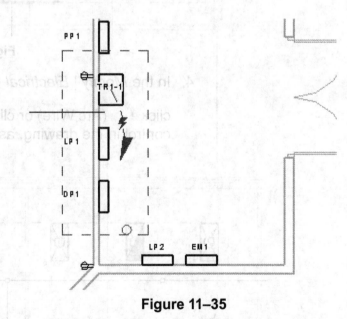

Figure 11–35

17. Click in the empty space to release the selection.

18. Save the project.

Task 6 - Show wire connections in a circuit.

1. Open the Electrical>Lighting> Floor Plans> **01 LIGHTING PLAN** view.

2. Zoom into the area near the electrical room but the nearby classroom should also be displayed.

3. Hover the cursor over one of the lights in the classroom and press < Tab> to highlight the circuit. Click to select it as shown in Figure 11–36.

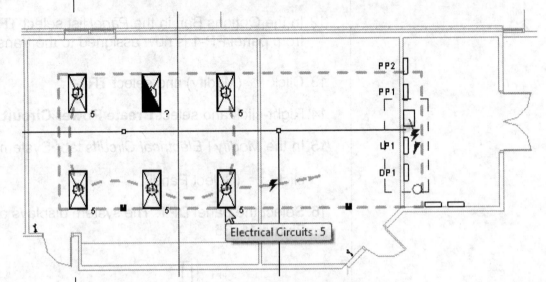

Figure 11–36

4. In the *Modify | Electrical Circuits* tab>Convert to Wire panel, click ✏ (Arc Wire) or click on the Generate arc type wiring control in the drawing, as shown in Figure 11–37.

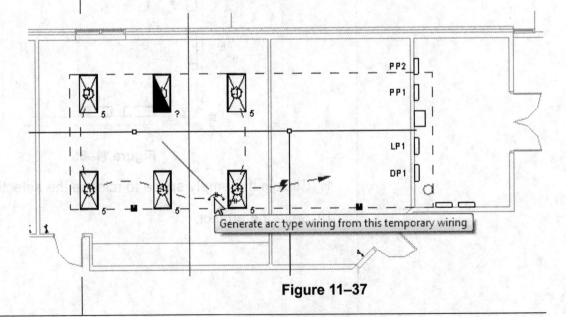

Figure 11–37

5. Wire displaying schematic routing of the circuit is automatically drawn. Adjust the wire arcs manually by pulling the blue control grips, as shown in Figure 11-38.

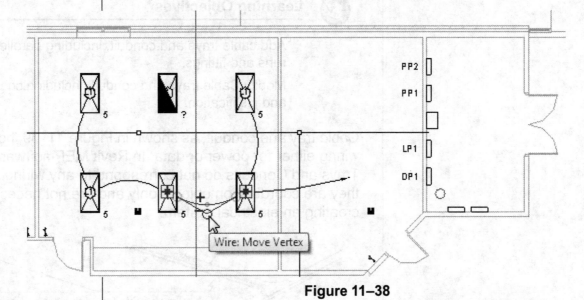

Figure 11-38

The fixture that remains in place is in the linked file.

6. Move a fixture and observe that the wire stays connected adjusting to the new fixture location. Wires are view specific.

7. If you have time you can also create a Switch System for the room.

8. Save the project.

11.4 Cable Trays and Conduit

 Learning Objectives

- Add cable trays and conduit, including parallel conduit runs and fittings.
- Modify Cable trays and conduit, including changing types and justification.

Cable tray and conduit, as shown in Figure 11–39, hold electrical wiring either for power or data. In Revit MEP software, Cable Trays and Conduits do not correspond to any wiring. As such, they are coordination objects only and are not necessary when creating an electrical system.

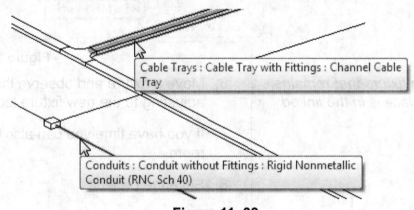

Cable Trays : Cable Tray with Fittings : Channel Cable Tray

Conduits : Conduit without Fittings : Rigid Nonmetallic Conduit (RNC Sch 40)

Figure 11–39

- The commands to create and place cable trays, conduits, and their appropriate fittings, are located in the *Systems* tab>Electrical panel, as shown in Figure 11–40.

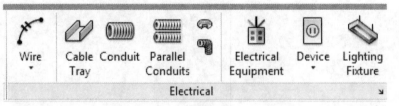

Wire | Cable Tray | Conduit | Parallel Conduits | Electrical Equipment | Device | Lighting Fixture

Electrical

Figure 11–40

- Cable trays, conduits, and fittings can be placed in any view, including plan, elevation, and 3D.

How To: Add Cable Tray or Conduit

1. Open the view where you want to place the cable tray or conduit.

2. In the *Systems* tab>Electrical panel, click ◢ (Cable Tray) or 🔘 (Conduit).

3. In Type Selector, select a type to insert. You can select a type that includes fittings, or a type that does not include fittings.

4. In the Options Bar, for Cable Tray, select the Level it is offset from and set the *Width*, *Height*, *Offset* and *Bend Radius*, as shown in Figure 11–41.

| Width: 12" ▼ | Height: 4" ▼ | Offset: 9' 0" ▼ | 🔒 | Apply | Bend Radius: 12" |

Figure 11–41

For Conduit, select the Level and set the *Diameter*, *Offset*, and *Bend Radius* values as shown in Figure 11–42.

| Diameter: 2" ▼ | Offset: 9' 0" ▼ | 🔒 | Apply | Bend Radius: 10 3/4" |

Figure 11–42

- Using 🔒 (Lock/unlock Specified Elevation) enables the locked segment elevations to maintain their current elevation. However, they cannot connect to segments on different elevations.

- To draw a vertical segment, specify a new *Offset* value in the Options Bar and click Apply .

5. In the Ribbon, adjust ⌐① (Tag on Placement) to required setting (selected to automatically tag the equipment is typically recommended). If required, in the Options Bar include a leader and its length.

6. Set the appropriate Placement Tools.

7. In the drawing, click at the required location to begin the cable tray or conduit run.

8. Move to a second location and click to place the other end point of the cable tray or conduit. Continue to click at other points to create additional cable tray segments starting from the last end point. Fittings are automatically added where needed.

9. Click ↖ (Modify) to end and exit the command.

When you snap to a connector, if Automatically Connect is not on, any changes in height and size are applied with the appropriate fittings.

- In the *Modify | Place Cable Tray (Conduit)* tab> Placement Tools panel, click ⬚ (Automatically Connect) if you want a cable tray or conduit to connect to a lower segment and put in all of the right fittings as shown in the background in Figure 11–43. Turn it off if you want to draw a tray that remains at the original elevation as shown in the foreground in Figure 11–43.

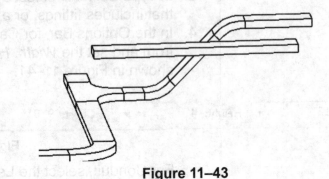

Figure 11–43

- To connect a conduit to a cable tray, start the conduit segment on a cable tray, regardless of elevation.

- For conduit, the **Placement Tools** option, ⌒ (Ignore Slope to Connect) draws conduit directly from a higher point to a lower point without any fittings, as shown on the right in Figure 11–44. If the option is off, then the conduit does not slope but bends down at the point of connection, as shown on the left in Figure 11–44.

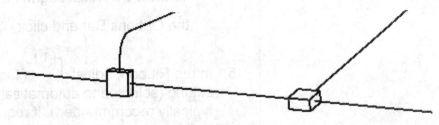

Figure 11–44

Cable Tray and Conduit With and Without Fittings

The process of placing cable tray and conduit is the same whether you select a type with fittings (separate elbows and tees) or a type without fittings (in the field the elements are bent to create curves and blends). In both cases, the software adds fitting components, but the one with fittings includes options to create tees and crosses, as shown on the left in Figure 11–45. The type without fittings does not, as shown on the right in Figure 11–45.

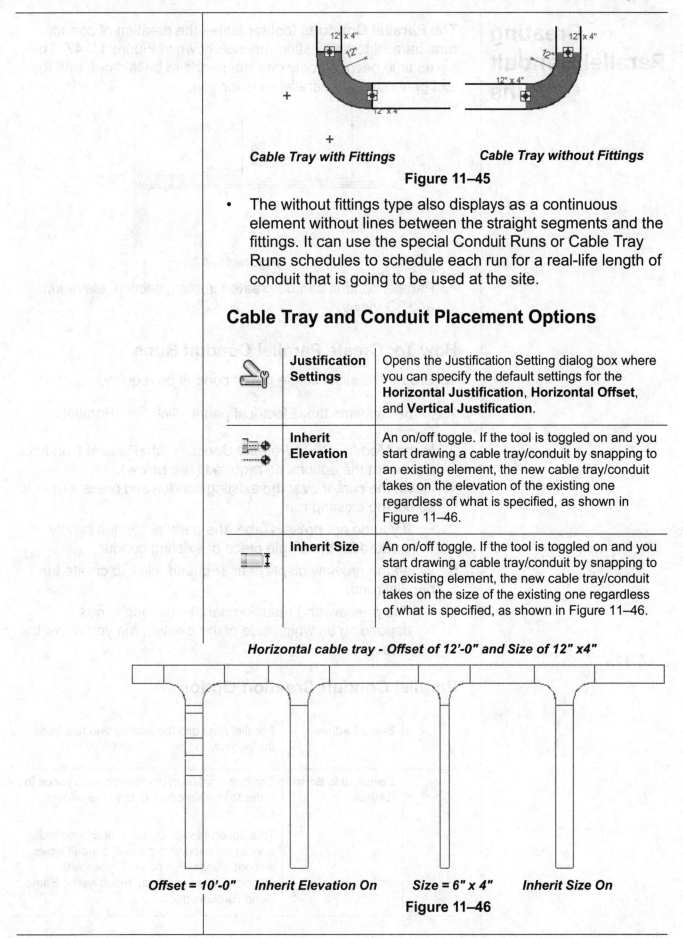

Cable Tray with Fittings   *Cable Tray without Fittings*

Figure 11–45

- The without fittings type also displays as a continuous element without lines between the straight segments and the fittings. It can use the special Conduit Runs or Cable Tray Runs schedules to schedule each run for a real-life length of conduit that is going to be used at the site.

Cable Tray and Conduit Placement Options

	Justification Settings	Opens the Justification Setting dialog box where you can specify the default settings for the **Horizontal Justification**, **Horizontal Offset**, and **Vertical Justification**.
	Inherit Elevation	An on/off toggle. If the tool is toggled on and you start drawing a cable tray/conduit by snapping to an existing element, the new cable tray/conduit takes on the elevation of the existing one regardless of what is specified, as shown in Figure 11–46.
	Inherit Size	An on/off toggle. If the tool is toggled on and you start drawing a cable tray/conduit by snapping to an existing element, the new cable tray/conduit takes on the size of the existing one regardless of what is specified, as shown in Figure 11–46.

Horizontal cable tray - Offset of 12'-0" and Size of 12" x4"

Offset = 10'-0"   Inherit Elevation On   Size = 6" x 4"   Inherit Size On

Figure 11–46

Creating Parallel Conduit Runs

The **Parallel Conduits** tool facilitates the creation of conduit runs parallel to an existing run, as shown in Figure 11–47. This saves time because only one run needs to be laid out, and the tool generates the parallel runs for you.

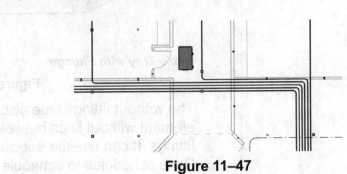

Figure 11–47

- Parallel conduit can be created in plan, section, elevation, and 3D views.

How To: Create Parallel Conduit Runs

1. Create the initial single run of conduit as required.
2. In the *Systems* tab>Electrical panel, click ⬚ (Parallel Conduits).
3. In the *Modify | Place Parallel Conduits* tab>Parallel Conduits panel, set the options as required (see below).
4. Hover the cursor over the existing conduit and press <Tab> to select the existing run.
   - If you do not press <Tab>, the parallel conduit is only created for the single piece of existing conduit.
5. When the preview displays as required, click to create the parallel runs.
   - The preview and resulting parallel conduit varies depending on which side of the existing run you hover the cursor.

Parallel Conduit Creation Options

⬚	**Bend Radius**	Parallel runs use the same bend radius as the original.
⬚	**Concentric Bend Radius**	The bend radius of the parallel runs varies in order to remain concentric to the original run.
		This option results in concentric bend radii only when used with parallel conduit types without fittings. For conduit types with fittings, it gives the same result as the Same Bend Radius option.

n/a	**Horizontal Number**	The total number of parallel conduit runs in the horizontal direction.
n/a	**Horizontal Offset**	The distance between parallel conduit runs in the horizontal direction.
n/a	**Vertical Number**	The total number of parallel conduit runs in the vertical direction.
n/a	**Vertical Offset**	The distance between parallel conduit runs in the vertical direction.

- In section and elevation views, horizontal refers to parallel to the view (visually up, down, left or right from the original conduit). Vertical creates parallel conduit runs perpendicular to the view, in the direction of the user.

Modifying Cable Tray and Conduit

Cable tray and conduit can be modified using a variety of standard modifying tools as well as changing type, modifying the justification and, in the case of conduit, ignoring slope to connect.

You can modify cable tray and conduit using universal methods by making changes in Properties, in the Options bar, and by using temporary dimensions, controls, and connectors. Modify tools, such as **Move**, **Rotate**, **Trim/Extend**, and **Align** enable you to place the elements in the correct locations.

Often a change using these tools automatically applies the correct fittings. For example, in Figure 11–48, the *Edit End Offset* control is changed from **12'-0"** on the left to **10'-0"** on the right and the appropriate cable tray fittings are automatically placed to facilitate the change in elevation.

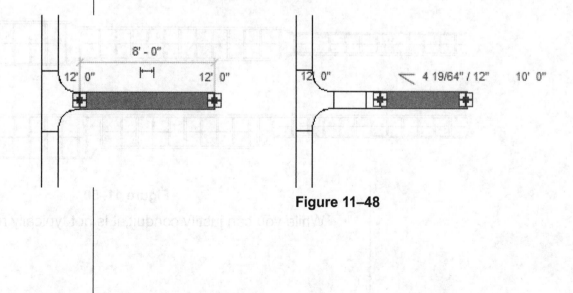

Figure 11–48

How To: Change the Type of Cable Tray and Conduit Runs

1. Select the cable tray or conduit run. Ensure that you filter out everything except related elements and fittings.

2. In the *Modify | Multi-Select* tab>Edit panel, click ⊞ (Change Type).

3. In the Type Selector, select a new type of conduit or cable tray. This changes the cable tray or conduit and also any related fittings. For example, as shown in Figure 11–49, a solid bottom cable tray is changed to a ladder cable tray.

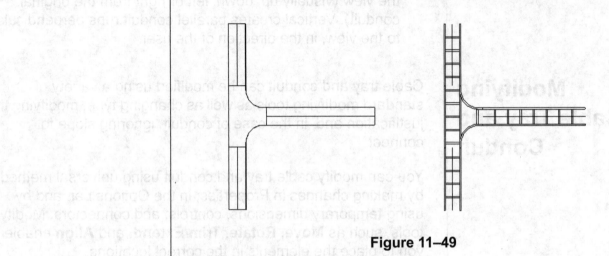

Figure 11–49

Modifying the Justification

If a cable tray or conduit run has different sizes along its run, you can modify the justification of the cable tray or conduit, as shown in Figure 11–50.

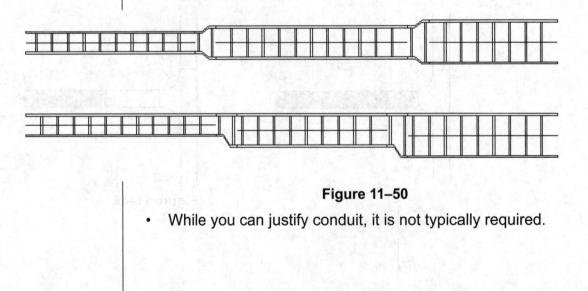

Figure 11–50

• While you can justify conduit, it is not typically required.

How To: Modify Cable Tray Justifications

1. Select the cable tray run.

2. In the *Modify | Multi-Select* tab>Edit Panel, click (Justify).

3. To specify the point on the cable tray you want to justify around, in the *Justification Editor* tab>Justify panel, click

   (Control Point) to cycle between the end point references. The alignment location displays as an arrow, as shown in Figure 11–51.

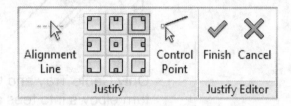

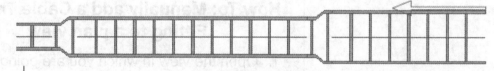

Figure 11–51

4. To indicate the required alignment, either click one of the nine alignment buttons in the Justify panel, or in a 3D view, use

   (Alignment Line) to select the required dashed line, as shown in Figure 11–52.

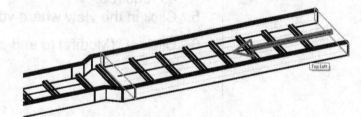

Figure 11–52

5. In the Justification Editor, click (Finish).

Adding Fittings

Revit MEP software automatically adds fittings to cable tray and conduit segments during their creation. It is also possible to manually add cable tray and conduit fittings to any existing segment or segment run. You can also use the controls on the fittings to modify the type, as shown in Figure 11–53.

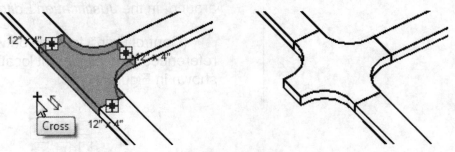

Figure 11–53

- Only Cable Tray and Conduit types with fittings display **+** to turn elbows into tees and tees into crosses.

How To: Manually add a Cable Tray or Conduit Fitting to a plan view

1. Open the view in which you are going to place the fitting.
2. In the *Systems* tab>Electrical panel, click either ⬭ (Cable Tray Fitting) or 🌀 (Conduit Fitting).
3. In the Type Selector, select the appropriate type you want to place.
4. In Properties, verify that the *Level* and *Offset* values are set as required.
5. Click in the view where you want to place the fitting.
6. Click ⬉ (Modify) to end and exit the command.

11.5 Electrical Panel Schedules

 Learning Objective

- Create and modify electrical panel schedules.

Panel schedules are used to concisely present information about panels and the components connected to them through their corresponding circuits. They also list the load values of these circuits, as shown in Figure 11–54. The Autodesk Revit MEP software can create these panel schedules and automatically update them as the panels circuits change.

Branch Panel: LP1

Location: ELECTRICAL 2500A	Volts: 480/277 Wye	A.I.C. Rating:
Supply From:	Phases: 3	Mains Type:
Mounting: Surface	Wires: 4	Mains Rating: 100 A
Enclosure: Type 3R		MCB Rating: 400 A

Notes:

CKT	Circuit Description	Trip	Poles	A		B		C		Poles	Trip	Circuit Description	CKT
1	Lighting - Dwelling Unit CLASSROOM 1509	20 A	1	496 VA	496 VA					1	20 A	Lighting - Dwelling Unit CLASSROOM 1507	2
3	Lighting - Dwelling Unit CLASSROOM 1505	20 A	1			496 VA	496 VA			1	20 A	Lighting - Dwelling Unit CLASSROOM 1503	4
5	Lighting - Dwelling Unit CLASSROOM 1501	20 A	1					496 VA	496 VA	1	20 A	Lighting - Dwelling Unit CLASSROOM 1508	6
7	Lighting - Dwelling Unit CLASSROOM 1506	20 A	1	496 VA	496 VA					1	20 A	Lighting - Dwelling Unit CLASSROOM 1504	8
9	Lighting - Dwelling Unit CLASSROOM 1502	20 A	1			496 VA	496 VA			1	20 A	Lighting - Dwelling Unit CLASSROOM 1500	10
11	Lighting - Dwelling Unit CLASSROOM 2009	20 A	1					496 VA	496 VA	1	20 A	Lighting - Dwelling Unit CLASSROOM 2007	12
13	Lighting - Dwelling Unit CLASSROOM 2005	20 A	1	496 VA	496 VA					1	20 A	Lighting - Dwelling Unit CLASSROOM 2003	14
15	Lighting - Dwelling Unit CLASSROOM 2001	20 A	1			496 VA	496 VA			1	20 A	Lighting - Dwelling Unit CLASSROOM 2008	16
17	Lighting - Dwelling Unit CLASSROOM 2006	20 A	1					496 VA	496 VA	1	20 A	Lighting - Dwelling Unit CLASSROOM 2004	18
19	Lighting - Dwelling Unit CLASSROOM 2002	20 A	1	496 VA	496 VA					1	20 A	Lighting - Dwelling Unit CLASSROOM 2000	20
21	Lighting - Dwelling Unit CLASSROOM 5009	20 A	1			496 VA	496 VA			1	20 A	Lighting - Dwelling Unit CLASSROOM 5008	22
23	Lighting - Dwelling Unit CLASSROOM 5004	20 A	1					496 VA	496 VA	1	20 A	Lighting - Dwelling Unit CLASSROOM 5003	24
25	Lighting - Dwelling Unit CLASSROOM 5000	20 A	1	496 VA	496 VA					1	20 A	Lighting - Dwelling Unit CLASSROOM 5010	26
27	Lighting - Dwelling Unit CLASSROOM 5007	20 A	1			496 VA	496 VA			1	20 A	Lighting - Dwelling Unit CLASSROOM 5006	28
29	Lighting - Dwelling Unit CLASSROOM 5002	20 A	1					496 VA	496 VA	1	20 A	Lighting - Dwelling Unit CLASSROOM 5001	30
31	Lighting - Dwelling Unit CLASSROOM 4509	20 A	1	496 VA	496 VA					1	20 A	Lighting - Dwelling Unit CLASSROOM 4508	32
33	Lighting - Dwelling Unit CLASSROOM 4504	20 A	1			496 VA	496 VA			1	20 A	Lighting - Dwelling Unit CLASSROOM 4503	34
35	Lighting - Dwelling Unit CLASSROOM 4500	20 A	1					496 VA	496 VA	1	20 A	Lighting - Dwelling Unit CLASSROOM 4510	36
37	Lighting - Dwelling Unit CLASSROOM 4507	20 A	1	496 VA	496 VA					1	20 A	Lighting - Dwelling Unit CLASSROOM 4506	38
39	Lighting - Dwelling Unit CLASSROOM 4502	20 A	1			496 VA	496 VA			1	20 A	Lighting - Dwelling Unit CLASSROOM 4501	40
41	Spare	0 A	1					0 VA					42
	Total Load:			6944 VA		6944 VA		5952 VA					
	Total Amps:			25 A		25 A		21 A					

Legend:

Load Classification	Connected Load	Demand Factor	Estimated Demand	Panel Totals	
Lighting	3840 VA	100.00%	3840 VA		
Lighting - Dwelling Unit	16000 VA	47.19%	7550 VA	Total Conn. Load:	19840 VA
				Total Est. Demand:	11390 VA
				Total Conn.:	24 A
				Total Est. Demand:	14 A

Figure 11–54

Create Panel Schedules

Panel schedules can be created for each panel in the model, and it can be created anytime before or after circuits are created for the panel. Once created, panel schedules are listed automatically in the Project Browser, in the **Panel Schedule** node, as shown in Figure 11–55.

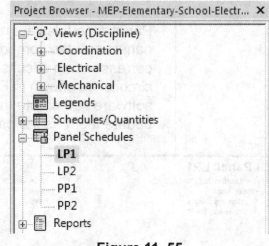

Figure 11–55

How To: Create a panel schedule

1. In a drawing view, select the panel that you want to create the panel for.

2. In the *Modify | Electrical Equipment* tab>Electrical panel, expand ![icon](Create Panel Schedule) and click ![icon](Use Default Template) to use the default panel template.

    *   You can also click ![icon](Choose a Template) to select a preexisting template to use.

3. A new panel schedule is created. Its view opens, and is listed in the Project Browser.

Modifying Panel Schedules

After a panel schedule has been created, its circuits can be modified. The circuits can be rearranged, locked, grouped, or renamed. Loads can be balanced across phases, and spares can be added.

How To: Modify a panel schedule

1. In the panel schedule view, select the particular circuit(s) or empty slot(s) that you want to modify.

2. In the *Modify Panel Schedule* tab, click the particular command that you want to conduct.

The various commands function as follows:

Icon	Command	Function
	Rebalance Loads	Rearranges the panels circuits to redistribute the loads evenly across each phase.
	Move Up, Down, Across	Moves the selected circuit up, down, or across on the circuit panel.
	Assign/Remove Spare/Space	Assigns a slot as either a spare or a space (and are automatically locked), or Removes a spare or space from a slot.
	Lock/Unlock	Locks or unlocks circuits, spares, or spaces in a specific slot location.
	Group/Ungroup	Groups single-pole circuits/spares together to act as a multi-pole circuit (or ungroups them).
	Update Names	Updates the names of the circuits on panel schedules.
	Edit Font	Opens the Edit Font dialog box where you can select a font and modify the font size, style, and color.
	Horizontally Align and Vertically Align	Select the alignment of the text in the selected cells

Practice 11b

Add Conduit and Panel Schedules

Estimated time for completion: 15 minutes

Learning Objectives

- Add conduit to a lighting plan.
- View and create panel schedules.

In this practice you will add conduit and a fitting to a project, as shown in Figure 11–56. You will also view an existing electrical panel schedule and create a new one.

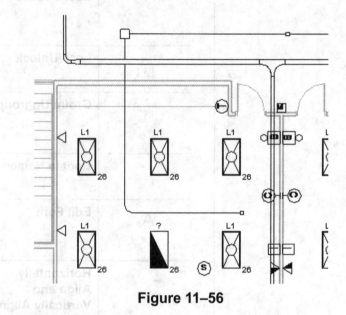

Figure 11–56

Task 1 - Add Conduit.

1. In the *C:\Autodesk Revit 2015 MEP Fundamentals Class Files\Electrical* folder, open **MEP-Elementary-School-Conduit.rvt**.

2. In the Electrical>Lighting>*Floor Plans*>**02 LIGHTING PLAN** view, zoom to the bottom left classroom in the north wing.

3. In the *Systems* tab>Electrical panel, click ⬚ (Conduit).

4. In the Type Selector, select **Conduit with Fittings - Rigid Nonmetallic Conduit (RNC Sch 40)**.

5. In Properties, set the *Reference Level* to **Level 2**, set the *Offset* to **9' 6"**, and click ⬚ Apply ⬚.

6. Start the first point of the conduit segment at the conduit junction box above the room, as shown in Figure 11–57.

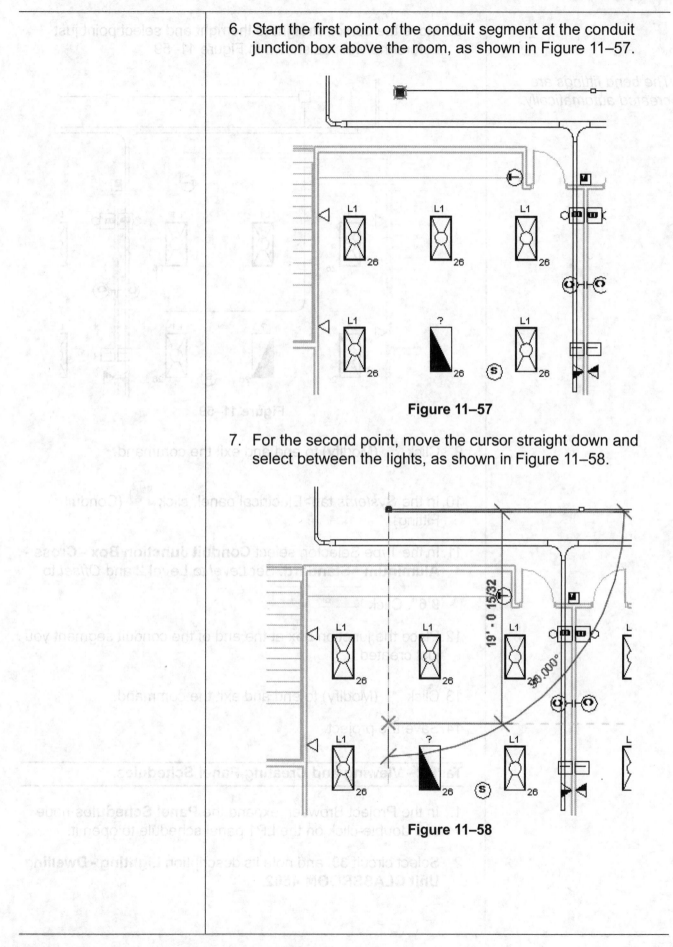

Figure 11–57

7. For the second point, move the cursor straight down and select between the lights, as shown in Figure 11–58.

Figure 11–58

The bend fittings are created automatically.

8. Move the cursor straight to the right and select point just before the wall, as shown in Figure 11–59.

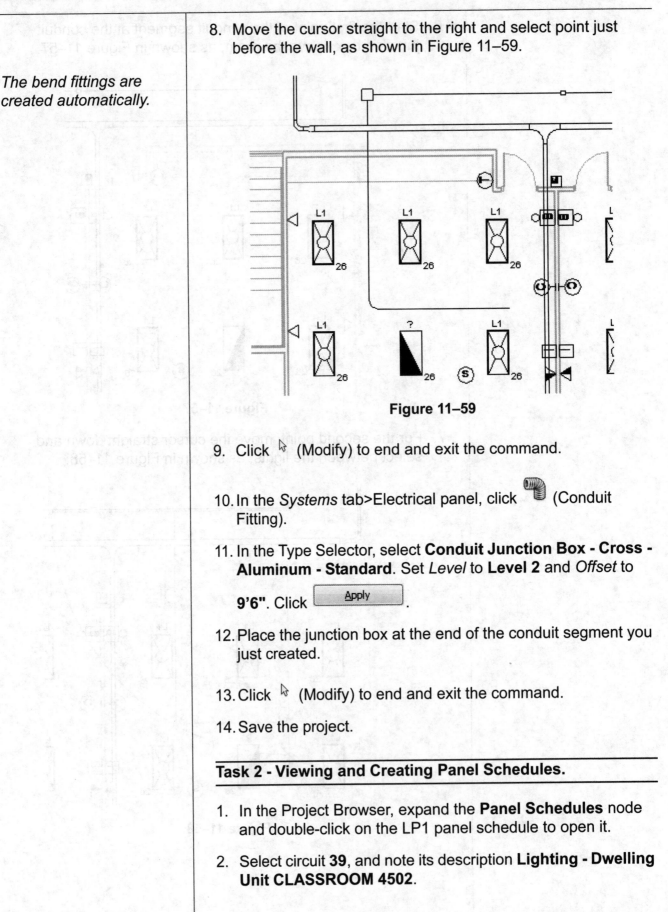

Figure 11–59

9. Click ⌖ (Modify) to end and exit the command.

10. In the *Systems* tab>Electrical panel, click 🔩 (Conduit Fitting).

11. In the Type Selector, select **Conduit Junction Box - Cross - Aluminum - Standard**. Set *Level* to **Level 2** and *Offset* to 9'6". Click 〔 Apply 〕 .

12. Place the junction box at the end of the conduit segment you just created.

13. Click ⌖ (Modify) to end and exit the command.

14. Save the project.

Task 2 - Viewing and Creating Panel Schedules.

1. In the Project Browser, expand the **Panel Schedules** node and double-click on the LP1 panel schedule to open it.

2. Select circuit **39**, and note its description **Lighting - Dwelling Unit CLASSROOM 4502**.

3. In the *Modify Panel Schedule* tab>Circuits panel, click

   ⊟ (Move Across). It switches place with circuit **40** on the right (**Lighting - Dwelling Unit CLASSROOM 4501**).

4. Continue to move it up, down, or across, and then **Lock** it and try to move others near it. The locked one will not move.

5. Select an empty circuit in the panel schedule.

6. Click ⌒ (Assign Spare) and a Spare is inserted into that circuit. Note that it is automatically **Locked**, but you can unlock it and move it if required.

7. Close Panel Schedule **LP1**.

8. In the **01 POWER PLAN** view, select the electrical panel **LP2**.

9. In the *Modify | Electrical Equipment* tab>Electrical panel, expand ▦ (Create Panel Schedules) and click ▦ (Use Default Template).

10. The Panel Schedule **LP2** is created and automatically opened, as shown in Figure 11–60. It is also listed in the Panel Schedules node in the Project Browser. Examine the values in the schedule.

Branch Panel: LP2

Location:	ELECTRICAL 2500A	Volts:	480/277 Wye	A.I.C. Rati
Supply From:		Phases:	3	Mains Ty
Mounting:	Surface	Wires:	4	Mains Rati
Enclosure:	Type 1			MCB Rati

Notes:

CKT	Circuit Description	Trip	Poles	A	B	C	Poles	Trip	
1									
3									
5									
7									
9									

Figure 11–60

11. Save the project.

Chapter Review Questions

1. Which of the following is NOT a type of system that can be created in the Autodesk Revit MEP software?

   a. Power

   b. Communications

   c. Low Voltage

   d. Lighting

2. Which of the following are types of electrical components that can be added to a project? (Select all that apply.)

   a. Electrical equipment

   b. Cable tray

   c. Lighting fixtures

   d. Electrical Devices

3. What happens to hosted lighting fixtures in an Autodesk Revit MEP project if the ceiling, as shown in Figure 11–61, is deleted and then a new one is added at a different height in the architectural linked model?

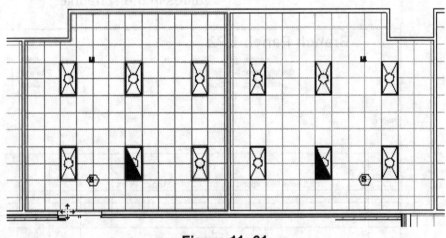

Figure 11–61

   a. The hosted lighting fixtures are deleted.

   b. A warning displays that you need a coordination review.

   c. A warning displays that the hosting element no longer exists in the linked model.

   d. Nothing happens, but in the 3D view, the light fixtures are not connected to the ceiling.

4. To change the type of a cable tray or conduit run, as shown in Figure 11–62, you must...

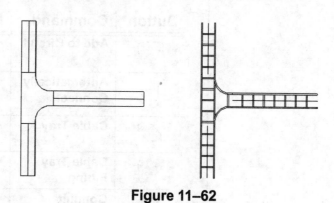

Figure 11–62

a. Redraw the run using the correct type.

b. Select one element in the run and change it in the Type Selector.

c. Select all of the elements in the run and change it in the Type Selector.

d. Select all the elements in the run and use **Change Type**.

5. Can a panel schedule, such as that shown in Figure 11–63, be modified once a circuit has been added to it?

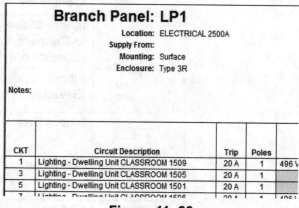

Branch Panel: LP1

Location: ELECTRICAL 2500A
Supply From:
Mounting: Surface
Enclosure: Type 3R

Notes:

CKT	Circuit Description	Trip	Poles	
1	Lighting - Dwelling Unit CLASSROOM 1509	20 A	1	496 V
3	Lighting - Dwelling Unit CLASSROOM 1505	20 A	1	
5	Lighting - Dwelling Unit CLASSROOM 1501	20 A	1	
7	Lighting - Dwelling Unit CLASSROOM 1508	20 A	1	496 V

Figure 11–63

a. Yes

b. No

6. How do you move a spare circuit in a panel schedule?

a. Select it and use the **Move** tool in the *Modify* tab.

b. Select it and use **Move Up**, **Move Down**, or **Move Across**.

c. Unlock it and use the **Move** tools in the Circuits panel.

d. Move the circuit in the plan view. The panel schedule updates accordingly.

Command Summary

Button	Command	Location
	Add to Circuit	• **Ribbon:** *Edit Circuit* tab>Edit Circuit panel
	Automatically Connect	• **Ribbon:** *Modify	Place Cable Tray* or *Place Conduit* tab>Placement Tools panel
	Cable Tray	• **Ribbon:** *Systems* tab>Electrical panel
	Cable Tray Fitting	• **Ribbon:** *Systems* tab>Electrical panel
	Conduit	• **Ribbon:** *Systems* tab>Electrical panel
	Conduit Fitting	• **Ribbon:** *Systems* tab>Electrical panel
	Create Panel Schedule	• **Ribbon:** *Modify	Electrical Equipment* tab>Electrical panel
Multiple buttons	**Device**	• **Ribbon:** *Systems* tab>Electrical panel
	Edit Circuit	• **Ribbon:** *Modify	Electrical Circuits* tab>System Tools panel
	Electrical Equipment	• **Ribbon:** *Systems* tab>Electrical panel
	Ignore Slope to Connect (Conduit only)	• **Ribbon:** *Modify	Place Conduit* tab>Placement Tools panel
	Inherit Elevation	• **Ribbon:** *Modify	Place Cable Tray* or *Place Conduit* tab>Placement Tools panel
	Inherit Size	• **Ribbon:** *Modify	Place Cable Tray* or *Place Conduit* tab>Placement Tools panel
	Justification	• **Ribbon:** *Modify	Place Cable Tray* or *Place Conduit* tab>Placement Tools panel
	Lighting Fixture	• **Ribbon:** *Systems* tab>Electrical panel
	Parallel Conduits	• **Ribbon:** *Systems* tab>Electrical panel
	Power	• **Ribbon:** *Modify	Lighting Fixtures* tab or *Modify Electrical Equipment* tab>Create Systems panel
	Remove from Circuit	• **Ribbon:** *Edit Circuit* tab>Edit Circuit panel
	Select Panel	• **Ribbon:** *Modify	Electrical Circuits* tab>System Tools panel

Chapter 12

Creating Construction Documents

In this chapter you learn how to setup construction documents by creating sheets with title blocks and adding views on the sheets. You also learn about printing the sheets.

This chapter contains the following topics:

- **Setting Up Sheets**
- **Placing and Modifying Views on Sheets**
- **Printing Sheets**

12.1 Setting Up Sheets

Learning Objectives

- Add Sheets to the project.
- Fill in title block information.

While you are working on a project, you should also be thinking about the working drawings that are needed to document it—that is, the printouts with details and annotation to guide construction. Any view, such as a floor plan, section, callout, or schedule, can be placed on a sheet. You can specify the scale for each view and add annotations and other detailing to the views or sheets, as shown in Figure 12–1.

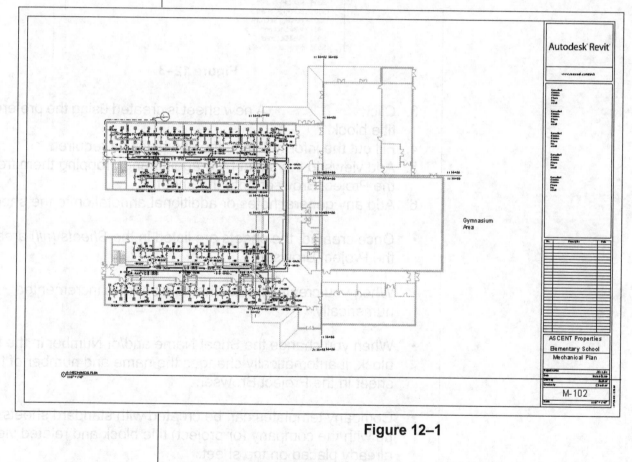

Figure 12–1

How To: Set Up Sheets

1. In the Project Browser, right-click on the *Sheets* area header and select **New Sheet...** or in the *View* tab>Sheet Composition panel, click [] (Sheet).

Click to load a sheet from the Library.

2. In the New Sheet dialog box, select a title block from the list as shown in Figure 12–2.

New Sheet

Select titleblocks: Load...

E1 30 x 42 Horizontal : E1 30x42 Horizontal
Syracuse Suites Cover Sheet : E1 30x42 Horizontal
Syracuse Suites E1 30 x 42 Horizontal : E1 30x42 Horizontal
None

Figure 12–2

- If you have a preset list of placeholder sheets, you can select the one that you want to use from the list, as shown in Figure 12–3.

Select placeholder sheets:

New
S202 - Ground Floor Plan
S203 - Typical Upper Floor Plan
S204 - Roof Plan
S301 - Building Sections
S302 - Building Sections
S401 - Wall Sections
S402 - Wall Sections
S501 - Structural Details

Figure 12–3

3. Click . A new sheet is created using the preferred title block.
4. Fill out the information in the title block as required.
5. Add views to the sheet by dragging and dropping them from the Project Browser onto the sheet.
6. Add any general notes or additional annotation to the sheet.

- Once created, the sheets are listed in the *Sheets (all)* area in the Project Browser.

- When you create sheets, the next sheet is incremented numerically.

- When you change the Sheet Name and/or Number in the title block, it automatically changes the name and number of the sheet in the Project Browser.

- Company templates can be created with standard sheets set up with the company (or project) title block and related views already placed on the sheet.

- You can also create placeholder sheets in a Sheet List schedule. A typical use of placeholder sheets in an architectural firm is to include the sheet names and numbers of the consultants sheets. This way they are listed in the sheet list even if they are not part of the architect's project and are not to be plotted by the architect.

- The plot stamp on the side of the sheet automatically updates according to the current date and time. The format of the display uses the regional settings of your computer.

- You can create your own title block using a template from the Autodesk® Revit® software (**Application Menu>New>Title Block**). Select the size that you want to work with and then add lines, text, labels, and imported files as required to create the title block.

Sheet (Title Block) Properties

A new sheet includes a title block. change the information in the title block, select the title block and click on any blue label you want to edit (e.g., Project Name, Project Number, etc.), as shown in Figure 12–4.

Figure 12–4

You can also change the title block information in Properties, as shown in Figure 12–5.

Figure 12–5

utodesk Revit 2015 MEP Fundamentals

- To set the properties that apply to all of the sheets, enter the Project Properties. In the *Manage* tab>Settings panel, click

  (Project Information). In the Project Properties dialog box (as shown in Figure 12–6), add the *Project Name*, *Client*, and other project based information.

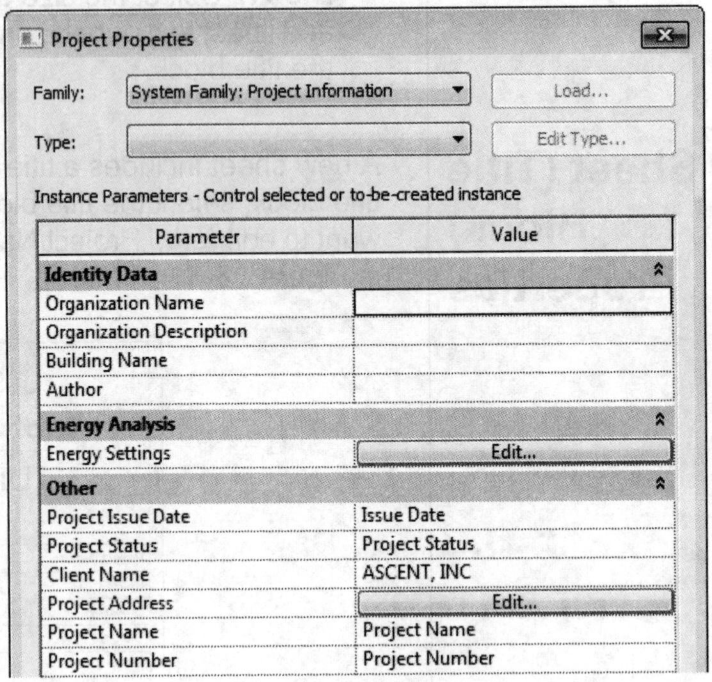

Project Properties	
Family:	System Family: Project Information ▼ Load...
Type:	▼ Edit Type...

Instance Parameters - Control selected or to-be-created instance

Parameter	Value
Identity Data	⌄
Organization Name	
Organization Description	
Building Name	
Author	
Energy Analysis	⌄
Energy Settings	Edit...
Other	⌄
Project Issue Date	Issue Date
Project Status	Project Status
Client Name	ASCENT, INC
Project Address	Edit...
Project Name	Project Name
Project Number	Project Number

Figure 12–6

12.2 Placing and Modifying Views on Sheets

Learning Objectives

- Place views on sheets including using Guide Grids to help place the views.
- Modify views on sheets including moving views and view titles, removing views, and resizing views.
- Activate views on sheets to make minor changes to them.

The process of adding views to a sheet is simple. Drag and drop a view from the Project Browser onto the sheet. The new view on the sheet is displayed at the scale specified in the original view. The view title displays the name, number, and scale of the view, as shown in Figure 12–7.

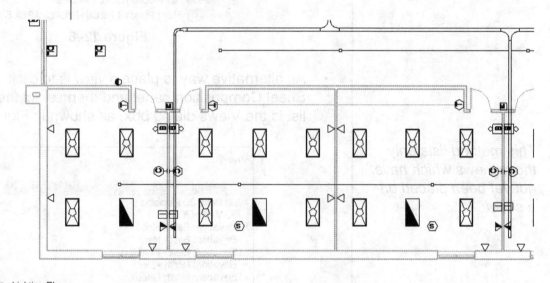

(1) Lighting Plan
1/8" = 1'-0"

Figure 12–7

How To: Place Views on Sheets

Alignment lines from existing views display to help you place additional views.

1. Set up the view as you want it to display on the sheet, including the scale and visibility of elements.
2. Create or open the sheet where you want to place the view.
3. Select the view in the Project Browser, and drag and drop it onto the sheet.
4. The center of the view is attached to the cursor. Position the view as required, and click to place it on the sheet.

- You cannot place a view more than once on your sheets. However, you can duplicate the view and place the copy on a sheet.

- Views on a sheet are associative. They automatically update to reflect changes to the project.

- Each view on a sheet is listed under the sheet name in the Project Browser, as shown in Figure 12–8.

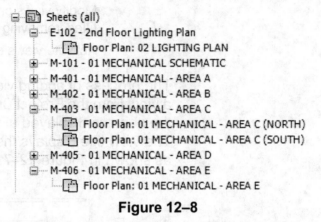

Figure 12–8

- An alternative way to place a view is to click (View) in the Sheet Composition panel and then select the view from the list in the Views dialog box, as shown in Figure 12–9.

This method lists only those views which have not yet been placed on a sheet.

Figure 12–9

- You can change the title of a view on a sheet without changing its name in the Project Browser. In Properties, in the *Identity Data* area, type a new title for the *Title on Sheet* parameter, as shown in Figure 12–10.

Identity Data	⌃
View Template	<None>
View Name	East - Plumbing
Dependency	Independent
Title on Sheet	East Elevation - Plumbing
Referencing Sheet	
Referencing Detail	

Figure 12–10

Working with Guide Grids

You can use a guide grid to help you place views on a sheet, as shown in Figure 12–11. Guide grids can be set up per sheet. You can also create different types with various grid spacings.

When moving a view to a guide grid, only orthogonal datum elements (levels and grids) and reference planes snap to the guide grid.

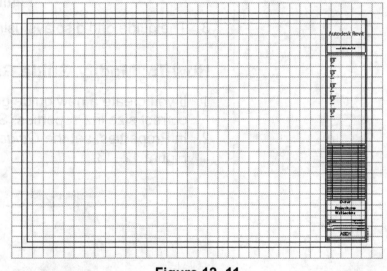

Figure 12–11

- You can move guide grids and resize them using controls.

How To: Add A Guide Grid

1. When a sheet is open, in the *View* tab>Sheet Composition panel, click ⠿ (Guide Grid).
2. In the Assign Guide Grid dialog box, select from existing guide grids (as shown in Figure 12–12), or create a new one and give it a name.

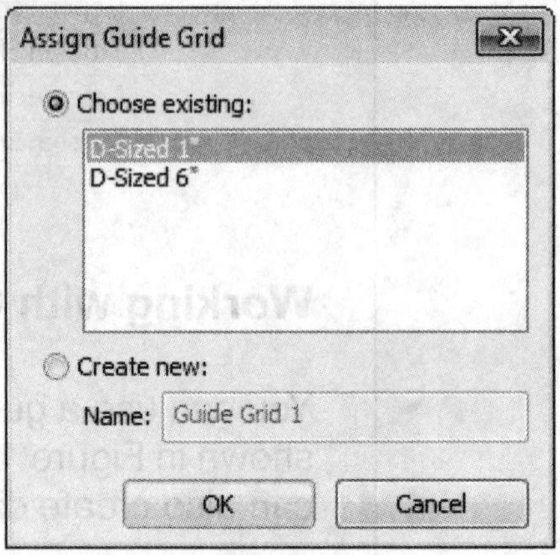

Figure 12–12

3. The guide grid displays using the specified sizing.

How To: Modify Guide Grid Sizing

1. If you create a new guide grid you need to update it to the correct size in Properties. Select the edge of the guide grid.
2. In Properties, set the *Guide Spacing*, as shown in Figure 12–13.

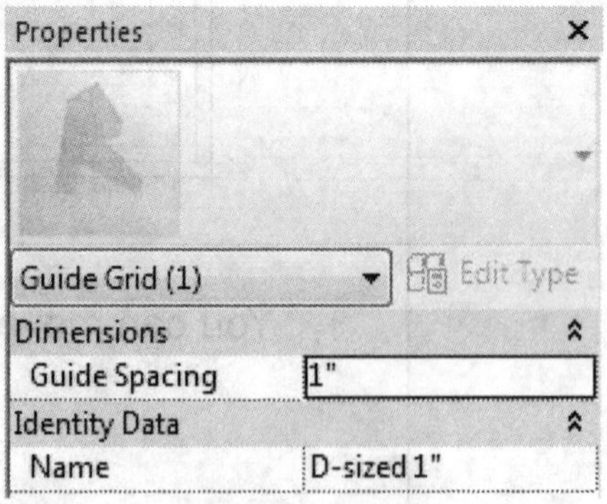

Figure 12–13

Modifying Views on Sheets

Views can be modified in several ways. You can move, delete, and rotate (90 degrees) views on a sheet. The view title can also be moved independently of the view. When you change any of the view properties of a view, they automatically update on the sheet.

- To show a specific portion of a model, use a callout view or modify the crop region in the view.

Moving Views and View Titles

*You can also use the **Move** command or the arrow keys to move a view.*

- To move a view on a sheet, select the edge of the viewport and drag it to a new location. The view title moves with the view.

- To move only the view title, select the title and drag it to the new location.

- To modify the length of the line under the title name, select the viewport and drag the controls, as shown in Figure 12–14.

1 North-South Entry
1/8" = 1'-0"

Figure 12–14

Deleting Views

- To remove a view from a sheet, select it and press <Delete>. Alternatively, select the view name under the sheet in the Project Browser, right-click, and select **Remove From Sheet**.

Rotating Views

- If you are creating a vertical sheet, you can rotate the view on the sheet by 90 degrees. Select the view and set the direction of rotation in the *Rotation on Sheet* drop-down list in the Options Bar, as shown in Figure 12–15.

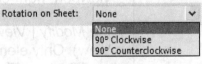

Rotation on Sheet: None
None
90° Clockwise
90° Counterclockwise

Figure 12–15

- If a view needs to be rotated to an angle other than 90 degrees, do this before you place it on a sheet. Turn on the crop region in the view and then select the view. In the Modify panel, click ↻ (Rotate) and change the rotation. The crop region remains as is, but the elements in the view rotate.

Resizing Views on Sheets

Each view displays the extents of the model or the elements contained in the crop region. If the view does not fit on a sheet, as shown in Figure 12–16, you might need to crop the view or move the elevation markers closer to the building.

If the extents of the view change dramatically based on a scale change or a crop region, it might be easier to delete the view on the sheet and drag it over again, rather than reworking the location of the view and title on the sheet.

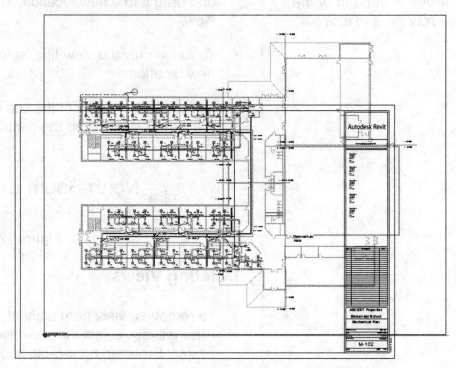

Figure 12–16

Working Inside Views

If you need to make small changes to a view while working on a sheet, you can work *through* the viewport on the model itself by activating a view.

Double-click inside the viewport to activate it or select the viewport, right-click and select **Activate View**. Alternatively, in the *Modify | Viewports* tab>Viewport panel, click ⬚ (Activate View). Only elements within the viewport are available for modification. The rest of the sheet is grayed out, as shown in Figure 12–17.

Only use this method for small changes. Significant changes should be made directly in the view.

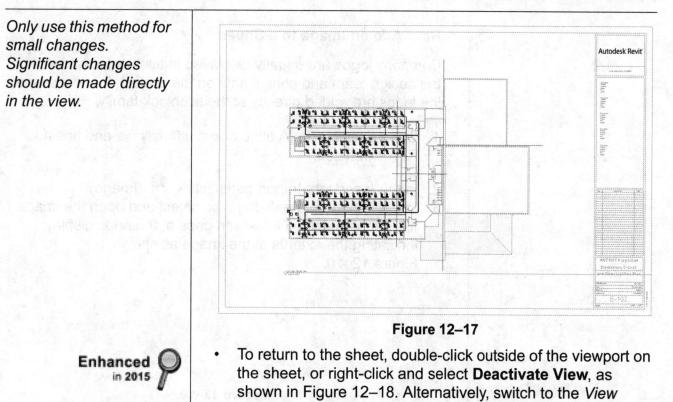

Figure 12–17

Enhanced
in 2015

- To return to the sheet, double-click outside of the viewport on the sheet, or right-click and select **Deactivate View**, as shown in Figure 12–18. Alternatively, switch to the *View* tab>Sheet Composition panel, expand (Viewports), and click (Deactivate View).

Figure 12–18

- Changes you make to elements when a view is activated also display in the original view.

Hint: Add an Image to a Sheet

Company logos are usually displayed in titleblocks to identify the design team and consultants on the project. In most cases, the logos are added directly to the titleblock family.

1. Open a titleblock. (A titleblock is a family file and has an RFA extension.)

2. In the *Insert* tab>Import panel, click 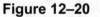 (Image).

3. In the Import Image dialog box, select and open the image file. Cross-hatching lines with grips at the ends display, indicating the extents of the image as shown in Figure 12–19.

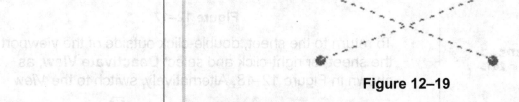

Figure 12–19

4. Place the image where you want it to be located within the titleblock.

5. The image is displayed. Pick one of the grips and extend it to modify the size of the image.

• In Properties, you can adjust the height and width and also set the *Draw Layer* to either **Background** or **Foreground**, as shown in Figure 12–20.

Dimensions		≫
Width	1' 5 185/256"	
Height	1' 1 41/64"	
Horizontal Scale	1.000000	
Vertical Scale	1.000000	
Lock Proportions	☑	
Other		≫
Draw Layer	Background	

Figure 12–20

• You can select more than one image at a time and move them as a group to the background or foreground.

Practice 12a

Create Construction Documents

Learning Objectives

- Add Project Information.
- Review existing sheets and create new sheets.
- Add views to the sheets.
- Place views on sheets.

Estimated time for completion: 20 minutes

In this practice you will specify project information that is used in title blocks and review existing sheets in the project. You will add new sheets individually and also by using placeholder sheets. You will then add views to sheets, such as the Lighting Plan sheet shown in Figure 12–21. Complete as many sheets as you have time for in class.

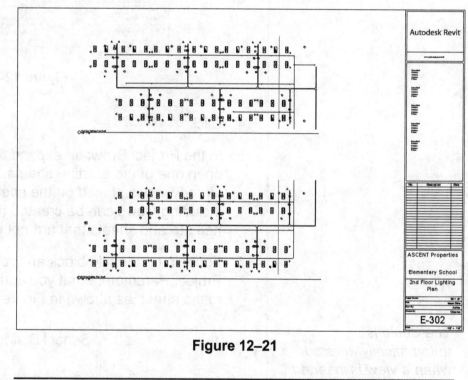

Figure 12–21

Task 1 - Setup Project Properties and review existing sheets.

1. In the *C:\Autodesk Revit 2015 MEP Fundamentals Class Files\Documents* folder, open **MEP-Elementary-School -Documents.rvt**.

2. In the *Manage* tab>Settings panel, click (Project Information).

3. In the Project Properties dialog box, add the following values, as shown in Figure 12–22.

    *   Client Name: **School District ABC**
    *   Project Name: **Elementary School**
    *   Project Number: **1234.56**

These values are added automatically to any sheet you create.

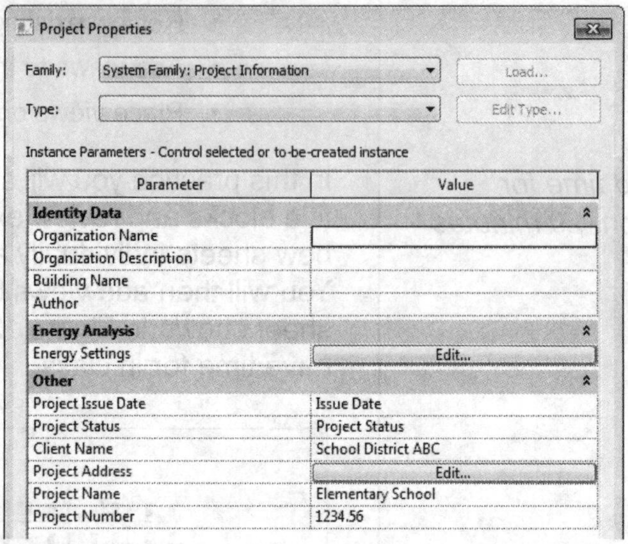

Figure 12–22

4. Click [OK] .

5. In the Project Browser, expand the *Sheets (all)* area and open one of the existing sheets. In this case, there are already views placed on the sheet. Sometimes such sheets including views can be created in the template. Then you need to add sheets that are not included.

6. Zoom in on the title block and review the contents. The Project Parameters that you added are automatically applied to the sheet, as shown in Figure 12–23.

The Scale is automatically entered when a view is inserted onto a sheet. If a sheet has multiple scales, the scale reads As Indicated.

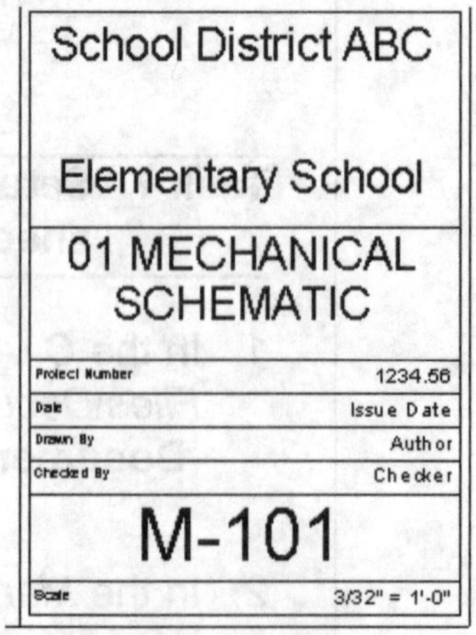

Figure 12–23

7. Set *Drawn by* to your initials. Leave the *Checked by* and *Issue Date* parameters as is.

8. Open another sheet. The project parameter values are repeated but note that the *Drawn By* value is not added because it is a by sheet parameter.

9. Review the other sheets and save the project.

Task 2 - Add Sheets.

1. In the *View* tab>Sheet Composition panel, click ⬚ (Sheet).

2. In the New Sheet dialog box, select the titleblock **E1 30 x42 Horizontal** and click [OK].

3. In the Project Browser, select the new sheet, right-click, and select **Rename**.

4. In the Sheet Title dialog box, set *Number* as **C-101**, *Name* as **Cover Sheet**, and click [OK]. The titleblock updates as shown in Figure 12–24.

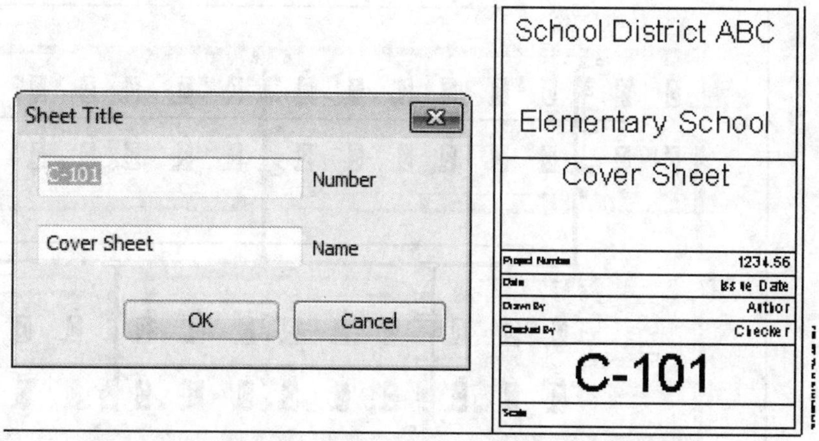

Figure 12–24

5. In the Project Browser, right-click on Sheets (all) and select **New Sheet....**

6. Using the same title block, create the following sheets:

   • E-302 - 2nd Floor Lighting Plan
   • E-303 - Power Panel Plan Detail
   • P-509 - Plumbing/Piping 3D

You can change the sheet number and name in the titleblock or by renaming it in the Project Browser.

7. Start the **Sheet** command by right-clicking on the *Sheets* node in the Project Browser, and selecting **New Sheet...**, or in the *View* tab>Sheets panel, by clicking 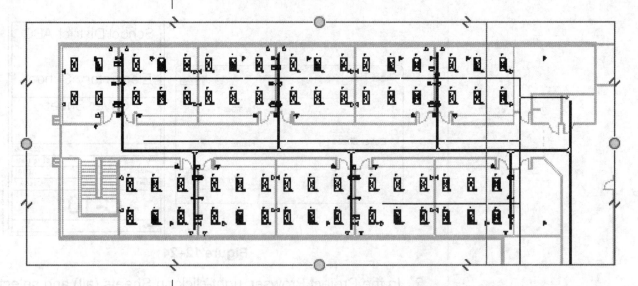 (Sheet). Select the placeholder sheets and click | OK |.

8. In the Project Browser, in the *Sheets (all)* area, note that these new sheets, the other sheets that you created, and the M-# sheets that were already created for you are displayed.

9. Save the project.

Task 3 - Set up and add views to sheets.

1. In the Project Browser, in the Electrical>Lighting Floor Plans, right click on the **02 LIGHTING PLAN** view and using **Duplicate as Dependent** create two copies. Name them as **02 LIGHTING PLAN - NORTH** and **02 LIGHTING PLAN - SOUTH**.

2. Open the **02 LIGHTING PLAN - NORTH** view, show the crop region, and resize it to fit the north classroom wing, as shown in Figure 12–25.

Figure 12–25

3. Turn the crop region off.

4. Repeat the steps with the **02 LIGHTING PLAN - SOUTH** view.

5. Open the **E-302 - 2nd Floor Lighting Plan** sheet and drag and drop the **2nd Floor Lighting Plan North** and **South** views you just created onto it.

6. Open the **E-303 - Power Panel Plan Detail** sheet and drag and drop the **Power Panel Callout** view onto it.

7. Repeat the process of adding views and schedules to sheets using the views and schedules you have available.

    - Modify crop regions and hide unnecessary elements in the views. Turn off crop regions after you have modified them.

    - Verify the scale of a view in Properties before placing it on a sheet.

    - Use alignment lines to help place multiple views on one sheet.

    - Change the view title if necessary to more accurately describe what is on the sheet.

    - To make minor changes to a view once it is on a sheet, right-click on the view and select Activate View. To return to the sheet, right-click on the view and select Deactivate View.

Your numbers might not exactly match the numbers in the example.

8. Switch to the **01 POWER PLAN** view. Zoom in on the callout marker by the power panels. Notice that it has now been automatically assigned a detail and sheet number, as shown in Figure 12–26.

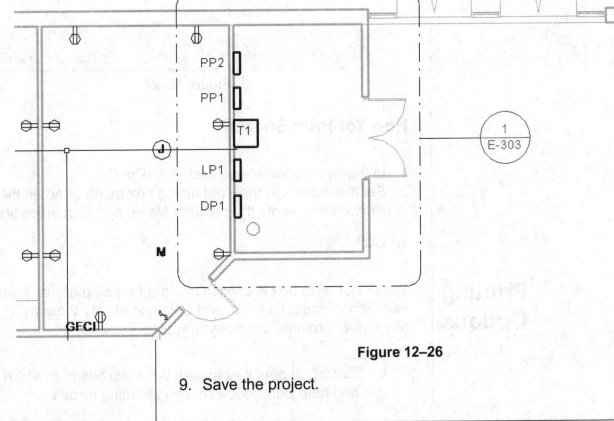

Figure 12–26

9. Save the project.

12.3 Printing Sheets

Learning Objective

- Print sheets using the default Print dialog box.

With the **Print** command, you can print individual sheets or a list of selected sheets. You can also print an individual view or a portion of a view for check prints or presentations. The Print dialog box is shown in Figure 12–27.

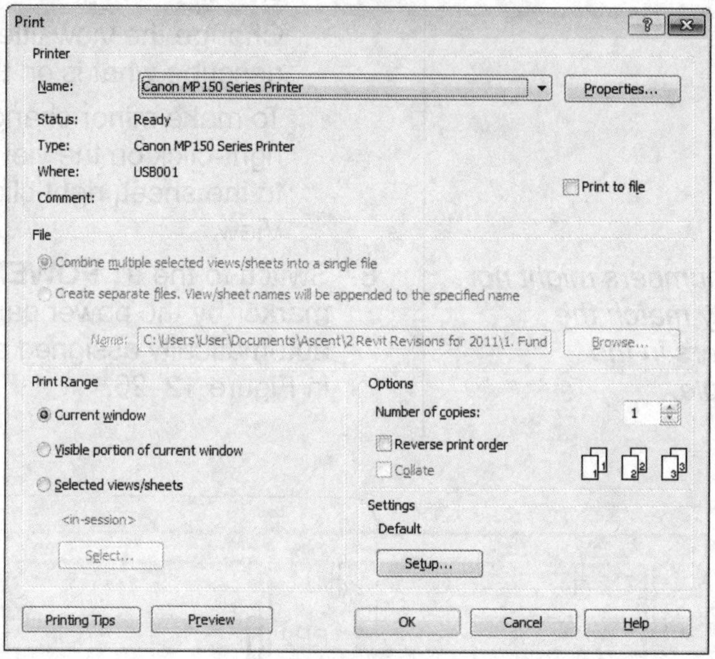

Figure 12–27

How To: Print Sheets

1. In the Application Menu, click 🖶 (Print).
2. Set the options in the Print dialog box as required. In the *Printer* area, verify the printer's *Name* and *Properties* first.

3. Click [OK]

Printing Options

The Print dialog box is divided into the following areas: *Printer*, *File*, *Print Range*, *Options*, and *Settings*. Modify them as required to produce the plot you want.

- [Printing Tips] opens Autodesk WikiHelp online in which you can find help with troubleshooting printing issues.

- Preview opens a preview of the print output so that you can see what is going to be printed.

Printer

Select from the list of available printers, as shown in Figure 12–28. Click Properties... to adjust the properties of the selected printer. The options vary according to the printer. Select the **Print to file** option to print to a file rather than directly to a printer. You can create .PLT or .PRN files.

If you do not have an Adobe PDF print driver installed on your system, you cannot print PDF files.

Figure 12–28

File

The *File* area is only available if the **Print to file** option has been selected in the *Printer* area. You can create one file or multiple files depending on the type of printer you are using, as shown in Figure 12–29.

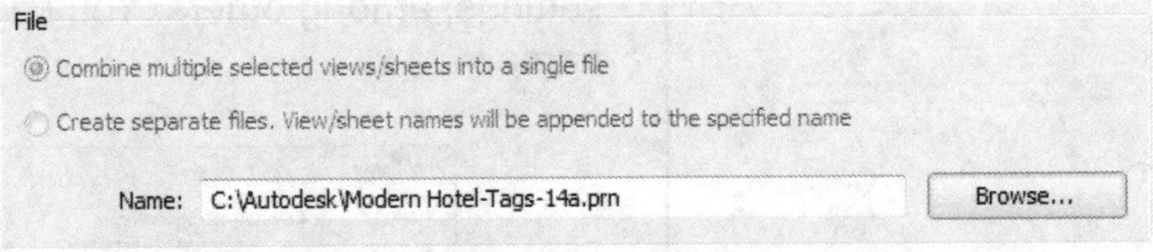

Figure 12–29

Options

If your printer supports multiple copies, you can specify the number in the *Options* area, as shown in Figure 12–30. You can also reverse the print order or collate your prints. These options are also available in the printer properties.

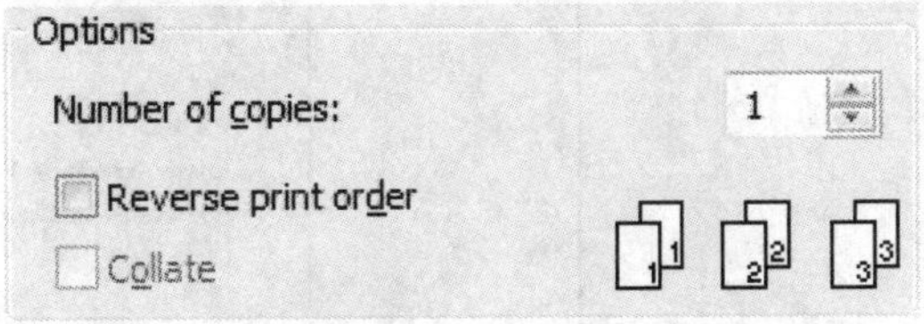

Figure 12–30

Print Range

The *Print Range* area, as shown in Figure 12–31, enables you to print individual views/sheets or sets of views/sheets. The **Current window** option prints the entire current sheet or view you have open. The **Visible portion of current window** option prints only what is displayed in the current sheet or view.

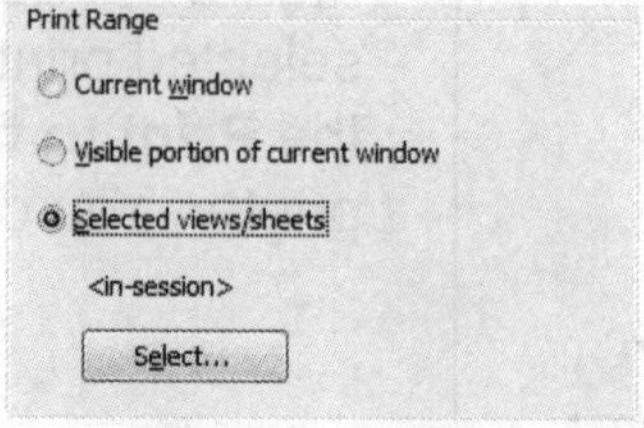

Figure 12–31

To print multiple sheets, select the **Selected views/sheets** option and click [Select...] to open the View/Sheet Set dialog box. Select each view or sheet to be included in the print set. You can save these sets by name so that you can more easily print the same group again.

Settings

Click [Setup...] to open the Print Setup dialog box, as shown in Figure 12–32. Here, you can specify the *Orientation* and *Zoom* settings, among others. You can also save these settings by name.

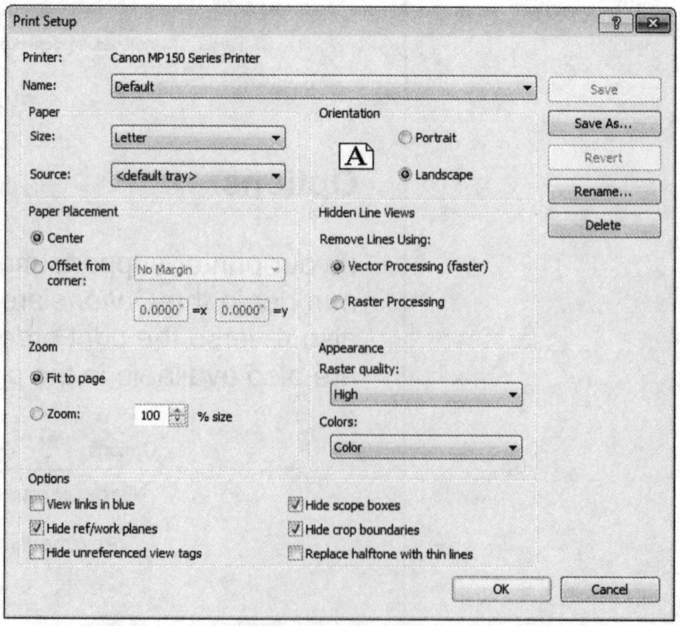

Figure 12–32

Chapter Review Questions

1. How do you specify the size of a sheet?

    a. In the Sheet Properties, specify the **Sheet Size**.

    b. In the Options Bar, specify the **Sheet Size**.

    c. In the New Sheet dialog box, select a title block to control the Sheet Size.

    d. In the Sheet view, right-click and select **Sheet Size**.

2. How is the title block information filled in as shown in Figure 12–33? (Select all that apply.)

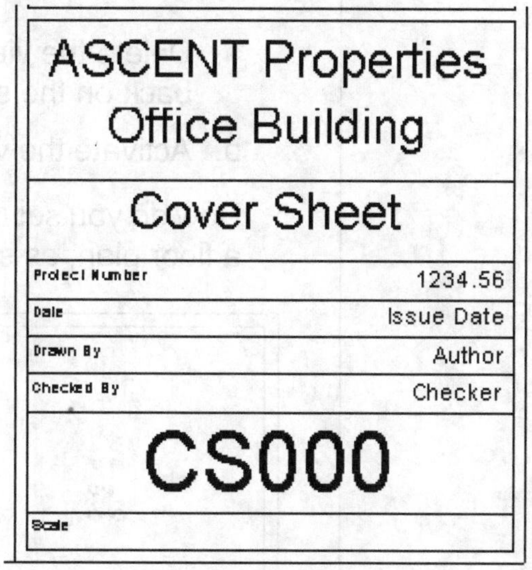

ASCENT Properties	
Office Building	
Cover Sheet	
Project Number	1234.56
Date	Issue Date
Drawn By	Author
Checked By	Checker
CS000	
Scale	

Figure 12–33

    a. Select the title block and select the label that you want to change.

    b. Select the title block and modify it in Properties.

    c. Right-click on the Sheet in the Project Browser and select **Information**.

    d. Some of the information is filled in automatically.

3. On how many sheets can a view be placed?

    a. 1

    b. 2-5

    c. 6+

    d. As many as you want.

4. Which of the following is the best method to use if the size of a view is too large for a sheet, as shown in Figure 12–34?

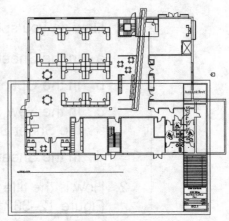

Figure 12–34

a. Delete the view, change the scale and place the view back on the sheet.

b. Activate the view and change the View Scale.

5. How do you set up a view on a sheet that only displays part of a floor plan, as shown in Figure 12–35?

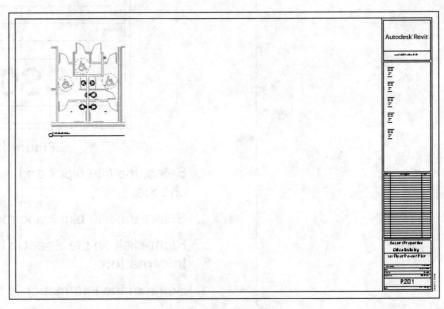

Figure 12–35

a. Drag and drop the view to the sheet and use the crop region to modify it.

b. Activate the view and rescale it.

c. Create a callout view displaying the part that you want to use and place the callout view on the sheet.

d. Open the view in the Project Browser and change the View Scale.

Command Summary

Button	Command	Location
	Activate View	• **Ribbon:** (*select the view*) *Modify | Viewports* tab>Viewport panel>Activate View • **Right-click:** (*on view*) Activate View
	Deactivate View	• **Ribbon:** *View* tab>Sheet Composition panel>expand Viewports>Deactivate View • **Right-click:** (*on view*) Deactivate View
	Guide Grid	• **Ribbon:** *View* tab>Sheet Composition panel>Guide Grid • **Properties:** (*when a sheet is selected*)
	Sheet	• **Ribbon:** *View* tab>Sheet Composition panel>Sheet
	View	• **Ribbon:** *View* tab>Sheet Composition panel>View

Chapter 13

Annotating Construction Documents

In this chapter you learn about adding dimensions and text to views used in construction documents. You learn how to add view specific detail lines and symbols to clarify design intent.You also learn how to create legends and add legend components.

This chapter contains the following topics:

- **Working with Dimensions**
- **Working With Text**
- **Adding Detail Lines and Symbols**
- **Creating Legends**

13.1 Working with Dimensions

 Learning Objectives

- Add a string of dimensions to walls and other elements and add dimensions to entire walls and their related elements.
- Add other dimensions, such as angular, radial, diameter, and arc length.
- Modify dimensions including the text and setting equal constraints.

You can create permanent dimensions using aligned, linear, angular, radial, and arc length dimensions. These can be individual or a string of dimensions, as shown in Figure 13–1. With aligned dimensions, you can also dimension entire walls with openings, grid lines, and/or intersecting walls.

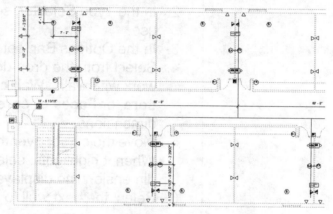

Figure 13–1

- Dimensions referencing model elements must be drawn on a model in an active view. You can dimension on sheets, but only to items drawn directly on the sheets.

- You can use permanent dimensions to modify elements. First, select the element being dimensioned and then edit the dimension value, as you would with temporary dimensions.

- Dimensions are available in the *Annotate* tab>Dimension panel and the *Modify* tab>Measure panel, as shown in Figure 13–2.

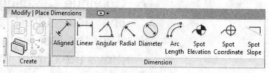

Figure 13–2

 (Aligned) is also located in the Quick Access Toolbar.

- The default template includes several dimension styles for each type of dimension. It also includes different styles with different leaders when you pull the text away from the dimension line. You can also create your own dimension styles with different text sizes, fonts, and arrowheads. including loop leaders, as shown in Figure 13–3.

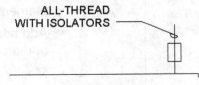

ALL-THREAD
WITH ISOLATORS

Figure 13–3

How To: Add Dimensions for a Series of Walls

1. In the Quick Access Toolbar or *Annotate* tab>Dimensions panel, click (Aligned) or use the shortcut by pressing <D> and then pressing <I>.
2. In the Type Selector, select the dimension type you want to use.
3. In the Options Bar, set *Pick* to **Individual References**.
4. Select from the drop-down list to define how the dimensions work with walls: **Wall centerlines**, **Wall faces**, **Center of core**, or **Faces of core**. This can be changed as you add dimensions.
5. Move the cursor over the first element you want to dimension. When it highlights, select the element. A ghost image of the dimension line displays.
6. Select the next wall to dimension, as shown in Figure 13–4.

When placing dimensions to and from Autodesk® Revit® MEP components, you can select either the edges or centers.

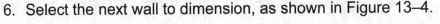
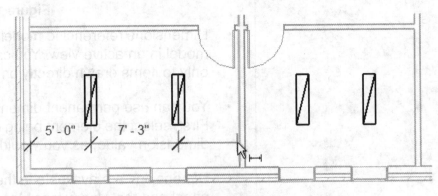

5' - 0"   7' - 3"

Figure 13–4

7. Continue selecting elements to dimension in a continuous line, as required.
8. After the last element to be dimensioned has been selected, move the cursor to a location for the dimension string. Click in an empty space to place it.

How To: Add Other Types of Dimensions

1. In the *Annotate* tab>Dimension panel, select a dimension method.

↗	**Aligned**	Most commonly used dimension type. Select individual elements or entire walls to dimension.
⊓	**Linear**	Used when you need to specify certain points on elements.
◁	**Angular**	Used to dimension the angle between two elements.
↖	**Radial**	Used to dimension the radius of circular elements.
⊘	**Diameter**	Used to dimension the diameter of circular elements.
⌒	**Arc Length**	Used to dimension the length of the arc of circular elements.

2. In the Type Selector, select the dimension type.
3. Follow the prompts for the selected method.

*When the **Dimension** command is active, the dimension methods are also accessible in the Modify | Place Dimensions tab> Dimension panel.*

Modifying Dimensions

Dimensions automatically update when you move the dimensioned elements. You can also modify the dimensions using various controls and constraints. While the dimension text is automatically updated you can still edit the dimension text, replace, or add to the dimension. There are also constraints for locking the dimension in place and to make dimensions equal.

When the **Modify** command is active and you select a dimension or dimension string, you can change several aspects of the dimension, as shown in Figure 13–5.

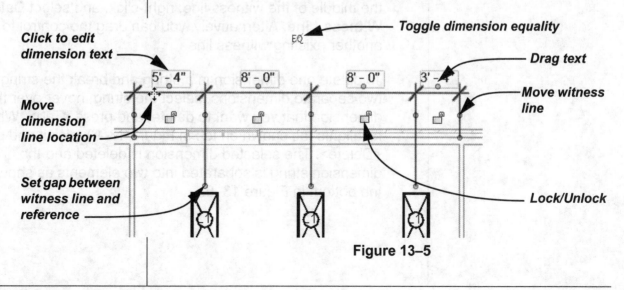

Figure 13–5

Modifying the Dimension Element

- To move the dimension text, select the **Drag text** control under the text and drag it to a new location. It automatically creates a leader from the dimension line if you drag it away. The style of the leader (arc or line) depends on the dimension style.

- To move the dimension line (the line parallel to the element being dimensioned), hover the cursor over the line until ⟷ (Move) displays. Drag the line to a new location.

- To change the gap between the witness line and the element being dimensioned, drag the control at the end of the witness line.

Modifying the Witness Lines

- To move the witness line (the line perpendicular to the element being dimensioned) to a different element or face of a wall, use the **Move Witness Line** control in the middle of the witness line. Click repeatedly to cycle through the various options. You can also drag this control to move the witness line to a different element, or right-click on the control and select **Move Witness Line**.

- To add a witness line to a string of dimensions, select the dimension and, in the Modify | Dimensions tab>Witness Lines panel, click ⊢ (Edit Witness Lines). Select the element(s) you want to add to the dimension. Click in space to finish.

- To delete a witness line, move the cursor over the control in the middle of the witness line, right-click, and select **Delete Witness Line**. Alternatively, you can drag the control to another existing witness line.

- To delete one dimension in a string and break the string into two separate dimensions, select the string, hover over the dimension that you want to delete, and press <Tab>. When it highlights (as shown on top in Figure 13–6), pick it and press <Delete>. The selected dimension is deleted and the dimension string is separated into two elements as shown on the bottom in Figure 13–6.

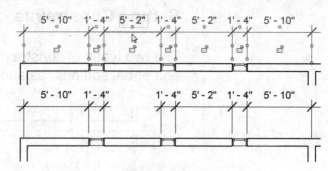

Figure 13–6

Modifying Dimension Text

The dimension text can be changed to a different value, though typically it is not recommended. Because the Autodesk® Revit® software is parametric, changing the dimension text without actually changing the elements dimensioned, can cause problems throughout the project especially if you use the project model to estimate materials or work with other disciplines. You can append the text, as shown in Figure 13–7, with prefixes and suffixes which is very useful in renovation projects.

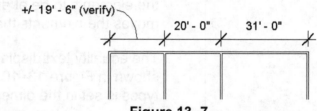

Figure 13–7

Double-click on the text to open the Dimension Text dialog box, as shown in Figure 13–8, and make modifications as required.

Figure 13–8

Setting Constraints

The two types of constraints that work with dimensions are locks and equal settings, as shown in Figure 13–9.

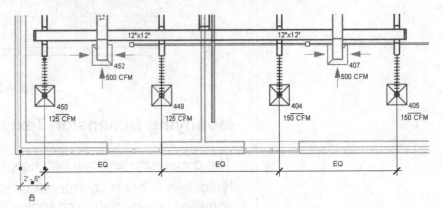

Figure 13–9

- When you lock a dimension, the value is set and you cannot make a change between it and the referenced elements. If it is unlocked, you can move it and change its value.

- For a string of dimensions, select the **EQ** symbol to constrain the elements to be at an equal distance apart. This actually moves the elements that are dimensioned.

- The equality text display can be changed in Properties as shown in Figure 13–10. The style for each of the display types is set in the dimension type.

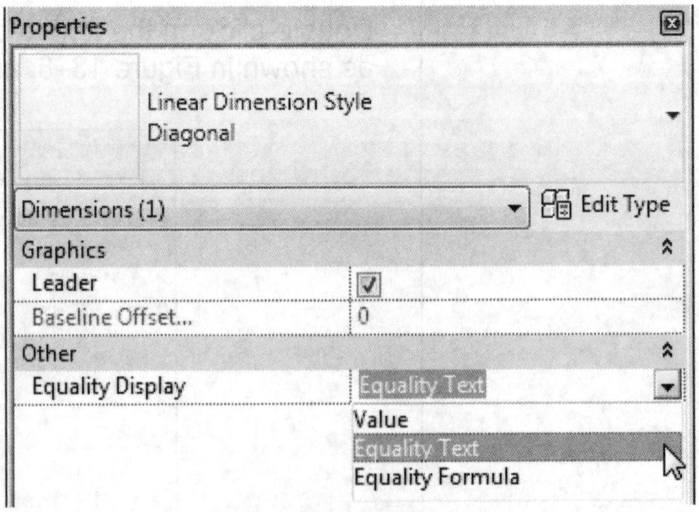

Figure 13–10

Practice 13a | Add Dimensions

 Learning Objective

Estimated time for completion: 10 minutes

- Add dimensions to a floor plan.

In this practice you will add dimensions to the duct branches, and then modify those dimensions, as shown in Figure 13–11.

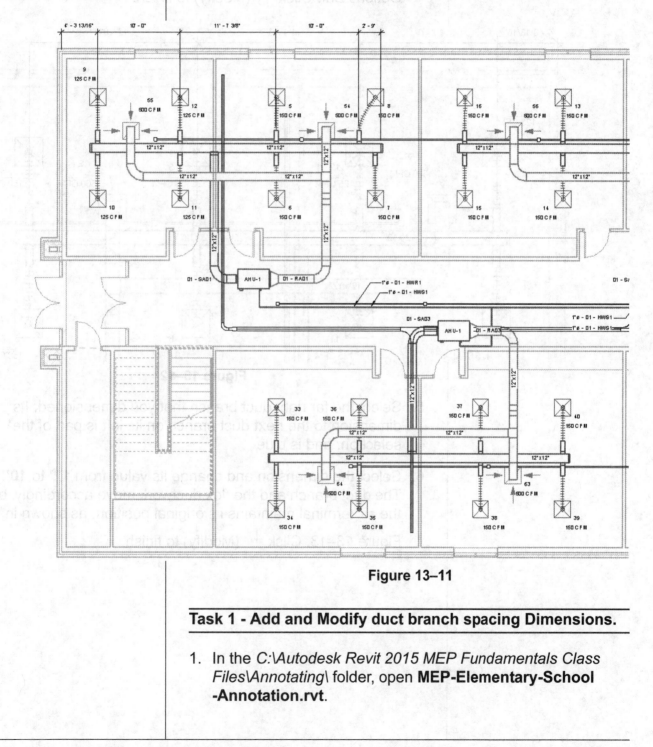

Figure 13–11

Task 1 - Add and Modify duct branch spacing Dimensions.

1. In the *C:\Autodesk Revit 2015 MEP Fundamentals Class Files\Annotating* folder, open **MEP-Elementary-School -Annotation.rvt**.

2. Open the Mechanical>HVAC>Floor Plans> **01 MECHANICAL PLAN** view.

3. In the *Annotate* tab>Dimension panel, click ✎ (Aligned).

4. Dimension the first four duct branches on the top side of the North wing, starting from the left side wall, as shown in Figure 13–12. Verify that the **Wall centerlines** is set in the Options Bar. Click ⬉ (Modify) to finish.

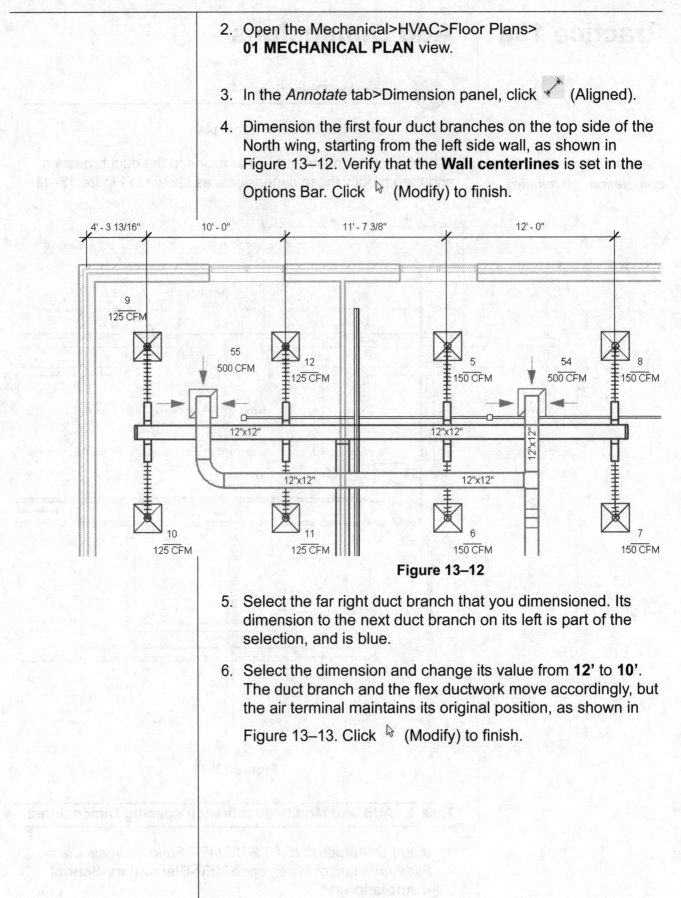

Figure 13–12

5. Select the far right duct branch that you dimensioned. Its dimension to the next duct branch on its left is part of the selection, and is blue.

6. Select the dimension and change its value from **12'** to **10'**. The duct branch and the flex ductwork move accordingly, but the air terminal maintains its original position, as shown in Figure 13–13. Click ⬉ (Modify) to finish.

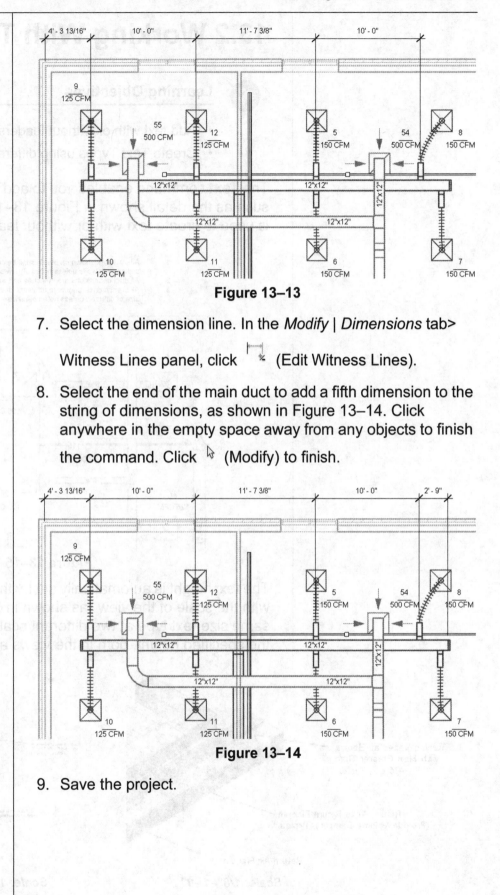

Figure 13–13

7. Select the dimension line. In the *Modify | Dimensions* tab> Witness Lines panel, click (Edit Witness Lines).

8. Select the end of the main duct to add a fifth dimension to the string of dimensions, as shown in Figure 13–14. Click anywhere in the empty space away from any objects to finish the command. Click (Modify) to finish.

Figure 13–14

9. Save the project.

13.2 Working With Text

Learning Objectives

- Add text with or without leaders.
- Create Text Types using different fonts and sizes.

The **Text** command enables you to add notes to views or sheets, such as the detail shown in Figure 13–15. The same command is used to create text with or without leaders.

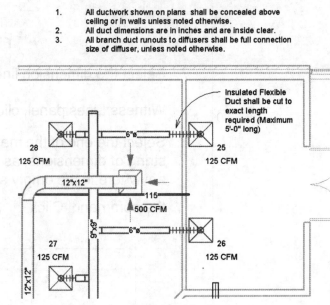

1. All ductwork shown on plans shall be concealed above ceiling or in walls unless noted otherwise.
2. All duct dimensions are in inches and are inside clear.
3. All branch duct runouts to diffusers shall be full connection size of diffuser, unless noted otherwise.

Insulated Flexible Duct shall be cut to exact length required (Maximum 5'-0" long)

Figure 13–15

The text height is automatically set by the text type in conjunction with the scale of the view (as shown in Figure 13–16), using the same size text type at two different scales. Text types display at the specified height, both in the views and on the sheet.

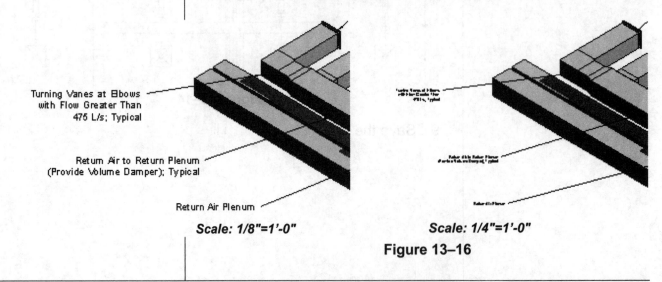

Turning Vanes at Elbows with Flow Greater Than 475 L/s; Typical

Return Air to Return Plenum (Provide Volume Damper); Typical

Return Air Plenum

Scale: 1/8"=1'-0"

Scale: 1/4"=1'-0"

Figure 13–16

How To: Add Text

1. In the *Annotate* tab>Text panel, click **A** (Text).
2. In the Type Selector, set the text type.
3. In the *Modify | Place Text* tab>Format panel, select the

   method you want to use: **A** (No Leader), **←A** (One

   Segment), **⤹A** (Two Segments), or **⤺A** (Curved).
4. In the Format panel, set the justification for the text and
   leader, as shown in Figure 13–17.

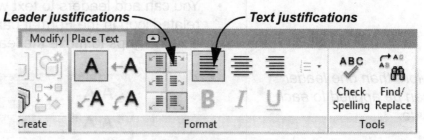

Figure 13–17

5. Select the location for the leader and text.
   - If the **No leader** option is selected, select the start point
     for the text and begin typing.
   - If using a leader, the first point places the arrow and you
     then select points for the leader. The text starts at the last
     leader point.
   - To set a word wrapping distance, click and drag to set the
     start and end points of the text.
6. Type the required text. In the Format panel, as shown in
   Figure 13–18, you can apply bold, italic, or underlined
   formatting to the text, as well as set a paragraph format.

Figure 13–18

7. Click outside the text box to complete the text element.
   - Pressing <Enter> after a line of text starts a new line of
     text in the same text window.

*The **Bold**, **Italic**, and **Underline** options only apply to that instance of text. If you want a specific type of text to have this formatting, create a new text type and select the new type in the Type Selector.*

8. Click in a new location to start another text element, or return to the **Modify** command to finish.

*   Use the controls shown in Figure 13–19 to position, rotate, or edit the text as required.

Figure 13–19

*   You can add leaders to text when it is selected. Click the related icon in the Format panel, as shown in Figure 13–20. Use the grips to move the leader once it is placed.

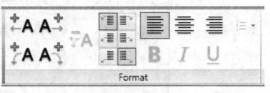

Figure 13–20

More than one leader can be applied to each side.

*   Several text types are included in the default template. These can be set in the Type Selector. You can also create your own text types.

*   When placing text, alignment lines help you align the text with other text elements based on the justification of the original text.

Setting the Paragraph Format

While entering text, you can set up individual lines of text using the paragraph formats shown in Figure 13–21. Change the text format option before you type the line of text. When you press <Enter> to start the next line, it continues to use the new format.

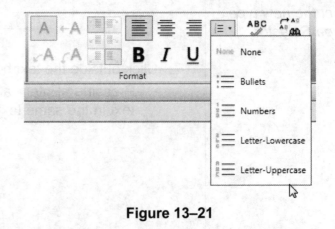

Figure 13–21

- To change a line that has already been typed, click anywhere on the line of text and change the paragraph format.

- You can also select several lines of text by dragging the cursor to highlight them and then change the paragraph format.

Hint: Model Text

Model text is different from annotation text. It is designed to create full-size text on the model itself. For example, you would use model text to create a sign on a door, as shown in Figure 13–22. One model text type, **24" Arial**, is included with the default template. You can create other types as required.

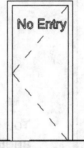

Figure 13–22

- Model text is found in the *Architecture* tab>Model panel, by

  clicking (Model Text).

Spell Checking

The Spelling dialog box displays any misspelled words in context and provides several options for changing them, as shown in Figure 13–23.

Figure 13–23

- To spell check all text in a view, in the *Annotate* tab>Text panel, click ABC✓ (Spelling) or press <F7>. As with other spell checkers, you can **Ignore**, **Add**, or **Change** the word.

- You can also check the spelling in selected text. With text selected, in the *Modify | Text Notes* tab>Tools panel, click ABC✓ (Spelling).

Creating Text Types

If you need new text types with a different text size or font (such as for a title or hand-lettering), you can create new ones, as shown in Figure 13–24. It is recommended that you create these in a project template so they are available in future projects.

General Notes

1. This project consists of
   furnishing and installing...

Figure 13–24

- You can copy and paste text types from one project to another or use **Transfer Project Standards**.

How To: Create Text Types

1. In the *Annotate* tab>Text panel, click **A** (Text). You can also start by selecting an existing text element.

2. In Properties, click ⊞ (Edit Type).

3. In the Type Properties dialog box, click [Duplicate].

4. In the Name dialog box, type a new name and click [OK].

5. Modify the text parameters as required. The parameters are shown in Figure 13–25.

Parameter	Value
Graphics	⌃
Color	■ Black
Line Weight	1
Background	Opaque
Show Border	☐
Leader/Border Offset	5/64"
Leader Arrowhead	Arrow 30 Degree
Text	⌃
Text Font	Arial
Text Size	1/4"
Tab Size	1/2"
Bold	☐
Italic	☐
Underline	☐
Width Factor	1.000000

The Show Border parameter, when selected, draws a rectangle around the text.

Figure 13–25

- In the *Graphics* area, click in the cell next to the **Color** parameter and select a color for the text in the Color dialog box. Typically, this remains black if you are creating working drawings. However, if you want to add color to a presentation, you can use the full range of True colors and Pantone colors.

- The **Background** parameter can be set to **Opaque** or **Transparent**. An opaque background includes a masking region that hides lines or elements beneath the text.

- In the *Text* area, the **Width Factor** parameter controls the width of the lettering, but does not affect the height. A width factor greater than **1** spreads the text out and a width factor less than **1** compresses it.

6. Click [OK] to close the Type Properties dialog box.

13.3 Adding Detail Lines and Symbols

 Learning Objectives

- Draw detail lines to display non model elements.
- Add 2D annotation symbols to specific views.

While annotating views for construction documents, you might need to add lines and symbols to clarify the design intent or show information, such as the life safety plan exit information, as shown in Figure 13–26.

Detail lines and symbols are view-specific, which means that they only display in the view in which they were created.

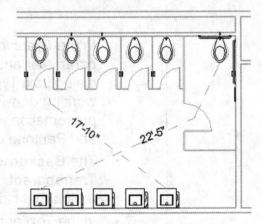

Figure 13–26

- Detail Lines and Symbols are also used to create detail views.

How To: Draw Detail Lines

1. In the *Annotation* tab>Detail panel, click (Detail Line).
2. In the *Modify | Place Detail Lines* tab>Line Style panel, select the type of line you want to use, as shown in Figure 13–27.

You can select from a variety of line styles including thin, medium, and wide lines, center lines, and demolition, hidden, and overhead lines. You can also create your own line styles.

Figure 13–27

3. Use the tools in the Draw panel to create the detail lines.

Using Symbols

Symbols are 2D elements that only display in one view, while components can be in 3D and display in many views.

Many of the annotations used in building design projects are frequently repeated. Several of them have been saved as symbols in the Autodesk Revit software, such as the North Arrow, Center Line, and Graphic Scale annotations as shown in Figure 13–28.

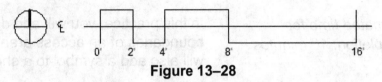

Figure 13–28

- You can also create or load custom annotation symbols.

How To: Place a Symbol

1. In the *Annotation* tab>Symbol panel, click ⊕ (Symbol).
2. In the Type Selector, select the symbol you want to use.
3. In the *Modify | Place Symbol* tab>Mode panel, click

    ⬇ (Load Family) if you want to load other symbols.
4. In the Options Bar, as shown in Figure 13–29, set the *Number of Leaders* and select the **Rotate after placement** option if you want to rotate the symbol as you insert it.

| Modify | Place Symbol | Number of Leaders: 0 ⇅ | ☐ Rotate after placement |

Figure 13–29

5. Place the symbol in the view. Rotate it if you selected the **Rotate after placement** option. If you specified leaders, use the controls to move them into place.

Practice 13b

Estimated time for completion: 10 minutes

Annotate Construction Documents

 Learning Objective

- Add detail lines and text in a callout view.

In this practice, you will add detail lines and text to show the boundaries of an access area, as shown in Figure 13–30. You will also add a symbol to a sheet.

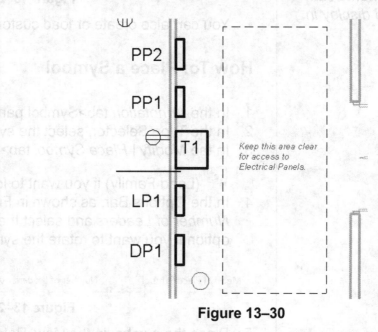

Figure 13–30

Task 1 - Add Detail Lines and Text.

1. In the *C:\Autodesk Revit 2015 MEP Fundamentals Class Files\Annotating* folder, open **MEP-Elementary-School -Annotation.rvt**.

2. Open the Electrical>Power>Floor Plans>**01 POWER PLAN** view, and zoom in on the Electrical Distribution Room in the upper right corner.

3. In the *Annotate* tab>Detail panel, click ⬛ (Detail Line).
4. In the *Modify | Place Detail Lines* tab>Line Style panel, set the *Line Style* to **MEP Hidden**.
5. Draw a rectangle from the upper left corner of the room to the lower right corner of the room, approximately **15' x 6'**, as

   shown in Figure 13–31. Click ⬚ (Modify) to finish.

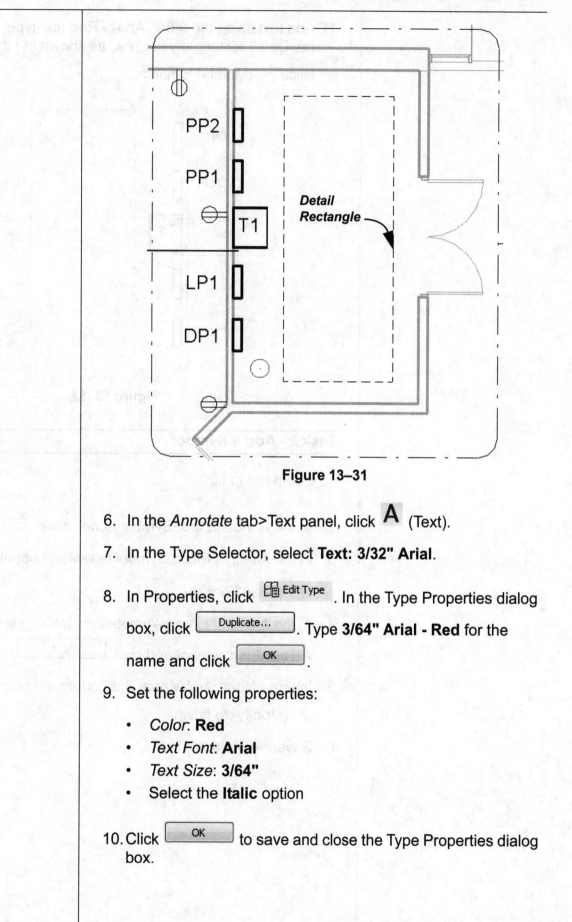

Figure 13–31

6. In the *Annotate* tab>Text panel, click **A** (Text).

7. In the Type Selector, select **Text: 3/32" Arial**.

8. In Properties, click ⊞ Edit Type . In the Type Properties dialog box, click [Duplicate...]. Type **3/64" Arial - Red** for the name and click [OK].

9. Set the following properties:

   • *Color*: **Red**
   • *Text Font*: **Arial**
   • *Text Size*: **3/64"**
   • Select the **Italic** option

10. Click [OK] to save and close the Type Properties dialog box.

11. Add text using the **3/64" Arial - Red** text type, to the inside of the Detail rectangle you drew, as shown in Figure 13–32. Click ⌨ (Modify) to finish.

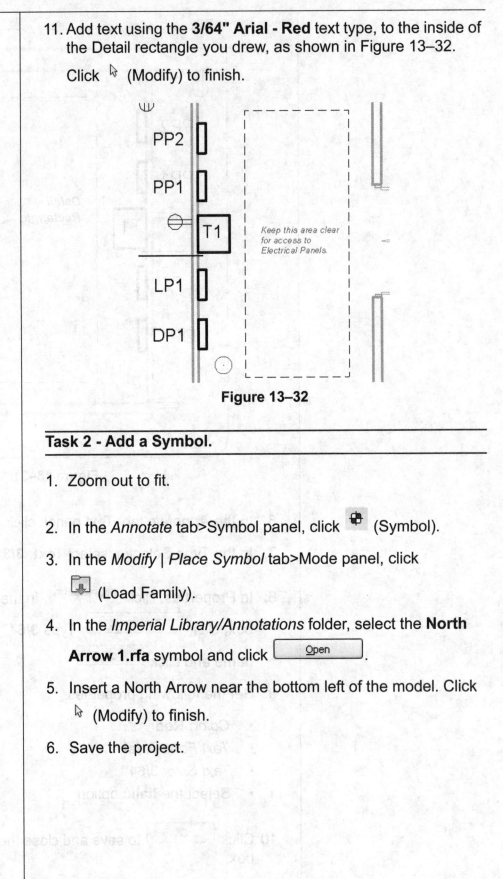

Figure 13–32

Task 2 - Add a Symbol.

1. Zoom out to fit.

2. In the *Annotate* tab>Symbol panel, click ⊕ (Symbol).

3. In the *Modify | Place Symbol* tab>Mode panel, click ⬇ (Load Family).

4. In the *Imperial Library/Annotations* folder, select the **North Arrow 1.rfa** symbol and click [Open].

5. Insert a North Arrow near the bottom left of the model. Click ⌨ (Modify) to finish.

6. Save the project.

13.4 Creating Legends

 Learning Objective

- Create legends in a legend view using detail lines, text, legend components, detail components, and symbols.

A legend is a separate view in which you can list the symbols used in your project and provide explanatory notes next to them. They are typically in a table format. Legends can include a list of all annotation symbols you use in your drawings, such as electrical switches (as shown in Figure 13–33), a list of materials, or items to remain or to be removed from a remodel.

Electrical Legend	
⊟	Dimmer Switch
⊟	3-Way Switch
⊠	Key Operated Switch
⊠	Manual Pull Fire Alarm

Figure 13–33

- You use ⌐ (Detail Lines) and **A** (Text) to create the table and explanatory notes. Once you have a legend view, you can use commands, such as ⌐ (Legend Component), ⊟ (Detail Component), and ⊕ (Symbol), to place elements in the drawing.

- Unlike other views, legend views can be attached to more than one sheet.

- You can set a legend's scale in the View Status Bar.

- Elements in legends can be dimensioned.

How To: Create a Legend

1. In the *View* tab>Create panel, expand ▦ (Legends) and click ▦ (Legend) or in the Project Browser, right-click on the *Legends* area title and select **New Legend**.

2. In the New Legend View dialog box, enter a name and select a scale for the legend, as shown in Figure 13–34, and click

$\boxed{\text{OK}}$.

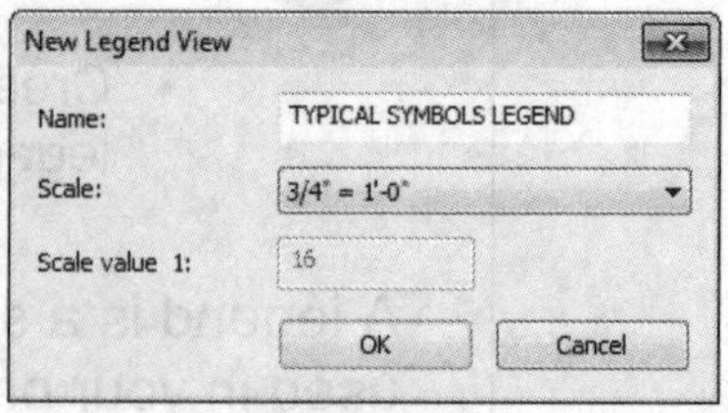

Figure 13–34

3. Place the components in the view first, and then sketch the outline of the table when you know the sizes. Use **Ref Planes** to line up the components.

How To: Use Legend Components

1. In the *Annotate* tab>Detail panel, expand ⬚ (Component) and click ⬚ (Legend Component).
2. In the Options Bar, select the *Family* type that you want to use, as shown in Figure 13–35. This list contains all of the elements in a drawing that can be used in a legend.

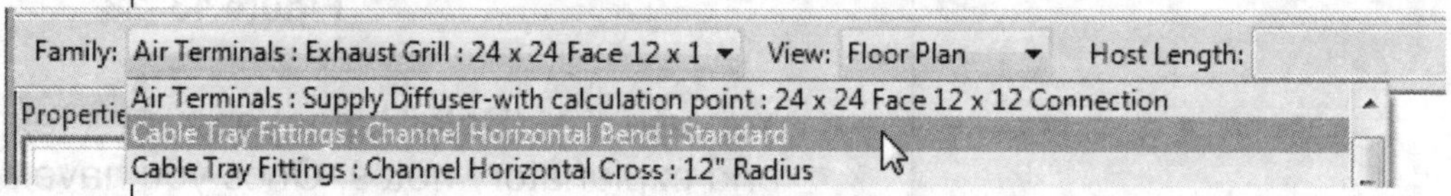

Figure 13–35

- The list of Families is limited to the ones that are loaded into the project, whether or not they have been used.
3. Select the *View* of the element that you want to use.
4. Place the component anywhere in the view.

 - Legend components are not counted in schedules and material takeoffs.
5. Add symbols (such as those shown in Figure 13–36), text, and detail lines to complete the legend.

Figure 13–36

- You can import an existing legend from a CAD file, but it is recommended to do a comparative check of the symbols in your model against the symbols in the imported CAD legend.

Practice 13c | Create Legends

 Learning Objective

- Create a legend using legend components, text, and detail lines

Estimated time for completion: 10 minutes

In this practice you will create a Plumbing Fixture legend using legend components, text and detail lines. You will then put the legend on a sheet, as shown in Figure 13–37

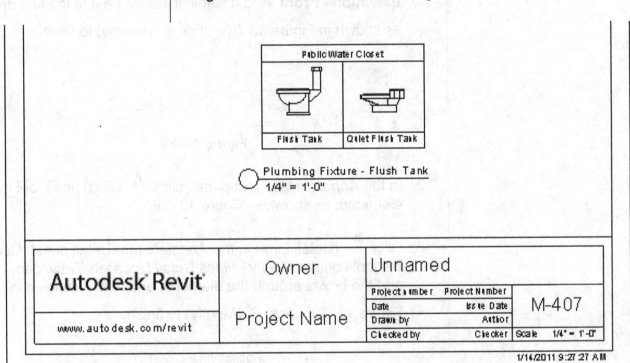

Figure 13–37

Task 1 - Add a Legend.

1. In the *C:\Autodesk Revit 2015 MEP Fundamentals Class Files\Annotating* folder, open **MEP-Elementary-School -Annotation.rvt**.

2. In the *View* tab>Create panel, expand ▦ (Legends) and click ▦ (Legend) to create a new Legend view.

3. Name the legend **Plumbing Fixture - Flush Tank** and set the *Scale* to **1/4"=1'-0"**. The new legend is created and placed in the *Legends* node of the Project Browser.

4. In the *Annotate* tab>Detail panel, expand ⬜ (Component) and click ⬛ (Legend Component).

5. In the Options Bar, set *Family* to **Plumbing Fixtures: Water Closet - Flush Tank: Public - 1.6 gpf** and set *View* to **Elevation - Front**. Add a single instance to the current Legend view.

6. In the Options Bar, set *Family* to **Plumbing Fixtures: Water Closet - Quiet Flush Tank: Public - 1.6 gpf**, and set *View* to **Elevation - Front**. Add a single instance next to the first one, as shown in Figure 13–38. Click ⌖ (Modify) to finish.

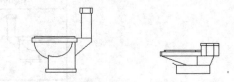

Figure 13–38

7. In the *Annotate* tab>Text panel, click **A** (Text) and label the elements, as shown in Figure 13–39.

8. Click ⬛ (Detail Line) in the *Annotate* tab>Detail panel. Use the tools on the *Modify | Place Detail Lines* tab>Draw panel to add the boxes around the elements and text, as shown in Figure 13–39. Click ⌖ (Modify) to finish.

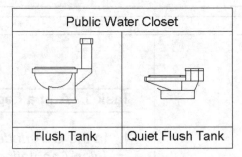

Figure 13–39

9. In the *View* tab>Sheet Composition panel, click ⬜ (Sheet) to create a new sheet. Use the **A 8.5 x 11 Vertical** titleblock, loading the titleblock if required.

10. Place the **Plumbing Fixture - Flush Tank** legend on the sheet, as shown at the beginning of the practice in Figure 13–37.

11. Save the project.

Chapter Review Questions

1. When a wall is moved (as shown in Figure 13–40), how do you update the dimension?

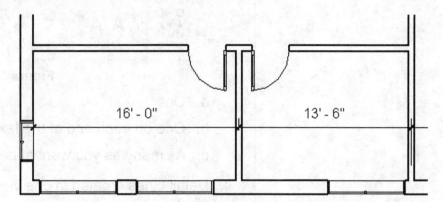

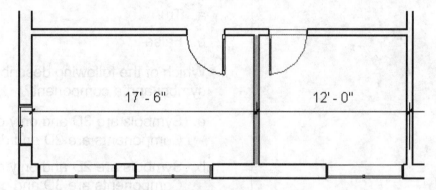

Figure 13–40

   a. Edit the dimension and move it over.

   b. Select the dimension and then click the **Update** button in the Options Bar.

   c. The dimension automatically updates.

   d. Delete the existing dimension and add a new one.

2. How do you create new text styles?

   a. Using the **Text Styles** command.

   b. Duplicate an existing type.

   c. They must be included in a template.

   d. Using the **Format Styles** command.

3. When you edit text, how many leaders can be added using the leader tools shown in Figure 13–41?

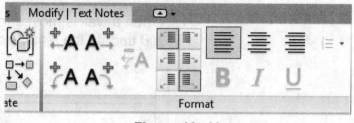

Figure 13–41

a. One

b. One on each end of the text.

c. As many as you want at each end of the text.

4. Detail Lines created in one view also display in the related view.

a. True

b. False

5. Which of the following describes the difference between a symbol and a component?

a. Symbols are 3D and only display in one view. Components are 2D and display in many views.

b. Symbols are 2D and only display in one view. Components are 3D and display in many views.

c. Symbols are 2D and display in many views. Components are 3D and only display in one view.

d. Symbols are 3D and display in many views. Components are 2D and only display in one view.

6. When creating a Legend, which of the following elements cannot be added? (Select all that apply.)

a. Legend Components

b. Tags

c. Rooms

d. Symbols

Command Summary

Button	Command	Location
	Aligned (Dimension)	• **Ribbon:** *Annotate* tab>Dimension panel>Aligned or *Modify* tab>Measure panel, expanded drop-down list • **Quick Access Toolbar** • **Shortcut:** \<D> and \<I>
	Angular (Dimension)	• **Ribbon:** *Annotate* tab>Dimension panel>Angular or *Modify* tab> Measure panel, expanded drop-down list
	Arc Length (Dimension)	• **Ribbon:** *Annotate* tab>Dimension panel>Arc Length or *Modify* tab> Measure panel, expanded drop-down list
	Diameter (Dimension)	• **Ribbon:** *Annotate* tab> Dimension panel>Diameter or *Modify* tab> Measure panel, expanded drop-down list
	Detail Line	• **Ribbon:** *Annotate* tab>Detail panel> Detail Line • **Shortcut:** \<D> and \<L>
	Linear (Dimension)	• **Ribbon:** *Annotate* tab>Dimension panel>Linear or *Modify* tab>Measure panel, expanded drop-down list
	Radial (Dimension)	• **Ribbon:** *Annotate* tab>Dimension panel>Radial or *Modify* tab>Measure panel, expanded drop-down list
	Stair Path	• **Ribbon:** *Annotate* tab>Symbol panel>Stair Path
	Symbol	• **Ribbon:** *Annotate* tab>Symbol panel>Symbol
	Text	• **Ribbon:** *Annotate* tab>Text panel> Text • **Shortcut:** \<T> and \<X>
	Legend	• **Ribbon:** *View* tab>Create panel> expand Legends>Legend
	Legend Component	• **Ribbon:** *Annotate* tab>Detail panel> expand Component>Legend Component

Chapter 14

Adding Tags and Schedules

In this chapter you learn how to add tags to individual and multiple elements. You also review schedules, how they update, and how to modify them in the schedule view and on a sheet.

This chapter contains the following topics:

- **Adding Tags**
- **Working with Schedules**

14.1 Adding Tags

Learning Objectives

- Add tags in 2D and 3D views individually or to all of the elements at the same time.
- Load tags that are needed for projects.

Tags identify elements that are listed in schedules. Many tags are added automatically if you use the **Tag on Placement** option when inserting an element. You can also add them later. Many different types of tags are available in the Autodesk® Revit® software, such as air terminal tags, lighting tags, and piping tags, as shown in Figure 14–1.

There are tags for many elements, including ducting and piping, mechanical and electrical equipment, electrical devices, and lighting fixtures. These tags are stored in the Annotations folder in the Library.

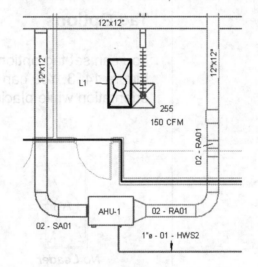

Figure 14–1

- The **Tag** command places all types of tags manually for most elements, except for a few that have separate commands.

You can place three types of tags, as follows:

- (Tag by Category): Tags according to the category of the element. It places door tags on doors and wall tags on walls.

- **(Multi-Category):** Tags elements belonging to multiple categories. The tags display information from parameters that they have in common.

- **(Material):** Tags that display the type of material. They are typically used in detailing.

How To: Add Tags

1. In the *Annotate* tab>Tag panel, click 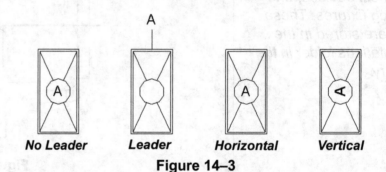 (Tag by Category), (Multi-Category), or (Material) depending on the type of tag you want to place.
2. In the Options Bar, set the options as required, as shown in Figure 14–2.

| Modify | Tag | Horizontal ▾ | Tags... | ☑ Leader | Attached End ▾ | ↦ 1/2" |

Figure 14–2

3. Select the element you want to tag. The appropriate tag is applied for the type of element selected. If the tag is not loaded, you are prompted to load it from the Library.

Tag Options

You can set tag options for leaders and tag rotation, as shown in Figure 14–3. You can also press the <Spacebar> to toggle the orientation while placing the tag or when modifying it.

No Leader   *Leader*   *Horizontal*   *Vertical*

Figure 14–3

• Leaders can have an **Attached End** or a **Free End**, as shown in Figure 14–4. The attached end must be connected to the element being tagged. A free end has an additional drag control where the leader touches the element.

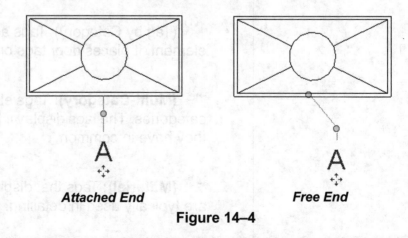

Attached End   *Free End*

Figure 14–4

- The **Length** option specifies the length of the leader in plotting units. It is grayed out if the **Leader** option is not selected or if a **Free End** leader is defined.

- If a tag is not loaded a warning box opens as shown in Figure 14–5. Click [Yes] to open the Load Family dialog box in which you can select the appropriate tag.

No Tag Loaded
There is no tag loaded for Duct Fittings. Do you want to load one now?
[Yes]   [No]

Figure 14–5

- To load tags, you can click [Tags...] in the Options Bar when a **Tag** command is active, or, in the *Annotate* tab, expand the Tag panel and click (Loaded Tags). This opens the Tags dialog box, which displays the tags that have been loaded and load additional tags, as shown in Figure 14–6. Most tags are stored in the *Annotations* folder in the Library.

Loaded Tags

Select an available Tag Family for each Family Category listed

Note: Multi-Category Tag Families are not shown below.

Filter list: <multiple>   Load Family...

Category	Loaded Tags
Air Terminals	Diffuser Tag
Areas	Area Tag
Assemblies	
Cable Tray Fittings	
Cable Trays	
Communication Devices	
Conduit Fittings	
Conduits	
Data Devices	Data Device Tag
Detail Items	
Duct Accessories	
Duct Fittings	

OK   Cancel   Help

Figure 14–6

Instance vs. Type Based Tags

Some elements are tagged in a numbered sequence, with each instance of the element having a separate tag number. Other elements are tagged by type, as shown in Figure 14–7. Changing the information in one tag changes all instances of that element.

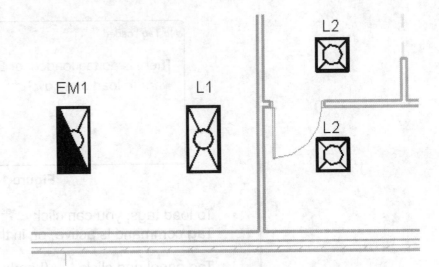

Figure 14–7

- In Properties or the Options Bar, change the *Leader* and *Orientation* of any type of tag.

- Tags can be letters or numbers, or a combination of the two.

- To modify the number of an instance tag you can double-click directly on the number in the tag and modify it. Alternatively, you can select the element (not the tag) and in Properties, in the *Identity Data* area, modify the *Mark* as shown in Figure 14–8. Only that one instance updates.

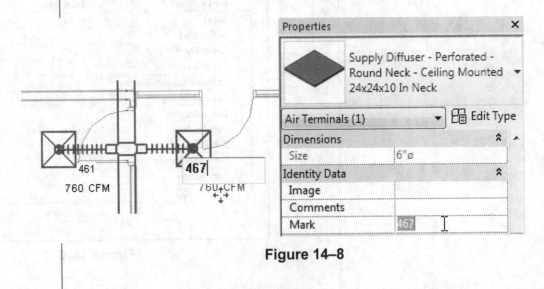

Figure 14–8

- To modify the number of a type tag, you can either click directly on the number in the tag and modify it, or select the element and, in Properties, click ⊞ (Edit Type). In the Type Properties dialog box, in the *Identity Data* area, modify the *Type Mark*, as shown in Figure 14–9. All instances of this element then update.

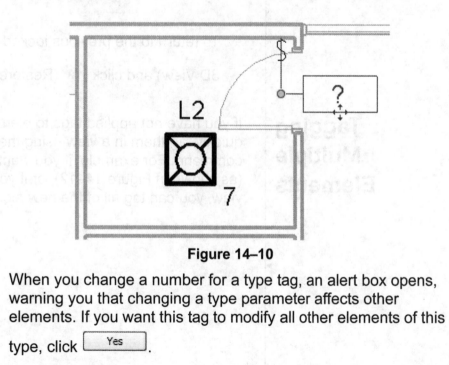

Figure 14–9

- Some tags come in empty, as shown in Figure 14–10. You can select the empty tag, click on the question mark, and type a number. Doing so changes all instances of the type in the project.

Figure 14–10

When you change a number for a type tag, an alert box opens, warning you that changing a type parameter affects other elements. If you want this tag to modify all other elements of this type, click Yes .

Tagging in 3D Views

You can add tags (and some dimensions) to 3D views, as shown in Figure 14–11, as long as the views are locked first. You can only add tags in isometric views.

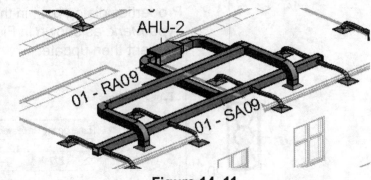

Figure 14–11

How To: Lock a 3D View

1. Open a 3D view and set it up as you want it to display.

2. In the View Control Bar, expand 🔓 (Unlocked 3D View) and click 🔒 (Save Orientation and Lock View).

- If you are using the default 3D view and it has not been saved, you are prompted to name and save the view first.

- You can modify the orientation of the view, expand 🔒 (Locked 3D View) and click 🔓 (Unlock View). This also removes any tags you have applied.

- To return to the previous locked view, expand 🔓 (Unlocked 3D View) and click 🔒 (Restore Orientation and Lock View).

Tagging Multiple Elements

If you have not applied tags to elements in a project, you can quickly tag them in a view using the **Tag All Not Tagged** command. For example, if you want to show tags in an elevation (as shown in Figure 14–12), or if you copy elements in a plan view, you can tag all of the new elements at the same time.

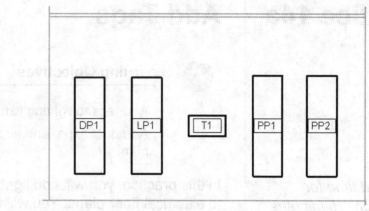

Figure 14–12

How To: Add Multiple Tags

1. In the *Annotate* tab>Tag panel, click (Tag All).
2. Select one or more categories that you want to tag, as shown in Figure 14–13. You can select more than one category by holding down <Shift> or <Ctrl>. Set the *Leader* and *Orientation* as required.

*To only tag some elements, select them before starting this command. In the Tag All Not Tagged dialog box, select the **Only selected objects in the current view** option.*

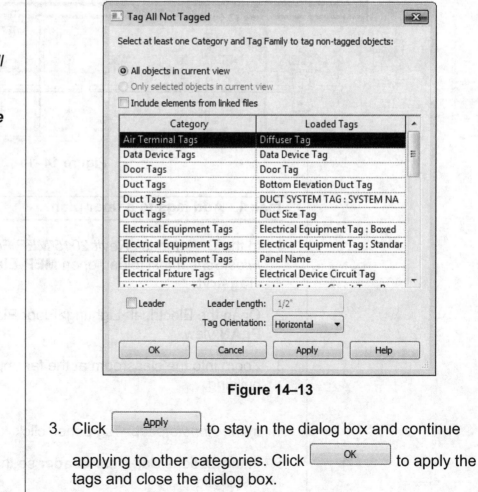

Figure 14–13

3. Click Apply to stay in the dialog box and continue applying to other categories. Click OK to apply the tags and close the dialog box.

Practice 14a | Add Tags

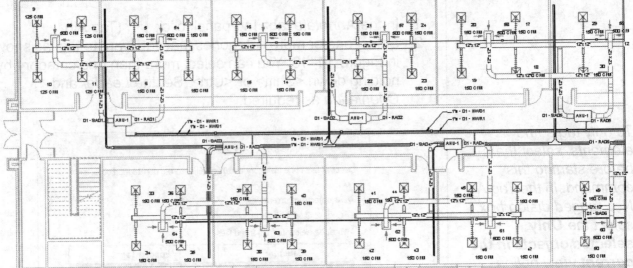

Learning Objectives

- Add tags to lighting fixtures and conduits in a floor plan.
- Add duct, pipe, and air terminal tags in a separate floor plan.

Estimated time for completion: 15 minutes

In this practice, you will add lighting fixture tags and conduit tags to electrical floor plans. You will then add duct, pipe, and air terminal tags to a mechanical floor plan, as shown in Figure 14–14.

Figure 14–14

Task 1 - Add tags to a floor plan.

1. In the *C:\Autodesk Revit 2015 MEP Fundamentals Class Files\Schedules* folder, open **MEP-Elementary-School -Tags.rvt**.

2. Open the Electrical>Lighting>Floor Plans>**01 LIGHTING PLAN** view.

3. Zoom into the classroom at the far upper left corner of the building.

4. In the *Annotate* tab>Tag panel, click 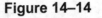 (Tag by Category).

5. In the Options Bar, clear **Leader** so that leaders are not displayed.

6. Tag the three light fixtures, as shown in Figure 14–15. The default **Lighting Fixture Tag: Standard** is used.

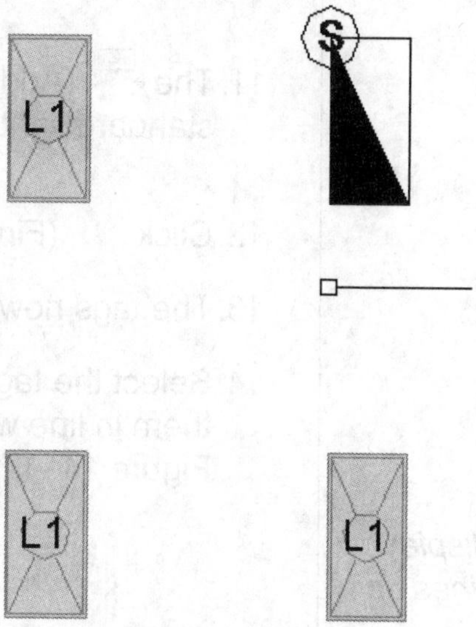

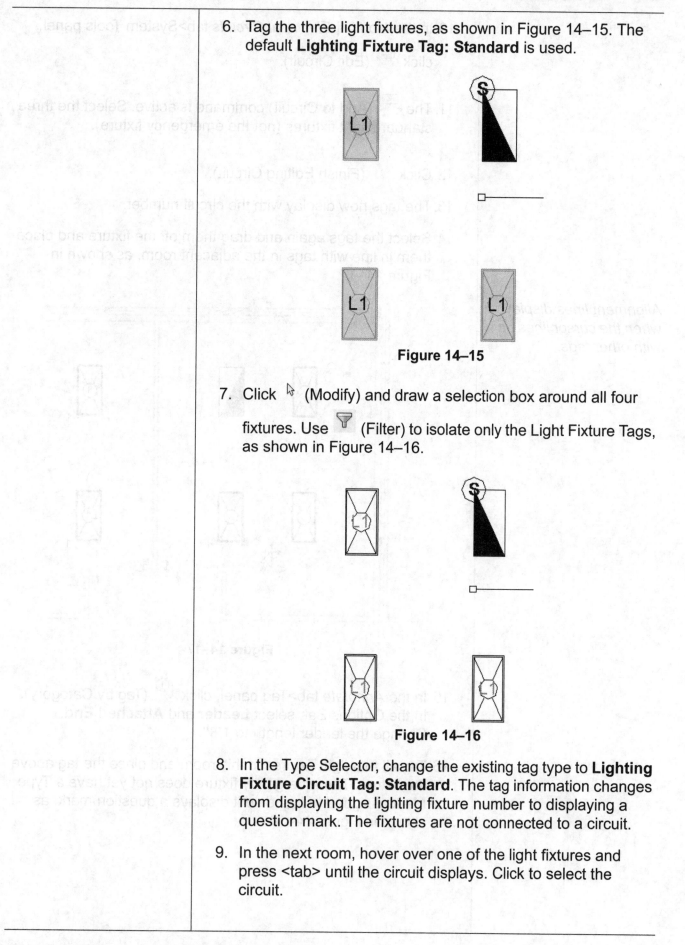

Figure 14–15

7. Click (Modify) and draw a selection box around all four fixtures. Use (Filter) to isolate only the Light Fixture Tags, as shown in Figure 14–16.

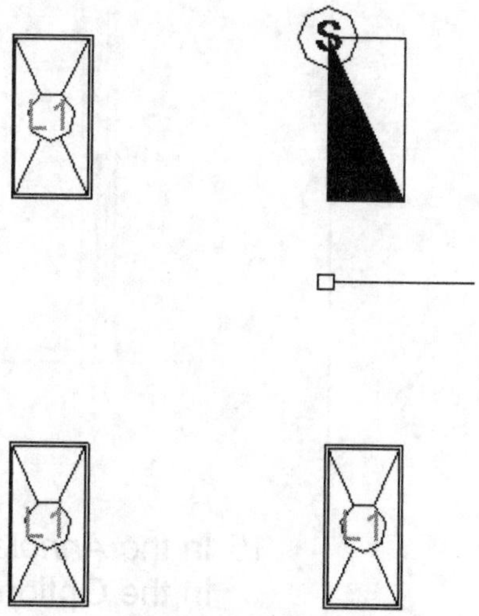

Figure 14–16

8. In the Type Selector, change the existing tag type to **Lighting Fixture Circuit Tag: Standard**. The tag information changes from displaying the lighting fixture number to displaying a question mark. The fixtures are not connected to a circuit.

9. In the next room, hover over one of the light fixtures and press <tab> until the circuit displays. Click to select the circuit.

10. In the *Modify | Electrical Circuits* tab>System Tools panel, click 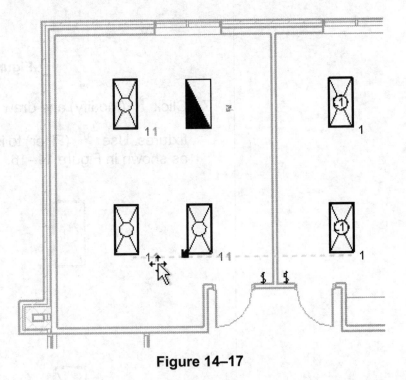 (Edit Circuit).

11. The (Add to Circuit) command is active. Select the three standard light fixtures (not the emergency fixture).

12. Click (Finish Editing Circuit).

13. The tags now display with the circuit number.

14. Select the tags again and drag them off the fixture and place them in line with tags in the adjacent room, as shown in Figure 14–17.

Alignment lines display when the cursor lines up with other tags.

Figure 14–17

15. In the *Annotate* tab>Tag panel, click (Tag by Category). In the Options Bar, select **Leader** and **Attached End**. Change the leader length to **1/8"**.

16. Tag all four light fixtures in this room and place the tag above the fixture. The emergency fixture does not yet have a Type Mark assigned to it and so it displays a question mark, as shown in Figure 14–18.

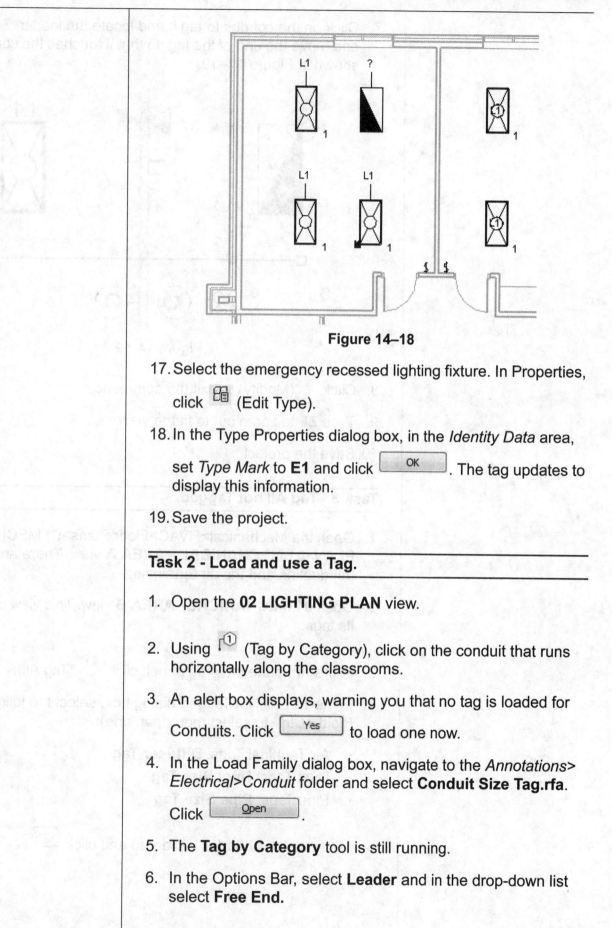

Figure 14–18

17. Select the emergency recessed lighting fixture. In Properties, click ⊞ (Edit Type).

18. In the Type Properties dialog box, in the *Identity Data* area, set *Type Mark* to **E1** and click [OK]. The tag updates to display this information.

19. Save the project.

Task 2 - Load and use a Tag.

1. Open the **02 LIGHTING PLAN** view.

2. Using ᐧ① (Tag by Category), click on the conduit that runs horizontally along the classrooms.

3. An alert box displays, warning you that no tag is loaded for Conduits. Click [Yes] to load one now.

4. In the Load Family dialog box, navigate to the *Annotations> Electrical>Conduit* folder and select **Conduit Size Tag.rfa**. Click [Open].

5. The **Tag by Category** tool is still running.

6. In the Options Bar, select **Leader** and in the drop-down list select **Free End**.

7. Click on the conduit to tag it and locate the leader. Zoom in and move the end of the tag so that it touches the conduit, as shown in Figure 14–19.

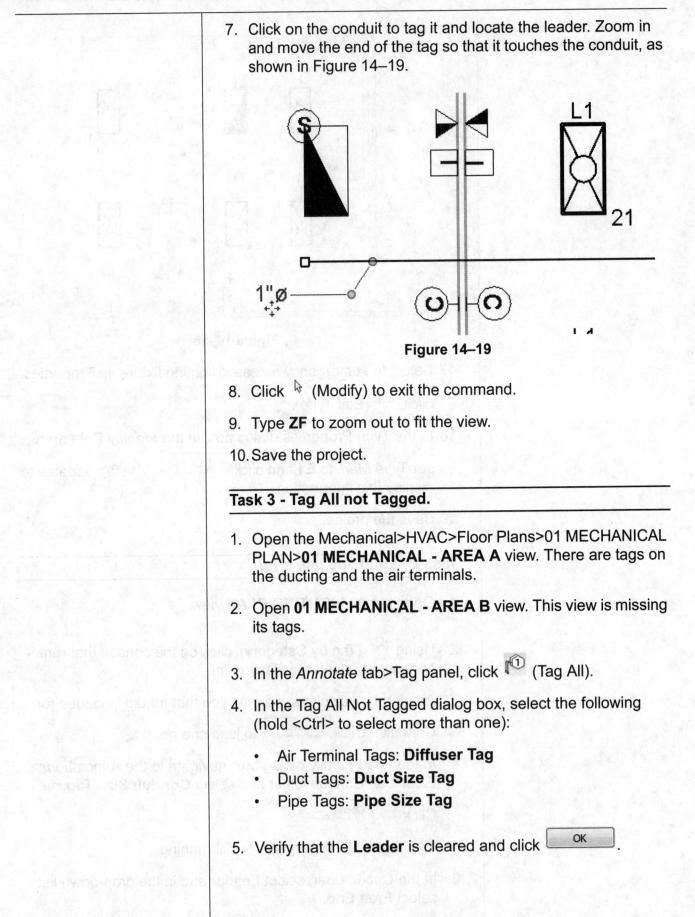

Figure 14–19

8. Click ⌖ (Modify) to exit the command.

9. Type **ZF** to zoom out to fit the view.

10. Save the project.

Task 3 - Tag All not Tagged.

1. Open the Mechanical>HVAC>Floor Plans>01 MECHANICAL PLAN>**01 MECHANICAL - AREA A** view. There are tags on the ducting and the air terminals.

2. Open **01 MECHANICAL - AREA B** view. This view is missing its tags.

3. In the *Annotate* tab>Tag panel, click 🔖 (Tag All).

4. In the Tag All Not Tagged dialog box, select the following (hold <Ctrl> to select more than one):

- Air Terminal Tags: **Diffuser Tag**
- Duct Tags: **Duct Size Tag**
- Pipe Tags: **Pipe Size Tag**

5. Verify that the **Leader** is cleared and click [OK].

6. If a warning box displays about Elements Have Hidden Tags, click OK .

7. All of the air terminals, pipes and ducts are now tagged in this view, as shown in part in Figure 14–20.

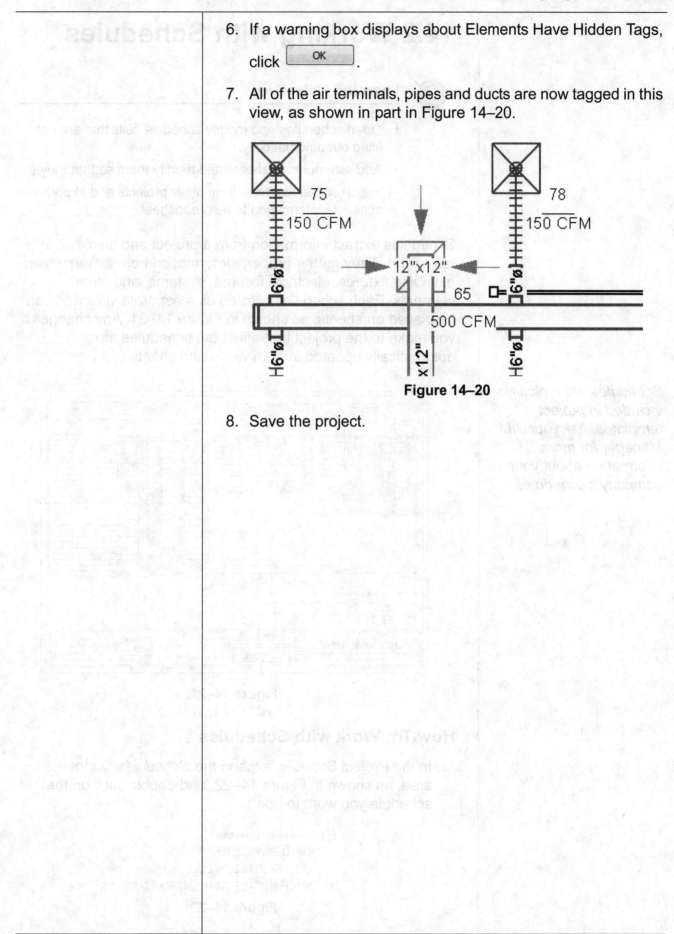

Figure 14–20

8. Save the project.

14.2 Working with Schedules

 Learning Objectives

- Open schedules and modify schedule cells that are not filled out automatically.
- Add schedules to sheets and modify them so that they fit.
- Import schedule styles from other projects and export schedule information to a spreadsheet.

Schedules extract information from a project and display it in table form. They gather property information from air terminals, plumbing fixtures, electrical fixtures, systems, and other elements. Each schedule is stored as a separate view and can be placed on sheets, as shown in Figure 14–21. Any changes you make to the project that affect the schedules are automatically updated in both views and sheets.

Schedules are typically included in project templates. Ask your BIM Manager for more information about your company's schedules.

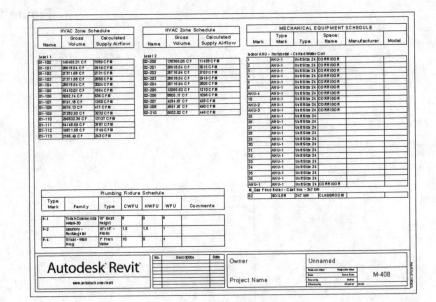

Figure 14–21

How To: Work with Schedules

1. In the Project Browser, expand the *Schedules/Quantities* area, as shown in Figure 14–22, and double-click on the schedule you want to open.

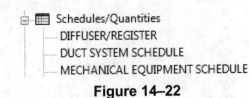

Figure 14–22

2. Schedules are automatically filled out with the information stored in the property parameters of related elements that are added to the model.
3. Fill out additional information in either the schedule or Properties. Some information is per instance and some is by type.
4. Drag and drop the schedule onto a sheet.

Modifying Schedules

When you make changes to scheduled elements (such as, changing the type of a plumbing or lighting fixture, or changing the flow of an air terminal), the schedule automatically updates. You can also change information in the cells of the schedule table, which automatically updates the elements in the project.

The tools in the *Modify Schedule/Quantities* tab (as shown in Figure 14–23), are used to further modify the schedule table. The available tools depend on what you have selected in the table: the title, headers, or cells. The other tools are grayed out.

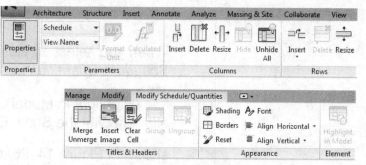

Figure 14–23

- Be careful about making changes using the Ribbon tools as you can easily alter the schedule that was created using the company or project standard.

How To: Modify Schedule Cells

1. Open the schedule view.
2. Select the cell you want to change. Some cells have drop-down lists, as shown in Figure 14–24. Others have edit fields.

A	B	C
SPACE NO.	NAME	Condition Type
DIFFUSER ID	DIFFUSER TYPE	DIFFUSER AIRFLOW
100	PLUMBING CHASE	Unconditioned
101	PLUMBING CHASE	Unconditioned
200	RECEPTION	Unconditioned
201	RESOURCE	Unconditioned
1500	SPECIAL ED	Heated and cooled
	STORAGE	150 CFM

Figure 14–24

3. Add the new information. The change is reflected in the schedule, on the sheet, and in the elements of the project.

- If you change a Type Property in the schedule, it applies to all elements of that type. If you change an Instance Property, it only applies to that instance.

- If you change a Type Property, an alert box opens as shown in Figure 14–25. Changing the schedule updates all related elements.

Revit ✕

This change will be applied to all elements of type
Supply Diffuser: 24 x 24 Face 12 x 12
Connection.

[OK]   [Cancel]

Figure 14–25

- When you select an element in a schedule, in the *Modify Schedule/Quantities* tab>Element panel, you can click

    (Highlight in Model). This opens a close-up view of the element with the Show Element(s) in View dialog box, as

    shown in Figure 14–26. Click [Show] to display more

    views of the element. Click [Close] to finish the command.

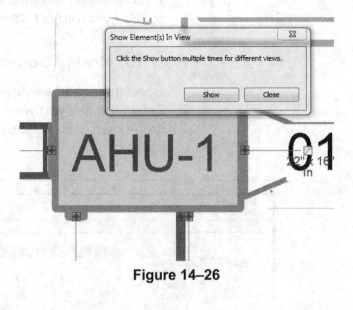

Figure 14–26

Modifying a Schedule on a Sheet

Once you have placed a schedule on a sheet, you can manipulate it to fit the information into the available space. Select the schedule to display the controls that enable you to modify it, as shown in Figure 14–27.

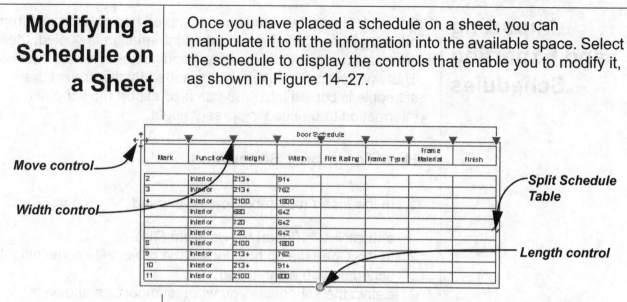

Move control

Width control

Split Schedule Table

Length control

Figure 14–27

- The blue triangles modify the width of each column.

- The break mark splits the schedule into two parts.

- In each part of a split schedule, additional blue controls are displayed. The arrows in the center enable you to drag that portion of the schedule. The bottom circle on the first schedule enables you to modify the length of the schedule, which automatically impacts the other part(s) of the split, as shown in Figure 14–28.

Room Schedule		
Level	Number	Name
Not Placed	1	Room
Not Placed	2	Room
Not Placed	3	Room
First Floor	101	Office
First Floor	102	Office
First Floor	103	Studio
First Floor	104	Product Library
First Floor	105	Mech/Elec
First Floor	106	Stair 2
First Floor	107	Print Room
First Floor	108	Storage

Room Schedule		
Level	Number	Name
First Floor	109	Men
First Floor	110	Women
First Floor	111	Conference
First Floor	112	Storage
First Floor	113	Shower
First Floor	114	Chiller Enclosure Area
First Floor	115	Stair 1
Second Floor	116	Room
Second Floor	117	Room

Figure 14–28

- To unsplit a schedule, drag the Move control from the side of the schedule that you want to unsplit back to the original column.

Importing and Exporting Schedules

Schedules are views and can be copied into your project from other projects. Only the formatting information is copied; the information about individually scheduled items is not included. That information is automatically added by the project the schedule is copied into. You can also export the schedule information to be used in spreadsheets.

How To: Import Schedules

1. In the *Insert* tab>Import panel, expand 🗋↓ (Insert From File) and click 🗗↓ (Insert Views From File).
2. In the Open dialog box, locate the project file containing the schedule you want to use.
3. Select the schedules you want to import, as shown in Figure 14–29.

*If the referenced project contains many types of views, change Views: to **Show schedules and reports only**.*

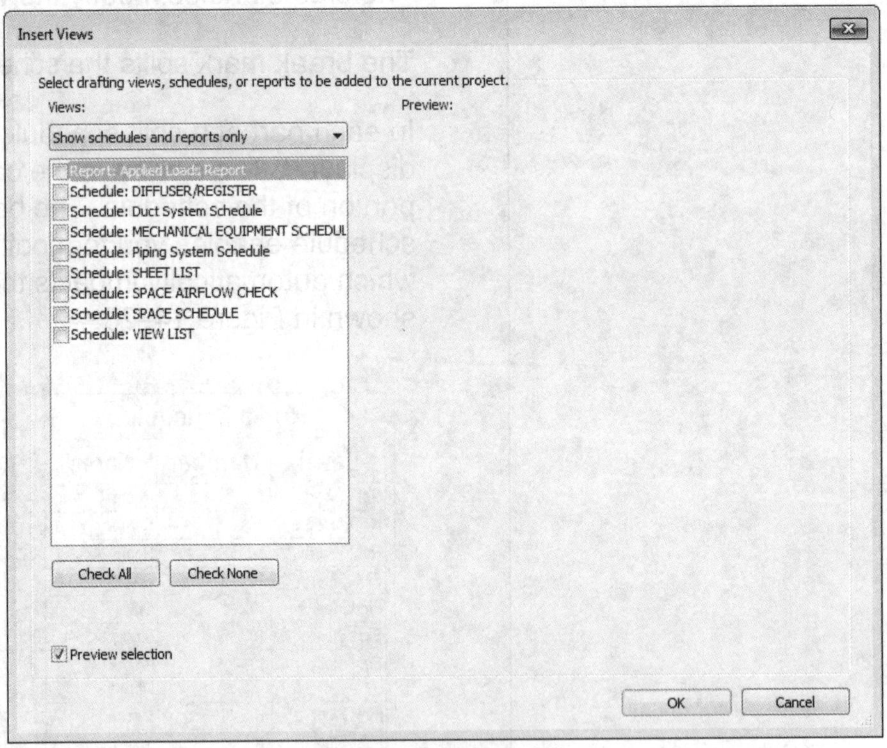

Figure 14–29

4. Click [OK].

How To: Export Schedule Information

1. Switch to the schedule view that you want to export.

2. In the Application Menu, click 🗗 (Export)> 📄 (Reports)> ▦ (Schedule).

3. Select a location and name for the text file in the Export Schedule dialog box and click [Save].

4. In the Export Schedule dialog box, set the options in the *Schedule appearance* and *Output options* areas that best suit your spreadsheet software, as shown in Figure 14–30.

Figure 14–30

5. Click [OK]. A new text file is created that you can open in a spreadsheet, as shown in Figure 14–31.

	A	B	C	D	E
1	DUCT SYSTEM SCHEDULE				
2	System Classification	System Name	Comment	Static Pressure	Flow
3					
4	Return Air	01 - RA01	RA	0.08 in-wg	1000 CFM
5	Return Air	01 - RA02	RA	0.08 in-wg	1000 CFM
6	Return Air	01 - RA03	RA	0.08 in-wg	1000 CFM
7	Return Air	01 - RA04	RA	0.08 in-wg	1000 CFM
8	Return Air	01 - RA05	RA	0.07 in-wg	1000 CFM

Figure 14–31

Practice 14b

Work with Schedules

 Learning Objective

- Update schedules and add schedules to sheets.

Estimated time for completion:10 minutes

In this practice you will update a schedule and place it on a sheet., as shown in Figure 14–32.

<MECHANICAL EQUIPMENT SCHEDULE>					
A	B	C	D	E	F
Type Mark	Mark	Space: Name	Manufacturer	Model	Comments
AHU-1	1	CORRIDOR	ME Unlimited	AHU-24-M	
AHU-1	2	CORRIDOR	ME Unlimited	AHU-24-M	
AHU-1	3	CORRIDOR	ME Unlimited	AHU-24-M	
AHU-1	4	CORRIDOR	ME Unlimited	AHU-24-M	
AHU-1	5	CORRIDOR	ME Unlimited	AHU-24-M	
AHU-1	6	CORRIDOR	ME Unlimited	AHU-24-M	
AHU-1	7	CORRIDOR	ME Unlimited	AHU-24-M	
AHU-1	8	CORRIDOR	ME Unlimited	AHU-24-M	
AHU-3	9	CORRIDOR	ME Unlimited	AHU-36-L	
AHU-1	10	CORRIDOR	ME Unlimited	AHU-24-M	
AHU-1	11	CORRIDOR	ME Unlimited	AHU-24-M	
AHU-1	12	CORRIDOR	ME Unlimited	AHU-24-M	
AHU-2	13	CORRIDOR	ME Unlimited	AHU-12-S	
HW-1	14	STORAGE	ME Unlimited	HWH-10-M	
HW-1	15	STORAGE	ME Unlimited	HWH-10-M	
HW-1	16	JNTR.	ME Unlimited	HWH-10-M	
HW-1	17	JNTR.	ME Unlimited	HWH-10-M	

Figure 14–32

Task 1 - Fill in schedules.

1. In the *C:\Autodesk Revit 2015 MEP Fundamentals Class Files\Schedules* folder, open **MEP-Elementary-School-Schedules.rvt**.

2. In the Project Browser, expand *Schedules/Quantities*. Several schedules have been added to this project.

3. Double-click on **MECHANICAL EQUIPMENT SCHEDULE** to open it. The schedule is already populated with some of the basic information, as shown in Figure 14–33.

<MECHANICAL EQUIPMENT SCHEDULE>					
A	B	C	D	E	F
Type Mark	Mark	Space: Name	Manufacturer	Model	Comments
AHU-1	1	CORRIDOR			
AHU-1	2	CORRIDOR			
AHU-1	3	CORRIDOR			
AHU-1	4	CORRIDOR			
AHU-1	5	CORRIDOR			
AHU-1	6	CORRIDOR			
AHU-1	7	CORRIDOR			
AHU-1	8	CORRIDOR			
AHU-1	9	CORRIDOR			
AHU-1	10	CORRIDOR			
AHU-1	11	CORRIDOR			
AHU-1	12	CORRIDOR			
	49	STORAGE			
	50	STORAGE			
	51	JNTR.			
	52	JNTR.			
AHU-1	53	CORRIDOR			

Figure 14–33

4. Several Type Marks are empty. Click in one of the empty *Type Mark* cells. In the *Modify Schedules/Quantities* tab> Element panel, click ▦ (Highlight in Model).

5. If an alert box displays about no open views, click

   [OK] to search and open a view.

6. In the view that comes up, click [Close] in the Show Element(s) in View dialog box.

7. Zoom out so that you can see the elements (i.e., a hot water heater) in context.

8. In Properties, click ▦ (Edit Type).

9. In the Type Properties dialog box, in the *Identity Data* area, set the *Type Mark* to **HW-1**.

10. Click [OK] to finish.

11. Return to the Mechanical Equipment Schedule. (Press <Ctrl>+<Tab> to switch between open windows.)

12. All of the hot water heaters in the project now have a *Type Mark* set, as shown in Figure 14–34.

<MECHANICAL EQUIPMENT SCHEDULE>					
A	B	C	D	E	F
Type Mark	Mark	Space: Name	Manufacturer	Model	Comments
AHU-1	1	CORRIDOR			
AHU-1	2	CORRIDOR			
AHU-1	3	CORRIDOR			
AHU-1	4	CORRIDOR			
AHU-1	5	CORRIDOR			
AHU-1	6	CORRIDOR			
AHU-1	7	CORRIDOR			
AHU-1	8	CORRIDOR			
AHU-1	9	CORRIDOR			
AHU-1	10	CORRIDOR			
AHU-1	11	CORRIDOR			
AHU-1	12	CORRIDOR			
HW-1	49	STORAGE			
HW-1	50	STORAGE			
HW-1	51	JNTR.			
HW-1	52	JNTR.			
AHU-1	53	CORRIDOR			

Figure 14–34

13. In the *Mark* column you can see that the numbers are out of sequence. The numbering of hot water heaters and one air handling unit (AHU-1) is incorrect, starting at 49.

14. Change the *Mark* of the incorrectly numbered AHU-1 to **13**.

15. Modify the *Mark* of the hot water heaters to match the sequence.

16. In the schedule view, change the name of the Manufacturer of one of the AHUs. An alert displays warning that changing this changes all of the elements of this type, as shown in Figure 14–35. Click .

<MECHANICAL EQUIPMENT SCHEDULE>					
A	B	C	D	E	F
Type Mark	Mark	Space: Name	Manufacturer	Model	Comments
AHU-1	1	CORRIDOR	ME Unlimited		
AHU-1	2	CORRIDOR			
AHU-1	3	CORRIDOR			
AHU-1	4	CORRIDOR			
AHU-1	5	CORRIDOR			
AHU-1	6				
AHU-1	7				
AHU-1	8				
AHU-1	9				
AHU-1	10				
AHU-1	11				
AHU-1	12				
AHU-1	13				
HW-1	14				
HW-1	15				
HW-1	16				
HW-1	17				

Revit

This change will be applied to all elements of type
Indoor AHU - Horizontal - Chilled Water Coil:
Unit Size 24.

OK   Cancel

Figure 14–35

17. Open the Mechanical>HVAC>Floor Plans>**01 MECHANICAL** view and zoom in on the office area.

18. Select the AHU that is connected to the Office duct system. In the Type Selector, change it to **Indoor AHU - Horizontal - Chilled Water Coil: Unit Size 12**.

19. While it is still selected, edit the type and set the *Type Mark* to **AHU-2**.

20. Press <Esc> to clear the selection when you are finished.

21. Switch back to the schedule view to see the change.

22. In the *Manufacturer* column, use the drop-down list to select the same *Manufacturer* for the modified AHU, as shown in Figure 14–36.

		<MECHANICAL EQUIPMENT SCHEDULE>			
A	B	C	D	E	F
Type Mark	Mark	Space: Name	Manufacturer	Model	Comments
AHU-1	1	CORRIDOR	ME Unlimited		
AHU-1	2	CORRIDOR	ME Unlimited		
AHU-1	3	CORRIDOR	ME Unlimited		
AHU-1	4	CORRIDOR	ME Unlimited		
AHU-1	5	CORRIDOR	ME Unlimited		
AHU-1	6	CORRIDOR	ME Unlimited		
AHU-1	7	CORRIDOR	ME Unlimited		
AHU-1	8	CORRIDOR	ME Unlimited		
AHU-1	9	CORRIDOR	ME Unlimited		
AHU-1	10	CORRIDOR	ME Unlimited		
AHU-1	11	CORRIDOR	ME Unlimited		
AHU-1	12	CORRIDOR	ME Unlimited		
AHU-2	13	CORRIDOR			
HW-1	14	STORAGE	ME Unlimited		
HW-1	15	STORAGE			
HW-1	16	JNTR.			
HW-1	17	JNTR.			

Figure 14–36

23. Fill in the other information.

24. Save the project.

Task 2 - Add schedules to a sheet.

---

1. In the Project Browser, right-click on Sheets (all) and select **New Sheet**. Select the E-sized title block and click OK.

2. In the Project Browser, right-click on the new sheet (which is bold) and select Rename. In the Sheet Title dialog box, set the *Number* to **M-801** and the *Name* to **Schedules** and click OK.

3. Drag and drop the **MECHANICALEQUIPMENT SCHEDULE** view onto the sheet, as shown in Figure 14–37.

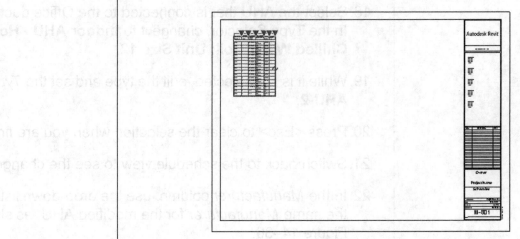

Figure 14–37

4. Zoom in and use the arrows at the top to modify the width of the columns so that the titles display correctly.

5. Click in empty space on the sheet to finish placing the schedule.

6. Switch back to the Mechanical>HVAC>Floor Plans> **01 MECHANICAL** view and select one of the Classroom AHUs.

7. In the Type Selector, change the size to **Unit Size 36**. In Type Properties add the *Model*, *Manufacturer*, and *Type Mark*.

8. Return to the Schedule sheet. The information is automatically populated, as shown in Figure 14–38.

MECHANICAL EQUIPMENT SCHEDULE					
Type Mark	Mark	Space: Name	Manufacturer	Model	Comments
AHU-1	1	CORRIDOR	ME Unlimited	AHU-24-M	
AHU-1	2	CORRIDOR	ME Unlimited	AHU-24-M	
AHU-1	3	CORRIDOR	ME Unlimited	AHU-24-M	
AHU-1	4	CORRIDOR	ME Unlimited	AHU-24-M	
AHU-1	5	CORRIDOR	ME Unlimited	AHU-24-M	
AHU-1	6	CORRIDOR	ME Unlimited	AHU-24-M	
AHU-1	7	CORRIDOR	ME Unlimited	AHU-24-M	
AHU-1	8	CORRIDOR	ME Unlimited	AHU-24-M	
AHU-3	9	CORRIDOR	ME Unlimited	AHU-36-L	
AHU-1	10	CORRIDOR	ME Unlimited	AHU-24-M	
AHU-1	11	CORRIDOR	ME Unlimited	AHU-24-M	
AHU-1	12	CORRIDOR	ME Unlimited	AHU-24-M	
AHU-2	13	CORRIDOR	ME Unlimited	AHU-12-S	
HW-1	14	STORAGE	ME Unlimited	HWH-10-M	
HW-1	15	STORAGE	ME Unlimited	HWH-10-M	
HW-1	16	JNTR.	ME Unlimited	HWH-10-M	
HW-1	17	JNTR.	ME Unlimited	HWH-10-M	

Figure 14–38

9. Save the project.

Chapter Review Questions

1. Which of the following elements cannot be tagged using **Tag by Category**?

   a. Spaces

   b. Ducts

   c. Plumbing Fixtures

   d. Communication Devices

2. What happens when you delete an air terminal in an Autodesk Revit model, as shown in Figure 14–39?

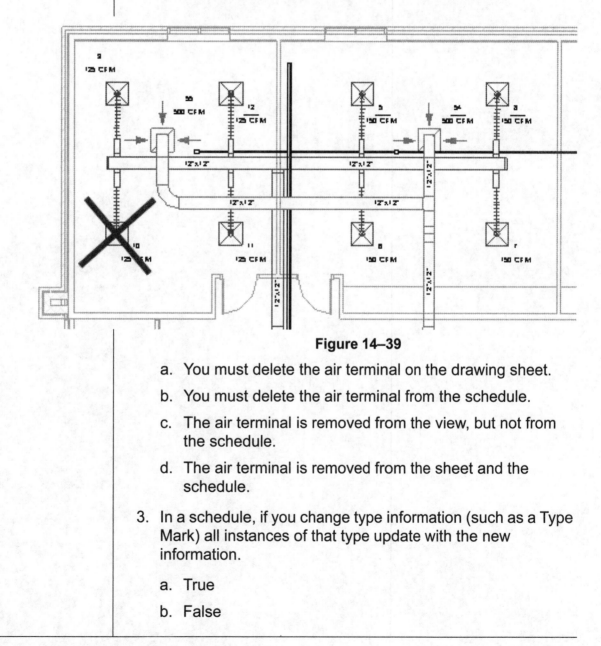

Figure 14–39

   a. You must delete the air terminal on the drawing sheet.

   b. You must delete the air terminal from the schedule.

   c. The air terminal is removed from the view, but not from the schedule.

   d. The air terminal is removed from the sheet and the schedule.

3. In a schedule, if you change type information (such as a Type Mark) all instances of that type update with the new information.

   a. True

   b. False

4. Which of the following commands enables you to reuse a schedule from another project?

    a. **Schedules>Schedule/Quantities**

    b. **Insert from File>Insert Views from File**

    c. **Insert from File>Insert 2D Elements from File**

    d. **Import Reports>Schedule**

Command Summary

Button	Command	Location
	Material Tag	**Ribbon:** *Annotate* tab>Tag panel> Material tag
	Multi-Category	**Ribbon:** *Annotate* tab>Tag panel> Multi-Category
	Tag All Not Tagged	**Ribbon:** *Annotate* tab>Tag panel> Tag All
	Tag by Category	**Ribbon:** *Annotate* tab>Tag panel> Tag by Category **Shortcut:** <T> and <G>

Chapter 15

Creating Details

In this chapter you learn how to set up detail views, add detail components, and annotate details.

This chapter contains the following topics:

- **Setting Up Detail Views**
- **Adding Detail Components**
- **Annotating Details**

15.1 Setting Up Detail Views

Learning Objectives

- Create 2D drafting views in which you can draw details indicating how parts of a building fit together.
- Link callout views to drafting views so that they are referenced correctly in the construction documents.
- Save drafting views so that you can use them in other projects.

Most of the work you do in the Autodesk® Revit® software is exclusively with *smart* elements that interconnect and work together in the model. However, the software does not automatically display how elements should be built to fit together. For this, you need to create detail drawings, as shown in Figure 15–1. There are a variety of tools that enable you to create details, including drafting views, detail lines, special components, filled regions, and insulation.

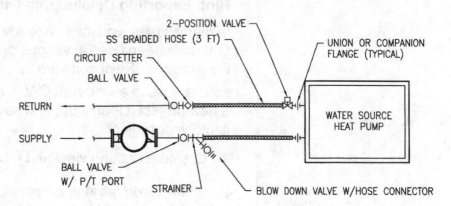

WATER SOURCE HEAT PUMP
PIPING DETAIL

Figure 15–1

- You can use detailing tools (such as detail lines and components, filled regions, and insulation) directly in a specially created *Drafting View*, or you can work in a callout from a plan, elevation, or section view.

- Drafting views are listed in their own section in the Project Browser

How To: Create a Drafting View

1. In the *View* tab>Create panel, click (Drafting View).
2. In the New Drafting View dialog box, enter a *Name* and set a *Scale*, as shown in Figure 15–2.

If you set the Scale to **Custom**, *you can type the Scale value. Otherwise, the Scale automatically controls the Scale value.*

New Drafting View	
Name:	Piping Detail
Scale:	1 1/2" = 1'-0" ▼
Scale value 1:	8
	OK Cancel

Figure 15–2

3. Click [OK]. A blank view is created with space in which you can draw.
4. Add detail lines, components, text, and dimensions as required.

Hint: Importing Details from Other CAD Software

In many cases, you might already have a set of standard details that have been used in various projects. You can reuse them in the Autodesk Revit software, even if they were created in other software, such as the AutoCAD® software. Import the detail into a new project, clean it up, and save it as a view before bringing it into your project.

1. Create a drafting view and make it active.

2. In the *Insert* tab>Import panel, click (Import CAD).
3. In the Import CAD dialog box, select the file to import. Most of the default values are what you need. You might want to change the *Layer/Level colors* to **Black and White**.
4. Click [Open].

- If you want to modify the detail, select the imported data. In the *Modify | [filename]* tab>Import Instance panel, expand (Explode) and click (Partial Explode) or (Full Explode). Click (Delete Layers) before you explode the detail. A full explode greatly increases the file size.

- Modify the detail using tools in the Modify panel. Change all of the text and line styles to Autodesk Revit specific elements.

How To: Create a Detail View from a Section

1. In the Quick Access Toolbar or the *View* tab>Create panel, click 🔾 (Section).
2. In the Type Selector select **Section:Detail**.
3. Draw the section detail, such as the example shown in Figure 15–3. The marker indicates that it is a detail, rather than a section, but it is still creating a section cut.

Callouts also have a Detail View Type that can be used in the same way.

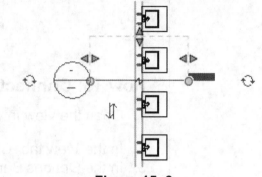

Figure 15–3

4. Open the new detail. Use the tools to draw on top of or add to the building elements.

- In this type of detail view when the building elements change, the detail changes as well, as shown in Figure 15–4.

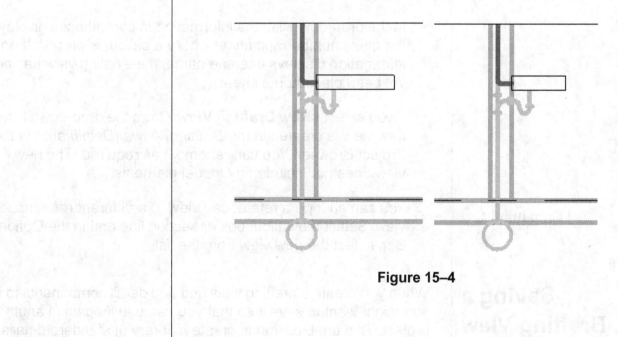

Figure 15–4

Connecting a Callout to a Drafting View

Once you have created a drafting view, you can link it to a callout in another view, as shown in Figure 15–5. For example, in a section view, you might want a callout that references a roof detail. You can reference drafting views, sections, elevations, and callouts.

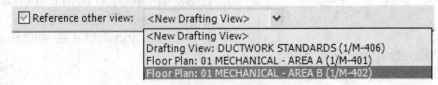

Figure 15–5

How To: Connect a Callout to a Drafting View

1. Open the view in which you want to place the callout.
2. In the *View* tab>Create panel, click (Callout).
3. In the Options Bar, select **Reference other view**. In the drop-down list, select **<New Drafting View>** or an existing drafting view.
4. Draw the callout box around the required area and move the bubble as required.
5. When you place the associated drafting view on a sheet, the callout bubble in this view updates with the appropriate information.

• In the drop-down list, the information in parentheses displays the detail number and sheet where a callout is placed. If no information displays after the name, the existing view has not yet been placed on a sheet.

• If you select **<New Drafting View>** from the drop-down list, a new view is created in the *Drafting Views (Detail)* area in the Project Browser. You can rename it as required. The new view does not include any model elements.

• You can change a referenced view to a different referenced view. Select the callout box or section line and in the Options Bar, select the new view from the list.

Enhanced in 2015

Saving a Drafting View

When you create a drafting view and add detail components to it, you might want to save it so that you can use it again in another project. This enables you to create a library of standard details that can be copied into a project and then modified to suit the new software.

Drafting views can be saved in two ways: save an individual drafting view to a new file or save all of the drafting views as a group in one new file.

How To: Save One Drafting View to a File

1. In the Project Browser, right-click on the drafting view you want to save and select **Save to New File...**, as shown in Figure 15–6.

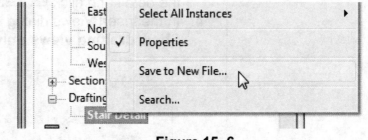

Figure 15–6

2. In the Save As dialog box, specify a name and location for the file and click [Save].

How To: Save a Group of Drafting Views to a File

1. In the Application Menu, expand 🖫 (Save As), expand ▦ (Library), and click ▢ (View).
2. In the Save Views dialog box, in the *Views:* pane, expand the list and select **Show drafting views only**.
3. Select the drafting views that you want to save as shown in Figure 15–7.

Save Views

Select views to save to a file.

Views:

Show drafting views only ▼

Preview:

☑ Drafting View: Floor Cleanout Detail
☐ Drafting View: Recessed Light Fixture Detail
☑ Drafting View: Trap Primer Detail

Figure 15–7

4. Click [OK].
5. In the Save As dialog box, specify a name and location for the file and click [Save].

You can save sheets, drafting views, model views (floor plans), schedules, and reports.

How To: Use a Saved Drafting View in another Project

1. Open the project to which you want to add the drafting view.

2. In the *Insert* tab>Import panel, expand ⬇ (Insert from File) and click ⬇ (Insert Views from File).

3. In the Open dialog box, select the project in which you saved the detail and click [Open].

4. In the Insert Views dialog box, limit the types of views to **Show drafting views only**, as shown in Figure 15–8.

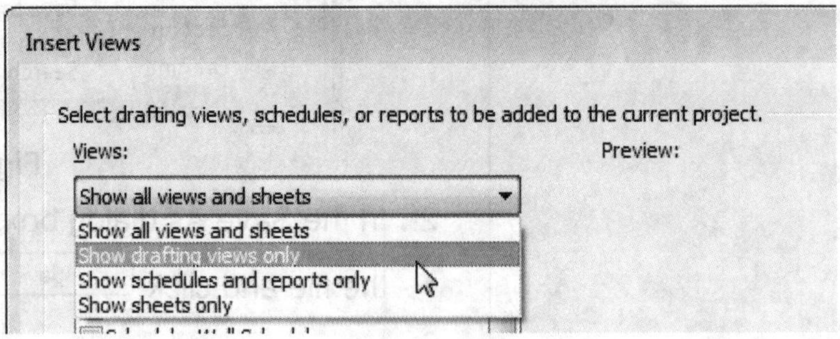

Figure 15–8

5. Select the view(s) that you want to insert and click [OK].

15.2 Adding Detail Components

Learning Objective

- Add detail components to a drafting view to create a 2D building detail.

Autodesk Revit elements, such as the heat pump detail shown on the left in Figure 15–9, typically require additional information to ensure that they are constructed correctly. To create details you add detail components, detail lines, and various annotation elements. These elements are drawn in a 2D drafting view, and are not directly connected to the full model.

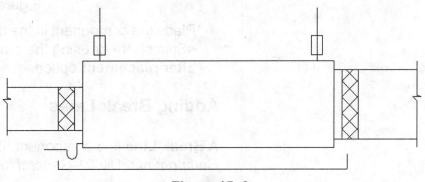

Figure 15–9

Detail Components

Detail components are 2D drawings made with detail sketch lines that are created in a detail component family. The Detail Library contains components for all disciplines, such as roof drains, cabinet sections, window heads, and jambs. The Library contains over 500 2D detail components organized by CSI format, as shown in Figure 15–10.

Figure 15–10

- Additional components can be created through Families.

How To: Add a Detail Component

1. In the *Annotate* tab>Detail panel, expand ⬜ (Component) and click ⬜ (Detail Component).
2. In the Type Selector, select the detail component type. You can load additional types from the Library.
3. Many detail components can be rotated as you insert them by pressing the <Spacebar>. If you know that the components do not rotate by this method, select the **Rotate after placement** option in the Options Bar, as shown in Figure 15–11.

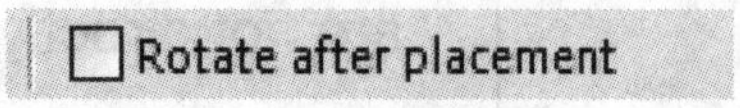

☐ Rotate after placement

Figure 15–11

4. Place the component in the drawing. Rotate it by pressing the <Spacebar> or using the prompts if you selected the **Rotate after placement** option.

Adding Break Lines

A **Break Line** is a component. It can be found in the *Detail Components>Div 01-General* folder, and is inserted using

⬜ (Detail Component). A break line consists of a rectangular area (shown highlighted in Figure 15–12) which is used to block out elements behind it. You can modify the size of the area that is covered and change the size of the cut line using controls.

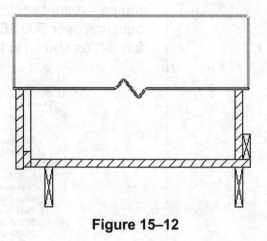

Figure 15–12

Hint: Working with the Draw Order of Details

When you select detail elements in a view, the *Modify | Detail Items* tab displays. In the Arrange panel, you can change the draw order of the elements. You can bring elements in front of other elements or place them behind elements, as shown in Figure 15–13.

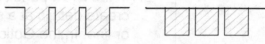

Figure 15–13

*   **(Bring to Front):** Places element in front of all other elements.

*   **(Send to Back):** Places element behind all other elements.

*   **(Bring Forward):** Moves element one step to the front.

*   **(Send Backward):** Moves element one step to the back.

*   You can select multiple detail elements and change the draw order of all of them in one step. If they are on different layers, they keep the relative order of the original selection.

Repeating Details

Details are often repeated, such as a brick or concrete block. Instead of having to insert a component multiple times, you can

use (Repeating Detail Component) and draw a string of components, as shown in Figure 15–14. One repeating detail is included with the standard template. You can also create custom details.

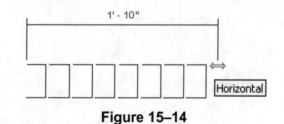

Figure 15–14

How To: Insert a Repeating Detail

1. In the *Annotate* tab>Detail panel, expand ⬚ (Component) and click ⯗ (Repeating Detail Component).
2. In the Type Selector, select the detail you want to use.

3. In the Draw panel, click ╱ (Line) or ⬩ (Pick Lines). You can create details at a specified distance from the selected points or line. In the Options Bar, type a value for the *Offset*.

   • If you click ╱ (Line), select two points on the screen and the components repeat.

   • If you click ⬩ (Pick Lines), select a detail line that exists in the view.

4. The components repeat as required to fit the length of the line, as shown in Figure 15–15. You can lock the components to the line.

Figure 15–15

15.3 Annotating Details

Learning Objective

- Use annotation tools including patterning and detail tags to annotate a 2D building detail.

After you have added components and drawn detail lines, you need to add annotations to the drawing. You can use standard annotation tools to place text notes, dimensions and symbols, as shown in Figure 15–16. You can also fill regions with a pattern and add detail tags to the region.

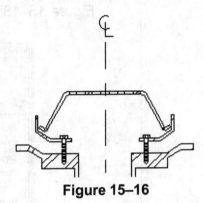

Figure 15–16

Creating Filled Regions

Many elements include material information that displays in plan and section views, while other elements need such details to be added. To add patterns manually for details, you create filled regions, as shown in Figure 15–17.

Figure 15–17

The patterns used in details are *drafting patterns*. They are scaled to the view scale and update if you modify it. You can also add full-size *model patterns*, such as a Flemish Bond brick pattern, to the surface of some elements.

- Fill patterns can be applied to all surfaces in a model. If the surface is warped, the patterns display as planar surfaces to keep the visual integrity of the geometry.

How To: Add a Filled Region

1. In the *Annotate* tab>Detail panel, expand ▢ (Region) and click ▢ (Filled Region).

2. In the *Modify | Create Filled Region Boundary* tab>Draw panel, click ╱ (Line) or ⬟ (Pick Lines) and outline the region (it must be a closed area).

3. In the Line Style panel, select the line type for the outside edge of the boundary.

4. Click ✓ (Finish Edit Mode).

5. In the Type Selector, select the fill type, as shown in Figure 15–18.

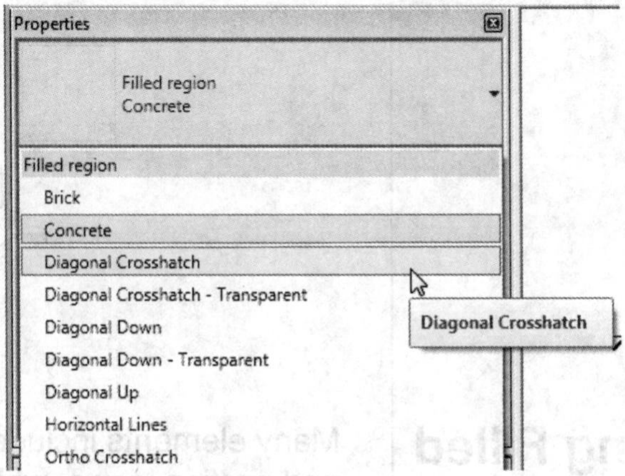

Figure 15–18

6. Click in empty space to finish.

- You can modify a region after it is added by selecting and changing the fill type in the Type Selector or by editing the sketch.

- Double-click on the filled region to edit the sketch. If you have the Selection option set to ⬚ (Select elements by face) you can select the pattern. If it is not toggled on, you need to select the edge of the filled region.

Hint: Creating a Filled Region Pattern Type

You can create a custom pattern by duplicating and editing an existing pattern type.

1. Select an existing region or create a boundary.

2. In Properties, click ⊞ (Edit Type).

3. In the Type Properties dialog box, click [Duplicate...] and name the new pattern.

4. Select a *Fill Pattern*, *Background*, *Line Weight*, and *Color*, as shown in Figure 15–19.

Graphics		⌃
Fill Pattern	Concrete [Drafting]	⋯
Background	Opaque	
Line Weight	1	
Color	■ Black	

Figure 15–19

5. Click [OK].

- You can select from two types of Fill Patterns: **Drafting**, as shown in Figure 15–20, and **Model**. Drafting fill patterns scale to the view scale factor. Model fill patterns display full scale on the model and are not impacted by the view scale factor.

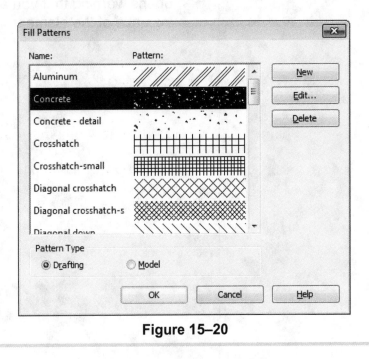

Figure 15–20

Adding Detail Tags

You can tag detail items, such as components, using 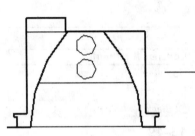 (Tag By Category). This is another way of annotating your details instead of using text and leaders. When you modify the tag name, you actually change the *Type Mark* that is set in the Type Parameters for that detail, as shown in Figure 15–21. This means that if you have more than one copy of the component in your drawing, you do not have to rename it each time you place its tag.

Reccessed Light Fixture

Type Parameters	
Parameter	Value
Identity Data	☆
Keynote	26 51 00.A1
Type Image	
Model	
Manufacturer	
Type Comments	
URL	
Description	
Assembly Code	
Cost	
Assembly Description	
Type Mark	Reccessed Light Fixture
OmniClass Number	
OmniClass Title	

Figure 15–21

- The **Detail Item Tag.rfa** tag is located in the *Annotations* folder in the Library.

- The first time you modify a *Type Mark* for a detail, an alert box opens warning that you are changing a type rather than an instance of the element.

Hint: Multiple Dimension Options

If you are creating details that show one element with multiple dimension values, as shown in Figure 15–22, you can easily modify the dimension text.

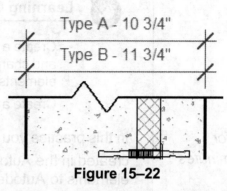

Figure 15–22

Select the dimension and then the dimension text. The Dimension Text dialog box opens. You can replace the text, as shown in Figure 15–23, or add text fields above or below, as well as a prefix or suffix.

Dimension Text

Note: this tool replaces or appends dimensions values with text and has no effect on model geometry.

Dimension Value

○ Use Actual Value   0' - 11 3/4"

● Replace With Text   Type A - 10 3/4"

Text Fields

Above:

Prefix: Value: Suffix:
                   0' - 11 3/4"

Below:

OK   Cancel   Apply

Figure 15–23

Practice 15a

Create a Detail Based on a CAD File

 Learning Objectives

- Create a detail based on an imported CAD file. Explode it and change all of the elements to Autodesk Revit specific elements, including text and filled regions.
- Create a view of the new detail and import it into a project.

Estimated time for completion: 15 minutes

In this practice you will create a detail based on an existing detail created in the AutoCAD® software, modifying the imported elements to Autodesk Revit MEP standard elements. You will create leaders and patterning and save it as a separate view. You will then bring the view into the main project, add a detail component and another text note and place the new view on a sheet, as shown in Figure 15–24.

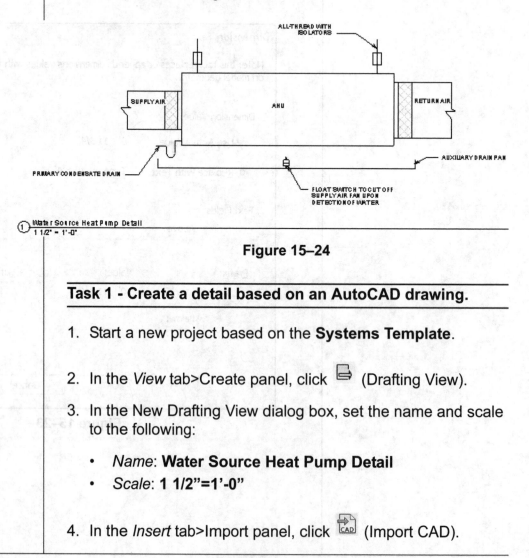

Figure 15–24

Task 1 - Create a detail based on an AutoCAD drawing.

1. Start a new project based on the **Systems Template**.

2. In the *View* tab>Create panel, click ⎙ (Drafting View).

3. In the New Drafting View dialog box, set the name and scale to the following:

- *Name*: **Water Source Heat Pump Detail**
- *Scale*: **1 1/2"=1'-0"**

4. In the *Insert* tab>Import panel, click 🗋 (Import CAD).

5. In the Import CAD Formats dialog box, select the AutoCAD drawing **WS-Heat-Pump-Detail.dwg** found in *Detailing* folder of your class files folder. Change the *Colors* to **Black and White**, as shown in Figure 15–25 and click [Open]

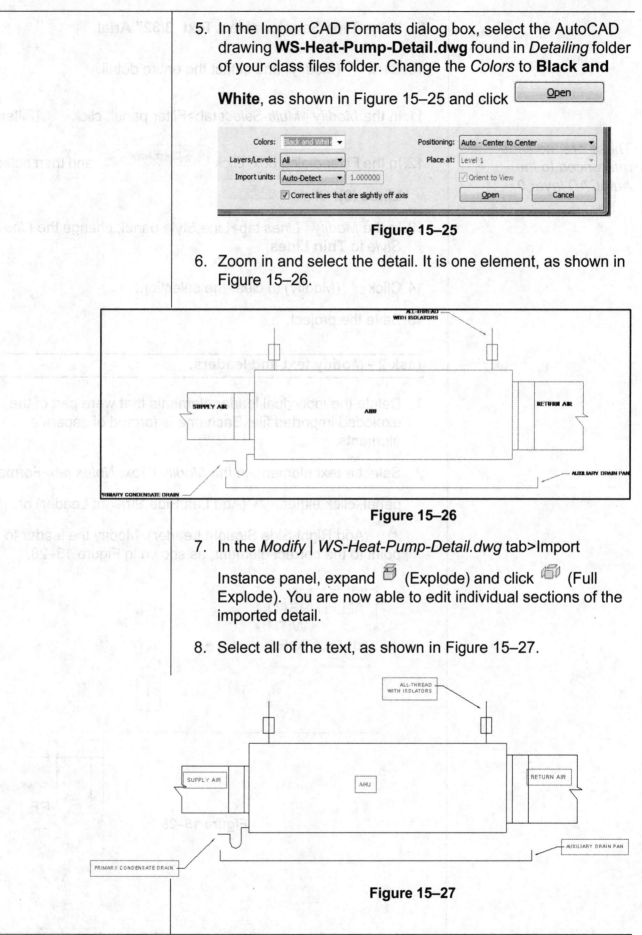

Colors:	Black and White ▼		Positioning:	Auto - Center to Center	▼
Layers/Levels:	All	▼	Place at:	Level 1	▼
Import units:	Auto-Detect ▼	1.000000		☑ Orient to View	
	☑ Correct lines that are slightly off axis			Open	Cancel

Figure 15–25

6. Zoom in and select the detail. It is one element, as shown in Figure 15–26.

Figure 15–26

7. In the *Modify | WS-Heat-Pump-Detail.dwg* tab>Import Instance panel, expand 🔲 (Explode) and click 🔳 (Full Explode). You are now able to edit individual sections of the imported detail.

8. Select all of the text, as shown in Figure 15–27.

Figure 15–27

9. In the Type Selector, select **Text: 3/32" Arial**.

10. Click (Modify) and select the entire detail.

11. In the *Modify | Multi-Select* tab>Filter panel, click (Filter).

12. In the Filter dialog box, click [Check None] and then select **Lines (0)**. Click [OK].

13. In the *Modify | Lines* tab>Line Style panel, change the *Line Style* to **Thin Lines**.

14. Click (Modify) to clear the selection.

15. Save the project.

These are the lines referenced to the AutoCAD layer 0.

Task 2 - Modify text and leaders.

1. Delete the individual leader elements that were part of the exploded imported file. Each one is formed of separate elements.

2. Select a text element. In the *Modify | Text Notes* tab>Format panel, click either $^+$A (Add Left Side Straight Leader) or A$^+$ (Add Right Side Straight Leader). Modify the leader to point to the correct element, as shown in Figure 15–28.

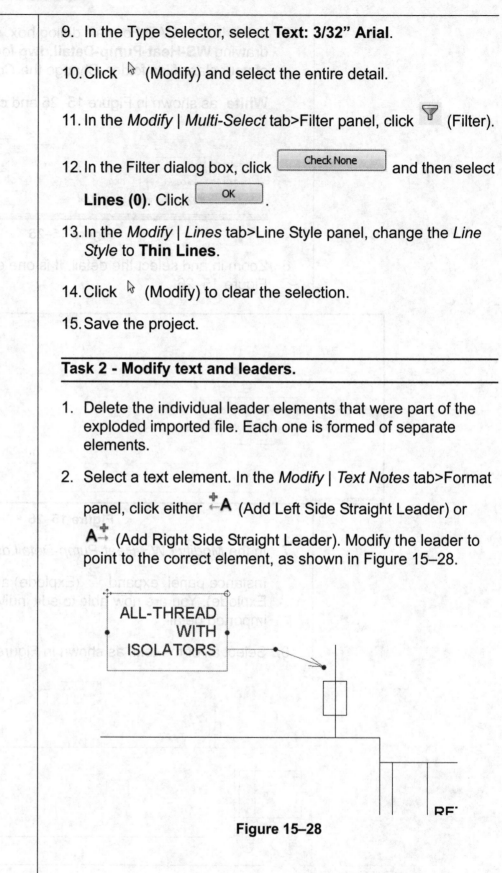

Figure 15–28

3. Repeat the process of adding leaders to the text, pointing to the appropriate parts of the detail, as shown in Figure 15–29.

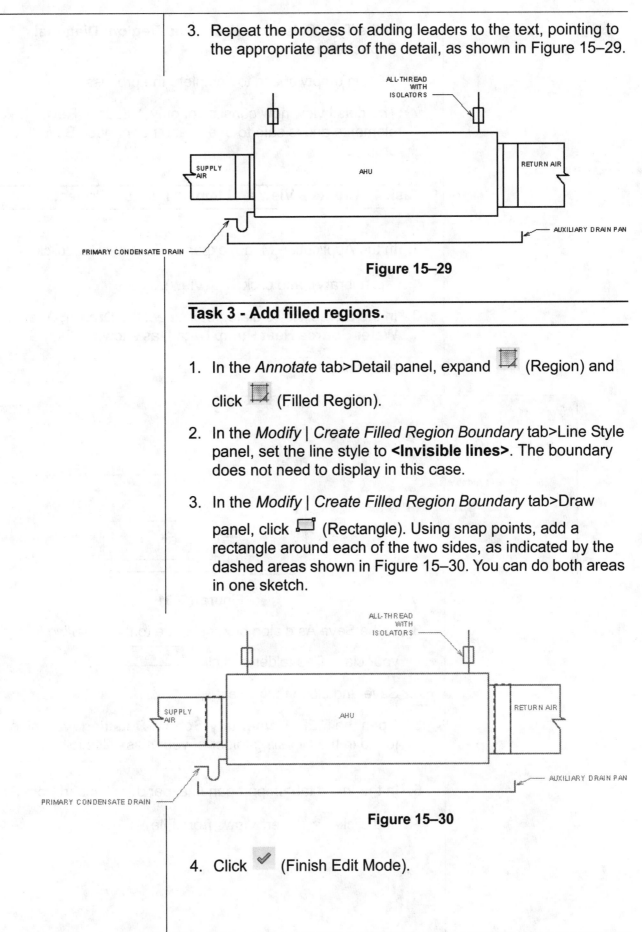

Figure 15–29

Task 3 - Add filled regions.

1. In the *Annotate* tab>Detail panel, expand ⬜ (Region) and click ⬜ (Filled Region).

2. In the *Modify | Create Filled Region Boundary* tab>Line Style panel, set the line style to **<Invisible lines>**. The boundary does not need to display in this case.

3. In the *Modify | Create Filled Region Boundary* tab>Draw panel, click ▭ (Rectangle). Using snap points, add a rectangle around each of the two sides, as indicated by the dashed areas shown in Figure 15–30. You can do both areas in one sketch.

Figure 15–30

4. Click ✓ (Finish Edit Mode).

5. In the Type Selector, select **Filled Region: Diagonal Crosshatch**.

6. Click in empty space to complete the process.

7. The detail view now consists of only Autodesk Revit MEP elements and is safe to use in another project. Save the project.

Task 4 - Create a View and Import it in to a Project.

1. In the Application Menu, expand ![save] (Save As), click ![library] (Library), and click ![view] (View).

2. In the Saved Views dialog box select the **Drafting View: Water Source Heat Pump Detail,** as shown in Figure 15–31 and click ![OK] OK .

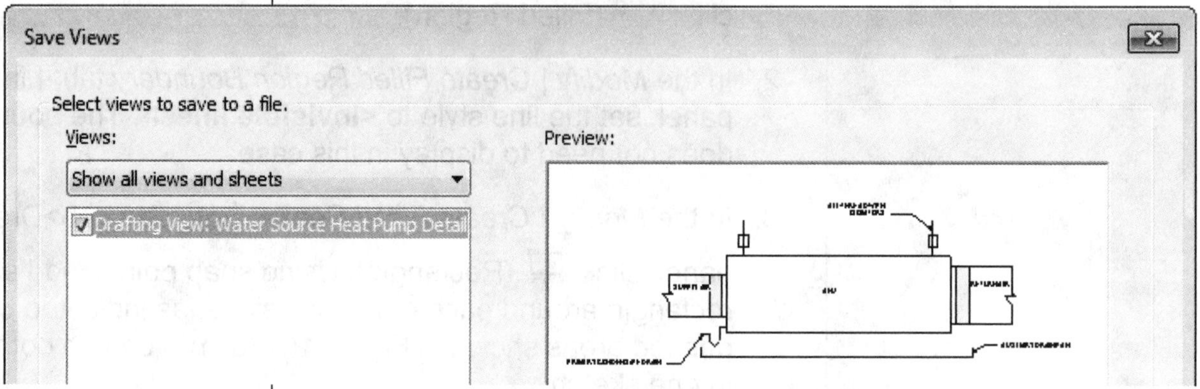

Figure 15–31

3. In the Save As dialog box, navigate to the *Detailing* folder of your class files folder and click ![Save] Save .

4. Save and close the project.

5. Open the **MEP-Elementary-School-Detailing.rvt** project found in the *Detailing* folder of your class files folder.

6. In the *Insert* tab>Import panel, expand ![insert] (Insert from File) and click ![insert views] (Insert Views from File).

7. In the Open dialog box navigate to the *Detailing* folder of your class files folder where you saved the view. Select the view you created, **Water Source Heat Pump Detail.rvt,** and click

    [Open] .

8. In the Insert Views dialog box only this view is available. Click

    [OK] .

9. Accept any warnings that might display about duplicate types. They do not impact the project.

Task 5 - Add a detail component and notes.

1. In the *Annotate* tab>Detail panel, expand as required and click (Detail Component).

2. In the *Modify | Place Detail Component* tab>Mode panel, click (Load Family).

3. In the Load Family dialog box navigate to the *Detailing* folder of your class files folder. Select **Float Switch.rfa** and click

    [Open] .

4. Place the detail component in the drain plan at the center of the AHU as shown in Figure 15–32.

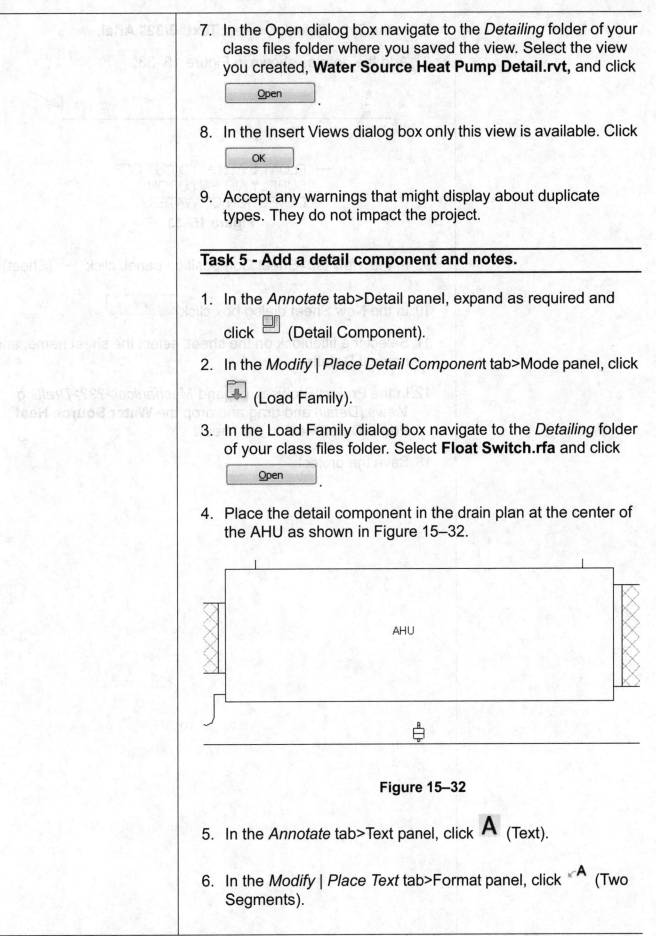

Figure 15–32

5. In the *Annotate* tab>Text panel, click **A** (Text).

6. In the *Modify | Place Text* tab>Format panel, click **A** (Two Segments).

7. In the Type Selector, select **Text: 3/32" Arial**.

8. Add the note as shown in Figure 15–33.

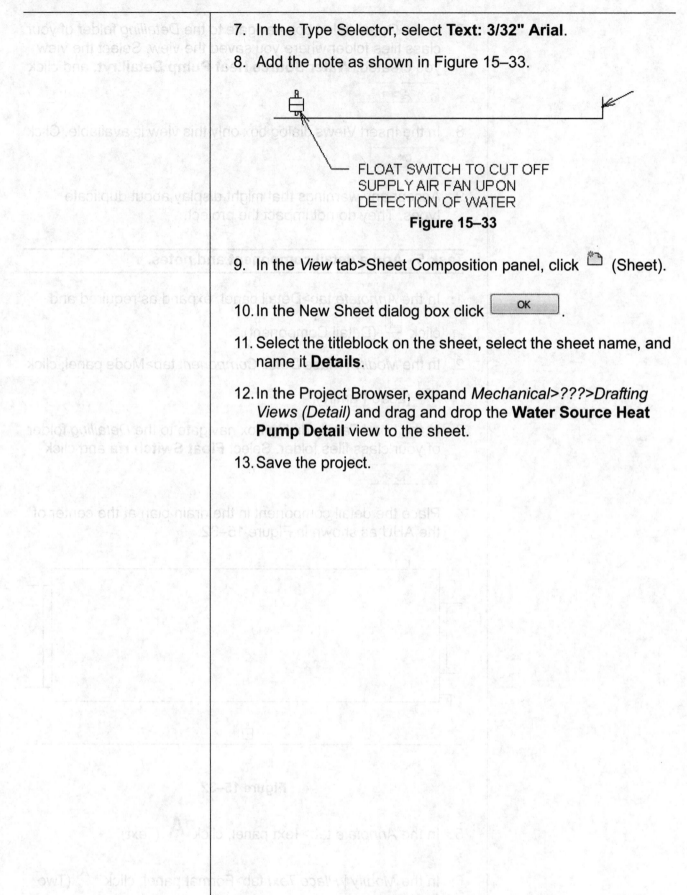

FLOAT SWITCH TO CUT OFF
SUPPLY AIR FAN UPON
DETECTION OF WATER

Figure 15–33

9. In the *View* tab>Sheet Composition panel, click (Sheet).

10. In the New Sheet dialog box click OK .

11. Select the titleblock on the sheet, select the sheet name, and name it **Details**.

12. In the Project Browser, expand *Mechanical>???>Drafting Views (Detail)* and drag and drop the **Water Source Heat Pump Detail** view to the sheet.

13. Save the project.

Chapter Review Questions

1. Which of the following are ways in which you can create a detail? (Select all that apply.)

   a. Make a callout of a section and draw over it.

   b. Draw all of the elements from scratch.

   c. Import a CAD detail and modify or draw over it.

   d. Insert an existing drafting view from another file.

2. In which type of view can you NOT add detail lines?

   a. Plans

   b. Elevations

   c. 3D views

   d. Legends

3. How is a detail component different from a building component?

   a. There is no difference.

   b. Detail components are made of 2D detail lines only.

   c. Detail components are made of building elements, but only display in detail views.

   d. Detail components are made of 2D and 3D elements.

4. When you draw detail lines they are...

   a. Always the same width.

   b. Vary in width according to the view.

   c. Display in all views associated with the detail.

   d. Display only in the view in which they were created.

5. Which command do you use to add a pattern to part of a detail?

   a. Region

   b. Filled Region

   c. Masking Region

   d. Pattern Region

Command Summary

Button	Command	Location
CAD Import Tools		
	Delete Layers	• **Ribbon:** *Modify	<imported filename>* tab>Import Instance panel
	Full Explode	• **Ribbon:** *Modify	<imported filename>* tab>Import Instance panel> expand Explode
	Import CAD	• **Ribbon:** *Insert* tab>Import panel
	Partial Explode	• **Ribbon:** *Modify	<imported filename>* tab>Import Instance panel> expand Explode
Detail Tools		
	Detail Component	• **Ribbon:** *Annotate* tab>Detail panel> expand Component
	Detail Line	• **Ribbon:** *Annotate* tab>Detail panel
	Insulation	• **Ribbon:** *Annotate* tab>Detail panel
	Region	• **Ribbon:** *Annotate* tab>Detail panel
	Repeating Detail Component	• **Ribbon:** *Annotate* tab>Detail panel> expand Component
View Tools		
	Bring Forward	• **Ribbon:** *Modify	Detail Items* tab> Arrange panel
	Bring to Front	• **Ribbon:** *Modify	Detail Items* tab> Arrange panel
	Drafting View	• **Ribbon:** *View* tab>Create panel
	Insert from File: Insert Views from File	• **Ribbon:** *Insert* tab>Import panel> expand Insert from File
	Send Backward	• **Ribbon:** *Modify	Detail Items* tab> Arrange panel
	Send to Back	• **Ribbon:** *Modify	Detail Items* tab> Arrange panel

Appendix A

Introduction to Worksets

In this chapter you learn about the purpose of worksharing and the basics of using worksets including how to open a local file, work in a local file, and synchronize with a central file.

This chapter contains the following topics:

- **Introduction to Worksets**

A.1 Introduction to Worksets

 Learning Objective

- Create a local file and synchronize it back to a central file.

When a project becomes too big for one person, it needs to be subdivided so that a team of people can work on it. Since Autodesk® Revit® projects include the entire building model in one file, the file needs to be separated into logical components, as shown in Figure A–1, without losing the connection to the whole. This process is called *worksharing* and the main components are worksets.

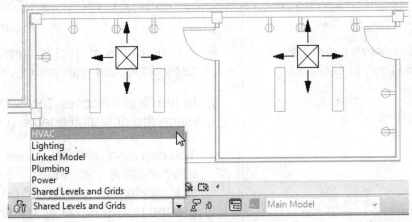

Figure A–1

When worksets are established in a project, there is one **central file** and as many **local files** as required for each person on the team to have a file, as shown in Figure A–2.

*The **central file** is created by the BIM Manager, Project Manager, or Project Lead, and is stored on a server, enabling multiple users to access it. A **local file** is a copy of the central file that is stored on your computer.*

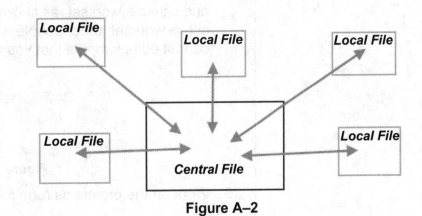

Figure A–2

- All local files are saved back to the central file, and updates to the central file are sent out to the local files. This way, all changes remain in one file, while the project, model, views, and sheets are automatically updated.

How To: Create a Local File

1. In the Application Menu or Quick Access Toolbar click

    📂 (Open). You must use this method to be able to create a local file from the central file.

2. In the Open dialog box, navigate to the central file server location, and select the central file. Do not work in this file. Select **Create New Local**, as shown in Figure A–3.

3. Verify that this option is selected and click [Open].

File name:	Modern Hotel-Central ▼
Files of type:	All Supported Files (*.rvt, *.rfa, *.rte, *.adsk) ▼

Worksharing

☐ Audit   ☐ Detach from Central   ☑ Create New Local   [Open] [▼]   [Cancel]

Figure A–3

User Names can be assigned in Options.

4. A copy of the project is created. It is named the same as the central file, but with your *User Name* added to the end.

5. In the Quick Access Toolbar, click 💾 (Save) to save the file using the default filename (i.e., *Central File Name-Local*.rvt).

*   You can also use 💾 (Save As) and name the file according to your office's standard. It should include *Local* in the name to indicate that it is saved on your local computer, or that you are the only one working with that version of the file.

How To: Work in a Workset-Related File

1. Open your local file.

2. In the Status Bar, expand the *Active Workset* drop-down list and select a workset, as shown in Figure A–4. By setting the active workset, other people can work in the project but cannot edit elements that you add to the workset.

HVAC
Interiors
Lighting
Shared Levels and Grids
Structure

Interiors ▼   🔒 :0   🗐

Figure A–4

3. Work on the project as required.

Saving Workset-Related Files

When you are using a workset-related file, you need to save the file locally and centrally.

- Save the local file frequently (every 15-30 minutes). In the Quick Access Toolbar, click 🖫 (Save) to save the local file just as you would any other project.

- Synchronize the local file with the central file periodically (every hour or two) or after you have made major changes to the project.

Hint: Set up Notifications to Save and Synchronize

You can set up reminders to save and synchronize files to the central file in the Options dialog box, on the *General* pane, as shown in Figure A–5.

Figure A–5

Synchronizing to the Central File

There are two methods for synchronizing to the central file. They are located in the Quick Access Toolbar or the *Collaborate* tab> Synchronize panel.

Click ⬡ (Synchronize Now) to update the central file and then the local file with any changes to the central file since the last synchronization. This does not prompt you for any thing. It automatically relinquishes elements borrowed from a workset used by another person, but retains worksets used by the current person.

Click (Synchronize and Modify Settings) to open the Synchronize with Central dialog box, as shown in Figure A–6, where you can set the location of the central file, add comments, save the file locally before and after synchronization, and set the options for relinquishing worksets and elements.

Figure A–6

- Always save the local file after you have synchronized the file with central. Changes from the central file might have been copied into your file.

- When you close a local file without saving to the central file, you are prompted with options, as shown in Figure A–7.

Figure A–7

Command Summary

Button	Command	Location
	Save	• **Quick Access Toolbar** • **Application Menu:** Save • **Shortcut:** <Ctrl>+<S>
	Synchronize and Modify Settings	• **Quick Access Toolbar** • **Ribbon:** *Collaborate* tab> Synchronize panel>expand Synchronize with Central
	Synchronize Now	• **Quick Access Toolbar** • **Ribbon:** *Collaborate* tab> Synchronize panel>expand Synchronize with Central

Appendix B

Additional Tools

In this appendix you learn how to annotate dependent views, setup system graphics, divide systems, create pressure loss reports, set up and use revisions, and create building component schedules.

This chapter contains the following topics:

- **Annotating Dependent Views**
- **Work with System Graphics**
- **Dividing Systems**
- **Pressure Loss Reports**
- **Revision Tracking**
- **Creating Building Component Schedules**

B.1 Annotating Dependent Views

Learning Objectives

- Duplicate dependent views so that a large building can be placed across several sheets.
- Add Matchlines and View References to indicate where the dependent views separate.

The **Duplicate as a Dependent** command creates a copy of the view and links it to the selected view. Changes made to the original view are also made in the dependent view and vice-versa. Use dependent views when the building model is so large you need to split the building up on separate sheets, with views that are all at the same scale. Having one overall view with dependent views makes viewing changes, such as to the scale or detail level, easier.

Dependent views display in the Project Browser under the top-level view, as shown in Figure B–1.

Figure B–1

How To: Duplicate Dependent Views

1. Select the view you want to use as the top-level view.
2. Right-click and select **Duplicate View>Duplicate as a Dependent**.
3. Rename the dependent views as required.

- If you want to separate a dependent view from the original view, right-click on the dependent view and select **Convert to independent view**.

Annotating Views

Annotation Crop Region and Matchlines can be used in any type of view.

When you work with a dependent view, you can use several tools to clarify and annotate the view, including **Matchlines** and **View References**, as shown in Figure B–2.

Figure B–2

How To: Add Matchlines

Matchlines are drawn in the primary view to specify where dependent views separate. They display in all related views, as shown in Figure B–3, and extend through all levels of the project by default.

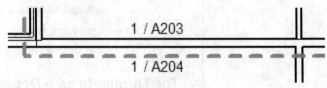

Figure B–3

1. In the *View* tab>Sheet Composition panel, click
   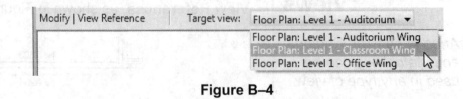 (Matchline).

2. In the Draw panel, click ✓ (Line) and draw the location of the matchline.

3. In the Matchline panel, click ✓ (Finish Edit Mode) when you are finished.

- To modify an existing matchline by selecting it and clicking

  🗐 (Edit Sketch) in the *Modify | Matchline* tab>Mode panel.

- In the *Manage* tab>Settings panel, click 🟦 (Object Styles) to open the Object Styles dialog box. In the *Annotation Objects* tab, you can make changes to Matchline properties including color, linetype, and line weight.

How To: Add View References

View references only work with primary or dependent views.

Once you have dependent views and a matchline in place, you might want to add view references on either side of the matchline.

1. In the *View* tab>Sheet Composition panel or *Annotate* tab>Tag panel, click 🔲 (View Reference).

2. In the Options Bar, set the *Target view*, as shown in Figure B–4.

The views listed are the dependent views of the primary view in which you are working.

Figure B–4

3. Place the tag on the side of the matchline that corresponds to the target view.
4. Select another target view from the list and place the tag on the other side of the matchline.
5. The tags display as empty dashes until the views are placed onto sheets. They then update to include the detail and sheet number, as shown in Figure B–5.

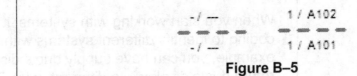

Figure B–5

- You can click on the view reference to open the associated view.

- If only a label named **REF** displays when you place a view reference, it means you need to load and update the tag. The **View Reference.rfa** tag is located in the *Annotations* folder. Once you have the tag loaded, in the Type Selector, select one of the view references and, in Properties, click 🗔 (Edit Type). Select the **View Reference** tag in the drop-down list, as shown in Figure B–6, and click [OK] to close the dialog box. The new tag displays.

Type Parameters	
Parameter	Value
Graphics	≋
View Reference Tag	View Reference ▾
	<none>
	View Reference

Figure B–6

B.2 Work with System Graphics

Learning Objective

- Set up and use duct and piping systems, graphic overrides, and filters.

When you start working with systems, it helps to have color coding to identify different systems within a discipline. For example, you can have supply ducts display in one color and return ducts display in a different color. These are setup by graphic overrides at the system level. You can also setup filters that help you display only the systems you want to see in a view. For example, in a section view, you might want to display the sanitary piping only and not the hot and cold water piping, as shown in Figure B–7.

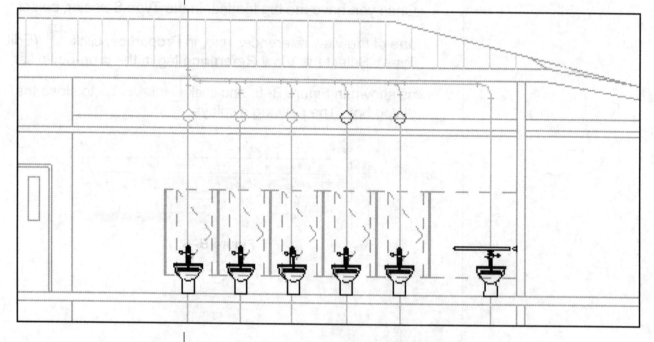

Figure B–7

Duct and Piping System Graphic Overrides

When you create Duct and Piping Systems, they are automatically assigned specific graphic overrides based on the system family settings. By default, for example, Return Air Systems are magenta and Supply Air Systems are blue. In this example the Hydronic Supply Systems are red, and Hydronic Return Systems are cyan.

The system colors display in all views including 3D views, as shown in Figure B–8.

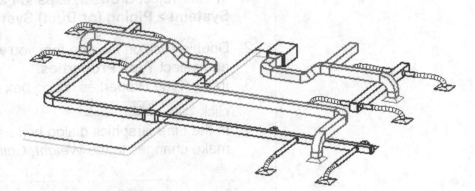

Figure B–8

The various Piping Systems, as shown in the Project Browser in Figure B–9, also have graphic overrides applied.

To create a new system family, in the Project Browser, right-click on an existing type and duplicate it.

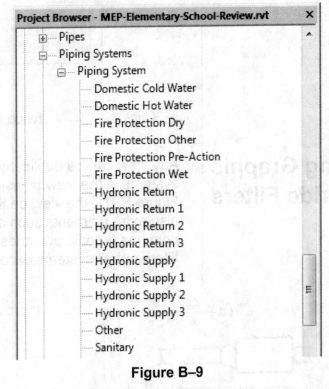

Figure B–9

Legacy drawings need to be updated.

- These graphic overrides are consistent across a project. They are not view dependent. This is a change from earlier versions of the Autodesk Revit software where the View Filters were applied individually to views.

How To: Setup System Graphic Overrides

1. In the Project Browser, expand **Families>Piping (or Duct) Systems> Piping (or Duct) System**.

2. Double-click on the one that you want to modify or right-click and select **Type Properties**.

3. In the Type Properties dialog box next to *Graphic Overrides*, click [Edit...].

4. In the Line Graphics dialog box as shown in Figure B–10, make changes to the *Weight*, *Color*, and/or *Pattern*.

Figure B–10

5. Click [OK] twice to apply the changes.

Using Graphic Override Filters

Any view can be duplicated and then set to display only specific systems in the view by using filters. In the example in Figure B–11, the view on the left displays all of the systems and also extra elements such as data components. The view on the right has graphic overrides that turn off extraneous elements and filters out all systems except duct and hydronic piping.

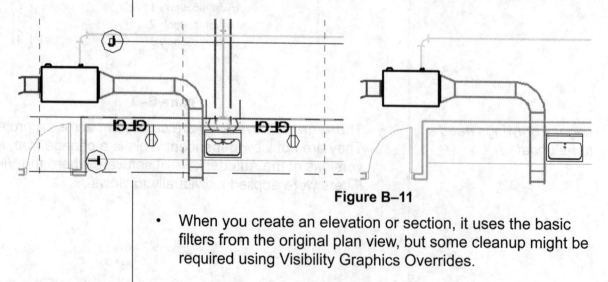

Figure B–11

- When you create an elevation or section, it uses the basic filters from the original plan view, but some cleanup might be required using Visibility Graphics Overrides.

How To: Apply a View Filter to Override a View

1. Type **VG** or **VV** to open the Visibility/Graphic Overrides dialog box.

2. In the dialog box, select the *Filters* tab. Some filters might be available.

3. To add a new filter to this view, click [Add].

4. In the Add Filters dialog box, as shown in Figure B–12, select the type of systems you want to modify and click [OK].

The list might vary depending on the filters that have been set up in the project.

Add Filters

Select one or more filters to insert.

Domestic
Domestic Cold Water
Domestic Hot Water
Hydronic
Hydronic Return
Hydronic Supply
Interior
Mechanical - Exhaust
Mechanical - Return
Mechanical - Supply
Sanitary

[Edit/New...]

[OK]   [Cancel]   [Help]

Figure B–12

5. In the *Filters* tab, select **Visibility** and any other overrides you might want to use. In the example in Figure B–13, the Domestic Cold and Hot Water have been turned off while only the Sanitary systems display.

Visibility/Graphic Overrides for Section: Section 3

| Model Categories | Annotation Categories | Analytical Model Categories | Imported Categories | Filters | Revit Links |

Name	Visibility	Projection/Surface		Cut		Halftone	Ghost S...	Transpar...
		Lines	Patterns	Lines	Patterns			
Sanitary	☑					☐	☐	☐
Domestic Cold Water	☐	Override...	Override...			☐	☐	☐
Domestic Hot Water	☐					☐	☐	☐

Figure B–13

6. Click [OK] to close the dialog box.

- You might also want to turn off other elements, such as levels or grids. You can use the other tabs in the Visibility/Graphics dialog box or use **Hide in View** or **Override Graphics in View**.

- View Filters override system graphics so any colors you set in this dialog box supersede those specified in the System Type.

- If you need to change information about the filter itself click [Edit/New...] in the Add Filters or Filters dialog box. Then modify the *Categories* or *Filter Rules*. For example, the Mechanical - Exhaust Filter does not include Air Terminals by default so you need to select it as shown in Figure B–14.

Figure B–14

B.3 Dividing Systems

 Learning Objective

- Break down a large system into several smaller systems

As you analyze the systems, there might be a large system, such as shown in Figure B–15, that needs to be broken up into subsystems. You can do this using (Divide Systems).

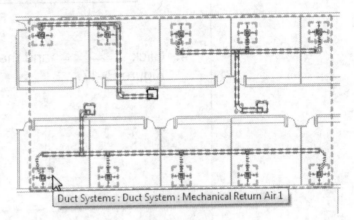

Duct Systems : Duct System : Mechanical Return Air 1

Figure B–15

- Systems can only be divided if they have more than one network of ducts or pipes. In the example shown in Figure B–15, there are three networks of ducts and each one is connected to a different air handling unit.

- If you needed to divide a system even further, add another piece of equipment and connect some of the air terminals or fixtures to it.

How To: Divide Systems

1. Select the system you want to divide.
2. In the *Modify | Duct (or Pipe) Systems* tab>System Tools panel, click (Divide System).

3. An alert box, as shown in Figure B–16, displays. It indicates the number of networks that are to be converted into individual systems.

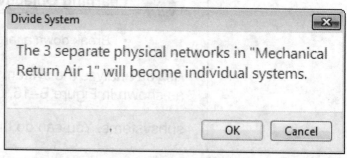

Figure B–16

4. Click and the systems are separated as shown in Figure B–17.

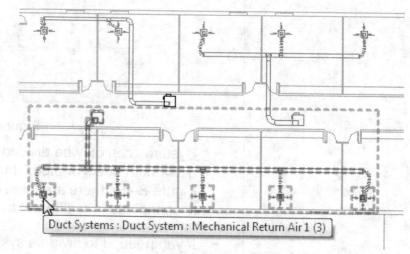

Figure B–17

B.4 Pressure Loss Reports

Learning Objective

- Create a pressure loss report for duct and pipe systems.

Pressure Loss Reports are HTML files (as shown in Figure B–18), that include all of the data that can be viewed dynamically in the System Inspector. The reports can be set up to export exactly the information you need. They can be created for Duct or Pipe systems. The analysis for each system includes total pressure loss for the system as well as detailed information for various sections of duct or pipe.

System Classification	Return Air
System Type	Return Air
System Name	01 - RA01
Abbreviation	

Total Pressure Loss Calculations by Sections

Section	Element	Flow	Size	Velocity	Velocity Pressure	Length	Loss Co
	Duct	500 CFM	12"x12"	500 FPM	-	3' - 11 1/2"	-
1	Fittings	500 CFM	-	500 FPM	0.02 in-wg	-	0.17
	Air Terminal	500 CFM	-	-	-	-	-
2	Duct	1000 CFM	12"x12"	1000 FPM	-	12' - 4 15/16"	-
	Fittings	1000 CFM	-	1000 FPM	0.06 in-wg	-	0.81490!
3	Fittings	1000 CFM	-	409 FPM	0.01 in-wg	-	0
	Equipment	1000 CFM	-	-	-	-	-
	Duct	500 CFM	12"x12"	500 FPM	-	24' - 7 1/2"	-
4	Fittings	500 CFM	-	500 FPM	0.02 in-wg	-	0.34
	Air Terminal	500 CFM	-	-	-	-	-

Critical Path : 4-2-3 ; Total Pressure Loss : 0.14 in-wg

Detail Information of Straight Segment by Sections

Section	Element ID	Flow	Size	Velocity	Velocity Pressure
1	250437	500 CFM	12"x12"	500 FPM	0.02 in-wg
	250440	500 CFM	12"x12"	500 FPM	0.02 in-wg
2	250623	1000 CFM	12"x12"	1000 FPM	0.06 in-wg
	252421	1000 CFM	12"x12"	1000 FPM	0.06 in-wg
	252430	1000 CFM	12"x12"	1000 FPM	0.06 in-wg
4	250445	500 CFM	12"x12"	500 FPM	0.02 in-wg
	250446	500 CFM	12"x12"	500 FPM	0.02 in-wg
	250449	500 CFM	12"x12"	500 FPM	0.02 in-wg

Figure B–18

How To: Create a Duct/Pipe Pressure Loss Report

1. When a system is selected, in the contextual *Modify Duct (Pipe) System* tab>Duct (Pipe) System Report panel, click

   (Duct Pressure Loss Report) or (Pipe Pressure Loss Report). These tools are also found in the *Analyze* tab>*Reports & Schedules* panel.

2. In the Duct (Pipe) Pressure Loss Report - System Selector dialog box (shown in Figure B–19), select the systems that you want to include in the report.

Figure B–19

- To limit the systems displayed in the System Selector, click [System Type Filter] to open the dialog box shown in Figure B–20. Select the types of systems you want to include in the report and click [OK] to return to the main dialog box.

Figure B–20

- Use [Select All] [Select None] [Invert Selection] to help with the selection as required.

3. When you have finished selecting the systems to include, click .

4. In the Duct/Pipe Pressure Loss Reports Settings dialog box, specify the type of Report Format and the Reports Fields, as well as other information as shown in Figure B–21.

Duct Pressure Loss Report Settings

Report Format: <default>   Save   Delete

Available Fields:

Diameter
Equivalent Diameter
Free Size
Height
Hydraulic Diameter
Overall Size
Reynolds number
Width

Add -->
<-- Remove

Report Fields (in order):

Flow
Size
Velocity
Velocity Pressure
Length
Loss Coefficient
Friction

Move Up   Move Down

☑ Display System Information

☑ Display Critical Path

☑ Display Detail Information of Straight Segment by Sections   Settings...

☑ Display Fitting and Accessory Loss Coefficient Summary by Sections   Settings...

☑ Open the Pressure Loss Report directly after it's created

Generate   Cancel

Figure B–21

5. Click Generate .

B.5 Revision Tracking

 Learning Objectives

- Add and tag revision clouds around areas that are changed on sheets.
- Create a revision table for the project or a template.
- Issue revisions for the record.

When a set of drawings has been put into production, you need to show where changes are made. Typically, these are shown on drawing sheets using a revision cloud. Each cloud is then tagged and the number is referenced elsewhere on the sheet with the description and date, as shown in Figure B–22. The Autodesk Revit software has created a process where the numbering and description are automatically applied to the title blocks when you associate a revision cloud with the information.

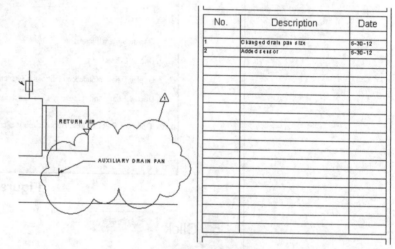

No.	Description	Date
1	Changed drain pan size	5-30-12
2	Added sensor	5-30-12

Figure B–22

The information is stored in a revision table. This table can be created before or after you start adding revision clouds to the project. Once the table is created, you can modify the **Revision** parameter of the cloud to match the corresponding information.

- More than one revision cloud can be associated with a revision number.

- The title blocks that come with the Autodesk Revit software already have a revision schedule inserted into the title area. It is recommended that you also add a revision schedule to your company title block.

Revision Clouds

Revision clouds can be added before or after you create a revision table that assigns the number and value.

When you add revision clouds to a project, you also need to assign the revision to the cloud and tag the cloud, as shown in Figure B–23.

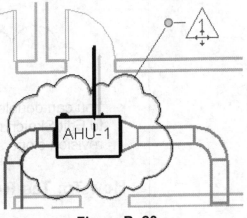

Figure B–23

How To: Add Revision Clouds

Enhanced in 2015

1. In the *Annotate* tab>Detail panel, click (Revision Cloud).
2. In the *Modify | Create Revision Cloud Sketch* tab>Draw panel, use the draw tools to create the cloud.
3. In the *Modify | Create Revision Cloud Sketch* tab>Mode panel, click (Finish Edit Mode).
4. In the Options Bar or Properties, expand the Revision drop-down list and select the Revision list, as shown in Figure B–24.

If the revision table has not be set up, you can do this at a later date.

Revision Clouds (1)	▼	⊞ Edit Type
Identity Data		⊗
Revision	Seq. 1 - Changed drain pan s ▼	
Revision Number	Seq. 1 - Changed drain pan size	
Revision Date	Seq. 2 - Added sensor	
Issued to		

Figure B–24

5. Click in empty space to release the selection.

- The *Revision Number* and *Date* are automatically assigned according to the specifications in the revision table.

Enhanced
in 2015

- The length of the arcs that form the revision cloud is controlled in the Sheet Issues/Revisions dialog box. It is an annotation element, and therefore is scaled according to the view scale.

- You can create an open cloud (e.g., as a tree line), as shown in Figure B–25.

Figure B–25

- You can double-click on the edge of revision cloud to switch to Edit Sketch mode and modify the size or location of the revision cloud arcs.

How To: Tag Revision Clouds

1. In the *Annotate* tab>Tag panel, click [1] (Tag By Category).
2. Select the revision cloud to tag. A tooltip containing the revision number and revision from the cloud properties displays when you hover the cursor over the revision cloud, as shown in Figure B–26.

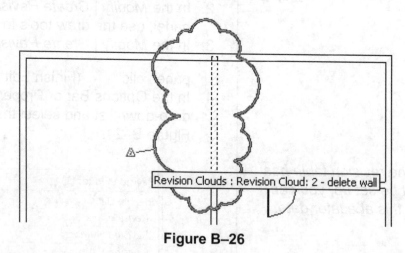

Revision Clouds : Revision Cloud: 2 - delete wall

Figure B–26

- If the revision cloud tag is not loaded, load **Revision Tag.rfa** from the *Annotations* folder in the Library.

Creating the Revision Table

As you add revisions, you need to create the table that specifies the revision tag number, revision date, and description.

- One revision is always available in a project.

- Revision clouds can be added before creating the revision table as required.

How To: Create a Revision Table

1. Open an existing project or a template,

2. In the *View* tab>Sheet Composition panel, click 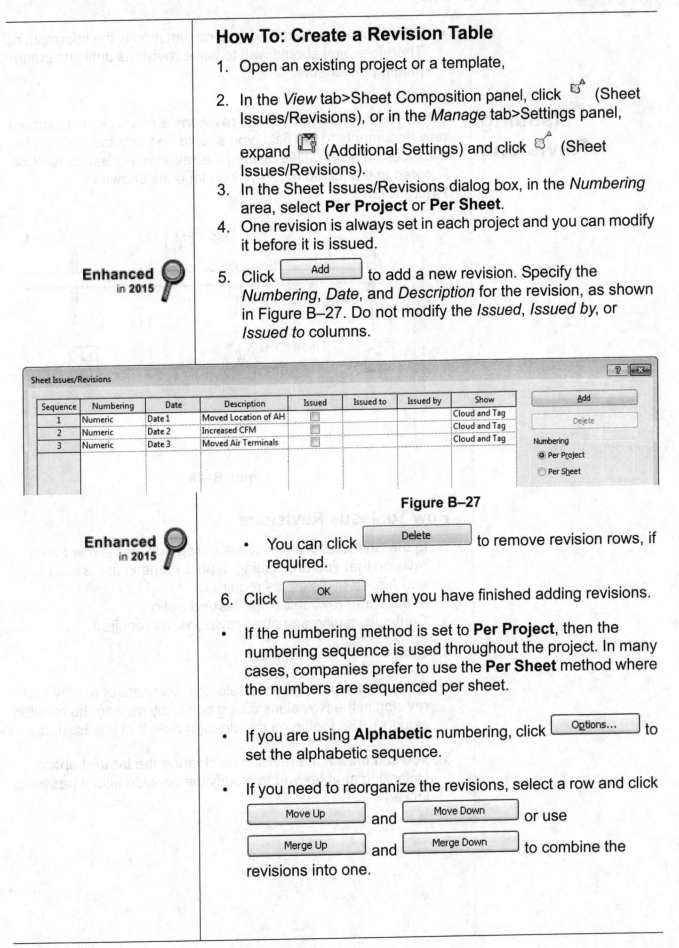 (Sheet Issues/Revisions), or in the *Manage* tab>Settings panel, expand (Additional Settings) and click (Sheet Issues/Revisions).

3. In the Sheet Issues/Revisions dialog box, in the *Numbering* area, select **Per Project** or **Per Sheet**.

4. One revision is always set in each project and you can modify it before it is issued.

Enhanced
in 2015

5. Click [Add] to add a new revision. Specify the *Numbering*, *Date*, and *Description* for the revision, as shown in Figure B–27. Do not modify the *Issued*, *Issued by*, or *Issued to* columns.

Sequence	Numbering	Date	Description	Issued	Issued to	Issued by	Show
1	Numeric	Date 1	Moved Location of AH	☐			Cloud and Tag
2	Numeric	Date 2	Increased CFM	☐			Cloud and Tag
3	Numeric	Date 3	Moved Air Terminals	☐			Cloud and Tag

Add

Delete

Numbering
◉ Per Project
○ Per Sheet

Figure B–27

Enhanced
in 2015

- You can click [Delete] to remove revision rows, if required.

6. Click [OK] when you have finished adding revisions.

- If the numbering method is set to **Per Project**, then the numbering sequence is used throughout the project. In many cases, companies prefer to use the **Per Sheet** method where the numbers are sequenced per sheet.

- If you are using **Alphabetic** numbering, click [Options...] to set the alphabetic sequence.

- If you need to reorganize the revisions, select a row and click [Move Up] and [Move Down] or use [Merge Up] and [Merge Down] to combine the revisions into one.

- When a revision is issued, you cannot modify the information. Therefore, you should wait to issue revisions until just before printing the sheets.

Issuing Revisions

When you have completed the revisions and are ready to submit new documents to the field, you should first lock the revision for the record. This is called issuing the revision. An issued revision is noted in the tooltip of a revision cloud, as shown in Figure B–28.

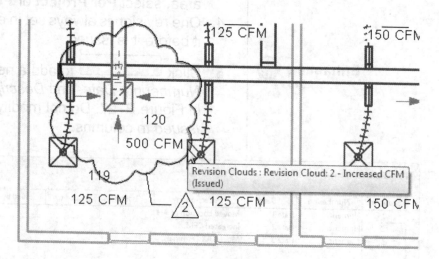

Figure B–28

How To: Issue Revisions

1. In the Sheet Issues/Revisions dialog box, in the row for the revision that you are issuing, type a name in the *Issued to* and *Issued by* fields, as required.
2. In the same row, select the **Issued** option.
3. Continue issuing any other revisions, as required.
4. Click to finish.

- Once the **Issued** option is selected, you cannot modify that revision in the Revisions dialog box or by moving the revision cloud(s). The tooltip on the cloud(s) note that it is **Issued**.

5. You can unlock the revision by clearing the **Issued** option. Unlocking enables you to modify the revision after it has been locked.

B.6 Creating Building Component Schedules

 Learning Objectives

- Schedule building components based on type and instance parameters of elements.
- Setup schedule tables using filters, sorting, grouping, formatting, and appearance.
- Access the Schedule Properties dialog box from the Properties palette

A Building Component schedule is a table view of the type and instance parameters of a specific element. You can specify the parameters (fields) you want to include in the schedule. All of the parameters found in the type of element you are scheduling are available to use. For example, an air terminal schedule (as shown in Figure B–29) can include instance parameters that are automatically filled in (such as **Flow**) and type parameters that might need to have the information assigned in the schedule or element type (such as **Type Mark**, **Manufacturer**, and **Model**).

Air Terminal Schedule					
Type Mark	Family	Type	Flow	Manufacturer	Model
RD-1	Return Diffuser - Hosted	Workplane-based Retur	500 CFM		
RD-2	Return Diffuser	24 x 24 Face 12 x 12 C	500 CFM		
SD-1	Supply Diffuser - Perforated - R	24x24x10 In Neck	100 CFM	Price	TBD2
SD-1	Supply Diffuser - Perforated - R	24x24x10 In Neck	123 CFM	Price	TBD2
SD-1	Supply Diffuser - Perforated - R	24x24x10 In Neck	124 CFM	Price	TBD2
SD-1	Supply Diffuser - Perforated - R	24x24x10 In Neck	125 CFM	Price	TBD2
SD-1	Supply Diffuser - Perforated - R	24x24x10 In Neck	150 CFM	Price	TBD2
SD-1	Supply Diffuser - Perforated - R	24x24x10 In Neck	760 CFM	Price	TBD2
SD-2	Supply Diffuser - Perforated - R	24x12x6 In Neck	275 CFM		
SD-3	Supply Diffuser - Perforated - R	24x24x12 In Neck	1100 CFM		

Figure B–29

How To: Create a Building Component Schedule

1. In the *View* tab>Create panel, expand ▦ (Schedules) and click ▦ (Schedule/Quantities) or in the Project Browser, right-click on the Schedule/Quantities node and select **New Schedule/Quantities**.

In the Filter list drop-down list, you can specify the discipline(s) to show only the categories that you want to display.

2. In the New Schedule dialog box, select the type of schedule you want to create (e.g., Mechanical Equipment or Fire Alarm Devices) from the *Category* list, as shown in Figure B–30.

Figure B–30

3. Type a new *Name*, if the default does not suit.
4. Select **Schedule building components.**
5. Specify the *Phase* as required.
6. Click [OK].
7. Fill out the information in the Schedule Properties dialog box. This includes the information in the *Fields*, *Filter*, *Sorting/Grouping*, *Formatting*, and *Appearance* tabs.
8. Once you have entering the schedule properties, click [OK]. A schedule report is created in its own view.

Schedule Properties – Fields Tab

In the *Fields* tab, you can select from a list of available fields and organize them in the order in which you want them to display in the schedule, as shown in Figure B–31.

Figure B–31

How To: Fill out the Fields Tab

1. In the *Available fields* list, select one or more fields you want to add to the schedule and click [Add -->]. The field(s) are placed in the *Scheduled fields (in order)* list.

You can also double-click on a field to move it from the Available Fields to the Scheduled Fields list.

2. Continue adding fields as required. If you add one you did not want to use, select it in the *Scheduled fields* list and click [<-- Remove] to move it back to the *Available fields* list.

3. Use [Move Up] and [Move Down] to change the order of the scheduled fields.

Other Fields Tab Options

Select available fields from	Enables you to select additional category fields for the specified schedule. The available list of additional fields depends on the original category of the schedule. Typically, they include room information.
Include elements in linked files	Includes elements that are in files linked to the current project, so that their elements can be included in the schedule.
[Add Parameter...]	Adds a new field according to your specification. New fields can be placed by instance or by type.
[Calculated Value...]	Enables you to create a field that uses a formula based on other fields.
[Edit...]	Enables you to edit custom fields. This is grayed out if you select a standard field.
[Delete]	Deletes selected custom fields. This is grayed out if you select a standard field.

Schedule Properties – Filter Tab

In the *Filter* tab, you can set up filters so that only elements meeting specific criteria are included in the schedule. For example, you might only want to show information for one level, as shown in Figure B–32. You can create filters for up to eight values. All values must be satisfied for the elements to display.

Enhanced in 2015

Figure B–32

- The parameter you want to use as a filter must be included in the schedule. You can hide the parameter once you have completed the schedule, if required.

Filter by	Specifies the field to filter. Not all fields are available to be filtered.
Condition	Specifies the condition that must be met. This includes options such as **equal**, **not equal**, **greater than**, and **less than**.
Value	Specifies the value of the element to be filtered. You can select from a drop-down list of appropriate values. For example, if you set *Filter By* to **Level**, it displays the list of levels in the project.

Schedule Properties – Sorting/Grouping Tab

In the *Sorting/Grouping* tab, you can set how you want the information to be sorted, as shown in Figure B–33. For example, you can sort by **Mark** (number) and then **Type**.

Figure B–33

Sort by	Enables you to select the field(s) you want to sort by. You can select up to four levels of sorting.
Ascending/ Descending	Sorts fields in **Ascending** or **Descending** order.

Header/Footer	Enables you to group similar information and separate it by a **Header** with a title and/or a **Footer** with quantity information.
Blank line	Adds a blank line between groups.
Grand totals	Selects which totals to display for the entire schedule. You can specify a name to display in the schedule for the Grand total.
Itemize every instance	If selected, displays each instance of the element in the schedule. If not selected, displays only one instance of each type, as shown in Figure B–34.

Enhanced
in 2015

<Air Terminal Schedule>

A	B	C	D
Mark	Family	Type	Flow
RD-1	Return Diffuser - Hosted	Workplane-based Return Diffuser	500 CFM
SD-1	Supply Diffuser - Perforated - Round Neck - Ceiling Mount	24x24x10 In Neck	
Grand total			

Figure B–34

Schedule Properties – Formatting Tab

In the *Formatting* tab, you can control how the headers of each field display, as shown in Figure B–35.

Figure B–35

Fields	Enables you to select the field for which you want to modify the formatting.
Heading	Enables you to change the heading of the field if you want it to be different from the field name. For example, you might want to replace **Mark** (a generic name) with the more specific **Door Number** in a door schedule.

Heading orientation	Enables you to set the heading on sheets to **Horizontal** or **Vertical**. This does not impact the schedule view.
Alignment	Aligns the text in rows under the heading to be **Left**, **Right**, or **Center**.
Field Format...	Sets the units format for the length, area, volume, angle, or number field. By default, this is set to use the project settings.
Conditional Format...	Sets up the schedule to display visual feedback based on the conditions listed.
Hidden field	Enables you to hide a field. For example, you might want to use a field for sorting purposes, but not have it display in the schedule. You can also modify this option in the schedule view later.
Show conditional format on sheets	Select if you want the color code set up in the Conditional Format dialog box to display on sheets.
Calculate totals	Displays the subtotals of numerical columns in a group.

Schedule Properties – Appearance Tab

In the *Appearance* tab, you can set the text style and grid options for a schedule, as shown in Figure B–36.

Figure B–36

Grid lines		Displays lines between each instance listed and around the outside of the schedule. Select the style of lines from the drop-down list; this controls all lines for the schedule, unless modified.
Grid in headers/footers/ spacers		Extends the vertical grid lines between the columns.
Outline		Specify a different line type for the outline of the schedule.
Blank row before data		Select this option if you want a blank row to be displayed before the data begins in the schedule.
Show Title/Show Headers		Select these options to include the text in the schedule.
Title text/Header text/Body Text		Select the text style for the title, header, and body text.

Schedule Properties

Schedule views have properties including the *View Name*, *Phases* and methods of returning to the Schedule Properties dialog box as shown in Figure B–37. In the *Other* area, select the button next to the tab that you want to open in the Schedule Properties dialog box. In the dialog box, you can switch from tab to tab and make any required changes to the overall schedule.

Figure B–37

Command Summary

Button	Command	Location
Annotations		
	Matchline	• **Ribbon:** *View* tab>Sheet Composition panel
	View Reference	• **Ribbon:** *View* tab>Sheet Composition panel or *Annotate* tab> Tag panel
Systems		
	Divide Systems	• **Ribbon:** *Modify | Duct (or Pipe) Systems* tab>System Tools panel.
	Duct Pressure Loss Report	• **Ribbon:** *Modify Duct System* tab>Duct System Report panel, *Analyze* tab>*Reports & Schedules* panel.
	Pipe Pressure Loss Report	• **Ribbon:** *Modify Pipe System* tab>Pipe System Report panel, *Analyze* tab>*Reports & Schedules* panel.
Revisions		
	Revision Cloud	• **Ribbon:** *Annotate* tab>Detail panel
	Sheet Issues/ Revisions	• **Ribbon:** *Manage* tab>Settings panel> expand Additional Settings
Schedules		
	Schedule/ Quantities	• **Ribbon:** *View* tab>Create panel> expand Schedules

Index